THE
MACMILLAN
READER

THE MACMILLAN READER

SIXTH EDITION

Judith Nadell

John Langan
Atlantic Community College

Eliza A. Comodromos
Rutgers, The State University of New Jersey

Longman

New York   San Francisco   Boston
London   Toronto   Sydney   Tokyo   Singapore   Madrid
Mexico City   Munich   Paris   Cape Town   Hong Kong   Montreal

Editor-in-Chief: Joseph Opiela
Vice President: Eben W. Ludlow
Marketing Manager: Carlise Paulson
Supplements Editor: Donna Campion
Senior Production Manager: Valerie Zaborski
Project Coordination, Text Design, and Electronic Page Makeup: Elm Street
　　Publishing Services, Inc.
Cover Designer/Manager: John Callahan
Cover Photo: Annapurna south face at dawn, courtesy FPG International
Manufacturing Buyer: Lucy Hebard
Printer and Binder: R.R. Donnelley & Sons, Harrisonburg
Cover Printer: Coral Graphic Services

For permission to use copyrighted material, grateful acknowledgment is made to the
copyright holders on pp. 737–741, which are hereby made part of this copyright page.

Library of Congress Cataloging-in-Publication Data
Nadell, Judith.
　　The Macmillan reader / Judith Nadell, John Langan, Eliza A. Comodromos—
6th ed.
　　　　p. cm.
　　Includes index.
　　ISBN 0-205-33463-6
　　1. College readers. 2. English language—Rhetoric—Problems, exercises, etc.
　　3. Report writing—Problems, exercises, etc. I. Langan, John, 1942– II.
Comodromos, Eliza A. III. Title.

PE1417.N33 2001
808'.0427—dc21　　　　　　　　　　　　　　　　　　　　　　2001029333

Please visit our website at http://www.ablongman.com

ISBN 0-205-33463-6

1 2 3 4 5 6 7 8 9 10—DOH—04 03 02 01

ABOUT THE AUTHORS

Judith Nadell was until several years ago Associate Professor of Communications at Rowan University (New Jersey). During her eighteen years at Rowan, she coordinated the introductory course in the Freshman Writing Sequence and served as Director of the Writing Lab. In the past several years, she has developed a special interest in grassroots literacy. Besides designing an adult-literacy project, a children's reading-enrichment program, and a family-literacy initiative, she has worked as a volunteer tutor and a tutor trainer in the programs. A Phi Beta Kappa graduate of Tufts University, she received a doctorate from Columbia University. She is author of *Becoming a Read-Aloud Coach* (Townsend Press) and coauthor of *Doing Well in College* (McGraw-Hill), *Vocabulary Basics* (Townsend Press), and *The Macmillan Writer*. The recipient of a New Jersey award for excellence in the teaching of writing, Judith Nadell lives with her coauthor husband, John Langan, near Philadelphia.

John Langan has taught reading and writing courses at Atlantic Community College near the New Jersey shore for more than twenty years. He earned an advanced degree in reading at Glassboro

State College and another in writing at Rutgers University. Active in a mentoring program, he designed a reading-enrichment program for inner-city high school students and recently wrote a motivational and learning skills guidebook, *Ten Skills You Really Need to Succeed in School,* for urban youngsters. Coauthor of *The Macmillan Writer* and author of a series of college textbooks on both reading and writing, he has published widely with McGraw-Hill Book Company, Townsend Press, and Longman. His books include *English Skills, Reading and Study Skills,* and *College Writing Skills.*

Eliza A. Comodromos has taught composition and developmental writing in the English Departments of both Rutgers University and John Jay College of Criminal Justice. After graduating with a B.A. in English and French from La Salle University, she did graduate work at the City University of New York Graduate School and went on to earn an advanced degree at Rutgers University, New Brunswick. A freelance editor and textbook consultant, Eliza Comodromos has delivered numerous papers at language and literature conferences around the country. Currently, she teaches composition at Rutgers University and lives near Philadelphia.

CONTENTS

3 DESCRIPTION   83

Gordon Parks   FLAVIO'S HOME   98
Having battled poverty and prejudice himself, writer-photogra-
pher Gordon Parks visits a Brazilian slum and finds, among the
wretched thousands forgotten by the outside world, a dying yet
smiling boy.

Russell Baker   IN MY DAY   108
The author visits his elderly mother in the hospital and muses
on the entwining of lives within a family.

Maya Angelou   SISTER FLOWERS   116
Hidden deep within herself after the trauma of a rape, a young
girl is escorted back into life by the grand lady of a small town.

E. B. White   ONCE MORE TO THE LAKE   125
Past, present, and future merge when White returns to a
beloved boyhood spot.

Judith Ortiz Cofer   A PARTIAL REMEMBRANCE
OF A PUERTO RICAN
CHILDHOOD   134
With wistful affection, the author recalls the laughter and les-
sons of the late-afternoon gathering of women in her family.

Additional Writing Topics   143

7   PROCESS ANALYSIS   325

12 COMBINING THE PATTERNS   659

THEMATIC CONTENTS

COMMUNICATION AND LANGUAGE

EDUCATION AND WORK

ETHICS AND MORALITY

FAMILY AND CHILDREN

GOVERNMENT AND LAW

HEALTH AND MEDICINE

HUMAN GROUPS AND SOCIETY

HUMOR AND SATIRE

MEANING IN LIFE

MEMORIES AND AUTOBIOGRAPHY

MEN AND WOMEN

NATURE AND SCIENCE

MEDIA AND TECHNOLOGY

PREFACE

Our bookshelves, and perhaps yours, sag under the weight of all the readers published over the years. Semester after semester, we used to switch texts because we wanted more than was offered. For one thing, we found that many of the readers contained an all-too-predictable blend of selections, with the same pieces cropping up from one book to the next. We also discovered that the books provided students with little guidance on ways to read, think, and write about the selections. And so, when we first began working on *The Macmillan Reader*, we aimed for a different kind of text—one that would offer fresh examples of professional prose, one that would take a more active role in helping students become stronger readers, thinkers, and writers.

As in the first five editions, our primary goal in the sixth edition has been to enliven the mix of selections commonly appearing in readers. Although *The Macmillan Reader* includes widely read and classic essays, a number of our selections have not yet appeared in other anthologies. Among these are Beth Johnson's "Bombs Bursting in Air," Gordon Parks's "Flavio's Home," Caroline Rego's "The Fine Art of Complaining," and Charles Sykes's "The 'Values'

Wasteland." We've been careful to choose selections that range widely in subject matter and approach, from the humorous to the informative, from personal meditation to polemic. We've also made sure that each selection captures students' interest and clearly illustrates a specific pattern of development or combination of patterns.

Our second concern has remained the quality of instruction in the book. As before, our objective has been to help students bridge the gap between the product and process approaches to reading and writing. Throughout, we describe possible sequences and structures but emphasize that such steps and formats are not meant to be viewed as rigid prescriptions; rather, they are strategies for helping students discover what works best in a particular situation. Buoyed by compliments about the previous editions' teachability, we haven't tinkered with the book's underlying format. Such a structure, we've been told, does indeed help students read more critically, think more logically, and write more skillfully. Here is the book's basic format:

- **Chapter 1, "The Reading Process,"** is designed to reflect current theories about the interaction of reading, thinking, and writing. The chapter provides guided practice in a three-part process for reading with close attention and a high level of interpretive skill. This step-by-step process sharpens students' understanding of the book's selections and promotes the rigorous thinking needed to write effective essays. An activity at the end of the chapter gives students a chance to use the three-step process. First, they read an essay by journalist Ellen Goodman. The essay has been annotated both to show students the reading process in action and to illustrate how close critical reading can pave the way to promising writing topics. Then they respond to sample questions and writing assignments, all similar to those accompanying each of the book's selections. The chapter thus does more than just tell students how to sharpen their reading abilities; it guides them through a clearly sequenced plan for developing critical reading skills.
- **Chapter 2, "The Writing Process,"** introduces students to essay writing. To make the composing process easier for students to grasp, we provide a separate section for each of the following stages: prewriting, identifying a thesis, supporting

the thesis with evidence, organizing the evidence, writing the first draft, and revising. From the start, we point out that the stages are fluid. Indeed, the case history of an evolving student paper illustrates just how recursive and individualized the writing process can be. Guided activities at the end of each section give students practice taking their essays through successive stages in the composing process.

To illustrate the link between reading and writing, the writing chapter presents the progressive stages of a student paper written in response to Ellen Goodman's "Family Counterculture," the selection presented in Chapter 1. An easy-to-spot symbol in the margin (✎) makes it possible to locate—at a glance—this evolving student essay. Commentary following the student paper highlights the essay's strengths and points out spots that could use additional work. In short, by the end of the second chapter, the entire reading-writing process has been illustrated, from reading a selection to writing about it.

- **Chapters 3–11** of *The Macmillan Reader* contain selections grouped according to **nine patterns of development**: description, narration, exemplification, division-classification, process analysis, comparison-contrast, cause-effect, definition, and argumentation-persuasion. The sequence progresses from the more personal and expressive patterns to the more public and analytic. However, because each chapter is self-contained, the patterns may be covered in any order. Instructors preferring a thematic approach will find the Thematic Contents list helpful.

The Macmillan Reader treats the patterns separately because such an approach helps students grasp the distinctive characteristics of each pattern. At the same time, the book continually shows the way writers usually combine patterns in their work. We also encourage students to view the patterns as strategies for generating and organizing ideas. Writers, we explain, rarely set out to compose an essay in a specific pattern. Rather, they choose a pattern or combination of patterns because it suits their purpose, audience, and subject.

Each of the nine pattern-of-development chapters follows this format:

1. **A detailed explanation of the pattern** begins the chapter. The explanation includes (a) a definition of the pattern, (b) a description of the way the pattern helps a writer accommodate his or her purpose and audience, and (c) step-by-step guidelines for using the pattern.

2. Next, we present **an annotated student essay** using the pattern. Written in response to one of the professional selections in the chapter, each essay illustrates the characteristic features of the pattern discussed in the chapter.

3. **Commentary** after each student essay points out the blend of patterns in the piece, identifies the paper's strengths, and locates areas needing improvement. "First draft" and "revised" versions of one section of the essay reveal how the student writer went about revising, thus illustrating the relationship between the final draft and the steps taken to produce it.

4. The **professional selections** in the pattern-of-development chapters are accompanied by these items:

   - *A biographical note and "Pre-Reading Journal Entry"* give students a perspective on the author and create interest in the piece.

   - *Questions for Close Reading* help students dig into and interpret the selection. The first question asks them to identify the selection's thesis; the last provides work on vocabulary development.

   - *Questions About the Writer's Craft* deal with such matters as purpose, audience, tone, organization, sentence structure, diction, and figures of speech. The first question in the series (labeled "The Pattern") focuses on the distinctive features of the pattern used in the selection. And usually there's another question (labeled "Other Patterns") that asks students to analyze the writer's use of additional patterns in the piece.

   - *Writing Assignments,* five in all, follow each selection. Packed with suggestions on how to proceed, the assignments use the selection as a springboard. The first two assignments ask students to write an essay using the same pattern as the one in the selection; the next two assignments encourage students to discover for themselves which combination of patterns would be most appropriate for an essay; the last assignment helps students turn the raw material in their journals into fully considered essays. Frequently, the assignments are preceded by the symbol ∞, indicating a cross-reference to at least one other selection in the book. By encouraging students to make connections among readings, such assignments broaden students' perspective and give them additional material to draw on when they write. These "paired assignments" will be especially welcome to instructors stressing recurring ideas and themes.

5. **Prewriting and revising activities**, placed in shaded boxes at the end of each chapter, help students understand the unique demands posed by the pattern being studied.

6. At the end of each pattern-of-development chapter are two sets of **Additional Writing Assignments:** "General Assignments" and "Assignments With a Specific Purpose and Audience." The first set provides open-ended topics that prompt students to discover the best way to use a specific pattern; the second set develops their sensitivity to rhetorical context by asking them to apply the pattern in a real-world situation.

• **Chapter 12, "Combining the Patterns,"** offers two essays each by three very different prose stylists. Annotations on one of the selections show how writers often blend patterns of development in their work. The chapter also provides guidelines to help students analyze this fusing of patterns.

• An **Appendix, "A Concise Guide to Finding and Documenting Sources,"** provides guidelines for conducting library and Internet research and for citing print and electronic sources.

The Macmillan Reader also includes a glossary that lists all the key terms presented in the text. In addition, a comprehensive *Instructor's Manual* contains the following: in-depth answers to the "Questions for Close Reading" and "Questions About the Writer's Craft"; suggested activities; pointers about using the book; a detailed syllabus; and an analysis of the blend of patterns in the selections in the "Combining the Patterns" chapter.

WHAT'S NEW IN THE SIXTH EDITION

In preparing this edition, we looked closely at scores of question-naires completed by instructors using the book. Their comments helped us identify new directions the book might take. Indeed, even a quick glance at the sixth edition of *The Macmillan Reader* reveals that this is a significant revision. Here are some of the new features of this edition of *The Macmillan Reader:*

- Most importantly, *every selection in the book* (both new and retained) *is framed by a new set of assignments: a "Pre-Reading Journal Entry" assignment before the piece and a "Writing Assignment Using a Journal Entry as a Starting Point" after the piece. Taken together, these two "bookend" assignments illustrate not only the connection between reading and writing but also the process involved in shaping a piece of writing.* The journal assignment "primes" students for the selection by encouraging them to explore—in a loose, unpressured way—their thoughts about an issue that will be raised in the selection. The journal entry thus motivates students to read the piece with extra care, attention, and per-sonal investment. The journal assignment also paves the way to the "Writing Assignment Using a Journal Entry as a Starting Point." The latter assignment helps students trans-late the raw material in their journals into a full-length essay. By the time students reach this final assignment, the rough ideas in their journal entry will have been enriched by a care-ful reading of the selection, setting the stage for a more rig-orously conceived essay.
- *Nearly one quarter of the selections are new.* Many of these readings were suggested by instructors across the country; others were chosen after a lengthy search through magazines, nonfiction collections, newspapers, autobiographies, and the like. Whether written by a well-known figure such as Joan Didion ("The Santa Ana") or a relative newcomer such as Beth Johnson ("Bombs Bursting in Air"), the new selections are bound to stimulate strong writing on a variety of topics—gender, family life, education, race, mass culture, and moral-ity, to name a few. When selecting new readings, we took special care to include humorous pieces (for example, Bill

Bryson's "Your New Computer") as well as those written from the third-person point of view (for example, James Gleick's "Life As Type A"). Honoring the requests of many instructors, we also made an effort to find compelling pieces on the way technology affects our everyday lives. Jonathan Coleman's "Is Technology Making Us Intimate Strangers?" is one of several such pieces.

- *A provocative new selection in the reading process chapter,* Ellen Goodman's "Family Counterculture," *provides the foundation for the student paper presented in the writing-process chapter.* Seeing such a direct connection between a selection and the writing it inspires helps students appreciate the *interdependence of the reading and writing process.*

- *Additional attention is given to the concept of peer review.* An expanded discussion provides students with guidelines for reacting to other students' work and for responding to the feedback they themselves receive. This emphasis on peer review encourages students to work together and learn from one another; it also helps students evaluate their own writing more incisively. For quick, easy reference, the inside back cover now features a checklist that can be used for peer review. And the book's companion website offers a peer-review checklist for each pattern of development.

- *Many assignments* (signaled by 💻) *suggest that students might want to conduct research in the library and/or on the Internet as part of their preparation for an essay.* Most of these assignments are worded in such a way that the essay can be written without visiting the library or going online, but the research option is there for instructors and students who think an essay would benefit from the citation of outside sources. The companion website provides links to Internet sites that students will find helpful if they supplement an essay with research.

- *The value of collaborative learning is underscored more than ever.* Many assignments encourage students to investigate various sides of an issue by brainstorming with classmates, questioning friends, speaking with family members, or interviewing "experts." Such assignments help students formulate sound, well-reasoned opinions and steer them away from reflexive, off-the-cuff positions.

- *A greater number of linked assignments* (indicated by ∞) *help students make connections between selections,* thus broadening their perspectives and giving them additional material to draw upon when they write.
- The *research paper* has been *updated* to reflect the *most recent MLA guidelines regarding the use of electronic sources.*
- *A new section, "A Concise Guide to Finding and Documenting Sources," has been added.* This Appendix now includes *up-to-date information on both library and Internet research.* The Internet section discusses the advantages and pitfalls of conducting research online, presents suggestions for using online time efficiently, and offers guidelines for evaluating online materials. The Appendix also shows how to document print and electronic sources.
- *A companion website, www.ablongman.com/nadell,* offers a number of helpful features, including additional activities and assignments, the address of relevant websites for assignments calling for Internet research, prewriting and peer review/revision checklists for each pattern of development, and a variety of supplementary activities.

The sixth edition of *The Macmillan Reader* has one more important new feature: Eliza A. Comodromos joins the book's original team of authors. A freelance editor and textbook consultant, Eliza has taught a variety of college writing courses; her special interest is in freshman composition. Eliza's considerable talents have helped shape this new edition of the book. Her presence is indeed welcome.

ACKNOWLEDGMENTS

At Longman, our thanks go to Eben Ludlow for his perceptive editorial guidance and continued enthusiasm for *The Macmillan Reader.* We're also indebted to Martha Beyerlein, Jonathan Lyzun, Rob Riley, and Irene Sotiroff of Elm Street Publishing Services, Inc., and Valerie Zaborski of Longman for their skillful handling of the never-ending complexities of the production process.

Over the years, many writing instructors have reviewed *The Macmillan Reader* and responded to detailed questionnaires about its selections and pedagogy. Their comments have guided our work every step of the way. To the following reviewers we are indeed grateful: Donald W. Adams, Chipola Junior College; James C. Addison, Jr., Western Carolina University; Rebecca L. Allen, Louisburg College; Ken Anania, Massasoit Community College; Chris Anson, University of Minnesota; Bruce J. Ardinger, Columbus State Community College; Constantina Rhodes Bailly, Hillsborough Community College; Mary Beth Bamforth, Wake Technical Community College; B. G. Bardin, Rogers State College; A. M. Belmont, Southern Arkansas University; Wilson C. Boynton, Holyoke Community College; John S. Capps, Virginia Western Community College; Ursula Carfagno, Montgomery County Community College; Barbara Carr, Stephen F. Austin State University; Bruce Coad, Mountain View College; David Cole, Quinnipaic College; Viralene J. Coleman, University of Arkansas, Pine Bluff; Howard J. Coughlin, Jr., Eastern Connecticut University; Charles R. Croghan, Jr., Indian River Community College; Michael Cross, Tulsa Junior College; F. Marino D'Amato, Manchester Community College; Betty Keating Dietz, Ohlone College; Benjamin B. Edwards, Tulsa Junior College; Mary Faraci, Florida Atlantic University; Benjamin Fiester, Wilkes College; Raymond W. Foster, Scottsdale Community College; Sister Pauline Fox, Mt. Mercy College; Margaret Franson, Valparaiso University; Lois Friesen, Butler County Community College; Ann Mace Futrell, Louisiana Technical University; Loris D. Galford, McNeese State University; Anita Gandolfo, West Virginia University; Michael G. Gessner, Central Arizona College; Casey Gilson, Broward Community College; Patricia Graves, Georgia State University; Michael Gress, Vincennes University; Chrysanthy M. Grieco, Seton Hall University; Gary Griswold, California State University, Long Beach; Mary M. Hatcher, Burlington County College; Betty Boyd Heard, Averett College; Angela Hilterbrand, Ashland Community College; Jean Hodgin, North Shore Community College; Patricia Hummel, Albright College; Ginger A. Hurajt, Northern Essex Community College; Eleanor D. James, Montgomery County Community College; Wanda L. Jared, Tennessee Technological University; Shakuntala Jayswal, University of New Haven; Kellie Jones, University of Tennessee at Martin; Sue V. Lape, Columbus State Community College; Stephen Larson, Wake Technical Community College; Robert Lesman, Northern Virginia Community College; Barry Maid, University of Arkansas at Little

Rock; Paul Marx, University of New Haven; Catherine Mau, Leeward Community College; Joseph F. McCadden, Burlington County College; Mary Ann McCandless, Butler County Community College; Brian McRea, University of Florida; Elizabeth Metzger, University of South Florida; Teresa Miller, Rogers State University; Kathy Mincey, Morehead State University; R. H. Moody, Madison Area Tech College; Roxanne Munch, Joliet Junior College; Steve Odden, University of Wisconsin at Stevens Point; Thomas B. O'Grady, University of Massachusetts, Boston; Michael G. O'Hara, Muscatine Community College; Barbara J. Porter, Canisius College; M. Cathleen Raymond, Florida Atlantic University; John Rogers, Vincennes University; Susan Schmeling, Vincennes University; Marcia Bundy Seabury, University of Hartford; Marie Secor, Pennsylvania State University; Carl Singleton, Fort Hays State University; Carolyn Smith, University of Florida; Eric R. Smith, SUNY College at Cortland; James Gregory Smith, Lamar University; Margo Smith, Rogers State College; Cynthia Somin, Long Beach City College; Charles Staats, Broward Community College–North; Judith Stanford, Merrimack College; Jacqueline Stark, Los Angeles Valley College; Virginia Stein, Community College of Allegheny County; Suzanne St. Laurent, Broward Community College; George Stoll, Broward Community College–North; Ralph Sturm, Edinboro University of Pennsylvania; John W. Taylor, South Dakota State University; Merle Thompson, North Virginia Community College; Robert Thompson, Macomb County Community College; Vivian Tortorici, Hudson Valley Community College; Larry K. Uffelman, Mansfield University; Cyrilla M. Vessey, Northern Virginia Community College; Anna Villegas, San Joaquin Delta College; Cheryl L. Ware, McNeese State University; Mildred J. White, Ohlone College; Samuel W. Whyte, Montgomery County Community College; David Wickham, Mountain View College; Dorena Allen Wright, Loyola Marymount University; Wei-hsiung Kitty Wu, Bowie State University; Donnie Yeilding, Central Texas College; and Sam Zahran, Fayetteville Technical Community College.

For help in preparing the sixth edition of *The Macmillan Reader*, we owe thanks to the insightful comments of these reviewers: Joseph A. Alvarez, Central Piedmont Community College; George Cox, Johnston Community College; Laurie Culbreth, Chipola Junior College; Nancy N. Frazer, Fairmont State College;

Casey Gilson, Broward Community College; Roberta Grantham, Chipola Junior College; Harrabeth A. Haidusek, Lamar University; Mary L. Hurst, Cuyahoga Community College; Eleanor James, Montgomery County Community College; David Kelly, Dyersburg State Community College; Teri Maddox, Jackson State Community College; Grace C. Ocasio, Central Piedmont Community College; Richard Pepp, Massasoit Community College; Lillian Polak, Nassau Community College; Patricia M. Price, Virginia Western Community College; Taryn Rice, Johnston Community College; Rhonda Lemke Sanford, Fairmont State College; Rita J. Self, Lamar University; Charles Swannell, Burlington County College; Victor Uszerowicz, Miami-Dade Community College; Patricia M. Wheeler, Central Piedmont Community College; and Donnie Yeilding, Central Texas College.

Our work on this edition was influenced too by the many students who took advantage of the questionnaire at the back of the fifth edition to tell us which selections they preferred.

Several individuals from our at-home office deserve special thanks. During the preparation of the sixth edition, Karen Beardslee and Frank Smigiel provided valuable assistance with the apparatus. And we're especially grateful to Janet M. Goldstein for the insight she provided when it came time to refine the journal-to-essay writing assignments. Finally, as always, we're thankful to our students. Their reaction to various drafts of material sharpened our thinking and helped focus our work. And we are especially indebted to the ten students whose essays are included in the book. Their thoughtful, carefully revised papers dramatize the potential of student writing and the power of the composing process.

Judith Nadell
John Langan
Eliza A. Comodromos

1

THE READING PROCESS

More than two hundred years ago, essayist Joseph Addison commented, "Of all the diversions of life, there is none so proper to fill
up its empty spaces as the reading of useful and entertaining
authors." Addison might have added that reading also challenges
our beliefs, deepens our awareness, and stimulates our imagination.

Why, then, don't more people delight in reading? After all,
most children feel great pleasure and pride when they first learn to
read. As children grow older, though, the initially magical world of
books is increasingly associated with homework, tests, and grades.
Reading turns into an anxiety-producing chore. Also, as demands
on a person's time accumulate throughout adolescence and adulthood, reading often gets pushed aside in favor of something that
takes less effort. It's easier simply to switch on the television and
passively view the ready-made images that flash across the screen. In
contrast, it's almost impossible to remain passive while reading.
Even a slick best-seller requires that the reader decode, visualize,
and interpret what's on the page. The more challenging the material, the more actively involved the reader must be.

The essays we selected for this book call for active reading. Representing a broad mix of styles and subjects, the essays range from the classic to the contemporary. They contain language that will move you, images that will enlarge your understanding of other people, ideas that will transform your views on complex issues.

The selections serve other purposes as well. For one thing, they'll help you develop a repertoire of reading skills—abilities that will benefit you throughout life. Second, as you become a better reader, your own writing style will become more insightful and polished. Increasingly, you'll be able to draw on the ideas presented in the selections and employ the techniques that professional writers use to express such ideas. As novelist Saul Bellow has observed, "A writer is a reader moved to emulation."

In the pages ahead, we outline a three-stage approach for getting the most out of this book's selections. Our suggestions will enhance your understanding of the book's essays, as well as help you read other material with greater ease and assurance.

STAGE 1: GET AN OVERVIEW OF THE SELECTION

Ideally, you should get settled in a quiet place that encourages concentration. If you can focus your attention while sprawled on a bed or curled up in a chair, that's fine. But if you find that being very comfortable is more conducive to daydreaming and dozing off than it is to studying, avoid getting too relaxed.

Once you're settled, it's time to read the selection. To ensure a good first reading, try the following hints:

- Start by reading the biographical note that precedes the selection. By providing background information about the author, the biographical note helps you evaluate the writer's credibility as well as his or her slant on the subject. For example, if you know that Deborah Tannen is a linguistics professor at Georgetown University, you can better assess whether she is a credible source for the analysis she presents in her essay "But What Do You Mean?" (page 313).
- Do the *Pre-Reading Journal Entry* assignment, which precedes the selection. This assignment "primes" you for the piece by helping you to explore—in an easy, unpressured way—your thoughts about a key point raised in the selection. By preparing

the journal entry, you're inspired to read the selection with special care, attention, and personal investment. (For more on pre-reading journal entries, see pages 16–18 and 728.)

- Consider the selection's title. A good title often expresses the essay's main idea, giving you insight into the selection even before you read it. For example, the title of Marie Winn's essay, "TV Addiction" (page 522), suggests that the piece will focus on television's negative effects. A title may also hint at a selection's tone. Paul Roberts's "How to Say Nothing in 500 Words" (page 365) points to an essay that's light in spirit, whereas George Orwell's "Shooting an Elephant" (page 167) suggests a piece with a serious mood.

- Read the selection straight through purely for pleasure. Allow yourself to be drawn into the world the author has created. Just as you first see a painting from the doorway of a room and form an overall impression without perceiving the details, you can have a preliminary, subjective feeling about a reading selection. Moreover, because you bring your own experiences and viewpoints to the piece, your reading will be unique. As Ralph Waldo Emerson said, "Take the book, my friend, and read your eyes out; you will never find there what I find."

- After this initial reading of the selection, focus your first impressions by asking yourself whether you like the selection. In your own words, briefly describe the piece and your reaction to it.

STAGE 2: DEEPEN YOUR SENSE OF THE SELECTION

At this point, you're ready to move further into the selection. A second reading will help you identify the specific features that triggered your initial reaction. Here are some suggestions on how to proceed:

- Mark off the selection's main idea, or thesis, often found near the beginning or end. If the thesis isn't stated explicitly, write down your own version of the selection's main idea.

- Locate the main supporting evidence used to develop the thesis. You may even want to number in the margin each key supporting point.

- Take a minute to write "Yes" or "No" beside points with which you strongly agree or disagree. Your reaction to these points often explains your feelings about the aptness of the selection's ideas.
- Return to any unclear passages you encountered during the first reading. The feeling you now have for the piece as a whole will probably help you make sense of initially confusing spots. However, this second reading may also reveal that, in places, the writer's thinking isn't as clear as it could be.
- Use your dictionary to check the meanings of any unfamiliar words.
- Ask yourself if your initial impression of the selection has changed in any way as a result of this second reading. If your feelings *have* changed, try to determine why you reacted differently on this reading.

STAGE 3: EVALUATE THE SELECTION

Now that you have a good grasp of the selection, you may want to read it a third time, especially if the piece is long or complex. This time, your goal is to make judgments about the essay's effectiveness. Keep in mind, though, that you shouldn't evaluate the selection until after you have a strong hold on it. A negative, even a positive reaction is valid only if it's based on an accurate reading.

At first, you may feel uncomfortable about evaluating the work of a professional writer. But remember: Written material set in type only *seems* perfect; all writing can be fine-tuned. By identifying what does and doesn't work in others' writing, you're taking an important first step toward developing your own power as a writer. You might find it helpful at this point to get together with other students to discuss the selection. Comparing viewpoints often opens up a piece, enabling you to gain a clearer perspective on the selection and the author's approach.

To evaluate the essay, ask yourself the following questions:

1. *Where does support for the selection's thesis seem logical and sufficient? Where does support seem weak?* Which of the author's supporting facts, arguments, and examples seem pertinent and convincing? Which don't?

2. *Is the selection unified? If not, why not?* Where does some-thing in the selection not seem relevant? Where are there any unnecessary digressions or detours?

3. *How does the writer make the selection move smoothly from beginning to end?* How does the writer create an easy flow between ideas? Are any parts of the essay abrupt and jarring? Which ones?

4. *Which stylistic devices are used to good effect in the selection?* Which pattern of development or combination of patterns does the writer use to develop the piece? Why do you think those patterns were selected? How do paragraph develop-ment, sentence structure, and word choice contribute to the piece's overall effect? What tone does the writer adopt? Where does the writer use figures of speech effectively? (The next chapter and the glossary explain these terms.)

5. *How does the selection encourage further thought?* What new per-spective on an issue does the writer provide? What ideas has the selection prompted you to explore in an essay of your own?

It takes some work to follow the three-step approach just described, but the selections in *The Macmillan Reader* are worth the effort. Bear in mind that none of the selections sprang full-blown from the pen of its author. Rather, each essay is the result of hours of work—hours of thinking, writing, rethinking, and revising. As a reader, you should show the same willingness to work with the selections, to read them carefully and thoughtfully. Henry David Thoreau, an avid reader and prolific writer, emphasized the impor-tance of this kind of attentive reading when he advised that "books must be read as deliberately and unreservedly as they were written."

To illustrate the multi-stage reading process just described, we've annotated the professional essay that follows: "Family Counterculture" by Ellen Goodman. Note that annotations are provided in the margin of the essay as well as at the end of the essay. As you read Goodman's essay, try applying the three-stage sequence. You can measure your ability to dig into the selection by making your own annotations on Goodman's essay and then com-paring them to ours. You can also see how well you evaluated the piece by answering the preceding five questions and then compar-ing your responses to ours on pages 9–11.

Ellen Goodman

The recipient of a Pulitzer Prize, Ellen Goodman (1941–) worked for *Newsweek* and the *Detroit Free Press* before joining the staff of the *Boston Globe* in the mid-1970s. A resident of the Boston area, Goodman writes a popular syndicated column that provides insightful commentary on life in the United States. Her pieces have appeared in a number of national publications, including *The Village Voice* and *McCalls*. Collections of her columns have been published in *Close to Home* (1979), *Turning Points* (1979), *At Large* (1981), *Keeping in Touch* (1985), *Making Sense* (1989), and *Value Judgments* (1993). Most recently, she coauthored *I Know Just What You Mean* (1999), a book that examines the complex nature of women's friendships. The following selection is from *Value Judgments*.

Pre-Reading Journal Entry

Television is often blamed for having a harmful effect on children. Do you think this criticism is merited? In what ways does TV exert a negative influence on children? In what ways does TV exert a positive influence on youngsters? Take a few minutes to respond to these questions in your journal.

Marginal Annotations

Family Counterculture

Interesting take on the term "counterculture"

Time frame established

1   Sooner or later, most Americans become card-carrying members of the counterculture. This is not an underground holdout of hippies. No beads are required. All you need to join is a child.

Light humor. Easy, casual tone

Time frame picked up

Thesis, developed overall by cause-effect pattern

2   At some point between Lamaze and the PTA, it becomes clear that one of your main jobs as a parent is to counter the culture. What the media delivers to children by the masses, you are expected to rebut one at a time.

First research-based example to support thesis

3   The latest evidence of this frustrating piece of the parenting job description came from pediatricians. This summer, the American Academy of Pediatrics called for a ban on television food ads. Their plea was hard on the heels of a study

showing that one Saturday morning of TV cartoons contained 202 junk-food ads.

4 The kids see, want, and nag. That is, after all, the theory behind advertising to children, since few six-year-olds have their own trust funds. The end result, said the pediatricians, is obesity and high cholesterol.

5 Their call for a ban was predictably attacked by the grocers' association. But it was also attacked by people assembled under the umbrella marked "parental responsibility." We don't need bans, said these "PR" people, we need parents who know how to say "no."

Relevant paragraph? Identifies Goodman as a parent, but interrupts flow

6 Well, I bow to no one in my capacity for naysaying. I agree that it's a well-honed skill of child raising. By the time my daughter was seven, she qualified as a media critic.

Transition doesn't work but would if ¶6 cut.

7 But it occurs to me now that the call for "parental responsibility" is increasing in direct proportion to the irresponsibility of the marketplace. Parents are expected to protect their children from an increasingly hostile environment.

Series of questions and brief answers consistent with overall casual tone.

8 Are the kids being sold junk food? Just say no. Is TV bad? Turn it off. Are there messages about sex, drugs, violence all around? Counter the culture.

Brief real-life examples support thesis.

9 Mothers and fathers are expected to screen virtually every aspect of their children's lives. To check the ratings on the movies, to read the labels on the CDs, to find out if there's MTV in the house next door. All the while keeping in touch with school and, in their free time, earning a living.

Fragments

10 In real life, most parents do a great deal of this monitoring and just-say-no-ing. Any trip to the supermarket produces at least one scene of a child grabbing for something only to have it returned to the shelf by a frazzled parent. An extraordinary number of the family arguments are over the goodies—sneakers, clothes, games—that the young know only because of ads.

More examples

Another weak transition—no contrast	But at times it seems that the media have become the mainstream culture in children's lives. Parents have become the alternative.
Restatement of thesis	Barbara Dafoe Whitehead, a research associate at the Institute for American Values, found this out in interviews with middle-class parents.
Second research-based example to support thesis	
Citing an expert reinforces thesis.	"A common complaint I heard from parents was their sense of being overwhelmed by the culture. They felt their voice was a lot weaker. And they felt relatively more helpless than their parents.
Restatement of thesis	"Parents," she notes, "see themselves in a struggle for the hearts and minds of their own children." It isn't that they can't say no. It's that there's so much more to say no to.
Comparison-contrast pattern—signaled by "once," "Today," "Once," and "Now"	Without wallowing in false nostalgia, there has been a fundamental shift. Americans once expected parents to raise their children in accordance with the dominant cultural messages. Today they are expected to raise their children in opposition.
	Once the chorus of cultural values was full of ministers, teachers, neighbors, leaders. They demanded more conformity, but offered more support. Now the messengers are Ninja Turtles, Madonna, rap groups, and celebrities pushing sneakers. Parents are considered "responsible" only if they are successful in their resistance.
Restatement of thesis	It's what makes child raising harder. It's why parents feel more isolated. It's not just that American families have less time with their kids. It's that we have to spend more of this time doing battle with our own culture.
Conveys the challenges that parents face	It's rather like trying to get your kids to eat their green beans after they've been told all day about the wonders of Milky Way. Come to think of it, it's exactly like that.

11
12
13
14
15
16
17

Annotations at End of Selection

Thesis: First stated in paragraph 2 (". . . it becomes clear that one of your main jobs as a parent is to counter the culture. What the media delivers to children by the masses, you are expected to rebut one at a time.") and then restated in paragraphs 11 ("the media have become the mainstream culture in children's lives. Parents have become the alternative."); 13 (Parents are frustrated, not because ". . . they can't say no. It's that there's so much more to say no to."); and 16 ("It's not just that American families have less time with their kids. It's that we have to spend more of this time doing battle with our own culture.").

First reading: A quick take on a serious subject. Informal tone and to-the-point style gets to the heart of the media vs. parenting problem. Easy to relate to.

Second and third readings:
1. Uses the findings of the American Academy of Pediatrics, a statement made by Barbara Dafoe Whitehead, and a number of brief examples to illustrate the relentless work parents must do to counter the culture.
2. Uses cause-effect overall to support thesis and comparison/contrast to show how parenting nowadays is more difficult than it used to be.
3. Not everything works (reference to her daughter as a media critic, repetitive and often inappropriate use of "but" as a transition), but overall the essay succeeds.
4. At first, the ending seems weak. But it feels just right after an additional reading. Shows how parents' attempts to counter the culture are as commonplace as their attempts to get kids to eat vegetables. It's an ongoing and constant battle that makes parenting more difficult than it has to be and less enjoyable than it should be.
5. Possible essay topics: A humorous paper about the strategies kids use to get around their parents' saying "no" or a serious paper on the negative effects on kids of another aspect of television culture (cable television, MTV, tabloid-style talk shows, and so on).

The following answers to the questions on pages 4–5 will help crystallize your reaction to Goodman's essay.

1. *Where does support for the selection's thesis seem logical and sufficient? Where does support seem weak?*

Goodman begins to provide evidence for her thesis when she cites the American Academy of Pediatrics' call for a "ban on television food ads" (paragraphs 3–5). The ban followed a study showing that kids are exposed to 202 junk-food ads during a single Saturday morning of television cartoons. Goodman further buoys her thesis with a list of brief "countering the culture" examples (8–10) and a slightly more detailed example (10) describing the parent-child conflicts that occur on a typical trip to the supermarket. By citing Barbara Dafoe Whitehead's findings later on (12–13), Goodman further reinforces her point that the need for constant rebuttal makes parenting especially frustrating: Because parents have to say "no" to virtually everything, more and more family time ends up being spent "doing battle" with the culture (16).

2. *Is the selection unified? If not, why not?*

In the first two paragraphs, Goodman identifies the problem and then provides solid evidence of its existence (3–4, 8–10). But Goodman's comments in paragraph 6 about her daughter's skill as a media critic seem distracting. Even so, paragraph 6 serves a purpose because it establishes Goodman's credibility by showing that she, too, is a parent and has been compelled to be a constant naysayer with her child. From paragraph 7 on, the piece stays on course by focusing on the way parents have to compete with the media for control of their children. The concluding paragraphs (16–17) reinforce Goodman's thesis by suggesting that parents' struggle to counteract the media is as common—and as exasperating—as trying to get children to eat their vegetables when all the kids want is to gorge on candy.

3. *How does the writer make the selection move smoothly from beginning to end?*

The first two paragraphs of Goodman's essay are clearly connected: The phrase "sooner or later" at the beginning of the first paragraph establishes a time frame that is then picked up at the beginning of the second paragraph with the phrase "at some point between Lamaze and the PTA." And Goodman's use in paragraph 3 of the word *this* ("The latest evidence of *this* frustrating piece of the parenting job description . . .") provides a link to the preceding paragraph. Other connecting strategies can be found in the piece. For example, the words *once, Today, Once,* and *Now* in paragraphs 14–15 provide an easy-to-follow contrast between parenting in earlier times and parenting in this era. However, because paragraph 6 contains a distracting aside, the contrast implied by the word *But* at the beginning of paragraph 7 doesn't work. Nor does Goodman's use of the word *But* at the beginning of paragraph 11 work; the point there emphasizes rather than contrasts with the one made in paragraph 10. From this point on, though, the essay is tightly written and moves smoothly along to its conclusion.

4. *Which stylistic devices are used to good effect in the selection?*

Goodman uses several patterns of development in her essay. The selection as a whole shows the *effect* of the mass media on kids and their parents. In paragraphs 3 and 12, Goodman provides *examples in the form of research data* to support her thesis, while paragraphs 8–10 provide a series of *brief real-life examples.* Paragraphs 12–15 use *contrast,* and paragraph 17 makes a *comparison* to punctuate Goodman's concluding point. Throughout, Goodman's *informal, conversational tone* draws readers in, and her *no-holds-barred style* drives her point home forcefully. In paragraph 8, she uses a *question and answer format* ("Are the kids being sold junk food? Just say no.") and *short sentences* ("Turn it off" and "Counter the culture") to illustrate how pervasive the situation is. And in paragraph 9, she uses *fragments* ("To check the ratings . . ." and "All the while keeping in touch with school . . .") to focus attention on the problem. These varied stylistic devices help make the essay a quick, enjoyable read. Finally, although Goodman is concerned about the corrosive effects of the media, she leavens her essay with dashes of *humor*. For example, the image of parents as counter-culturists (1) and the comments about green beans and Milky Ways (17) probably elicit smiles or gentle laughter from most readers.

5. *How does the selection encourage further thought?*

Goodman's essay touches on a problem most parents face at some time or another—having to counter the culture in order to protect their children. Her main concern is how difficult it is for parents to say "no" to virtually every aspect of the culture. Although Goodman offers no immediate solutions, her presentation of the issue urges us to decide for ourselves which aspects of the culture should be countered and which should not.

If, for each essay you read in this book, you consider the preceding questions, you'll be able to respond thoughtfully to the *Questions for Close Reading* and *Questions About the Writer's Craft* presented after each selection. Your responses will, in turn, prepare you for the writing assignments that follow the questions. Interesting and varied, the assignments invite you to examine issues raised by the selections and encourage you to experiment with various writing styles and organizational patterns.

Following are some sample questions and writing assignments based on the Goodman essay; all are similar to the sort that appear later in this book. Note that the final writing assignment paves the way for a student essay, the stages of which are illustrated in Chapter 2.

Questions for Close Reading

1. According to Goodman, what does it mean to "counter the culture"? Why is it harder now than ever before?
2. Which two groups, according to Goodman, protested the American Academy of Pediatrics's ban on television food ads? Which of these two groups does she take more seriously? Why?

Questions About the Writer's Craft

1. What audience do you think Goodman had in mind when she wrote this piece? How do you know? Where does she address this audience directly?
2. What word appears four times in paragraph 16? Why do you think Goodman repeats this word so often? What is the effect of this repetition?

Writing Assignments

1. Goodman believes that parents are forced to say "no" to almost everything the media offer. Write an essay illustrating the idea that not everything the media present is bad for children.
2. Goodman implies that, in some ways, today's world is hostile to children. Do you agree? Drawing upon but not limiting yourself to the material in your pre-reading journal, write an essay in which you support or reject this viewpoint.

The benefits of active reading are many. Books in general and the selections in *The Macmillan Reader* in particular will bring you face to face with issues that concern all of us. If you study the selections and the questions that follow them, you'll be on the way to discovering ideas for your own papers. Chapter 2, "The Writing Process," offers practical suggestions for turning those ideas into well-organized, thoughtful essays.

2

THE WRITING PROCESS

Not many people retire at age thirty-eight. But Michel Montaigne, a sixteenth-century French attorney, did exactly that. Montaigne retired at a young age because he wanted to read, think, and write about all the subjects that interested him. After spending years getting his ideas down on paper, Montaigne finally published his short prose pieces. He called them *essays*—French for "trials" or "attempts."

In fact, all writing is an attempt to transform ideas into words, thus giving order and meaning to life. By using the term *essais*, Montaigne acknowledged that a written piece is never really finished. Of course, writers have to stop at some point, especially if they have deadlines to meet. But, as all experienced writers know, even after they dot the final *i*, cross the final *t*, and say "That's it," there's always something that could have been explored further or expressed a little better.

Because writing is a process, shaky starts and changes in direction aren't uncommon. Although there's no way to eliminate the work needed to write effectively, certain approaches can make the process more manageable and rewarding. This chapter describes a sequence of steps for writing essays. Familiarity with a specific sequence develops your awareness of strategies and choices, making you feel more confident when it comes time to write. You're less likely to look at a blank piece of paper and think, "Help! Now what do I do?" During the sequence, you do the following:

1. Prewrite
2. Identify the thesis
3. Support the thesis with evidence
4. Organize the evidence
5. Write the first draft
6. Revise the essay

We present the sequence as a series of stages, but we urge you not to view it as a rigid formula that must be followed step by unchanging step. Most people develop personalized approaches to the writing process. Some writers mull over a topic in their heads, then move quickly into a promising first draft; others outline their essays in detail before beginning to write. Between these two extremes are any number of effective approaches. The sequence here can be streamlined, juggled around, or otherwise altered to fit individual writing styles as well as the requirements of specific assignments.

STAGE 1: PREWRITE

Prewriting refers to strategies you can use to generate ideas *before* starting the first draft of a paper. Prewriting techniques are like the warm-ups you do before going out to jog—they loosen you up, get you moving, and help you to develop a sense of well-being and confidence. Since prewriting techniques encourage imaginative exploration, they also help you discover what interests you most about your subject. Having such a focus early in the writing process keeps you from plunging into your initial draft without first giving some thought to what you want to say.

Prewriting can help in other ways, too. When we write, we often sabotage our ability to generate material because we continually critique what we put down on paper. During prewriting, you deliberately ignore your internal critic. Your purpose is simply to get ideas down on paper *without evaluating* their effectiveness. Writing without immediately judging what you produce can be liberating. Once you feel less pressure, you'll probably find that you can generate a good deal of material. And that can make your confidence soar.

Keep a Journal

Of all the prewriting techniques, keeping a journal (daily or almost daily) is the one most likely to make writing a part of your life. Some journal entries focus on a single theme; others wander from topic to topic. Your starting point may be a dream, a snippet of overheard conversation, a video on MTV, a political cartoon, an issue raised in class or in your reading—anything that surprises, interests, angers, depresses, confuses, or amuses you. You may also use a journal to experiment with your writing style—say, to vary your sentence structure if you tend to use predictable patterns.

Here is a fairly focused excerpt from a student's journal:

Today I had to show Paul around school. He and Mom got here by 9. I didn't let on that this was the earliest I've gotten up all semester! He got out of the car looking kind of nervous. Maybe he thought his big brother would be different after a couple of months of college. I walked him around part of the campus and then he went with me to Am. Civ. and then to lunch. He met Greg and some other guys. Everyone seemed to like him. He's got a nice, quiet sense of humor. When I went to Bio., I told him that he could walk around on his own since he wasn't crazy about sitting in on a science class. But he said "I'd rather stick with you." Was he flattering me or was he just scared? Anyway it made me feel good. Later when he was leaving, he told me he's definitely going to apply. I guess that'd be kind of nice, having him here. Mom thinks it's great and she's pushing it. I don't know. I feel kind of like it would invade my privacy. I found this school and have made a life for myself here. Let him find his own school! But it could be great having my kid brother here. I guess this is a classic case of what my psych teacher calls ambivalence. Part of me wants him to come, and part of me doesn't! (November 10)

Although some instructors collect students' journals, you needn't be overly concerned with spelling, grammar, sentence structure, or organization. While journal writing is typically more structured than freewriting (see page 25), you don't have to strive for entries that read like mini-essays. In fact, sometimes you may find it helpful to use a simple list (see the journal entry on page 24) when recording your thoughts about a subject. The important thing is to let your journal writing prompt reflection and new insights, providing you with material to draw upon in your writing. It is, then, a good idea to reread each week's entries to identify recurring themes and concerns. Keep a list of these issues at the back of your journal, under a heading like "Possible Essay Subjects." Here, for instance, are a few topics suggested by the preceding journal entry: deciding which college to attend, leaving home, sibling rivalry. Each of these topics could be developed in a full-length essay.

The Pre-Reading Journal.   To reinforce the value of journal writing, we've included a journal assignment before every selection in the book. This assignment, called *Pre-Reading Journal Entry*, "primes" you for the piece by encouraging you to explore—in a tentative fashion—your thoughts about an issue that will be raised in the selection. Here, once again, is the *Pre-Reading Journal Entry* assignment that precedes Ellen Goodman's "Family Counterculture" (page 6):

> Television is often blamed for having a harmful effect on children. Do you think this criticism is merited? In what ways does TV exert a negative influence on children? In what ways does TV exert a positive influence on youngsters? Take a few minutes to respond to these questions in your journal.

The following journal entry shows how one student, Harriet Davids, responded to the journal assignment. A thirty-eight-year-old college student and mother of two young teenagers, Harriet was understandably intrigued by the assignment. As you'll see, Harriet used a listing strategy to prepare her journal entry. She found that lists were perfect for dealing with the essentially "for or against" nature of the journal assignment.

TV's Negative Influence on Kids	TV's Positive Influence on Kids
Teaches negative behaviors (violence, sex, swearing, drugs, alcohol, etc.)	Teaches important educational concepts (Sesame Street, shows on The Learning Channel, etc.)
Cuts down on imagination and creativity	Exposes kids to new images and worlds (Reading Rainbow, Mister Rogers' Neighborhood)
Cuts down on time spent with parents (talking, reading, playing games together)	Can inspire important discussions (about morals, sexuality, drugs, etc.) between kids and parents
Encourages parents' lack of involvement with kids	Gives parents a needed break from kids
Encourages isolation (watching screen rather than interacting with other kids)	Creates common ground among kids, basis of conversations and games
De-emphasizes reading and creates need for constant stimulation	Encourages kids to slow down and read books based on a TV series or show (the Arthur and the Clifford, the Big Red Dog series, The Bookworm Bunch, etc.)
Promotes materialism (commercials)	Can be used by parents to teach kids that they can't have everything they see

The journal assignment and subsequent journal entry do more than prepare you to read a selection with extra care and attention; they also pave the way to a full-length essay. Here's how. The final assignment following each selection is called *Writing Assignment Using a Journal Entry as a Starting Point*. This assignment helps you to translate the raw material in your journal entry into a thoughtful, well-considered essay. By the time you get to the assignment, the rough ideas in your journal entry will have been enriched by your reading of the selection. (For an example of a writing assignment that draws upon material in a pre-reading journal entry, turn to page 107.)

As you've just seen, journal writing can stimulate thinking in a loose, unstructured way; journal writing can also prompt the focused thinking required by a specific writing assignment. When you have a specific piece to write, you should approach prewriting in a purposeful, focused manner. You need to:

- Understand the boundaries of the assignment.
- Determine your purpose, audience, and tone.
- Discover your essay's limited subject.
- Generate raw material about your limited subject.
- Organize the raw material.

We'll discuss each of these steps in turn. But first, here's a practical tip: If you don't use a word processor during the prewriting stage, try using a pencil and scrap paper. They're less intimidating than pen, typewriter, and "official" paper; they also reinforce the notion that prewriting is tentative and exploratory.

Understand the Boundaries of the Assignment

You shouldn't start writing a paper until you know what's expected. First, clarify the *kind of paper* the instructor has in mind. Assume the instructor asks you to discuss the key ideas in an assigned reading. What does the instructor want you to do? Should you include a brief summary of the selection? Should you compare the author's ideas with your own view of the subject? Should you determine if the author's view is supported by valid evidence?

If you're not sure about an assignment, ask your instructor—not the student next to you, who may be as confused as you—to make the requirements clear. Most instructors are more than willing to provide an explanation. They would rather take a few minutes of class time to explain the assignment than spend hours reading dozens of student essays that miss the mark.

Second, find out *how long* the paper is expected to be. Many instructors will indicate the approximate length of the papers they assign. If no length requirements are provided, discuss with the instructor what you plan to cover and indicate how long you think your paper will be. The instructor will either give you the go-ahead or help you refine the direction and scope of your work.

Determine Your Purpose, Audience, and Tone

Once you understand the requirements for a writing assignment, you're ready to begin thinking about the essay. What is its *purpose*? For what *audience* will it be written? What *tone* will you use? Later on, you may modify your decisions about these issues. That's fine. But you need to understand the way these considerations influence your work in the early phases of the writing process.

Purpose.   The papers you write in college are usually meant to *inform* or *explain,* to *convince* or *persuade,* and sometimes to *entertain*. In practice, writing often combines purposes. You might, for example, write an essay trying to *convince* people to support a new trash recycling program in your community. But before you win readers over, you most likely would have to *explain* something about current waste disposal technology.

When purposes blend this way, the predominant one determines the essay's content, organization, emphasis, and choice of words. Assume you're writing about a political campaign. If your primary goal is to *entertain,* to take a gentle poke at two candidates, you might start with several accounts of one candidate's "foot-in-mouth" disease and then describe the attempts of the other candidate, a multimillionaire, to portray himself as an average Joe. Your language, full of exaggeration, would reflect your objective. But if your primary purpose is to *persuade* readers that the candidates are incompetent and shouldn't be elected, you might adopt a serious, straightforward style. Rather than poke fun at one candidate's gaffes, you would use them to illustrate her insensitivity to important issues. Similarly, the other candidate's posturing would be presented, not as a foolish pretension, but as evidence of his lack of judgment.

Audience.   To write effectively, you need to identify who your readers are and to take their expectations and needs into account. An essay about the artificial preservatives in the food served by the campus cafeteria would take one form if submitted to your chemistry professor and a very different one if written for the college newspaper. The chemistry paper would probably be formal and technical, complete with chemical formulations and scientific data: "Distillation revealed sodium benzoate particles suspended in a gelatinous medium." But such technical material would be inappropriate in a newspaper column intended for general readers. In this case, you might provide specific examples of cafeteria foods containing additives—"Those deliciously smoky cold cuts are loaded with nitrates and nitrites, both known to cause cancer in laboratory animals"—and suggest ways to eat more healthily—"Pass by the deli counter and fill up instead on vegetarian pizza and fruit juices."

Ask yourself the following questions when analyzing your audience:

- What are my readers' age, sex, and educational level?
- What are their political, religious, and other beliefs?
- What interests and needs motivate my audience?
- How much do my readers already know about my subject?
- Do they have any misconceptions?
- What biases do they have about me, my subject, my opinion?
- How do my readers expect me to relate to them?
- What values do I share with my readers that will help me communicate with them?

Tone.   Just as your voice may project a range of feelings, your writing can convey one or more *tones,* or emotional states: enthusiasm, anger, resignation, and so on. Tone is integral to meaning; it permeates writing and reflects your attitude toward yourself, your purpose, your subject, and your readers. How do you project tone? You pay close attention to sentence structure and word choice.

Sentence structure refers to the way sentences are shaped. Although the two paragraphs that follow deal with exactly the same subject, note how differences in sentence structure create sharply dissimilar tones:

> During the 1960s, many inner-city minorities considered the police an occupying force and an oppressive agent of control. As a result, violence against police grew in poorer neighborhoods, as did the number of residents killed by police.

An occupying force. An agent of control. An oppressor. That's how many inner-city minorities in the '60s viewed the police. Violence against police soared. Police killings of residents mounted.

Informative in its approach, the first paragraph projects a neutral, almost dispassionate tone. The sentences are fairly long, and clear transitions ("During the 1960s"; "As a result") mark the progression of thought. But the second paragraph, with its dramatic, almost alarmist tone, seems intended to elicit a strong emotional response; its short sentences, fragments, and abrupt transitions reflect the turbulence of earlier times.

Word choice also plays a role in establishing the tone of an essay. Words have *denotations,* neutral dictionary meanings, as well as *connotations,* emotional associations that go beyond the literal meaning. The word *beach,* for instance, is defined in the dictionary as "a nearly level stretch of pebbles and sand beside a body of water." This definition, however, doesn't capture individual responses to the word. For some, *beach* suggests warmth and relaxation; for others, it calls up images of hospital waste and sewage washed up on a once-clean stretch of shoreline.

Since tone and meaning are tightly bound, you must be sensitive to the emotional nuances of words. In a respectful essay about police officers, you wouldn't refer to *cops, narcs,* or *flatfoots;* such terms convey a contempt inconsistent with the tone intended. Your words must also convey tone clearly. Suppose you're writing a satirical piece criticizing a local beauty pageant. Dubbing the participants "livestock on view" leaves no question about your tone. But if you simply referred to the participants as "attractive young women," readers might be unsure of your attitude. Remember, readers can't read your mind, only your paper.

Discover Your Essay's Limited Subject

Once you have a firm grasp of the assignment's boundaries and have determined your purpose, audience, and tone, you're ready to focus on a limited aspect of the general assignment. Because too broad a subject can result in a diffuse, rambling essay, be sure to restrict your general subject before starting to write.

The following examples show the difference between general subjects that are too broad for an essay and limited subjects that are appropriate and workable. The examples, of course, represent only a few among many possibilities.

General Subject	Less General	Limited
Education	Computers in education	Computers in elementary school arithmetic classes
	High school education	High school electives
Transportation	Low-cost travel	Hitchhiking
	Getting around a metropolitan area	The transit system in a nearby city
Work	Planning for a career	College internships
	Women in the work force	Women's success as managers

How do you move from a general to a narrow subject? Imagine that you're asked to prepare a straightforward, informative essay for your writing class. The assignment, prompted by Ellen Goodman's essay "Family Counterculture" (page 6), is an extension of the journal-writing assignment on page 12.

> Goodman implies that, in some ways, today's world is hostile to children. Do you agree? Drawing upon but not limiting yourself to the material in your pre-reading journal, write an essay in which you support or reject this viewpoint.

You might feel unsure about how to proceed. But two techniques can help you limit such a general assignment. Keeping your purpose, audience, and tone in mind, you may *question* or *brainstorm* the general subject. These two techniques have a paradoxical effect. Although they encourage you to roam freely over a subject, they also help restrict the discussion by revealing which aspects of the subject interest you most.

1. Question the general subject.   One way to narrow a subject is to ask a series of *who, how, why, where, when,* and *what* questions.

The following example shows how Harriet Davids, the mother of two young teenagers, used this technique to limit the Goodman assignment.

You may recall that, before reading Goodman's essay, Harriet had used her journal to explore TV's effect on children (see page 17). After reading "Family Counterculture," Harriet concluded that she essentially agreed with Goodman; like Goodman, she felt that parents nowadays are indeed forced to raise their kids in an "increasingly hostile environment." She was pleased that the writing assignment gave her an opportunity to expand preliminary ideas she had jotted down in her journal.

Harriet soon realized that she had to narrow the Goodman assignment. She started by asking a number of pointed questions about the general topic. As she proceeded, she was aware that the same questions could have led to different limited subjects—just as other questions would have.

General Subject: We live in a world that is difficult, even hostile to children.

Question	Limited Subject
Where do kids go to escape?	Television, which makes the world seem even more dangerous (violence, sex, etc.). Also malls and the Internet
Who is to blame for the difficult conditions under which children grow up?	Parents' casual attitude toward child-rearing
How have schools contributed to the problems children face?	Not enough counseling programs for kids in distress
Why do children feel frightened?	Divorce
When are children most vulnerable?	The special problems of adolescents
What dangers or fears should parents discuss with their children?	AIDS, drugs, alcohol, war, terrorism

2. Brainstorm the general subject.   Another way to focus on a limited subject is to list quickly everything about the general topic that pops into your mind. Working vertically down the page, jot down brief words, phrases, and abbreviations to capture your free-floating thoughts. Writing in complete sentences will slow you down. Don't try to organize or censor your ideas. Even the most fleeting, random, or seemingly outrageous thoughts can be productive.

Here's an example of the brainstorming that Harriet Davids generated in an effort to gather even more material on the Goodman assignment:

General Subject: We live in a world that is difficult, even hostile to children.

- TV--shows corrupt politicians, casual sex, drugs, alcohol, foul language, violence
- Kids babysat by TV
- Not enough guidance from parents
- Kids raise themselves
- Too many divorces
- Parents squabbling over material goods in settlements
- Money too important
- Kids feel unimportant
- Families move a lot
- I moved in fourth grade--hated it
- Rootless feeling
- Nobody graduates from high school in the same district they went to kindergarten in
- Drug abuse all over, in little kids' schools
- Pop music glorifies drugs
- Kids not innocent--know too much
- Single-parent homes
- Day care problems
- Abuse of little kids in day care
- TV coverage of day care abuse frightens kids
- Perfect families on TV make kids feel inadequate

As you can see, questioning and brainstorming suggest many possible limited subjects. To identify especially promising ones, reread your material. What arouses your interest, anger, or curiosity? What themes seem to dominate and cut to the heart of the matter? Star or circle ideas with potential.

After marking the material, write several phrases or sentences summarizing the most promising limited subjects. These, for example, are just a few that emerged from Harriet Davids's questioning and brainstorming for the Goodman assignment:

- TV partly to blame for children having such a hard time
- Relocation stressful to children
- Schools also at fault
- The special problems that parents face raising children today

Harriet decided to write on the last of these limited subjects— the special problems that parents face raising children today. This topic, in turn, is the focus of our discussion in the pages ahead.

Generate Raw Material About Your Limited Subject

When a limited subject strikes you as having possibilities, your next step is to see if you have enough interesting and insightful things to say about the subject to write an effective essay. To find out if you do, you may use any or all of the following techniques:

1. Freewrite on your limited subject.   *Freewriting* means jotting down in rough sentences or phrases everything that comes to mind. To capture this continuous stream of thought, write nonstop for ten minutes or more. Don't censor anything; put down whatever pops into your head. Don't reread, edit, or pay attention to organization, spelling, or grammar. If your mind goes blank, repeat words until another thought emerges.

Here is part of the freewriting that Harriet Davids generated about her limited subject, "The special problems that parents face raising children today":

Parents today have tough problems to face. Lots of dangers. Drugs and alcohol for one thing. Also crimes of violence against kids. Parents also have to keep up with cost of living, everything costs more, kids want and expect more. Television? The Internet? Another thing is Playboy, Penthouse. Internet sites featuring sex. Sexy ads on TV, movies deal with sex. Kids grow up too fast, too fast. Drugs. Little kids can't handle knowing too much at an early age. Both parents at work much of the day. Finding good day care a real problem. Lots of latchkey kids. Another problem is getting kids to do homework, lots of other things to do. Especially playing on the computer and going to the mall! When I was young, we did homework after dinner, no excuses accepted by my parents.

2. Brainstorm your limited subject.   Let your mind wander freely, as you did when using brainstorming to narrow your subject. This time, though, list every idea, fact, and example that occurs to you about your limited subject. Use brief words and phrases so you don't get bogged down writing full sentences. For now, don't worry whether ideas fit together or whether the points listed make sense.

To gather additional material on her limited subject for the Goodman assignment ("The special problems that parents face raising children today"), Harriet Davids brainstormed the following list:

- Trying to raise kids when both parents work
- Prices of everything outrageous, even when both parents work
- Commercials make kids want <u>more</u> of everything
- Clothes so important
- Day care not always the answer--cases of abuse
- Day care very expensive
- Sex everywhere--TV, movies, magazines
- Sexy clothes on little kids. Absurd!
- Sexual abuse of kids
- Violence against kids when parents abuse drugs
- Acid, "Ecstasy," heroin, AIDS
- Schools have to teach kids about these things
- Schools doing too much--not as good as they used to be
- Not enough homework assigned--kids unprepared
- Distractions from homework--malls, TV, phones, stereos, MTV, Internet, computer games

3. Use group brainstorming.   Brainstorming can also be conducted as a group activity. Thrashing out ideas with other people stretches the imagination, revealing possibilities you may not have considered on your own. Group brainstorming doesn't have to be conducted in a formal classroom situation. You can bounce ideas around with friends and family anywhere—over lunch, at the student center, and so on.

4. Map out the limited subject.   If you're the kind of person who doodles while thinking, you may want to try *mapping*, sometimes called *diagramming* or *clustering*. Like other prewriting techniques, mapping proceeds rapidly and encourages the free flow of ideas. Begin by expressing your limited subject in a crisp phrase and placing it in the center of a blank sheet of paper. As ideas come to you, put them along lines or in boxes or circles around the limited subject. Draw arrows and lines to show the relationships among ideas. Don't stop there, however. Focus on each idea; as subpoints and details come to you, connect them to their source idea, again using boxes, lines, circles, or arrows to clarify how everything relates.

5. Use the patterns of development.   Throughout this book, we show how writers use various patterns of development (narration, process analysis, definition, and so on), singly or in combination, to develop and organize their ideas. Because each pattern has its own distinctive logic, the patterns encourage you, when you prewrite, to think about a subject in different ways, causing insights to surface that might otherwise remain submerged.

The various patterns of development are discussed in detail in Chapters 3–11. At this point, though, you should find the following chart helpful. It not only summarizes the broad purpose of each pattern but also shows the way each pattern can generate different raw material for the limited subject of Harriet Davids's essay:

Limited Subject: The special problems that parents face raising children today.

Pattern	Purpose	Raw Material
Description	To detail what a person, place, or object is like	Detail the sights and sounds of a glitzy mall that attracts kids
Narration	To relate an event	Recount what happened when neighbors tried to forbid their kids from going to a rock concert
Exemplification	To provide specific instances or examples	Offer examples of family arguments. Can a friend known to use drugs visit? Can a child go to a party where alcohol will be served? Can parents outlaw MTV?

Pattern	Purpose	Raw Material
Division-classification	To divide something into parts or to group related things in categories	Identify components of a TV commercial that distorts kids' values
		Classify the kinds of commercials that make it difficult to teach kids values
Process analysis	To explain how something happens or how something is done	Explain step by step how family life can disintegrate when parents have to work all the time to make ends meet
Comparison-contrast	To point out similarities and/or dissimilarities	Contrast families today with those of a generation ago
Cause-effect	To analyze reasons and consequences	Explain why parents are not around to be with their kids: Industry's failure to provide day care and inflexibility about granting time off for parents with sick kids
		Explain the consequences of absentee parents: Kids feel unloved; they're undisciplined; they take on adult responsibility too early
Definition	To explain the meaning of a term or concept	What is meant by "tough love"?
Argumentation-persuasion	To win people over to a point of view	Convince parents to work with schools to develop programs that make kids feel safer and more secure

(For more on ways to use the patterns of development in different phases of the writing process, see pages 38–39, 46–47, and 659–661.)

6. Conduct research.   Depending on your topic, you may find it helpful to visit the library and/or to go online to identify books and articles about your limited subject. (See pages 691–705 for hints on conducting research.) At this point, you don't need to read closely the material you find. Just skim and perhaps take a few brief notes on ideas and points that could be useful.

If researching the Goodman assignment, for instance, Harriet Davids could look under such headings and subheadings as the following:

> Day care
> Drug abuse
> Family
> Parent-child relationship
> > Child abuse
> > Children of divorced parents
> > Children of working mothers
> School and home

Organize the Raw Material

Once you generate the raw material for your limited subject, you're ready to shape your rough, preliminary ideas. Preparing a *scratch outline* or *scratch list* is an effective strategy. On pages 50–53, we talk about the more formal outline you may need later on in the writing process. Here we show how a rough outline or scratch list can impose order on the tentative ideas generated during prewriting.

Reread your exploratory thoughts about the limited subject. Cross out anything not appropriate for your purpose, audience, and tone; add points that didn't originally occur to you. Star or circle compelling items that warrant further development. Then draw arrows between related items, your goal being to group such material under a common heading. Finally, determine what seems to be the best order for those headings.

By giving you a sense of the way your free-form material might fit together, a scratch outline makes the writing process more manageable. You're less likely to feel overwhelmed once you actually start writing because you'll already have some idea about how to shape your material into a meaningful statement. Remember, though, the scratch outline can, and most likely will, be modified along the way.

The following scratch outline shows how Harriet Davids began to shape her brainstorming (page 24) into a more organized format. Note the way she eliminated some items (for example, the point about outrageous prices), added others (for example, the point about video arcades), and grouped the brainstormed items under four main headings, with the appropriate details listed underneath. (If you'd like to see Harriet's more formal outline and her first draft, turn to pages 52–53 and 67–68.)

Limited Subject: The special problems that parents face raising children today.

1. Day care for two-career families
   - Expensive
   - Before-school problems
   - After-school problems

2. Distractions from homework
   - Stereos, televisions, and computers in room at home
   - Places to go--malls, video arcades, fast-food restaurants, rock concerts

3. Sexually explicit materials
   - Magazines and books
   - Television shows
   - Internet
   - MTV
   - Movies
   - Rock posters

4. Life-threatening dangers
   - AIDS
   - Drugs
   - Drinking
   - Violence against children (by sitters, in day care, etc.)

The prewriting strategies just described provide a solid foundation for the next stages of your work. But invention and imaginative exploration don't end when prewriting is completed. As you'll see, remaining open to new ideas is crucial during all phases of the writing process.

Activities: Prewrite

1. Number the items in each set from 1 (*broadest subject*) to 5 (*most limited subject*):

Set A	Set B
Abortion	Business Majors

Controversial social issue	Students' majors
Cutting state abortion funds	College students
Federal funding of abortions	Kinds of students on campus
Social issues	Why many students major in business

2. Which of the following topics are too broad for an essay of two to five typewritten pages: soap operas' appeal to college students; day care; trying to "kick" the junk-food habit; male and female relationships; international terrorism?

3. Use the techniques indicated in parentheses to limit each general topic listed below. Then, identify a specific purpose, audience, and tone for the one limited subject you consider most interesting. Next, with the help of the patterns of development, generate raw material about that limited subject. (You may find it helpful to work with others when developing this material.) Finally, shape your raw material into a scratch outline—crossing out, combining, and adding ideas as needed. (Save your scratch outline so you can work with it further after reading about the next stage in the writing process.)

Friendship (*journal writing*)
Malls (*mapping*)
Leisure (*freewriting*)
Television (*brainstorming*)
Required courses (*group brainstorming*)
Manners (*questioning*)

STAGE 2: IDENTIFY THE THESIS

The process of prewriting—discovering a limited subject and generating ideas about it—prepares you for the next stage in writing an essay: identifying the paper's *thesis*, or controlling idea. Presenting your opinion on a subject, the thesis should focus on an interesting and significant issue, one that engages your energies and merits your consideration. You may think of the thesis as the essay's hub—the central point around which all the other material revolves. Your thesis determines what does and does not belong in the essay. The thesis, especially when it occurs early in an essay, also helps focus the reader on the piece's central point.

Sometimes the thesis emerges early in the prewriting stage, particularly if a special angle on your limited topic sparks your interest or becomes readily apparent. Often, though, you'll need to do some work to determine your thesis. For some topics, you may need to do some library research. For others, the best way to identify a promising thesis is to look through your prewriting and ask yourself questions such as these: "What statement does all this prewriting support? What aspect of the limited subject is covered in most detail? What is the focus of the most provocative material?"

For a look at the process of finding the thesis within prewriting material, glance back at the scratch outline (page 30) that Harriet Davids prepared for the limited subject "The special problems that parents face raising children today." Harriet devised the following thesis to capture the focus of this prewriting: "Being a parent today is much more difficult than it was a generation ago." (The full outline for Harriet's paper appears on pages 52–53; the first draft on pages 67–68; the final draft on pages 75–77.)

Writing an Effective Thesis

What makes a thesis effective? Generally expressed in one or two sentences, a thesis statement often has two parts. One part presents your paper's *limited subject;* the other presents your *point of view,* or *attitude,* about that subject. Here are some examples of the way you might move from general subject to limited subject to thesis statement. In each thesis statement, the limited subject is underlined once and the attitude twice.

General Subject	Limited Subject	Thesis
Education	Computers in elementary school arithmetic classes	Computer programs in arithmetic can individualize instruction more effectively than the average elementary schoolteacher can.
Transportation	A metropolitan transit system	Although the city's transit system still has problems, it has become safer and more efficient in the last two years.

General Subject	Limited Subject	Thesis
Work	College internships	College internships provide valuable opportunities to students uncertain about what to do after graduation.
Our anti-child world	Special problems that parents face raising children today	Being a parent today is much more difficult than it was a generation ago.

(*Reminder:* The last of these thesis statements is the one that Harriet Davids devised for the essay she planned to write in response to the assignment on page 12. Harriet's prewriting appears on pages 24 and 30. You can find her first draft on pages 67–68.)

Because identifying your thesis statement is an important step in writing a sharply focused essay, you need to avoid three common problems that lead to an ineffective thesis.

Don't make an announcement.   Some writers use the thesis statement merely to announce the limited subject of their paper and forget to indicate their attitude toward the subject. Such statements are announcements of intent, not thesis statements.

Compare the following three announcements with the thesis statements beside them.

Announcements	Thesis Statements
My essay will discuss whether a student pub should exist on campus.	This college should not allow a student pub on campus.
Handgun legislation is the subject of this paper.	Banning handguns is the first step toward controlling crime in the United States.
I want to discuss cable television.	Cable television has not delivered on its promise to provide an alternative to network programming.

Don't make a factual statement.   Your thesis and thus your essay should focus on an issue capable of being developed. If a fact is used as a thesis, you have no place to go; a fact generally doesn't invite much discussion.

Notice the difference between these factual statements and thesis statements:

Factual Statements	Thesis Statements
Many businesses pollute the environment.	Tax penalties should be levied against businesses that pollute the environment.
Nowadays, many movies are violent.	Movie violence provides a healthy outlet for aggression.
The population of the United States is growing older.	The aging of the U.S. population will eventually create a crisis in the delivery of health-care services.

Don't make a broad statement.   Avoid stating your thesis in vague, general, or sweeping terms. Broad statements make it difficult for readers to grasp your essay's point. Moreover, if you start with a broad thesis, you're saddled with the impossible task of trying to develop a book-length idea in an essay that runs only several pages.

The following examples contrast statements that are too broad with thesis statements that are focused effectively

Broad Statements	Thesis Statements
Nowadays, high school education is often meaningless.	High school diplomas have been devalued by grade inflation.
Newspapers cater to the taste of the American public.	The success of *USA Today* indicates that people want newspapers that are easy to read and entertaining.
The computer revolution is not all that we have been led to believe it is.	Home computers are still an impractical purchase for many people.

You have considerable freedom regarding the placement of the thesis in an essay. The thesis is often stated near the beginning, but it may be delayed, especially if you need to provide background information before it can be understood. Sometimes the thesis is reiterated—using fresh words—in the essay's conclusion or elsewhere.

You may even leave the thesis unstated, relying on strong evidence to convey the essay's central idea.

One final point: Once you start writing your first draft, some feelings, thoughts, and examples may emerge that qualify, even contradict, your initial thesis. Don't resist these new ideas; they frequently move you toward a clearer statement of your main point. Remember, though, your essay must have a thesis. Without this central concept, you have no reason for writing.

Activities: Identify the Thesis

1. For each of the following limited subjects, four possible thesis statements are given. Indicate whether each is an announcement (*A*), a factual statement (*FS*), too broad a statement (*TB*), or an effective thesis (*OK*). Then, for each effective thesis, identify a possible purpose, audience, and tone.

   Limited Subject: The ethics of treating severely handicapped infants

   Some babies born with severe handicaps have been allowed to die.
   There are many serious issues involved in the treatment of handicapped newborns.
   The government should pass legislation requiring medical treatment for handicapped newborns.
   This essay will analyze the controversy surrounding the treatment of severely handicapped babies who would die without medical care.

   Limited Subject: Privacy and computerized records

   Computers raise some significant and crucial questions for all of us. Computerized records keep track of consumer spending habits, credit records, travel patterns, and other personal information. Computerized records have turned our private lives into public property.
   In this paper, the relationship between computerized records and the right to privacy will be discussed.

2. Each of the following sets lists the key points in an essay. Based on the information provided, prepare a possible thesis for each essay.

   Set A
   • One evidence of this growing conservatism is the reemerging popularity of fraternities and sororities.

- Beauty contests, ROTC training, and corporate recruiting—once rejected by students on many campuses—are again popular.
- Most important, many students no longer choose risky careers that enable them to contribute to society but select, instead, safe fields with moneymaking potential.

Set B
- We do not know how engineering new forms of life might affect the earth's delicate ecological balance.
- Another danger of genetic research is its potential for unleashing new forms of disease.
- Even beneficial attempts to eliminate genetic defects could contribute to the dangerous idea that only perfect individuals are entitled to live.

3. Following are four pairs of general and limited subjects. Generate an appropriate thesis statement for each pair. Select one thesis, and determine which pattern of development would support it most effectively. Use that pattern to draft a paragraph developing the thesis. (Save the paragraph so you can work with it further after reading about the next stage in the writing process.)

General Subject	Limited Subject
Psychology	The power struggles in a classroom
Health	Doctors' attitudes toward patients
U.S. politics	Television's coverage of presidential campaigns
Work	Minimum-wage jobs for young people

4. Return to the scratch outline you prepared for activity 3 on page 31. After examining the outline, identify a thesis that conveys the central idea behind most of the raw material. Then, ask others to evaluate your thesis in light of the material in the outline. Finally, keeping the thesis—as well as your purpose, audience, and tone—in mind, refine the scratch outline by deleting inappropriate items, adding relevant ones, and indicating where more material is needed. (Save your refined scratch outline and thesis so you can work with them further after reading about the next stage in the writing process.)

STAGE 3: SUPPORT THE THESIS WITH EVIDENCE

After identifying a preliminary thesis, you should develop the evidence needed to support the central idea. Such supporting material grounds your essay, showing readers you have good reason for feeling as you do about your subject. Your evidence also adds interest and color to your writing. In college essays of five hundred to fifteen hundred words, you usually need at least three major points of evidence to develop your thesis. These major points—each focusing on related but separate aspects of the thesis—eventually become the supporting paragraphs in the body of the essay.

What Is Evidence?

By *evidence,* we mean a number of different kinds of support. *Examples* are just one option. To develop your thesis, you might also include *reasons, facts, details, statistics, anecdotes,* and *quotations from experts.* Imagine you're writing an essay with the thesis, "People normally unconcerned about the environment can be galvanized to constructive action if they feel personally affected by an environmental problem." You could support this thesis with any combination of the following types of evidence:

- *Examples* of successful recycling efforts in several neighborhoods.
- *Reasons* why people got involved in a neighborhood recycling effort.
- *Facts* about other residents' efforts to preserve the quality of their well water.
- *Details* about the steps that people can take to get involved in environmental issues.
- *Statistics* showing the number of Americans concerned about the environment.
- An *anecdote* about your involvement in environmental efforts.
- A *quotation* from a well-known scientist about the impact that citizens can have on environmental legislation.

Where Do You Find Evidence?

Where do you find the examples, anecdotes, details, and other types of evidence needed to support your thesis? As you saw when you followed Harriet Davids's strategies for gathering material for an essay (pages 22–29), a good deal of evidence is generated during the prewriting stage. In this phase of the writing process, you tap into your personal experiences, draw upon other people's observations, perhaps interview a person with special knowledge about your subject. The library, with its abundant material, is another rich source of supporting evidence. In addition, the various patterns of development are a valuable source of evidence.

How the Patterns of Development Help Generate Evidence

On pages 27–28, we discussed the way patterns of development help generate material about a limited subject. The same patterns also help develop support for a thesis. The following chart shows how they generate evidence for this thesis: "To those who haven't done it, babysitting looks easy. In practice, though, babysitting can be difficult, frightening, even dangerous."

Pattern	Evidence Generated
Description	Details about a child who, while being babysat, was badly hurt.
Narration	Story about the time a friend babysat an ill child whose condition was worsened by the babysitter's actions.
Exemplification	Examples of potential babysitting problems: an infant rolls off a changing table; a toddler sticks objects in an electric outlet; a school-age child is bitten by a neighborhood dog.
Division-classification	A typical babysitting evening divided into stages: playing with the kids; putting them to bed; dealing with their nighttime fears once they're in bed.
	Classify kids' nighttime fears: of monsters under their beds; of bad dreams; of being abandoned by their parents.

Pattern	Evidence Generated
Process analysis	Step-by-step account of what a babysitter should do if a child becomes ill or injured.
Comparison-contrast	Contrast between two babysitters: one well-prepared, the other unprepared.
Cause-effect	Why children have temper tantrums; the effect of such tantrums on an unskilled babysitter.
Definition	What is meant by a *skilled* babysitter?
Argumentation-persuasion	A proposal for a babysitting training program.

(For more on ways to use the patterns of development in different phases of the writing process, see pages 27–28, 46–47, and 659–661.)

Characteristics of Evidence

No matter how it is generated, all types of supporting evidence share the characteristics described in the following sections. You should keep these characteristics in mind as you review your thesis and scratch outline. That way, you can make the changes needed to strengthen the evidence gathered earlier. As you'll see shortly, Harriet Davids focused on many of these issues as she worked with the evidence she collected during the prewriting phase.

The evidence is relevant and unified.   All the evidence in an essay must clearly support the thesis. It makes no difference how riveting material might be; if it doesn't *relate directly* to the essay's central point, the evidence should be eliminated. Irrelevant material can weaken your position by implying that no relevant support exists. It also distracts readers from your controlling idea, thus disrupting the paper's overall unity.

The following paragraph, taken from an essay illustrating recent changes in Americans' television-viewing habits, demonstrates the importance of unified evidence. The paragraph focuses on people's reasons for switching from network to cable television. As you'll see, the paragraph lacks unity because it contains points (underlined) unrelated to its main idea. Specifically, the comments about cable's foul language should be deleted. Although these observations bring up interesting points, they shift the paragraph's focus. If the writer wants to present a balanced view of the pros and cons of cable and network television, these points *should* be covered, but in *another paragraph.*

Nonunified Support

Many people consider cable TV an improvement over network television. For one thing, viewers usually prefer the movies on cable. Unlike network films, cable movies are often only months old, they have not been edited by censors, and they are not interrupted by commercials. Growing numbers of people also feel that cable specials are superior to the ones the networks grind out. Cable viewers may enjoy such pop stars as Billy Joel, Mariah Carey, or Chris Rock in concert, whereas the networks continue to broadcast tired Bob Hope variety shows and boring awards ceremonies. There is, however, one problem with cable comedians. The foul language many of them use makes it hard to watch these cable specials with children. The networks, in contrast, generally present "clean" shows that parents and children can watch together. Then, too, cable TV offers viewers more flexibility since it schedules shows at various times over the month. People working night shifts or attending evening classes can see movies in the afternoon, and viewers missing the first twenty minutes of a show can always catch them later. It's not surprising that cable viewership is growing while network ratings have taken a plunge.

Early in the writing process, Harriet Davids was aware of the importance of relevant evidence. Take a moment to compare Harriet's brainstorming (pages 24 and 26) and her scratch outline (page 30). Even though Harriet hadn't identified her thesis when she prepared the scratch outline, she realized she should delete a number of items on the reshaped version of her brainstorming—for example, the second item and third-to-last item ("prices of everything outrageous" and "schools doing too much"). Harriet eliminated these points because they weren't consistent with the focus of her limited subject.

The evidence is specific.   When evidence is vague and general, readers lose interest in what you're saying, become skeptical of your ideas' validity, and feel puzzled about your meaning. In contrast, *specific, concrete evidence* provides sharp *word pictures* that engage your readers, persuade them that your thinking is sound, and clarify meaning.

Consider, for example, the differences between the following two sentences: "The young man had trouble lifting the box out of an old car" and "Joe, only twenty years old but more than fifty pounds overweight, struggled to lift the heavy wooden crate out of the rusty, dented Chevrolet." The first sentence, filled with generalities, is fuzzy and imprecise while the second sentence, filled with specifics, is crisp and clear.

As the preceding sentences illustrate, three strategies can be used, singly or in combination, to make writing specific. First, you can provide answers to *who, which, what,* and similar *questions.* (The question "How does the car look?" prompts a change in which "an old car" becomes "a rusty, dented Chevrolet.") Second, you can use *vigorous verbs* ("had trouble lifting" becomes "struggled to lift"). Finally, you can replace *vague, abstract* nouns with *vivid, concrete* nouns or phrases ("the young man" becomes "Joe, only twenty years old but more than fifty pounds overweight").

Following are two versions of a paragraph from an essay about trends in the business community. Although both paragraphs focus on one such trend—flexible working hours—note how the first version's bland language fails to engage the reader and how its vague generalities leave the meaning unclear. What, for example, is meant by the term "flex-time scheduling"? The second paragraph answers this question (as well as several others) with clear specifics; it also uses strong, energetic language. As a result, the second paragraph is more informative and more interesting than the first.

Nonspecific Support

More and more companies have begun to realize that flex-time scheduling offers advantages. Several companies outside Boston have tried flex-time scheduling and are pleased with the way the system reduces the difficulties their employees face getting to work. Studies show that flex-time scheduling also increases productivity, reduces on-the-job conflict, and minimizes work-related accidents.

Specific Support

More and more companies have begun to realize that flex-time scheduling offers advantages over a rigid 9-to-5 routine. Along suburban Boston's Route 128, such companies as Compugraphics and Consolidated Paper now permit employees to schedule their arrival any time between 6 A.M. and 11 A.M. The corporations report that the number of rush-hour jams and accidents has fallen dramatically. As a result, employees no longer arrive at work weighed down by tension induced by choking clouds of exhaust fumes and the blaring horns of gridlocked drivers. Studies sponsored by the journal <u>Business Quarterly</u> show that this more mellow state of mind benefits corporations. Traffic-stressed employees begin their workday anxious and exasperated, still grinding their teeth at their fellow commuters, their frustration often spilling over into their performance at work. By contrast, stress-free employees work more productively and take fewer days off. They are more tolerant of coworkers and customers, and less likely to balloon minor irritations into major confrontations. Perhaps most importantly, employees arriving at work relatively free of stress can focus their attention on working safely. They rack up significantly fewer on-the-job accidents, such as falls and injuries resulting from careless handling of dangerous equipment. Flex-time improves employee well-being, and as well-being rises, so do company profits.

At this point, it will be helpful to compare once again Harriet Davids's brainstorming (page 24 and 26) and her scratch outline (page 30). Note the way she added new details to make her brainstorming more specific. For example, to the item "Distractions from homework," she added the new examples "video arcades," "fast-food restaurants," and "rock concerts." And, as you'll see when you read Harriet's first and final drafts (pages 67–68 and 75–77), she added many more vigorous specifics during later stages of the writing process.

The evidence is adequate.   Readers won't automatically accept your thesis; you need to provide *enough specific evidence* to support your viewpoint. On occasion, a single extended example will suffice. Generally, though, you'll need a variety of evidence: facts, examples, reasons, personal observations, expert opinion, and so on.

Following are two versions of a paragraph from a paper showing how difficult it is to get personal, attentive service nowadays at gas stations, supermarkets, and department stores. Both paragraphs focus on the problem at gas stations, but one paragraph is much more effective. As you'll see, the first paragraph starts with good specific support, yet fails to provide enough of it. The second paragraph offers additional examples, descriptive details, and dialogue—all of which make the writing stronger and more convincing.

Inadequate Support

Gas stations are a good example of this impersonal attitude. At many stations, attendants have even stopped pumping gas. Motorists pull up to a combination convenience store and gas island where an attendant is enclosed in a glass booth with a tray for taking money. The driver must get out of the car, pump the gas, and walk over to the booth to pay. That's a real inconvenience, especially when compared with the way service stations used to be run.

Adequate Support

Gas stations are a good example of this impersonal attitude. At many stations, attendants have even stopped pumping gas. Motorists pull up to a combination convenience store and gas island where an attendant is enclosed in a glass booth with a tray for taking money. The driver must get out of the car, pump the gas, and walk over to the booth to pay. Even at stations that still have "pump jockeys," employees seldom ask, "Check your oil?" or wash windshields, although they may grudgingly point out the location of the bucket and squeegee. And customers with a balky engine or a nonfunctioning heater are usually out of luck. Why? Many gas stations have eliminated on-duty mechanics. The skillful mechanic who could replace a belt or fix a tire in a few minutes has been replaced by a teenager in a jumpsuit who doesn't know a carburetor from a charge card and couldn't care less.

Now take a final look at Harriet Davids's scratch outline (page 30). You'll see that Harriet realized she needed more than one block of supporting material to develop her limited subject; that's why she identified four separate blocks of evidence (day care, homework distractions, sexual material, and dangers). When Harriet prepared her first and final drafts (pages 67–68 and 75–77), she decided to eliminate the material about day care. But she added so many more specific and dramatic details that her evidence was more than sufficient.

The evidence is accurate.   When you have a strong belief and want readers to see things your way, you may be tempted to overstate or downplay facts, disregard information, misquote, or make up details. Suppose you plan to write an essay making the point that dormitory security is lax. You begin supporting your thesis by narrating the time you were nearly mugged in your dorm hallway. Realizing the essay would be more persuasive if you also mentioned other episodes, you decide to invent some material. Perhaps you describe several supposed burglaries on your dorm floor or exaggerate the amount of time it took campus security to respond to an emergency call from a residence hall. Yes, you've supported your point—but at the expense of truth.

The evidence is representative.   Using representative evidence means that you rely on the typical, the usual, to show that your point is valid. Contrary to the maxim, exceptions don't prove the rule. Perhaps you plan to write an essay contending that the value of seat belts has been exaggerated. To support your position, you mention a friend who survived a head-on collision without wearing a seat belt. Such an example isn't representative because the facts and figures on accidents suggest your friend's survival was a fluke.

Borrowed evidence is documented.   If you include evidence from outside sources (books, articles, interviews), you need to acknowledge where that information comes from. If you don't, readers may consider your evidence nothing more than your point of view, or they may regard as dishonest your failure to cite your indebtedness to others for ideas that obviously aren't your own.

For help in documenting sources in brief, informal papers, turn to page 546. For information on acknowledging sources in longer, more formal papers, refer to the Appendix (pages 705–718).

Strong supporting evidence is at the heart of effective writing. Without it, essays lack energy and fail to convey the writer's perspective. Such lifeless writing is more apt to put readers to sleep than to engage their interest and convince them that the points being made are valid. Taking the time to accumulate solid supporting material is, then, a critical step in the writing process.

Activities: Support the Thesis With Evidence

1. Each of the following sets includes a thesis statement and four points of support. In each set, identify the one point that is off target.

   Set A

   Thesis: Colleges should put less emphasis on sports.

   Encourages grade fixing
   Creates a strong following among former graduates
   Distracts from real goals of education
   Causes extensive and expensive injuries

   Set B

   Thesis: The United States is becoming a homogenized country.

Regional accents vanishing
Chain stores blanket country
Americans proud of their ethnic identities
Metropolitan areas almost indistinguishable from one another

2. For each of the following thesis statements, develop three points of relevant support. Then use the patterns of development to generate evidence for each point of support.

   Thesis: The trend toward disposable, throwaway products has gone too far.
   Thesis: The local (or college) library fails to meet the needs of those it is supposed to serve.
   Thesis: Television portrays men as incompetent creatures.

3. Choose one of the following thesis statements. Then identify an appropriate purpose, audience, and tone for an essay with this thesis. Using freewriting, mapping, or the questioning technique, generate at least three supporting points for the thesis. Last, write a paragraph about one of the points, making sure your evidence reflects the characteristics discussed in these pages. Alternatively, you may go ahead and prepare the first draft of an essay having the selected thesis. (If you choose the second option, you may want to turn to page 66 to see a diagram showing how to organize a first draft.) Save whatever you prepare so you can work with it further after reading about the next stage in the writing process.

   - Winning the lottery may not always be a blessing.
   - All of us can take steps to reduce the country's trash crisis.
   - Drug education programs in public schools are (or are not) effective.

4. Select one of the following thesis statements. Then determine your purpose, audience, and tone for an essay with this thesis. Next, use the patterns of development to generate at least three supporting points for the thesis. Finally, write a paragraph about one of the points, making sure that your evidence demonstrates the characteristics discussed in these pages. Alternatively, you may go ahead and prepare a first draft of an essay having the thesis selected. (If you choose the latter option, you may want to turn to page 66 to see a diagram showing how to organize a first draft.) Save whatever you prepare so you can work with it further after reading about the next stage in the writing process.

   - Teenagers should (or should not) be able to obtain birth-control devices without their parents' permission.

> • The college's system for awarding student loans needs to be overhauled.
> • VCRs have changed for the worse (or the better) the way Americans entertain themselves.
>
> 5. Retrieve the paragraph you wrote in response to activity 3 on page 36. Keeping in mind the characteristics of effective evidence discussed in pages 39–44, make whatever changes are needed to strengthen the paragraph. (Save the paragraph so you can work with it further after reading about the next stage in the writing process.)
>
> 6. Look at the thesis and refined scratch outline you prepared in response to activity 4 on page 36. Where do you see gaps in the support for your thesis? By brainstorming with others, generate material to fill these gaps. If some of the new points generated suggest that you should modify your thesis, make the appropriate changes now. (Save this material so you can work with it further after reading about the next stage in the writing process.)

STAGE 4: ORGANIZE THE EVIDENCE

After you've generated supporting evidence, you're ready to *organize* that material. Even highly compelling evidence won't illustrate the validity of your thesis or achieve your purpose if readers have to plow through a maze of chaotic evidence. Some writers can move quickly from generating support to writing a clearly structured first draft. (They usually say they have sequenced their ideas in their heads.) Most, however, need to spend some time sorting out their thoughts on paper before starting the first draft; otherwise, they tend to lose their way in a tangle of ideas.

When moving to the organizing stage, you should have in front of you your scratch outline (see pages 29–30) and thesis plus any supporting material you've accumulated since you did your prewriting. To find a logical framework for all this material, you'll need to (1) determine which pattern of development is implied in your evidence, (2) select one of four basic approaches for organizing your evidence, and (3) outline your evidence. These issues are discussed in the pages ahead.

Use the Patterns of Development

As you saw on pages 27–28 and 38–39, the patterns of development (definition, narration, process analysis, and others) can help you develop prewriting material and generate evidence for a thesis. In the organizing stage, the patterns provide frameworks for presenting evidence in an orderly, accessible way. Here's how.

Each pattern of development has its own internal logic that makes it appropriate for some writing purposes but not for others. (You may find it helpful at this point to turn to pages 27–28 so you can review the broad purpose of each pattern.) Once you see which pattern (or combination of patterns) is implied by your purpose, you can block out your paper's general structure. Imagine that you're writing an essay *explaining why* some students drop out of college during the first semester. You might organize the essay around a three-part discussion of the key *causes* contributing to the difficulty that students have adjusting to college: (1) they miss friends and family, (2) they take inappropriate courses, and (3) they experience conflicts with roommates. As you can see, your choice of pattern of development significantly influences your essay's content and organization.

Some essays follow a single pattern, but most blend them, with a predominant pattern providing the piece's organizational framework. In our example essay, you might include a brief *description* of an overwhelmed first-year college student; you might *define* the psychological term "separation anxiety"; you might end the paper by briefly explaining a *process* for making students' adjustment to college easier. Still, the essay's overall organizational pattern would be *cause-effect* since the paper's primary purpose is to explain why students drop out of college. (For more information on the way patterns often blend in writing, see Chapter 12, "Combining the Patterns.")

Although writers often combine the patterns of development, your composition instructor may ask you to write an essay organized according to a single pattern. Such an assignment helps you understand a particular pattern's unique demands. Keep in mind, though, that most writing begins not with a specific pattern but with a specific *purpose*. The pattern or combination of patterns used to develop and organize an essay evolves out of that purpose.

Select an Organizational Approach

No matter which pattern(s) of development you select, you need to know four general approaches for organizing supporting evidence. These are explained below.

Chronological approach.   When an essay is organized *chronologically,* supporting material is arranged in a clear time sequence, usually starting with what happened first and ending with what happened last. Occasionally, chronological sequences can be rearranged to create flashback or flashforward effects, two techniques discussed in Chapter 4 on narration. Essays using narration (for example, an experience with prejudice) or process analysis (for instance, how to deliver an effective speech) are most likely to be organized chronologically. The paper on public speaking might use a time sequence to present its points: how to prepare a few days before the presentation is due; what to do right before the speech; what to concentrate on during the speech itself. (For examples of chronologically arranged student essays, turn to pages 154 and 334.)

Spatial approach.   When you arrange supporting evidence *spatially,* you discuss details as they occur in space, or from certain locations. This strategy is particularly appropriate for description. Imagine that you plan to write an essay describing the joyous times you spent as a child playing by a towering old oak tree in the neighborhood park. Using spatial organization, you start by describing the rich animal life (the plump earthworms, swarming anthills, and numerous animal tracks) you observed while hunkered down *at the base* of the tree. Next, you recreate the contented feeling you experienced sitting on a branch *in the middle* of the tree. Finally, you end by describing the glorious view of the world you had *from the top* of the tree.

Although spatial arrangement is flexible (you could, for instance, start with a description from the top of the tree), you should always proceed systematically. And once you select a particular spatial order, you should usually maintain that sequence throughout the essay; otherwise, readers may get lost along the way. (A spatially arranged student essay appears on page 90.)

Emphatic approach.   In *emphatic* order, the most compelling evidence is saved for last. This arrangement is based on the psychological principle that people remember best what they experience last. Emphatic order has built-in momentum because it starts with the least important point and builds to the most significant. This method is especially effective in argumentation-persuasion essays, in papers developed through examples, and in pieces involving comparison-contrast, division-classification, or causal analysis.

Consider an essay analyzing the negative effect that workaholic parents can have on their children. The paper might start with a brief discussion of relatively minor effects such as the family's eating mostly frozen or takeout foods. Paragraphs on more serious effects might follow: children get no parental help with homework; they try to resolve personal problems without parental advice. Finally, the essay might close with a detailed discussion of the most significant effect—children's lack of self-esteem because they feel unimportant in their parents' lives. (The student essays on pages 206, 397, and 496 all use an emphatic arrangement.)

Simple-to-complex approach.   A final way to organize an essay is to proceed from relatively *simple* concepts to more *complex* ones. By starting with easy-to-grasp, generally accepted evidence, you establish rapport with your readers and assure them that the essay is firmly grounded in shared experience. In contrast, if you open with difficult or highly technical material, you risk confusing and alienating your audience.

Assume you plan to write a paper arguing that your college has endangered students' health by not making an all-out effort to remove asbestos from dormitories and classroom buildings. It probably wouldn't be a good idea to begin with a medically sophisticated explanation of precisely how asbestos damages lung tissue. Instead, you might start with an observation that is likely to be familiar to your readers—one that is part of their everyday experience. You could, for example, open with a description of asbestos—as readers might see it—wrapped around air ducts and furnaces or used as electrical insulation and fireproofing material. Having provided a basic, easy-to-visualize description, you could then go on to explain the complicated process by which asbestos can cause chronic lung inflammation. (See page 447 for an example of a student essay using the simple-to-complex arrangement.)

Depending on your purpose, any one of these four organizational approaches might be appropriate. For example, assume that you planned to write an essay developing Harriet Davids's thesis: "Being a parent today is much more difficult than it was a generation ago." To emphasize that the various stages in children's lives present parents with different difficulties, you'd probably select a *chronological* sequence. To show that the challenges that parents face vary depending on whether children are at home, at school, or in the world at large, you'd probably choose a *spatial* sequence. To stress the range of problems that parents face (from less to more serious), you'd probably use an *emphatic* sequence. To illustrate today's confusing array of theories for raising children, you might take a *simple-to-complex* approach, moving from the basic to the most sophisticated theories.

Prepare an Outline

Do you, if asked to submit an outline, prepare it *after* you've written the essay? If you do, we hope to convince you that having an outline—a skeletal version of your paper—*before* you begin the first draft makes the writing process much more manageable. The outline helps you organize your thoughts beforehand, and it guides your writing as you work on the draft. Even though ideas continue to evolve during the draft, an outline clarifies how ideas fit together, which points are major, which should come first, and so on. An outline may also reveal places where evidence is weak, underscoring the need, perhaps, for more prewriting.

Like previous stages in the writing process, outlining is individualized. Some people prepare highly structured outlines; others make only a few informal jottings. Sometimes outlining will go quickly, with points falling easily into place; at other times you'll have to work hard to figure out how points are related. If that happens, be glad you caught the problem while outlining rather than while writing the first draft.

To prepare an effective outline, you should reread and evaluate your scratch outline and thesis as well as any other evidence you've generated since the prewriting stage. Then decide which pattern of development (description, cause-effect, and so on) seems to be suggested by your evidence. Also determine whether your evidence lends itself to a chronological, a spatial, an emphatic, or a simple-to-complex order. Having done all that, you're ready to identify and sequence your main and supporting points.

The amount of detail in an outline will vary according to the paper's length and the instructor's requirements. A scratch outline (like the one on page 30) is often sufficient, but for longer papers, you'll probably need a more detailed and formal outline. In such cases, the suggestions in the accompanying checklist will help you develop a sound plan. Feel free to modify these guidelines to suit your needs.

Outlining Checklist

- Write your purpose, audience, tone, and thesis at the top of the outlining page.

- Below the thesis, enter the pattern of development that seems to be implied by the evidence you've accumulated.
- Also record which of the four organizational approaches would be most effective in sequencing your evidence.
- Reevaluate your supporting material. Delete anything that doesn't develop the thesis or that isn't appropriate for your purpose, audience, and tone.
- Add any new points or material. Group related items together. Give each group a heading that represents a main topic in support of your thesis.
- Label these main topics with roman numerals (I, II, III, and so on). Let the order of the numerals indicate the best sequence.
- Identify subtopics and group them under the appropriate main topics. Indent and label these subtopics with capital letters (A, B, C, and so on). Let the order of the letters indicate the best sequence.
- Identify supporting points (often, reasons and examples) and group them under the appropriate subtopics. Indent and label these supporting points with Arabic numbers (1, 2, 3, and so on). Let the numbers indicate the best sequence.
- Identify specific details (secondary examples, facts, statistics, expert opinions, quotations) and group them under the appropriate supporting points. Indent and label these specific details with lowercase letters (a, b, c, and so on). Let the letters indicate the best sequence.
- Examine your outline, looking for places where evidence is weak. Where appropriate, add new evidence.
- Double-check that all main topics, subtopics, supporting points, and specific details develop some aspect of the thesis. Also confirm that all items are arranged in the most logical order.

The sample outline that follows develops the thesis "Being a parent today is much more difficult than it was a generation ago." You may remember that this is the thesis that Harriet Davids devised for the essay she planned to write in response to the assignment on page 12. Harriet's scratch list appears on page 26. When you compare Harriet's scratch list and outline, you'll find some differences. On the whole, the outline contains more specifics, but it doesn't include all the material in the scratch list. For example, after reconsidering her purpose, audience, tone, and thesis, Harriet decided to omit from her outline the section on day care and the points about rock concerts, MTV, rock posters, and AIDS.

The plan shown below is called a *topic outline* because it uses phrases, or topics, for each entry. For a lengthier or more complex paper, a *sentence outline* would be more appropriate.

Purpose: To inform

Audience: Instructor as well as class members, most of whom are 18-20 years old

Tone: Serious and straightforward

Thesis: Being a parent today is much more difficult than it was a generation ago.

Pattern of development: Exemplification

Organizational approach: Emphatic order

I. Distractions from homework
   A. At home
      1. Stereos, radios, tapes
      2. Television--esp. on MTV
      3. Computers
   B. Outside home
      1. Malls
      2. Video arcades
      3. Fast-food restaurants

II. Sexually explicit materials
   A. In print
      1. Sex magazines
         a. Playboy
         b. Penthouse
      2. Pornographic books
   B. In movies
      1. Seduction scenes
      2. Casual sex
   C. On television
      1. Soap operas
      2. R-rated comedians
      3. R-rated movies on cable
   D. Internet
      1. Easy-to-access adult chat rooms

2. Easy-to-access pornographic websites

III. Increased dangers
A. Drugs--peer pressure
B. Alcohol--peer pressure
C. Violent crimes against children

(If you'd like to see the first draft that resulted from Harriet's outline, turn to pages 67–68. Hints for moving from an outline to a first draft appear on pages 55–56.)

Before starting to write your first draft, show your outline to several people (your instructor, friends, classmates). Their reactions will indicate whether your proposed organization is appropriate for your thesis, purpose, audience, and tone. Their comments can also highlight areas needing additional work. After making whatever changes are needed, you're in a good position to go ahead and write the first draft of your essay.

Activities: Organize the Evidence

1. The thesis statement below is followed by a scrambled list of supporting points. Prepare an outline for a potential essay, making sure to distinguish between major and secondary points.

   Thesis: Our schools, now in crisis, could be improved in several ways.

   Certification requirements for teachers
   Schedules
   Teachers
   Longer school year
   Merit pay for outstanding teachers
   Curriculum
   Better textbooks for classroom use
   Longer school days
   More challenging content in courses

2. Assume you plan to write an essay based on the following brief outline, which consists of a thesis and several points of support. Determine which pattern of development (pages 46–47) you would probably use for the essay's overall framework. Also identify which organizational approach (pages 47–50) you would most likely adopt to sequence the points of support listed. Then, use one or more patterns of development to generate material to support those points. Having done that, review the material generated,

deleting, adding, combining, and arranging ideas in logical order. Finally, make an outline for the body of the essay. (Save your outline so you can work with it further after reading about the next stage in the writing process.)

Thesis: Friends of the opposite sex fall into one of several categories: the pal, the confidant, or the pest.

- Frequently, an opposite-sex friend is simply a "pal."
- Sometimes, though, a pal turns, step by step, into a confidant.
- If a confidant begins to have romantic thoughts, he or she may become a pest, thus disrupting the friendship.

3. Retrieve the writing you prepared in response to activity 3, 4, or 5 on pages 45–46. As needed, reshape that material, applying the organizational principles discussed in these pages. Be sure, for example, that you select the approach (chronological, spatial, emphatic, or simple-to-complex) that would be most appropriate, given your main idea, purpose, audience, and tone. (Save whatever you prepare so you can work with it further after reading about the next stage in the writing process.)

4. Look again at the thesis and scratch outline you refined and elaborated in response to activity 6 on page 46. Reevaluate this material by deleting, adding, combining, and rearranging ideas as needed. Also, keeping your purpose, audience, and tone in mind, consider whether a chronological, a spatial, an emphatic, or a simple-to-complex approach will be most appropriate. Now prepare an outline of your ideas. Finally, ask at least one person to evaluate your organizational plan. (Save your outline. After reading about the next stage in the writing process, you can use it to write the essay's first draft.)

STAGE 5: WRITE THE FIRST DRAFT

After prewriting, deciding on a thesis, and developing and organizing evidence, you're ready to write a *first draft*—a rough, provisional version of your essay. Because of your work in the preceding stages, the first draft may flow quite smoothly. But don't be discouraged if it doesn't. You may find that your thesis has to be reshaped, that a point no longer fits, that you need to return to a prewriting activity to generate additional material. Such stopping and starting is to be expected. Writing the first draft is a process of discovery, involving the continual clarification and refining of ideas.

How to Proceed

There's no single right way to prepare a first draft. Some writers rely heavily on their scratch lists or outlines; others glance at them only occasionally. Some people write the first draft in longhand; others use a typewriter or a computer.

However you choose to proceed, consider the following suggestions when moving from an outline or scratch list to a first draft:

- Make the outline's *main topics* (I, II, III) the *topic sentences* of the essay's supporting paragraphs. (Topic sentences are discussed later on page 57.)
- Make the outline's *subtopics* (A, B, C) the *subpoints* in each paragraph.
- Make the outline's *supporting points* (1, 2, 3) the key *examples* and *reasons* in each paragraph.
- Make the outline's *specific details* (a, b, c) the *secondary examples, facts, statistics, expert opinions,* and *quotations* in each paragraph.

(To see how one student, Harriet Davids, moved from outline to first draft, turn to pages 66–68.)
Although outlines and lists are valuable for guiding your work, don't be so dependent on them that you shy away from new ideas that surface during your writing of the first draft. If promising new thoughts pop up, jot them down in the margin. Then, at the appropriate point, go back and evaluate them: Do they support your thesis? Are they appropriate for your essay's purpose, audience, and tone? If so, go ahead and include the material in your draft.

It's easy to get bogged down while preparing the first draft if you try to edit as you write. Remember: A draft isn't intended to be perfect. For the time being, adopt a relaxed, noncritical attitude. Working as quickly as you can, don't stop to check spelling, correct grammar, or refine sentence structure. Save these tasks for later. One good way to help remind you that the first draft is tentative is to use scrap paper and pencil. Writing on alternate lines also underscores your intention to revise later on, when the extra space will make it easier to add and delete material. Similarly, writing on only one side of the paper can prove helpful if, during revision, you decide to move a section to another part of the paper.

What should you do if you get stuck while writing your first draft? Stay calm and try to write something—no matter how awkward or imprecise it may seem. Just jot a reminder to yourself in the margin ("Fix this," "Redo," or "Ugh!") to fine-tune the section later. Or leave a blank space to hold a spot for the right words when they finally break loose. It may also help to reread—out loud is best—what you've already written. Regaining a sense of the larger context is often enough to get you moving again. You might also try talking your way through a troublesome section. By speaking aloud, you tap your natural oral fluency and put it to work in your writing.

If a section of the essay strikes you as particularly difficult, don't spend time struggling with it. Move on to an easier section, write that, and then return to the challenging part. If you're still getting nowhere, take a break. Watch television, listen to music, talk with friends. While you're relaxing, your thoughts may loosen up and untangle the knotty section.

Because you read essays from beginning to end, you may assume that writers work the same way, starting with the introduction and going straight through to the conclusion. Often, however, this isn't the case. In fact, since an introduction depends so heavily on everything that follows, it's usually best to write the introduction *after* the essay's body.

When preparing your first draft, you may find it helpful to follow this sequence:

1. Write the supporting paragraphs.
2. Connect ideas in the supporting paragraphs.
3. Write the introduction.
4. Write the conclusion.
5. Write the title.

Write the Supporting Paragraphs

Drawn from the main sections in your outline or scratch list, each *supporting paragraph* should develop an aspect of your essay's thesis. Besides containing relevant, concrete, and sufficient evidence (see pages 37–44), a strong supporting paragraph is (1) often focused by a topic sentence and (2) organized around one or more patterns of development. We'll focus on both features in the pages ahead. As you read our discussion, though, keep in mind that you shouldn't expect your draft paragraphs to be perfect; you'll have a chance to revise them later on.

Use topic sentences.   Frequently, each supporting paragraph in an essay is focused by a *topic sentence* that functions as a kind of mini-thesis for the paragraph. Generally one or two sentences in length, the topic sentence usually appears at or near the beginning of the paragraph. However, it may also appear at the end, in the middle, or—with varied wording—several times within the paragraph.

Regardless of its length or location, the topic sentence states the paragraph's main idea. The other sentences in the paragraph provide support for this central point in the form of examples, facts, expert opinion, and so on. Like a thesis statement, the topic sentence *signals the paragraph's subject* and frequently *indicates the writer's attitude* toward that subject. In the topic sentences that follow, the subject of the paragraph is underlined once and the attitude toward that subject is underlined twice:

> Some students select a particular field of study for the wrong reasons.
> The ocean dumping of radioactive waste is a ticking time bomb.
> Several contemporary rock groups show unexpected sensitivity to social issues.
> Political candidates are sold like slickly packaged products.

As you work on the first draft, you may find yourself writing paragraphs without paying too much attention to topic sentences. That's fine, as long as you evaluate the paragraphs later on. When revising, you can provide a topic sentence for a paragraph that needs a sharper focus, recast a topic sentence for a paragraph that ended up taking an unexpected turn, even eliminate a topic sentence altogether if a paragraph's content is sufficiently unified to imply its point.

Use the patterns of development.   As you saw on pages 46–47, an entire essay can be organized around one or more patterns of development (narration, process analysis, definition, and so forth). These patterns can also provide the organizational framework for an essay's supporting paragraphs. Assume you're writing an article for your town newspaper with the thesis "Year-round residents of an ocean community must take an active role in safeguarding the seashore environment." Your supporting paragraphs could develop this thesis through a variety of patterns, with each paragraph's topic sentence suggesting a specific pattern or combination of patterns. For example, one paragraph might start with the topic sentence "In a nearby ocean community, signs of environmental danger are everywhere" and go on to *describe* a seaside town with polluted waters, blighted trees, and diseased marine life. The next paragraph might have the topic sentence "Fortunately, not all seaside towns are plagued by such environmental problems" and continue by *contrasting* the troubled community with another, more ecologically sound shore town. A later paragraph, focused by the topic sentence "Residents can get involved in a variety of pro-environment activities," might use *division-classification* to elaborate on activities at the neighborhood, town, and municipal levels.

Connect Ideas in the Supporting Paragraphs

While writing the supporting paragraphs, you can try to smooth out the progression of ideas within and between paragraphs. In a *coherent* essay, the relationship between points is clear; readers can easily follow the development of your thoughts. (Sometimes, working on coherence causes a first draft to get bogged down; if this happens, move on, and wait until the revision stage to focus on such matters.)

The following paragraph lacks coherence for two main reasons. First, it sequences ideas improperly. (The idea about the toll attendants' being cut off from coworkers is introduced, dropped, then picked up again. References to motorists are similarly scattered throughout the paragraph.) Second, it doesn't indicate how individual ideas are related. (What, for example, is the connection between drivers who pass by without saying anything and attendants who have to work at night?)

Incoherent Support

Collecting tolls on the turnpike must be one of the loneliest jobs in the world. Each toll attendant sits in his or her booth, cut off from other attendants. Many drivers pass by each booth. None stays long enough for a brief "hello." Most don't acknowledge the attendant at all. Many toll attendants work at night, pushing them "out of synch" with the rest of the world. And sometimes the attendants have to deal with rude drivers who treat them like non-people, swearing at them for the long lines at the tollgate. Attendants also dislike how cut off they feel from their coworkers. Except for infrequent breaks, they have little chance to chat with each other and swap horror stories--small pleasures that would make their otherwise routine jobs bearable.

Coherent Support

Collecting tolls on the turnpike must be one of the loneliest jobs in the world. First of all, although many drivers pass by the attendants, none stays long enough for more than a brief "hello." Most drivers, in fact, don't acknowledge the toll collectors at all, with the exception of those rude drivers who treat the attendants like non-people, swearing at them for the long lines at the tollgate. Then, too, many toll attendants work at night, pushing them further "out of synch" with the rest of the world. Worst of all, attendants say, is how isolated they feel from their coworkers. Each attendant sits in his or her booth, cut off from other attendants. Except for infrequent breaks, they have little chance to chat with each other and swap horror stories--small pleasures that would make their otherwise routine jobs bearable.

To avoid the kinds of problems found in the incoherent paragraph, use—as the revised version does—two key strategies: (1) a clearly *chronological, spatial, emphatic* (*"Worst of all,* attendants say . . ."), or *simple-to-complex* approach and (2) *signal devices* (*"First of all,* although many drivers pass by . . .") to show how ideas are connected. For a discussion of the four organizational approaches, see pages 47–50. The following paragraphs describe signal devices.

Once you determine a logical approach for presenting your points, you need to make sure readers can follow the progression of those points. Signal devices provide readers with cues, reminding them where they have been and indicating where they are going.

Aim to include some signals—however awkward or temporary—in your first draft. If you find you *can't*, that's probably a warning that your ideas may not be arranged logically. A light touch should be your goal with such signals. Too many call attention to themselves, making the essay mechanical and plodding. In any case, here are some signaling devices to consider:

1. Transitions.   Words and phrases that ease readers from one idea to another are called *transitions*. Among such signals are the following:

Time	Space	Addition	Examples
first	above	moreover	for instance
next	below	also	for example
now	next to	furthermore	to illustrate
finally	behind	in addition	specifically

Contrast		Comparison	Summary
but		similarly	therefore
however		also	thus
otherwise		likewise	in short
on the one/other hand		too	in conclusion

Here's an earlier paragraph from this chapter. Note how the italicized transitions show readers how ideas fit together.

> *After* you've generated supporting evidence, you're ready to organize that material. Even highly compelling evidence won't illustrate the validity of your thesis or achieve your purpose if the readers have to plow through a maze of chaotic evidence. Some writers can move quickly from generating support to writing a clearly structured first draft. (They usually say they have sequenced their ideas in their heads.) Most, *however,* need to spend some time sorting out their thoughts on paper before starting the first draft; *otherwise,* they tend to lose their way in a tangle of ideas.

2. Bridging sentences.   Although bridging sentences may be used within a paragraph, they are more often used to move readers from one paragraph to the next. Look again at the first sentence in the preceding paragraph. Note that the sentence consists of two parts: The first part reminds readers that the previous discussion focused on techniques for generating evidence; the second part tells readers that the focus will now be the organization of such evidence.

3. Repeated words, synonyms, and pronouns.   The repetition of important words maintains continuity, reassures readers that they are on the right track, and highlights key ideas. Synonyms—words similar in meaning to key words or phrases—also provide coherence, while making it possible to avoid unimaginative and tedious repetitions. Finally, pronouns (*he, she, it, they, this, that*) enhance coherence by causing readers to think back to the original word the pronoun replaces (antecedent). When using pronouns, however, be sure there is no ambiguity about antecedents.

Reprinted here is another paragraph from this chapter. Repeated words have been underlined once, synonyms underlined twice, and pronouns printed in italic type to illustrate how these techniques were used to integrate the paragraph's ideas.

> The process of prewriting—discovering a limited subject and generating ideas about *it*—prepares you for the next stage in writing an essay: identifying the paper's thesis or controlling idea. Presenting your opinion on a subject, the thesis should focus on an interesting and significant issue, *one* that engages your energies and merits your consideration. You may think of the thesis as the essay's hub—the central point around which all the other material revolves. Your thesis determines what does and does not belong in the essay. The thesis, especially when *it* occurs early in an essay, also helps focus the reader on the piece's central point.

Write the Introduction

Many writers don't prepare an introduction until they have started to revise; others feel more comfortable if their first draft includes in basic form all parts of the final essay. If that's how you feel, you'll probably write the introduction as you complete your first draft. No matter when you prepare it, keep in mind how crucial the introduction is to your essay's success. Specifically, the introduction serves three distinct functions: It arouses readers' interest, introduces your subject, and presents your thesis.

The length of your introduction will vary according to your paper's scope and purpose. Most essays you write, however, will be served best by a one- or two-paragraph beginning. To write an effective introduction, use any of the following methods, singly or in combination. The thesis statement in each sample introduction is underlined.

Broad Statement Narrowing to a Limited Subject

For generations, morality has been molded primarily by parents, religion, and schools. Children traditionally acquired their ideas about what is right and wrong, which goals are important in life, and how other people should be treated from these three sources collectively. But in the past few decades, a single force--television--has undermined the beneficial influence that parents, religion, and school have on children's moral development. Indeed, television often implants in children negative values about sex, work, and family life.

Brief Anecdote

At a local high school recently, students in a psychology course were given a hint of what it is like to be the parents of a newborn. Each "parent" had to carry a raw egg around at all times to symbolize the responsibilities of parenthood. The egg could not be left alone; it limited the "parents'" activities; it placed a fulltime emotional burden on "Mom" and "Dad." This class exercise illustrates a common problem facing the majority of new mothers and fathers. Most people receive little preparation for the job of being parents.

Idea That Is the Opposite of the One Developed

We hear a great deal about divorce's disastrous impact on children. We are deluged with advice on ways to make divorce as painless as possible for youngsters; we listen to heartbreaking stories about the confused, grieving children of divorced parents. Little attention has been paid, however, to a different kind of effect that divorce may have on children. Children from divorced families may become skilled manipulators, playing off one parent against the other, worsening an already painful situation.

Series of Short Questions

What happens if a child is caught vandalizing school property? What happens if a child goes for a joyride in a stolen car and accidentally hits a pedestrian? Should parents be liable for their children's mistakes? Should parents have to pay what might be hundreds of thousands of dollars in damages? Adults have begun to think seriously about such questions because the laws concerning the limits of parental responsibility are changing rapidly. With unfortunate frequency, courts have begun to hold parents legally and financially accountable for their children's misdeeds.

Quotation

Educator Neil Postman believes that television has blurred the line between childhood and adulthood. According to Postman, "All the secrets that a print culture kept from children . . . are revealed all at once by media that do not, and cannot, exclude any audience." <u>This media barrage of information, once intended only for adults, has changed childhood for the worse.</u>

Refutation of a Common Belief

Adolescents care only about material things; their lives revolve around brand-name sneakers, designer jeans, the latest fad in stereo equipment. They resist education, don't read, barely know who is president, mainline rock 'n' roll, experiment with drugs, and exist on a steady diet of Ring-Dings, nachos, and beer. This is what many adults, including parents, seem to believe about the young. <u>The reality is, however, that young people today show more maturity and common sense than most adults give them credit for.</u>

Dramatic Fact or Statistic

Seventy percent of the respondents in a poll conducted by columnist Ann Landers stated that if they could live their lives over, they would choose not to have children. This startling statistic makes one wonder what these people believed parenthood would be like. <u>Most parents, it seems, have unrealistic expectations about their children.</u> Parents want their children to accept their values, follow their paths, and succeed where they failed.

Introductory paragraphs sometimes end with a *plan of development:* a quick preview of the essay's major points in the order in which those points will be discussed. The plan of development may be part of the thesis (as in the first sample introduction) or it may immediately follow the thesis (as in the last sample introduction). Because the plan of development outlines the essay's organizational structure, it helps prepare the reader for the essay's progression of ideas. In a brief essay, readers can often keep track of the ideas without this extra help. In a longer paper, though, a plan of development can be an effective unifying device since it highlights the main ideas the essay will develop.

Write the Conclusion

You may have come across essays that ended with jarring abruptness because they had no conclusions at all. Other papers may have had conclusions, but they sputtered to a weak close, a sure sign that the writers had run out of steam and wanted to finish as quickly as possible. Just as satisfying closes are an important part of everyday life (we feel cheated if dinner doesn't end with dessert or if a friend leaves without saying goodbye), a strong conclusion is an important part of an effective essay. Generally one or two paragraphs in length, the conclusion should give the reader a feeling of completeness and finality. One way to achieve this sense of "rounding off" is to return to an image, idea, or anecdote from the introduction. Because people tend to remember most clearly the points they read last, the conclusion is also a good place to remind readers of your thesis. You may also use the conclusion to make a final point about your subject. Be careful, though, not to open an entirely new line of thought at the essay's close.

Illustrated briefly here are several strategies for writing sound conclusions. These techniques may be used singly or in combination. The first strategy, the summary conclusion, can be especially helpful in long, complex essays since readers may appreciate a review of your points. Tacked onto a short essay, though, a summary conclusion often seems boring and mechanical.

Summary

Contrary to what many adults think, most adolescents are not only aware of the important issues of the times but also deeply concerned about them. They are sensitive to the plight of the homeless, the destruction of the environment, and the pitfalls of rampant materialism. Indeed, today's young people are not less mature and sensible than their parents were. If anything, they are more so.

Prediction

The growing tendency on the part of the judicial system to hold parents responsible for the actions of their wayward children can have a disturbing impact on all of us. Parents will feel bitter toward their own children and cynical about a system that holds them accountable for the actions of minors. Children, continuing to escape the consequences of their actions, will become even more lawless and destructive. Society cannot afford two such possibilities.

Quotation

The comic W. C. Fields is reputed to have said, "Anyone who hates children and dogs can't be all bad." Most people do not share Fields's cynicism. Viewing childhood as a time of purity, they are alarmed at the way television exposes children to the seamy side of life, stripping youngsters of their innocence and giving them a glib sophistication that is a poor substitute for wisdom.

Statistic

Granted, divorce may, in some cases, be the best thing for families torn apart by parents who battle one another. However, in longitudinal studies of children from divorced families, psychologist Judith Wallerstein found that only 10 percent of the youngsters felt relief at their parents' divorce; the remaining 90 percent felt devastated. Such statistics surely call into question parents' claims that they are divorcing for their children's sake.

Recommendation or Call for Action

It is a mistake to leave parenting to instinct. Instead, we should make parenting skills a required course in schools. In addition, a nationwide hotline should be established to help parents deal with crises. Such training and continuing support would help adults deal more effectively with many of the problems they face as parents.

Write the Title

Some writers say that they began a certain piece with only a title in mind. But for most people, writing a title is a finishing touch. Although creating a title for your paper is usually one of the last steps in writing an essay, it shouldn't be done haphazardly. It may take time to write an effective title—one that hints at the essay's thesis and snares the reader's interest.

Good titles may make use of the following techniques: repetition of sounds ("Affirmative Action: The Price of Preference"); questions ("Are the Homeless Crazy?"), and humor ("How to Say Nothing in 500 Words"). More often, though, titles are straightforward phrases derived from the essay's subject or thesis: "Shooting an Elephant" and "TV Addiction," for example.

Pull It All Together

Now that you know how to prepare a first draft, you might find it helpful to examine the accompanying illustration to see how the different parts of a draft can fit together. Keep in mind that not every essay you write will take this shape. As your purpose, audience, and tone change, so will your essay's structure. An introduction or conclusion, for instance, may be developed in more than one paragraph; the thesis statement may be implied or delayed until the essay's middle or end; not all paragraphs may have topic sentences; and several supporting paragraphs may be needed to develop a single topic sentence. Even so, the basic format presented here offers a strategy for organizing a variety of writing assignments—from term papers to lab reports. Once you feel comfortable with the structure, you have a foundation on which to base your variations. (This book's student and professional essays illustrate some possibilities.) Even when using a specific format, you always have room to give your spirit and imagination free play. The language you use, the details you select, the perspective you offer are uniquely yours. They are what make your essay different from everyone else's.

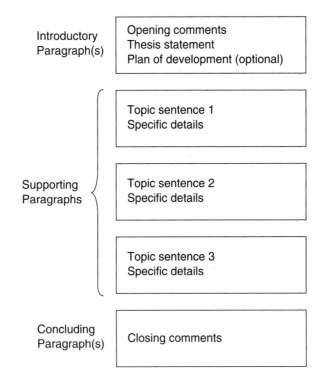

Introductory Paragraph(s)
- Opening comments
- Thesis statement
- Plan of development (optional)

Supporting Paragraphs
- Topic sentence 1
  Specific details
- Topic sentence 2
  Specific details
- Topic sentence 3
  Specific details

Concluding Paragraph(s)
- Closing comments

Sample First Draft

Here is the first draft of Harriet Davids's essay. (The assignment and prewriting for the essay appear on pages 22, 23–26, and 30.) Harriet wrote the draft in one sitting. Working at a computer, she started by typing her thesis at the top of the first page. Then, following the guidelines on page 55, she moved the material in her outline (pages 52–53) to her draft. Harriet worked rapidly; she started with the first body paragraph and wrote straight through to the last supporting paragraph.

By moving quickly, Harriet got down her essay's basic text rather easily. Once she felt she had captured in rough form what she wanted to say, she reread her draft to get a sense of how she might open and close the essay. Then she drafted her introduction and conclusion; both appear here, together with the body of the essay. The commentary following the draft will give you a clearer sense of how Harriet proceeded.

Challenges for Today's Parents
by Harriet Davids

Thesis: Being a parent today is much more difficult than it was a generation ago.

Raising children used to be much simpler in the '50s and '60s. I remember TV images from that era showing that parenting involved simply teaching kids to clean their rooms, do their homework, and _____(ADD SPECIFICS). But being a parent today is much more difficult because nowadays parents have to shield/protect kids from lots of things, like distractions from schoolwork, from sexual material, from dangerous situations.

Parents have to control all the new distractions/temptations that turn kids away from schoolwork. These days many kids have stereos, computers, and televisions in their rooms. Certainly, my girls can't resist the urge to listen to MTV and go online, especially if it's time to do homework. Unfortunately, though, kids aren't assigned much homework and what is assigned too often is busywork. And there are even more distractions outside the home. Teens no longer hang out/congregate on the corner where Dad and Mom can yell to them to come home and do homework. Instead they hang out at the mall, in video arcades, and fast-food restaurants. Obviously, parents and school can't compete with all this.

Also (WEAK TRANS.) parents have to help kids develop responsible sexual values even though sex is everywhere. Kids see sex magazines and dirty paperbacks in the corner store where they used to get candy and comic books. And instead of the artsy nude shots of the past, kids see ronchey (SP?), explicit shots in <u>Playboy</u> and <u>Penthouse</u>. And movies have sexy stuff in them today. Teachers seduce students and people treat sex casually/as a sport. Not exactly traditional values. TV is no better. Kids see soap-opera characters in bed and cable shows full of nudity by just flipping the dial (FIX). Even worse is what's on the Internet. Too easy for kids to access chat rooms and websites dealing with adult, sometimes pornographic material. The situation has gotten so out of hand that maybe the government should establish guidelines on what's permissible.

Worst of all are the life-threatening dangers that parents must help children fend off over the years. With older kids, drugs fall into place as a main concern (AWK). Peer pressure to try drugs is bigger (WRONG WORD) to kids than their parents' warnings. Other kinds of warnings are common when children are small. Then parents fear violence since news shows constantly report stories of little children being abused (ADD SPECIFICS). And when kids aren't much older, they have to resist the pressure to drink. Alcohol has always attracted kids, but nowadays they are drinking more and this can be deadly, especially when drinking is combined with driving (REDO).

Most adults love their children and want to be good parents. But it's difficult because the world seems stacked against young people. Even Holden Caufield (SP?) had trouble dealing with society's confusing pressures. Parents must give their children some freedom but not so much that the kids lose sight of what's important.

Commentary

As you can see, Harriet's draft is rough. Because she knew she would revise later on (page 69), she "zapped out" the draft in an informal, colloquial style. For example, she occasionally expressed her thoughts in fragments ("Not exactly traditional values"), relied heavily on "and" as a transition, and used slangy expressions such as "kids," "dirty paperbacks," and "lots of things." Similarly, rather than fine-tuning, Harriet simply used capital letters to type parenthetic notes to herself: "REDO" or "FIX" to signal awkward sentences; "ADD SPECIFICS" to mark overly general statements; "WRONG WORD" after an imprecise word; "SP?" to remind herself to check spelling in the dictionary; "WEAK TRANS." to indicate where a stronger signaling device was needed. Note, too, that she used slashes between alternative word choices and left a blank space when wording just wouldn't come. (Harriet's final draft appears on pages 75–77.)

Writing a first draft may seem like quite a challenge, but the tips offered in these pages should help you proceed with confidence.

Indeed, as you work on the draft, you may be surprised how much you enjoy writing. After all, this is your chance to get down on paper something you want to say.

Activities: Write the First Draft

1. Retrieve the writing you prepared in response to activity 3 on page 54. Applying the principles just presented, rework that material. If you wrote a single paragraph earlier, expand the material into a full essay draft. If you prepared an essay, strengthen what you wrote. In both cases, remember to consider your purpose, audience, and tone as you write the body of the essay as well as its introduction and conclusion. (Save your draft so you can rework it even further after reading about the next stage in the writing process.)

2. Referring to the outline you prepared in response to activity 2 or activity 4 on pages 53–54, draft the body of your essay, making your evidence as strong as possible. As you work, keep your purpose, audience, and tone in mind. After reading what you've prepared, go ahead and draft a rough introduction, conclusion, and title. Finally, ask at least one other person to react to your draft by listing its strengths and weaknesses. (Save the draft so you can work with it further after reading about the next stage in the writing process.)

STAGE 6: REVISE THE ESSAY

By now, you've probably abandoned any preconceptions you might have had about good writers sitting down and creating a finished product in one easy step. Alexander Pope's comment that "true ease in writing comes from art, not chance" is as true today as it was more than two hundred years ago. Writing that seems effortlessly clear is often the result of sustained work, not of good luck or even inborn talent. And much of this work takes place during the final stage of the writing process when ideas, paragraphs, sentences, and words are refined and reshaped.

Professional writers—novelists, journalists, textbook authors— seldom submit a piece of writing that hasn't been revised. They recognize that rough, unpolished work doesn't do them justice. What's more, they often look forward to revising. Columnist Ellen Goodman puts it this way: "What makes me happy is rewriting. . . . It's like cleaning house, getting rid of all the junk, getting things in the right order, tightening up."

In a sense, revision occurs throughout the writing process: At some earlier stage, you may have dropped an idea, overhauled your thesis, or shifted paragraph order. What, then, is different about the rewriting that occurs in the revision stage? The answer has to do with the literal meaning of the word *revision*—to resee, or to see again. Genuine revision involves casting clear eyes on your work, viewing it as though you're a reader rather than the writer. Revision means that you go through your paper looking for trouble, ready to pick a fight with your own writing. And then you must be willing to sit down and make the changes needed for your writing to be as effective as possible.

Revision is not, as some believe, simply touch-up work—changing a sentence here or a word there, eliminating spelling errors, typing a neat final copy. Revision means cutting deadwood, rearranging paragraphs, substituting new words for old ones, recasting sentences, improving coherence, even generating new material when appropriate. Because such work is challenging, you may resist revision or feel shaky about how to proceed.

Strategies to Make Revision Easier

The following pointers should help get you going if you balk at or feel overwhelmed by revising.

- *Set your draft aside for a while* before revising. When you pick up your paper again, you'll have a fresh, more objective point of view.
- *Work from typed material* whenever possible. Having your essay in neutral typed letters instead of in your own familiar writing helps you see the paper impartially, as if someone else had written it. Each time you make major changes, try to retype that section so that you can see it anew.
- *Read your draft aloud* as often as you can. Hearing how your writing sounds helps you pick up problems that passed you by before: places where sentences are awkward, meaning is ambiguous, words are imprecise. Even better, have another person read aloud to you what you have written. If the reader slows to a crawl over a murky paragraph or trips over a convoluted sentence, you know where you have to do some rewriting.

- *Participate in peer review.* Many instructors include in-class or at-home peer review as a regular part of a composition course. Peer review—the critical reading of another person's writing with the intention of suggesting changes—accomplishes several important goals. First, peer review helps you gain a more objective perspective on your work. When you write something, you're often too close to what you've prepared to evaluate it fairly; you may have trouble seeing where the writing is strong and where it needs to be strengthened. Peer review supplies the fresh, neutral perspective you need. Second, reviewing your classmates' work broadens your own composing options. You may be inspired to experiment with a technique you admired in a classmate's writing but wouldn't have thought of on your own. Finally, peer review trains you to be a better reader and critic of your *own* writing. When you get into the habit of critically reading other students' writing, you become more adept at critiquing your own.

  An important note: Preparing a helpful peer review is a skill that takes time to develop. At first, you, like many students, may be too easy or too critical. Effective peer review calls for rigor and care; you should give classmates the conscientious feedback that you hope for in return. Peer review also requires tact and kindness; feedback should always be constructive and include observations about what works well in a piece of writing. People have difficulty mustering the energy to revise if they feel there's nothing worth revising.

  If your instructor doesn't require peer review, you can set up peer review sessions on your own, adapting the suggestions here to fit your needs. Start by selecting readers who are objective (not a love-struck admirer or doting grandparent) and skilled enough to provide useful commentary. To ensure that you leave peer review sessions with specific observations about what does and doesn't work in your writing, give your readers a clear sense of what you want from them. If you simply ask, "How's this?" you may receive a vague comment like "It's not very effective." What you want are concrete observations and suggestions: "I'm confused because what you say in the fifth sentence contradicts what you say in the second."

To promote such specific responses, ask your readers targeted (preferably written) questions like "I'm having trouble moving from my second to my third point. How can I make the transition smoother?" Such questions require more than "yes" or "no" responses; they encourage readers to dig into your writing where you sense it needs work. You may develop your own questions, or you may adapt the checklist on pages 73–75 and at the front of the book. (If it's feasible, encourage readers to *write* their responses to your questions.)

If you're most concerned about your draft's overall meaning (pages 73–74), readers don't necessarily need a copy of your essay. The draft can be read aloud so everyone can hear it. However, if you want feedback on individual paragraphs (page 74) or on specific sentences and words (pages 74–75), you should supply readers with copies of your draft.

- *Evaluate and respond to peer review.* Accepting criticism isn't easy (even if you asked for it), and not all peer reviewers will be diplomatic. Even so, try to listen with an open mind to those giving you feedback. Take notes on their oral observations and/or have them fill out the checklist described above. Later, when you're ready to revise your paper, reread your notes. Which reviewer remarks seem valid? Which don't? Rank the problems and solutions that your reviewers identified, designating the most critical as number 1. Based on the peer feedback, enter your own notes for revising in the margins of a clean copy of your draft. This way, you'll know exactly what changes need to be made in your draft as you proceed. Then, keeping the problems and remedies in mind, start revising. If you've been working on a computer, type in your changes, or handwrite changes directly on the draft above the appropriate line. (Rework extensive sections on a separate piece of paper.) When revising, always keep in mind that you may not agree with every reviewer suggestion. That's fine. It's *your* paper, and it's *your* decision to implement or reject the suggestions made by your peers.

- *Evaluate and respond to instructor feedback.* Most likely, your peers won't be the only ones giving you feedback. Your instructor will also react to your early or final draft. Like many students, you may be tempted to look only briefly at your instructor's comments. Perhaps you've "had it" with the essay and don't want to think about revising it to reflect the instructor's remarks. And if there's a grade on the essay, you may think that's the only thing that counts. But remember: Although grades are important, comments are even more so. They can help you *improve* your writing—if not in this paper, then in the next one. If you don't understand or agree with the instructor's observations, don't hesitate to request a conference. Getting together gives both you and the instructor a chance to clarify your respective points of view.

- *View revision as a series of steps.* Don't try to tackle all of a draft's problems at once; instead, proceed step by step. (The feedback chart and annotation system described above will help you do just that.) Whenever possible, read your draft several times, each time focusing on different issues and asking yourself different questions. Move from a broad view of the draft to an up close look at its mechanics.

The following checklist describes a number of questions you and your readers can ask when moving through the various steps in the revising process. (To see how one student, Harriet Davids, used the checklist when revising, turn to pages 79–80.) Keep in mind, though, that there are no hard-and-fast rules about the revision steps outlined here. Everyone approaches revision differently. There are bound to be occasions when you have time for only one quick pass over a draft. And with experience, you'll learn how to streamline the process so you can focus on the most critical issues for a particular piece of writing. Feel free, then, to adapt our suggestions to your individual needs.

Peer Review/Revision Checklist

First Step: Revise Overall Meaning and Structure

- Considering the essay's purpose, audience, and tone (pages 19–21), in what ways does or doesn't the paper accomplish what was intended?
- What is the essay's thesis (pages 32–35)? Is it stated explicitly, or is it implied? If the perceived thesis isn't what was intended, what changes need to be made?
- What are the essay's main points of support (pages 37–38)? If any of these stray from or contradict the thesis (pages 39–40), what changes need to be made?

- Are the main points arranged in a chronological, spatial, emphatic, or simple-to-complex sequence (pages 47–49)? How does this organizational format reinforce the thesis?
- Which patterns of development (pages 46–47) provide the essay's organizational framework? How do these patterns reinforce the thesis?

Second Step: Revise Paragraph Development

- Where in each paragraph does support seem irrelevant, vague, insufficient, inaccurate, or nonrepresentative (pages 39–44)? What could be done to remedy these problems?
- By what organizational principles (pages 47–49) are the ideas in each paragraph arranged? Why is this the most effective arrangement?
- What signal devices (pages 59–61) are used to connect ideas within and between paragraphs? Where are there too few signals or too many?
- What strategies are used to open (pages 61–63) and close (pages 63–65) the essay? How could the introduction and conclusion be made more effective?

Third Step: Revise Sentences and Words

- Which sentences seem inconsistent with the essay's intended tone (pages 20–21)? How could the problem be corrected?
- Where does sentence structure become monotonous and predictable (pages 90 and 152)? How could a different sentence pattern add variety?
- Which words are vague and overly general (pages 88–90 and 150–152)? How could the language be made more vigorous and concrete?
- Where does gender-biased language (pages 726–727) appear? How could the problem be eliminated?

Fourth Step: Proofread for Grammar, Punctuation, and Typing Errors

- A note about proofreading: Although proofing seems to involve relatively minor matters, an accumulation of small errors—misspellings, typos, misplaced commas—can distract readers and sabotage an otherwise strong essay. So before handing in the final draft of your essay, proofread it closely, keeping a dictionary and English handbook nearby. When proofing, people tend to see what they think is on the page rather than what really is there. Reading the essay out loud and backwards, starting with the last word first, can highlight errors that otherwise might slip by.

STUDENT ESSAY

In this chapter, we've taken you through the various stages in the writing process. You've seen how Harriet Davids used prewriting (pages 23–26 and 30) and outlining (pages 52–54) to arrive at her first draft (pages 67–68). In the following pages, you'll look at Harriet's final draft—the paper she submitted to her instructor.

Harriet, a thirty-eight-year-old college student and mother of two teenagers, wanted to write an informative paper with a straightforward, serious tone. While preparing her essay, she kept in mind that her audience would include her course instructor as well as her classmates, many of them considerably younger than she. This is the assignment that prompted Harriet's essay:

> Goodman implies that, in some ways, today's world is hostile to children. Do you agree? Drawing upon but not limiting yourself to the material in your pre-reading journal, write an essay in which you support or reject this viewpoint.

Harriet's essay is annotated so that you can see how it illustrates the essay format described on page 66. As you read her essay, try to determine how well it reflects the principles of effective writing. The commentary following the paper will help you look at the essay more closely and give you some sense of the way Harriet went about revising her first draft.

Challenges for Today's Parents
by Harriet Davids

Introduction	Reruns of situation comedies from the 1950s and early 1960s dramatize the kinds of problems that parents used to have with their children. The Cleavers scold Beaver for not washing his hands before dinner; the Andersons ground Bud for not doing his	1

homework; the Nelsons dock little Ricky's allowance because he keeps forgetting to clean his room. But times have changed dramatically. Being a parent today is much more difficult than it was a generation ago. Parents nowadays must protect their children from a growing number of distractions, from sexually explicit material, and from life-threatening situations.

Today's parents must try, first of all, to control all the new distractions that tempt children away from schoolwork. At home, a child may have a room furnished with a stereo, television, and computer. Not many young people can resist the urge to listen to CDs, go online, play computer games, or watch MTV--especially if it is time to do schoolwork. Outside the home, the distractions are even more alluring. Children no longer "hang out" on a neighborhood corner within earshot of Mom or Dad's reminder to come in and do homework. Instead, they congregate in vast shopping malls, buzzing video arcades, and gleaming fast-food restaurants. Parents and school assignments have obvious difficulty competing with such enticing alternatives.

Besides dealing with these distractions, parents have to shield their children from a flood of sexually explicit materials. Today, children can find sex magazines and pornographic paperbacks in the same corner store that once offered only comics and candy. Children will not see the fuzzily photographed nudes that a previous generation did but will encounter the hard-core raunchiness of Playboy or Penthouse. Moreover, the movies young people attend often focus on highly sexual situations. It is difficult to teach children traditional values when films show teachers seducing students and young people treating sex as a casual sport. Unfortunately, television, with its often heavily sexual content, is no better. With just a flick of the dial, children can see soap-opera stars cavorting in bed or watch cable programs where nudity is common. But the sexually graphic content of TV shows is nothing compared to the seamy material on the Internet. Many parents report that their children, sometimes without intending to, access pornographic chat rooms and websites that haunt the youngsters for months afterward.

Margin annotations:

- Thesis
- Plan of development
- First supporting paragraph
- Topic sentence
- Second supporting paragraph
- Topic sentence with link to previous paragraph

Paragraph numbers: 2, 3

Third supporting paragraph

Topic sentence with emphasis signal

Most disturbing to parents today, however, is the increase in life-threatening dangers that face young people. When children are small, parents fear that their youngsters may be victims of violence. Every news program seems to carry a report about a mass murderer who preys on young girls, a deviant who has buried six boys in his cellar, or an organized child pornography ring that molests preschoolers. When children are older, parents begin to worry about their kids' use of drugs. Peer pressure to experiment with drugs is often stronger than parents' warnings. This pressure to experiment can be fatal. Finally, even if young people escape the hazards associated with drugs, they must still resist the pressure to drink. Although alcohol has always held an attraction for teenagers, reports indicate that they are drinking more than ever before. As many parents know, the consequences of this attraction can be deadly--especially when drinking is combined with driving.

Conclusion

References to TV shows recall introduction

Within one generation, the world as a place to raise children has changed dramatically. One wonders how yesterday's parents would have dealt with today's problems. Could the Andersons have kept Bud away from MTV? Could the Nelsons have shielded little Ricky from sexually explicit material on the Internet? Could the Cleavers have protected Beaver from drugs and alcohol? Parents must be aware of all these distractions and dangers yet be willing to give their children the freedom they need to become responsible adults. It is not an easy task.

COMMENTARY

Introduction and thesis.   The opening paragraph attracts readers' interest by recalling several vintage television shows that have almost become part of our cultural heritage. Harriet begins with these examples from the past because they offer such a sharp contrast to the present, thus underscoring the idea expressed in her *thesis:* "Being a parent today is much more difficult than it was a generation ago." Opening in this way, with material that serves as a striking contrast to what follows, is a common and effective strategy. Note, too, that Harriet's thesis states the paper's subject (being a parent) as well as her attitude toward the subject (the job is more demanding than it was years ago).

Plan of development.   Harriet follows her thesis with a *plan of development* that anticipates the three major points to be covered in the essay's supporting paragraphs. Unfortunately, this particular plan of development is somewhat mechanical, with the major points being trotted past the reader in one long, awkward sentence. To deal with the problem, Harriet could have rewritten the sentence or eliminated the plan of development altogether, ending the introduction with her thesis.

Patterns of development.   Although Harriet develops her thesis primarily through *examples,* she also draws on two other patterns of development. The whole paper implies a *contrast* between the way life is now and the way it used to be. The essay also contains an element of *causal analysis* since all the factors that Harriet cites affect children and the way they are raised.

Purpose, audience, and tone.   Given the essay's *purpose* and *audience,* Harriet adopts a serious *tone,* providing no-nonsense evidence to support her thesis. But assume she had been asked by her daughters' school newspaper to write a humorous column about the trials and tribulations that parents face raising children. Aiming for a different tone, purpose, and audience, Harriet would have taken another approach. Drawing on her experience as a mother of two teenage daughters, she might have confessed how she survives MTV's flash and dazzle, as well as the din of stereos blasting rock music at all hours: she stuffs her ears with cotton, hides her daughters' tapes, and cuts off the electricity. This material—with its personalized perspective, exaggeration, and light tone—would be appropriate.

Organization.   Structuring the essay around a series of *relevant* and *specific examples,* Harriet uses *emphatic order* to sequence the paper's three main points: that a growing number of distractions, sexually explicit materials, and life-threatening situations make parenting difficult nowadays. The third supporting paragraph begins with the words "Most disturbing to parents today . . . ," signaling that Harriet feels particular concern about the physical dangers children face. Moreover, she uses basic organizational strategies to sequence the supporting examples within each paragraph. The details in the first supporting paragraph are organized *spatially*, starting with distractions at home and moving to those outside the home. The second supporting paragraph arranges examples *emphatically*. Harriet starts with sexually explicit publications and ends with the "seamy material on the Internet," which is even more disturbing than TV's "heavily sexual content." The third and final supporting paragraph is organized *chronologically*; it begins by discussing dangers to small children and concludes by talking about teenagers.

The essay also displays Harriet's familiarity with other kinds of organizational strategies. Each supporting paragraph opens with a *topic sentence*. Further, *signal devices* are used throughout the paper to show how ideas are related to one another: *transitions* ("Instead, they congregate in vast shopping malls"; "Moreover, the movies young people attend often focus on highly sexual situations"); *repetition* ("sexual situations" and "sexual content"); *synonyms* ("distractions . . . enticing alternatives" and "life-threatening . . . fatal"); *pronouns* ("young people . . . they"); and *bridging sentences* ("Besides dealing with these distractions, parents have to shield their children from a flood of sexually explicit material").

Two minor problems.   Harriet's efforts to write a well-organized essay result in a somewhat predictable structure. It might have been better had she rewritten one of the paragraphs, perhaps embedding the topic sentence in the middle of the paragraph or saving it for the end. Similarly, Harriet's signal devices are a little heavy-handed. Even so, an essay with a sharp focus and clear signals is preferable to one with a confusing or inaccessible structure. As she gains more experience, Harriet can work on making the structure of her essays more subtle.

Conclusion.   Harriet brings the essay to a satisfying *close* by reminding readers of the paper's central idea and three main points. The final paragraph also extends the essay's scope by introducing a new but related issue: that parents have to strike a balance between their need to provide limitations and their children's need for freedom.

Revising the first draft.   With the help of several classmates, Harriet reworked her essay a number of times. Using the checklist on pages 73–75 to focus their feedback, Harriet's revising team offered various suggestions to strengthen the paper. To get a sense of Harriet's revising process, compare the final version of her conclusion (page 77) with the original version reprinted here.

Original Version of Conclusion

Most adults love their children and want to be good parents. But it's difficult because the world seems stacked against young people. Even Holden Caulfield had trouble dealing with society's pressures. Parents must give their children some freedom but not so much that kids lose sight of what's important.

As soon as Harriet heard her paper read aloud during a group session, she realized the conclusion didn't work at all, but she wisely waited to rework the conclusion until after she had fine-tuned the rest of the essay. At that point, she made marginal annotations summarizing the problems that she and her editing group detected in the conclusion. Together, they identified three problems, numbered in order of importance. First, the conclusion seemed tacked on, rather like a tired afterthought. Second, the allusion to *The Catcher in the Rye* misrepresented the essay's focus since Harriet discusses children of all ages, not just teens. Third, the first sentence in the conclusion was bland and boring.

Keeping these points in mind, Harriet decided to scrap her original conclusion. Working at a word processor, she prepared a much stronger concluding paragraph. Besides eliminating the distracting reference to Holden Caulfield, she replaced the shopworn opening sentence ("Most adults love their children . . . ") with three interesting and rhythmical questions ("Could the Andersons . . . ? Could the Nelsons . . . ? Could the Cleavers . . . ?"). Because these questions recall the essay's main points and echo the introduction's reference to vintage television shows, they help unify Harriet's paper and bring it to a satisfying close.

These are just a few of the changes Harriet made when reworking her essay. Realizing that writing is a process, she left herself enough time to revise. She was gratified by her classmates' responses to what she had written and pleased by the lively discussion her essay provoked. Early in her composition course, Harriet learned that attention to the various stages in the writing process yields satisfying results, for writer and reader alike.

Activity: Revise the Essay

Return to the draft you wrote in response to either activity 1 or activity 2 on page 69. Also look at any written feedback you received on the draft. To identify any further problems in the draft, get together with several people (classmates, friends, or family members) and request that one of them read the draft aloud to you. Then ask your audience focused questions about the areas you sense need work, or use the checklist on pages 73–75 to focus the feedback. In either case, summarize and rank the comments on a feedback chart or in marginal annotations. Then, using the comments as a guide, go ahead and revise the draft. Either type a new version or do your revising by hand, perhaps on a photocopy of the draft. Don't forget to proofread closely before submitting the paper to your instructor.

3

DESCRIPTION

WHAT IS DESCRIPTION?

All of us respond in a strong way to sensory stimulation. The sweet perfume of a candy shop takes us back to childhood; the blank white walls of the campus infirmary remind us of long vigils at a hospital where a grandmother lay dying; the screech of a subway car sets our nerves on edge.

Without any sensory stimulation, we sink into a less-than-human state. Neglected babies, left alone with no human touch, no colors, no lullabies, become withdrawn and unresponsive. And prisoners dread solitary confinement, knowing that the sensory deprivation can be unbearable, even to the point of madness.

Because sensory impressions are so potent, descriptive writing has a unique power and appeal. *Description* can be defined as the expression, in vivid language, of what the five senses experience. A richly rendered description freezes a subject in time, evoking sights, smells, sounds, textures, and tastes in such a way that readers become one with the writer's world.

HOW DESCRIPTION FITS YOUR
PURPOSE AND AUDIENCE

Description can be a supportive technique that develops part of an essay, or it can be the dominant technique used throughout an essay. Here are some examples of the way description can help you meet the objective of an essay developed chiefly through another pattern of development:

- In a *causal analysis* showing the *consequences* of pet overpopulation, you might describe the desperate appearance of a pack of starving stray dogs.
- In an *argumentation-persuasion* essay urging more rigorous handgun control, you might start with a description of a violent family confrontation that ended in murder.
- In a *process analysis* explaining the pleasure of making ice cream at home, you might describe the beauty of an old-fashioned, hand-cranked ice-cream maker.
- In a *narrative essay* recounting a day in the life of a street musician, you might describe the musician's energy and the joyous appreciation of passersby.

In each case, the essay's overall purpose would affect the amount of description needed.

Your readers also influence how much description to include. As you write, ask yourself, "What do my particular readers need to know to understand and experience keenly what I'm describing? What descriptive details will they enjoy most?" Your answers to these and similar questions will help you tailor your description to specific readers. Consider an article intended for professional horticulturists; its purpose is to explain a new technique for controlling spider mites. Because of readers' expertise, there would be little need for a lengthy description of the insects. Written for a college newspaper, however, the article would probably provide a detailed description of the mites so student gardeners could distinguish between the pesky parasites and flecks of dust.

While your purpose and audience define *how much* to describe, you have great freedom deciding *what* to describe. Description is especially suited to objects (your car or desk, for example), but you can also describe a person, an animal, a place, a time, and a phenomenon or concept. You might write an effective description about a friend who runs marathons (person), a pair of ducks who return each year to a neighbor's pond (animals), the kitchen of a fast-food restaurant (place), a period when you were unemployed (time), the "fight or flight" response to danger (phenomenon or concept).

Description can be divided into two types: *objective* and *subjective*. In an objective description, you describe the subject in a straightforward and literal way, without revealing your attitude or feelings. Reporters, as well as technical and scientific writers, specialize in objective description; their jobs depend on their ability to detail experiences without emotional bias. For example, a reporter may write an unemotional account of a township meeting that ended in a fistfight. Or a marine biologist may write a factual report describing the way sea mammals are killed by the plastic refuse (sandwich wrappings, straws, fishing lines) that humans throw into the ocean.

In contrast, when writing a subjective description, you convey a highly personal view of your subject and seek to elicit a strong emotional response from your readers. Such subjective descriptions often take the form of reflective pieces or character studies. For example, in an essay describing the rich plant life in an inner-city garden, you might reflect on people's longing to connect with the soil and express admiration for the gardeners' hard work—an admiration you'd like readers to share. Or, in a character study of your grandfather, you might describe his stern appearance and gentle behavior, hoping that the contradiction will move readers as much as it moves you.

The *tone* of a subjective description is determined by your purpose, your attitude toward the subject, and the reader response you wish to evoke. Consider an essay about a dynamic woman who runs a center for disturbed children. If your goal is to make readers admire the woman, your tone will be serious and appreciative. But if you want to criticize the woman's high-pressure tactics and create distaste for her management style, your tone will be disapproving and severe.

The language of a descriptive piece also depends, to a great extent, on whether your purpose is primarily objective or subjective. If the description is objective, the language is straightforward, precise, and factual. Such *denotative* language consists of neutral dictionary meanings. If you want to describe as dispassionately as possible fans' violent behavior at a football game, you might write about the "large crowd" and its "mass movement onto the field." But if you are shocked by the fans' behavior and want to write a subjective piece that inspires similar outrage in readers, then you might write about the "swelling mob" and its "rowdy stampede onto the field." In the latter case, the language used would be *connotative* and emotionally charged so that readers would share your feelings.

Subjective and objective descriptions often overlap. Sometimes a single sentence contains both objective and subjective elements: "Although his hands were large and misshapen by arthritis, they were gentle to the touch, inspiring confidence and trust." Other times, part of an essay may provide a factual description (the physical appearance of a summer cabin your family rented), while another part of the essay may be highly subjective (how you felt in the cabin, sitting in front of a fire on a rainy day).

SUGGESTIONS FOR USING DESCRIPTION IN AN ESSAY

The following suggestions will be helpful whether you use description as a dominant or a supportive pattern of development.

1. Focus a descriptive essay around a dominant impression. Like other kinds of writing, a descriptive essay must have a thesis, or main point. In a descriptive essay with a subjective slant, the thesis usually centers on the *dominant impression* you have about your subject. Suppose you decide to write an essay on your ninth-grade history teacher, Ms. Hazzard. You want the paper to convey how unconventional and flamboyant she was. The essay could, of course, focus on a different dominant impression—how insensitive she could be to students, for example. What's important is that you establish—early in the paper—the dominant impression you intend to convey. Although descriptive essays often imply, rather than explicitly state, the dominant impression, that impression should be unmistakable.

2. Select the details to include. The power of description hinges on your ability to select from all possible details only those that support the dominant impression. All others, no matter how vivid or interesting, must be left out. If you're describing how flamboyant Ms. Hazzard could be, the details in the following paragraph would be appropriate.

A large-boned woman, Ms. Hazzard wore her bright red hair piled on top of her head, where it perched precariously. By the end of class, wayward strands of hair tumbled down and fell into eyes fringed by spiky false eyelashes. Ms. Hazzard's nails, filed into crisp points, were painted either bloody burgundy or neon pink. Plastic bangle bracelets, also either burgundy or pink, clattered up and down her ample arms as she scrawled on the board the historical dates that had, she claimed, "changed the world."

Such details—the heavy eye makeup, stiletto nails, gaudy bracelets—contribute to the impression of a flamboyant, unusual person. Even if you remembered times that Ms. Hazzard seemed perfectly conventional and understated, most likely you wouldn't describe those times since they contradict the dominant impression.

You must also be selective in the *number of details* you include. Having a dominant impression helps you eliminate many details gathered during prewriting, but there still will be choices to make. For example, it would be inappropriate to describe in exhaustive detail everything in a messy room:

The brown desk, made of a grained plastic laminate, is directly under a small window covered by a torn yellow-and-gold plaid curtain. In the left corner of the desk are four crumbled balls of blue-lined yellow paper, three red markers, two fine-point blue pens, an ink eraser, and four letters, two bearing special wildlife stamps. A green down-filled vest and a red cable-knit sweater are thrown over the back of the bright blue metal bridge chair pushed under the desk. Under the chair is an oval braided rug, its once brilliant blues and greens spotted by old coffee stains.

Readers will be reluctant to wade through such undifferentiated specifics. Even more important, such excessive detailing dilutes the focus of the essay. You end up with a seemingly endless list of specifics rather than with a carefully crafted picture in words. In this regard, sculptors and writers are similar—what they take away is as important as what they leave in.

Perhaps you're wondering how to generate the details that support your dominant impression. As you can imagine, you have to develop heightened powers of observation and recall. To sharpen these key faculties, it can be helpful to make up a chart with separate columns for each of the five senses. If you can observe your subject directly, enter in the appropriate columns what you see, hear, taste, and so on. If you're attempting to remember something from the past, try to recollect details under each of these sense headings. Ask yourself questions ("How did it smell? What did I hear?") and list each memory recaptured. You'll be surprised how this simple technique can tune you in to your experiences and help uncover the specific details needed to develop your dominant impression.

3. Organize the descriptive details. Select the organizational pattern (or combination of patterns) that best supports your dominant impression. The paragraphs in a descriptive essay are usually sequenced *spatially* (from top to bottom, interior to exterior, near to far) or *chronologically* (as the subject is experienced in time). But the paragraphs can also be ordered *emphatically* (ending with your subject's most striking elements) or by *sensory impression* (first smell, then taste, then touch, and so on).

You might, for instance, use a *spatial* pattern to organize a description of a large city as you viewed it from the air, a taxi, and a subway car. A description of your first day on a new job might move *chronologically*, starting with how you felt the first hour on the job and proceeding through the rest of the day. In a paper describing a bout with the flu, you might arrange details *emphatically*, beginning with a description of your low-level aches and pains and concluding with an account of your raging fever. An essay about a neighborhood garbage dump, euphemistically called an "ecology landfill" by its owners, could be organized by *sensory impressions:* the sights of the dump, its smells, its sounds. Regardless of the organizational pattern you use, provide enough *signal devices* (for example, *about, next, worst of all*) so that readers can follow the description easily.

Finally, although descriptive essays don't always have conventional topic sentences, each descriptive paragraph should have a clear focus. Often this focus is indicated by a sentence early in the paragraph that names the scene, object, or individual to be described. Such a sentence functions as a kind of *informal topic sentence;* the paragraph's descriptive details then develop that topic sentence.

4. Use vivid sensory language and varied sentence structure. The connotative language typical of subjective description should be richly evocative. The words you select must etch in readers' minds the same picture that you have in yours. For this reason, rather than relying on vague generalities, you must use language that involves readers' senses. Consider the difference between the following paired descriptions:

Vague	Vivid
The food was unappetizing.	The stew congealed into an oval pool of milky-brown fat.
The toothpaste was refreshing.	The toothpaste, tasting minty sweet, felt good against slippery teeth, free finally from braces.
Filled with passengers and baggage, the car moved slowly down the road.	Burdened with its load of clamoring children and well-worn suitcases, the car labored down the interstate on bald tires and worn shocks, emitting puffs of blue exhaust and an occasional backfire.

Unlike the *concrete, sensory-packed* sentences on the right, the sentences on the left fail to create vivid word pictures that engage readers. While all good writing blends abstract and concrete language, descriptive writing demands an abundance of specific sensory language.

Keep in mind, too, that *verbs pack more of a wallop* than adverbs. The following sentence has to rely on adverbs (italicized) because its verbs are so weak: "She walked *casually* into the room and *deliberately* tried not to pay much attention to their stares." Rewritten, so that verbs (italicized), not adverbs, do the bulk of the work, the sentence becomes more powerful: "She *strolled* into the room and *ignored* their stares."

Figures of speech—nonliteral, imaginative comparisons between two basically dissimilar things—are another way to enliven descriptive writing. *Similes* use the words *like* or *as* when comparing; *metaphors* state or imply that two things being compared are alike; and *personification* attributes human characteristics to inanimate things.

The examples that follow show how effective figurative language can be in descriptive writing.

Moving as jerkily as a marionette on strings, the old man picked himself up off the sidewalk and staggered down the street. (*simile*)

Stalking their prey, the hall monitors remained hidden in the corridors, motionless and ready to spring on any unsuspecting student who dared to sneak into class late. (*metaphor*)

The scoop of vanilla ice cream, plain and unadorned, cried out for hot-fudge sauce and a sprinkling of sliced pecans. (*personification*)

Finally, when writing descriptive passages, you need to *vary sentence structure*. Don't use the same subject-verb pattern in all sentences. The second example above, for instance, could have been written as follows: "The hall monitors stalked their prey. They hid in the corridors. They remained motionless and ready to spring on any unsuspecting student who tried to sneak into class late." But the sentence is richer and more interesting when the descriptive elements are embedded, eliminating what would otherwise have been a clipped and predictable subject-verb pattern.

STUDENT ESSAY

The following student essay was written by Marie Martinez in response to this assignment:

The essay "Once More to the Lake" is an evocative piece about a spot that had special meaning in E. B. White's life. Write an essay about a place that holds rich significance for you, centering the description on a dominant impression.

While reading Marie's paper, try to determine how well it applies the principles of description. The annotations on Marie's paper and the commentary following it will help you look at the essay more closely.

Salt Marsh
by Marie Martinez

Introduction   In one of his journals, Thoreau told of the difficul-   1
ty he had escaping the obligations and cares of society: "It sometimes happens that I cannot easily shake off the village. The thought of some work will run in

my head and I am not where my body is--I am out of my senses. In my walks I . . . return to my senses." All of us feel out of our senses at times. Overwhelmed by problems or everyday annoyances, we lose touch with sensory pleasures as we spend our days in noisy cities and stuffy classrooms. Just as Thoreau walked in the woods to return to his senses, I have a special place where I return to mine: the salt marsh behind my grandparents' house.

Dominant impression (thesis)

My grandparents live on the East Coast, a mile or so inland from the sea. Between the ocean and the mainland is a wide fringe of salt marsh. A salt marsh is not a swamp, but an expanse of dark, spongy soil threaded with saltwater creeks and clothed in a kind of grass called salt meadow hay. All the water in the marsh rises and falls daily with the ocean tides, an endless cycle that changes the look of the marsh-- partly flooded or mostly dry--as the day progresses.

Informal topic sentence: Definition paragraph

Heading out to the marsh from my grandparents' house, I follow a short path through the woods. As I walk along, a sharp smell of salt mixed with the rich aroma of peaty soil fills my nostrils. I am always amazed by the way the path changes with the seasons. Sometimes I walk in the brilliant green of spring, sometimes in the tawny gold of autumn, sometimes in the grayish tan of winter. No matter the season, the grass flanking the trail is often flattened into swirls, like thick Van Gogh brush strokes that curve and recurve in circular patterns. No people come here. The peacefulness heals me like a soothing drug.

Informal topic sentence: First paragraph in a four-part spatial sequence

Simile

After a few minutes, the trail suddenly opens up to a view that calms me no matter how upset or discouraged I might be: a line of tall waving reeds bordering and nearly hiding the salt marsh creek. To get to the creek, I part the reeds.

Informal topic sentence: Second paragraph in the spatial sequence

The creek is a narrow body of water no more than fifteen feet wide, and it ebbs and flows as the ocean currents sweep toward the land or rush back toward the sea. The creek winds in a sinuous pattern so that I cannot see its beginning or end, the places where it trickles into the marsh or spills into the open ocean. Little brown birds dip in and out of the reeds on the far shore of the creek, making a special

Informal topic sentence: Third paragraph in the spatial sequence

2

3

4

5

"tweep-tweep" sound peculiar to the marsh. When I stand at low tide on the shore of the creek, I am on a miniature cliff, for the bank of the creek falls abruptly and steeply into the water. Below me, green grasses wave and shimmer under the water while tiny minnows flash their silvery sides as they dart through the underwater tangles.

Informal topic sentence: Last paragraph in the spatial sequence

6   The creek water is often much warmer than the ocean, so I can swim there in three seasons. Sitting on the edge of the creek, I scoop some water into my hand, rub my face and neck, then ease into the water. Where the creek is shallow, my feet sink into a foot of

Simile

muck that feels like mashed potatoes mixed with motor oil. But once I become accustomed to it, I enjoy squishing the slimy mud through my toes. Sometimes I feel brushing past my legs the blue crabs that live in the creek. Other times, I hear the splash of a turtle or an otter as it slips from the shore into the water. Otherwise, it is silent. The salty water is buoyant and lifts my spirits as I stroke through it to reach the middle of the creek. There in the center, I float weightlessly, surrounded by tall reeds that reduce the world to water and sky. I am at peace.

Conclusion

7   The salt marsh is not the kind of dramatic landscape found on picture postcards. There are no soaring mountains, sandy beaches, or lush valleys. The marsh is a flat world that some consider dull and uninviting. I am glad most people do not respond to the marsh's subtle beauty because that means I can be alone there.

Echo of idea in introduction

Just as the rising tide sweeps over the marsh, floating debris out to the ocean, the marsh washes away my concerns and restores me to my senses.

COMMENTARY

The dominant impression.   Marie responded to the assignment by writing a moving tribute to a place having special meaning for her—the salt marsh near her grandparents' home. Like most descriptive pieces, Marie's essay is organized around a *dominant impression:* the marsh's peaceful solitude and gentle, natural beauty. The essay's introduction provides a context for the dominant impression by comparing the pleasure Marie experiences in the marsh to the happiness Thoreau felt in his walks around Walden Pond.

Other patterns of development.   Before developing the essay's dominant impression, Marie uses the second paragraph to *define* a salt marsh. An *objective description,* the definition clarifies that a salt marsh—with its spongy soil, haylike grass, and ebbing tides—is not to be confused with a swamp. Because Marie offers such a factual definition, readers have the background needed to enjoy the personalized view that follows.

Besides the definition paragraph and the comparison in the opening paragraph, the essay contains a strong element of *causal analysis:* Throughout, Marie describes the marsh's effect on her.

Sensory language.   At times, Marie develops the essay's dominant impression explicitly, as when she writes "No people come here" (paragraph 3) and "I am at peace" (6). But Marie generally uses the more subtle techniques characteristic of *subjective description* to convey the dominant impression. First of all, she fills the essay with strong *connotative language,* rich with *sensory images.* The third paragraph describes what she smells (the "sharp smell of salt mixed with the rich aroma of peaty soil") and what she sees ("brilliant green," "tawny gold," and "grayish tan"). In the fifth paragraph, she tells us that she hears the chirping sounds of small birds. And the sixth paragraph includes vigorous descriptions of how the marsh feels to Marie's touch. She splashes water on her face and neck; she digs her toes into the mud at the bottom of the creek; she delights in the delicate brushing of crabs against her legs.

Figurative language, vigorous verbs, and varied sentence structure.   You might also have noted that *figurative language, energetic verbs,* and *varied sentence patterns* contribute to the essay's descriptive power. Marie develops a *simile* in the third paragraph when she compares the flattened swirls of swamp grass to the brush strokes in a painting by Van Gogh. Later she uses another simile when she writes that the creek's thick mud feels "like mashed potatoes mixed with motor oil." Moreover, throughout the essay, she uses lively verbs ("shimmer," "flash") to capture the marsh's magical quality. Similarly, Marie enhances descriptive passages by varying the length of her sentences. Long, fairly elaborate sentences are interspersed with short, dramatic statements. In the third paragraph, for example, the long sentence describing the circular swirls of swamp grass is followed by the brief statement "No people come here." And the sixth paragraph uses two short sentences ("Otherwise, it is silent" and "I am at peace") to punctuate the paragraph's longer sentences.

Organization.   We can follow Marie's journey through the marsh because she uses an easy-to-follow combination of *spatial, chronological,* and *emphatic* patterns to sequence her experience. The essay relies primarily on a spatial arrangement since the four body paragraphs focus on the different spots that Marie reaches: first, the path behind her grandparents' house (paragraph 3); then the area bordering the creek (4); next, her view of the creek (5); last, the creek itself (6). Each stage of her walk is signaled by an *informal topic sentence* near the start of each paragraph. Furthermore, *signal devices* (marked by italics here) indicate not only her location but also the chronological passage of time: "*As* I walk along, a sharp smell . . . fills my nostrils" (3); "*After* a few minutes, the trail suddenly opens up . . ." (4); "*Below* me, green grasses wave . . ." (5). And to call attention to the creek's serene beauty, Marie saves for last the description of the peace she feels while floating in the creek.

An inappropriate figure of speech.   Although the four body paragraphs focus on the distinctive qualities of each location, Marie runs into a minor problem in the third paragraph. Take a moment to reread that paragraph's last sentence. Comparing the peace of the marsh to the effect of a "soothing drug" is jarring. The effectiveness of Marie's essay hinges on her ability to create a picture of a pure, natural world. A reference to drugs is inappropriate. Now, reread the paragraph aloud, stopping after "No people come here." Note how much more in keeping with the essay's dominant impression the paragraph is when the reference to drugs is omitted.

Conclusion.   The concluding paragraph brings the essay to a graceful close. The powerful *simile* found in the last sentence contains an implied reference to Thoreau and to Marie's earlier statement about the joy to be found in special places having restorative powers. Such an allusion echoes, with good effect, the paper's opening comments.

Revising the first draft.   When Marie met with some classmates during a group feedback session, the students agreed that Marie's first draft was strong and moving. But they also said that they had difficulty following her route through the marsh; they found her third paragraph especially confusing. Marie kept track of her classmates' comments on a separate piece of paper and then entered them, numbered in order of importance, in the margin of her first draft. Reprinted here is the original version of Marie's third paragraph.

Original Version of the Third Paragraph

As I head out to the marsh from the house, I follow a short trail through the woods. A smell of salt mixed with the aroma of soil fills my nostrils. The end of the trail suddenly opens up to a view that calms me no matter how upset or discouraged I might be: a line of tall waving reeds bordering the salt marsh creek. Civilization seems far away as I walk the path of flattened grass and finally reach my goal, the salt marsh creek hidden behind the tall waving reeds. The path changes with the seasons; sometimes I walk in the brilliant green of spring, sometimes in the tawny gold of autumn, sometimes in the quiet grayish tan of winter. In some areas, the grass is flattened into swirls that make the marsh resemble one of those paintings by Van Gogh. No people come here. The peacefulness heals me like a soothing drug. The path stops at the line of tall waving reeds, standing upright at the border of the creek. I part the reeds to get to the creek.

When Marie looked more carefully at the paragraph, she agreed it was confusing. For one thing, the paragraph's third and fourth sentences indicated that she had come to the path's end and had reached the reeds bordering the creek. In the following sentences, however, she was on the path again. Then, at the end, she was back at the creek, as if she had just arrived there. Marie resolved this confusion by breaking the single paragraph into two separate ones—the first describing the walk along the path, the second describing her arrival at the creek. This restructuring, especially when combined with clearer transitions, eliminated the confusion.

While revising her essay, Marie also intensified the sensory images in her original paragraph. She changed the "smell of salt and soil" to the "sharp smell of salt mixed with the rich aroma of peaty soil." And when she added the phrase "thick Van Gogh brush strokes that curve and recurve in circular patterns," she made the comparison between the marsh grass and a Van Gogh painting more vivid.

These are just some of the changes Marie made while rewriting her paper. Her skillful revisions provided the polish needed to make an already strong essay even more evocative.

ACTIVITIES: DESCRIPTION

Prewriting Activities

1. Imagine you're writing two essays: One explains the *process* by which students get "burned out"; the other *argues* that being a spendthrift is better (or worse) than being frugal. Jot down ways you might use description in each essay.

2. Go to a place on campus where students congregate. In preparation for an *objective* description of this place, make notes of various sights, sounds, smells, and textures, as well as the overall "feel" of the place. Then, in preparation for a *subjective* description, observe and take notes on another sheet of paper. Compare the two sets of material. What differences do you see in word choice and selection of details?

Revising Activities

3. Revise each of the following sentence sets twice. The first time, create an unmistakable mood; the second time, create a sharply contrasting mood. To convey atmosphere, vary sentence structure, use vigorous verbs, provide rich sensory details, and pay special attention to words' connotations.
   a. The card players sat around the table. The table was old. The players were, too.
   b. A long line formed outside the movie theater. People didn't want to miss the show. The movie had received a lot of attention recently.
   c. A girl walked down the street in her first pair of high heels. This was a new experience for her.

4. The following descriptive paragraph is from the first draft of an essay showing that personal growth may result when romanticized notions and reality collide. How effective is the paragraph in illustrating the essay's thesis? Which details are powerful? Which could be more concrete? Which should be deleted? Where should sentence structure be more varied? How could the description be made more coherent? Revise the paragraph, correcting any problems you

discover and adding whatever sensory details are needed to enliven the description. Feel free to break the paragraph into two or more separate ones.

As a child, I was intrigued by stories about the farm in Harrison County, Maine, where my father spent his teens. Being raised on a farm seemed more interesting than growing up in the suburbs. So about a year ago, I decided to see for myself what the farm was like. I got there by driving on Route 334, a surprisingly easy-to-drive, four-lane highway that had recently been built with matching state and federal funds. I turned into the dirt road leading to the farm and got out of my car. It had been washed and waxed for the occasion. Then I headed for a dirt-colored barn. Its roof was full of huge, rotted holes. As I rounded the bushes, I saw the house. It too was dirt-colored. Its paint must have worn off decades ago. A couple of dead-looking old cars were sprawled in front of the barn. They were dented and windowless. Also by the barn was an ancient refrigerator, crushed like a discarded accordion. The porch steps to the house were slanted and wobbly. Through the open windows came a stale smell and the sound of television. Looking in the front door screen, I could see two chickens jumping around inside. Everything looked dirty both inside and out. Secretly grateful that no one answered my knock, I bolted down the stairs, got into my clean, shiny car, and drove away.

Gordon Parks

The son of deeply religious tenant farmers, Gordon Parks (1912–) grew up in Kansas knowing both the comforts of familial love and the torments of poverty and racism. Sent as a teenager to live with his sister in Minnesota after his mother's death, Parks was thrown out on his own in a frigid winter by his brother-in-law. To support himself, Parks worked as a janitor in a flophouse and as a piano player in a bordello. These and other odd jobs gave Parks the means to buy his first camera. Fascinated by photographic images, Parks studied the masters and eventually developed his own powers as a photographer. So evocative were his photographic studies that both *Life* and *Vogue* brought him on staff, the first Black photographer to be hired by the two magazines. Parks's prodigious creativity has found expression in filmmaking (*Shaft* in 1971), musical composition (both classical and jazz), fiction, nonfiction, and poetry (titles include *The Learning Tree, A Choice of Weapons, To Smile in Autumn, Arias in Silence,* and *Glimpses Toward Infinity,* published, respectively, in 1986, 1987, 1988, 1994, and 1996). But it is Parks's photographic essays, covering five decades of American life, that have brought him the most acclaim. In the following essay, taken from his 1990 autobiography, *Voices in the Mirror,* Parks tells the story behind one of his most memorable photographic works—that of a twelve-year-old boy and his family, living in the slums of Rio de Janeiro.

Pre-Reading Journal Entry

The problem of poverty has provoked a wide array of proposed solutions. One controversial proposal argues that the government should pay poor women financial incentives to use birth control. What do you think of this proposal? Why is such a policy controversial? Use your journal to explore your thinking on this issue.

Flavio's Home

I've never lost my fierce grudge against poverty. It is the most   1
savage of all human afflictions, claiming victims who can't mobilize their efforts against it, who often lack strength to digest what little food they scrounge up to survive. It keeps growing, multiplying, spreading like a cancer. In my wanderings I attack it wherever I can—in barrios, slums and favelas.

Catacumba was the name of the favela[1] where I found Flavio da 2
Silva. It was wickedly hot. The noon sun baked the mud-rot of the
wet mountainside. Garbage and human excrement clogged the
open sewers snaking down the slopes. José Gallo, a *Life* reporter,
and I rested in the shade of a jacaranda tree halfway up Rio de
Janeiro's most infamous deathtrap. Below and above us were a maze
of shacks, but in the distance alongside the beach stood the gleaming white homes of the rich.

Breathing hard, balancing a tin of water on his head, a small boy 3
climbed toward us. He was miserably thin, naked but for filthy
denim shorts. His legs resembled sticks covered with skin and
screwed into his feet. Death was all over him, in his sunken eyes,
cheeks and jaundiced coloring. He stopped for breath, coughing,
his chest heaving as water slopped over his bony shoulders. Then
jerking sideways like a mechanical toy, he smiled a smile I will never
forget. Turning, he went on up the mountainside.

The detailed *Life* assignment in my back pocket was to find an 4
impoverished father with a family, to examine his earnings, political
leanings, religion, friends, dreams and frustrations. I had been sent
to do an essay on poverty. This frail boy bent under his load said
more to me about poverty than a dozen poor fathers. I touched
Gallo, and we got up and followed the boy to where he entered a
shack near the top of the mountainside. It was a leaning crumpled
place of old plankings with a rusted tin roof. From inside we heard
the babblings of several children. José knocked. The door opened
and the boy stood smiling with a bawling naked baby in his arms.

Still smiling, he whacked the baby's rump, invited us in and 5
offered us a box to sit on. The only other recognizable furniture was
a sagging bed and a broken baby's crib. Flavio was twelve, and with
Gallo acting as interpreter, he introduced his younger brothers and
sisters: "Mario, the bad one; Baptista, the good one; Albia, Isabel
and the baby Zacarias." Two other girls burst into the shack,
screaming and pounding on one another. Flavio jumped in and parted them. "Shut up, you two." He pointed at the older girl. "That's
Maria, the nasty one." She spit in his face. He smacked her and
pointed to the smaller sister. "That's Luzia. She thinks she's pretty."

Having finished the introductions, he went to build a fire under 6
the stove—a rusted, bent top of an old gas range resting on several

[1]Slums on the outskirts of Rio de Janeiro, Brazil, inhabited by seven hundred thousand people (editors' note).

bricks. Beneath it was a piece of tin that caught the hot coals. The shack was about six by ten feet. Its grimy walls were a patchwork of misshapen boards with large gaps between them, revealing other shacks below stilted against the slopes. The floor, rotting under layers of grease and dirt, caught shafts of light slanting down through spaces in the roof. A large hole in the far corner served as a toilet. Beneath that hole was the sloping mountainside. Pockets of poverty in New York's Harlem, on Chicago's south side, in Puerto Rico's infamous El Fungito seemed pale by comparison. None of them had prepared me for this one in the favela of Catacumba.

Flavio washed rice in a large dishpan, then washed Zacarias's   7
feet in the same water. But even that dirty water wasn't to be wasted. He tossed in a chunk of lye soap and ordered each child to wash up. When they were finished he splashed the water over the dirty floor, and, dropping to his knees, he scrubbed the planks until the black suds sank in. Just before sundown he put beans on the stove to warm, then left, saying he would be back shortly. "Don't let them burn," he cautioned Maria. "If they do and Poppa beats me, you'll get it later." Maria, happy to get at the licking spoon, switched over and began to stir the beans. Then slyly she dipped out a spoonful and swallowed them. Luzia eyed her. "I see you. I'm going to tell on you for stealing our supper."

Maria's eyes flashed anger. "You do and I'll beat you, you little   8
bitch." Luzia threw a stick at Maria and fled out the door. Zacarias dropped off to sleep. Mario, the bad one, slouched in a corner and sucked his thumb. Isabel and Albia sat on the floor clinging to each other with a strange tenderness. Isabel held onto Albia's hair and Albia clutched at Isabel's neck. They appeared frozen in an act of quiet violence.

Flavio returned with wood, dumped it beside the stove and sat   9
down to rest for a few minutes, then went down the mountain for more water. It was dark when he finally came back, his body sagging from exhaustion. No longer smiling, he suddenly had the look of an old man and by now we could see that he kept the family going. In the closed torment of that pitiful shack, he was waging a hopeless battle against starvation. The da Silva children were living in a coffin.

When at last the parents came in, Gallo and I seemed to be part   10
of the family. Flavio had already told them we were there. "Gordunn Americano!" Luzia said, pointing at me. José, the father, viewed us

with skepticism. Nair, his pregnant wife, seemed tired beyond speaking. Hardly acknowledging our presence, she picked up Zacarias, placed him on her shoulder and gently patted his behind. Flavio scurried about like a frightened rat, his silence plainly expressing the fear he held of his father. Impatiently, José da Silva waited for Flavio to serve dinner. He sat in the center of the bed with his legs crossed beneath him, frowning, waiting. There were only three tin plates. Flavio filled them with black beans and rice, then placed them before his father. José da Silva tasted them, chewed for several moments, then nodded his approval for the others to start. Only he and Nair had spoons; the children ate with their fingers. Flavio ate off the top of a coffee can. Afraid to offer us food, he edged his rice and beans toward us, gesturing for us to take some. We refused. He smiled, knowing we understood.

Later, when we got down to the difficult business of obtaining permission from José da Silva to photograph his family, he hemmed and hawed, wallowing in the pleasant authority of the decision maker. He finally gave in, but his manner told us that he expected something in return. As we were saying good night Flavio began to cough violently. For a few moments his lungs seemed to be tearing apart. I wanted to get away as quickly as possible. It was cowardly of me, but the bluish cast of his skin beneath the sweat, the choking and spitting were suddenly unbearable. 11

Gallo and I moved cautiously down through the darkness trying not to appear as strangers. The Catacumba was no place for strangers after sundown. Desperate criminals hid out there. To hunt them out, the police came in packs, but only in daylight. Gallo cautioned me. "If you get caught up here after dark it's best to stay at the da Silvas' until morning." As we drove toward the city the large white buildings of the rich loomed up. The world behind us seemed like a bad dream. I had already decided to get the boy Flavio to a doctor, and as quickly as possible. 12

The plush lobby of my hotel on the Copacabana waterfront was crammed with people in formal attire. With the stink of the favela in my clothes, I hurried to the elevator hoping no passengers would be aboard. But as the door was closing a beautiful girl in a white lace gown stepped in. I moved as far away as possible. Her escort entered behind her, swept her into his arms and they indulged in a kiss that lasted until they exited on the next floor. Neither of them seemed to realize that I was there. The room I returned to seemed to be 13 oversized; the da Silva shack would have fitted into one corner of it. The steak dinner I had would have fed the da Silvas for three days.

Billowing clouds blanketed Mount Corcovado as we approached   14
the favela the following morning. Suddenly the sun burst through, silhouetting Cristo Redentor, the towering sculpture of Christ with arms extended, its back turned against the slopes of Catacumba. The square at the entrance to the favela bustled with hundreds of favelados. Long lines waited at the sole water spigot. Others waited at the only toilet on the entire mountainside. Women, unable to pay for soap, beat dirt from their wash at laundry tubs. Men, burdened with lumber, picks and shovels and tools important to their existence threaded their way through the noisy throngs. Dogs snarled, barked and fought. Woodsmoke mixed with the stench of rotting things. In the mist curling over the higher paths, columns of favelados climbed like ants with wood and water cans on their heads.

We came upon Nair bent over her tub of wash. She wiped away   15
sweat with her apron and managed a smile. We asked for her husband and she pointed to a tiny shack off to her right. This was José's store, where he sold kerosene and bleach. He was sitting on a box, dozing. Sensing our presence, he awoke and commenced complaining about his back. "It kills me. The doctors don't help because I have no money. Always talk and a little pink pill that does no good. Ah, what is to become of me?" A woman came to buy bleach. He filled her bottle. She dropped a few coins and as she walked away his eyes stayed on her backside until she was out of sight. Then he was complaining about his back again.

"How much do you earn a day?" Gallo asked.   16
"Seventy-five cents. On a good day maybe a dollar."   17
"Why aren't the kids in school?"   18
"I don't have money for the clothes they need to go to school."   19
"Has Flavio seen a doctor?"   20
He pointed to a one-story wooden building. "That's the clinic   21
right there. They're mad because I built my store in front of their place. I won't tear it down so they won't help my kids. Talk, talk, talk and pink pills." We bid him good-bye and started climbing, following mud trails, jutting rock, slime-filled holes and shack after shack propped against the slopes on shaky pilings. We sidestepped a dead cat covered with maggots. I held my breath for an instant, only to inhale the stench of human excrement and garbage. Bare feet and

legs with open sores climbed above us—evils of the terrible soil they trod every day, and there were seven hundred thousand or more afflicted people in favelas around Rio alone. Touching me, Gallo pointed to Flavio climbing ahead of us carrying firewood. He stopped to glance at a man descending with a small coffin on his shoulder. A woman and a small child followed him. When I lifted my camera, grumbling erupted from a group of men sharing beer beneath a tree.

"They're threatening," Gallo said. "Keep moving. They fear   22
cameras. Think they're evil eyes bringing bad luck." Turning to watch the funeral procession, Flavio caught sight of us and waited. When we took the wood from him he protested, saying he was used to carrying it. He gave in when I hung my camera around his neck. Then, beaming, he climbed on ahead of us.

The fog had lifted and in the crisp morning light the shack   23
looked more squalid. Inside the kids seemed even noisier. Flavio smiled and spoke above their racket. "Someday I want to live in a real house on a real street with good pots and pans and a bed with sheets." He lit the fire to warm leftovers from the night before. Stale rice and beans—for breakfast and supper. No lunch; midday eating was out of the question. Smoke rose and curled up through the ceiling's cracks. An air current forced it back, filling the place and Flavio's lungs with fumes. A coughing spasm doubled him up, turned his skin blue under viscous sweat. I handed him a cup of water, but he waved it away. His stomach tightened as he dropped to his knees. His veins throbbed as if they would burst. Frustrated, we could only watch; there was nothing we could do to help. Strangely, none of his brothers or sisters appeared to notice. None of them stopped doing whatever they were doing. Perhaps they had seen it too often. After five interminable minutes it was over, and he got to his feet, smiling as though it had all been a joke. "Maria, it's time for Zacarias to be washed!"

"But there's rice in the pan!"   24

"Dump it in another pan—and don't spill water!"   25

Maria picked up Zacarias, who screamed, not wanting to be   26
washed. Irritated, Maria gave him a solid smack on his bare bottom. Flavio stepped over and gave her the same, then a free-for-all started with Flavio, Maria and Mario slinging fists at one another. Mario got one in the eye and fled the shack calling Flavio a dirty son-of-a-bitch. Zacarias wound up on the floor sucking his thumb and escaping his

washing. The black bean and rice breakfast helped to get things back to normal. Now it was time to get Flavio to the doctor.

The clinic was crowded with patients—mothers and children   27
covered with open sores, a paralytic teenager, a man with an ear in a state of decay, an aged blind couple holding hands in doubled darkness. Throughout the place came wailings of hunger and hurt. Flavio sat nervously between Gallo and me. "What will the doctor do to me?" he kept asking.

"We'll see. We'll wait and see."   28

In all, there were over fifty people. Finally, after two hours, it   29
was Flavio's turn and he broke out in a sweat, though he smiled at the nurse as he passed through the door to the doctor's office. The nurse ignored it; in this place of misery, smiles were unexpected.

The doctor, a large, beady-eyed man with a crew cut, had an air   30
of impatience. Hardly acknowledging our presence, he began to examine the frightened Flavio. "Open your mouth. Say 'Ah.' Jump up and down. Breathe out. Take off those pants. Bend over. Stand up. Cough. Cough louder. Louder." He did it all with such cold efficiency. Then he spoke to us in English so Flavio wouldn't understand. "This little chap has just about had it." My heart sank. Flavio was smiling, happy to be over with the examination. He was handed a bottle of cough medicine and a small box of pink pills, then asked to step outside and wait.

"This the da Silva kid?"   31
"Yes."   32
"What's your interest in him?"   33
"We want to help in some way."   34
"I'm afraid you're too late. He's wasted with bronchial asthma,   35
malnutrition and, I suspect, tuberculosis. His heart, lungs and teeth are all bad." He paused and wearily rubbed his forehead. "All that at the ripe old age of twelve. And these hills are packed with other kids just as bad off. Last year ten thousand died from dysentery alone. But what can we do? You saw what's waiting outside. It's like this every day. There's hardly enough money to buy aspirin. A few wealthy people who care help keep us going." He was quiet for a moment. "Maybe the right climate, the right diet, and constant medical care might . . ." He stopped and shook his head. "Naw. That poor lad's finished. He might last another year—maybe not." We thanked him and left.

"What did he say?" Flavio asked as we scaled the hill.   36

"Everything's going to be all right, Flav. There's nothing to   37
worry about."

It had clouded over again by the time we reached the top. The   38
rain swept in, clearing the mountain of Corcovado. The huge Christ
figure loomed up again with clouds swirling around it. And to it I
said a quick prayer for the boy walking beside us. He smiled as if he
had read my thoughts. "Papa says 'El Cristo' has turned his back on
the favela."

"You're going to be all right, Flavio."   39

"I'm not scared of death. It's my brothers and sisters I worry   40
about. What would they do?"

"You'll be all right, Flavio."² 41

----

²Parks's photo-essay on Flavio generated an unprecedented response from *Life* readers. Indeed, they sent so much money to the da Silvas that the family was able to leave
the *favela* for better living conditions. Parks brought Flavio to the United States for
medical treatment, and the boy's health was restored. However, Flavio's story didn't
have an unqualifiedly happy ending. Although he overcame his illness and later married and had a family, Flavio continuously fantasized about returning to the United
States, convinced that only by returning to America could he improve his life. His
obsession eventually eroded the promise of his life in Brazil (editors' note).

Questions for Close Reading

1. What is the selection's thesis (or dominant impression)? Locate the sen-
   tence(s) in which Parks states his main idea. If he doesn't state the thesis explicitly, express it in your own words.
2. What is Flavio's family like? Why does Flavio have so much responsibility in the household?
3. What are some of the distinctive characteristics of Flavio's neighborhood
   and home?
4. What seems to be the basis of Flavio's fear of giving food to Parks and
   Gallo? What did Parks and Gallo understand that led them to refuse?
5. Refer to your dictionary as needed to define the following words used in
   the selection: *barrios* (paragraph 1), *jacaranda* (2), *jaundiced* (3), and
   spigot (14).

Questions About the Writer's Craft

1. **The pattern.** Without stating it explicitly, Parks conveys a dominant
   impression about Flavio. What is that impression? What details create it?

2. **Other patterns.** When relating how Flavio performs numerous household tasks, Parks describes several processes. How do these step-by-step explanations reinforce Parks's dominant impression of Flavio?

3. Parks provides numerous sensory specifics to depict Flavio's home. Look closely, for example, at the description in paragraph 6. Which words and phrases convey strong sensory images? How does Parks use transitions to help the reader move from one sensory image to another?

4. Paragraph 13 includes a scene that occurs in Parks's hotel. What's the effect of this scene? What does it contribute to the essay that the most detailed description of the *favela* could not?

Writing Assignments Using Description as a Pattern of Development

∞ 1. Parks paints a wrenching portrait of a person who remains vibrant and hopeful even though he is suffering greatly—from physical illness, poverty, overwork, and worry. Write a description about someone you know who has shown courage or other positive qualities during a time of personal trouble. Include, as Parks does, plentiful details about the person's appearance and behavior so that you don't have to state directly what you admire about the person. Maya Angelou's "Sister Flowers" (page 116) shows how one writer conveys the special quality of an admirable individual.

2. Parks presents an unforgettable description of the *favela* and the living conditions there. Write an essay about a region, city, neighborhood, or building that also projects an overwhelming negative feeling. Include only those details that convey your dominant impression, and provide—as Parks does— vivid sensory language to convey your attitude toward your subject.

Writing Assignments Using Other Patterns of Development

∞ 3. The doctor reports that a few wealthy people contribute to the clinic, but the reader can tell from the scene in Parks's hotel that most people are insensitive to those less fortunate. Write an essay describing a specific situation that you feel reflects people's tendency to ignore the difficulties of others. Analyze why people distance themselves from the problem; then present specific steps that could be taken to sensitize them to the situation. Gloria Naylor's "Mommy, What Does 'Nigger' Mean?" (page 587) and Mark Twain's "The Damned Human Race" (page 516) will provide some perspective on the way people harden themselves to the pain of others.

4. Although Parks celebrates Flavio's generosity of spirit, the writer also illustrates the brutalizing effect of an impoverished environment. Prepare an essay in which you also show that setting, architecture, even furnishings can influence mood and behavior. You may, as Parks does, focus on the corrosive effect of a negative environment, or you may write about the nurturing effect of a positive environment. Possible subjects include a park in the middle of a city, a bus terminal, and a college library.

Writing Assignments Using a Journal Entry as a Starting Point

5. Write an essay explaining why you think impoverished women should—or should not—be paid financial incentives to practice birth control. To help define your position, review your pre-reading journal entry, and interview classmates, friends, and family members to get their opinions. Consider supplementing this informal research with material gathered in the library and/or on the Internet. Weigh all the evidence carefully before formulating your position.

Russell Baker

Currently the host of the popular PBS series *Masterpiece Theatre,* Baker writes a column "The Observer" for the *New York Times.* In the column, he applies his unique brand of humor to social commentary. Born in Virginia in 1925, Baker received his B.A. from Johns Hopkins University and spent several years working as a reporter for the *Baltimore Sun* before joining the *Times* in the mid-1950s. In 1979, Baker won a Pulitzer Prize, journalism's highest honor. Baker's columns have been collected in several books, including *No Cause for Panic* (1969), *Poor Russell's Almanac* (1972), *So This Is Depravity* (1980), and *There's a Country in My Cellar* (1990). He also edited the book *Russell Baker's Book of American Humor.* Baker has written a widely read and critically acclaimed two-volume autobiography, *Growing Up* (1982), which was awarded a Pulitzer Prize, and *The Good Times* (1989). He co-edited *Inventing the Truth: The Art and Craft of Memoir* (1995).The following selection is taken from *Growing Up.*

Pre-Reading Journal Entry

Life expectancy continues to rise in the United States, with more people being "senior citizens" than ever before. What is life like for this segment of the populace? In your journal, list the challenges that people typically face as they become older. As you write, reflect on your experiences with the elderly—those you know well and those you've observed.

In My Day

At the age of eighty my mother had her last bad fall, and after that her mind wandered free through time. Some days she went to weddings and funerals that had taken place half a century earlier. On others she presided over family dinners cooked on Sunday afternoons for children who were now gray with age. Through all this she lay in bed but moved across time, traveling among the dead decades with a speed and ease beyond the gift of physical science. 1

"Where's Russell?" she asked one day when I came to visit at the nursing home. 2

"I'm Russell," I said. 3

She gazed at this improbably overgrown figure out of an incon- 4
ceivable future and promptly dismissed it.

"Russell's only this big," she said, holding her hand, palm 5
down, two feet from the floor. That day she was a young country
wife with chickens in the backyard and a view of hazy blue Virginia
mountains behind the apple orchard, and I was a stranger old
enough to be her father.

Early one morning she phoned me in New York. "Are you com- 6
ing to my funeral today?" she asked.

It was an awkward question with which to be awakened. "What 7
are you talking about, for God's sake?" was the best reply I could
manage.

"I'm being buried today," she declared briskly, as though 8
announcing an important social event.

"I'll phone you back," I said and hung up, and when I did 9
phone back she was all right, although she wasn't all right, of course,
and we all knew she wasn't.

She had always been a small woman—short, light-boned, deli- 10
cately structured—but now, under the white hospital sheet, she was
becoming tiny. I thought of a doll with huge, fierce eyes. There had
always been a fierceness in her. It showed in that angry, challenging
thrust of the chin when she issued an opinion, and a great one she
had always been for issuing opinions.

"I tell people exactly what's on my mind," she had been fond of 11
boasting. "I tell them what I think, whether they like it or not."
Often they had not liked it. She could be sarcastic to people in
whom she detected evidence of the ignoramus or the fool.

"It's not always good policy to tell people exactly what's on 12
your mind," I used to caution her.

"If they don't like it, that's too bad," was her customary reply, 13
"because that's the way I am."

And so she was. A formidable woman. Determined to speak her 14
mind, determined to have her way, determined to bend those who
opposed her. In that time when I had known her best, my mother
had hurled herself at life with chin thrust forward, eyes blazing, and
an energy that made her seem always on the run.

She ran after squawking chickens, an axe in her hand, deter- 15
mined on a beheading that would put dinner in the pot. She ran
when she made the beds, ran when she set the table. One
Thanksgiving she burned herself badly when, running up from the
cellar oven with the ceremonial turkey, she tripped on the stairs and

tumbled back down, ending at the bottom in the debris of giblets, hot gravy, and battered turkey. Life was combat, and victory was not to the lazy, the timid, the slugabed, the drugstore cowboy, the libertine, the mushmouth afraid to tell people exactly what was on his mind whether people liked it or not. She ran.

But now the running was over. For a time I could not accept the   16
inevitable. As I sat by her bed, my impulse was to argue her back to reality. On my first visit to the hospital in Baltimore, she asked who I was.

"Russell," I said.   17
"Russell's way out west," she advised me.   18
"No, I'm right here."   19
"Guess where I came from today?" was her response.   20
"Where?"   21
"All the way from New Jersey."   22
"When?"   23
"Tonight."   24
"No. You've been in the hospital for three days," I insisted.   25
"I suggest the thing to do is calm down a little bit," she replied.   26
"Go over to the house and shut the door."

Now she was years deep into the past, living in the neighbor-   27
hood where she had settled forty years earlier, and she had just been talking with Mrs. Hoffman, a neighbor across the street.

"It's like Mrs. Hoffman said today: The children always wander   28
back to where they come from," she remarked.
"Mrs. Hoffman has been dead for fifteen years."   29
"Russ got married today," she replied.   30
"I got married in 1950," I said, which was the fact.   31
"The house is unlocked," she said.   32

So it went until a doctor came by to give one of those oral quizzes   33
that medical men apply in such cases. She failed catastrophically, giving wrong answers or none at all to "What day is this?" "Do you know where you are?" "How old are you?" and so on. Then, a surprise.

"When is your birthday?" he asked.   34
"November 5, 1897," she said. Correct. Absolutely correct.   35
"How do you remember that?" the doctor asked.   36
"Because I was born on Guy Fawkes Day," she said.   37
"Guy Fawkes?" asked the doctor. "Who is Guy Fawkes?"   38
She replied with a rhyme I had heard her recite time and again   39
over the years when the subject of her birth date arose:

"Please to remember the Fifth of November,
Gunpowder treason and plot.
I see no reason why gunpowder treason
Should ever be forgot."

Then she glared at this young doctor so ill informed about Guy Fawkes' failed scheme to blow King James off his throne with barrels of gunpowder in 1605. She had been a schoolteacher, after all, and knew how to glare at a dolt. "You may know a lot about medicine, but you obviously don't know any history," she said. Having told him exactly what was on her mind, she left us again.

The doctors diagnosed a hopeless senility. Not unusual, they said. "Hardening of the arteries" was the explanation for laymen. I thought it was more complicated than that. For ten years or more the ferocity with which she had once attacked life had been turning to a rage against the weakness, the boredom, and the absence of love that too much age had brought her. Now, after the last bad fall, she seemed to have broken chains that imprisoned her in a life she had come to hate and to return to a time inhabited by people who loved her, a time in which she was needed. Gradually I understood. It was the first time in years I had seen her happy.

She had written a letter three years earlier which explained more than "hardening of the arteries." I had gone down from New York to Baltimore, where she lived, for one of my infrequent visits and, afterwards, had written her with some banal advice to look for the silver lining, to count her blessings instead of burdening others with her miseries. I suppose what it really amounted to was a threat that if she was not more cheerful during my visits I would not come to see her very often. Sons are capable of such letters. This one was written out of a childish faith in the eternal strength of parents, a naive belief that age and wear could be overcome by an effort of will, that all she needed was a good pep talk to recharge a flagging spirit. It was such a foolish, innocent idea, but one thinks of parents differently from other people. Other people can become frail and break, but not parents.

She wrote back in an unusually cheery vein intended to demonstrate, I suppose, that she was mending her ways. She was never a woman to apologize, but for one moment with the pen in her hand she came very close. Referring to my visit, she wrote: "If I seemed unhappy to you at times—" Here she drew back, reconsidered, and said something quite different:

"If I seemed unhappy to you at times, I am, but there's real-   43
ly nothing anyone can do about it, because I'm just so very tired
and lonely that I'll just go to sleep and forget it." She was then
seventy-eight.

Now, three years later, after the last bad fall, she had managed   44
to forget the fatigue and loneliness and, in these free-wheeling
excursions back through time, to recapture happiness. I soon
stopped trying to wrest her back to what I considered the real world
and tried to travel along with her on those fantastic swoops into the
past. One day when I arrived at her bedside she was radiant.

"Feeling good today," I said.   45

"Why shouldn't I feel good?" she asked. "Papa's going to take   46
me up to Baltimore on the boat today."

At that moment she was a young girl standing on a wharf at   47
Merry Point, Virginia, waiting for the Chesapeake Bay steamer with
her father, who had been dead sixty-one years. William Howard Taft
was in the White House, Europe still drowsed in the dusk of the
great century of peace, America was a young country, and the future
stretched before it in beams of crystal sunlight. "The greatest country on God's green earth," her father might have said, if I had been
able to step into my mother's time machine and join him on the
wharf with the satchels packed for Baltimore.

I could imagine her there quite clearly. She was wearing a blue   48
dress with big puffy sleeves and long black stockings. There was a
ribbon in her hair and a big bow tied on the side of her head. There
had been a childhood photograph in her bedroom which showed all
this, although the colors of course had been added years later by a
restorer who tinted the picture.

About her father, my grandfather, I could only guess, and   49
indeed, about the girl on the wharf with the bow in her hair, I was
merely sentimentalizing. Of my mother's childhood and her people, of their time and place, I knew very little. A world had lived
and died, and though it was part of my blood and bone I knew little more about it than I knew of the world of the pharaohs. It was
useless now to ask for help from my mother. The orbits of her
mind rarely touched present interrogators for more than a
moment.

Sitting at her bedside, forever out of touch with her, I wondered   50
about my own children, and their children, and children in general,
and about the disconnections between children and parents that prevent them from knowing each other. Children rarely want to know

who their parents were before they were parents, and when age finally stirs their curiosity there is no parent left to tell them. If a parent
does lift the curtain a bit, it is often only to stun the young with some
exemplary tale of how much harder life was in the old days.

I had been guilty of this when my children were small in the   51
early 1960s and living the affluent life. It galled me that their child-
hoods should be, as I thought, so easy when my own had been, as I
thought, so hard. I had developed the habit, when they complained
about the steak being overcooked or the television being cut off, of
lecturing them on the harshness of life in my day.

"In my day all we got for dinner was macaroni and cheese, and   52
we were glad to get it."

"In my day we didn't have any television."   53

"In my day . . ."   54

"In my day . . ."   55

At dinner one evening a son had offended me with an inade-   56
quate report card, and as I leaned back and cleared my throat to lecture, he gazed at me with an expression of unutterable resignation
and said, "Tell me how it was in your days, Dad."

I was angry with him for that, but angrier with myself for hav-   57
ing become one of those ancient bores whose highly selective memories of the past become transparently dishonest even to small children. I tried to break the habit, but must have failed. A few years
later my son was referring to me when I was out of earshot as "the
old-timer." Between us there was a dispute about time. He looked
upon the time that had been my future in a disturbing way. My
future was his past, and being young, he was indifferent to the past.

As I hovered over my mother's bed listening for muffled signals   58
from her childhood, I realized that this same dispute had existed
between her and me. When she was young, with life ahead of her, I
had been her future and resented it. Instinctively, I wanted to break
free, cease being a creature defined by her time, consign her future
to the past, and create my own. Well, I had finally done that, and
then with my own children I had seen my exciting future become
their boring past.

These hopeless end-of-the-line visits with my mother made me   59
wish I had not thrown off my own past so carelessly. We all come
from the past, and children ought to know what it was that went
into their making, to know that life is a braided cord of humanity
stretching up from time long gone, and that it cannot be defined by
the span of a single journey from diaper to shroud.

Questions for Close Reading

1. What is the selection's thesis (or dominant impression)? Locate the sentence(s) in which Baker states his main idea. If he doesn't state the thesis explicitly, express it in your own words.
2. What was Mrs. Baker's philosophy of life? How did it change in her old age?
3. Why does Baker feel "forever out of touch" with his mother? Does he feel equally out of touch with his children?
4. Why does Baker stop trying to get his eighty-year-old mother to return to the real world? Is he being kind or unkind?
5. Refer to your dictionary as needed to define the following words used in the selection: *inconceivable* (paragraph 4), *libertine* (15), *banal* (41), *wrest* (44), *exemplary* (50), *galled* (51), and *consign* (58).

Questions About the Writer's Craft

1. **The pattern.**   How does the series of scenes in "In My Day" develop the essay's dominant impression?
2. Baker describes his mother by using details about her actions and her appearance, as well as by quoting things she said. Both are typical techniques for revealing character in a descriptive piece. Which technique is more effective in conveying Mrs. Baker's personality?
3. In paragraph 15, Baker repeats the word *ran* when describing his mother's energy. He also speaks several times of her *falls.* What do you think might have been Baker's purpose for repeating these words? What do they suggest about the pattern of his mother's life?
4. If something is *ironic,* there is a discrepancy between what is said and what is known. In paragraph 28, Mrs. Baker says, "The children always wander back to where they come from." How is this comment by Baker's mother ironic? Find some other examples of irony in the essay.

Writing Assignments Using Description as a Pattern of Development

∞ 1. Write a description of a parent or relative at a certain age, for example, "My Brother at Fourteen" or "My Mother at Fifty-Five." Your description should create a dominant impression by conveying the person's characteristic approach to life. Be sure to select lively details that support this dominant impression. Before planning your paper, you might want to read Judith Ortiz Cofer's "A Partial Remembrance of a Puerto Rican Childhood" (page 134), and Maya Angelou's "Sister Flowers" (page 116), two essays that pay loving tribute to indomitable figures.

2. Describe one or more active, vital older people who have not retreated into the past to find happiness. Your examples could be people you know, people you have heard about, or people in the public eye. Choose vivid details that show how such people's actions and attitudes keep them "young." Draw some conclusions about what older people can do to stay involved with life.

Writing Assignments Using Other Patterns of Development

3. Russell Baker's essay concerns a crisis in his family. Write an essay about a crisis situation in a family—your own or someone else's. The crisis might be a divorce, serious or chronic illness, loss of a job, financial difficulties, or some other serious problem. Your essay might explore the causes and/or effects of the crisis; it might outline the steps the family has taken to deal with the crisis; it might be a narrative that points to some conclusion about how people deal with crises.

4. In the past, most elderly parents lived in an extended family—children, grandchildren, and other relatives were all part of a single household. Today, though, many old people are isolated from families. In addition, many people feel our society—unlike some others—doesn't seem to revere older people; indeed, we often disregard their experience, wisdom, and traditions. Write an essay showing how society's attitude toward older people affects the lives of both the old and the young.

Writing Assignments Using a Journal Entry as a Starting Point

5. Review your pre-reading journal entry, selecting *one* especially difficult challenge that elderly people face. Then write an essay illustrating, with several strong examples, the extent of the problem. At the end of your essay, describe briefly the steps that might be taken to alleviate the difficulty. To lend authority to your discussion, consider interviewing others (especially senior citizens) and conducting research in the library and/or on the Internet.

Maya Angelou

Born Marguerite Johnson in 1928, Maya Angelou spent her childhood in Stamps, Arkansas, with her brother, Bailey, and her grandmother, "Momma." Although her youth was difficult—she was raped at age eight and a mother at sixteen—Angelou somehow managed to thrive. Multi-talented, she later worked as a professional dancer, starred in an off-Broadway play, appeared in the television miniseries *Roots*, served as a coordinator for the Southern Christian Leadership Conference, and wrote several well-received volumes of poetry—among them *Oh Pray My Wings Are Gonna Fit Me Well* (1975) and *And Still I Rise* (1996). She has also written children's books, including *My Painted House, My Friendly Chicken, and Me* (1994) and *Kofi and His Magic* (1996) and, most recently, wrote a collection of essays called *Even the Stars Look Lonesome* (1997). A professor at Wake Forest University since 1991, Angelou delivered at the 1993 presidential inauguration a stirring poem written for the occasion. The recipient of numerous honorary doctorates, Angelou is best known for her series of five autobiographical books, starting with *I Know Why the Caged Bird Sings* (1970) and concluding with *All God's Children Need Traveling Shoes* (1986). The following essay is taken from *I Know Why the Caged Bird Sings*.

Pre-Reading Journal Entry

Growing up isn't easy. In your journal, list several challenges you've had to face in your life. In each case, was there someone who served as a "lifeline," providing you with crucial guidance and support? Who was that individual? How did this person steer you through the difficulty?

Sister Flowers

For nearly a year [after I was raped], I sopped around the house, 1 the Store, the school and the church, like an old biscuit, dirty and inedible. Then I met, or rather got to know, the lady who threw me my first life line.

Mrs. Bertha Flowers was the aristocrat of Black Stamps. She had 2 the grace of control to appear warm in the coldest weather, and on the Arkansas summer days it seemed she had a private breeze which swirled around, cooling her. She was thin without the taut look of wiry people, and her printed voile dresses and flowered hats were as right for her as denim overalls for a farmer. She was our side's answer to the richest white woman in town.

Her skin was a rich black that would have peeled like a plum if 3 snagged, but then no one would have thought of getting close enough to Mrs. Flowers to ruffle her dress, let alone snag her skin. She didn't encourage familiarity. She wore gloves too.

I don't think I ever saw Mrs. Flowers laugh, but she smiled 4 often. A slow widening of her thin black lips to show even, small white teeth, then the slow effortless closing. When she chose to smile on me, I always wanted to thank her. The action was so graceful and inclusively benign.

She was one of the few gentlewomen I have ever known, and 5 has remained throughout my life the measure of what a human being can be.

Momma had a strange relationship with her. Most often when 6 she passed on the road in front of the Store, she spoke to Momma in that soft yet carrying voice, "Good day, Mrs. Henderson." Momma responded with "How you, Sister Flowers?"

Mrs. Flowers didn't belong to our church, nor was she 7 Momma's familiar. Why on earth did she insist on calling her Sister Flowers? Shame made me want to hide my face. Mrs. Flowers deserved better than to be called Sister. Then, Momma left out the verb. Why not ask, "How *are* you, *Mrs.* Flowers?" With the unbalanced passion of the young, I hated her for showing her ignorance to Mrs. Flowers. It didn't occur to me for many years that they were as alike as sisters, separated only by formal education.

Although I was upset, neither of the women was in the least 8 shaken by what I thought an unceremonious greeting. Mrs. Flowers would continue her easy gait up the hill to her little bungalow, and Momma kept on shelling peas or doing whatever had brought her to the front porch.

Occasionally, though, Mrs. Flowers would drift off the road and 9 down to the Store and Momma would say to me, "Sister, you go on and play." As she left I would hear the beginning of an intimate conversation. Momma persistently using the wrong verb, or none at all.

"Brother and Sister Wilcox is sho'ly the meanest—" "Is," 10 Momma? "Is"? Oh, please, not "is," Momma, for two or more. But they talked, and from the side of the building where I waited for the ground to open up and swallow me, I heard the soft-voiced Mrs. Flowers and the textured voice of my grandmother merging and melting. They were interrupted from time to time by giggles that must have come from Mrs. Flowers (Momma never giggled in her life). Then she was gone.

She appealed to me because she was like people I had never met   11
personally. Like women in English novels who walked the moors (whatever they were) with their loyal dogs racing at a respectful distance. Like the women who sat in front of roaring fireplaces, drinking tea incessantly from silver trays full of scones and crumpets. Women who walked over the "heath" and read morocco-bound books and had two last names divided by a hyphen. It would be safe to say that she made me proud to be Negro, just by being herself.

She acted just as refined as whitefolks in the movies and books   12
and she was more beautiful, for none of them could have come near that warm color without looking gray by comparison.

It was fortunate that I never saw her in the company of   13
powhitefolks. For since they tend to think of their whiteness as an evenizer, I'm certain that I would have had to hear her spoken to commonly as Bertha, and my image of her would have been shattered like the unmendable Humpty-Dumpty.

One summer afternoon, sweet-milk fresh in my memory, she   14
stopped at the Store to buy provisions. Another Negro woman of her health and age would have been expected to carry the paper sacks home in one hand, but Momma said, "Sister Flowers, I'll send Bailey up to your house with these things."

She smiled that slow dragging smile, "Thank you, Mrs.   15
Henderson. I'd prefer Marguerite, though." My name was beautiful when she said it. "I've been meaning to talk to her, anyway." They gave each other age-group looks.

Momma said, "Well, that's all right then. Sister, go and change   16
your dress. You going to Sister Flowers's."

The chifforobe was a maze. What on earth did one put on to go   17
to Mrs. Flowers's house? I knew I shouldn't put on a Sunday dress. It might be sacrilegious. Certainly not a house dress, since I was already wearing a fresh one. I chose a school dress, naturally. It was formal without suggesting that going to Mrs. Flowers's house was equivalent to attending church.

I trusted myself back into the Store.   18

"Now, don't you look nice." I had chosen the right thing, for   19
once. . . .

There was a little path beside the rocky road, and Mrs. Flowers   20
walked in front swinging her arms and picking her way over the stones.

She said, without turning her head, to me, "I hear you're doing   21
very good school work, Marguerite, but that it's all written. The
teachers report that they have trouble getting you to talk in class."
We passed the triangular farm on our left and the path widened to
allow us to walk together. I hung back in the separate unasked and
unanswerable questions.

"Come and walk along with me, Marguerite." I couldn't have   22
refused even if I wanted to. She pronounced my name so nicely. Or
more correctly, she spoke each word with such clarity that I was certain a foreigner who didn't understand English could have understood her.

"Now no one is going to make you talk—possibly no one can.   23
But bear in mind, language is man's way of communicating with his
fellow man and it is language alone which separates him from the
lower animals." That was a totally new idea to me, and I would need
time to think about it.

"Your grandmother says you read a lot. Every chance you get.   24
That's good, but not good enough. Words mean more than what is
set down on paper. It takes the human voice to infuse them with the
shades of deeper meaning."

I memorized the part about the human voice infusing words. It   25
seemed so valid and poetic.

She said she was going to give me some books and that I not   26
only must read them, I must read them aloud. She suggested that I
try to make a sentence sound in as many different ways as possible.

"I'll accept no excuse if you return a book to me that has been   27
badly handled." My imagination boggled at the punishment I
would deserve if in fact I did abuse a book of Mrs. Flowers's. Death
would be too kind and brief.

The odors in the house surprised me. Somehow I had never   28
connected Mrs. Flowers with food or eating or any other common
experience of common people. There must have been an outhouse,
too, but my mind never recorded it.

The sweet scent of vanilla had met us as she opened the door.   29

"I made tea cookies this morning. You see, I had planned to   30
invite you for cookies and lemonade so we could have this little chat.
The lemonade is in the icebox."

It followed that Mrs. Flowers would have ice on an ordinary   31
day, when most families in our town bought ice late on Saturdays
only a few times during the summer to be used in the wooden ice-
cream freezers.

She took the bags from me and disappeared through the   32
kitchen door. I looked around the room that I had never in my
wildest fantasies imagined I would see. Browned photographs leered
or threatened from the walls and the white, freshly done curtains
pushed against themselves and against the wind. I wanted to gobble
up the room entire and take it to Bailey, who would help me analyze and enjoy it.

"Have a seat, Marguerite. Over there by the table." She carried   33
a platter covered with a tea towel. Although she warned that she
hadn't tried her hand at baking sweets for some time, I was certain
that like everything else about her the cookies would be perfect.

They were flat round wafers, slightly browned on the edges and   34
butter-yellow in the center. With the cold lemonade they were sufficient for childhood's lifelong diet. Remembering my manners, I
took nice little lady-like bites off the edges. She said she had made
them expressly for me and that she had a few in the kitchen that I
could take home to my brother. So I jammed one whole cake in my
mouth and the rough crumbs scratched the insides of my jaws, and
if I hadn't had to swallow, it would have been a dream come true.

As I ate she began the first of what we later called "my lessons   35
in living." She said that I must always be intolerant of ignorance but
understanding of illiteracy. That some people, unable to go to
school, were more educated and even more intelligent than college
professors. She encouraged me to listen carefully to what country
people called mother wit. That in those homely sayings was couched
the collective wisdom of generations.

When I finished the cookies she brushed off the table and   36
brought a thick, small book from the bookcase. I had read *A Tale
of Two Cities* and found it up to my standards as a romantic novel.
She opened the first page and I heard poetry for the first time in
my life.

"It was the best of times and the worst of times . . ." Her voice   37
slid in and curved down through and over the words. She was nearly singing. I wanted to look at the pages. Were they the same that I
had read? Or were there notes, music, lined on the pages, as in a
hymn book? Her sounds began cascading gently. I knew from listening to a thousand preachers that she was nearing the end of her
reading, and I hadn't really heard, heard to understand, a single
word.

"How do you like that?"   38

It occurred to me that she expected a response. The sweet vanil-   39
la flavor was still on my tongue and her reading was a wonder in my
ears. I had to speak.

I said, "Yes, ma'am." It was the least I could do, but it was the   40
most also.

"There's one more thing. Take this book of poems and memo-   41
rize one for me. Next time you pay me a visit, I want you to recite."

I have tried often to search behind the sophistication of years for   42
the enchantment I so easily found in those gifts. The essence escapes
but its aura remains. To be allowed, no, invited, into the private lives
of strangers, and to share their joys and fears, was a chance to
exchange the Southern bitter wormwood for a cup of mead with
Beowulf[1] or a hot cup of tea and milk with Oliver Twist.[2] When I
said aloud, "It is a far, far better thing that I do, than I have ever
done . . ."[3] tears of love filled my eyes at my selflessness.

On that first day, I ran down the hill and into the road (few cars   43
ever came along it) and had the good sense to stop running before
I reached the Store.

I was liked, and what a difference it made. I was respected not   44
as Mrs. Henderson's grandchild or Bailey's sister but for just being
Marguerite Johnson.

Childhood's logic never asks to be proved (all conclusions are   45
absolute). I didn't question why Mrs. Flowers had singled me out
for attention, nor did it occur to me that Momma might have asked
her to give me a little talking to. All I cared about was that she had
made tea cookies for *me* and read to *me* from her favorite book. It
was enough to prove that she liked me.

---

[1]The hero of an Old English epic poem dating from the eighth century (editors'
note).
[2]The main character in Charles Dickens's novel *Oliver Twist* (1837) (editors' note).
[3]The last words of Sydney Carton, the selfless hero of Charles Dickens's novel *A
Tale of Two Cities* (1859) (editors' note).

Questions for Close Reading

1. What is the selection's thesis (or dominant impression)? Locate the sen-
   tence(s) in which Angelou states her main idea. If she doesn't state the
   thesis explicitly, express it in your own words.

2. Angelou states that Mrs. Flowers "has remained throughout my life the measure of what a human being can be" (paragraph 5). What does Angelou admire about Mrs. Flowers?

3. Why is young Angelou so ashamed of Momma when Mrs. Flowers is around? How do Momma and Mrs. Flowers behave with each other?

4. What are the "lessons in living" that Angelou receives from Mrs. Flowers during their first visit? How do you think these lessons might have subsequently influenced Angelou?

5. Refer to your dictionary as needed to define the following words used in the selection: *taut* (paragraph 2), *voile* (2), *benign* (4), *unceremonious* (8), *gait* (8), *moors* (11), *incessantly* (11), *scones* (11), *crumpets* (11), *heath* (11), *chifforobe* (17), *sacrilegious* (17), *infuse* (24), *couched* (35), and *aura* (42).

Questions About the Writer's Craft

1. **The pattern.** Reread the essay, focusing on the descriptive passages first of Mrs. Flowers and then of Angelou's visit to Mrs. Flowers's house. To what senses does Angelou appeal in these passages? What method of organization (see pages 47–49) does she use to order these sensory details?

2. To enrich the description of her eventful encounter with Mrs. Flowers, Angelou draws upon figures of speech (see pages 89–90). Consider, for example, the similes in paragraphs 1 and 11. How do these figures of speech contribute to the essay's dominant impression?

3. **Other patterns.**   Because Angelou's description has a strong narrative component, it isn't surprising that there's a considerable amount of dialogue in the selection. For example, in paragraphs 7 and 10, Angelou quotes Momma's incorrect grammar. She then provides an imagined conversation in which the young Angelou scolds Momma and corrects her speech. What do these imagined scoldings of Momma reveal about young Angelou? How do they relate to Mrs. Flowers's subsequent "lessons in life"?

4. Although it's not the focus of this selection, the issue of race remains in the background of Angelou's portrait of Mrs. Flowers. Where in the selection does Angelou imply that race was a fact of life in her town? How does this specter of racism help Angelou underscore the significance of her encounter with Mrs. Flowers?

Writing Assignments Using Comparison-Contrast as a Method of Development

1. At one time or another, just about all of us have met someone who taught us to see ourselves more clearly and helped us understand what

we wanted from life. Write an essay describing such a person. Focus on the individual's personal qualities, as a way of depicting the role he or she played in your life. Be sure not to limit yourself to an objective description. Subjective description, filled with lively language and figures of speech, will serve you well as you provide a portrait of this special person.

∞ 2. Thrilled by the spectacle of Mrs. Flowers's interesting home, Angelou says she wanted to "gobble up the room entire" and share it with her brother. Write an essay describing in detail a place that vividly survives in your memory. You may describe a setting that you visited only once or a familiar setting that holds a special place in your heart. Before you write, list the qualities and sensory impressions you associate with this special place; then refine the list so that all details support your dominant impression. You may want to read E. B. White's "Once More to the Lake" (page 125) to see how a professional writer evokes the qualities of a special place in his life.

Writing Assignments Using Other Patterns of Development

∞ 3. When the young Angelou discovers, thanks to Mrs. Flowers, the thrill of acceptance, she experiences a kind of *epiphany*—a moment of enlightenment. Write an essay about an event in your life that represented a kind of epiphany. You might write about a positive discovery, such as when you realized you had a special talent for something, or about a negative discovery, such as when you realized that a beloved family member had a serious flaw. To make the point that the moment was a turning point in your life, start by describing what kind of person you were before the discovery. Then narrate the actual incident, using vivid details and dialogue to make the event come alive. End by discussing the importance of this epiphany in your life. For additional accounts of personal epiphanies, you might read Audre Lorde's "The Fourth of July" (page 160), Langston Hughes's "Salvation" (page 183), and Beth Johnson's "Bombs Bursting in Air" (page 242).

4. Think of an activity that engages you completely, one that provides—as reading does for Angelou—an opportunity for growth and expansion. Possibilities include reading, writing, playing an instrument, doing crafts, dancing, hiking, playing a sport, cooking, or traveling. Write an essay in which you argue the merits of your chosen pastime. Assume that some of your readers are highly skeptical. To win them over, you'll need to provide convincing examples that demonstrate the pleasure and benefits you have discovered in the activity.

Writing Assignments Using a Journal Entry
as a Starting Point

∞ 5. Write an essay about a time when someone threw you a much-needed "lifeline" at a challenging time. Review your pre-reading journal entry, selecting *one* time when a person's encouragement and support made a great difference in your life. Be sure to describe the challenge you faced before recounting the specific details of the person's help. Dialogue and descriptive details will help you recreate the power of the experience. You should consider reading "Beauty: When the Other Dancer Is the Self" (page 467), in which Alice Walker shows how loving guidance made a world of difference in her life.

E. B. White

Elwyn Brooks White (1899–1985) is considered one of America's finest essayists. For many years, White was a member of the *New Yorker* magazine staff and wrote the magazine's popular column, "The Talk of the Town." He also wrote children's books, including the classic *Charlotte's Web* (1952), and was the coauthor with William Strunk, Jr., of the renowned guide for writers, *The Elements of Style* (1959). But most memorable are the essays White produced during his life—gems of clarity, wit, and heartfelt expression. White's contribution to literature earned him many awards, including the Presidential Medal of Freedom and the National Medal for Literature. The classic essay reprinted here is taken from *The Essays of E. B. White* (1977).

Pre-Reading Journal Entry

In your journal, list at least two occasions—either serious or humorous—that made you keenly aware that you were growing older. What was it about each situation that forced this realization upon you? How did the realization affect you? Did it please or distress you? Jot down as many details about each instance as you can.

Once More to the Lake

One summer, along about 1904, my father rented a camp on a lake in Maine and took us all there for the month of August. We all got ringworm from some kittens and had to rub Pond's Extract on our arms and legs night and morning, and my father rolled over in a canoe with all his clothes on; but outside of that the vacation was a success and from then on none of us ever thought there was any place in the world like that lake in Maine. We returned summer after summer—always on August 1 for one month. I have since become a salt-water man, but sometimes in summer there are days when the restlessness of the tides and the fearful cold of the sea water and the incessant wind that blows across the afternoon and into the evening make me wish for the placidity of a lake in the woods. A few weeks ago this feeling got so strong I bought myself a couple of bass hooks

1

and a spinner and returned to the lake where we used to go, for a week's fishing and to revisit old haunts.

I took along my son, who had never had any fresh water up his   2
nose and who had seen lily pads only from train windows. On the journey over to the lake I began to wonder what it would be like. I wondered how time would have marred this unique, this holy spot—the coves and streams, the hills that the sun set behind, the camps and the paths behind the camps. I was sure that the tarred road would have found it out, and I wondered in what other ways it would be desolated. It is strange how much you can remember about places like that once you allow your mind to return into the grooves that lead back. You remember one thing, and that suddenly reminds you of another thing. I guess I remembered clearest of all the early mornings, when the lake was cool and motionless, remembered how the bedroom smelled of the lumber it was made of and of the wet woods whose scent entered through the screen. The partitions in the camp were thin and did not extend clear to the top of the rooms, and as I was always the first up I would dress softly so as not to wake the others, and sneak out into the sweet outdoors and start out in the canoe, keeping close along the shore in the long shadows of the pines. I remembered being very careful never to rub my paddle against the gunwale for fear of disturbing the stillness of the cathedral.

The lake had never been what you would call a wild lake. There   3
were cottages sprinkled around the shores, and it was in farming country although the shores of the lake were quite heavily wooded. Some of the cottages were owned by nearby farmers, and you would live at the shore and eat your meals at the farmhouse. That's what our family did. But although it wasn't wild, it was a fairly large and undisturbed lake and there were places in it that, to a child at least, seemed infinitely remote and primeval.

I was right about the tar: it led to within half a mile of the shore.   4
But when I got back there, with my boy, and we settled into a camp near a farmhouse and into the kind of summertime I had known, I could tell that it was going to be pretty much the same as it had been before—I knew it, lying in bed the first morning, smelling the bedroom and hearing the boy sneak quietly out and go off along the shore in a boat. I began to sustain the illusion that he was I, and therefore, by simple transposition, that I was my father. This sensation persisted, kept cropping up all the time we were there. It was

not an entirely new feeling, but in this setting it grew much stronger. I seemed to be living a dual existence. I would be in the middle of some simple act, I would be picking up a bait box or laying down a table fork, or I would be saying something, and suddenly it would be not I but my father who was saying the words or making the gesture. It gave me a creepy sensation.

We went fishing the first morning. I felt the same damp moss covering the worms in the bait can, and saw the dragonfly alight on the tip of my rod as it hovered a few inches from the surface of the water. It was the arrival of this fly that convinced me beyond any doubt that everything was as it always had been, that the years were a mirage and that there had been no years. The small waves were the same, chucking the rowboat under the chin as we fished at anchor, and the boat was the same boat, the same color green and the ribs broken in the same places, and under the floorboards the same fresh-water leavings and débris—the dead helgramite, the wisps of moss, the rusty discarded fishhook, the dried blood from yesterday's catch. We stared silently at the tips of our rods, at the dragonflies that came and went. I lowered the tip of mine into the water, tentatively, pensively dislodging the fly, which darted two feet away, poised, darted two feet back, and came to rest again a little farther up the rod. There had been no years between the ducking of this dragonfly and the other one—the one that was part of memory. I looked at the boy, who was silently watching his fly, and it was my hands that held his rod, my eyes watching. I felt dizzy and didn't know which rod I was at the end of.

We caught two bass, hauling them in briskly as though they were mackerel, pulling them over the side of the boat in a businesslike manner without any landing net, and stunning them with a blow on the back of the head. When we got back for a swim before lunch, the lake was exactly where we had left it, the same number of inches from the dock, and there was only the merest suggestion of a breeze. This seemed an utterly enchanted sea, this lake you could leave to its own devices for a few hours and come back to, and find that it had not stirred, this constant and trustworthy body of water. In the shallows, the dark, water-soaked sticks and twigs, smooth and old, were undulating in clusters on the bottom against the clean ribbed sand, and the track of the mussel was plain. A school of minnows swam by, each minnow with its small individual shadow, doubling the attendance, so clear and sharp in the sunlight. Some of the

5

6

other campers were in swimming, along the shore, one of them with a cake of soap, and the water felt thin and clear and unsubstantial. Over the years there had been this person with the cake of soap, this cultist, and here he was. There had been no years.

Up to the farmhouse to dinner through the teeming, dusty field, the road under our sneakers was only a two-track road. The middle track was missing, the one with the marks of the hooves and the splotches of dried, flaky manure. There had always been three tracks to choose from in choosing which track to walk in; now the choice was narrowed down to two. For a moment I missed terribly the middle alternative. But the way led past the tennis court, and something about the way it lay there in the sun reassured me; the tape had loosened along the backline, the alleys were green with plantains and other weeds, and the net (installed in June and removed in September) sagged in the dry noon, and the whole place steamed with midday heat and hunger and emptiness. There was a choice of pie for dessert, and one was blueberry and one was apple, and the waitresses were the same country girls, there having been no passage of time, only the illusion of it as in a dropped curtain—the waitresses were still fifteen; their hair had been washed, that was the only difference—they had been to the movies and seen the pretty girls with the clean hair.   7

Summertime, oh, summertime, pattern of life indelible, the fade-proof lake, the woods unshatterable, the pasture with the sweetfern and the juniper forever and ever, summer without end; this was the background, and the life along the shore was the design, the cottagers with their innocent and tranquil design, their tiny docks with the flagpole and the American flag floating against the white clouds in the blue sky, the little paths over the roots of the trees leading from camp to camp and the paths leading back to the outhouses and the can of lime for sprinkling, and at the souvenir counters at the store the miniature birch-bark canoes and the post-cards that showed things looking a little better than they looked. This was the American family at play, escaping the city heat, wondering whether the newcomers in the camp at the head of the cove were "common" or "nice," wondering whether it was true that the people who drove up for Sunday dinner at the farmhouse were turned away because there wasn't enough chicken.   8

It seemed to me, as I kept remembering all this, that those times and those summers had been infinitely precious and worth saving.   9

There had been jollity and peace and goodness. The arriving (at the beginning of August) had been so big a business in itself, at the railway station the farm wagon drawn up, the first smell of the pine-laden air, the first glimpse of the smiling farmer, and the great importance of the trunks and your father's enormous authority in such matters, and the feel of the wagon under you for the long ten-mile haul, and at the top of the last long hill catching the first view of the lake after eleven months of not seeing this cherished body of water. The shouts and cries of the other campers when they saw you, and the trunks to be unpacked, to give up their rich burden. (Arriving was less exciting nowadays, when you sneaked up in your car and parked it under a tree near the camp and took out the bags and in five minutes it was all over, no fuss, no loud wonderful fuss about trunks.)

Peace and goodness and jollity. The only thing that was wrong   10
now, really, was the sound of the place, an unfamiliar nervous sound of the outboard motors. This was the note that jarred, the one thing that would sometimes break the illusion and set the years moving. In those other summertimes all motors were inboard; and when they were at a little distance, the noise they made was a sedative, an ingredient of summer sleep. They were one-cylinder and two-cylinder engines, and some were make-and-break and some were jump-spark, but they all made a sleepy sound across the lake. The one-lungers throbbed and fluttered, and the twin-cylinder ones purred and purred, and that was a quiet sound, too. But now the campers all had outboards. In the daytime, in the hot mornings, these motors made a petulant, irritable sound; at night, in the still evening when the afterglow lit the water, they whined about one's ears like mosquitoes. My boy loved our rented outboard, and his great desire was to achieve single-handed mastery over it, and authority, and he soon learned the trick of choking it a little (but not too much), and the adjustment of the needle valve. Watching him I would remember the things you could do with the old one-cylinder engine with the heavy flywheel, how you could have it eating out of your hand if you got really close to it spiritually. Motorboats in those days didn't have clutches, and you would make a landing by shutting off the motor at the proper time and coasting in with a dead rudder. But there was a way of reversing them, if you learned the trick, by cutting the switch and putting it on again exactly on the final dying revolution of the flywheel, so

that it would kick back against compression and begin reversing. Approaching a dock in a strong following breeze, it was difficult to slow up sufficiently by the ordinary coasting method, and if a boy felt he had complete mastery over his motor, he was tempted to keep it running beyond its time and then reverse it a few feet from the dock. It took a cool nerve, because if you threw the switch a twentieth of a second too soon you would catch the flywheel when it still had speed enough to go up past center, and the boat would leap ahead, charging bullfashion at the dock.

We had a good week at the camp. The bass were biting well and 11 the sun shone endlessly, day after day. We would be tired at night and lie down in the accumulated heat of the little bedrooms after the long hot day and the breeze would stir almost imperceptibly outside and the smell of the swamp drift in through the rusty screens. Sleep would come easily and in the morning the red squirrel would be on the roof, tapping out his gay routine. I kept remembering everything, lying in bed in the mornings—the small steamboat that had a long rounded stern like the lip of a Ubangi, and how quietly she ran on the moonlight sails, when the older boys played their mandolins and the girls sang and we ate doughnuts dipped in sugar, and how sweet the music was on the water in the shining night, and what it had felt like to think about girls then. After breakfast we would go up to the store and the things were in the same place—the minnows in a bottle, the plugs and spinners disarranged and pawed over by the youngsters from the boys' camp, the Fig Newtons and the Beeman's gum. Outside, the road was tarred and cars stood in front of the store. Inside, all was just as it had always been, except there was more Coca-Cola and not so much Moxie and root beer and birch beer and sarsaparilla. We would walk out with the bottle of pop apiece and sometimes the pop would backfire up our noses and hurt. We explored the streams, quietly, where the turtles slid off the sunny logs and dug their way into the soft bottom; and we lay on the town wharf and fed worms to the tame bass. Everywhere we went I had trouble making out which was I, the one walking at my side, the one walking in my pants.

One afternoon while we were there at the lake a thunderstorm 12 came up. It was like the revival of an old melodrama that I had seen long ago with childish awe. The second-act climax of the drama of the electrical disturbance over a lake in America had not changed in any important respect. This was the big scene, still the big scene. The whole thing was so familiar, the first feeling of oppression and heat and a general air around camp of not wanting to go very far away. In midafternoon (it was all the same) a curious darkening of the sky, and a lull in everything that had made life tick; and then the way the boats suddenly swung the other way at their moorings with the coming of a breeze out of the new quarter, and premonitory rumble. Then the kettle drum, then the snare, then the bass drum and cymbals, then cackling light against the dark, and the gods grinning and licking their chops in the hills. Afterward the calm, the rain steadily rustling in the calm lake, the return of light and hope and spirits, and the campers running out in joy and relief to go swimming in the rain, their bright cries perpetuating the deathless joke about how they were getting simply drenched, and the children screaming with delight at the new sensation of bathing in the rain, and the joke about getting drenched linking the generations in a strong indestructible chain. And the comedian who waded in carrying an umbrella.

When the others went swimming, my son said he was going in, 13 too. He pulled his dripping trunks from the line where they had hung all through the shower and wrung them out. Languidly, and with no thought of going in, I watched him, his hard little body, skinny and bare, saw him wince slightly as he pulled up around his vitals the small, soggy, icy garment. As he buckled the swollen belt, suddenly my groin felt the chill of death.

Questions for Close Reading

1. What is the selection's thesis (or dominant impression)? Locate the sentence(s) in which White states his main idea. If he doesn't state the thesis explicitly, express it in your own words.
2. Why does White return to the lake in Maine he had visited as a child? Why do you think he has waited to revisit it until he has a young son to bring along?
3. Several times in the essay, White notes that he felt as if he were his own father—and that his son became his childhood self. What event first prompts this sensation? What actions and thoughts cause it to recur?
4. How is the latest visit to the lake similar to White's childhood summers? What differences does White notice? What effects do the differences have on him?
5. Refer to your dictionary as needed to define the following words used in the selection: *incessant* (paragraph 1), *placidity* (1), *primeval* (3), *transposition* (4), *undulating* (6), *indelible* (8), *petulant* (10), and *languidly* (13).

Questions About the Writer's Craft

1. **The pattern.** Through vivid language, descriptive writing evokes sensory experiences. In "Once More to the Lake," White overlays two sets of sensory details: those of the present-day lake and those of the lake as it was in his boyhood. Which set of details is more objective? Which seems sharper and more powerful? Why?

2. To describe the lake, White chooses many words and phrases with religious connotations. Give some examples. What might have been his purpose in using such language?

3. **Other patterns.** In paragraph 12, White uses a metaphor to describe a thunderstorm. To what does he compare a thunderstorm? Why does he make this comparison?

4. White refers to "the chill of death" in the final paragraph. What brings on this feeling? Why does he feel it "in his groin"? Where has this idea been hinted at previously in the essay?

Writing Assignments Using Description as a Pattern of Development

∞ 1. Write an essay describing a special place in your life. The place need not be a natural setting like White's lake; it could be a city or building that has meant a great deal to you. Use sensory details and figurative language, as White does, to enliven your description and convey the place's significance for you. Before writing, read Maya Angelou's "Sister Flowers" (page 116) to see how a professional writer conveys the special qualities of a memorable childhood place.

∞ 2. White was fortunate that his lake had remained virtually unchanged. But many other special spots have been destroyed or are threatened with destruction. Write an essay describing a place (a park, a school, an old-fashioned ice-cream parlor) that is "infinitely precious and worth saving." For your dominant theme, show which aspects of your subject make it worthy of being preserved for future generations. Before writing your essay, you might want to read Rachel Carson's "A Fable for Tomorrow" (page 405), an essay that laments the loss of a special place.

Writing Assignments Using Other Patterns of Development

3. Sometimes, we, like White, are suddenly reminded of the nearness of death: a crushed animal lies in the road, a politician is assassinated, a classmate is killed in a car crash. Write an essay about a time you were forced to think about mortality. Explain what happened and describe your thoughts and feelings afterwards.

∞ **4.** Have your older relatives attempted to share with you some special experiences of their younger years? Have you done the same thing with your own children, nephews, or nieces? You may have taken loved ones to a special place, as White did, or listened to stories or looked at photographs. Write an essay recounting such an experience. Explain the motivations of the older generation and the effects on the younger one. Judith Ortiz Cofer's "A Partial Remembrance of a Puerto Rican Childhood" (page 134) will spark some thoughts about special family times.

Writing Assignments Using a Journal Entry as a Starting Point

∞ **5.** Write an essay narrating an incident that reminded you that you weren't as young as you used to be. Review your pre-reading journal entry, selecting the *one* occasion you would most enjoy writing about. Draw upon the specifics in your journal, providing additional details about both external circumstances and your internal state of mind. End your essay by discussing how your realization affected your subsequent thoughts and actions. Before you write, consider reading "In My Day" (page 108), Russell Baker's account of his sobering realization that he's growing older.

Judith Ortiz Cofer

Born in Puerto Rico, raised both on her native island and in the United States, and educated in sites that included Oxford University in England, Judith Ortiz Cofer (1952–) knows what it is to move between cultures, absorbing from each while keeping mindful of her own heritage. Cofer earned a master's degree in English from the University of Florida before spending a year in graduate study at Oxford. Following a stint as a bilingual teacher, Cofer taught English at several colleges and universities. She has published collections of poetry, including *Peregrine* (1986), *Terms of Survival* (1995), and *Reaching for the Mainland and Selected New Poems* (1995); a novel, *The Line of the Sun* (1989); and three books of essays, *Silent Dancing: A Partial Remembrance of a Puerto Rican Childhood* (1990), *The Latin Deli: Telling the Lives of Barrio Women* (1993), and *An Island Like You: Stories of the Barrio* (1995). The following essay is taken from *Silent Dancing*.

Pre-Reading Journal Entry

Everyone loves a good story. But stories do more than merely entertain us. Use your journal to reflect on two or more stories that adults told you in your childhood as a way to teach an important lesson about life. In addition to sketching out the stories themselves, outline the circumstances of hearing the stories: who told them, where you were when you heard the stories, why the stories were recounted.

A Partial Remembrance of a Puerto Rican Childhood

At three or four o'clock in the afternoon, the hour of *café con leche*,[1] the women of my family gathered in Mamá's living room to speak of important things and retell familiar stories meant to be overheard by us young girls, their daughters. In Mamá's house (everyone called my grandmother Mamá) was a large parlor built by my grandfather to his wife's exact specifications so that it was always

1

---

[1]Spanish for "coffee with milk" (editors' note).

cool, facing away from the sun. The doorway was on the side of the house so no one could walk directly into her living room. First they had to take a little stroll through and around her beautiful garden where prize-winning orchids grew in the trunk of an ancient tree she had hollowed out for that purpose. This room was furnished with several mahogany rocking chairs, acquired at the births of her children, and one intricately carved rocker that had passed down to Mamá at the death of her own mother.

It was on these rockers that my mother, her sisters, and my   2 grandmother sat on these afternoons of my childhood to tell their stories, teaching each other, and my cousin and me, what it was like to be a woman, more specifically, a Puerto Rican woman. They talked about life on the island, and life in *Los Nueva Yores,* their way of referring to the United States from New York City to California: the other place, not home, all the same. They told real-life stories though, as I later learned, always embellishing them with a little or a lot of dramatic detail. And they told *cuentos,* the morality and cautionary tales told by the women in our family for generations: stories that became a part of my subconscious as I grew up in two worlds, the tropical island and the cold city, and that would later surface in my dreams and in my poetry.

One of these tales was about the woman who was left at the   3 altar. Mamá liked to tell that one with histrionic intensity. I remember the rise and fall of her voice, the sighs, and her constantly gesturing hands, like two birds swooping through her words. This particular story usually would come up in a conversation as a result of someone mentioning a forthcoming engagement or wedding. The first time I remember hearing it, I was sitting on the floor at Mamá's feet, pretending to read a comic book. I may have been eleven or twelve years old, at that difficult age when a girl was no longer a child who could be ordered to leave the room if the women wanted freedom to take their talk into forbidden zones, nor really old enough to be considered a part of their conclave. I could only sit quietly, pretending to be in another world, while absorbing it all in a sort of unspoken agreement of my status as silent auditor. On this day, Mamá had taken my long, tangled mane of hair into her ever-busy hands. Without looking down at me and with no interruption of her flow of words, she began braiding my hair, working at it with the quickness and determination that characterized all her actions.

My mother was watching us impassively from her rocker across the room. On her lips played a little ironic smile. I would never sit still for *her* ministrations, but even then, I instinctively knew that she did not possess Mamá's matriarchal power to command and keep everyone's attention. This was never more evident than in the spell she cast when telling a story.

"It is not like it used to be when I was a girl," Mamá   4
announced. "Then, a man could leave a girl standing at the church altar with a bouquet of fresh flowers in her hands and disappear off the face of the earth. No way to track him down if he was from another town. He could be a married man, with maybe even two or three families all over the island. There was no way to know. And there were men who did this. *Hombres*[2] with the devil in their flesh who would come to a *pueblo*,[3] like this one, take a job at one of the *haciendas*,[4] never meaning to stay, only to have a good time and to seduce the women."

The whole time she was speaking, Mamá would be weaving my   5
hair into a flat plait that required pulling apart the two sections of hair with little jerks that made my eyes water; but knowing how grandmother detested whining and *boba* (sissy) tears, as she called them, I just sat up as straight and stiff as I did at La Escuela San Jose, where the nuns enforced good posture with a flexible plastic ruler they bounced off of slumped shoulders and heads. As Mamá's story progressed, I noticed how my young Aunt Laura lowered her eyes, refusing to meet Mamá's meaningful gaze. Laura was seventeen, in her last year of high school, and already engaged to a boy from another town who had staked his claim with a tiny diamond ring, then left for Los Nueva Yores to make his fortune. They were planning to get married in a year. Mamá had expressed serious doubts that the wedding would ever take place. In Mamá's eyes, a man set free without a legal contract was a man lost. She believed that marriage was not something men desired, but simply the price they had to pay for the privilege of children and, of course, for what no decent (synonymous with "smart") woman would give away for free.

"María La Loca was only seventeen when *it* happened to her."   6
I listened closely at the mention of this name. María was a town character, a fat middle-aged woman who lived with her old mother

---

[2]Spanish for "men" (editors' note).
[3]Spanish for "community" (editors' note).
[4]Spanish for "large estate" or "ranch" (editors' note).

on the outskirts of town. She was to be seen around the pueblo delivering the meat pies the two women made for a living. The most peculiar thing about María, in my eyes, was that she walked and moved like a little girl though she had the thick body and wrinkled face of an old woman. She would swing her hips in an exaggerated, clownish way, and sometimes even hop and skip up to someone's house. She spoke to no one. Even if you asked her a question, she would just look at you and smile, showing her yellow teeth. But I had heard that if you got close enough, you could hear her humming a tune without words. The kids yelled out nasty things at her, calling her *La Loca*,[5] and the men who hung out at the *bodega*[6] playing dominoes sometimes whistled mockingly as she passed by with her funny, outlandish walk. But María seemed impervious to it all, carrying her basket of *pasteles*[7] like a grotesque Little Red Riding Hood through the forest.

María La Loca interested me, as did all the eccentrics and crazies of our pueblo. Their weirdness was a measuring stick I used in my serious quest for a definition of normal. As a Navy brat shuttling between New Jersey and the pueblo, I was constantly made to feel like an oddball by my peers, who made fun of my two-way accent: a Spanish accent when I spoke English, and when I spoke Spanish I was told that I sounded like a *Gringa*.[8] Being the outsider had already turned my brother and me into cultural chameleons. We developed early on the ability to blend into a crowd, to sit and read quietly in a fifth story apartment building for days and days when it was too bitterly cold to play outside, or, set free, to run wild in Mamá's realm, where she took charge of our lives, releasing Mother for a while from the intense fear for our safety that our father's absences instilled in her. In order to keep us from harm when Father was away, Mother kept us under strict surveillance. She even walked us to and from Public School No. 11, which we attended during the months we lived in Paterson, New Jersey, our home base in the States. Mamá freed all three of us like pigeons from a cage. I saw her as my liberator and my model. Her stories were parables from which to glean the *Truth*.

7

[5]Spanish for "crazy one" (editors' note).
[6]Spanish for a neighborhood grocery store (editors' note).
[7]Spanish for "pastries" (editors' note).
[8]A negatively charged Latin American slang expression for a female foreigner (editors' note).

"María La Loca was once a beautiful girl. Everyone thought she   8
would marry the Méndez boy." As everyone knew, Rogelio Méndez
was the richest man in town. "But," Mamá continued, knitting my
hair with the same intensity she was putting into her story, "this
macho made a fool out of her and ruined her life." She paused for the
effect of her use of the word "macho," which at that time had not
yet become a popular epithet for an unliberated man. This word had
for us the crude and comical connotation of "male of the species,"
stud; a *macho* was what you put in a pen to increase your stock.

I peeked over my comic book at my mother. She too was under   9
Mamá's spell, smiling conspiratorially at this little swipe at men. She
was safe from Mamá's contempt in this area. Married at an early age,
an unspotted lamb, she had been accepted by a good family of strict
Spaniards whose name was old and respected, though their fortune
had been lost long before my birth. In a rocker Papá had painted sky
blue sat Mamá's oldest child, Aunt Nena. Mother of three children,
stepmother of two more, she was a quiet woman who liked books
but had married an ignorant and abusive widower whose main interest in life was accumulating wealth. He too was in the mainland
working on his dream of returning home rich and triumphant to
buy the *finca*[9] of his dreams. She was waiting for him to send for
her. She would leave her children with Mamá for several years while
the two of them slaved away in factories. He would one day be a rich
man, and she a sadder woman. Even now her life-light was dim-
ming. She spoke little, an aberration in Mamá's house, and she read
avidly, as if storing up spiritual food for the long winters that await-
ed her in Los Nueva Yores without her family. But even Aunt Nena
came alive to Mamá's words, rocking gently, her hands over a thick
book in her lap.

Her daughter, my cousin Sara, played jacks by herself on the tile   10
porch outside the room where we sat. She was a year older than I.
We shared a bed and all our family's secrets. Collaborators in search
of answers, Sara and I discussed everything we heard the women say,
trying to fit it all together like a puzzle that, once assembled, would
reveal life's mysteries to us. Though she and I still enjoyed taking
part in boys' games—chase, volleyball, and even *vaqueros,* the island
version of cowboys and Indians involving cap-gun battles and violent shoot-outs under the mango tree in Mamá's backyard—we

[9]Spanish for "farm" or "ranch" (editors' note).

loved best the quiet hours in the afternoon when the men were still at work, and the boys had gone to play serious baseball at the park. Then Mamá's house belonged only to us women. The aroma of coffee perking in the kitchen, the mesmerizing creaks and groans of the rockers, and the women telling their lives in *cuentos* are forever woven into the fabric of my imagination, braided like my hair that day I felt my grandmother's hands teaching me about strength, her voice convincing me of the power of storytelling.

That day Mamá told how the beautiful María had fallen prey to   11
a man whose name was never the same in subsequent versions of the story; it was Juan one time, José, Rafael, Diego, another. We understood that neither the name or any of the *facts* were important, only that a woman had allowed love to defeat her. Mamá put each of us in María's place by describing her wedding dress in loving detail: how she looked like a princess in her lace as she waited at the altar. Then, as Mamá approached the tragic denouement of her story, I was distracted by the sound of my Aunt Laura's violent rocking. She seemed on the verge of tears. She knew the fable was intended for her. That week she was going to have her wedding gown fitted, though no firm date had been set for the marriage. Mamá ignored Laura's obvious discomfort, digging out a ribbon from the sewing basket she kept by her rocker while describing María's long illness, "a fever that would not break for days." She spoke of a mother's despair: "that woman climbed the church steps on her knees every morning, wore only black as a *promesa* to the Holy Virgin in exchange for her daughter's health." By the time María returned from her honeymoon with death, she was ravished, no longer young or sane. "As you can see, she is almost as old as her mother already," Mamá lamented while tying the ribbon to the ends of my hair, pulling it back with such force that I just knew I would never be able to close my eyes completely again.

"That María's getting crazier every day." Mamá's voice would   12
take a lighter tone now, expressing satisfaction, either for the perfection of my braid, or for a story well told—it was hard to tell. "You know that tune María is always humming?" Carried away by her enthusiasm, I tried to nod, but Mamá still had me pinned between her knees.

"Well, that's the wedding march." Surprising us all, Mamá sang   13
out, "Da, da, dara . . . da, da, dara." Then lifting me off the floor by my skinny shoulders, she would lead me around the room in an

impromptu waltz—another session ending with the laughter of women, all of us caught up in the infectious joke of our lives.

Questions for Close Reading

1. What is the selection's thesis (or dominant impression)? Locate the sentence(s) in which Cofer states her main idea. If she doesn't state the thesis explicitly, express it in your own words.
2. Who are the women who participate in the storytelling sessions? Why is Cofer allowed to join them? Why aren't men or boys part of the group?
3. What lessons about men and women does Mamá intend the story of María La Loca to teach?
4. What information does Cofer provide about her aunts and her mother? What similarities and/or differences are there between each of their lives and the story of María La Loca?
5. Refer to your dictionary as needed to define the following words used in the selection: *intricately* (paragraph 1), *embellishing* (2), *cautionary* (2), *histrionic* (3), *conclave* (3), *auditor* (3), *impassively* (3), *ministrations* (3), *matriarchal* (3), *quest* (7), *chameleons* (7), *surveillance* (7), *conspiratorially* (9), *aberration* (9), *mesmerizing* (10), *denouement* (11), *ravished* (11), and *impromptu* (13).

Questions About the Writer's Craft

1. **The pattern.** Of all the women mentioned in the essay, only María La Loca is described in detail. What descriptive details does Cofer offer about her? Why do you suppose Cofer provides so much description about this particular woman?
2. In paragraph 7, Cofer provides some specifics about her childhood as a "Navy brat." What would have been lost if Cofer hadn't included this material?
3. **Other patterns.** Reread paragraphs 4, 6, 8, and 11–13, where Cofer recounts her grandmother's story. Why do you think Cofer doesn't tell the story straight through, without interruptions? What purpose do the interruptions serve? How does Cofer signal when she is moving away from the story or back to it?
4. Why might Cofer have mentioned in several spots the braiding of her hair, which goes on the whole time Mamá tells María's story? What similarities are there between the braiding and the storytelling session? What similarities are there between the braiding and Cofer's descriptive style (consider especially the last sentence of paragraph 10)?

Writing Assignments Using Description as a Pattern of Development

1. Cofer paints a vivid picture of a childhood ritual: the telling of stories among the women in her family. Think of a specific scene, event, or ritual from your own childhood or youth that has special meaning for you. Then write a descriptive essay conveying the distinctive flavor of that occasion. Draw upon vivid sensory language to capture your dominant impression of that time. Consider using dialogue, as Cofer does, to texturize your description and to reveal character.

2. To Cofer, Mamá was a "liberator" and a "model." Think of a person in your life who served as a role model or opened doors for you, and write an essay describing that person. Like Cofer, place the person in a characteristic setting and supply vigorous details about the person's actions, speech, looks, and so forth. Make sure that all the descriptive details reinforce your dominant impression of the individual. You may want to read Maya Angelou's "Sister Flowers" (page 116) to see how one especially skilled writer describes a powerful, influential person.

Writing Assignments Using Other Patterns of Development

3. Cofer's family is close-knit, but family life nowadays is more likely to be fragmented, with everyone going separate ways. Write an essay explaining what steps families could take to offset this tendency toward fragmentation. You might want to focus on a particular area of family life, such as mealtimes, after-supper hours, or vacations. Be sure to spend some time discussing the expected outcomes of the steps you propose. You might benefit from conducting research in the library and/or on the Internet into how to increase the quality and quantity of family time.

4. The stories Cofer heard taught her "what it was like to be a woman." What information and experiences shaped your understanding of your gender? Write an essay showing how your perception of your gender identity was influenced by what you heard, witnessed, and experienced as a child. Before writing your paper, you may wish to read some of the following essays, each of which provides insight into gender expectations: Barbara Ehrenreich's "What I've Learned From Men" (page 249), Deborah Tannen's "But What Do You Mean?" (page 313), Dave Barry's "The Ugly Truth About Beauty" (page 422), Camille Paglia's "Rape: A Bigger Danger Than Feminists Know" (page 615), and Susan Jacoby's "Common Decency" (page 622).

Writing Assignments Using a Journal Entry as a Starting Point

5. Write an essay narrating an experience that put to the test the moral of a story you were told when you were young. Select from your pre-reading journal entry the *one* story whose "truth" was most memorably validated *or* discredited by an experience later in your life. Your tone might be serious or humorous. In either case, be sure to make clear how you felt about the truth of the story after it was "tested" by experience.

Additional Writing Topics

DESCRIPTION

General Assignments

Write an essay using description to develop any of the following topics. Remember that an effective description focuses on a dominant impression and arranges details in a way that best supports that impression. Your details—vivid and appealing to the senses—should be carefully chosen so that the essay isn't overburdened with material of secondary importance. When writing, keep in mind that varied sentence structure and imaginative figures of speech are ways to make a descriptive piece compelling.

1. A favorite item of clothing
2. A school as a young child might see it
3. A hospital room you visited or stayed in
4. An individualist's appearance
5. A coffee shop, a bus shelter, a newsstand, or some other small place
6. A parade or victory celebration
7. A banana, a squash, or another fruit or vegetable
8. A particular drawer in a desk or bureau
9. A houseplant
10. A "media event"
11. A dorm room
12. An elderly person
13. An attractive man or woman
14. A prosthetic device or wheelchair
15. A TV, film, or music celebrity
16. A student lounge
17. A once-in-a-lifetime event
18. The inside of something, such as a cave, boat, car, shed, or machine
19. A friend, a roommate, or another person you know well
20. An essential gadget or a useless gadget

Assignments With a Specific Purpose and Audience

1. For an audience of incoming first-year students, prepare a speech describing registration day at your college. Use specific details to help prepare students for the actual event. Choose an adjective that represents your dominant impression of the experience, and keep that word in mind as you write.

2. As a subscriber to a dating service, you've been asked to submit a description of the kind of person you'd like to meet. Describe your ideal date. Focus on specifics about physical appearance, personal habits, character traits, and interests.

3. Your college has decided to replace an old campus structure (for example, a dorm or dining hall) with a new version. Write a letter of protest to the administration, describing the place so vividly and appealingly that its value and need for preservation are unquestionable.

4. As a staff member of the campus newspaper, you have been asked to write a weekly column of social news and gossip. For your first column, you plan to describe a recent campus event—a dance, party, concert, or other social activity. With a straightforward or tongue-in-cheek tone, describe where the event was held, the appearance of the people who attended, and so on.

5. Students at your college have complained that the course catalog is inaccurate. Its course descriptions are often brief, misleading, or just plain incorrect. You're part of a student-faculty group responsible for revising the catalog. Write a full and accurate description of a course with which you're familiar. Tell exactly what the course is about, who teaches it, and how it is run.

6. As a resident of a particular town, you're angered by the appearance of a certain spot and by the activities that take place there. Write a letter to the town council, describing in detail the undesirable nature of this place (a video arcade, an adult bookstore, a bar, a bus station, a neglected park or beach). End with some suggestions about ways to improve the situation.

4

NARRATION

WHAT IS NARRATION?

Human beings are instinctively storytellers. In prehistoric times, our ancestors huddled around campfires to hear tales of hunting and magic. In ancient times, warriors gathered in halls to listen to bards praise in song the exploits of epic heroes. Things are no different today. Boisterous children invariably settle down to listen when their parents read to them; millions of people tune in day after day to the ongoing drama of their favorite soap operas; vacationers sit motionless on the beach, caught up in the latest best-sellers; and all of us enjoy saying, "Just listen to what happened to me today." Our hunger for storytelling is a basic part of us.

Narration means telling a single story or several related stories. The story can be a means to an end, a way to support a main idea or thesis. For instance, to demonstrate that television has become the constant companion of many children, you might narrate a typical child's day in front of the television—starting with frantic cartoons in the morning and ending with dizzy situation comedies at night.

Or to support the point that the college registration process should be reformed, you could tell the tale of a chaotic morning spent trying to enroll in classes.

Narration is powerful. Every public speaker, from politician to classroom teacher, knows that stories capture the attention of listeners as nothing else can. Narration speaks to us strongly because it is about us; we want to know what happened to others, not simply because we're curious, but because their experiences shed light on the nature of our own lives. Narration lends force to opinions, triggers the flow of memory, and evokes places and times in ways that are compelling and affecting.

HOW NARRATION FITS YOUR PURPOSE AND AUDIENCE

Because narratives tell a story, you may think they are found only in novels or short stories. But narration can also appear in essays, sometimes as a supplemental pattern of development. For example, if your purpose in a paper is to *persuade* apathetic readers that airport security regulations must be followed strictly, you might lead off with a brief account of an armed terrorist who easily boarded a plane. In a paper *defining* good teaching, you might keep readers engaged by including satirical anecdotes about one hapless instructor, the antithesis of an effective teacher. An essay on the *effects* of an overburdened judicial system might provide—in an attempt to involve readers—a dramatic account of the way one clearly guilty murderer plea-bargained his way to freedom.

In addition to providing effective support in one section of your paper, narration can also serve as an essay's dominant pattern of development. In fact, most of this chapter shows you how to use a single extended narrative to convey a central point and share with readers your view of what happened. You might choose to narrate the events of a day spent with your three-year-old nephew as a way of revealing how you rediscovered the importance of family life. Or you might relate the story of your roommate's mugging, evoking the powerlessness and terror of being a victim. Any story can form the basis for a narrative essay as long as you convey the essence of the experience and evoke its meaning.

SUGGESTIONS FOR USING NARRATION IN AN ESSAY

The following suggestions will be helpful whether you use narration as a dominant or a supportive pattern of development.

1. Identify the conflict in the event. The power of many narratives is rooted in a special kind of tension that "hooks" readers and makes them want to follow the story to its end. This narrative tension is often a by-product of some form of *conflict* within the story. Many narratives revolve around an internal dilemma experienced by a key person in the story. Or the conflict may be between people in the story or between a pivotal character and some social institution or natural phenomenon.

2. Identify the point of the narrative. In *The Adventures of Huckleberry Finn*, Mark Twain warned: "Persons attempting to find a motive in this narrative will be prosecuted; persons attempting to find a moral in it will be banished; persons attempting to find a plot in it will be shot." Twain was, of course, being ironic; his novel's richness lies in its "motives" and "morals." Similarly, when you recount a narrative, it's your responsibility to convey the event's *significance* or *meaning*. In other words, be sure readers are clear about your *narrative point*, or thesis.

Suppose you decide to write about the time you got locked in a mall late at night. Your narrative might focus on the way the mall looked after hours and the way you struggled with mounting terror. But you would also use the narrative to make a point. Perhaps you want to emphasize that fear can be instructive. Or your point might be that malls have a disturbing, surreal underside. You could state this thesis explicitly. ("After hours, the mall shed its cheerful daytime demeanor and took on a more sinister quality.") Or you could refrain from stating the thesis directly, relying on your details and language to convey the point of the narrative: "The mannequins stared at me with glazed eyes and frozen smiles" and "The steel grates pulled over each store's entrance glinted in the cold light, making each shop look like a prison cell."

3. Develop only those details that advance the narrative point. You know from experience that nothing is more boring than a storyteller who gets sidetracked and drags out a story with nonessential details. If a friend started to tell about the time his car broke down in the middle of an expressway—but interrupted his story to complain at length about the slipshod work done by his auto repair shop—you might clench your teeth in annoyance, wishing your friend would hurry up and get back to the interesting part of the story.

Brainstorming ("What happened? When? Where? Who was involved? Why did it happen?") can be valuable for helping you amass narrative details. Then, after generating the specifics, you cull out the nonessential and devote your energies to the key specifics needed to advance your narrative point. When telling a story, you maintain an effective narrative pace by focusing on that point and eliminating details that don't support it. A good narrative depends not only on what is included, but also on what has been left out.

But how do you determine which specifics to omit, which to treat briefly, and which to emphasize? Having a clear sense of your narrative point and knowing your audience are crucial. Assume you're writing a narrative about a disastrous get-acquainted dance sponsored by your college the first week of the academic year. In addition to telling what happened, you want to make a point; perhaps you want to emphasize that, despite the college's good intentions, such official events actually make it difficult to meet people. With this purpose in mind, you might write about how stiff and unnatural students seemed, all dressed up in their best clothes; you might narrate snatches of strained conversation you overheard; you might describe the way males gathered on one side of the room, females on the other—reverting to behaviors supposedly abandoned in fifth grade. All these details would support your narrative point.

Because you don't want to get waylaid by detours that lead away from that point, you would leave out details about the top-notch band and the appetizing refreshments at the dance. The music and food may have been surprisingly good, but since these details don't advance the point you want to make, they should be omitted.

You also need to keep your audience in mind when selecting narrative details. If the audience consists of your instructor and other students—all of them familiar with the new student center where the dance was held—specific details about the center probably wouldn't have to be provided. But imagine that the essay is going to appear in the quarterly magazine published by the college's community relations office. Many of the magazine's readers are former graduates who haven't been on campus for several years. They may need some additional specifics about the student center: its location, how many people it holds, how it is furnished.

As you write, keep asking yourself, "Is this detail or character or snippet of conversation essential? Does my audience need this detail to understand the conflict in the situation? Does this detail advance or intensify the narrative action?" Summarize details that have some importance but do not deserve lengthy treatment ("Two hours went by . . ."). And try to limit *narrative commentary*—statements that tell rather than show what happened—since such remarks interrupt the narrative flow. Focus instead on the specifics that propel action forward in a vigorous way.

Sometimes, especially if the narrative re-creates an event from the past, you won't be able to remember what happened detail for detail. In such a case, you should take advantage of what is called *dramatic license*. Using as a guide your powers of recall as well as the perspective you now have of that particular time, feel free to reshape events to suit your narrative point.

4. Organize the narrative sequence. All of us know the traditional beginning of fairy tales: "Once upon a time. . . ." Every narrative begins somewhere, presents a span of time, and ends at a certain point. Frequently, you'll want to use a straightforward time order, following the event *chronologically* from beginning to end: first this happened, next this happened, finally this happened.

But sometimes a strict chronological recounting may not be effective—especially if the high point of the narrative gets lost somewhere in the middle of the time sequence. To avoid that possibility, you may want to disrupt chronology, plunge the reader into the middle of the story, and then return in a *flashback* to the beginning of the tale. You're probably familiar with the way flashback is used on television and in film. You see someone appealing to the main character for financial help, then return to an earlier time when both were students in the same class, before learning how the rest of the story unfolds. Narratives can also use *flashforward*. You give readers a glimpse of the future (the main character being jailed) before the story continues in the present (the events leading to the arrest). These techniques shift the story onto several planes and keep it from becoming a step-by-step, predictable account. Reserve flashforwards and flashbacks, however, for crucial incidents only, since breaking out of chronological order acts as emphasis. Here are examples of how flashback and flashforward can be used in narrative writing:

Flashback

Standing behind the wooden counter, Greg wielded his knife expertly as he shucked clams--one every ten seconds--with practiced ease. The scene contrasted sharply with his first day on the job, when his hands broke out in blisters and when splitting each shell was like prying open a safe.

Flashforward

Rushing to move my car from the no-parking zone, I waved a quick goodbye to Karen as she climbed the steps to the bus. I didn't know then that by the time I picked her up at the bus station later that day, she had made a decision that would affect both our lives.

Whether or not you choose to include flashbacks or flashforwards in an essay, remember to limit the time span covered by the narrative. Otherwise, you will have trouble generating the details needed to give the story depth and meaning. Also, regardless of the time sequence you select, organize the tale so that it drives toward a strong finish. Be careful that your story doesn't trail off into minor, anticlimactic details.

5. Make the narrative easy to follow.   Describing each distinct action in a separate paragraph helps readers grasp the flow of events. Although narrative essays don't always have conventional topic sentences, each narrative paragraph should have a clear focus. Often this focus is indicated by a sentence early in the paragraph that directs attention to the action taking place. Such a sentence functions as a kind of *informal topic sentence;* the rest of the paragraph then develops that topic sentence. You should also be sure to use time signals when narrating a story. Words like *now, then, next, after,* and *later* ensure that your reader won't get lost as the story progresses.

6. Make the narrative vigorous and immediate.   A compelling narrative provides an abundance of specific details, making readers feel as if they're experiencing the story being told. Readers must be able to see, hear, touch, smell, and taste the event you're narrating. *Vivid sensory description* is, therefore, an essential part of an effective narrative. Not only do specific sensory details make writing a pleasure to read—we all enjoy learning the particulars about people,

places, and things—but they also give the narrative the stamp of
reality. The specifics convince the reader that the event being
described actually did, or could, occur.

Compare the following excerpts from a narrative essay. The first
version is lifeless and dull; the revised version, packed with sensory
images, grabs readers with its sense of foreboding:

That eventful day started out like every other summer day. My sister Tricia and I made several elaborate mud pies, which we decorated
with care. A little later on, as we were spraying each other with the garden hose, we heard my father walk up the path.

That sad summer day started out uneventfully enough. My sister
Tricia and I spent a few hours mixing and decorating mud pies. Our
hands caked with dry mud, we sprinkled each lopsided pie with alter-
nating rows of dandelion and clover petals. Later when the sun got hot-
ter, we tossed our white T-shirts over the red picket fence--forgetting
my grandmother's frequent warnings to be more ladylike. Our sweaty
backs bared to the sun, we doused each other with icy sprays from the
garden hose. Caught up in the primitive pleasure of it all, we barely
heard my father as he walked up the garden path, the gravel crunching
under his heavy work boots.

A caution: Sensory language enlivens narration, but it also
slows the pace. Be sure that the slower pace suits your purpose. For
example, a lengthy description fits an account of a leisurely summer
vacation but is inappropriate in a tale about a frantic search for a
misplaced wallet.

Another way to create an aura of narrative immediacy is to use
dialogue while telling a story. Our sense of other people comes, in
part, from what they say and from the way they sound. Conversational exchanges allow the reader to experience characters directly.
Compare the following fragments of a narrative, one with dialogue
and one without, noting how much more energetic the second version is.

When I finally found my way back to the campsite, the trail guide
commented on my disheveled appearance.

When I finally found my way back to the campsite, the trail guide
took one look at me and drawled, "What on earth happened to you,
Daniel Boone? You look as though you've been dragged through a
haystack backwards."

"I'd look a lot worse if I hadn't run back here. When a bullet whizzes by me, I don't stick around to see who's doing the shooting."

Note that, when using dialogue, you generally begin a new paragraph to indicate a shift from one person's speech to another's (as in the second example above).

Using *varied sentence structure* is another strategy for making narratives lively and vigorous. Sentences that plod along predictably (subject-verb, subject-verb) put readers to sleep. Experiment with your sentences by juggling length and sentence type; mix long and short sentences, simple and complex. Compare the following original and revised versions to get an idea of how effective varied sentence rhythm can be in narrative writing.

Original

The store manager went to the walk-in refrigerator every day. The heavy metal door clanged shut behind her. I had visions of her freezing to death among the hanging carcasses. The shiny door finally swung open. She waddled out.

Revised

Each time the store manager went to the walk-in refrigerator, the heavy metal door clanged shut behind her. Visions of her freezing to death among the hanging carcasses crept into my mind until the shiny door finally swung open and she waddled out.

Original

The yellow-and-blue-striped fish struggled on the line. Its scales shimmered in the sunlight. Its tail waved frantically. I saw its desire to live. I decided to let it go.

Revised

Scales shimmering in the sunlight, tail waving frantically, the yellow-and-blue-striped fish struggled on the line. Seeing its desire to live, I let it go.

Finally, *vigorous verbs* lend energy to narratives. Use active verb forms ("The boss *yelled at* him") rather than passive ones ("He *was yelled at* by the boss"), and try to replace anemic *to be* verbs ("She *was* a good basketball player") with more dynamic constructions ("She *played* basketball well").

7. Keep your point of view and verb tense consistent. All stories have a *narrator,* the person who tells the story. If you, as narrator, tell a story as you experienced it, the story is written in the *first-person point of view* ("*I* saw the dog pull loose"). But if you observed the event (or heard about it from others) and want to tell how someone else experienced the incident, you would use the *third-person point of view* ("*Anne* saw the dog pull loose"). Each point of view has advantages and limitations. First person allows you to express ordinarily private thoughts and to re-create an event as you actually experienced it. This point of view is limited, though, in its ability to depict the inner thoughts of other people involved in the event. By way of contrast, third person makes it easier to provide insight into the thoughts of all the participants. However, its objective, broad perspective may undercut some of the subjective immediacy typical of the "I was there" point of view. No matter which point of view you select, stay with that vantage point throughout the entire narrative.

Knowing whether to use the *past* or *present tense* ("I *strolled* into the room" as opposed to "I *stroll* into the room") is important. In most narrations, the past tense predominates, enabling the writer to span a considerable period of time. Although more rarely used, the present tense can be powerful for events of short duration—a wrestling match or a medical emergency, for instance. A narrative in the present tense prolongs each moment, intensifying the reader's sense of participation. Be careful, though; unless the event is intense and fast-paced, the present tense can seem contrived. Whichever tense you choose, avoid shifting midstream—starting, let's say, in the past tense ("she skated") and switching to present ("she runs").

STUDENT ESSAY

The following student essay was written by Paul Monahan in response to this assignment.

> In "Shooting an Elephant," George Orwell tells about an incident that forced him to act in a manner that ran counter to his better instincts. Write a narrative about a time when you faced a disturbing conflict and ended up doing something you later regretted.

While reading Paul's paper, try to determine how well it applies the principles of narration. The annotations on Paul's paper and the commentary following it will help you look at the essay more closely.

If Only
by Paul Monahan

Introduction

Having worked at a 7-Eleven store for two years, I thought I had become successful at what our manager calls "customer relations." I firmly believed that a friendly smile and an automatic "sir," "ma'am," and "thank you" would see me through any situation that might arise, from soothing impatient or unpleasant people to apologizing for giving out the wrong change. But the other night an old woman shattered my belief that a glib response could smooth over the rough spots of dealing with other human beings.   1

Narrative Point (thesis)

Informal topic sentence

The moment she entered, the woman presented a sharp contrast to our shiny store with its bright lighting and neatly arranged shelves. Walking as if each step were painful, she slowly pushed open the glass door and hobbled down the nearest aisle. She coughed dryly, wheezing with each breath. On a forty-degree night, she was wearing only a faded print dress, a thin, light beige sweater too small to button, and black vinyl slippers with the backs cut out to expose calloused heels. There were no stockings or socks on her splotchy, blue-veined legs.   2

Sensory details

After strolling around the store for several minutes, the old woman stopped in front of the rows of canned vegetables. She picked up some corn niblets and stared with a strange intensity at the label. At that point, I decided to be a good, courteous employee and asked her if she needed help. As I stood close to her, my smile became harder to maintain; her red-rimmed eyes were partially closed by yellowish crusts; her hands were covered with layer upon layer of grime, and the stale smell of sweat rose in a thick vaporous cloud from her clothes.   3

Informal topic sentence

Sensory details

Start of dialogue

"I need some food," she muttered in reply to my bright "Can I help you?"   4

"Are you looking for corn, ma'am?"   5

"I need some food," she repeated. "Any kind."   6

"Well, the corn is ninety-five cents," I said in my   7
most helpful voice. "Or, if you like, we have a special
on bologna today."

"I can't pay," she said.   8

Conflict established → For a second, I was tempted to say, "Take the   9
corn." But the employee rules flooded into my mind:
Remain polite, but do not let customers get the best
of you. Let them know that you are in control. For a
moment, I even entertained the idea that this was
some sort of test, and that this woman was someone
from the head office, testing my loyalty. I responded
dutifully, "I'm sorry, ma'am, but I can't give away
anything free."

Informal topic sentence → The old woman's face collapsed a bit more, if   10
that were possible, and her hands trembled as she
put the can back on the shelf. She shuffled past me
toward the door, her torn and dirty clothing barely
covering her bent back.

Conclusion   Moments after she left, I rushed out the door   11
with the can of corn, but she was nowhere in sight.
For the rest of my shift, the image of the woman
haunted me. I had been young, healthy, and smug.
Echoing of narrative point in the introduction She had been old, sick, and desperate. Wishing with
all my heart that I had acted like a human being
rather than a robot, I was saddened to realize how
fragile a hold we have on our better instincts.

COMMENTARY

Point of view, tense, and conflict.   Paul chose to write "If Only"
from the *first-person point of view,* a logical choice because he
appears as a main character in his own story. Using the *past tense,*
Paul recounts an incident filled with *conflicts*—between him and the
woman and between his fear of breaking the rules and his human
instinct to help someone in need.

Narrative point.   It isn't always necessary to state the *narrative
point* of an essay; it can be implied. But Paul decided to express the
controlling idea of his narrative in two places—in the introduction
("But the other night an old woman shattered my belief that a glib

response could smooth over the rough spots of dealing with other human beings") and again in the conclusion, where he expands his idea about rote responses overriding impulses of independent judgment and compassion. All of the essay's *narrative details* contribute to the point of the piece; Paul does not include any extraneous information that would detract from the central idea he wants to convey.

Organization and other patterns of development.   The narrative is *organized chronologically,* from the moment the woman enters the store to Paul's reaction after she leaves. Paul limits the narrative's time span. The entire incident probably occurs in under ten minutes, yet the introduction serves as a kind of *flashback* by providing some necessary background about Paul's past experiences. To help the reader follow the course of the narrative, Paul uses *time signals:* "*The moment* she entered, the woman presented a sharp contrast" (paragraph 2); "*At that point,* I decided to be a good, courteous employee" (3); "*For the rest of my shift,* the image of the woman haunted me" (11).

The paragraphs (except for those consisting solely of dialogue) also contain *informal topic sentences* that direct attention to the specific stage of action being narrated. Indeed, each paragraph focuses on a distinct event: the elderly woman's actions when she first enters the store, the encounter between Paul and the woman, Paul's resulting inner conflict, the woman's subsequent response, and Paul's delayed reaction.

This chain of events, with one action leading to another, illustrates that the *cause-effect* pattern underlies the essay's basic structure. And another pattern—*description*—gives dramatic immediacy to the events being recounted. Throughout, rich sensory details engage the reader's interest. For instance, the sentence "her red-rimmed eyes were partially closed by yellowish crusts" (3) vividly recreates the woman's appearance while also suggesting Paul's inner reaction to the woman.

Dialogue and sentence structure.   Paul uses other techniques to add energy and interest to his narrative. For one thing, he dramatizes his conflict with the woman through *dialogue* that crackles with tension. And he achieves a vigorous narrative pace by *varying the length and structure of his sentences.* In the second paragraph, a short sentence ("There were no stockings or socks on her splotchy, blue-veined legs") alternates with a longer one ("On a forty-degree night, she was wearing only a faded print dress, a thin, light beige sweater too small to button, and black vinyl slippers with the backs cut out to expose calloused heels"). Some sentences in the essay open with a subject and verb ("She coughed dryly"), while others start with dependent clauses or participial phrases ("As I stood close to her, my smile became harder to maintain"; "Walking as if each step were painful, she slowly pushed open the glass door") or with a prepositional phrase ("For a second, I was tempted").

Revising the first draft.   Comparing the final version of the essay's third paragraph, shown above, with the preliminary version reprinted below reveals some of the changes Paul made while revising the essay.

Original Version of the Third Paragraph

After sneezing and hacking her way around the store, the old woman stopped in front of the vegetable shelves. She picked up a can of corn and stared at the label. She stayed like this for several minutes. Then I walked over to her and asked if I could be of help.

After putting the original draft aside for a while, Paul reread his paper aloud and realized the third paragraph especially lacked power. So he decided to add compelling descriptive details about the woman ("the stale smell of sweat," for example). When revising, he also worked to reduce the paragraph's choppiness. By expanding and combining sentences, he gave the paragraph an easier, more graceful rhythm. Much of the time, revision involves paring down excess material. In this case, though, Paul made the right decision to elaborate his sentences. Furthermore, he added the following comment to the third paragraph: "I decided to be a good, courteous employee." These few words introduce an appropriate note of irony and serve to echo the essay's controlling idea.

Finally, Paul decided to omit the words "sneezing and hacking" because he realized they were too comic or light for his subject. Still, the first sentence in the revised paragraph is somewhat jarring. The word *strolling* isn't quite appropriate since it implies a leisurely grace inconsistent with the impression he wants to convey. Replacing *strolling* with, say, *shuffling* would bring the image more into line with the essay's overall mood.

Despite this slight problem, Paul's revisions are right on the mark. The changes he made strengthened his essay, turning it into a more evocative, more polished piece of narrative writing.

ACTIVITIES: NARRATION

Prewriting Activities

1. Imagine you're writing two essays: One analyzes the *effect* of insensitive teachers on young children; the other *argues* the importance of family traditions. With the help of your journal or freewriting, identify different narratives you could use to open each essay.

2. For each of the situations below, identify two different conflicts that would make a story worth relating. Then prepare six to ten lines of natural-sounding dialogue for each potential conflict in *one* of the situations.
   a. Going to the supermarket with a friend
   b. Telling your parents which college you've decided to attend
   c. Participating in a demonstration
   d. Preparing for an exam in a difficult course

Revising Activities

3. Revise each of the following narrative sentence groups twice: once with words that carry negative connotations, and again with words that carry positive connotations. Use varied sentence structure, sensory details, and vigorous verbs to convey mood.
   a. The bell rang. It rang loudly. Students knew the last day of class was over.
   b. Last weekend, our neighbors burned leaves in their yard. We went over to speak with them.
   c. The sun shone in through my bedroom window. It made me sit up in bed. Daylight was finally here, I told myself.

4. The following paragraph is the introduction from the first draft of an essay proposing harsher penalties for drunk drivers. Revise this narrative paragraph to make it more effective. How can you make sentence structure less predictable? Which details should you delete? As you revise, provide language that conveys the event's sights, smells, and sounds. Also, clarify the chronological sequence.

As I drove down the street in my bright blue sports car, I saw a car coming rapidly around the curve. The car didn't slow down as it headed toward the traffic light. The light turned yellow and then red. A young couple, dressed like models, started crossing the street. When the woman saw the car, she called out to her husband. He jumped onto the shoulder. The man wasn't hurt but, seconds later, it was clear the woman was. I ran to a nearby emergency phone and called the police. The ambulance arrived, but the woman was already dead. The driver, who looked terrible, failed the sobriety test, and the police found out that he had two previous offenses. It's apparent that better ways have to be found for getting drunk drivers off the road.

Audre Lorde

Named poet laureate of the state of New York in 1991, Audre Lorde (1934–92) was a New Yorker born of African-Caribbean parents. After earning degrees at Hunter College and Columbia University, Lorde held numerous teaching positions throughout the New York City area. She later toured the world as a lecturer, forming women's rights coalitions in the Caribbean, Africa, and Europe. Best known as a feminist theorist, Lorde combined social criticism and personal revelation in her writing on such topics as race, gender relations, and sexuality. Her numerous poems and nonfiction pieces were published in a variety of magazines and literary journals. Her books include *The Black Unicorn: Poems* (1978), *Sister Outsider: Essays and Speeches* (1984), and *A Burst of Light* (1988). The following selection is an excerpt from her autobiography, *Zami: A New Spelling of My Name* (1982).

Pre-Reading Journal Entry

When you were a child, what beliefs about the United States did you have? List these beliefs. For each, indicate whether subsequent experience maintained or shattered your childhood understanding of these beliefs. Take a little time to explore these issues in your journal.

The Fourth of July

The first time I went to Washington, D.C., was on the edge of 1 the summer when I was supposed to stop being a child. At least that's what they said to us all at graduation from the eighth grade. My sister Phyllis graduated at the same time from high school. I don't know what she was supposed to stop being. But as graduation presents for us both, the whole family took a Fourth of July trip to Washington, D.C., the fabled and famous capital of our country.

It was the first time I'd ever been on a railroad train during the 2 day. When I was little, and we used to go to the Connecticut shore, we always went at night on the milk train, because it was cheaper.

Preparations were in the air around our house before school 3 was even over. We packed for a week. There were two very large suitcases that my father carried, and a box filled with food. In fact, my first trip to Washington was a mobile feast; I started eating as soon as we were comfortably ensconced in our seats, and did not stop until somewhere after Philadelphia. I remember it was Philadelphia because I was disappointed not to have passed by the Liberty Bell.

My mother had roasted two chickens and cut them up into 4 dainty bite-size pieces. She packed slices of brown bread and butter and green pepper and carrot sticks. There were little violently yellow iced cakes with scalloped edges called "marigolds," that came from Cushman's Bakery. There was a spice bun and rock-cakes from Newton's, the West Indian bakery across Lenox Avenue from St. Mark's School, and iced tea in a wrapped mayonnaise jar. There were sweet pickles for us and dill pickles for my father, and peaches with the fuzz still on them, individually wrapped to keep them from bruising. And, for neatness, there were piles of napkins and a little tin box with a washcloth dampened with rosewater and glycerine for wiping sticky mouths.

I wanted to eat in the dining car because I had read all about 5 them, but my mother reminded me for the umpteenth time that dining car food always cost too much money and besides, you never could tell whose hands had been playing all over that food, nor where those same hands had been just before. My mother never mentioned that Black people were not allowed into railroad dining cars headed south in 1947. As usual, whatever my mother did not like and could not change, she ignored. Perhaps it would go away, deprived of her attention.

I learned later that Phyllis's high school senior class trip had 6 been to Washington, but the nuns had given her back her deposit in private, explaining to her that the class, all of whom were white, except Phyllis, would be staying in a hotel where Phyllis "would not be happy," meaning, Daddy explained to her, also in private, that they did not rent rooms to Negroes. "We will take you to Washington, ourselves," my father had avowed, "and not just for an overnight in some measly fleabag hotel."

American racism was a new and crushing reality that my parents 7 had to deal with every day of their lives once they came to this country. They handled it as a private woe. My mother and father believed that they could best protect their children from the realities of race in america and the fact of american racism by never giving them name, much less discussing their nature. We were told we must never trust white people, but *why* was never explained, nor the nature of their ill will. Like so many other vital pieces of information in my childhood, I was supposed to know without being told. It always seemed like a very strange injunction coming from my mother, who looked so much like one of those people we were never supposed to trust. But something always warned me not to ask my mother why she wasn't white, and why Auntie Lillah and Auntie Etta weren't, even though they were all that same problematic color so different from my father and me, even from my sisters, who were somewhere in-between.

In Washington, D.C., we had one large room with two double   8 beds and an extra cot for me. It was a back-street hotel that belonged to a friend of my father's who was in real estate, and I spent the whole next day after Mass squinting up at the Lincoln Memorial where Marian Anderson[1] had sung after the D.A.R.[2] refused to allow her to sing in their auditorium because she was Black. Or because she was "Colored," my father said as he told us the story. Except that what he probably said was "Negro," because for his time, my father was quite progressive.

I was squinting because I was in that silent agony that charac-   9 terized all of my childhood summers, from the time school let out in June to the end of July, brought about by my dilated and vulnerable eyes exposed to the summer brightness.

I viewed Julys through an agonizing corolla of dazzling white-   10 ness and I always hated the Fourth of July, even before I came to realize the travesty such a celebration was for Black people in this country.

My parents did not approve of sunglasses, nor of their expense.   11

I spent the afternoon squinting up at monuments to freedom   12 and past presidencies and democracy, and wondering why the light and heat were both so much stronger in Washington, D.C., than back home in New York City. Even the pavement on the streets was a shade lighter in color than back home.

Late that Washington afternoon my family and I walked back   13 down Pennsylvania Avenue. We were a proper caravan, mother

[1](1902–93) Acclaimed African-American opera singer, famed for her renderings of Black spirituals (editors' note).
[2]Daughters of the American Revolution. A society, founded in 1890, for women who can prove direct lineage to soldiers or others who aided in winning American independence from Great Britain during the Revolutionary War (1775–83) (editors' note).

bright and father brown, the three of us girls step-standards in-between. Moved by our historical surroundings and the heat of the early evening, my father decreed yet another treat. He had a great sense of history, a flair for the quietly dramatic and the sense of specialness of an occasion and a trip.

"Shall we stop and have a little something to cool off, Lin?"   14

Two blocks away from our hotel, the family stopped for a dish   15
of vanilla ice cream at a Breyer's ice cream and soda fountain. Indoors, the soda fountain was dim and fan-cooled, deliciously relieving to my scorched eyes.

Corded and crisp and pinafored, the five of us seated ourselves   16
one by one at the counter. There was I between my mother and father, and my two sisters on the other side of my mother. We settled ourselves along the white mottled marble counter, and when the waitress spoke at first no one understood what she was saying, and so the five of us just sat there.

The waitress moved along the line of us closer to my father and   17
spoke again. "I said I kin give you to take out, but you can't eat here. Sorry." Then she dropped her eyes looking very embarrassed, and suddenly we heard what it was she was saying all at the same time, loud and clear.

Straight-backed and indignant, one by one, my family and I got   18
down from the counter stools and turned around and marched out of the store, quiet and outraged, as if we had never been Black before. No one would answer my emphatic questions with anything other than a guilty silence. "But we hadn't done anything!" This wasn't right or fair! Hadn't I written poems about Bataan and freedom and democracy for all?

My parents wouldn't speak of this injustice, not because they   19
had contributed to it, but because they felt they should have anticipated it and avoided it. This made me even angrier. My fury was not going to be acknowledged by a like fury. Even my two sisters copied my parents' pretense that nothing unusual and anti-american had occurred. I was left to write my angry letter to the president of the united states all by myself, although my father did promise I could type it out on the office typewriter next week, after I showed it to him in my copybook diary.

The waitress was white, and the counter was white, and the ice   20
cream I never ate in Washington, D.C., that summer I left childhood was white, and the white heat and the white pavement and the

white stone monuments of my first Washington summer made me
sick to my stomach for the whole rest of that trip and it wasn't much
of a graduation present after all.

Questions for Close Reading

1. What is the selection's thesis (or narrative point)? Locate the sentence(s)
   in which Lorde states her main idea. If she doesn't state the thesis explicitly, express it in your own words.
2. In paragraph 4, Lorde describes the elaborate picnic her mother prepared for the trip to Washington, D.C. Why did Lorde's mother make
   such elaborate preparations? What do these preparations tell us about
   Lorde's mother?
3. Why does Lorde have trouble understanding her parents' dictate that she
   "never trust white people" (paragraph 7)?
4. In general, how do Lorde's parents handle racism? How does the family as a whole deal with the racism they encounter in the ice-cream parlor? How does the family's reaction to the ice-cream parlor incident
   make Lorde feel?
5. Refer to your dictionary as needed to define the following words used in
   the selection: *fabled* (paragraph 1), *injunction* (7), *progressive* (8), *dilated* (9), *vulnerable* (9), *travesty* (10), *decreed* (13), and *pretense* (19).

Questions About the Writer's Craft

1. **The pattern.** What techniques does Lorde use to help readers follow
   the unfolding of the story as it occurs in both time and space?
2. When telling a story, skilled writers limit narrative commentary—statements that tell rather than show what happened—because such commentary tends to interrupt the narrative flow. Lorde, however, provides
   narrative commentary in several spots. Find these instances. How is the
   information she provides in these places essential to her narrative?
3. In paragraphs 7 and 19, Lorde uses all lowercase letters when referring to America/American and to the President of the United States.
   Why do you suppose she doesn't follow the rules of capitalization? In
   what ways does her rejection of these rules reinforce what she is trying to convey through the essay's title?
4. What key word does Lorde repeat in paragraph 20? What effect do you
   think she hopes the repetition will have on readers?

Writing Assignments Using Comparison-Contrast as a Method of Development

1. Lorde recounts an incident during which she was treated unfairly. Write
   a narrative about a time when either you were treated unjustly or you

treated someone else in an unfair manner. Like Lorde, use vivid details to make the incident come alive and to convey how it affected you. Essays including George Orwell's "Shooting an Elephant" (page 167) and Sophronia Liu's "So Tsi-Fai" (page 188) will prompt some ideas worth exploring.

2. Write a narrative about an experience that dramatically changed your view of the world. The experience might have been jarring and painful, or it may have been positive and uplifting. In either case, recount the incident with compelling narrative details. To illustrate the shift in your perspective, begin with a brief statement of the way you viewed the world before the experience. The following essays provide insight into the way a single experience can alter one's understanding of the world: Maya Angelou's "Sister Flowers" (page 116), Langston Hughes's "Salvation" (page 183), Sophronia Liu's "So Tsi-Fai" (page 188), and Alice Walker's "Beauty: When the Other Dancer Is the Self" (page 467).

Writing Assignments Using Other Patterns of Development

3. Lorde suggests that her parents use the coping mechanism of denial to deal with life's harsh realities. For example, she writes that whatever her mother "did not like and could not change, she ignored." Refer to a psychology textbook to learn more about denial as a coping mechanism. When is it productive? When is it counterproductive? Drawing upon your own experiences as well as those of friends, family, and classmates, write an essay contrasting effective and ineffective uses of denial. Near the end of the paper, present brief guidelines that will help readers identify when denial may be detrimental.

4. In her essay, Lorde decries and by implication takes a strong stance against racial discrimination. Brainstorm with friends, family members, and classmates to identify other injustices in American society. To prompt discussion, you might begin by considering attitudes toward the elderly, the overweight, the physically disabled; the funding of schools in poor and affluent neighborhoods; the portrayal of a specific ethnic group on television; and so on. Focusing on *one* such injustice, write an essay arguing that such an injustice indeed exists. To document the nature and extent of the injustice, use the library and/or Internet research as well as your own and other people's experiences. Acknowledge and, when you can, dismantle the views of those who think there isn't a problem.

Writing Assignments Using a Journal Entry as a Starting Point

5. Write an essay comparing and/or contrasting the beliefs you had about the United States as a child with those you have as an adult. Review your

pre-reading journal entry, and select *one* American belief to focus on. Provide strong, dramatic examples that show why your childhood belief in this concept has been strengthened or weakened. Before writing, you should consider reading Gloria Naylor's "Mommy, What Does 'Nigger' Mean?" (page 516) and Juh Ji-Yeon's "Let's Tell the Story of All America's Cultures" (page 581), two powerful accounts of personal disillusionment with American ideals.

George Orwell

Born Eric Blair in the British colony of India, George Orwell (1903–50) is probably best known for his two novels, *Animal Farm* (1946) and *1984* (1949), both searing depictions of totalitarian societies. Orwell was also the author of numerous books and essays, many based on his diverse life experiences. He served with the Indian imperial police in Burma, worked at various jobs in London and Paris, and fought in the Spanish Civil War. His experiences in Burma provide the basis for the following essay, which is taken from his collection, *Shooting an Elephant and Other Essays* (1950).

Pre-Reading Journal Entry

Think of times when you were keenly aware of institutional injustice—an action, law, or regulation that is legally in the right but that you felt was wrong. In your journal, record several such examples. Why do you consider them wrong? Have you always felt that way? If not, what changed your opinion?

Shooting an Elephant

In Moulmein, in Lower Burma, I was hated by large numbers of people—the only time in my life that I have been important enough for this to happen to me. I was sub-divisional police officer of the town, and in an aimless, petty kind of way anti-European feeling was very bitter. No one had the guts to raise a riot, but if a European woman went through the bazaars alone somebody would probably spit betel juice over her dress. As a police officer I was an obvious target and was baited whenever it seemed safe to do so. When a nimble Burman tripped me up on the football field and the referee (another Burman) looked the other way, the crowd yelled with hideous laughter. This happened more than once. In the end the sneering yellow faces of young men that met me everywhere, the insults hooted after me when I was at a safe distance, got badly on my nerves. The young Buddhist priests were the worst of all. There were several thousand of them in the town and none of them seemed to have anything to do except stand on street corners and jeer at Europeans.

1

All this was perplexing and upsetting. For at that time I had   2
already made up my mind that imperialism was an evil thing and the
sooner I chucked up my job and got out of it the better.
Theoretically—and secretly, of course—I was all for the Burmese and
all against their oppressors, the British. As for the job I was doing, I
hated it more bitterly than I can perhaps make clear. In a job like that
you see the dirty work of Empire at close quarters. The wretched
prisoners huddling in the stinking cages of the lock-ups, the grey,
cowed faces of the long-term convicts, the scarred buttocks of the
men who had been flogged with bamboos—all these oppressed me
with an intolerable sense of guilt. But I could get nothing into perspective. I was young and ill-educated and I had had to think out my
problems in the utter silence that is imposed on every Englishman in
the East. I did not even know that the British Empire is dying, still
less did I know that it is a great deal better than the younger empires
that are going to supplant it. All I knew was that I was stuck between
my hatred of the empire I served and my rage against the evil-spirit-
ed little beasts who tried to make my job impossible. With one part
of my mind I thought of the British Raj as an unbreakable tyranny,
as something clamped down, in *saecula saeculorum*,[1] upon the will
of prostrate peoples; with another part I thought that the greatest
joy in the world would be to drive a bayonet into a Buddhist priest's
guts. Feelings like these are the normal by-products of imperialism;
ask any Anglo-Indian official, if you can catch him off duty.

One day something happened which in a roundabout way was   3
enlightening. It was a tiny incident in itself, but it gave me a better
glimpse than I had had before of the real nature of imperialism—the
real motives for which despotic governments act. Early one morning
the sub-inspector at a police station at the other end of the town
rang me up on the 'phone and said that an elephant was ravaging the
bazaar. Would I please come and do something about it? I did not
know what I could do, but I wanted to see what was happening and
I got onto a pony and started out. I took my rifle, an old .44
Winchester and much too small to kill an elephant, but I thought the
noise might be useful *in terrorem*.[2] Various Burmans stopped me on
the way and told me about the elephant's doings. It was not, of
course, a wild elephant, but a tame one which had gone "must." It
had been chained up, as tame elephants always are when their attack

[1] For ever and ever (editors' note).
[2] As a warning (editors' note).

of "must" is due, but on the previous night it had broken its chain and escaped. Its mahout, the only person who could manage it when it was in that state, had set out in pursuit, but had taken the wrong direction and was now twelve hours' journey away, and in the morning the elephant had suddenly reappeared in the town. The Burmese population had no weapons and were quite helpless against it. It had already destroyed somebody's bamboo hut, killed a cow and raided some fruit-stalls and devoured the stock; also it had met the municipal rubbish van and, when the driver jumped out and took to his heels, had turned the van over and inflicted violence upon it.

The Burmese sub-inspector and some Indian constables were 4 waiting for me in the quarter where the elephant had been seen. It was a very poor quarter, a labyrinth of squalid bamboo huts, thatched with palm-leaf, winding all over a steep hillside. I remember that it was a cloudy, stuffy morning at the beginning of the rains. We began questioning the people as to where the elephant had gone and, as usual, failed to get any definite information. That is invariably the case in the East; a story always sounds clear enough at a distance, but the nearer you get to the scene of events the vaguer it becomes. Some of the people said that the elephant had gone in one direction, some said that he had gone in another, some professed not even to have heard of any elephant. I had almost made up my mind that the whole story was a pack of lies, when we heard yells a little distance away. There was a loud, scandalized cry of "Go away, child! Go away this instant!" and an old woman with a switch in her hand came round the corner of a hut, violently shooing away a crowd of naked children. Some more women followed, clicking their tongues and exclaiming; evidently there was something that the children ought not to have seen. I rounded the hut and saw a man's dead body sprawling in the mud. He was an Indian, a black Dravidian coolie, almost naked, and he could not have been dead many minutes. The people said that the elephant had come suddenly upon him round the corner of the hut, caught him with its trunk, put its foot on his back and ground him into the earth. This was the rainy season and the ground was soft, and his face had scored a trench a foot deep and a couple of yards long. He was lying on his belly with arms crucified and head sharply twisted to one side. His face was coated with mud, the eyes wide open, the teeth bared and grinning with an expression of unendurable agony. (Never tell me, by the way, that the dead look peaceful. Most of the corpses I have seen looked devilish.) The friction of the great beast's foot had stripped the skin from his back as neatly as one skins a rabbit. As soon as I saw the dead man I sent an orderly to a friend's house nearby to borrow an elephant rifle. I had already sent back the pony, not wanting it to go mad with fright and throw me if it smelt the elephant.

The orderly came back in a few minutes with a rifle and five car-   5 tridges, and meanwhile some Burmans had arrived and told us that the elephant was in the paddy fields below, only a few hundred yards away. As I started forward practically the whole population of the quarter flocked out of the houses and followed me. They had seen the rifle and were all shouting excitedly that I was going to shoot the elephant. They had not shown much interest in the elephant when he was merely ravaging their homes, but it was different now that he was going to be shot. It was a bit of fun to them, as it would be to an English crowd; besides they wanted the meat. It made me vague-ly uneasy. I had no intention of shooting the elephant—I had mere-ly sent for the rifle to defend myself if necessary—and it is always unnerving to have a crowd following you. I marched down the hill, looking and feeling a fool, with the rifle over my shoulder and an ever-growing army of people jostling at my heels. At the bottom, when you got away from the huts, there was a metalled road and beyond that a miry waste of paddy fields a thousand yards across, not yet ploughed but soggy from the first rains and dotted with coarse grass. The elephant was standing eight yards from the road, his left side towards us. He took not the slightest notice of the crowd's approach. He was tearing up bunches of grass, beating them against his knees to clean them and stuffing them into his mouth.

I had halted on the road. As soon as I saw the elephant I knew   6 with perfect certainty that I ought not to shoot him. It is a serious matter to shoot a working elephant—it is comparable to destroying a huge and costly piece of machinery—and obviously one ought not to do it if it can possibly be avoided. And at that distance, peacefully eat-ing, the elephant looked no more dangerous than a cow. I thought then and I think now that his attack of "must" was already passing off; in which case he would merely wander harmlessly about until the mahout came back and caught him. Moreover, I did not in the least want to shoot him. I decided that I would watch him for a little while to make sure that he did not turn savage again, and then go home.   7

But at that moment I glanced round at the crowd that had fol-lowed me. It was an immense crowd, two thousand at the least and growing every minute. It blocked the road for a long distance on either side. I looked at the sea of yellow faces above the garish clothes—faces all happy and excited over this bit of fun, all certain that the elephant was going to be shot. They were watching me as they would watch a conjurer about to perform a trick. They did not like me, but with the magical rifle in my hands I was momentarily worth watching. And suddenly I realized that I should have to shoot the elephant after all. The people expected it of me and I had got to do it; I could feel their two thousand wills pressing me forward, irresistibly. And it was at this moment, as I stood there with the rifle in my hands, that I first grasped the hollowness, the futility of the white man's dominion in the East. Here was I, the white man with his gun, standing in front of the unarmed native crowd—seemingly the leading actor of the piece; but in reality I was only an absurd puppet pushed to and fro by the will of those yellow faces behind. I perceived in this moment that when the white man turns tyrant it is his own freedom that he destroys. He becomes a sort of hollow, posing dummy, the conventionalized figure of a sahib. For it is the condition of his rule that he shall spend his life in trying to impress the "natives," and so in every crisis he has got to do what the "natives" expect of him. He wears a mask, and his face grows to fit it. I had got to shoot the elephant. I had committed myself to doing it when I sent for the rifle. A sahib has got to act like a sahib; he has got to appear resolute, to know his own mind and do definite things. To come all that way, rifle in hand, with two thousand people marching at my heels, and then to trail feebly away, having done nothing—no, that was impossible. The crowd would laugh at me. And my whole life, every white man's life in the East, was one long struggle not be laughed at.

But I did not want to shoot the elephant. I watched him beat- 8 ing his bunch of grass against his knees, with that preoccupied grandmotherly air that elephants have. It seemed to me that it would be murder to shoot him. At that age I was not squeamish about killing animals, but I had never shot an elephant and never wanted to. (Somehow it always seems worse to kill a *large* animal.) Besides, there was the beast's owner to be considered. Alive, the elephant was worth at least a hundred pounds; dead, he would only be worth the value of his tusks, five pounds, possibly. But I had got to act quickly. I turned to some experienced-looking Burmans who had been there when we arrived, and asked them how the elephant had been behaving. They all said the same thing: he took no notice of you if you left him alone, but he might charge if you went too close to him.

It was perfectly clear to me what I ought to do. I ought to walk   9
up to within, say, twenty-five yards of the elephant and test his
behavior. If he charged, I could shoot; if he took no notice of me, it
would be safe to leave him until the mahout came back. But also I
knew that I was going to do no such thing. I was a poor shot with a
rifle and the ground was soft mud into which one would sink at
every step. If the elephant charged and I missed him, I should have
about as much chance as a toad under a steam-roller. But even then
I was not thinking particularly of my own skin, only of the watchful
yellow faces behind. For at that moment, with the crowd watching
me, I was not afraid in the ordinary sense, as I would have been if I
had been alone. A white man mustn't be frightened in front of
"natives"; and so, in general, he isn't frightened. The sole thought
in my mind was that if anything went wrong those two thousand
Burmans would see me pursued, caught, trampled on and reduced
to a grinning corpse like that Indian up the hill. And if that happened
it was quite probable that some of them would laugh. That would
never do. There was only one alternative. I shoved the cartridges
into the magazine and lay down on the road to get a better aim.

The crowd grew very still, and a deep, low, happy sigh, as of   10
people who see the theatre curtain go up at last, breathed from
innumerable throats. They were going to have their bit of fun after
all. The rifle was a beautiful German thing with cross-hair sights. I
did not then know that in shooting an elephant one would shoot to
cut an imaginary bar running from ear-hole to ear-hole. I ought,
therefore, as the elephant was sideway on, to have aimed straight at
his ear-hole; actually I aimed several inches in front of this, thinking
the brain would be further forward.

When I pulled the trigger I did not hear the bang or feel the   11
kick—one never does when a shot goes home—but I heard the devilish roar of glee that went up from the crowd. In that instant, in too
short a time, one would have thought, even for the bullet to get
there, a mysterious, terrible change had come over the elephant. He
neither stirred nor fell, but every line of his body had altered. He
looked suddenly stricken, shrunken, immensely old, as though the
frightful impact of the bullet had paralyzed him without knocking
him down. At last, after what seemed a long time—it might have
been five seconds, I dare say—he sagged flabbily to his knees. His
mouth slobbered. An enormous senility seemed to have settled
upon him. One could have imagined him thousands of years old. I

fired again into the same spot. At the second shot he did not collapse but climbed with desperate slowness to his feet and stood
weakly upright, with legs sagging and head drooping. I fired a third
time. That was the shot that did for him. You could see the agony
of it jolt his whole body and knock the last remnant of strength from
his legs. But in falling he seemed for a moment to rise, for as his
hind legs collapsed beneath him he seemed to tower upward like a
huge rock toppling, his trunk reaching skywards like a tree. He
trumpeted, for the first and only time. And then down he came, his
belly towards me, with a crash that seemed to shake the ground even
where I lay.

I got up. The Burmans were already racing past me across the   12
mud. It was obvious that the elephant would never rise again, but
he was not dead. He was breathing very rhythmically with long rat-
tling gasps, his great mound of a side painfully rising and falling. His
mouth was wide open—I could see far down into caverns of pale
pink throat. I waited a long time for him to die, but his breathing
did not weaken. Finally I fired my two remaining shots into the spot
where I thought his heart must be. The thick blood welled out of
him like red velvet, but still he did not die. His body did not even
jerk when the shots hit him, the tortured breathing continued without a pause. He was dying, very slowly and in great agony, but in
some world remote from me where not even a bullet could damage
him further. I felt that I had got to put an end to that dreadful noise.
It seemed dreadful to see the great beast lying there, powerless to
move and yet powerless to die, and not even to be able to finish him.
I sent back for my small rifle and poured shot after shot into his
heart and down his throat. They seemed to make no impression.
The tortured gasps continued as steadily as the ticking of a clock.

In the end I could not stand it any longer and went away. I   13
heard later that it took him half an hour to die. Burmans were bringing dahs and baskets even before I left, and I was told they had
stripped the body almost to the bones by the afternoon.

Afterwards, of course, there were endless discussions about the   14
shooting of the elephant. The owner was furious, but he was only
an Indian and could do nothing. Besides, legally I had done the
right thing, for a mad elephant has to be killed, like a mad dog, if its
owner fails to control it. Among the Europeans opinion was divided. The older men said I was right, the younger men said it was a
damn shame to shoot an elephant for killing a coolie, because an

elephant was worth more than any damn Coringhee coolie. And afterwards I was very glad that the coolie had been killed; it put me legally in the right and it gave me a sufficient pretext for shooting the elephant. I often wondered whether any of the others grasped that I had done it solely to avoid looking a fool.

Questions for Close Reading

1. What is the selection's thesis (or narrative point)? Locate the sentence(s) in which Orwell states his main idea. If he doesn't state the thesis explicitly, express it in your own words.
2. How does Orwell feel about the Burmans? What words does he use to describe them?
3. What reasons does Orwell give for shooting the elephant?
4. In paragraph 3, Orwell says that the elephant incident gave him a better understanding of "the real motives for which despotic governments act." What do you think he means? Before you answer, reread paragraph 7 carefully.
5. Refer to your dictionary as needed to define the following words used in the selection: *imperialism* (paragraph 2), *prostrate* (2), *despotic* (3), *mahout* (3), *miry* (5), *conjurer* (7), *futility* (7), and *sahib* (7).

Questions About the Writer's Craft

1. **The pattern.** Most effective narratives encompass a restricted time span. How much time elapses from the moment Orwell gets his gun to the death of the elephant? What time signals does Orwell provide to help the reader follow the sequence of events in this limited time span?
2. Orwell doesn't actually begin his narrative until the third paragraph. What purposes do the first two paragraphs serve?
3. **Other patterns.** In paragraph 6, Orwell says that shooting a working elephant "is comparable to destroying a huge and costly piece of machinery." This kind of comparison is called an *analogy*—describing something unfamiliar, often abstract, in terms of something more familiar and concrete. Find at least three additional analogies in Orwell's essay. What effect do they have?
4. **Other patterns.** Much of the power of Orwell's narrative comes from his ability to convey sensory impressions—what he saw, heard, smelled. Orwell's description becomes most vivid when he writes about the death of the elephant in paragraphs 11 and 12. Find some evocative words and phrases that give the description its power.

Writing Assignments Using Narration as a Pattern of Development

1. Orwell recounts a time he acted under great pressure. Write a narrative about an action you once took simply because you felt pressured. Perhaps you were attempting to avoid ridicule or to fulfill someone else's expectations. Like Orwell, use vivid details to bring the incident to life and to convey its effect on you. Langston Hughes's "Salvation" (page 183) may lead you to some insights about the way stress influences behavior.

2. Write a narrative essay about an experience that gave you, like Orwell, a deeper insight into your own nature. You may have discovered, for instance, that you can be surprisingly naive, compassionate, petty, brave, rebellious, or good at something. Consider first reading Annie Dillard's "The Chase" (page 176), an essay showing how the author's response to a challenge revealed much about her character.

Writing Assignments Using Other Patterns of Development

3. Was Orwell justified in shooting the elephant? Write an essay arguing that Orwell was either justified *or* not justified. To develop your thesis, cite several specific reasons, each supported by details drawn from the essay. Here are some points you might consider: the legality of Orwell's act, the elephant's temperament, the crowd's presence, the aftermath of the elephant's death, the death itself.

4. Orwell's essay concerns, in part, the tendency to conceal indecision and confusion behind a facade of authority. Focusing on one or two groups of people (parents, teachers, doctors, politicians, and so on), write an essay about the way people in authority sometimes *pretend* to know what they're doing so that subordinates won't suspect their insecurity or incompetence. Part of your essay should focus on the consequences of such behaviors.

Writing Assignments Using a Journal Entry as a Starting Point

5. Review your pre-reading journal entry, and select *one* action, law, or regulation that you consider indefensible. Interview friends, family, and classmates in an effort to gather views on all sides of the issue. Also consider supplementing this informal research with information gathered in the library and/or on the Internet. After weighing all your material, formulate a thesis; then write an essay convincing readers of the validity of your position.

Annie Dillard

Pilgrim at Tinker Creek (1974) is probably Annie Dillard's best-known work. A collection of lyrical observations and reflections about the natural world, *Pilgrim* was awarded a Pulitzer Prize for general nonfiction. Born in 1945, Dillard is currently Adjunct Professor at Wesleyan University in Connecticut and a contributing editor at Harper's. Over the years, she has published a variety of books: *Tickets for a Prayer Wheel* (1974), a book of poetry; *Holy the Firm* (1978), *Teaching a Stone to Talk* (1982), *The Annie Dillard Reader* (1994), and *Mornings Like This* (1995), collections of essays; *Living by Fiction* (1982), literary criticism; *Encounters With Chinese Writers* (1984) and *For the Time Being* (1999), narrative nonfiction; *An American Childhood* (1987), an autobiography; and *The Writing Life* (1989), miscellaneous reflections on writing. Her first novel, *The Living*, was published to critical acclaim in 1992. The following selection is from *An American Childhood*.

Pre-Reading Journal Entry

Use your journal to reminisce about several of your memorable childhood and/or adolescent adventures that involved a confrontation with an adult. Some events may be amusing, while others may be serious. What happened? Who was involved? What was the outcome? Writing quickly, immerse yourself in your memories, recapturing as best you can your thoughts and feelings at the time of the incident.

The Chase

Some boys taught me to play football. This was fine sport. You 1
thought up a new strategy for every play and whispered it to the others. You went out for a pass, fooling everyone. Best, you got to throw yourself mightily at someone's running legs. Either you brought him down or you hit the ground flat out on your chin, with your arms empty before you. It was all or nothing. If you hesitated in fear, you would miss and get hurt: you would take a hard fall while the kid got away, or you would get kicked in the face while the kid got away. But if you flung yourself wholeheartedly at the back of his knees—if you gathered and joined body and soul and pointed them

diving fearlessly—then you likely wouldn't get hurt, and you'd stop the ball. Your fate, and your team's score, depended on your concentration and courage. Nothing girls did could compare with it.

Boys welcomed me at baseball, too, for I had, through enthusiastic practice, what was weirdly known as a boy's arm. In winter, in the snow, there was neither baseball or football, so the boys and I threw snowballs at passing cars. I got in trouble throwing snowballs, and have seldom been happier since.

On one weekday morning after Christmas, six inches of new snow had just fallen. We were standing up to our boot tops in snow on a front yard on trafficked Reynolds Street, waiting for cars. The cars traveled Reynolds Street slowly and evenly; they were targets all but wrapped in red ribbons, cream puffs. We couldn't miss.

I was seven; the boys were eight, nine, and ten. The oldest two Fahey boys were there—Mikey and Peter—polite blond boys who lived near me on Lloyd Street, and who already had four brothers and sisters. My parents approved Mikey and Peter Fahey. Chickie McBride was there, a tough kid, and Billy Paul and Mackie Kean too, from across Reynolds, where the boys grew up dark and furious, grew up skinny, knowing, and skilled. We had all drifted from our houses that morning looking for action, and had found it here on Reynolds Street.

It was cloudy but cold. The cars' tires laid behind them on the snowy street a complex trail of beige chunks like crenellated castle walls. I had stepped on some earlier; they squeaked. We could have wished for more traffic. When a car came, we all popped it one. In the intervals between cars we reverted to the natural solitude of children.

I started making an iceball—a perfect iceball, from perfectly white snow, perfectly spherical, and squeezed perfectly translucent so no snow remained all the way through. (The Fahey boys and I considered it unfair actually to throw an iceball at somebody, but it had been known to happen.)

I had just embarked on the iceball project when we heard tire chains come clanking from afar. A black Buick was moving toward us down the street. We all spread out, banged together some regular snowballs, took aim, and, when the Buick drew nigh, fired.

A soft snowball hit the driver's windshield right before the driver's face. It made a smashed star with a hump in the middle.

Often, of course, we hit our target, but this time, the only time in all of life, the car pulled over and stopped. Its wide black door opened; a man got out of it, running. He didn't even close the car door.

He ran after us, and we ran away from him, up the snowy   10
Reynolds sidewalk. At the corner, I looked back; incredibly, he was still after us. He was in city clothes: a suit and tie, street shoes. Any normal adult would have quit, having sprung us into flight and made his point. This man was gaining on us. He was a thin man, all action. All of a sudden, we were running for our lives.

Wordless, we split up. We were on our turf; we could lose our-   11
selves in the neighborhood backyards, everyone for himself. I paused and considered. Everyone had vanished except Mikey Fahey, who was just rounding the corner of a yellow brick house. Poor Mikey, I trailed him. The driver of the Buick sensibly picked the two of us to follow. The man apparently had all day.

He chased Mikey and me around the yellow house and up a   12
backyard path we knew by heart: under a low tree, up a bank, through a hedge, down some snowy steps, and across the grocery store's delivery driveway. We smashed through a gap in another hedge, entered a scruffy backyard and ran around its back porch and tight between houses to Edgerton Avenue; we ran across Edgerton to an alley and up our own sliding woodpile to the Halls' front yard; he kept coming. We ran up Lloyd Street and wound through mazy backyards toward the steep hilltop at Willard and Lang.

He chased us silently, block after block. He chased us silently   13
over picket fences, through thorny hedges, between houses, around garbage cans, and across streets. Every time I glanced back, choking for breath, I expected he would have quit. He must have been as breathless as we were. His jacket strained over his body. It was an immense discovery, pounding into my hot head with every sliding, joyous step, that this ordinary adult evidently knew what I thought only children who trained at football knew: that you have to fling yourself at what you're doing, you have to point yourself, forget yourself, aim, dive.

Mikey and I had nowhere to go, in our own neighborhood or   14
out of it, but away from this man who was chasing us. He impelled us forward; we compelled him to follow our route. The air was cold; every breath tore my throat. We kept running, block after block; we kept improvising, backyard after backyard, running a frantic course and choosing it simultaneously, failing always to find small places or hard places to slow him down, and discovering always, exhilarated,

dismayed, that only bare speed could save us—for he would never give up, this man—and we were losing speed.

He chased us through the backyard labyrinths of ten blocks   15
before he caught us by our jackets. He caught us and we all stopped.

We three stood staggering, half blinded, coughing, in an   16
obscure hilltop backyard: a man in his twenties, a boy, a girl. He had released our jackets, our pursuer, our captor, our hero: he knew we weren't going anywhere. We all played by the rules. Mikey and I unzipped our jackets. I pulled off my sopping mittens. Our tracks multiplied in the backyard's new snow. We had been breaking new snow all morning. We didn't look at each other. I was cherishing my excitement. The man's lower pants legs were wet; his cuffs were full of snow, and there was a prow of snow beneath them on his shoes and socks. Some trees bordered the little flat backyard, some messy winter trees. There was no one around: a clearing in a grove, and we the only players.

It was a long time before he could speak. I had some difficulty   17
at first, recalling why we were there. My lips felt swollen; I couldn't see out of the sides of my eyes; I kept coughing.

"You stupid kids," he began perfunctorily.   18

We listened perfunctorily indeed, if we listened at all, for the   19
chewing out was redundant, a mere formality, and beside the point. The point was that he had chased us passionately without giving up, and so he had caught us. Now he came down to earth. I wanted the glory to last forever.

But how could the glory have lasted forever? We could have run   20
through every backyard in North America until we got to Panama. But when he trapped us at the lip of the Panama Canal, what precisely could he have done to prolong the drama of the chase and cap its glory? I brooded about this for the next few years. He could only have fried Mikey Fahey and me in boiling oil, say, or dismembered us piecemeal, or staked us to anthills. None of which I really wanted, and none of which any adult was likely to do, even in the spirit of fun. He could only chew us out there in the Panamanian jungle, after months or years of exalting pursuit. He could only begin, "You stupid kids," and continue in his ordinary Pittsburgh accent with his normal righteous anger and the usual common sense.

If in that snowy backyard the driver of the black Buick had cut   21
off our heads, Mikey's and mine, I would have died happy, for nothing has required so much of me since as being chased all over

Pittsburgh in the middle of winter—running terrified, exhausted—by this sainted, skinny, furious redheaded man who wished to have a word with us. I don't know how he found his way back to his car.

Questions for Close Reading

1. What is the selection's thesis (or narrative point)? Locate the sentence(s) in which Dillard states her main idea. If Dillard doesn't state the thesis explicitly, express it in your own words.
2. In the first paragraph, Dillard describes football as a "fine sport." Which aspects of the sport does she refer to when illustrating her point? Which aspect is most important? Why?
3. Why was the driver's decision to follow Dillard and Mikey "sensible"?
4. Dillard dubs her pursuer "our hero" (paragraph 16) and says he was "sainted" (21). What is it about the man that merits these words of praise?
5. Refer to your dictionary as needed to define the following words used in the selection: *crenellated* (paragraph 5), *spherical* (6), *translucent* (6), *embarked* (7), *simultaneously* (14), *dismayed* (14), *labyrinths* (15), *prow* (16), *perfunctorily* (18), and *redundant* (19).

Questions About the Writer's Craft

1. **The pattern.** Dillard draws upon sensory details, play-by-play action, varied sentence length, and repetition to create a narrative filled with drama and suspense. Locate examples of each of these techniques and explain how the strategy keeps readers on the edge of their seats.
2. What key word does Dillard repeat in paragraph 6? Why do you suppose she repeats this word? What is the effect?
3. **Other patterns.** In paragraphs 12 and 13, Dillard provides a number of spatial signals to help readers track the path she and Mikey followed. Identify the signals and comment on their effectiveness.
4. There is only one place in the essay where someone actually speaks. Locate this instance of dialogue. Why do you think Dillard chose to include only this one piece of dialogue?

Writing Assignments Using Narration as a Pattern of Development

1. The chase tested Dillard—and she rose to the challenge. In a narrative of your own, write about a challenge that you responded to in a way that made you feel proud. Perhaps you triumphed over a serious illness, succeeded in a difficult sporting event, or worked hard not to lash out

verbally at someone who had hurt you. Like Dillard, use vivid narrative details to convey how you reacted and why you felt good about your reaction.

2. Like Dillard, most of us—at some point in our lives—have done something that crossed traditional gender lines. If you're female, you might have built some bookshelves. If you're male, you might have prepared a special dinner for friends. Write an essay about a time you engaged in what might be considered a "gender-bending" activity. Where appropriate, use sensory details and dialogue to convey how you and others felt about what you did. Before writing, you may want to read one or more of the following essays exploring gender-based behaviors: Barbara Ehrenreich's "What I've Learned From Men" (page 249), Deborah Tannen's "But What Do You Mean?" (page 313), Dave Barry's "The Ugly Truth About Beauty" (page 422), and Virginia Woolf's "Professions for Women" (page 669).

Writing Assignments Using Other Patterns of Development

3. Dillard believes that there are times we should "fling" ourselves at an experience and "dive" in with abandon. In an essay, argue the opposing point of view. Defend the position that there are times in life when a measured, thoughtful response is called for even though the common tendency is to act impulsively. Select convincing examples to support your position, showing how a more spontaneous approach could be harmful or counterproductive.

4. At one time or another, all children do things they shouldn't. Focus on *one* negative thing that children do in the classroom, at home, or in a public place, and write an essay showing that adults' typical response to the behavior is far from effective. Contrast adults' usual response with what you think adults should do to handle the problem behavior more effectively. Before writing, you might consider investigating your topic in the library and/or on the Internet.

Writing Assignments Using a Journal Entry as a Starting Point

5. Reread your pre-reading journal entry, and choose the *one* memory that conveys most dramatically a collision between the world of children (or adolescents) and the world of adults. Write an essay about this event. Make the conflict real and immediate by providing rich sensory details about the place and people involved. Reveal, either implicitly or explicitly, your current perspective on the event. Before you begin writing,

read Audre Lorde's "The Fourth of July" (page 160) and Langston Hughes's "Salvation" (page 183) for inspiration in depicting this clash between child and adult worlds.

Langston Hughes

One of the foremost members of the 1920s literary movement known as the Harlem Renaissance, Langston Hughes (1902–67) committed himself to portraying the richness of Black life in the United States. A poet and a writer of short stories, Hughes was greatly influenced by the rhythms of blues and jazz. In his later years, he published two autobiographical works, *The Big Sea* (1940) and *I Wonder as I Wander* (1956), and he wrote a history of the National Association for the Advancement of Colored People (NAACP). The following selection is from *The Big Sea*.

Pre-Reading Journal Entry

Young people often feel pressured by family and community to adopt certain values, beliefs, or traditions. In your journal, reflect on some of the pressures that you've experienced. What was your response to these pressures? What have been the consequences of your response? Do you think your experience with these family or community pressures was unique or fairly common?

Salvation

I was saved from sin when I was going on thirteen. But not really saved. It happened like this. There was a big revival at my Auntie Reed's church. Every night for weeks there had been much preaching, singing, praying, and shouting, and some very hardened sinners had been brought to Christ, and the membership of the church had grown by leaps and bounds. Then just before the revival ended, they held a special meeting for children, "to bring the young lambs to the fold." My aunt spoke of it for days ahead. That night I was escorted to the front row and placed on the mourners' bench with all the other young sinners, who had not yet been brought to Jesus. 1

My aunt told me that when you were saved you saw a light, and something happened to you inside! And Jesus came into your life! And God was with you from then on! She said you could see and hear and feel Jesus in your soul. I believed her. I had heard a great many old people say the same thing and it seemed to me they ought 2 to know. So I sat there calmly in the hot, crowded church, waiting for Jesus to come to me.

The preacher preached a wonderful rhythmical sermon, all moans and shouts and lonely cries and dire pictures of hell, and then he sang a song about the ninety and nine safe in the fold, but one little lamb was left out in the cold. Then he said: "Won't you come? Won't you come to Jesus? Young lambs, won't you come?" And he held out his arms to all us young sinners there on the mourners' bench. And the little girls cried. And some of them jumped up and went to Jesus right away. But most of us just sat there.   3

A great many older people came and knelt around us and prayed, old women with jet-black faces and braided hair, old men with work-gnarled hands. And the church sang a song about the lower lights are burning, some poor sinners to be saved. And the whole building rocked with prayer and song.   4

Still I kept waiting to *see* Jesus.   5

Finally all the young people had gone to the altar and were saved, but one boy and me. He was a rounder's son named Westley. Westley and I were surrounded by sisters and deacons praying. It was very hot in the church, and getting late now. Finally Westley said to me in a whisper: "God damn! I'm tired o' sitting here. Let's get up and be saved." So he got up and was saved.   6

Then I was left all alone on the mourners' bench. My aunt came and knelt at my knees and cried, while prayers and songs swirled all around me in the little church. The whole congregation prayed for me alone, in a mighty wail of moans and voices. And I kept waiting serenely for Jesus, waiting, waiting—but he didn't come. I wanted to see him, but nothing happened to me. Nothing! I wanted something to happen to me, but nothing happened.   7

I heard the songs and the minister saying: "Why don't you come? My dear child, why don't you come to Jesus? Jesus is waiting for you. He wants you. Why don't you come? Sister Reed, what is this child's name?"   8

"Langston," my aunt sobbed.   9

"Langston, why don't you come? Why don't you come and be saved? Oh, Lamb of God! Why don't you come?"   10

Now it was really getting late. I began to be ashamed of myself, holding everything up so long. I began to wonder what God thought about Westley, who certainly hadn't seen Jesus either, but who was now sitting proudly on the platform, swinging his knickerbockered   11 legs and grinning down at me, surrounded by deacons and old women on their knees praying. God had not struck Westley dead for taking his name in vain or for lying in the temple. So I decided that maybe to save further trouble, I'd better lie, too, and say that Jesus had come, and get up and be saved.

So I got up. 12

Suddenly the whole room broke into a sea of shouting, as they 13 saw me rise. Waves of rejoicing swept the place. Women leaped in the air. My aunt threw her arms around me. The minister took me by the hand and led me to the platform.

When things quieted down, in a hushed silence, punctuated by 14 a few ecstatic "Amens," all the new young lambs were blessed in the name of God. Then joyous singing filled the room.

That night, for the last time in my life but one—for I was a big 15 boy twelve years old—I cried. I cried, in bed alone, and couldn't stop. I buried my head under the quilts, but my aunt heard me. She woke up and told my uncle I was crying because the Holy Ghost had come into my life, and because I had seen Jesus. But I was really crying because I couldn't bear to tell her that I had lied, that I had deceived everybody in the church, and I hadn't seen Jesus, and that now I didn't believe there was a Jesus any more, since he didn't come to help me.

Questions for Close Reading

1. What is the selection's thesis (or narrative point)? Locate the sentence(s) in which Hughes states his main idea. If Hughes doesn't state the thesis explicitly, express it in your own words.
2. During the revival meeting, what pressures are put on the young Langston to get up and be saved?
3. How does Westley's attitude differ from Hughes's?
4. Does the narrator's Auntie Reed really understand him? Why can't he tell her the truth about his experience in the church?
5. Refer to your dictionary as needed to define the following words used in the selection: *revival* (paragraph 1), *knickerbockered* (11), *punctuated* (14), and *ecstatic* (14).

Questions About the Writer's Craft

1. **The pattern.** A narrative's power can often be traced to a conflict within the event being recounted. What conflict does the narrator of

"Salvation" experience? How does Hughes create tension about this conflict?

2. What key role does Westley serve in the resolution of the narrator's dilemma? How does Hughes's inclusion of Westley in the story help us to understand the narrator better?

3. **Other Patterns.** The thirteenth paragraph presents a metaphor of the church as an ocean. What images develop this metaphor? What does the metaphor tell us about Hughes's feelings and those of the church people?

4. The singing of hymns is a major part of this religious service. Why do you think Hughes has the narrator reveal the subjects and even the lyrics of some of the hymns?

Writing Assignments Using Narration as a Pattern of Development

1. Like Hughes, we sometimes believe that deception is our best alternative. Write a narrative about a time you felt deception was the best way either to protect those you care about or to maintain the respect of those important to you.

∞ 2. Write a narrative essay about a chain of events that caused you to become disillusioned about a person or institution you had previously regarded highly. Begin as Hughes does by presenting your initial beliefs. Relate the sequence of events that changed your evaluation of the person or organization. In the conclusion, explain the short- and long-term effects of the incident. For more accounts of childhood disillusionment, read Audre Lorde's "The Fourth of July" (page 160), Sophronia Liu's "So Tsi-Fai" (page 188), Beth Johnson's "Bombs Bursting in Air" (page 242), and Gloria Naylor's "Mommy, What Does 'Nigger' Mean?" (page 516).

Writing Assignments Using Other Patterns of Development

3. Hughes writes, "My aunt told me that when you were saved, you saw a light, and something happened to you inside! And Jesus came into your life!" What causes people to change their beliefs? Do such changes come from waiting calmly, as Hughes tried to do in church, or must they come from a more active process? Write an essay explaining your viewpoint. You may use process analysis, causal analysis, or some other organizational pattern to develop your thesis. Be sure to include specific examples to support your understanding of the way beliefs change.

∞ 4. Write a persuasive essay arguing either that lying is sometimes right or that lying is always wrong. Apply your thesis to particular situations and show how lying is or is not the right course of action. Remember to acknowledge the opposing viewpoint. Lewis Thomas's "The Lie

Detector" (page 477) and William Lutz's "Doublespeak" (page 296) may help you define your position. You might even mention these authors' perspectives in your essay.

Writing Assignments Using a Journal Entry as a Starting Point

5. Review your pre-reading journal entry, and select *one* family or community pressure with which you've had to contend. Then write an essay examining the effect that this pressure has had on you. Refer to your journal as you prepare to explain the values, beliefs, or traditions that you were expected to adopt. Discuss your response to this pressure and how your reaction has affected you.

Sophronia Liu

In 1973, at the age of twenty, Sophronia Liu came to the United States from her native Hong Kong. She earned a bachelor's degree in English and French and a master's degree in English from the University of South Dakota. She now makes her home in the Minneapolis-St. Paul area, where she is active as an organizer and educational consultant within the Asian-American community. An actress as well as a writer, Liu is a founding member of The Asian American Renaissance, a grassroots organization dedicated to building the Asian-American community through the arts. For her community work, she received a Governor's Award from the State of Minnesota. Liu's writing has appeared in *Colors Magazine, Making More Waves, Asian American Renaissance Journal,* and other publications. Currently, she is completing a memoir and her first full-length play, based on her family's stories. Initially written in response to a class assignment, the selection below was published in the feminist journal *Hurricane Alice* in 1986.

Pre-Reading Journal Entry

Think of at least two times in your childhood or adolescence when you witnessed—as an observer, participant, or victim—someone being bullied. In each case, reflect, in your journal, on these questions: What do you think made the person a target for bullying? Who were the offenders? What do you think provoked the bullying? What impact did this incident have on the people involved?

So Tsi-Fai

Voices, images, scenes from the past—twenty-three years ago, when I was in sixth grade: 1

"Let us bow our heads in silent prayer for the soul of So Tsi-fai. Let us pray for God's forgiveness for this boy's rash taking of his own life . . ." Sister Marie (Mung Gu-liang). My sixth-grade English teacher. Missionary nun from Paris. Principal of The Little Flower's School. Disciplinarian, perfectionist, authority figure: awesome and awful in my ten-year-old eyes. 2

"I don't need any supper. I have drunk enough insecticide." So   3
Tsi-fai. My fourteen-year-old classmate. Daredevil; good-for-noth-
ing lazybones (according to Mung Gu-liang). Bright black eyes,
disheveled hair, defiant sneer, creased and greasy uniform, dirty
hands, careless walk, shuffling feet. Standing in the corner for being
late, for forgetting his homework, for talking in class, for using foul
language. ("Shame on you! Go wash your mouth with soap!" Mung
Gu-liang's sharp command. He did, and came back with a grin.) So
Tsi-fai: Sticking his tongue out behind Mung Gu-liang's back, passing secret notes to his friends, kept behind after school, sent to the
Principal's office for repeated offenses. So Tsi-fai: incorrigible, hopeless, and without hope.

It was a Monday in late November when we heard of his death,   4
returning to school after the weekend with our parents' signatures
on our midterm reports. So Tsi-fai also showed his report to his
father, we were told later. He flunked three out of the fourteen subjects: English Grammar, Arithmetic, and Chinese Dictation. He
missed each one by one to three marks. That wasn't so bad. But he
was a hopeless case. Overaged, stubborn, and uncooperative; a
repeated offender of school rules, scourge of all teachers; who was
going to give him a lenient passing grade? Besides, being a few
months over the maximum age—fourteen—for sixth graders, he
wasn't even allowed to sit for the Secondary School Entrance Exam.

All sixth graders in Hong Kong had to pass the SSE before they   5
could obtain a seat in secondary school. In 1964 when I took the
exam, there were more than twenty thousand candidates. About
seven thousand of us passed: four thousand were sent to government and subsidized schools, the other three thousand to private
and grant-in-aid schools. I came in around no. 2000; I was lucky.
Without the public exam, there would be no secondary school for
So Tsi-fai. His future was sealed.

Looking at the report card with three red marks on it, his father   6
was furious. So Tsi-fai was the oldest son. There were three younger
children. His father was a vegetable farmer with a few plots of land
in Wong Juk-hang, by the sea. His mother worked in a local factory. So Tsi-fai helped in the fields, cooked for the family, and washed
his own clothes. ("Filthy, dirty boy!" gasped Mung Gu-liang.
"Grime behind the ears, black rims on the fingernails, dirty collar,
crumpled shirt. Why doesn't your mother iron your shirt?") Both

his parents were illiterate. So Tsi-fai was their biggest hope: He made it to the sixth grade.

Who woke him up for school every morning and had breakfast waiting for him? Nobody. ("Time for school! Get up! Eat your rice!" Ma nagged and screamed. The aroma of steamed rice and Chinese sausages spread all over the house. "Drink your tea! Eat your oranges! Wash your face! And remember to wash behind your ears!") And who helped So Tsi-fai do his homework? Nobody. Did he have older brothers like mine who knew all about the arithmetic of rowing a boat against the currents or with the currents, how to count the feet of chickens and rabbits in the same cage, the present perfect continuous tense of "to live" and the future perfect tense of "to succeed"? None. Nil. So Tsi-fai was a lost cause.   7

I came in first in both terms that year, the star pupil. So Tsi-fai was one of the last in the class: He was lazy; he didn't care. Or did he?   8

When his father scolded him, So Tsi-fai left the house. When he showed up again, late for supper, he announced, "I don't need any supper. I have drunk enough insecticide." Just like another one of his practical jokes. The insecticide was stored in the field for his father's vegetables. He was rushed to the hospital; dead upon arrival.   9

"He gulped for a last breath and was gone," an uncle told us at the funeral. "But his eyes wouldn't shut. So I said in his ear, 'You go now and rest in peace.' And I smoothed my hand over his eyelids. His face was all purple."   10

His face was still purple when we saw him in his coffin. Eyes shut tight, nostrils dilated and white as if fire and anger might shoot out, any minute.   11

In class that Monday morning, Sister Marie led us in prayer. "Let us pray that God will forgive him for his sins." We said the Lord's Prayer and the Hail Mary. We bowed our heads. I sat in my chair, frozen and dazed, thinking of the deadly chill in the morgue, the smell of disinfectant, ether, and dead flesh.   12

"Bang!" went a gust of wind, forcing open a leaf of the double door leading to the back balcony. "Flap, flap, flap." The door swung in the wind. We could see the treetops by the hillside rustling to and fro against a pale blue sky. An imperceptible presence had drifted in with the wind. The same careless walk and shuffling feet, the same daredevil air—except that the eyes were lusterless, dripping blood; the tongue hanging out, gasping for air. As usual, he was late. But he had come back to claim his place.   13

"I died a tragic death," his voice said. "I have as much right as 14
you to be here. This is my seat." We heard him; we knew he was back.
. . . So Tsi-fai: Standing in the corner for being late, for for- 15
getting his homework, for talking in class, for using foul language.
So Tsi-fai: Palm outstretched, chest sticking out, holding his
breath: "Tat. Tat. Tat." Down came the teacher's wooden ruler,
twenty times on each hand. Never batting an eyelash: then back to
facing the wall in the corner by the door. So Tsi-fai: grimy shirt,
disheveled hair, defiant sneer. So Tsi-fai. Incorrigible, hopeless, and
without hope.

The girls in front gasped and shrank back in their chairs. Mung 16
Gu-liang went to the door, held the doorknob in one hand, poked
her head out, and peered into the empty balcony. Then, with a
determined jerk, she pulled the door shut. Quickly crossing herself,
she returned to the teacher's desk. Her black cross swung upon the
front of her gray habit as she hurried across the room. "Don't be
silly!" she scolded the frightened girls in the front row.

What really happened? After all these years, my mind is still 17
haunted by this scene. What happened to So Tsi-fai? What happened
to me? What happened to all of us that year in sixth grade, when we
were green and young and ready to fling our arms out for the world?
All of a sudden, death claimed one of us and he was gone.

Who arbitrates between life and death? Who decides which life 18
is worth preserving and prospering, and which to nip in its bud?
How did it happen that I, at ten, turned out to be the star pupil, the
lucky one, while my friend, a peasant's son, was shoveled under the
heap and lost forever? How could it happen that this world would
close off a young boy's life at fourteen just because he was poor,
undisciplined, and lacked the training and support to pass his exams?
What really happened?

Today, twenty-three years later, So Tsi-fai's ghost still haunts 19
me. "I died a tragic death. I have as much right as you to be here.
This is my seat." The voice I heard twenty-three years ago in my
sixth-grade classroom follows me in my dreams. Is there anything I
can do to lay it to rest?

Questions for Close Reading

1. What is the selection's thesis (or narrative point)? Locate the sentence(s)
   in which Liu states her main idea. If she doesn't state the narrative point
   explicitly, express it in your own words.

2. What is the immediate cause of So Tsi-fai's suicide? What other factors also come into play? Why might he have chosen the method to kill himself that he did?

3. How did Liu's home life compare to that of So Tsi-fai? What connections do you see between each one's family life and academic progress?

4. What does So Tsi-fai say when he returns as a ghost? What do his words indicate about his perception of the educational system—and of his place in it?

5. Refer to your dictionary as needed to define the following words used in the selection: *defiant* (paragraph 3), *incorrigible* (3), *scourge* (4), *subsidized* (5), *dilated* (11), *ether* (12), *imperceptible* (13), *lusterless* (13), and *arbitrates* (18).

Questions About the Writer's Craft

1. **The pattern.** Most narratives establish a conflict and then move to its resolution. In "So Tsi-Fai," however, the reader knows by paragraph 2 that the boy will commit suicide; flashbacks and flashforwards comprise the rest of the essay. Locate these flashbacks and flashforwards. How does Liu signal these time shifts?

2. Liu describes a number of relationships filled with conflict. Identify as many of these conflicted relationships as you can. How do they heighten the essay's narrative tension?

3. In paragraphs 3, 6, and 7, Liu calls attention to certain conversations by placing quotations in parentheses. How do these parenthetical quotations reinforce the contrast between the different ways the author and So Tsi-fai were treated?

4. Throughout the essay, Liu repeats significant material. For example, she repeats the boy's last words twice (3 and 9) as well as whole passages of description (3 and 15). What effect do you think Liu intended these repetitions to have? How do they support her narrative point?

Writing Assignments Using Narration as a Pattern of Development

1. The death of So Tsi-fai marks the end of the author's childhood, the end of the time when she was "green and young and ready to fling [her] arms out for the world." Write an essay about a time when you were forced to grow up suddenly or were faced with a sobering reality. Your moment of lost innocence might have occurred when you were a child; perhaps you had to cope with illness or divorce. Or your moment of loss may have come when you were an adult; maybe you learned about a relative's unsavory business practices or a respected boss's discriminatory hiring practices. Use vivid description and revealing dialogue to convey

the tension and conflict you felt in the moment of discovery. Remember, though, to include only those details that reinforce your narrative point. Before writing, you may want to read Audre Lorde's "The Fourth of July" (page 160) and Langston Hughes's "Salvation" (page 183) for their powerful depiction of lost innocence.

2. Liu depicts the unfairness of an educational system that penalizes children simply because they are disadvantaged. Brainstorm with others to identify injustices that exist in our educational system. You might, for example, decide that teachers single out males for discipline, that students with learning disabilities get a second-rate education, that student athletes receive preferential treatment at grading time. Focusing on a specific educational level, select *one* such type of unfairness, and write an essay recounting two or three dramatic incidents of this inequity. To depict each incident fully, you'll need to reconstruct conversations and provide vivid narrative details, always keeping in mind the narrative point you want to make.

Writing Assignments Using Other Patterns of Development

3. Liu writes, "After all these years, my mind is still haunted by this scene." All of us have witnessed dramatic events that continue to exert power over us even though they occurred in the past. Write an essay showing the effects of such an event on your life, behavior, attitudes, and values. Begin with a brief account of the event; then explain its consequences for you, making sure your discussion honors the inevitable complexity of cause-effect relationships.

4. Liu's teacher clearly has no concern for her students' self-esteem, a factor that many consider crucial to children's well-being and success. Brainstorm with others to identify as many strategies as possible that elementary school teachers could use to strengthen students' self-image. Select what you consider to be the most compelling strategies, and categorize them into types, such as "group work," "independent study," "leadership experiences," "teacher-student conferences," and so on. Then write an essay explaining the techniques and their value. Be sure to illustrate the strategies with specific examples drawn from your own and other people's experiences. Maya Angelou's "Sister Flowers" (page 116), Alice Walker's "Beauty: When the Other Dancer Is the Self" (page 467), and Mary Sherry's "In Praise of the 'F' Word" (page 576) will provide insight into the development of a healthy self-esteem.

Writing Assignments Using a Journal Entry
as a Starting Point

5. Review your pre-reading journal entry, and select the most dramatic instance of bullying you witnessed as a child or adolescent. Then write an essay in which you analyze the causes and effects of the bullying incident. At the end of the essay, suggest ways that the bullying might have been prevented. To deepen your understanding of the bullying phenomenon, consider doing some research in the library and/or on the Internet.

Additional Writing Topics

NARRATION

General Assignments

Prepare an essay on any of the following topics, using narration as the paper's dominant method of development. Be sure to select details that advance the essay's narrative purpose; you may even want to experiment with flashback or flashforward. In any case, keep the sequence of events clear by using transitional cues. Within the limited time span covered, use vigorous details and varied sentence structure to enliven the narrative. Tell the story from a consistent point of view.

1. An emergency that brought out the best or worst in you
2. The hazards of taking children out to eat
3. An incident that made you believe in fate
4. Your best or worst day at school or work
5. A major decision
6. An encounter with a machine
7. An important learning experience
8. A narrow escape
9. Your first date, first day on the job, or first anything
10. A memorable childhood experience
11. A fairy tale the way you would like to hear it told
12. A painful moment
13. An incredible but true story
14. A significant family event
15. An experience in which a certain emotion (pride, anger, regret, or some other) was dominant

Assignments With a Specific Purpose and Audience

1. As the fund-raiser for a particular organization (for example, Red Cross, SPCA, Big Brothers/Big Sisters), you're sending a newsletter to contributors. Support your cause by telling the story of a time when your organization made all the difference—the blood donation that saved a life, the animal that was rescued from abuse, and so on.
2. A friend of yours has seen someone cheat on a test, shoplift, or violate an employer's trust. In a letter, convince this friend to inform the instructor, store owner, or employer by narrating an incident in which a witness did (or did not) speak up in such a situation. Tell what happened as a result.

3. You have had a disturbing encounter with one of the people who seem to have "fallen through the cracks" of society—a street person, an unwanted child, or anyone else who is alone and abandoned. Write a letter to the local newspaper describing this encounter. Your purpose is to arouse people's indignation and compassion and to get help for such unfortunates.

4. Write an article for your old high school newspaper. The article will be read primarily by seniors who are planning to go away to college next year. In the article, narrate a story that points to some truth about the "breaking away" stage of life.

5. A close friend has written a letter to you telling about a bad experience that he or she had with a teacher, employer, doctor, repairperson, or some other professional. On the basis of that single experience, your friend now negatively stereotypes the entire profession. Write a letter to your friend balancing his or her cynical picture by narrating a story that shows the "flip side" of this profession—someone who made every effort to help.

6. Your younger brother, sister, relative, or neighborhood friend can't wait to be your age. By narrating an appropriate story, show the young person that your age isn't as wonderful as he or she thinks. Be sure to select a story that the person can understand and appreciate.

5

EXEMPLIFICATION

WHAT IS EXEMPLIFICATION?

If someone asked you, "Have you been to any good restaurants lately?" you probably wouldn't answer "Yes" and then immediately change the subject. Most likely, you would go on to illustrate with *examples*. Perhaps you'd give the names of restaurants you've enjoyed and talk briefly about the specific things you liked: the attractive prices, the tasty main courses, the pleasant service, the tempting desserts. Such examples and details are needed to convince others that your opinion—in this or any matter—is valid. Similarly, when you talk about larger and more important issues, people won't pay much attention to your opinion if all you do is string together vague generalizations: "We have to do something about acid rain. It's had disastrous consequences for the environment. Its negative effects increase every year. Action must be taken to control the problem." To be taken seriously and to convince others that your point is well-founded, you must provide specific supporting examples: "The forests in the Adirondacks are dying"; "Yesterday's rainfall was fifty times more acidic than normal"; "Pine Lake, in the northern part of the state, was once a great fishing spot but now has no fish population."

Examples are equally important when you write an essay. It's not fuzzy generalities and highfalutin abstractions that make writing impressive. Just the opposite is true. Facts, anecdotes, statistics, details, opinions, and observations are at the heart of effective writing, giving your work substance and solidity.

HOW EXEMPLIFICATION FITS YOUR PURPOSE AND AUDIENCE

The wording of assignments and essay exam questions may signal the need for specific examples:

> Soap operas, whether shown during the day or in the evening, are among the most popular television programs. Why do you think this is so? Provide specific examples to support your position.

> Some observers claim that college students are less interested in learning than in getting ahead in their careers. Cite evidence to support or refute this claim.

> A growing number of people feel that parents should not allow young children to participate in highly competitive team sports. Basing your conclusion on your own experiences and observations, indicate whether you think this point of view is reasonable.

Such phrases as "Provide specific examples," "Cite evidence," and "Basing your conclusion on your own experiences and observations" signal that each essay would be developed through examples.

Usually, though, you won't be told so explicitly to provide examples. Instead, as you think about the best way to achieve your essay's purpose, you'll see the need for illustrative details—no matter which patterns of development you use. For instance, to *persuade* skeptical readers that the country needs a national health system, you might mention specific cases to dramatize the inadequacy of our current health-care system: a family bankrupted by medical bills; an uninsured accident victim turned away by a hospital; a chronically ill person rapidly deteriorating because he didn't have enough money to visit a doctor. Or imagine a lightly satiric piece that pokes fun at cat lovers. Insisting that "cat people" are pretty strange creatures, you might make your point—and make readers chuckle—with a series of examples *contrasting* cat lovers and dog lovers: the qualities admired by each group (loyalty in dogs versus independence in cats) and the different expectations each group has for its pets (dog lovers want Fido to be obedient and lovable, whereas cat lovers are satisfied with Felix's occasional spurts of docility and affection). Similarly, you would supply examples in a *causal analysis* speculating on the likely impact of a proposed tuition hike at your college. To convince the college administration of the probable negative effects of such a hike, you might cite the following examples: articles reporting a nationwide upswing in student transfers to less expensive schools; statistics indicating a significant drop in grades among already employed students forced to work more hours to pay increased tuition costs; interviews with students too financially strapped to continue their college education.

Whether you use examples as the primary or a supplemental method of development, they serve a number of important purposes. For one thing, examples make writing *interesting*. Assume you're writing an essay showing that television commercials are biased against women. Your essay would be lifeless and boring if all it did was repeat, in a general way, that commercials present stereotyped views of women.

An anti-female bias is rampant in television commercials. It is very much alive, yet most viewers seem to take it all in stride. Few people protest the obviously sexist characters and statements in such commercials. Surely, these commercials misrepresent the way most of us live.

Without interesting particulars, readers may respond, "Who cares?" But if you provide specific examples, you'll attract your readers' attention:

Sexism is rampant in television commercials. Although millions of women hold responsible jobs outside the home, commercials continue to portray women as simple creatures who spend most of their time thinking about wax buildup, cottony-soft bathroom tissue, and static-free clothes. Men, apparently, have better things to do than fret over such mundane household matters. How many commercials can you recall that depict men proclaiming the virtues of squeaky-clean dishes or sparkling bathrooms? Not many.

Examples also make writing *persuasive*. Most writing conveys a point, but many readers are reluctant to accept someone else's point of view unless evidence demonstrates its validity. Imagine you're writing an essay showing that latchkey children are more self-sufficient and emotionally secure than children who return from school to a home where a parent awaits them. Your thesis is obviously controversial. Without specific examples—from your own experience, personal observations, or research studies—your readers would undoubtedly question your position's validity.

Further, examples *help explain* difficult, abstract, or unusual ideas. Suppose you're assigned an essay on a complex subject such as inflation, zero population growth, or radiation exposure. As a writer, you have a responsibility to your readers to make these difficult concepts concrete and understandable. If writing an essay on radiation exposure in everyday life, you might start by providing specific examples of home appliances that emit radiation—color televisions, computers, and microwave ovens—and tell exactly how much radiation we absorb in a typical day from such equipment. To illustrate further the extent of our radiation exposure, you could also provide specifics about unavoidable sources of natural radiation (the sun, for instance) and details about the widespread use of radiation in medicine (X rays, radiation therapy). These examples would ground your discussion, making it immediate and concrete, preventing it from flying off into the vague and theoretical.

Finally, examples *help prevent unintended ambiguity*. All of us have experienced the frustration of having someone misinterpret what we say. In face-to-face communication, we can provide on-the-spot clarification. In writing, however, instantaneous feedback isn't available, so it's crucial that meaning be as unambiguous as possible. Examples will help.

Assume you're writing an essay asserting that ineffective teaching is on the rise in today's high schools. To clarify what you mean by "ineffective," you provide examples: the instructor who spends so much time disciplining unruly students that he never gets around to teaching; the moonlighting teacher who is so tired in class that she regularly takes naps during tests; and the teacher who accepts obviously plagiarized reports because he's grateful that students hand in something. Without such concrete examples, your readers will supply their own ideas—and these may not be what you had in mind. Readers might imagine "ineffective" to mean harsh and punitive, whereas your concrete examples would show that you intend it to mean out of control and irresponsible. Such specifics help prevent misunderstanding.

SUGGESTIONS FOR USING EXEMPLIFICATION IN AN ESSAY

The following suggestions will be helpful whether you use examples as a dominant or a supportive pattern of development.

1. Generate examples. Where do you get the examples to develop your essay? The first batch of examples is generated during the prewriting stage. With your purpose and thesis in mind, you make a broad sweep for examples, using brainstorming, freewriting, the mapping technique—whichever prewriting technique you prefer. During this preliminary search for examples, you may also read through your journal for relevant specifics, interview other people, or conduct library research.

Examples can take several forms, including specific names (of people, places, products, and so on), anecdotes, personal observations, expert opinion, as well as facts, statistics, and case studies gathered through research. While prewriting, try to generate more examples than you think you'll need. Starting with abundance—and then picking out the strongest examples—will give you a firm base on which to build the essay. If you have a great deal of trouble finding examples to support your thesis, you may need to revise the thesis; you may be trying to support an idea that has little validity. On the other hand, while prewriting, you may unearth numerous examples but find that many of them contradict the point you started out to support. If that happens, don't hesitate to recast your central point, always remembering that your thesis and examples must fit.

2. Select the examples to include. Once you've used prewriting to generate as many examples as possible, you're ready to limit your examples to the strongest ones. Keeping your purpose, thesis, and audience in mind, ask yourself several key questions: "Which examples support my thesis? Which do not? Which are most convincing? Which are most likely to interest readers and clarify meaning?"

You may include several brief examples within a single sentence:

The French people's fascination with some American literary figures, such as Poe and Hawthorne, is understandable, but their great respect for "artists" like comedian Jerry Lewis is a mystery.

Or you may develop a paragraph with a number of "for instances":

> A uniquely American style of movie-acting reached its peak in the 1950s. Certain charismatic actors completely abandoned the stage techniques and tradition that had been the foundation of acting up to that time. Instead of articulating their lines clearly, the actors mumbled; instead of making firm eye contact with their colleagues, they hung their heads, shifted their eyes, even talked with their eyes closed. Marlon Brando, Montgomery Clift, and then James Dean were three actors who exemplified this new trend.

As the preceding paragraph shows, *several examples* are usually needed to make a point. An essay with the thesis "Rock videos are dangerously violent" wouldn't be convincing if you gave only one example of a violent rock video. Several strong examples would be needed for readers to feel you had illustrated your point sufficiently.

As a general rule, you should strive for variety in the kinds of examples you include. For instance, you might choose a *personal-experience example* drawn from your own life or from the life of someone you know. Such examples pack the wallop of personal authority and lend drama to writing. Or you might include a *typical-case example*, an actual event or situation that did occur—but not to you or to anyone you know. (Perhaps you learned about the event through a magazine article, newspaper account, or television report.) The objective nature of such cases makes them especially convincing. You might also include a speculative or *hypothetical example* ("Imagine how difficult it must be for an elderly person to carry bags of groceries from the market to a bus stop several blocks away"). You'll find that hypothetical cases are effective for clarifying and dramatizing key points, but be sure to acknowledge that the example is indeed invented ("*Suppose* that . . ." or "Let's for a moment *assume* that . . ."). Make certain, too, that the invented situation is easily imagined and could conceivably happen. Finally, you might create a *generalized example*—one that is a composite of the typical or usual. Such generalized examples are often signaled by words that involve the reader ("*All of us*, at one time or another, have been driven to distraction by a trivial annoyance like the buzzing of a fly or the sting of a paper cut"), or they may refer to humanity in general ("When *most people* get a compliment, they perk up, preen, and think the praise-giver is blessed with astute powers of observation").

Occasionally, *one extended example*, fully developed with many details, can support an essay. It might be possible, for instance, to support the thesis "Federal legislation should raise the legal drinking age to twenty-one" with a single compelling, highly detailed example of the effects of one teenager's drunken-driving spree.

The examples you choose must also be *relevant;* that is, they must have direct bearing on the point you want to make. You would have a hard time convincing readers that Americans have callous attitudes toward the elderly if you described the wide range of new programs, all staffed by volunteers, at a well-financed center for senior citizens. Because these examples *contradict*, rather than support, your thesis, readers are apt to dismiss what you have to say.

Make certain, too, that your examples are *accurate*. Exercise special caution when using statistics. An old saying warns that there are lies, damned lies, and statistics—meaning that statistics can be misleading. A commercial may claim, "In a taste test, 80 percent of those questioned indicated that they preferred Fizzy Cola." Impressed? Don't be—at least, not until you find out how the test was conducted. Perhaps the subjects had to choose between Fizzy Cola and battery acid, or perhaps there were only five subjects, all Fizzy Cola vice presidents.

Finally, select *representative* examples. Picking the oddball, one-in-a-million example to support a point—and passing it off as typical—is dishonest. Consider an essay with the thesis "Part-time jobs contribute to academic success." Citing only one example of a student who works at a job twenty-five hours a week while earning straight As isn't playing fair. Why not? You've made a *hasty generalization* based on only one case. To be convincing, you need to show how holding down a job affects *most* students' academic performance. (For more on hasty generalizations, see page 553.)

3. Develop your examples sufficiently.   To ensure that you get your ideas across, your examples must be *specific*. An essay on the types of heroes in American movies wouldn't succeed if you simply strung together a series of undeveloped examples in paragraphs like this one:

Heroes in American movies usually fall into types. One kind of hero is the tight-lipped loner, men like Clint Eastwood and Humphrey Bogart. Another movie hero is the quiet, shy, or fumbling type who has appeared in movies since the beginning. The main characteristic of this hero is lovableness, as seen in actors like Jimmy Stewart. Perhaps the most one-dimensional and predictable hero is the superman who battles tough odds. This kind of hero is best illustrated by Sylvester Stallone as Rocky and Rambo.

If you developed the essay in this way—if you moved from one undeveloped example to another—you would be doing little more than making a list. To be effective, key examples must be expanded in sufficient detail. The examples in the preceding paragraph could be developed in paragraphs of their own. You could, for instance, develop the first example this way:

Heroes can be tight-lipped loners who appear out of nowhere, form no permanent attachments, and walk, drive, or ride off into the sunset. In many of his Westerns, from the low-budget "spaghetti Westerns" of the 1960s to Unforgiven in 1992, Clint Eastwood personifies this kind of hero. He is remote, mysterious, and untalkative. Yet he guns down an evil sheriff, runs other villains out of town, and helps a handicapped girl--acts that cement his heroic status. The loner might also be Sam Spade as played by Humphrey Bogart. Spade solves the crime and sends the guilty off to jail, yet he holds his emotions in check and has no permanent ties beyond his faithful secretary and shabby office. One gets the feeling that he could walk away from these, too, if necessary. Even in The Right Stuff, an account of the United States's early astronauts, the scriptwriters mold Chuck Yeager, the man who broke the sound barrier, into a classic loner. Yeager, portrayed by the aloof Sam Shepard, has a wife, but he is nevertheless insular. Taking mute pride in his ability to distance himself from politicians, bureaucrats, even colleagues, he soars into space, dignified and detached.

(For hints on ways to make writing specific, see pages 40–41.)

4. Organize the examples. If, as is usually the case, several examples support your point, be sure that you present the examples in an *organized* manner. Often you'll find that other patterns of development (cause-effect, comparison-contrast, definition, and so on) suggest ways to sequence examples. Let's say you're writing an essay showing that stay-at-home vacations offer numerous opportunities to relax. You might begin the essay with examples that *contrast* stay-at-home and get-away vacations. Then you might move to a *process analysis* that illustrates different techniques for unwinding at home.

The essay might end with examples showing the *effect* of such leisurely at-home breaks.

Finally, you need to select an *organizational approach consistent* with your *purpose* and *thesis*. Imagine you're writing an essay about students' adjustment during the first months of college. The supporting examples could be arranged *chronologically*. You might start by illustrating the ambivalence many students feel the first day of college when their parents leave for home; you might then offer an anecdote or two about students' frequent calls to Mom and Dad during the opening weeks of the semester; the essay might close with an account of students' reluctance to leave campus at the midyear break.

Similarly, an essay demonstrating that a room often reflects the character of its occupant might be organized *spatially:* from the empty soda cans on the floor to the spitballs on the ceiling. In an essay illustrating the kinds of skills taught in a composition course, you might move from *simple* to *complex* examples: starting with relatively matter-of-fact skills such as spelling and punctuation and ending with more conceptually difficult skills such as formulating a thesis and organizing an essay. Last, the *emphatic sequence*—in which you lead from your first example to your final, most significant one—is another effective way to organize an essay with many examples. A paper about Americans' characteristic impatience might progress from minor examples (dependence on fast food, obsession with ever faster mail delivery) to more disturbing manifestations of impatience (using drugs as quick solutions to problems, advocating simple answers to complex international problems: "Bomb them!").

5. Choose a point of view. Many essays developed by illustration place the subject in the foreground and the writer in the background. Such an approach calls for the *third-person point of view*. For example, even if you draw examples from your own personal experience, you can present them without using the *first-person* "I." You might convert such personal material into generalized examples (see page 202), or you might describe the personal experience as if it happened to someone else. Of course, you may use the first person if the use of "I" will make the example more believable and dramatic. But remember: Just because an event happened to you personally doesn't mean you have to use the first-person point of view.

STUDENT ESSAY

The following student essay was written by Michael Pagano in response to this assignment:

> In "The 'Values' Wasteland," Charles Sykes contends that the American educational system fails to provide students with firm guidelines for making moral choices. In an essay of your own, critique another aspect of American society, using—as Sykes does—numerous compelling examples to support your viewpoint.

While reading Michael's paper, try to determine how effectively it applies the principles of exemplification. The annotations on Michael's paper and the commentary following it will help you look at the essay more closely.

Pursuit of Possessions
by Michael Pagano

Introduction

Anne Morrow Lindbergh, a well-known novelist, essayist, and poet, once wrote that Americans "who could choose simplicity, choose complication." Lindbergh herself was a prime example of this phenomenon. Often in the spotlight as the wife of the famed aviation pioneer Charles Lindbergh, she also negotiated the demands of being a mother as well as a writer. Not surprisingly, Lindbergh sought to simplify her life. In one of her best-known essays, "Channelled Whelk," she describes her escape to a beach cottage, bare except for driftwood and seashells. There she was happy. But few of us Americans would be willing to simplify our lives as Lindbergh did. Instead, we choose to clutter our

Thesis
lives with a stream of material possessions. And what is the result of this mania for possessions?

Plan of
development
Much of our time goes to buying new things, dealing with the complications they create, and working madly to buy more things or pay for the things we already have.

Topic sentence
We devote a great deal of our lives to acquiring the material goods we imagine are essential to our

1

2

The first of three paragraphs in a chronological sequence

well-being. Hours are spent planning and thinking about our future purchases. We window-shop for designer jogging shoes; we leaf through magazines looking at ads for elaborate stereo equipment; we research back issues of Consumer Reports to find out about recent developments in exercise equipment. Moreover, once we find what we are looking for, more time is taken up when we decide to actually buy the items. How do we find this time? That's easy. We turn evenings, weekends, and holidays--time that used to be set aside for family and friends--into shopping expeditions. No wonder family life is deteriorating and children spend so much time in front of television sets. Their parents are seldom around.

Topic sentence

The second paragraph in the chronological sequence

A paragraph with many specific examples

As soon as we take our new purchases home, they begin to complicate our lives. A sleek new sports car has to be washed, waxed, and vacuumed. A fashionable pair of skintight jeans can't be thrown in the washing machine but has to be taken to the dry cleaner. New stereo equipment has to be connected with a tangled network of cables to the TV, radio, and cassette deck. Eventually, of course, the inevitable happens. Our indispensable possessions break down and need to be repaired. The home computer starts to lose data, the microwave has to have its temperature controls adjusted, and the videotape recorder has to be serviced when a cassette becomes jammed in the machine.   3

Topic sentence

The third paragraph in the chronological sequence

After more time has gone by, we sometimes discover that our purchases don't suit us anymore, and so we decide to replace them. Before making our replacement purchases, though, we have to find ways to get rid of the old items. If we want to replace our black-and-white 19-inch television set with a 25-inch color set, we have to find time to put an ad in the classified section of the paper. Then we have to handle phone calls and set up times people can come to look at the TV. We could store the set in the basement--if we are lucky enough to find a spot that isn't already filled with other discarded purchases.   4

Topic sentence with emphasis signal

Worst of all, this mania for possessions often influences our approach to work. It is not unusual for   5 people to take a second or even a third job to pay off the debt they fall into because they have over-bought. After paying for food, clothing, and shelter, many people see the rest of their paycheck go to Visa, MasterCard, department store charge accounts, and time payments. Panic sets in when they realize there simply is not enough money to cover all their expenses. Just to stay afloat, people may have to work overtime or take on additional jobs.

Conclusion

It is clear that many of us have allowed the pursuit of possessions to dominate our lives. We are so busy buying, maintaining, and paying for our worldly goods that we do not have much time to think about what is really important. We should try to step back from our compulsive need for more of everything and get in touch with the basic values that are the real point of our lives.

6

COMMENTARY

Thesis, other patterns of development, and plan of development.   In "Pursuit of Possessions," Michael analyzes the American mania for acquiring material goods. He begins with a quotation from Anne Morrow Lindbergh and briefly explains Lindbergh's strategy for simplifying her life. The reference to Lindbergh gives Michael a chance to *contrast* the way she tried to lead her life with the acquisitive and frenzied way many Americans lead theirs. This contrast leads logically to the essay's *thesis:* "We choose to clutter our lives with a stream of material possessions."

Besides introducing the basic contrast at the heart of the essay, Michael's opening paragraph helps readers see that the essay contains an element of *causal analysis.* Michael asks, "What is the result of this mania for possessions?" and then answers that question in the next sentence. This sentence also serves as the essay's *plan of development* and reveals that Michael feels the pursuit of possessions negatively affects our lives in three key ways.

Essays of this length often don't need a plan of development. But since Michael's paper is filled with many *examples,* the plan of development helps readers see how all the details relate to the essay's central point.

Evidence.   Support for the thesis consists of numerous examples presented in the *first-person-plural point of view* ("*We* choose to clutter our lives . . .," "*We* devote a great deal of our lives . . ." and so on). Many of these examples seem drawn from Michael's, his friends', or his family's experiences; however, to emphasize the events' universality, Michael converts these essentially personal examples into generalized ones that "we" all experience.

These examples, in turn, are organized around the three major points signaled by the plan of development. Michael uses one paragraph to develop his first and third points and two paragraphs to develop his second point. Each of the four supporting paragraphs is focused by a *topic sentence* that appears at the start of the paragraph. The transitional phrase "Worst of all" (paragraph 5) signals that Michael has sequenced his major points *emphatically,* saving for last the issue he considers most significant: how the "mania for possessions . . . influences our approach to work."

Organizational strategies.   Emphatic order isn't Michael's only organizational technique. When reading the paper, you probably felt that there was an easy flow from one supporting paragraph to the next. How does Michael achieve such *coherence between paragraphs?* For one thing, he sequences paragraphs 2–4 *chronologically:* what happens before a purchase is made; what happens afterward. Secondly, topic sentences in paragraphs 3 and 4 include *signal devices* that indicate this passage of time. The topic sentences also strengthen coherence by *linking back* to the preceding paragraph: "*As soon as we take our new purchases home,* they . . . complicate our lives" and "*After more time has gone by,* we . . . discover that our purchases don't suit us anymore."

The same organizing strategies are used *within paragraphs* to make the essay coherent. Details in paragraphs 2 through 4 are sequenced chronologically, and to help readers follow the chronology, Michael uses *signal devices: "Moreover, once* we find what we are looking for, more time is taken up . . ." (2); "*Eventually,* of course, the inevitable happens" (3); "*Then* we have to handle phone calls . . ." (4).

Problems with paragraph development.   You probably recall that an essay developed primarily through exemplification must include examples that are *relevant, interesting, convincing, representative, accurate,* and *specific.* On the whole, Michael's examples

meet these requirements. The third and fourth paragraphs, especially, include vigorous details that show how our mania for buying things can govern our lives. We may even laugh with self-
recognition when reading about "skintight jeans [that] can't be
thrown in the washing machine" or a basement "filled with other
discarded purchases."

The fifth paragraph, however, is underdeveloped. We know that
this paragraph presents what Michael considers his most significant
point, but the paragraph's examples are rather *flat* and *unconvincing*. To make this final section more compelling, Michael could
mention specific people who overspend, revealing how much they
are in debt and how much they have to work to become solvent
again. Or he could cite a television documentary or magazine article dealing with the issue of consumer debt. Such specifics would
give the paragraph the solidity it now lacks.

Shift in tone.   The fifth paragraph has a second, more subtle
problem; *a shift in tone.* Although Michael has, up to this point,
been critical of our possession-mad culture, he has poked fun at our
obsession and kept his tone conversational and gently satiric. In this
paragraph, though, he adopts a serious tone and, in the next paragraph, his tone becomes even weightier, almost preachy. It is, of
course, legitimate to have a serious message in a lightly satiric piece.
In fact, most satiric writing has such an additional layer of meaning.
But because Michael has trouble blending these two moods, there's
a jarring shift in the essay.

Shift in focus.   The second paragraph shows another kind of
shift—in *focus*. The paragraph's controlling idea is that too much
time is spent acquiring possessions. However, starting with "No
wonder family life is deteriorating," Michael includes two sentences
that introduce a complex issue beyond the scope of the essay. Since
these last two sentences disrupt the paragraph's unity, they should
be deleted.

Revising the first draft.   Although the final version of the essay
needs work in spots, it's much stronger than Michael's first draft. To
see how Michael went about revising the draft, compare his paper's
second and third supporting paragraphs with his draft version reprinted here.

Original Version of the Second Paragraph

Our lives are spent not only buying things but in dealing with the inevitable complications that are created by our newly acquired possessions. First, we have to find places to put all the objects we bring home. More clothes demand more closets; a second car demands more garage space; a home entertainment center requires elaborate shelving. We shouldn't be surprised that the average American family moves once every three years. A good many families move simply because they need more space to store all the things they buy. In addition, our possessions demand maintenance time. A person who gets a new car will spend hours washing it, waxing it, and vacuuming it. A new pair of jeans has to go to the dry cleaners. New stereo systems have to be connected to already existing equipment. Eventually, of course, the inevitable happens. Our new items need to be repaired. Or we get sick of them and decide to replace them. Before making our replacement purchases, though, we have to get rid of the old items. That can be a real inconvenience.

When Michael looked more closely at this paragraph, he realized it rambled and lacked energy. He started to revise the paragraph by tightening the first sentence, making it more focused and less awkward. Certainly, the revised sentence ("As soon as we take our new purchases home, they begin to complicate our lives") is crisper than the original. Next, he decided to omit the discussion about finding places to put new possessions; these sentences about inadequate closet, garage, and shelf space were so exaggerated that they undercut the valid point he wanted to make. He also chose to eliminate the sentences about the mobility of American families. This was, he felt, an interesting point, but it introduced an issue too complex to be included in the paragraph.

Michael strengthened the rest of the paragraph by making his examples more specific. A "new car" became a "sleek new sports car," and a "pair of jeans" became a "fashionable pair of skintight jeans." Michael also realized he had to do more than merely write, "Eventually, . . . our new items need to be repaired." This point had to be dramatized by sharp, convincing details. Therefore, Michael added lively examples to describe how high-tech possessions—microwaves, home computers, VCRs—break down. Similarly, Michael realized it wasn't enough simply to say, as he had in the original, that we run into problems when we try to replace out-of-favor purchases. Vigorous details were again needed to illustrate the point. Michael thus used a typical "replaceable" (an old black-and-white TV) as his key example and showed the annoyance involved in handling phone calls and setting up appointments so people could see the TV.

After adding these specifics, Michael realized he had enough material to devote a separate paragraph to the problems associated with replacing old purchases. By dividing his original paragraph, Michael ended up with two well-focused paragraphs, neither of which has the rambling quality found in the original.

In short, Michael strengthened his essay through substantial revision. Another round of rewriting would have made the essay stronger still. Even without this additional work, Michael's essay provides an interesting perspective on an American preoccupation.

ACTIVITIES: EXEMPLIFICATION

Prewriting Activities

1. Imagine you're writing two essays: One is a serious paper analyzing the factors that *cause* large numbers of public school teachers to leave the profession each year; the other is a light essay *defining* "preppie," "head banger," or some other slang term used to describe a kind of person. Jot down ways you might use examples in each essay.

2. Use mapping or another prewriting technique to gather examples illustrating the truth of *one* of the following familiar sayings. Then, using the same or a different prewriting technique, accumulate examples that counter the saying. Weigh both sets of examples to determine the saying's validity. After developing an appropriate thesis, decide which examples you would elaborate in an essay.

    a. Haste makes waste.

    b. There's no use crying over spilled milk.

    c. A bird in the hand is worth two in the bush.

Revising Activities

3. The following paragraph is from the first draft of an essay about the decline of small-town shopping districts. The paragraph is meant to show what small towns can do to revitalize business. Revise the paragraph, strengthening it with specific and convincing examples.

A small town can compete with a large new mall for shoppers. But merchants must work together, modernizing the stores and making the town's main street pleasant, even fun to walk. They should also copy the malls' example by including attention-getting events as often as possible.

4.   Reprinted here is a paragraph from the first draft of a light-spirited essay showing that Americans' pursuit of change for change's sake has drawbacks. The paragraph is meant to illustrate that infatuation with newness costs consumers money yet leads to no improvement in product quality. How effective is the paragraph? Which examples are specific and convincing? Which are not? Do any seem nonrepresentative, offensive, or sexist? How could the paragraph's organization be improved? Consider these questions as you rewrite the paragraph. Add specific examples where needed. Depending on the way you revise, you may want to break this one paragraph into several.

We end up paying for our passion for the new and improved. Trendy clothing styles convince us that last year's oufits are outdated, even though our old clothes are fine. Women are especially vulnerable in this regard. What, though, about items that have to be replaced periodically, like shampoo? Even slight changes lead to new formulations requiring retooling of the production process. That means increased manufacturing costs per item--all of which get passed on to us, the consumer. Then there are those items that tout new, trend-setting features that make earlier versions supposedly obsolete. Some manufacturers, for example, boast that their stereo or CD systems transmit an expanded-frequency range. The problem is that humans can't even hear such frequencies. But the high-tech feature dazzles men who are too naive to realize they're being hoodwinked.

Charles Sykes

A journalist whose work has appeared in the *New York Times*, the *Wall Street Journal*, and other leading newspapers, Charles Sykes (1954–) usually writes about education issues. His books include *ProfScam: Professors and the Demise of Higher Education* (1988), *The Hollow Men: Politics and Corruption in Higher Education* (1990), *A Nation of Victims: The Decay of the American Character* (1992), and *The End of Privacy* (1999). A senior fellow at the Wisconsin Policy Research Institute and host of a popular Milwaukee radio show, Sykes lectures widely on topics having to do with what he sees as the collapse of standards in American culture. The following excerpt is from Sykes's 1995 book, *Dumbing Down Our Kids: Why America's Children Feel Good About Themselves But Can't Read, Write, or Add.*

Pre-Reading Journal Entry

Recent studies reveal that sexual misbehavior, drug use, shoplifting, and cheating are on the rise among young people. In your journal, explore your thinking about young people's misconduct in two of these (or other) areas. Why do you think young people engage in such risky behavior?

The "Values" Wasteland

Eric Richardson was a seventeen-year-old member of the Spur Posse, a group of boys accused of raping girls as young as ten years old. After their arrests, the posse members reportedly returned to school as heroes, applauded for their exploits by their fellow students. In talk show appearances and media interviews, the boys were unrepentant. "They pass out condoms, teach sex education and pregnancy this and pregnancy that," Eric said after polishing off a Nacho Supreme and necking with his girlfriend in a booth at the Taco Bell. "But they don't teach us any rules."[1] His response was too glib and too convenient; it wasn't our fault, he was saying, you taught us to be like this. No school, however misguided, can ever be

---

[1] Jane Gross, "Where 'Boys will be Boys,' And Adults Are Bewildered," *New York Times*, 29 March 1993.

blamed for a piece of work like Eric Richardson. Even so, the evidence suggests that his ethical compass is not an isolated aberration.

A 1988 study of more than 2,000 Rhode Island students in grades six through nine found that two-thirds of the boys and half of the girls thought that "it was acceptable for a man to force sex on a woman" if they had been dating six months or more.[2] A write-in survey of 126,000 teenagers found that 25 to 40 percent of teens see nothing wrong with cheating on exams, stealing from employers, or keeping money that wasn't theirs. A seventeen-year-old high school senior explained: "A lot of it is a gray area. It's everybody doing their own thing."[3]

A 1992 survey by the Josephson Institute for Ethics of nearly 7,000 high school and college students, most of them from middle- and upper middle-class backgrounds, found the equivalent of a "hole in the moral ozone" among American youth.

- A third of high school students and 16 percent of college students said they have shoplifted in the last year. Nearly the same number (33 percent of high school students and 11 percent of college students) said they have stolen from their parents or relatives at least once.[4]
- One in eight college students admitted to committing an act of fraud, including borrowing money they did not intend to repay, and lying on financial aid or insurance forms.
- A third of high school and college students said they would lie to get a job. One in six said they have already done so at least once.
- More than 60 percent of high school students said they had cheated at least once on an exam.
- Forty percent of the high school students who participated in this survey admitted that they "were not completely honest" on at least one or two questions—meaning that they may have lied on a survey about lying.[5]

[2]J. Kikuchi, "Rhode Island Develops Successful Intervention Program for Adolescents," *National Coalition Against Sexual Assault Newsletter*, Fall 1988.
[3]*USA Weekend*, 21–22 August 1992.
[4]Gary Abrams, "Youth Gets Bad Marks in Morality," *Los Angeles Times*, 12 November 1992.
[5]Ibid.

"I think it's very easy to get through high school and college   4
these days and hardly ever hear, 'That's wrong,'" commented Patrick
McCarthy of Pasadena's Jefferson Center for Character Education.
Michael Josephson, the president of the Josephson Institute of
Ethics, describes a large and growing population as the "I-Deserve-
Its," or IDIs. "Their IDI-ology is exceptionally and dangerously self-
centered, preoccupied with personal needs, wants, don't-wants and
rights." In pursuit of success, or comfort, or self-gratification, the
IDIs are blithely willing to jettison traditional ethical restraints, and
as a result "IDIs are more likely to lie, cheat and engage in irresponsible behavior when it suits their purposes. IDIs act as if they need
whatever they want and deserve whatever they need. . . ."6 American
youth's culture of entitlement cannot, of course, be laid solely at the
feet of the schools. If there has been an ethical meltdown among
young Americans we need to look first to their parents, communities,
the media, and even the churches for explanations. Society's shift
from a culture of self-control to one of self-gratification, self-actualization, and self-realization, and its changing norms regarding personal responsibility and character, was not restricted to the arena of
public education. Even so, the ethical state of America's young people may, at least in part, have something to do with the way our
schools teach them about right and wrong.

At one time, American students used to study historical role   5
models like Benjamin Franklin, Florence Nightingale, Thomas
Edison, Madame Curie, Abraham Lincoln, and George
Washington—whose stories were used to provide object lessons in
inventiveness, character, compassion, curiosity, and truthfulness.
Following Aristotle, ethicists recognized that humanity does not
become virtuous simply by precept, but by "nature, habit, rational principle." "We become just by the practice of just actions,"
Aristotle observed, "self-controlled by exercising self-control."
This process was most effectively begun by placing examples of
such virtues in front of young people for them to emulate. But
while Asian children continue to read about stories of perseverance, hard work, loyalty, duty, prudence, heroism, and honesty,

6Michael Josephson, "Young American Is Looking Out for No. 1," *Los Angeles
Times,* 16 October 1990.

[educational researcher] Harold Stevenson finds that "For the most part, such cultural models have been displaced in the United States today."[7] In its place, we provide children a jumbled smorgasbord of moral choices.

How Do You *Feel* About Cheating?

The course is officially about "citizenship," but the subject is values.[8] Specially prepared for students in the fourth to sixth grades, the class is designed to help students clarify and discover their own values on issues like lying and cheating. As a group or by secret ballot, the fourth, fifth, and sixth graders are asked: "How many of you . . .   6

Think children should have to work for their allowances?
Think most rules are dumb?
Think that there are times when cheating is ok?
Wish you didn't have grades in school?
Think prizes should be awarded for everything?"

The section on cheating asks students: "What are your attitudes toward cheating?" They are asked to complete the following statements:

Tests are _____
Grades are _____
The bad thing about cheating is _____
The good thing about cheating is _____
If there were no such things as grades, would your attitude toward cheating change?
Is school the only place cheating takes place? Where else does cheating take place?
Is it ever OK to cheat? When?

It is not clear whether there are ever any right and wrong answers to these questions. The class takes a similar approach to lying. Students are asked, "Lying, What's Your View?". . . Children   7

---

[7]Harold W. Stevenson and James W. Stigler, *The Learning Gap* (New York: Summit Books, 1992), pp. 85–86.
[8]"Citizenship: 4th–6th Grade," xeroxed worksheets, undated. Several copies were provided to me by parents whose children had been given the assignment during class.

in the class are . . . presented with a series of ethical problems. They are not asked to define right and wrong or moral or immoral. Instead, they are asked to say which actions are "acceptable . . . and . . . which are . . . unacceptable. Do any of the situations involve lying?"

> A factory worker oversleeps and is late for work. He tells his supervisor that he was involved in a minor traffic accident.
>
> Janine just can't face a big history exam for which she hasn't studied. She convinces her mother that she has a terrible sore throat and must stay home.
>
> Bill runs into a friend he hasn't seen in months. The friend asks how he is. Bill smiles and answers "great!" even though his dog just died, he's flunking English, and he just broke up with his girlfriend....

Such nonjudgmentalism is a feature of the approach known as "values clarification," in which, as [journalist] William Kirk Kilpatrick writes, classroom discussions are turned into "'bull sessions' where opinions go back and forth but conclusions are never reached.". . . Many of these classes seem to be based on the rather fantastic notion that since none of the civilizations anywhere in the world throughout the entire sweep of human history has been able to work out a moral code of conduct worthy of being passed on, we should therefore leave it to fourth graders to work out questions of right and wrong on their own.   8

The Values Clarifiers

The developers of Values Clarification and other nonjudgmental approaches to moral decision making often claimed to be value-free, but their agenda was quite specific. Their bête noir was "moralizing" in any form. "Moralizing," the authors of *Values Clarification: A Handbook of Practical Strategies for Teachers and Students* wrote in 1978, "is the direct, although sometimes subtle inculcation of the adults' values upon the young."9 For the authors of the new curriculum, this was not merely authoritarian and stifling,   9

9Sidney B. Simon, Leland W. Howe, and Howard Kirschenbaum, *Values Clarification: A Handbook of Practical Strategies for Teachers and Students* (New York: Hart Publishing, 1972), p. 15.

but also dangerous to the ethical health of children. By passing on a set of moral values, they argued, parents were hampering the ability of children to come up with their own values. "Young people brought up by moralizing adults are not prepared to make their own responsible choices," they warned.[10] In any case, moralizing was no longer practical. Children were bombarded with so many different sets of values and parents were only some of the many voices they heard. In the end, they argue, every child had to make his own choices. That, of course, is true—making choices is the essence of free will. But where values clarification departed from older moral philosophies was in its contention that children do not need to be grounded in value systems or provided with moral road maps before they are asked to make such choices. Values clarifiers also did not care what values the child chose to follow. Specifically, values clarification did not concern itself with inculcating values such as self-control, honesty, responsibility, loyalty, prudence, duty, or justice. In its purest form, values clarification did not even argue that these virtues were superior or preferable to their opposites and had little to say about concepts of right and wrong. The goal of values clarification was not to create a virtuous young person, or young adult with character or probity; its goal was empowering youngsters to make their own decisions, *whatever those decisions were. . . .*

The assumption behind such programs was that children had 10
the capacity to develop character on their own; that students as young as third grade had the knowledge, insight, and cognitive abilities to wrestle through difficult dilemmas and thorny moral paradoxes without the benefit of a moral compass, either from parents or teachers. . . .

At the heart of the values clarification program was the effort to 11
have students develop an individual identity. One exercise was "Are You Someone Who . . ." followed by a long list of options, including: "is likely to marry someone of another religion?"; "is likely to grow a beard?"; "would consider joining the John Birch Society?"; "is apt to go out of your way to have a black (white) neighbor?"; "will subscribe to *Playboy* magazine?"; will change your religion?"; "will be likely to win a Nobel Peace Prize?"; "is apt to experiment with pot?"; "would get therapy on your own initiative?"; "will make a faithless husband? wife?"

[10]Ibid., p. 16.

The authors explain that such questions will cause students "to consider more thoughtfully what they value, what they want out of life and what type of persons they want to become."[11] But the questions send another message as well by treating the various options simply as different choices of apparently equal weight, like choices on a personality buffet line: Will you win the Nobel Prize or experiment with pot? Subscribe to *Playboy* or change your religion? There is no suggestion that growing a beard or cheating on your wife might be decisions that carry rather different moral weights. 12

Ultimately, the values clarification approach reduces moral choice to a matter of personal taste with no more basis in objective reality than a preference for a red car rather than a blue one. There is no right or wrong answer and no real ground to regard your own choice either as better or more valid than any other. 13

But is this really a process of working out moral values or is it simply a process of rationalization? Humans rationalize because it is convenient and it suits our interests. If we choose, we can shape morality to meet our inclinations and impulses, rather than try to shape our inclinations to accord with moral law. Moral reasoning, in contrast, involves asking whether an act is good, whether it is made with right intent, and examining the act's circumstances. To make such judgments requires an understanding of what the moral law might be, not simply how we feel about the act. But to take the subjective state of mind and make it the sole test of morality is to rationalize and call it moral reasoning. Checking one's inclinations is not the same as examining one's conscience, precisely because the conscience needs to be educated. 14

One would never get that idea from watching a values clarification "simulation" of a moral choice. In one popular exercise, students have to imagine that their class has been trapped in a cave-in. In the exercise, students are asked to imagine that they have to form a single line to work their way out of the cave. At any moment, another rock slide may close the way out. Those at the head of the line are therefore the most likely to survive. In the class exercise, each member of the class must give the reason he or she should be at the head of the line. The teacher tells them: "Your reasons can be of two kinds. You can tell us what you want to live for or what you have yet to get out of life that is important to you. Or you can talk 15

[11]Ibid., p. 366.

about what you have to contribute to others in the world that would justify your being near the front of the line." After hearing all of the pleas, the class then decides the order in which they will file out of the cave.[12]

Like other values clarification chestnuts, youngsters are asked to make life-and-death decisions. But what are the practical implications? Do students emerge from the class more empathetic? More willing to sacrifice for others? Are they likely to treat their peers with more respect? Show more self-restraint in the presence of their parents? Or are they likely to have a keener sense of their own egos? . . . 16

Other exercises ask students to choose who should be allowed to stay in a fallout shelter (and who should be left to die) during a nuclear attack; to decide whether it is morally permissible for a poor man to steal a drug that his desperately ill wife needs; to work through the dilemma of trapped settlers who must decide whether to turn to cannibalism or starve to death; to put themselves in the place of a mother who must choose which of her two children she will save; and consider the ethical dilemma of a doctor who must decide to operate on an injured child despite the religious objections of the parents. "Like a roller-coaster ride," William Kilpatrick writes, "the dilemma approach can leave its passengers a bit breathless. That is one of its attractions. But like a roller-coaster ride, it may also leave them a bit disoriented—or more than a bit."[13] As entertaining as such problems may be, they are hardly a guide for developing a moral code; morality is more than solving a complex and perhaps even unsolvable puzzle. Take the case of the man whose wife is dying of an incurable illness and who needs a rare and expensive drug. Kilpatrick wonders whether youngsters who spend a diverting and lively class period debating whether stealing is right or wrong in this case would be less likely to steal themselves? Or lie? Or cheat? Or will they come to the conclusion that moral questions are inevitably so complicated, so fraught with doubt, that no one answer is necessarily ever any better than any other and that all moral questions come down in the end simply to a matter of opinion? Or will they get the idea that it is less important whether one steals or not than that one has developed a system of "valuing" with which one is comfortable? 17

[12]Ibid., p. 288.
[13]William Kirk Kilpatrick, *Why Johnny Can't Tell Right From Wrong* (New York: Simon & Schuster, 1992), p. 84.

One of the striking things about spending time with high school   18
students is the near universality of this notion that values are something they work out on their own. One frequent speaker on ethical
issues recounts his experience with high school students in which he
presents them with a typical values clarification dilemma. They must
imagine that they are on a lifeboat with another person and their
family dog; the students can save only one, so they must choose
either the human being, who is a complete stranger, or the beloved
and cherished family dog. Typically, some of the students choose to
save the dog and allow the man to die; most students choose to save
the human being. But then the speaker asks them what they thought
of their classmates who had opted for the dog over the man. Almost
never, says the speaker, do students say that those choices were
"wrong" or morally objectionable.[14] Even for those who made the
correct moral choice, it was merely a matter of personal opinion, and
they refuse to be judgmental toward those who put the dog's life
ahead of the human being's. The concept that there might be universal and objective moral principles at stake is completely alien to
these youngsters.

Questions for Close Reading

1. What is the selection's thesis? Locate the sentence(s) in which Sykes
   states his main idea. If he doesn't state it directly, express it in your own
   words.
2. What, according to Sykes, is the difference between contemporary
   American education and American education in the past?
3. What group of people does Sykes blame for the erosion of morality in
   American education? What justification do these people provide for their
   approach?
4. Reread paragraphs 15 and 18. In each, Sykes describes a classroom exercise in "values clarification." What is the educational intent of the two
   exercises? How are they similar? How do they differ? What is Sykes's
   opinion of the two exercises?
5. Refer to your dictionary as needed to define the following words used in
   the selection: *unrepentant* (paragraph 1), *self-actualization* (4), *precept*
   (5), *emulate* (5), *perseverance* (5), *smorgasbord* (5), *bête noir* (9), *moralizing* (9), *cognitive* (10), *rationalization* (14), and *fraught* (17).

[14]Dennis Prager, conversation with author.

Questions About the Writer's Craft

1. **The pattern.** In the first three paragraphs of his essay, Sykes provides numerous examples to illustrate what he considers the moral looseness of young people. Why do you think he starts with the example of the seventeen-year-old rapist? In what ways is this example different from the examples he provides in paragraphs 2 and 3?
2. Why do you suppose Sykes entitles his essay "The 'Values' Wasteland"? Consider what each word means. Why do you think he puts quotation marks around the word "Values"?
3. In paragraphs 2 and 3, Sykes makes heavy use of statistics. Why do you suppose he cites statistics only in the beginning of the essay?
4. **Other patterns.** How would you characterize Sykes's tone? How does this tone reinforce his argument?

Writing Assignments Using Exemplification as a Pattern of Development

1. Sykes contends that modern education fails to teach morality. Do you agree? Write an essay illustrating the point that contemporary schooling blunts *or* enhances young people's moral sense. In either case, offer convincing examples from your own and other people's schooling to support your point of view. Consider opening your essay, as Sykes does, with a highly dramatic example.
2. Sykes believes that the moral fiber of young people has deteriorated. Interview classmates, friends, and family members of varying ages to see if they think that young people today are less moral than they were in earlier times. Ask each person to supply at least one example to illustrate his or her opinion. Review the examples, and decide whether you agree with or reject Sykes's position. Then write an essay in which you support your opinion, using the most compelling examples from your interviews as well as your own experiences and observations.

Writing Assignments Using Other Patterns of Development

3. Sykes believes that there are "universal and objective moral principles." Write an essay narrating a time when you faced a moral dilemma but knew deep down that there was only one moral way to act—even though such an action might have been to your personal disadvantage. Describe the situation, the conflict you experienced, and how you resolved the conflict. Before writing, read one or more of the following essays for insight into humans' moral impulse: George Orwell's "Shooting an Elephant" (page 167), Langston Hughes's "Salvation" (page 183), and Lewis Thomas's "The Lie Detector" (page 477).

4. Sykes writes that "we need to look first to . . . parents, communities, the media, and even the churches" to explain the "ethical meltdown" in young people. Focus on *one* of these forces, and write an essay analyzing the positive and negative effects it can have on young people's moral sense. To support your analysis, draw upon your own observations as well as those of friends, classmates, and family members.

Writing Assignments Using a Journal Entry as a Starting Point

5. Reread your pre-reading journal entry, and decide which *one* type of misconduct you think is most prevalent among young people nowadays. Then write an essay in which you illustrate the extent of the impropriety, using several persuasive examples to make your point. One section of the essay should explore causes of the misbehavior; another should discuss consequences. Brainstorming with others will help you identify examples, causes, and effects of the misbehavior. At the end of your essay, you might suggest steps that could be taken to set young people in the right direction. Also, consider supplementing your observations with information about your topic gathered in the library and/or on the Internet.

Alleen Pace Nilsen

A specialist in sexist language and children's literature, Alleen Pace Nilsen (1936–) teaches at Arizona State University. Nilsen's doctoral dissertation concerned linguistic sexism in books written for children. Coauthor of the text *Literature for Today's Young Adults* (1993) and the *Encyclopedia of 20th Century American Humor* (2000), she has written several books on language, including *Language Play: An Introduction to Language* (1983) and *The Language of Humor/The Humor of Language* (1985). In addition, she edited a collection of essays, *Censorship in Children's Literature* (2000). The following selection is from *Sexism and Language* (1977), a collection of essays published by the National Council of Teachers of English.

Pre-Reading Journal Entry

Some people believe that words like *policeman, chairman,* and *freshman* render females invisible. They argue that such gender-biased language, which gives the impression that males are the norm, should be changed to gender-neutral terms like *police officer, chairperson,* and *first-year student.* Do you agree? Why or why not? Use your journal to address this question.

Sexism and Language[1]

Over the last hundred years, American anthropologists have travelled to the corners of the earth to study primitive cultures. They either became linguists themselves or they took linguists with them to help in learning and analyzing languages. Even if the culture was one that no longer existed, they were interested in learning its language because besides being tools of communication, the vocabulary and structure of a language tell much about the values held by its speakers. 1

However, the culture need not be primitive, nor do the people making observations need to be anthropologists and linguists. Anyone living in the United States who listens with a keen ear or 2

[1]If you'd like some advice on ways to avoid sexist language in your writing, turn to the *gender-biased language* entry in the Glossary (editors' note).

reads with a perceptive eye can come up with startling new insights about the way American English reflects our values.

Animal Terms for People—Mirrors of the Double Standard

If we look at just one semantic area of English, that of animal   3
terms in relation to people, we can uncover some interesting insights into how our culture views males and females. References to identical animals can have negative connotations when related to a female, but positive or neutral connotations when related to a male. For example, a *shrew* has come to mean "a scolding, nagging, evil-tempered woman," while *shrewd* means "keen-witted, clever, or sharp in practical affairs; astute . . . businessman, etc." (*Webster's New World Dictionary of the American Language*, 1964).

A *lucky dog* or a *gay dog* may be a very interesting fellow, but   4
when a woman is a *dog*, she is unattractive, and when she's a *bitch* she's the personification of whatever is undesirable in the mind of the speaker. When a man is self-confident, he may be described as *cocksure* or even *cocky*, but in a woman this same self-confidence is likely to result in her being called a *cocky bitch*, which is not only a mixed metaphor, but also probably the most insulting animal metaphor we have. *Bitch* has taken on such negative connotations—children are taught it is a swear word—that in everyday American English, speakers are hesitant to call a female dog a *bitch*. Most of us feel that we would be insulting the dog. When we want to insult a man by comparing him to a dog, we call him a *son of a bitch*, which quite literally is an insult to his mother rather than to him.

If the female is called a *vixen* (a female fox), the dictionary says   5
this means she is "an ill-tempered, shrewish, or malicious woman." The female seems both to attract and to hold on longer to animal metaphors with negative connotations. A *vampire* was originally a corpse that came alive to suck the blood of living persons. The word acquired the general meaning of an unscrupulous person such as a blackmailer and then, the specialized meaning of "a beautiful but unscrupulous woman who seduces men and leads them to their ruin." From this latter meaning we get the word *vamp*. The popularity of this term and of the name *vampire bat* may contribute to the idea that a female being is referred to in a phrase such as *the old bat*.

Other animal metaphors do not have definitely derogatory con- 6
notations for the female, but they do seem to indicate frivolity or
unimportance, as in *social butterfly* and *flapper*. Look at the differences between the connotations of participating in a *hen party* and
in a *bull session*. Male metaphors, even when they are negative in
connotation, still relate to strength and conquest. Metaphors related to aggressive sex roles, for example, *buck, stag, wolf,* and *stud*, will
undoubtedly remain attached to males. Perhaps one of the reasons
that in the late sixties it was so shocking to hear policemen called
pigs was that the connotations of *pig* are very different from the
other animal metaphors we usually apply to males.

When I was living in Afghanistan, I was surprised at the cruelty 7
and unfairness of a proverb that said, "When you see an old man, sit
down and take a lesson; when you see an old woman, throw a
stone." In looking at Afghan folk literature, I found that young girls
were pictured as delightful and enticing, middle-aged women were
sometimes interesting but more often just tolerable, while old
women were always grotesque and villainous. Probably the reason
for the negative connotation of old age in women is that women are
valued for their bodies while men are valued for their accomplishments and their wisdom. Bodies deteriorate with age but wisdom
and accomplishments grow greater.

When we returned home from Afghanistan, I was shocked to 8
discover that we have remnants of this same attitude in America. We
see it in our animal metaphors. If both the animal and the woman
are young, the connotation is positive, but if the animal and the
woman are old, the connotation is negative. Hugh Hefner might
never have made it to the big time if he had called his girls *rabbits*
instead of *bunnies*. He probably chose *bunny* because he wanted
something close to, but not quite so obvious as *kitten* or *cat*—the
all-time winners for connoting female sexuality. Also *bunny*, as in the
skiers' *snow bunny*, already had some of the connotations Hefner
wanted. Compare the connotations of *filly* to *old nag; bird* to *old
crow* or *old bat;* and *lamb* to *crone* (apparently related to the early
modern Dutch *kronje, old ewe* but now *withered old woman*).

Probably the most striking examples of the contrast between 9
young and old women are animal metaphors relating to cats and
chickens. A young girl is encouraged to be *kittenish,* but not *catty*.
And though most of us wouldn't mind living next door to a *sex kitten,* we wouldn't want to live next door to a *cat house*. Parents might

name their daughter *Kitty* but not *Puss* or *Pussy*, which used to be a fairly common nickname for girls. It has now developed such sexual connotations that it is used mostly for humor, as in the James Bond movie featuring Pussy Galore and her flying felines.

In the chicken metaphors, a young girl is a *chick*. When she gets   10
old enough she marries and soon begins feeling *cooped up*. To relieve the boredom she goes to *hen parties* and *cackles* with her friends. Eventually she has her *brood*, begins to *henpeck* her husband, and finally turns into an *old biddy*.

How English Glorifies Maleness

Throughout the ages physical strength has been very important,   11
and because men are physically stronger than women, they have been valued more. Only now in the machine age, when the difference in strength between males and females pales into insignificance in comparison to the strength of earth-moving machinery, airplanes, and guns, males no longer have such an inherent advantage. Today a man of intellect is more valued than a physical laborer, and since women can compete intellectually with men, their value is on the rise. But language lags far behind cultural changes, so the language still reflects this emphasis on the importance of being male. For example, when we want to compliment a male, all we need to do is stress the fact that he is male by saying he is a *he-man*, or he is *manly*, or he is *virile*. Both *virile* and *virtuous* come from the Latin *vir*, meaning *man*.

The command or encouragement that males receive in sen-   12
tences like "Be a man!" implies that *to be a man* is to be honorable, strong, righteous, and whatever else the speaker thinks desirable. But in contrast to this, a girl is never told to be a *woman*. And when she is told to be a *lady*, she is simply being encouraged to "act feminine," which means sitting with her knees together, walking gracefully, and talking softly.

The armed forces, particularly the Marines, use the positive   13
masculine connotation as part of their recruitment psychology. They promote the idea that to join the Marines (or the Army, Navy, or Air Force) guarantees that you will become a man. But this brings up a problem, because much of the work that is necessary to keep a large organization running is what is traditionally thought of as *women's work*. Now, how can the Marines ask someone who has signed up for a *man-sized job* to do *women's work*? Since they can't, they

euphemize and give the jobs titles that either are more prestigious or, at least, don't make people think of females. Waitresses are called *orderlies*, secretaries are called *clerk-typists*, nurses are called *medics*, assistants are called *adjutants*, and cleaning up an area is called *policing* the area. The same kind of word glorification is used in civilian life to bolster a man's ego when he is doing such tasks as cooking and sewing. For example, a *chef* has higher prestige than a cook and a *tailor* has higher prestige than a *seamstress*.

Little girls learn early in life that the boy's role is one to be 14 envied and emulated. Child psychologists have pointed out that experimenting with the role of the opposite sex is much more acceptable for little girls than it is for little boys. For example, girls are free to dress in boys' clothes, but certainly not the other way around. Most parents are amused if they have a daughter who is a *tomboy*, but they are genuinely distressed if they have a son who is a *sissy*. The names we give to young children reflect this same attitude. It is all right for girls to have boys' names, but pity the boy who has a girl's name! Because parents keep giving boys' names to girls, the number of acceptable boys' names keeps shrinking. Currently popular names for girls include *Jo, Kelly, Teri, Chris, Pat, Shawn, Toni*, and *Sam* (short for *Samantha*). *Evelyn, Carroll, Gayle, Hazel, Lynn, Beverley, Marion, Francis*, and *Shirley* once were acceptable names for males. But as they were given to females, they became less and less acceptable. Today, men who are stuck with them self-consciously go by their initials or by abbreviated forms such as *Haze, Shirl, Frank*, or *Ev*. And they seldom pass these names on to their sons.

Many common words have come into the language from people's names. These lexical items again show the importance of maleness compared to the triviality of the feminine activities being described. Words derived from the names of women include *Melba toast*, named for the Australian singer Dame Nellie Melba; *Sally Lunn cakes*, named after an eighteenth-century woman who first made them; *pompadour*, a hair style named after Madame Pompadour; and the word *maudlin*, as in *maudlin sentiment*, from Mary Magdalene, who was often portrayed by artists as displaying exaggerated sorrow.

There are trivial items named after men—*teddy bear* after 16 Theodore Roosevelt and *sideburns* after General Burnside—but most words that come from men's names relate to significant inventions or developments. These include *pasteurization* after Louis

Pasteur, *sousaphone* after John Philip Sousa, *mason jar* after John L. Mason, *boysenberry* after Rudolph Boysen, *pullman car* after George M. Pullman, *braille* after Louis Braille, *franklin stove* after Benjamin Franklin, *diesel engine* after Rudolf Diesel, *ferris wheel* after George W. G. Ferris, and the verb *to lynch* after William Lynch, who was a vigilante captain in Virginia in 1780.

The latter is an example of a whole set of English words dealing   17 with violence. These words have strongly negative connotations. From research using free association and semantic differentials, with university students as subjects, James Ney concluded that English reflects both an anti-male and an anti-female bias because these biases exist in the culture (*Etc.: A Review of General Semantics,* March 1976, pp. 67–76). The students consistently marked as masculine such words as *killer, murderer, robber, attacker, fighter, stabber, rapist, assassin, gang, hood, arsonist, criminal, hijacker, villain,* and *bully,* even though most of these words contain nothing to specify that they are masculine. An example of bias against males, Ney observed, is the absence in English of a pejorative term for women equivalent to *rapist.* Outcomes of his free association test indicated that if "English speakers want to call a man something bad, there seems to be a large vocabulary available to them but if they want to use a term which is good to describe a male, there is a small vocabulary available. The reverse is true for women."

Certainly we do not always think positively about males; witness   18 such words as *jerk, creep, crumb, slob, fink,* and *jackass.* But much of what determines our positive and negative feelings relates to the roles people play. We have very negative feelings toward someone who is hurting us or threatening us or in some way making our lives miserable. To be able to do this, the person has to have power over us and this power usually belongs to males.

On the other hand, when someone helps us or makes our life   19 more pleasant, we have positive feelings toward that person or that role. *Mother* is one of the positive female terms in English, and we see such extensions of it as *Mother Nature, Mother Earth, mother lode, mother superior,* etc. But even though a word like *mother* is positive, it is still not a word of power. In the minds of English speakers being female and being powerless or passive are so closely related that we use the terms *feminine* and *lady* either to mean female or to describe a certain kind of quiet and unobtrusive behavior.

Words Labeling Women as Things

Because of our expectations of passivity, we like to compare 20
females to items that people acquire for their pleasure. For example, in a . . . commercial for the television show *Happy Days,* one of
the characters announced that in the coming season they were
going to have not only "cars, motorcycles, and girls," but also a
band. Another example of this kind of thinking is the comparison
of females to food since food is something we all enjoy, even
though it is extremely passive. We describe females as such delec-
table morsels as a *dish,* a *cookie,* a *tart, cheesecake, sugar and spice,* a
cute tomato, honey, a *sharp cookie,* and *sweetie pie.* We say a particular girl has a *peaches and cream complexion* or "she looks good
enough to eat." And parents give their daughters such names as
Candy and *Cherry.*

Other pleasurable items that we compare females to are toys. 21
Young girls are called *little dolls* or *China dolls,* while older girls—if
they are attractive—are simply called *dolls.* We might say about a
woman, "She's pretty as a picture," or "She's a fashion plate." And
we might compare a girl to a plant by saying she is a *clinging vine,*
a *shrinking violet,* or a *wallflower.* And we might name our daughters after plants such as *Rose, Lily, Ivy, Daisy, Iris,* and *Petunia.*
Compare these names to boys' names such as *Martin* which means
warlike, *Ernest* which means resolute fighter, *Nicholas* which means
victory, *Val* which means strong or valiant, and *Leo* which means
lion. We would be very hesitant to give a boy the name of something
as passive as a flower although we might say about a man that he is
a *late-bloomer.* This is making a comparison between a man and the
most active thing a plant can do, which is to bloom. The only other
familiar plant metaphor used for a man is the insulting *pansy,* implying that he is like a woman.

Questions for Close Reading

1. What is the selection's thesis? Locate the sentence(s) in which Nilsen
   states her main idea. If she doesn't state the thesis explicitly, express it in
   your own words.
2. According to Nilsen, what do animal metaphors usually imply when used
   to describe women? What do male animal metaphors imply?
3. Why, according to Nilsen, do some professions have different names
   depending on whether the job is performed by a male or female? What

is suggested by the existence of two different terms for the same occupation?

4. When positive terms are used for women, what personality characteristics do such terms suggest? Why are words connoting violence most
often applied to men?

5. Refer to your dictionary as needed to define the following words used in
the selection: *unscrupulous* (paragraph 5), *enticing* (7), *connotation* (8),
virile (11), *lexical* (15), *maudlin* (15), and *vigilante* (16).

Questions About the Writer's Craft

1. **The pattern.** Why does Nilsen use so many examples to illustrate each
type of sexism in the English language? What point of view is she trying
to anticipate and counteract?

2. What three main sexist motifs in English does Nilsen examine? How
does she signal her movement from one to the next?

3. Why do you think Nilsen begins by discussing animal terms for humans?
What effect does placing this section first have on the reader?

4. What is Nilsen's tone? What terms and expressions reveal her personal
viewpoint on sexism in our language?

Writing Assignments Using Exemplification as a Pattern of Development

1. Nilsen claims that our language glorifies maleness and denigrates female-
ness. Are there other areas of our lives where typical male behavior and
attitudes are valued more than typical female roles or characteristics?
Consider such areas as dating, marriage, sports, clothing, and occupations. Focusing on a single area, write an essay showing that our culture
glorifies one sex over the other. Try to include in your paper points made
in one of the following essays: Barbara Ehrenreich's "What I've Learned
From Men" (page 249), Deborah Tannen's "But What Do You Mean?"
(page 313), or Virginia Woolf's "Professions for Women" (page 669).

2. The English language embodies many prejudices besides sexism. Many
words and expressions, for example, reflect prejudice against skin color,
old age, youth, left-handedness, shortness, fatness, and so on. Focusing
on one such area, write an essay using specific examples of prejudicial
language to show how the words we use reflect our stereotypes and biases. Gloria Naylor's "Mommy, What Does 'Nigger' Mean?" (page 516)
and William Raspberry's "The Handicap of Definition" (page 529) will
develop further your understanding of the way language influences attitudes.

Writing Assignments Using Other Patterns of Development

∞ **3.** Would your life have been different if you had been born the opposite sex? Would you have been treated differently by your parents, teachers, and friends? Are there any specific experiences or events that would have turned out differently had you been a different sex? Write an essay persuading readers that your life would have been essentially the same *or* very different had you been born exactly as you were except for your sex. Deborah Tannen's "But What Do You Mean?" (page 313) and Virginia Woolf's "Professions for Women" (page 669) should spark some interesting ideas worth exploring in your paper.

∞ **4.** Gender-based stereotyping exists in many areas of our culture besides language. Imagine you're a visitor to the United States and know nothing about the culture—perhaps you're a visitor from Mars. You observe people, watch television for a week, and study several issues of a popular general-interest magazine, such as *People, Time,* or *Newsweek.* Then you send a report to your home about the differences between males and females in the United States. Providing numerous examples to explain the dissimilarities, cover one or two of the following in your analysis: occupations, recreational activities, friendships, and so forth. Barbara Ehrenreich's "What I've Learned From Men" (page 249), Deborah Tannen's "But What Do You Mean?" (page 313), and Dave Barry's "The Ugly Truth About Beauty" (page 422) highlight some issues to consider.

Writing Assignments Using a Journal Entry as a Starting Point

5. Write an essay arguing that English should *or* should not be modified to eliminate gender-biased language. Overall, you need to determine whether sensitivity to gendered language is justified—or unwarranted. To help you formulate your argument, refer to your pre-reading journal entry and, when appropriate, to Nilsen's essay. Also, brainstorming with others will expose you to a variety of viewpoints that will inform your argument.

James Thurber

American humorist James Thurber (1894–1961) is perhaps best known as the author of "The Secret Life of Walter Mitty." Thurber often wrote about people's longings, using his skill as a satirist to portray the humor and poignancy of the human condition. He was able to give his wit—which often bordered on the acerbic—full play during his long career at the *New Yorker*, where he wrote satiric essays and drew cartoons. He also wrote several humorous books, including *Is Sex Necessary?* (1929), which he coauthored with E. B. White; *Fables for Our Time* (1940); *My World and Welcome to It* (1942); and *Thurber Country* (1953). The following selection first appeared in *My Life and Hard Times* (1933).

Pre-Reading Journal Entry

What do you think of college so far? Use your journal to jot down your reactions to your college experience. What has surprised you—pleasantly or unpleasantly—about college life? What had you expected before you enrolled? Consider such aspects of college life as professors and classmates, course requirements and content, and school resources and facilities.

University Days

I passed all the other courses that I took at my university, but I could never pass botany. This was because all botany students had to spend several hours a week in a laboratory looking through a microscope at plant cells, and I could never see through a microscope. I never once saw a cell through a microscope. This used to enrage my instructor. He would wander around the laboratory pleased with the progress all the students were making in drawing the involved and, so I am told, interesting structure of flower cells, until he came to me. I would just be standing there. "I can't see anything," I would say. He would begin patiently enough, explaining how anybody can see through a microscope, but he would always end up in a fury, claiming that I could *too* see through a microscope but just pretended that I couldn't. "It takes away from the beauty of flowers anyway," I used to tell him. "We are not concerned with beauty in

1

this course," he would say. "We are concerned solely with what I may call the *mechanics* of flars." "Well," I'd say, "I can't see anything." "Try it just once again," he'd say, and I would put my eye to the microscope and see nothing at all, except now and again a nebulous milky substance—a phenomenon of maladjustment. You were supposed to see a vivid, restless clockwork of sharply defined plant cells. "I see what looks like a lot of milk," I would tell him. This, he claimed, was the result of my not having adjusted the microscope properly, so he would readjust it for me, or rather, for himself. And I would look again and see milk.

I finally took a deferred pass, as they called it, and waited a year   2
and tried again. (You had to pass one of the biological sciences or you couldn't graduate.) The professor had come back from vacation brown as a berry, bright-eyed, and eager to explain cell-structure again to his classes. "Well," he said to me, cheerily, when we met in the first laboratory hour of the semester, "we're going to see cells this time, aren't we?" "Yes, sir," I said. Students to right of me and to left of me and in front of me were seeing cells; what's more, they were quietly drawing pictures of them in their notebooks. Of course, I didn't see anything.

"We'll try it," the professor said to me, grimly, "with every   3
adjustment of the microscope known to man. As God is my witness, I'll arrange this glass so that you see cells through it or I'll give up teaching. In twenty-two years of botany, I—" He cut off abruptly for he was beginning to quiver all over, like Lionel Barrymore, and he genuinely wished to hold onto his temper; his scenes with me had taken a great deal out of him.

So we tried it with every adjustment of the microscope known   4
to man. With only one of them did I see anything but blackness or the familiar lacteal opacity, and that time I saw, to my pleasure and amazement, a variegated constellation of flecks, specks, and dots. These I hastily drew. The instructor, noting my activity, came back from an adjoining desk, a smile on his lips and his eyebrows high in hope. He looked at my cell drawing. "What's that?" he demanded, with a hint of a squeal in his voice. "That's what I saw," I said. "You didn't, you didn't, you *didn't!*" he screamed, losing control of his temper instantly, and he bent over and squinted into the microscope. His head snapped up. "That's your eye!" he shouted. "You've fixed the lens so that it reflects! You've drawn your eye!"

Another course that I didn't like, but somehow managed to   5
pass, was economics. I went to that class straight from the botany
class, which didn't help me any in understanding either subject. I
used to get them mixed up. But not as mixed up as another student
in my economics class who came there direct from a physics laboratory. He was a tackle on the football team, named Bolenciecwcz. At
that time Ohio State University had one of the best football teams
in the country, and Bolenciecwcz was one of its outstanding stars.
In order to be eligible to play it was necessary for him to keep up in
his studies, a very difficult matter, for while he was not dumber than
an ox he was not any smarter. Most of his professors were lenient
and helped him along. None gave him more hints in answering
questions or asked him simpler ones than the economics professor,
a thin, timid man named Bassum. One day when we were on the
subject of transportation and distribution, it came Bolenciecwcz's
turn to answer a question. "Name one means of transportation," the
professor said to him. No light came into the big tackle's eyes. "Just
any means of transportation," said the professor. Bolenciecwcz sat
staring at him. "That is," pursued the professor, "any medium,
agency, or method of going from one place to another."
Bolenciecwcz had the look of a man who is being led into a trap.
"You may choose among steam, horse-drawn, or electrically propelled vehicles," said the instructor. "I might suggest the one which
we commonly take in making long journeys across land." There was
a profound silence in which everybody stirred uneasily, including
Bolenciecwcz and Mr. Bassum. Mr. Bassum abruptly broke this
silence in an amazing manner. "Choo-choo-choo," he said, in a low
voice, and turned instantly scarlet. He glanced appealingly around
the room. All of us, of course, shared Mr. Bassum's desire that
Bolenciecwcz should stay abreast of the class in economics, for the
Illinois game, one of the hardest and most important of the season,
was only a week off. "Toot, toot, too-toooooot!" some student
with a deep voice moaned, and we all looked encouragingly at
Bolenciecwcz. Somebody else gave a fine imitation of a locomotive
letting off steam. Mr. Bassum himself rounded off the little show.
"Ding, dong, ding, dong," he said, hopefully. Bolenciecwcz was
staring at the floor now, trying to think, his great brow furrowed,
his huge hands rubbing together, his face red.

"How did you come to college this year, Mr. Bolenciecwcz?"   6
asked the professor. "*Chuffa* chuffa, *chuffa* chuffa."

"M'father sent me," said the football player.   7

"What on?" asked Bassum.   8

"I git an 'lowance," said the tackle, in a low, husky voice, obvi-   9
ously embarrassed.

"No, no," said Bassum. "Name a means of transportation.   10
What did you *ride* here on?"

"Train," said Bolenciecwcz.   11

"Quite right," said the professor. "Now, Mr. Nugent, will you   12
tell us—"

If I went through anguish in botany and economics—for differ-   13
ent reasons—gymnasium work was even worse. I don't even like to
think about it. They wouldn't let you play games or join in the exercises with your glasses on and I couldn't see with mine off. I
bumped into professors, horizontal bars, agricultural students, and
swinging iron rings. Not being able to see, I could take it but I
couldn't dish it out. Also, in order to pass gymnasium (and you had
to pass it to graduate) you had to learn to swim if you didn't know
how. I didn't like the swimming pool, I didn't like swimming, and
I didn't like the swimming instructor, and after all these years I still
don't. I never swam but I passed my gym work anyway, by having
another student give my gymnasium number (978) and swim across
the pool in my place. He was a quiet, amiable blond youth, number
473, and he would have seen through a microscope for me if we
could have got away with it, but we couldn't get away with it.
Another thing I didn't like about gymnasium work was that they
made you strip the day you registered. It is impossible for me to be
happy when I am stripped and being asked a lot of questions. Still,
I did better than a lanky agricultural student who was cross-exam-
ined just before I was. They asked each student what college he was
in—that is, whether Arts, Engineering, Commerce, or Agriculture.
"What college are you in?" the instructor snapped at the youth in
front of me. "Ohio State University," he said promptly.

It wasn't that agricultural student but it was another a whole lot   14
like him who decided to take up journalism, possibly on the ground
that when farming went to hell he could fall back on newspaper
work. He didn't realize, of course, that that would be very much like
falling back full-length on a kit of carpenter's tools. Haskins didn't
seem cut out for journalism, being too embarrassed to talk to anybody and unable to use a typewriter, but the editor of the college
paper assigned him to the cow barns, the sheep house, the horse

pavilion, and the animal husbandry department generally. This was a genuinely big "beat," for it took up five times as much ground and got ten times as great a legislative appropriation as the College of Liberal Arts. The agricultural student knew animals, but nevertheless his stories were dull and colorlessly written. He took all afternoon on each of them, on account of having to hunt for each letter on the typewriter. Once in a while he had to ask somebody to help him hunt. "C" and "L," in particular, were hard letters for him to find. His editor finally got pretty much annoyed at the farmer-journalist because his pieces were so uninteresting. "See here, Haskins," he snapped at him one day, "why is it we never have anything hot from you on the horse pavilion? Here we have two hundred head of horses on this campus—more than any other university in the Western Conference except Purdue—and yet you never get any real lowdown on them. Now shoot over to the horse barns and dig up something lively." Haskins shambled out and came back in about an hour; he said he had something. "Well, start it off snappily," said the editor. "Something people will read." Haskins set to work and in a couple of hours brought a sheet of typewritten paper to the desk; it was a two-hundred-word story about some disease that had broken out among the horses. Its opening sentence was simple but arresting. It read: "Who has noticed the sores on the tops of the horses in the animal husbandry building?"

Ohio State was a land grant university and therefore two years   15
of military drill was compulsory. We drilled with old Springfield rifles and studied the tactics of the Civil War even though the World War was going on at the time. At 11 o'clock each morning thousands of freshmen and sophomores used to deploy over the campus, moodily creeping up on the old chemistry building. It was good training for the kind of warfare that was waged at Shiloh but it had no connection with what was going on in Europe. Some people used to think there was German money behind it, but they didn't dare say so or they would have been thrown in jail as German spies. It was a period of muddy thought and marked, I believe, the decline of higher education in the Middle West.

As a soldier I was never any good at all. Most of the cadets were   16
glumly indifferent soldiers, but I was no good at all. Once General Littlefield, who was commandant of the cadet corps, popped up in front of me during regimental drill and snapped, "You are the main trouble with this university!" I think he meant that my type was the

main trouble with the university but he may have meant me individually. I was mediocre at drill, certainly—that is, until my senior year. By that time I had drilled longer than anybody else in the Western Conference, having failed at military at the end of each preceding year so that I had to do it all over again. I was the only senior still in uniform. The uniform which, when new, had made me look like an interurban railway conductor, now that it had become faded and too tight made me look like Bert Williams in his bellboy act. This had a definitely bad effect on my morale. Even so, I had become by sheer practice little short of wonderful at squad maneuvers.

One day General Littlefield picked our company out of the 17 whole regiment and tried to get it mixed up by putting it through one movement after another as fast as we could execute them: squads right, squads left, squads on right into line, squads right about, squads left front into line, etc. In about three minutes one hundred and nine men were marching in one direction and I was marching away from them at an angle of forty degrees, all alone. "Company, halt!" shouted General Littlefield. "That man is the only man who has it right!" I was made a corporal for my achievement.

The next day General Littlefield summoned me to his office. He 18 was swatting flies when I went in. I was silent and he was silent too, for a long time. I don't think he remembered me or why he had sent for me, but he didn't want to admit it. He swatted some more flies, keeping his eyes on them narrowly before he let go with the swatter. "Button up your coat!" he snapped. Looking back on it now I can see that he meant me although he was looking at a fly, but I just stood there. Another fly came to rest on a paper in front of the general and began rubbing its hind legs together. The general lifted the swatter cautiously. I moved restlessly and the fly flew away. "You startled him!" barked General Littlefield, looking at me severely. I said I was sorry. "That won't help the situation!" snapped the General, with cold military logic. I didn't see what I could do except offer to chase some more flies toward his desk, but I didn't say anything. He stared out the window at the faraway figures of co-eds crossing the campus toward the library. Finally, he told me I could go. So I went. He either didn't know which cadet I was or else he forgot what he wanted to see me about. It may have been that he wished to apologize for having called me the main trouble with the university; or maybe he had decided to compliment me on my brilliant drilling of the day before and then at the last minute decided not to. I don't know. I don't think about it much any more.

Questions for Close Reading

1. What is the selection's thesis? Locate the sentence(s) in which Thurber states his main idea. If he doesn't state the thesis explicitly, express it in your own words.
2. In his writings and cartoons, Thurber reveals a distaste for authority. Find evidence of such an attitude in this selection.
3. Thurber passes gym class by having another student assume his identification number. What does this fact indicate about his gym class in particular and about his university in general?
4. Thurber sets up a comparison between himself and the fly in General Littlefield's office. How is this comparison related to Thurber's thesis?
5. Refer to your dictionary as needed to define the following words used in the selection: *nebulous* (paragraph 1), *lacteal* (4), *opacity* (4), *variegated* (4), *husbandry* (14), and *appropriation* (14).

Questions About the Writer's Craft

1. **The pattern.** Thurber develops his piece through a series of examples, each in the form of a brief anecdote. Which two anecdotes does Thurber develop in most detail? What might have been his reason for proceeding in this way?
2. *Satire* uses humor to criticize a situation and create awareness of the need for change. One satiric technique is *caricature:* an oversimplified description in which one quality of an individual is exaggerated, resulting in a distorted stereotype. Where in "University Days" does Thurber employ caricature? What is he satirizing?
3. Thurber often uses dialogue rather than commentary to convey humor. Find several places in the essay where dialogue is especially effective in enhancing the essay's humor.
4. The inability to see is a recurrent theme in Thurber's essay. Locate instances of such difficulty. What might this inability symbolize?

Writing Assignments Using Exemplification as a Pattern of Development

∞ 1. Read William Zinsser's "College Pressures" (page 285). Zinsser sees college students as overly ambitious, driven to achieve credentials that will lead to financial success. But Thurber shows students too dull or apathetic to make much effort to move in any direction. Which view of students is more accurate? Using concrete examples of students you know or have observed, write an essay developing the point that college students are either too competitive or too lackadaisical. Save for last your most convincing example.

2. With great relish, Thurber illustrates ineptitude, showing people unable to master even the simplest of tasks. Write an essay illustrating excellence. Give several vivid examples of skill, even virtuosity, by depicting individuals engaged in tasks they have fully mastered. You might recall a rock musician you heard in concert, an Olympic gymnast you saw on television, a mechanic you watched repair a car. The people cited, though at first glance possibly quite dissimilar, should share one common trait: their basic excellence. Jacques D'Amboise's "Showing What Is Possible" (page 460) provides insights into the concept of excellence.

Writing Assignments Using Other Patterns of Development

3. Thurber and his instructors have different views about what's important. Write an essay recounting one or more occasions when your sense of what was important clashed with someone else's. How was the disagreement resolved? You might want to conclude with some generalization about the type of individual with whom you tend to come into conflict.

4. Thurber's instructors show varying degrees of patience, empathy, and success in dealing with their recalcitrant students. In a serious or playful essay, contrast a teacher you consider excellent with one you consider inferior. Address the same aspects of each teacher's style—for example, patience, command of subject matter, ability to create and maintain interest. No matter which tone you select, the essay should make clear those traits you consider most essential to excellent teaching.

Writing Assignments Using a Journal Entry as a Starting Point

5. Write an essay comparing and/or contrasting your expectations of college with the reality you've experienced. From your pre-reading journal entry, select *one* or *two* aspects of college life to focus on. To illustrate your pre-college expectations, you might describe brochure, website, or catalog information you received before attending. Be sure to make clear whether, in general, you are pleased or displeased with college life.

Beth Johnson

Beth Johnson (1956–) is a writer, occasional college teacher, and freelance editor. A graduate of Goshen College and Syracuse University, Johnson is the author of several college texts, including *Everyday Heroes* (1996). Containing profiles of men and women who have triumphed over obstacles to achieve personal and academic success, the book has provided a motivational boost to college students nationwide. She lives with her husband and three children in Lederach, Pennsylvania. The following piece is one of several that Johnson has written about the complexities and wonders of life.

Pre-Reading Journal Entry

When you were young, did adults acknowledge the existence of life's tragedies, or did they deny such harsh truths? In your journal, list several difficult events that you observed or experienced firsthand as a child. How did the adults in your life explain these hardships? In each case, do you think the adults acted appropriately? If not, how should they have responded?

Bombs Bursting in Air

It's Friday night and we're at the Olympics, the Junior Olympics, that is. My son is on a relay-race team competing against fourth-graders from all over the school district. His little sister and I sit high in the stands, trying to pick Isaac out from the crowd of figures milling around on the field during these moments of pre-game confusion. The public address system sputters to life and summons our attention. "And now," the tinny voice rings out, "please join together in the singing of our national anthem." 1

"Oh saaay can you seeeeee," we begin. My arm rests around Maddie's shoulders. I am touching her a lot today, and she notices. "Mom, you're *squishing* me," she chides, wriggling from my grip. I content myself with stroking her hair. News that reached me today makes me need to feel her near. We pipe along, squeaking out the impossibly high note of "land of the freeeeeeeee." Maddie clowns, half-singing, half-shouting the lyrics, hitting the "b's" explosively on "bombs bursting in air." 2

Bombs indeed, I think, replaying the sound of my friend's voice   3
over the phone that afternoon: "Bumped her head sledding. Took
her in for an x-ray, just to make sure. There was something strange,
so they did more tests . . . a brain tumor . . . Children's Hospital in
Boston Tuesday . . . surgery, yes, right away. . . ." Maddie's playmate
Shannon, only five years old. We'd last seen her at Halloween,
dressed in her blue princess costume, and we'd talked of Furby and
Scooby-Doo and Tootsie Rolls. Now her parents were hurriedly
learning a new vocabulary—CAT scans, glioma, pediatric neuro-
surgery, and frontal lobe.[1] A bomb had exploded in their midst, and,
like troops under attack, they were rallying in response.

The games over, the children and I edge our way out of the   4
school parking lot, bumper to bumper with other parents ferrying
their families home. I tell the kids as casually as I can about
Shannon. "She'll have to have an operation. It's lucky, really, that
they found it by accident this way while it's small."

"I want to send her a present," Maddie announces. "That'd be   5
nice," I say, glad to keep the conversation on a positive note.

But my older son is with us now. Sam, who is thirteen, says,   6
"She'll be OK, though, right?" It's not a question, really; it's a statement that I must either agree with or contradict. I want to say yes.
I want to say of course she'll be all right. I want them to inhabit a
world where five-year-olds do not develop silent, mysterious
growths in their brains, where "malignancy" and "seizure" are
words for *New York Times* crossword puzzles, not for little girls.
They would accept my assurance; they would believe me and sleep
well tonight. But I can't; the bomb that exploded in Shannon's
home has sent splinters of shrapnel into ours as well, and they cannot be ignored or lied away. "We hope she'll be just fine," I finally
say. "She has very good doctors. She has wonderful parents who are
doing everything they can. The tumor is small. Shannon's strong
and healthy."

"*She'll* be OK," says Maddie matter-of-factly. "In school we   7
read about a little boy who had something wrong with his leg and
he had an operation and got better. Can we go to Dairy Queen?"

---

[1]A CAT scan is a computerized cross-sectional image of an internal body structure;
a glioma is a tumor in the brain or spinal cord; pediatric neurosurgry is surgery performed on the nerves, brain, or spinal cord of a child; the frontal lobe is the largest
section of the brain (editors' note).

Bombs on the horizon don't faze Maddie. Not yet. I can just   8
barely remember from my own childhood the sense that still surrounds her, that feeling of being cocooned within reassuring walls
of security and order. Back then, Monday meant gym, Tuesday was
pizza in the cafeteria, Wednesday brought clarinet lessons. Teachers
stood in their familiar spots in the classrooms, telling us with reassuring simplicity that World War II happened because Hitler, a very
bad man, invaded Poland. Midterms and report cards, summer vacations and new notebooks in September gave a steady rhythm to the
world. It wasn't all necessarily happy—through the years there were
poor grades, grouchy teachers, exclusion from the desired social
group, dateless weekends when it seemed the rest of the world was
paired off—but it was familiar territory where we felt walled off
from the really bad things that happened to other people.

There were hints of them, though, even then. Looking back, I   9
recall the tiny shock waves, the tremors from far-off explosions that
occasionally rattled our shelter. There was the little girl who was
absent for a week and when she returned wasn't living with her
mother and stepfather anymore. There was a big girl who threw up
in the bathroom every morning and then disappeared from school.
A playful, friendly custodian was suddenly fired, and it had something to do with an angry parent. A teacher's husband had a heart
attack and died. These were interesting tidbits to report to our families over dinner, mostly out of morbid interest in seeing our parents
bite their lips and exchange glances.

As we got older, the bombs dropped closer. A friend's sister was   10
arrested for selling drugs; we saw her mother in tears at church that
Sunday. A boy I thought I knew, a school clown with a sweet
crooked grin, shot himself in the woods behind his house. A car full
of senior boys, going home from a dance where I'd been sent into
ecstasy when the cutest of them all greeted me by name, rounded a
curve too fast and crashed, killing them. We wept and hugged each
other in the halls. Our teachers listened to us grieve and tried to
comfort us, but their words came out impatient and almost angry. I
realize now that what sounded like anger was a helplessness to teach
us lessons we were still too young or too ignorant to learn. For
although our sorrow was real, we still had some sense of a protective curtain between us and the bombs. If only, we said. If only she
hadn't used drugs. If only he'd told someone how depressed he was.
If only they'd been more careful. *We* weren't like them; we were

careful. Like magical incantations, we recited the things that we would or wouldn't do in order to protect ourselves from such sad, unnecessary fates.

And then my best friend, a beautiful girl of sixteen, went to   11
sleep one January night and never woke up. I found myself shaken to the core of my being. My grief at the loss of my vibrant, laughing friend was great. But what really tilted my universe was the nakedness of my realization that there was no "if only." There were no drugs, no careless action, no crime, no accident, nothing I could focus on to explain away what had happened. She had simply died. Which could only mean that there was no magic barrier separating me and my loved ones from the bombs. We were as vulnerable as everyone else. For months the shock stayed with me. I sat in class watching my teachers draw diagrams of Saturn, talk about Watergate,[2] multiply fractions, and wondered at their apparent cheer and normalcy. Didn't they *know* we were all doomed? Didn't they know it was only a matter of time until one of us took a direct hit? What was the point of anything?

But time moved on, and I moved with it. College came and   12
went, graduate school, adulthood, middle age. My heightened sense of vulnerability began to subside, though I could never again slip fully into the soothing security of my younger days. I became more aware of the intertwining threads of joy, pain, and occasional tragedy that weave through all our lives. College was stimulating, exciting, full of friendship and challenge. I fell in love for the first time, reveled in its sweetness, then learned the painful lesson that love comes with no guarantee. A beloved professor lost two children to leukemia, but continued with skill and passion to introduce students to the riches of literature. My father grew ill, but the last day of his life, when I sat by his bed holding his hand, remains one of my sweetest memories. The marriage I'd entered into with optimism ended in bitter divorce, but produced three children whose existence is my daily delight. At every step along the way, I've seen that the most rewarding chapters of my life have contained parts that I not only would not have chosen, but would

[2]In June, 1972, supporters of Republican President Richard Nixon were caught breaking into the Democratic campaign headquarters in the Watergate office complex in Washington, D.C. The resulting investigation of the White House connection to the break-in led to President Nixon's eventual resignation in August, 1974 (editors' note).

have given much to avoid. But selecting just the good parts is not an option we are given.

The price of allowing ourselves to truly live, to love and be loved, is (and it's the ultimate irony) the knowledge that the greater our investment in life, the larger the target we create. Of course, it is within our power to refuse friendship, shrink from love, live in isolation, and thus create for ourselves a nearly impenetrable bomb shelter. There are those among us who choose such an existence, the price of intimacy being too high. Looking about me, however, I see few such examples. Instead, I am moved by the courage with which most of us, ordinary folks, continue soldiering on. We fall in love, we bring our children into the world, we forge our friendships, we give our hearts, knowing with increasing certainty that we do so at our own risk. Still we move ahead with open arms, saying yes, yes to life.   13

Shannon's surgery is behind her; the prognosis is good. Her mother reports that the family is returning to its normal routines, laughing again and talking of ordinary things, even while they step more gently, speak more quietly, are more aware of the precious fragility of life and of the blessing of every day that passes without explosion.   14

Bombs bursting in air. They can blind us, like fireworks at the moment of explosion. If we close our eyes and turn away, all we see is their fiery image. But if we have the courage to keep our eyes open and welcoming, even bombs finally fade against the vastness of the starry sky.   15

Questions for Close Reading

1. What is the selection's thesis? Locate the sentence(s) in which Johnson states her main idea. If she doesn't state the thesis explicitly, express it in your own words.
2. In paragraph 2, Johnson describes her "need to feel her [daughter] near." What compels her to want to be physically close to her daughter? Why do you think Johnson responds this way?
3. In describing her family's responses to Shannon's illness, Johnson presents three reactions: Maddie's, Sam's, and her own. How do these responses differ? In what ways do Maddie's, Sam's, and Johnson's reactions typify the age groups to which they belong?
4. In paragraph 13, Johnson describes two basic ways people respond to life's inevitable "bombs." What are these ways? Which response does Johnson endorse?

5. Refer to your dictionary as needed to define the following words used in the selection: *ferrying* (paragraph 4), *shrapnel* (6), *faze* (8), *cocooned* (8), *tremors* (9), *incantations* (10), *vulnerable* (11), *intertwining* (12), *impenetrable* (13), *soldiering on* (13), *prognosis* (14), and *fragility* (14).

Questions About the Writer's Craft

1. The pattern. Although Johnson provides many examples of life's "bombs," she gives more weight to some examples than to others. Which examples does she emphasize? Which ones receive less attention? Why?

2. Other patterns. What important contrast does Johnson develop in paragraph 6? How does this contrast reinforce the essay's main idea?

3. Writers generally vary sentence structure in an effort to add interest to their work. But in paragraphs 9 and 10, Johnson employs a repetitive sentence structure. Where is the repetition in these two paragraphs? Why do you think she uses this technique?

4. Johnson develops her essay by means of an extended metaphor (see pages 89–90), using bombs as her central image. Identify all the places where Johnson draws upon language and imagery related to bombs and battles. What do you think Johnson hopes to achieve with this sustained metaphor?

Writing Assignments Using Exemplification as a Pattern of Development

1. In paragraphs 9 and 10, Johnson catalogues a number of events that made her increasingly aware of life's bombs. Write an essay of your own, illustrating how you came to recognize the inevitability of painful life events. Start by listing the difficult events you've encountered. Select the three most compelling occurrences, and do some freewriting to generate details about each. Before writing, decide whether you will order your examples chronologically or emphatically; use whichever illustrates more effectively your dawning realization of life's complexity. End with some conclusions about your ability to cope with difficult times.

2. Johnson describes her evolving understanding of life. In an essay of your own, show the way several events combined to change your understanding of a specific aspect of your life. Perhaps a number of incidents prompted you to reconsider career choices, end a relationship, or appreciate the importance of family. Cite only those events that illustrate your emerging understanding. Your decision to use either chronological or emphatic sequence depends on which illustrates more dramatically the change in your perception. To see how other writers describe their journeys of self-discovery, read Maya Angelou's "Sister Flowers" (page 116), Richard Rodriguez's "Workers" (page 414), Jacques D'Amboise's

"Showing What Is Possible" (page 460), and Alice Walker's "Beauty: When the Other Dancer Is the Self" (page 467).

Writing Assignments Using Other Patterns of Development

∞ 3. Johnson explores the lasting impact the death of her friend had on her life. Write an essay about the effect of a *single* bomb on your life. You might discuss getting left back in school, losing a loved one, seeing the dark side of someone you admired, and so on. Your causal analysis should make clear how the event affected your life. Perhaps the event had painful short-term consequences but positive long-term repercussions. Langston Hughes's "Salvation" (page 183), Sophronia Liu's "So Tsi-Fai" (page 188), and Jacques D'Amboise's "Showing What Is Possible" (page 460) provide helpful models for examining the effects of a life-changing event.

🖳 4. In an essay, offer readers a guide to surviving a specific life calamity. You might, for instance, explain how to survive a pet's death, a painful breakup, a financial hardship. Consider doing some library and/or Internet research on your subject. Combining your own insights with any material gathered through research, describe fully the steps readers should take to recover from the devastating events.

Writing Assignments Using a Journal Entry as a Starting Point

∞ 5. Johnson asserts that painful truths shouldn't "be ignored or lied away" by adults. Do you agree? Write an essay explaining why you think adults should protect children from harsh realities—or why they should present the whole truth, even when it's painful. Review your pre-reading journal entry, searching for strong examples to support your position. Discussing this topic with others will also help you shape your point of view, as will reading Audre Lorde's "The Fourth of July" (page 160), Gloria Naylor's "Mommy, What Does 'Nigger' Mean?" (page 516), and Yuh Ji-Yeon's "Let's Tell the Story of All America's Cultures" (page 581).

Barbara Ehrenreich

Barbara Ehrenreich (1941–) has been a college professor, investigative reporter, magazine editor, and social activist. A graduate of Reed College, Ehrenreich received her Ph.D. in biology from Rockefeller University. She has cowritten several books, including *For Her Own Good: 150 Years of the Experts' Advice to Women* (1978) and *Remaking Love: The Feminization of Sex* (1986). Her more recent books include *Fear of Falling: The Inner Life of the Middle Class* (1989), *The Worst Years of Our Lives* (1990), *Snarling Citizen: Essays* (1995), and the novel *Kipper's Game* (1993). A regular columnist for *Time, The Guardian,* and *The Nation,* Ehrenreich has published articles in many other magazines, such as *Esquire, Vogue,* and the *New Republic.* "What I've Learned From Men" first appeared in *Ms.* in 1985.

Pre-Reading Journal Entry

Drawing upon childhood experiences and recent observations, reflect in your journal about the way children's gender identity is formed. What traits do parents and society tend to encourage in boys? In girls? How do these gendered characteristics benefit and/or hinder boys and girls later in life?

What I've Learned From Men

For many years I believed that women had only one thing to learn from men: how to get the attention of a waiter by some means short of kicking over the table and shrieking. Never in my life have I gotten the attention of a waiter, unless it was an off-duty waiter whose car I'd accidentally scraped in a parking lot somewhere. Men, however, can summon a maître d' just by thinking the word "coffee," and this is a power women would be well-advised to study. What else would we possibly want to learn from them? How to interrupt someone in mid-sentence as if you were performing an act of conversational euthanasia? How to drop a pair of socks three feet from an open hamper and keep right on walking? How to make those weird guttural gargling sounds in the bathroom? 1

But now, at mid-life, I am willing to admit that there are some real and useful things to learn from men. Not from all men—in fact, we may have the most to learn from some of the men we like the 2 least. This realization does not mean that my feminist principles have gone soft with age: what I think women could learn from men is how to get *tough*. After more than a decade of consciousness-raising, assertiveness training, and hand-to-hand combat in the battle of the sexes, we're still too ladylike. Let me try that again—we're just too *damn* ladylike.

Here is an example from my own experience, a story that I 3 blush to recount. A few years ago, at an international conference held in an exotic and luxurious setting, a prestigious professor invited me to his room for what he said would be an intellectual discussion on matters of theoretical importance. So far, so good. I showed up promptly. But only minutes into the conversation—held in all-too-adjacent chairs—it emerged that he was interested in something more substantial than a meeting of minds. I was disgusted, but not enough to overcome 30-odd years of programming in ladylikeness. Every time his comments took a lecherous turn, I chattered distractingly; every time his hand found its way to my knee, I returned it as if it were something he had misplaced. This went on for an unconscionable period (as much as 20 minutes); then there was a minor scuffle, a dash for the door, and I was out—with nothing violated but my self-esteem. I, a full-grown feminist, conversant with such matters as rape crisis counseling and sexual harassment at the workplace, had behaved like a ninny—or, as I now understand it, like a lady.

The essence of ladylikeness is a persistent servility masked as 4 "niceness." For example, we (women) tend to assume that it is our responsibility to keep everything "nice" even when the person we are with is rude, aggressive, or emotionally AWOL. (In the above example, I was so busy taking responsibility for preserving the veneer of "niceness" that I almost forgot to take responsibility for myself.) In conversations with men, we do almost all the work: sociologists have observed that in male-female social interactions it's the woman who throws out leading questions and verbal encouragements ("So how did you *feel* about that?" and so on) while the man, typically, says "Hmmmm." Wherever we go, we're perpetually smiling—the on-cue smile, like the now-outmoded curtsy, being one of our culture's little rituals of submission. We're trained to feel embarrassed if we're praised, but if we see a criticism coming at us from miles down the road, we rush to acknowledge it. And when we're feeling aggressive or angry or resentful, we just tighten up our smiles

or turn them into rueful little moues. In short, we spend a great deal
of time acting like wimps.

For contrast, think of the macho stars we love to watch. Think, 5
for example, of Mel Gibson facing down punk marauders in "The
Road Warrior". . . John Travolta swaggering his way through the
early scenes of "Saturday Night Fever". . . or Marlon Brando shrug-
ging off the local law in "The Wild One." Would they simper their
way through tight spots? Chatter aimlessly to keep the conversation
going? Get all clutched up whenever they think they might—just
might—have hurt someone's feelings? No, of course not, and there-
in, I think, lies their fascination for us.

The attraction of the "tough guy" is that he has—or at least 6
seems to have—what most of us lack, and that is an aura of power
and control. In an article, feminist psychiatrist Jean Baker Miller
writes that "a woman's using self-determined power for herself is
equivalent to selfishness [and] destructiveness"—an equation that
makes us want to avoid even the appearance of power. Miller cites
cases of women who get depressed just when they're on the verge
of success—and of women who do succeed and then bury their
achievement in self-deprecation. As an example, she describes one
company's periodic meetings to recognize outstanding salespeople:
when a woman is asked to say a few words about her achievement,
she tends to say something like, "Well, I really don't know how it
happened. I guess I was just lucky this time." In contrast, the men
will cheerfully own up to the hard work, intelligence, and so on, to
which they owe their success. By putting herself down, a woman
avoids feeling brazenly powerful and potentially "selfish"; she also
does the traditional lady's work of trying to make everyone else feel
better ("She's not really so smart, after all, just lucky").

So we might as well get a little tougher. And a good place to 7
start is by cutting back on the small acts of deference that we've been
programmed to perform since girlhood. Like unnecessary smiling.
For many women—waitresses, flight attendants, receptionists—smiling is an occupational requirement, but there's no reason for anyone
to go around grinning when she's not being paid for it. I'd suggest
that we save our off-duty smiles for when we truly feel like sharing
them, and if you're not sure what to do with your face in the meantime, study Clint Eastwood's expressions—both of them.

Along the same lines, I think women should stop taking respon- 8
sibility for every human interaction we engage in. In a social

encounter with a woman, the average man can go 25 minutes saying nothing more than "You don't say?" "Izzat so?" and, of course,
"Hmmmm." Why should we do all the work? By taking so much
responsibility for making conversations go well, we act as if we had
much more at stake in the encounter than the other party—and that
gives him (or her) the power advantage. Every now and then, we
deserve to get more out of a conversation than we put into it: I'd
suggest not offering information you'd rather not share ("I'm really terrified that my sales plan won't work") and not, out of sheer
politeness, soliciting information you don't really want ("Wherever
did you get that lovely tie?"). There will be pauses, but they don't
have to be awkward for *you*.

It is true that some, perhaps most, men will interpret any   9
decrease in female deference as a deliberate act of hostility. Omit the
free smiles and perky conversation-boosters and someone is bound
to ask, "Well, what's come over *you* today?" For most of us, the first
impulse is to stare at our feet and make vague references to a termi-
nally ill aunt in Atlanta, but we should have as much right to be taciturn as the average (male) taxi driver. If you're taking a vacation
from smiles and small talk and some fellow is moved to inquire
about what's "bothering" you, just stare back levelly and say, the
international debt crisis, the arms race, or the death of God.

There are all kinds of ways to toughen up—and potentially   10
move up—at work, and I leave the details to the purveyors of
assertiveness training. But Jean Baker Miller's study underscores a
fundamental principle that anyone can master on her own. We can
stop acting less capable than we actually are. For example, in the
matter of taking credit when credit is due, there's a key difference
between saying "I was just lucky" and saying "I had a plan and it
worked." If you take the credit you deserve, you're letting people
know that you were confident you'd succeed all along, and that you
fully intend to do so again.

Finally, we may be able to learn something from men about   11
what to do with anger. As a general rule, women get irritated: men
get *mad*. We make tight little smiles of ladylike exasperation; they
pound on desks and roar. I wouldn't recommend emulating the full
basso profundo male tantrum, but women do need ways of expressing justified anger clearly, colorfully, and, when necessary, crudely. If
you're not just irritated, but *pissed off*, it might help to say so.

I, for example, have rerun the scene with the prestigious pro- 12
fessor many times in my mind. And in my mind, I play it like Bogart.
I start by moving my chair over to where I can look the professor
full in the face. I let him do the chattering, and when it becomes
evident that he has nothing serious to say, I lean back and cross my
arms, just to let him know that he's wasting my time. I do not smile,
neither do I nod encouragement. Nor, of course, do I respond to
his blandishments with apologetic shrugs and blushes. Then, at the
first flicker of lechery, I stand up and announce coolly, "All right,
I've had enough of this crap." Then I walk out—slowly, deliberately, confidently. Just like a man.

Or—now that I think of it—just like a woman.   13

Questions for Close Reading

1. What is the selection's thesis? Locate the sentence(s) in which
   Ehrenreich states her main idea. If she doesn't state the thesis explicitly,
   express it in your own words.
2. Why did Ehrenreich handle the lecherous professor as she did? In retrospect, how does she wish she had dealt with the situation? How does her
   current perspective of the way she should have behaved reinforce her
   thesis in the essay?
3. What does "behaving like a lady" mean, according to Ehrenreich? What
   is her opinion of "ladylike" behavior?
4. Why, in Ehrenreich's view, do we like "macho stars" (paragraph 5)?
   What can we learn from them?
5. Refer to your dictionary as needed to define the following words used in
   the selection: *euthanasia* (paragraph 1), *guttural* (1), *lecherous* (3), *distractingly* (3), *unconscionable* (3), *ninny* (3), *servility* (4), *veneer* (4), *moues*
   (4), *marauders* (5), *aura* (6), *brazenly* (6), *deference* (9), *taciturn* (9), *purveyors* (10), *emulating* (11), *basso profundo* (11), and *blandishments* (12).

Questions About the Writer's Craft

1. **The pattern.** In paragraphs 3 and 12, Ehrenreich uses her own personal experience as a key example. Why do you think she chooses to include
   this example? Why do you suppose she presents it so early in the essay
   and then returns to it at the end?
2. **Other patterns.** Locate places in the essay where Ehrenreich uses examples to contrast the different responses and behaviors of males and
   females. How do these contrasts help the writer develop her main idea?

3. Do you think that Ehrenreich is speaking primarily to a male or to a female audience? What in the essay makes you feel this way? Do you think that the author expects her audience to be positive, hostile, or neutral toward her ideas? What in the essay leads you to this conclusion?

4. In her attack on "ladylikeness," Ehrenreich deliberately avoids using a "ladylike" or "nice" tone. Which of her phrases or expressions seem to defy stereotypes about the way "ladies" should express themselves?

Writing Assignments Using Exemplification as a Pattern of Development

∞ 1. If, as Ehrenreich suggests, women have much to learn from men, is it also true that men could learn from women? Write an essay illustrating your belief that men would indeed be better off if they acquired some attitudes and behaviors traditionally associated with women. Be sure to provide numerous examples from your own experience and observations. You may take a humorous or serious approach when showing that men should—in some respects—become more like women. Deborah Tannen's "But What Do You Mean?" (page 313) and Dave Barry's "The Ugly Truth About Beauty" (page 422) may spark some insight into characteristically male and female behavioral patterns.

∞ 2. Ehrenreich points to the popularity of several "macho stars": Mel Gibson in *The Road Warrior,* John Travolta in *Saturday Night Fever,* Marlon Brando in *The Wild One,* and Clint Eastwood in anything. Choose several female characters from film or television who you feel provide positive role models for both males and females. Write an essay in which you use these characters as examples of the way that men and women should conduct their lives. Before writing, consider reading Maya Angelou's "Sister Flowers" (page 116), a loving portrait of a memorable female role-model.

Writing Assignments Using Other Patterns of Development

∞ 3. Ehrenreich suggests that some of the problems women experience in relationships and careers are of their own making—they smile too much, are too deferential, and fail to claim their own achievements. Pick one or two areas in which women tend to experience difficulty and write an essay arguing either that women sabotage themselves or that they are sabotaged by society's attitudes and expectations. Brainstorm with others to gather ideas for your paper. For other perspectives, you may want to read one or more of the following essays: Alleen Pace Nilsen's "Sexism and Language" (page 225), Deborah Tannen's "But What Do You Mean?" (page 313), Dave Barry's "The Ugly Truth About Beauty" (page 422), Camille Paglia's "Rape: A Bigger Danger Than Feminists Know" (page 615), Susan Jacoby's "Common Decency" (page 622), and Virginia Woolf's "Professions for Women" (page 669).

∞ 4. Like Ehrenreich, most of us have been subjected at one time or another to the inappropriate or unpleasant behavior of others: slurs on our abilities, interests, or appearance; derision about our sex or sexual preference; taunts about our race, religion, or ethnic background. Focus on *one* kind of insult, and brainstorm with others to identify ways for dealing with such an affront. Then write an essay describing different strategies for coping with the offensive behavior. Reach some conclusions about which approach is most effective. Deborah Tannen's "But What Do You Mean?" (page 313) and Caroline Rego's "The Fine Art of Complaining" (page 380) may spark some ideas worth exploring.

Writing Assignments Using a Journal Entry as a Starting Point

▢ 5. Drawing upon your pre-reading journal entry, write an essay in which you compare and/or contrast the qualities that parents and the culture at large nurture in boys with those they nurture in girls. Brainstorming with others will help you identify telling examples. Reach some conclusions about the long-term effects on children of these parental and societal influences. Consider supplementing your informal research with library and/or Internet information about the formation of children's gender identity.

Additional Writing Topics

EXEMPLIFICATION

General Assignments

Use examples to develop any one of the following topics into a well-organized essay. When writing the paper, choose enough relevant examples to support your thesis. Organize the material into a sequence that most effectively illustrates the thesis, keeping in mind that emphatic order is often the most compelling way to present specifics.

1. Many of today's drivers have dangerous habits.
2. Drug and alcohol abuse is (or is not) a serious problem among many young people.
3. One rule of restaurant dining is "Management often seems oblivious to problems that are perfectly obvious to customers."
4. Children today are not encouraged to use their imaginations.
5. The worst kind of hypocrite is a religious hypocrite.
6. The best things in life are definitely not free.
7. A part-time job is an important experience that every college student should have.
8. Many TV and magazine ads use sexual allusions to sell their products.
9. _____ (name someone you know well) is a _____ (use a quality: open-minded, dishonest, compulsive, reliable, gentle, and so on) person.
10. Television commercials stereotype the elderly (or another minority group).
11. Today, salespeople act as if they're doing you a favor by taking your money.
12. Most people behave decently in their daily interactions with each other.
13. Pettiness, jealousy, and selfishness abound in our daily interactions with each other.
14. You can tell a lot about people by observing what they wear and eat.
15. Too many Americans are overly concerned with being physically fit.
16. There are several study techniques that will help a student learn more efficiently.
17. Some teachers seem to enjoy turning tests into ordeals.
18. "How to avoid bad eating habits" is one course all college students should take.
19. More needs to be done to eliminate obstacles faced by the physically handicapped.
20. Some of the best presents are those that cost the least.

Assignments With a Specific Purpose and Audience

1. A friend of yours has taken a job in a big city or moved to a small town. To prepare your friend for this new environment, write a letter giving examples of what life in a big city or small town is like. You might focus on the benefits or dangers with which your friend is unlikely to be familiar.

2. Shopping for a new car, you become annoyed at how many safety features are available only as expensive options. Write a letter of complaint to the auto manufacturer, citing at least three examples of such options. Avoid sounding hostile.

3. Lately, many people at your college or workplace have been experiencing stress. As a member of the Campus (or Company) Committee on Morale, you've been asked to prepare a pamphlet illustrating different strategies for reducing stress. Decide what strategies you'll discuss and explain them with helpful examples.

4. Assume that you're an elementary school principal planning to give a speech in which you'll try to convince parents that television distorts children's perceptions of reality. Write the speech, illustrating your point with vivid examples.

5. A pet food company is having an annual contest to choose a new animal to feature in its advertising. To win the contest, you must convince the company that your pet is personable, playful, unique. Write an essay giving examples of your pet's special qualities.

6. For your college humor magazine, write an article on what you consider to be the "three best consumer products of the past twenty-five years." Support your opinion with lively, engaging specifics that are consistent with the magazine's offbeat and slightly ironic tone.

6

DIVISION-CLASSIFICATION

WHAT IS DIVISION-CLASSIFICATION?

Imagine what life would be like if this is how an average day unfolded:

> You plan to stop at the supermarket for only five items, but your marketing takes over an hour because all the items in the store are jumbled together. Clerks put new shipments anywhere they please; the milk might be with the vegetables on Monday but with laundry detergent on Thursday. Next, you go to the drugstore to pick up some photos you left to be developed. You don't have time, though, to wait while the cashier roots through the large carton into which all the pickup envelopes have been thrown. You return to your car and decide to stop at the town hall to pay a parking ticket. But the town hall baffles you. The offices are unmarked, and there's not even a directory to tell you on which floor the Violations Bureau can be found. Annoyed,

you get back into your car and, minutes later, end up colliding with another car, which is driving toward you in your lane. When you wake up in the hospital, you find there are three other patients in your room: a middle-aged man with a heart problem, a young boy ready to have his tonsils removed, and a woman about to go into labor.

Such a muddled world, lacking the most basic forms of organization, would make daily life chaotic. All of us instinctively look for ways to order our environment. Without systems, categories, or sorting mechanisms, we'd be overwhelmed by life's complexity. An organization such as a college or university, for example, is made manageable by being divided into various schools (Liberal Arts, Performing Arts, Engineering, and so on). The schools are then separated into departments (English, History, Political Science), and each department's offerings are grouped into distinct categories—English, for instance, into Literature and Composition—before being further divided into specific courses.

The kind of ordering system we've been discussing is called *division-classification,* a logical way of thinking that allows us to make sense of a complex world. Division and classification, though separate processes, are often used together as complementary techniques. *Division* involves taking a single unit or concept, breaking the unit down into its parts, and then analyzing the connections among the parts and between the parts and the whole. For instance, if we wanted to organize the chaotic hospital described at the start of the chapter, we might think about how the single concept "a hospital" could be broken down into its components. We might come up with the following breakdown: pediatric wing, cardiac wing, maternity wing, and so on.

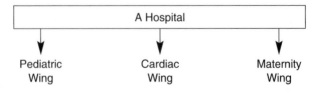

What we have just done involves division: We've taken a single entity (a hospital) and divided it into some of its component parts (wings), each with its own facilities and patients.

In contrast, *classification* brings two or more related items together and categorizes them according to type or kind. If the disorganized supermarket described earlier were to be restructured, the clerks would have to classify the separate items arriving at the loading dock. Cartons of lettuce, tomatoes, cucumbers, butter, yogurt, milk, shampoo, conditioner, and setting lotion would be assigned to the appropriate categories:

Lettuce	Butter	Shampoo
Tomatoes	Yogurt	Conditioner
Cucumbers	Milk	Setting Lotion
↓	↓	↓
Produce	Dairy	Hair Products

HOW DIVISION-CLASSIFICATION FITS YOUR PURPOSE AND AUDIENCE

The reorganized hospital and supermarket show the way division and classification work in everyday life. But division and classification also come into play during the writing process. Because division involves breaking a subject into parts, it can be a helpful strategy during prewriting, especially if you're analyzing a broad, complex subject: the structure of a film; the motivation of a character in a novel; the problem your community has with vandalism; the controversy surrounding school prayer. An editorial examining a recent hostage crisis, for example, might divide the crisis into three areas: how the hostages were treated by (1) their captors, (2) the governments negotiating their release, and (3) the media. The purpose of the editorial might be to show readers that the governments' treatment of the hostages was particularly exploitative.

Classification can be useful for imposing order on the hodgepodge of ideas generated during prewriting. You examine that material to see which of your rough ideas are alike and which are dissimilar, so that you can cluster related items in the same category. Classification would, then, be a helpful strategy in analyzing topics like these: techniques for impressing teachers; comic styles of talk-show hosts; views on abortion; reasons for the current rise in volunteerism. You might, for instance, use classification in a paper showing that Americans are undermining their health through their obsessive pursuit of various diets. Perhaps you begin by brainstorming all the diets that have gained popularity in recent years (Weight Watchers', Slim-Fast, Jenny Craig, whatever). Then you categorize the diets according to type: high-fiber, low-protein, high-carbohydrate, and so on. Once the diets are grouped, you can discuss the problems within each category, demonstrating to readers that none of the diets is safe or effective.

Division-classification can be crucial when responding to college assignments like the following:

> Based on your observations, what kinds of appeals do television advertisers use when selling automobiles? In your view, are any of these appeals morally irresponsible?

> Analyze the components that go into being an effective parent. Indicate those you consider most vital for raising confident, well-adjusted children.

> Describe the hierarchy of the typical high school clique, identifying the various parts of the hierarchy. Use your analysis to support or refute the view that adolescence is a period of rigid conformity.

> Many social commentators have observed that discourtesy is on the rise. Indicate whether you think this is a valid observation by characterizing the types of everyday encounters you have with people.

These assignments suggest division-classification through the use of such words as *kinds, components, parts,* and *types.* Generally, though, you won't receive such clear signals to use division-classification. Instead, the broad purpose of the essay—and the point you want to make—will lead you to the analytical thinking characteristic of division-classification.

Sometimes division-classification will be the dominant technique for structuring an essay; other times it will be used as a supplemental pattern in an essay organized primarily according to another pattern of development. Let's look at some examples. Say you want to write a paper *explaining a process* (surviving divorce; creating a hit record; shepherding a bill through Congress; using the Heimlich maneuver on people who are choking).

You could *divide* the process into parts or stages, showing, for instance, that the Heimlich maneuver is an easily mastered skill that readers should acquire. Or perhaps you plan to write a light-spirited essay analyzing the *effect* that increased awareness of sexual stereotypes has had on college students' social lives. In such a case, you might use *classification*. To show readers that shifting gender roles make young men and women comically self-conscious, you could categorize the places where students scout each other out: in class, at the library, at parties, in dorms. You could then show how students—not wishing to be macho or coyly feminine—approach each other with laughable tentativeness in these four environments.

Now imagine that you're writing an *argumentation-persuasion* essay urging that the federal government prohibit the use of growth-inducing antibiotics in livestock feed. The paper could begin by *dividing* the antibiotics cycle into stages: the effects of antibiotics on livestock; the short-term effects on humans who consume the animals; the possible long-term effects of consuming antibiotic-tainted meat. To increase readers' understanding of the problem, you might also discuss the antibiotics controversy in terms of an even larger issue: the dangerous ways food is treated before being consumed. In this case, you would consider the various procedures (use of additives, preservatives, artificial colors, and so on), *classifying* these treatments into several types—from least harmful (some additives or artificial colors, perhaps) to most harmful (you might slot the antibiotics here). Such an essay would be developed using both division *and* classification: first, the division of the antibiotics cycle and then the classification of the various food treatments. Frequently, this interdependence will be reversed, and classification will precede rather than follow division.

SUGGESTIONS FOR USING DIVISION-CLASSIFICATION IN AN ESSAY

The following suggestions will be helpful whether you use division-classification as a dominant or a supportive pattern of development.

1. Select a principle of division-classification consistent with your purpose. Most subjects can be divided or classified according to a *number of different principles*. For example, when writing about an ideal vacation, you could divide your subject according to any of these principles: location, cost, recreation available. Similarly, when analyzing students at your college, you could base your classification on a variety of principles: students' majors, their racial or ethnic background, whether they belong to a fraternity or sorority. In all cases, though, the principle of division-classification you select must meet one stringent requirement: It must help you meet your overall purpose and reinforce your central point.

Sometimes a principle of division-classification seems so attractive that you latch on to it without examining whether it's consistent with your purpose. Suppose you want to write a paper asserting that several episodes of a new television comedy are destined to become classics. Here's how you might go wrong.

You begin by doing some brainstorming about the episodes. Then, as you start to organize the prewriting material, you hit on a possible principle of classification: grouping the characters in the show according to the frequency with which they appear (main characters appearing in every show, supporting characters appearing in most shows, and guest characters appearing once or twice). You name the characters and explain which characters fit where. But is this principle of classification significant? Has it anything to do with why the shows will become classics? No, it hasn't. Such an essay would be little more than a meaningless exercise in classifying things just to classify them.

In contrast, a significant principle of classification might involve categorizing a number of shows according to the easily recognized human types portrayed: the Pompous Know-It-All, the Boss Who's Out of Control, the Lovable Grouch, the Surprisingly Savvy Innocent. You might illustrate the way certain episodes offer delightful twists on these stock figures, making such shows models of comic plotting and humor.

When you write an essay that uses division-classification as its primary method of development, a *single principle* of division-classification provides the foundation for each major section of the paper. Imagine you're writing an essay showing that the success of contemporary music groups has less to do with musical talent than with the groups' ability to market themselves to a distinct segment of the listening audience. To develop your point, you might categorize several performers according to the age ranges they appeal to (preteens, adolescents, people in their late twenties) and then analyze the marketing strategies the musicians use to gain their fans' support. The essay's logic would be undermined if you switched, in the middle of your analysis, to another principle of classification—say, the influence of earlier groups on today's music scene.

Don't, however, take this caution to mean that essays can never use more than one principle of division-classification as they unfold. They can—as long as the *shift from one principle to another* occurs in *different parts* of the paper. Imagine you want to write about widespread disillusionment with student government leaders at your college. You could develop this point by breaking down the dissatisfaction into the following: disappointment with the students' qualifications for office; disenchantment with their campaign tactics; frustration with their performance once elected. That section of the essay completed, you might move to a second principle of division—how students can get involved in campus government. Perhaps you break the proposed involvement into the following possibilities: serving on nominating committees; helping to run candidates' campaigns; attending open sessions of the student government.

2. Apply the principle of division-classification logically. In an essay using division-classification, you need to demonstrate to readers that your analysis is the result of careful thought. First of all, your division-classification should be as *complete* as possible. Your analysis should include—within reason—all the parts into which you can divide your subject, or all the types into which you can categorize your subjects. Let's say you're writing an essay showing that where college students live is an important factor in determining how satisfied they are with college life. Keeping your purpose in mind, you classify students according to where they live: with parents, in dorms, in fraternity and sorority houses. But what about all the students who live in rented apartments, houses, or rooms off campus? If these places of residence are ignored, your classification won't be complete; you will lose credibility with your readers because they'll probably realize that you have overlooked several important considerations.

Your division-classification should also be *consistent:* The parts into which you break your subject or the groups into which you place your subjects should be as mutually exclusive as possible. The parts or categories should not be mixed, nor should they overlap. Assume you're writing an essay describing the animals at the zoo in a nearby city. You decide to describe the zoo's mammals, reptiles, birds, and endangered species. But such a classification is inconsistent. You begin by categorizing the animals according to scientific class (mammals, birds, reptiles), then switch to another principle when you classify some animals according to whether they are endangered. Because you drift over to a different principle of classification, your categories are no longer mutually exclusive: Endangered species could overlap with any of the other categories. In which section of the paper, for instance, would you describe an exotic parrot that is obviously a bird but is also nearly extinct? And how would you categorize the zoo's rare mountain gorilla? This impressive creature is a mammal, but it is also an endangered species. Such overlapping categories undercut the logic that gives an essay its integrity.

A helpful tip: A solid outline is invaluable when you use division-classification. The outline encourages you to do the rigorous thinking needed to arrive at divisions and classifications that are logical, complete, and consistent.

3. Prepare an effective thesis. If your essay uses division-classification as its dominant method of development, it might be helpful to prepare a thesis that does more than signal the paper's subject and suggest your attitude toward that general subject. You might also want the thesis to state the principle of division-classification at the heart of the essay. Furthermore, you might want the thesis to reveal which part or category you regard as most important.

Consider the two thesis statements that follow:

As the observant beachcomber moves from the tidal area to the upper beach to the sandy dunes, rich variations in marine life become apparent.

Although most people focus on the dangers associated with the disposal of toxic waste in the land and ocean, the incineration of toxic matter may pose an even more serious threat to human life.

The first thesis statement makes clear that the writer will organize the paper by classifying forms of marine life according to location. Because the purpose of the essay is to inform as objectively as possible, the thesis doesn't suggest the writer's opinion about which category is most significant.

The second thesis signals that the essay will evolve by dividing the issue of toxic waste according to methods of disposal. Moreover, because the paper takes a stance on a controversial subject, the thesis is worded to reveal which aspect of the topic the writer considers most important. Such a clear statement of the writer's position is an effective strategy in an essay of this kind.

You may have noted that each thesis statement also signals the paper's plan of development. The first essay, for example, will use specific facts, examples, and details to describe the kinds of marine life found in the tidal area, upper beach, and dunes. However, thesis statements in papers developed primarily through division-classification don't have to be so structured. If a paper is well written, your principle of division-classification, your opinion about which part or category is most important, and the essay's plan of development will become apparent as the essay unfolds.

4. Organize the paper logically.   Whether your paper is developed wholly or in part by division-classification, it should have a logical structure. As much as possible, you should try to discuss *comparable points* in each section of the paper. In the essay on seashore life, for example, you might describe life in the tidal area by discussing the mollusks, crustaceans, birds, and amphibians that live or feed there. You would then follow through, as much as you could, with this arrangement in the paper's other sections (upper beach and dune). Forgetting to describe the birdlife thriving in the dunes, especially when you had discussed birdlife in the tidal and upper-beach areas, would compromise the paper's structure. Of course, perfect parallelism is not always possible—there are no mollusks in the dunes, for instance. You should also use *signal devices* to connect various parts of the paper: "*Another* characteristic of marine life battered by the tides"; "A *final* important trait of both tidal and upper-beach crustaceans"; "*Unlike* the creatures of the tidal area and the upper beach." Such signals clarify the connections among the essay's ideas.

5. State any conclusions or recommendations in the paper's final section.   The analytic thinking that occurs during division-classification often leads to surprising insights. Such insights may be introduced early on, or they may be reserved for the end, where they are stated as conclusions or recommendations. A paper might categorize different kinds of coaches—from inspiring to incompetent—and make the point that athletes learn a great deal about human relations simply by having to get along with their coaches, regardless of the coaches' skills. Such a paper might conclude that participation in a team sport teaches more about human nature than several courses in psychology. Or the essay might end with a pro-posal: Rookies and seasoned team members should be paired so that novice players can get advice on dealing with coaching eccentricities.

STUDENT ESSAY

The following student essay was written by Gail Oremland in response to this assignment:

> In "Propaganda Techniques in Today's Advertising," Ann McClintock describes the flaws in many of the persuasive strategies used by advertisers. Choose another group of people whose job is also to communicate—for example, parents, bosses, teachers. Then, in an essay of your own, divide the group into types according to the flaws they make when communicating.

While reading Gail's paper, try to determine how effectively it applies the principles of division-classification. The annotations on Gail's paper and the commentary following it will help you look at the essay more closely.

The Truth About College Teachers
by Gail Oremland

Introduction

A recent TV news story told about a group of   1
college professors from a nearby university who were hired by a local school system to help upgrade the teaching in the community's public schools. The professors were to visit classrooms, analyze teachers' skills, and then conduct workshops to help the teachers become more effective at their jobs. But after the first round of workshops, the superintendent of schools decided to cancel the whole project. He fired the learned professors and sent them back to their ivory tower. Why did the project fall apart? There was a simple reason. The college professors, who were supposedly going to show the public school teachers how to be more effective, were themselves poor teachers. Many college students could have predicted such a disas-trous outcome. They know, firsthand, that college

Thesis

teachers are strange. They know that professors often exhibit bizarre behaviors, relating to students in ways that make it difficult for students to stay awake, or--if awake--to learn.

One type of professor assumes, legitimately enough, that her function is to pass on to students the vast store of knowledge she has acquired. But because the "Knowledgeable One" regards herself as an expert and her students as the ignorant masses, she adopts an elitist approach that sabotages learning. The Knowledgeable One enters a lecture hall with a self-important air, walks to the podium, places her yellowed-with-age notes on the stand, and begins her lecture at the exact second the class is officially scheduled to begin. There can be a blizzard or hurricane raging outside the lecture hall; students can be running through freezing sleet and howling winds to get to class on time. Will the Knowledgeable One wait for them to arrive before beginning her lecture? Probably not. The Knowledgeable One's time is precious. She's there, set to begin, and that's what matters.

Topic sentence

The first of three paragraphs on the first category of teacher

The first paragraph in a three-part chronological sequence: What happens *before* class

2

Topic sentence

The second paragraph on the first category of teacher

The second paragraph in the chronological sequence: What happens *during* class

Once the monologue begins, the Knowledgeable One drones on and on. The Knowledgeable One is a fact person. She may be the history prof who knows the death toll of every Civil War battle, the biology prof who can diagram all the common biological molecules, the accounting prof who enumerates every clause of the federal tax form. Oblivious to students' glazed eyes and stifled yawns, the Knowledgeable One delivers her monologue, dispensing one dry fact after another. The only advantage to being on the receiving end of this boring monologue is that students do not have to worry about being called on to question a point or provide an opinion; the Knowledgeable One is not willing to relinquish one minute of her time by giving students a voice. Assume for one improbable moment that a student actually manages to stay awake during the monologue and is brave enough to ask a question. In such a case, the Knowledgeable One will address the questioning student as "Mr." or "Miss." This formality does not, as some students mistakenly suppose, indicate respect for

3

the student as a fledgling member of the academic community. Not at all. This impersonality represents the Knowledgeable One's desire to keep as wide a distance as possible between her and her students.

Topic sentence ⟶ The Knowledgeable One's monologue always   4 comes to a close at the precise second the class is scheduled to end. No sooner has she delivered her last forgettable word than the Knowledgeable One packs up her notes and shoots out the door, heading back to the privacy of her office, where she can pursue her specialized academic interests--free of any possible interruption from students. The Knowledgeable One's hasty departure from the lecture hall makes it clear she has no desire to talk with students. In her eyes, she has met her obligations; she has taken time away from her research to transmit to students what she knows. Any closer contact might mean she would risk contagion from students, that great unwashed mass. Such a danger is to be avoided at all costs.

The third paragraph on the first category of teacher

The final paragraph in the chronological sequence: What happens after *class*

Unlike the Knowledgeable One, the "Leader of   5 Intellectual Discussion" seems to respect students. Emphasizing class discussion, the Leader encourages students to confront ideas ("What is Twain's view of morality?" "Was our intervention in Vietnam justified?" "Should big business be given tax breaks?") and discover their own truths. Then, about three weeks into the semester, it becomes clear that the Leader wants students to discover <u>his</u> version of the truth. Behind the Leader's democratic guise lurks a dictator. When a student voices an opinion that the Leader accepts, the student is rewarded by hearty nods of approval and "Good point, good point." But if a student is rash enough to advance a conflicting viewpoint, the Leader responds with killing politeness: "Well, yes, that's an interesting perspective. But don't you think that . . . ?" Grade-conscious students soon learn not to chime in with their viewpoint. They know that when the Leader, with seeming honesty, says, "I'd be interested in hearing what you think. Let's open this up for discussion," they had better figure out what the Leader wants to hear before advancing their own

Topic sentence ⟶

Paragraph on the second category of teacher

theories. "Me-tooism" rather than independent thinking, they discover, guarantees good grades in the Leader's class.

Topic sentence ⟶ Then there is the professor who comes across   6
Paragraph on the third category of teacher
as the students' "Buddy." This kind of professor does not see himself as an imparter of knowledge or a leader of discussion but as a pal, just one in a community of equals. The Buddy may start his course this way. "All of us know that this college stuff--grades, degrees, exams, required reading--is a game. So let's not play it, okay?" Dressed in jeans, sweatshirt, and scuffed sneakers, the Buddy projects a relaxed, casual attitude. He arranges the class seats in a circle (he would never take a position in front of the room) and insists that students call him by his first name. He uses no syllabus and gives few tests, believing that such constraints keep students from directing their own learning. A free spirit, the Buddy often teaches courses like "The Psychology of Interpersonal Relations" or "The Social Dynamics of the Family." If students choose to use class time to discuss the course material, that's fine. If they want to discuss something else, that's fine, too. It's the self-expression, the honest dialogue, that counts. In fact, the Buddy seems especially fond of digressions from academic subjects. By talking about his political views, his marital problems, his tendency to drink one too many beers, the Buddy lets students see that he is a regular guy--just like them. At first, students look forward to classes with the Buddy. They enjoy the informality, the chitchat, the lack of pressure. But after a while, they wonder why they are paying for a course where they learn nothing. They might as well stay home and watch the soaps.

Conclusion

Echoes opening anecdote
Obviously, some college professors are excel-   7
lent. They are learned, hardworking, and imaginative; they enjoy their work and like being with students. On the whole, though, college professors are a strange lot. Despite their advanced degrees and their own exposure to many different kinds of teachers, they do not seem to understand how to relate to students. Rather than being hired as consultants to help others upgrade their teaching

skills, college professors should themselves hire consultants to tell them what they are doing wrong and how they can improve. Who should these consultants be? That's easy: the people who know them best--their students.

COMMENTARY

Introduction and thesis.   After years of being graded by teachers, Gail took special pleasure in writing an essay that gave her a chance to evaluate her teachers—in this case, her college professors. Even the essay's title, "The Truth About College Teachers," implies that Gail is going to have fun knocking profs down from their ivory towers. To introduce her subject, she uses a timely news story. This brief anecdote leads directly to the essay's *thesis:* "Professors often exhibit bizarre behaviors, relating to students in ways that make it difficult for students to stay awake, or—if awake—to learn." Note that Gail's thesis isn't highly structured; it doesn't, for example, name the specific categories to be discussed. Still, her thesis suggests that the essay is going to *categorize* a range of teaching behaviors, using as a *principle of classification* the strange ways that college profs relate to students.

Purpose.   As with all good papers developed through division-classification, Gail's essay doesn't use classification as an end in itself. Gail uses classification because it helps her achieve a broader *purpose*. She wants to *convince* readers—without moralizing or abandoning her humorous tone—that such teaching styles inhibit learning. In other words, there's a serious underside to her essay. This additional layer of meaning is characteristic of satiric writing.

Categories and topic sentences.   The essay's body, consisting of five paragraphs, presents the three categories that make up Gail's analysis. According to Gail, college teachers can be categorized as the Knowledgeable One (paragraphs 2–4), the Leader of Intellectual Discussion (5), or the Buddy (6). Obviously, there are other ways professors might be classified. But given Gail's purpose, audience, tone, and point of view, her categories are appropriate; they are reasonably *complete, consistent,* and *mutually exclusive.* Note, too, that Gail uses *topic sentences* near the beginning of each category to help readers see which professorial type she's discussing.

Overall organization and paragraph structure.   Gail is able to shift smoothly and easily from one category to the next. How does she achieve such graceful transitions? Take a moment to reread the sentences that introduce her second and third categories (paragraphs 5 and 6). Look at the way each sentence's beginning (in italics here) links back to the preceding category or categories: "*Unlike the Knowledgeable One,* the 'Leader of Intellectual Discussion' seems to respect students"; and "[the Buddy] . . . *does not see himself as an imparter of knowledge or a leader of discussion* but as a pal. . . ."

Gail is equally careful about providing an easy-to-follow structure within each section. She uses a *chronological sequence* to organize her three-paragraph discussion of the Knowledgeable One. The first paragraph deals with the beginning of the Knowledgeable One's lecture; the second, with the lecture itself; the third, with the end of the lecture. And the paragraphs' *topic sentences* clearly indicate this passage of time. Similarly, *transitions* are used in the paragraphs on the Leader of Intellectual Discussion and the Buddy to ensure a logical progression of points: "*Then,* about three weeks into the semester, it becomes clear that the Leader wants students to discover *his* version of the truth" (5) and "*At first,* students look forward to classes with the Buddy. . . . But *after a while,* they wonder why they are paying for a course where they learn nothing" (6).

Tone.   The essay's unity can also be traced to Gail's skill in sustaining her satiric tone. Throughout the essay, Gail selects details that fit her gently mocking attitude. She depicts the Knowledgeable One lecturing from "yellowed-with-age notes . . . , oblivious to students' glazed eyes and stifled yawns," unwilling to wait for students who "run . . . through freezing sleet and howling winds to get to class on time." Then she presents another tongue-in-cheek description, this one focusing on the way the Leader of Intellectual Discussion conducts class: "Good point, good point. . . . Well, yes, that's an interesting perspective. But don't you think that . . .?" Finally, with similar killing accuracy, Gail portrays the Buddy, democratically garbed in "jeans, sweatshirt, and scuffed sneakers."

Other patterns of development.   Gail's satiric depiction of her three professorial types employs a number of techniques associated with *narrative* and *descriptive writing:* vigorous images, highly connotative language, and dialogue. *Definition, exemplification, causal* *analysis,* and *comparison-contrast* also come into play. Gail defines the characteristics of each type of professor; she provides numerous examples to support her categories; she explains the effects of the different teaching styles on students; and, in her description of the Leader of Intellectual Discussion, she contrasts the appearance of democracy with the dictatorial reality.

Unequal development of categories.   Although Gail's essay is unified, organized, and well-developed, you may have felt that the first category outweighs the other two. There is, of course, no need to balance the categories exactly. But Gail's extended treatment of the first category sets up an expectation that the others will be treated as fully. One way to remedy this problem would be to delete some material from the discussion of the Knowledgeable One. Gail might, for instance, omit the last five sentences in the third paragraph (about the professor's habit of addressing students as "Mr." or "Miss"). Such a change could be made without taking the bite out of her portrayal. Even better, Gail could simply switch the order of her sections, putting the portrait of the Knowledgeable One at the essay's end. Here, the extended discussion wouldn't seem out of proportion. Instead, the sections would appear in *emphatic order,* with the most detailed category saved for last.

Revising the first draft.   It's apparent that an essay as engaging as Gail's must have undergone a good deal of revising. That was in fact the case. Gail made many changes in the body of the essay, but it's particularly interesting to review what happened to the introduction as she revised the paper. Reprinted here is Gail's original introduction.

Original Version of the Introduction

Despite their high IQs, advanced degrees, and published papers, some college professors just don't know how to teach. Found in almost any department, in tenured and untenured positions, they prompt student apathy. They fail to convey ideas effectively and to challenge or inspire students. Students thus finish their courses having learned very little. Contrary to popular opinion, these professors' ineptitude is not simply a matter of delivering boring lectures or not caring about students. Many of them care a great deal. Their failure actually stems from their unrealistic perceptions of what a teacher should be. Specifically, they adopt teaching styles or roles that alienate students and undermine learning. Three of the most common ones are "The Knowledgeable One," "The Leader of Intellectual Discussion," and "The Buddy."

When Gail showed the first draft of the essay to her composition instructor, he laughed—and occasionally squirmed—as he read what she had prepared. He was enthusiastic about the paper but felt that there was a problem with the introduction's tone; it was too serious when compared to the playful, lightly satiric mood of the rest of the essay. When Gail reread the paragraph, she agreed, but she was uncertain about the best way to remedy the problem. After revising other sections of the essay, she decided to let the paper sit for a while before going back to rewrite the introduction.

In the meantime, Gail switched on the TV. The timing couldn't have been better; she tuned into a news story about several supposedly learned professors who had been fired from a consulting job because they had turned out to know so little about teaching. This was exactly the kind of item Gail needed to start her essay. Now she was able to prepare a completely new introduction, making it consistent in spirit with the rest of the paper.

With this stronger introduction and the rest of the essay well in hand, Gail was ready to write a conclusion. Now, as she worked on the concluding paragraph, she deliberately shaped it to recall the story about the fired consultants. By echoing the opening anecdote in her conclusion, Gail was able to end the paper with another poke at professors—a perfect way to close her clever and insightful essay.

ACTIVITIES: DIVISION-CLASSIFICATION

Prewriting Activities

1. Imagine you're writing two essays: One is a humorous paper outlining a *process* for impressing college instructors; the other is a serious essay examining the *causes* of the recent rise in volunteerism. What about the topics might you divide and/or classify?

2. Use group brainstorming to identify three principles of division for *one* of the topics in Set A below. Focusing on one of the principles, decide what your thesis might be if you were writing an essay. That done, use group brainstorming to identify three principles of classification that might provide the structure for *one* of the topics in Set

B. Focusing on one of the principles, decide what your thesis might be if you were writing an essay.

Set A
- Rock music
- A shopping mall
- A good horror movie

Set B
- Why people get addicted to computers
- How fast-food restaurants affect family life
- Why long-term relationships break up

Revising Activities

3. Following is a scratch outline for an essay developed through division-classification. On what principle of division-classification is the essay based? What problem do you see in the way the principle is applied? How could the problem be remedied?

   Thesis: The same experience often teaches opposite things to different people.

   - What working as a fast-food cook teaches: Some learn responsibility; others learn to take a "quick and dirty" approach.
   - What a negative experience teaches optimists: Some learn from their mistakes; others continue to maintain a positive outlook.
   - What a difficult course teaches: Some learn to study hard; others learn to avoid demanding courses.
   - What the breakup of a close relationship teaches: Some learn how to negotiate differences; others learn to avoid intimacy.

4. Following is a paragraph from the first draft of an essay urging that day care centers adopt play programs tailored to children's developmental needs. What principle of division-classification focuses the paragraph? Is the principle applied consistently and logically? Are parts/categories developed sufficiently? Revise the paragraph, eliminating any problems you discover and adding specific details where needed.

   Within a few years, preschool children move from self-absorbed to interactive play. Babies and toddlers engage in solitary play. Although they sometimes prefer being near other children, they focus primarily on their own actions. This is very different from the highly interactive play of the elementary school years. Sometime in children's second year, solitary play is replaced by parallel play, during which children engage in similar activities near one another. However, they interact only occasionally. By age three, most children show at least some cooperative play, a form that involves interaction and cooperative role-taking. Such role-taking can be found in the "pretend" games that children play to explore adult relationships (games of "Mommy and Daddy") and anatomy (games of "Doctor"). Additional signs of youngsters' growing awareness of peers can be seen at about age four. At this age, many children begin showing a special devotion to one other child and may want to play only with that child. During this time, children also begin to take special delight in physical activities such as running and jumping, often going off by themselves to expend their abundant physical energy.

Judith Viorst

A contributing editor at *Redbook,* Judith Viorst (1936–) is perhaps best known for her column in that magazine. She has also written several children's books, including *Alexander and the Terrible, Horrible, No Good, Very Bad Day* (1982) and *Sad Underwear and Other Complications* (1995); a number of volumes of light verse, including *It's Hard to Be Hip Over Thirty and Other Tragedies of Modern Life* (1970), *How Did I Get to Be Forty and Other Atrocities* (1984), and *Suddenly Sixty and Other Shocks of Later Life* (2000); a novel, *Murdering Mr. Monti: A Merry Little Tale of Sex and Violence* (1994); and the serious, nonfictional *Necessary Losses* (1986) and *Imperfect Control* (1998). Viorst's writing style, which often combines deeply felt emotion and wry humor, has made her works popular and widely read. The following selection first appeared in *Redbook* in 1977.

Pre-Reading Journal Entry

In your journal, explore your thoughts on the topic of friendship. In one column, focus on your childhood perspective of friendship. What did you value in and expect from your friends? In another column, respond to the same questions, this time from an adult perspective. In each case, jot down examples illustrating your values and expectations.

Friends, Good Friends— Such Good Friends

Women are friends, I once would have said, when they totally love 1 and support and trust each other, and bare to each other the secrets of their souls, and run—no questions asked—to help each other, and tell harsh truths to each other (no, you can't wear that dress unless you lose ten pounds first) when harsh truths must be told.

Women are friends, I once would have said, when they share the 2 same affection for Ingmar Bergman, plus train rides, cats, warm rain, charades, Camus, and hate with equal ardor Newark and Brussels sprouts and Lawrence Welk[1] and camping.

---

[1]Ingmar Bergman, a Swedish filmmaker noted for his deep probings into the darkness of the human soul; Albert Camus, a French writer whose essays and novels depict the human capacity for moral and responsible action in an otherwise pointless world; Lawrence Welk, a television band leader whose bubbly "champagne" music was often criticized as being bland and homogenized (editors' note).

In other words, I once would have said that a friend is a friend   3
all the way, but now I believe that's a narrow point of view. For the
friendships I have and the friendships I see are conducted at many
levels of intensity, serve many different functions, meet different
needs and range from those as all-the-way as the friendship of the
soul sisters mentioned above to that of the most nonchalant and
casual playmates.

Consider these varieties of friendship: 4

1. Convenience friends. These are women with whom, if our   5
paths weren't crossing all the time, we'd have no particular reason
to be friends: a next-door neighbor, a woman in our car pool, the
mother of one of our children's closest friends or maybe some
mommy with whom we serve juice and cookies each week at the
Glenwood Co-op Nursery.

Convenience friends are convenient indeed. They'll lend us   6
their cups and silverware for a party. They'll drive our kids to soccer
when we're sick. They'll take us to pick up our car when we need a
lift to the garage. They'll even take our cats when we go on vacation. As we will for them.

But we don't, with convenience friends, ever come too close or   7
tell too much; we maintain our public face and emotional distance.
"Which means," says Elaine, "that I'll talk about being overweight
but not about being depressed. Which means I'll admit being mad
but not blind with rage. Which means that I might say that we're
pinched this month but never that I'm worried sick over money."

But which doesn't mean that there isn't sufficient value to be   8
found in these friendships of mutual aid, in convenience friends.

2. Special-interest friends. These friendships aren't intimate,   9
and they needn't involve kids or silverware or cats. Their value lies
in some interest jointly shared. And so we may have an office friend
or a yoga friend or a tennis friend or a friend from the Women's
Democratic Club.

"I've got one woman friend," says Joyce, "who likes, as I do, to   10
take psychology courses. Which makes it nice for me—and nice for
her. It's fun to go with someone you know and it's fun to discuss
what you've learned, driving back from the classes." And for the
most part, she says, that's all they discuss.

"I'd say that what we're doing is *doing* together, not being   11
together," Suzanne says of her Tuesday-doubles friends. "It's main-

ly a tennis relationship, but we play together well. And I guess we all need to have a couple of playmates."

I agree.   12

My playmate is a shopping friend, a woman of marvelous taste,   13
a woman who knows exactly *where* to buy *what,* and furthermore is
a woman who always knows beyond a doubt what one ought to be
buying. I don't have the time to keep up with what's new in eyeshadow, hemlines and shoes and whether the smock look is in or finished already. But since (oh, shame!) I care a lot about eyeshadow,
hemlines and shoes, and since I don't *want* to wear smocks if the
smock look is finished, I'm very glad to have a shopping friend.

3. Historical friends. We all have a friend who knew us when . . .   14
maybe way back in Miss Meltzer's second grade, when our family
lived in that three-room flat in Brooklyn, when our dad was out of
work for seven months, when our brother Allie got in that fight
where they had to call the police, when our sister married the
endodontist from Yonkers and when, the morning after we lost our
virginity, she was the first, the only, friend we told.

The years have gone by and we've gone separate ways and we've   15
little in common now, but we're still an intimate part of each other's
past. And so whenever we go to Detroit we always go to visit this
friend of our girlhood. Who knows how we looked before our teeth
were straightened. Who knows how we talked before our voice got
un-Brooklyned. Who knows what we ate before we learned about
artichokes. And who, by her presence, puts us in touch with an earlier part of ourself, a part of ourself it's important never to lose.

"What this friend means to me and what I mean to her," says   16
Grace, "is having a sister without sibling rivalry. We know the texture of each other's lives. She remembers my grandmother's cabbage soup. I remember the way her uncle played the piano. There's
simply no other friend who remembers those things."

4. Crossroads friends. Like historical friends, our crossroads   17
friends are important for *what was*—for the friendship we shared at a
crucial, now past, time of life. A time, perhaps, when we roomed in
college together; or worked as eager young singles in the Big City
together; or went together, as my friend Elizabeth and I did, through
pregnancy, birth and that scary first year of new motherhood.

Crossroads friends forge powerful links, links strong enough to   18
endure with not much more contact than once-a-year letters at

Christmas. And out of respect for those crossroads years, for those dramas and dreams we once shared, we will always be friends.

5. Cross-generational friends. Historical friends and crossroads   19
friends seem to maintain a special kind of intimacy—dormant but always ready to be revived—and though we may rarely meet, whenever we do connect, it's personal and intense. Another kind of intimacy exists in the friendships that form across generations in what one woman calls her daughter-mother and her mother-daughter relationships.

Evelyn's friend is her mother's age—"but I share so much more   20
than I ever could with my mother"—a woman she talks to of music, of books and of life. "What I get from her is the benefit of her experience. What she gets—and enjoys—from me is a youthful perspective. It's a pleasure for both of us."

I have in my own life a precious friend, a woman of 65 who has   21
lived very hard, who is wise, who listens well; who has been where I am and can help me understand it; and who represents not only an ultimate ideal mother to me but also the person I'd like to be when I grow up.

In our daughter role we tend to do more than our share of self-   22
revelation; in our mother role we tend to receive what's revealed. It's another kind of pleasure—playing wise mother to a questing younger person. It's another very lovely kind of friendship.

6. Part-of-a-couple friends. Some of the women we call our   23
friends we never see alone—we see them as part of a couple at couples' parties. And though we share interests in many things and respect each other's views, we aren't moved to deepen the relationship. Whatever the reason, a lack of time or—and this is more likely—a lack of chemistry, our friendship remains in the context of a group. But the fact that our feeling on seeing each other is always, "I'm *so* glad she's here" and the fact that we spend half the evening talking together says that this too, in its own way, counts as a friendship.

(Other part-of-a-couple friends are the friends that came with   24
the marriage, and some of these are friends we could live without. But sometimes, alas, she married our husband's best friend; and sometimes, alas, she *is* our husband's best friend. And so we find ourself dealing with her, somewhat against our will, in a spirit of what I'll call *reluctant* friendship.)

7. Men who are friends. I wanted to write just of women 25
friends, but the women I've talked to won't let me—they say I must
mention man-woman friendships too. For these friendships can be
just as close and as dear as those that we form with women. Listen
to Lucy's description of one such friendship:

"We've found we have things to talk about that are different 26
from what he talks about with my husband and different from what
I talk about with his wife. So sometimes we call on the phone or
meet for lunch. There are similar intellectual interests—we always
pass on to each other the books that we love—but there's also something tender and caring too."

In a couple of crises, Lucy says, "he offered himself for talking 27
and for helping. And when someone died in his family he wanted me
there. The sexual, flirty part of our friendship is very small, but
some—just enough to make it fun and different." She thinks—and I
agree—that the sexual part, though small, is always *some*, is always
there when a man and a woman are friends.

It's only in the past few years that I've made friends with men, 28
in the sense of a friendship that's *mine*, not just part of two couples.
And achieving with them the ease and the trust I've found with
women friends has value indeed. Under the dryer at home last week,
putting on mascara and rouge, I comfortably sat and talked with a
fellow named Peter. Peter, I finally decided, could handle the shock
of me minus mascara under the dryer. Because we care for each
other. Because we're friends.

8. There are medium friends, and pretty good friends, and very 29
good friends indeed, and these friendships are defined by their level
of intimacy. And what we'll reveal at each of these levels of intimacy is calibrated with care. We might tell a medium friend, for example, that yesterday we had a fight with our husband. And we might
tell a pretty good friend that this fight with our husband made us so
mad that we slept on the couch. And we might tell a very good
friend that the reason we got so mad in that fight that we slept on
the couch had something to do with that girl who works in his
office. But it's only to our very best friends that we're willing to tell
all, to tell what's going on with that girl in his office.

The best of friends, I still believe, totally love and support and 30
trust each other, and bare to each other the secrets of their souls,
and run—no questions asked—to help each other, and tell harsh
truths to each other when they must be told.

But we needn't agree about everything (only 12-year-old girl 31
friends agree about *everything*) to tolerate each other's point of view.
To accept without judgment. To give and to take without ever keeping score. And to *be* there, as I am for them and as they are for me,
to comfort our sorrows, to celebrate our joys.

Questions for Close Reading

1. What is the selection's thesis? Locate the sentence(s) in which Viorst
   states her main idea. If she doesn't state the thesis explicitly, express it in
   your own words.
2. Viorst's view of what constitutes a friendship has changed over time.
   What did she once believe was the essence of friendship? How and why
   has her definition of friendship changed?
3. According to Viorst, what do historical and crossroads friends have in
   common? How are they different?
4. What does Viorst mean when she writes that the intimacy level of our
   relationships is "calibrated with care" (paragraph 29)?
5. Refer to your dictionary as needed to define the following words used in
   the selection: *ardor* (paragraph 2), *nonchalant* (3), *sibling* (16), *calibrated* (29).

Questions About the Writer's Craft

1. **The pattern.**   What principle of division-classification does Viorst use
   to sequence the "varieties of friendship"?
2. **Other patterns.**   What is Viorst's purpose in this essay? What other
   patterns of development besides division-classification does she use to
   achieve this purpose?
3. Examine the essay's introduction and conclusion. What idea appears in
   both sections? What idea appears only in the conclusion? Why do you
   think Viorst ends with this idea?
4. How would you describe Viorst's tone in this essay? What words and
   phrases help create this tone? What effect do you think Viorst intends
   this tone to have on her readers?

Writing Assignments Using Division-Classification
as a Pattern of Development

1. Enlarge upon Viorst's analysis by interviewing some males about the
   types of friendships they typically form. Describe men's friendships in an
   essay, pointing out in the introduction or conclusion any differences
   you've discovered in the way males and females approach friendship.

Before writing the paper, you may want to read Deborah Tannen's "But What Do You Mean?" (page 313) and Dave Barry's "The Ugly Truth About Beauty" (page 422) for observations about the dissimilarities in men's and women's interpersonal styles.

2. Viorst writes about various kinds of friends. Following Viorst's lead, choose another group of people (for example, bosses, salespeople, or parents) and write an essay about the different types of individuals within that broad category. Your tone may be light or serious, but you should, as Viorst does, reach some conclusions about the types of people you describe.

Writing Assignments Using Other Patterns of Development

3. As Viorst indicates, friends survive disagreements by being tolerant and accepting of each other "without judgment." Sometimes, though, friendships erupt into conflict. Write an essay describing a process by which friends who are having a significant disagreement can restore the harmony of their relationship. Caroline Rego's "The Fine Art of Complaining" (page 380) and Deborah Tannen's "But What Do You Mean?" (page 313) offer some suggestions for resolving conflict.

4. Viorst suggests that women and men can be friends without there being a distracting sexual element. Think about the opposite-sex friendships you have had, and talk about such friendships with some people you know well. Then decide whether you believe that nonromantic opposite-sex friendship is possible. Write an essay arguing either that all such friendships are tinged with significant sexual overtones or that pure friendship can occur between males and females. Remember to acknowledge the opposing viewpoint, and include plentiful examples from your own and others' experience to support your position.

Writing Assignments Using a Journal Entry as a Starting Point

5. Write an essay comparing and/or contrasting your childhood and adult views of friendship. Review your pre-reading journal entry to identify ideas worth developing. Also consider brainstorming with others to gain insight into the ways that friendships change—or remain the same—as people get older.

William Zinsser

Currently executive editor of the Book-of-the-Month Club and instructor at the New School for Social Research, William Zinsser has written news journalism, drama criticism, magazine columns, and several books on U.S. culture. Born in 1922 in New York, Zinsser attended Princeton University and worked for the *New York Herald Tribune, Life,* and *Look*. In 1970, Zinsser designed a course in nonfiction writing for Yale University. Based on what he learned at Yale about the way college students approach the writing process, Zinsser wrote the popular guide *On Writing Well* (1976). His other books include *The City Dwellers* (1962), *Pop Goes America* (1966), *The Lunacy Boom* (1970), *Writing With a Word Processor* (1982), *American Places: A Writer's Pilgrimage to 15 of This Country's Most Visited and Cherished Sites* (1992) and *Speaking of Journalism* (1994). He also co-edited *Inventing the Truth: The Art & Craft of Memoir* (1995). The following essay first appeared in the magazine *Country Journal* in 1979.

Pre-Reading Journal Entry

Many students feel pressured by college graduation requirements. Do you? What courses are you required to take that you wouldn't ordinarily choose? What courses would you like to take but don't have time for? Should colleges require students to take courses that aren't part of their majors? Why or why not? Use your journal to respond to these questions.

College Pressures

Dear Carlos: I desperately need a dean's excuse for my chem midterm which will begin in about 1 hour. All I can say is that I totally blew it this week. I've fallen incredibly, inconceivably behind.

Carlos: Help! I'm anxious to hear from you. I'll be in my room and won't leave it until I hear from you. Tomorrow is the last day for . . .

Carlos: I left town because I started bugging out again. I stayed up all night to finish a take-home make-up exam & am typing it to hand in on the 10th. It was due on the 5th. P.S. I'm going to the dentist. Pain is pretty bad.

Carlos: Probably by Friday I'll be able to get back to my studies. Right now I'm going to take a long walk. This whole thing has taken a lot out of me.

Carlos: I'm really up the proverbial creek. The problem is I really *bombed* the history final. Since I need that course for my major I . . .

Carlos: Here follows a tale of woe. I went home this weekend, had to help my Mom, & caught a fever so didn't have much time to study. My professor . . .

Carlos: Aargh! Trouble. Nothing original but everything's piling up at once. To be brief, my job interview . . .

Hey Carlos, good news! I've got mononucleosis.

Who are these wretched supplicants, scribbling notes so laden   1
with anxiety, seeking such miracles of postponement and balm? They are men and women who belong to Branford College, one of the twelve residential colleges at Yale University, and the messages are just a few of the hundreds that they left for their dean, Carlos Hortas—often slipped under his door at 4 A.M.—last year.

But students like the ones who wrote those notes can also be   2
found on campuses from coast to coast—especially in New England and at many other private colleges across the country that have high academic standards and highly motivated students. Nobody could doubt that the notes are real. In their urgency and their gallows humor they are authentic voices of a generation that is panicky to succeed.

My own connection with the message writers is that I am mas-   3
ter of Branford College. I live in its Gothic quadrangle and know the students well. (We have 485 of them.) I am privy to their hopes and fears—and also to their stereo music and their piercing cries in the dead of the night ("Does anybody *ca-a-are?*"). If they went to

Carlos to ask how to get through tomorrow, they come to me to ask how to get through the rest of their lives.

Mainly I try to remind them that the road ahead is a long one 4
and that it will have more unexpected turns than they think. There will be plenty of time to change jobs, change careers, change whole attitudes and approaches. They don't want to hear such liberating news. They want a map—right now—that they can follow unswervingly to career security, financial security, Social Security and, presumably, a prepaid grave.

What I wish for all students is some release from the clammy 5
grip of the future. I wish them a chance to savor each segment of their education as an experience in itself and not as a grim preparation for the next step. I wish them the right to experiment, to trip and fall, to learn that defeat is as instructive as victory and is not the end of the world.

My wish, of course, is naïve. One of the few rights that America 6
does not proclaim is the right to fail. Achievement is the national god, venerated in our media—the million-dollar athlete, the wealthy executive—and glorified in our praise of possessions. In the presence of such a potent state religion, the young are growing up old.

I see four kinds of pressure working on college students today: 7
economic pressure, parental pressure, peer pressure, and self-induced pressure. It is easy to look around for villains—to blame the colleges for charging too much money, the professors for assigning too much work, the parents for pushing their children too far, the students for driving themselves too hard. But there are no villains; only victims.

"In the late 1960s," one dean told me, "the typical question 8
that I got from students was 'Why is there so much suffering in the world?' or 'How can I make a contribution?' Today it's 'Do you think it would look better for getting into law school if I did a double major in history and political science, or just majored in one of them?'" Many other deans confirmed this pattern. One said: "They're trying to find an edge—the intangible something that will look better on paper if two students are about equal."

Note the emphasis on looking better. The transcript has become 9
a sacred document, the passport to security. How one appears on paper is more important than how one appears in person. *A* is for Admirable and *B* is for Borderline, even though, in Yale's official

system of grading, *A* means "excellent" and *B* means "very good." Today, looking very good is no longer good enough, especially for students who hope to go on to law school or medical school. They know that entrance into the better schools will be an entrance into the better law firms and better medical practices where they will make a lot of money. They also know that the odds are harsh. Yale Law School, for instance, matriculates 170 students from an applicant pool of 3,700; Harvard enrolls 550 from a pool of 7,000.

It's all very well for those of us who write letters of recommen-   10
dation for our students to stress the qualities of humanity that will make them good lawyers or doctors. And it's nice to think that admission officers are really reading our letters and looking for the extra dimension of commitment or concern. Still, it would be hard for a student not to visualize these officers shuffling so many transcripts studded with *A*s that they regard a *B* as positively shameful.

The pressure is almost as heavy on students who just want to   11
graduate and get a job. Long gone are the days of the "gentleman's *C*," when students journeyed through college with a certain relaxation, sampling a wide variety of courses—music, art, philosophy, classics, anthropology, poetry, religion—that would send them out as liberally educated men and women. If I were an employer I would rather employ graduates who have this range and curiosity than those who narrowly pursued safe subjects and high grades. I know countless students whose inquiring minds exhilarate me. I like to hear the play of their ideas. I don't know if they are getting *A*s or *C*s, and I don't care. I also like them as people. The country needs them, and they will find satisfying jobs. I tell them to relax. They can't.

Nor can I blame them. They live in a brutal economy. Tuition,   12
room, and board at most private colleges now comes to at least $7,000 [in 1979], not counting books and fees. This might seem to suggest that the colleges are getting rich. But they are equally battered by inflation. Tuition covers only 60 percent of what it costs to educate a student, and ordinarily the remainder comes from what colleges receive in endowments, grants, and gifts. Now the remainder keeps being swallowed by the cruel costs—higher every year—of just opening the doors. Heating oil is up. Insurance is up. Postage is up. Health-premium costs are up. Everything is up. Deficits are up. We are witnessing in America the creation of a brotherhood of paupers—colleges, parents, and students, joined by the common bond of debt.

Today it is not unusual for a student, even if he works part time 13
at college and full time during the summer, to accrue $5,000 in
loans after four years—loans that he must start to repay within one
year after graduation. Exhorted at commencement to go forth into
the world, he is already behind as he goes forth. How could he not
feel under pressure throughout college to prepare for this day of
reckoning? I have used "he," incidentally, only for brevity. Women
at Yale are under no less pressure to justify their expensive education
to themselves, their parents, and society. In fact, they are probably
under more pressure. For although they leave college superbly
equipped to bring fresh leadership to traditionally male jobs, society hasn't yet caught up with this fact.

Along with economic pressure goes parental pressure. 14
Inevitably, the two are deeply intertwined.

I see many students taking pre-medical courses with joyless 15
tenacity. They go off to their labs as if they were going to the dentist. It saddens me because I know them in other corners of their life
as cheerful people.

"Do you want to go to medical school?" I ask them. 16

"I guess so," they say, without conviction, or "Not really." 17

"Then why are you going?" 18

"Well, my parents want me to be a doctor. They're paying all 19
this money and . . ."

Poor students, poor parents. They are caught in one of the old- 20
est webs of love and duty and guilt. The parents mean well; they are
trying to steer their sons and daughters toward a secure future. But
the sons and daughters want to major in history or classics or philosophy—subjects with no "practical" value. Where's the payoff on
the humanities? It's not easy to persuade such loving parents that
the humanities do indeed pay off. The intellectual faculties developed by studying subjects like history and classics—an ability to synthesize and relate, to weigh cause and effect, to see events in perspective—are just the faculties that make creative leaders in business
or almost any general field. Still, many fathers would rather put their
money on courses that point toward a specific profession—courses
that are pre-law, pre-medical, pre-business, or, as I sometimes heard
it put, "pre-rich."

But the pressure on students is severe. They are truly torn. One 21
part of them feels obligated to fulfill their parents' expectations;

after all, their parents are older and presumably wiser. Another part tells them that the expectations that are right for their parents are not right for them.

I know a student who wants to be an artist. She is very obvi- 22 ously an artist and will be a good one—she has already had several modest local exhibits. Meanwhile she is growing as a well-rounded person and taking humanistic subjects that will enrich the inner resources out of which her art will grow. But her father is strongly opposed. He thinks that an artist is a "dumb" thing to be. The student vacillates and tries to please everybody. She keeps up with her art somewhat furtively and takes some of the "dumb" courses her father wants her to take—at least they are dumb courses for her. She is a free spirit on a campus of tense students—no small achievement in itself—and she deserves to follow her muse.

Peer pressure and self-induced pressure are also intertwined, 23 and they begin almost at the beginning of freshman year.

"I had a freshman student I'll call Linda," one dean told me, 24 "who came in and said she was under terrible pressure because her roommate, Barbara, was much brighter and studied all the time. I couldn't tell her that Barbara had come in two hours earlier to say the same thing about Linda."

The story is almost funny—except that it's not. It's sympto- 25 matic of all the pressures put together. When every student thinks every other student is working harder and doing better, the only solution is to study harder still. I see students going off to the library every night after dinner and coming back when it closes at midnight. I wish they would sometimes forget about their peers and go to a movie. I hear the clacking of typewriters in the hours before dawn. I see the tension in their eyes when exams are approaching and papers are due: *"Will I get everything done?"*

Probably they won't. They will get sick. They will get 26 "blocked." They will sleep. They will oversleep. They will bug out. *Hey, Carlos, help!*

Part of the problem is that they do more than they are expect- 27 ed to do. A professor will assign five-page papers. Several students will start writing ten-page papers to impress him. Then more students will write ten-page papers, and a few will raise the ante to fifteen. Pity the poor student who is still just doing the assignment.

"Once you have twenty or thirty percent of the student popu- 28 lation deliberately overexerting," one dean points out, "it's bad for everybody. When a teacher gets more and more effort from his class, the student who is doing normal work can be perceived as not doing well. The tactic works, psychologically."

Why can't the professor just cut back and not accept longer papers? He can, and he probably will. But by then the term will be half over and the damage done. Grade fever is highly contagious and not easily reversed. Besides, the professor's main concern is with his course. He knows his students only in relation to the course and doesn't know that they are also overexerting in their other courses. Nor is it really his business. He didn't sign up for dealing with the student as a whole person and with all the emotional baggage the student brought along from home. That's what deans, masters, chaplains, and psychiatrists are for.   29

To some extent this is nothing new: a certain number of professors have always been self-contained islands of scholarship and shyness, more comfortable with books than with people. But the new pauperism has widened the gap still further, for professors who actually like to spend time with students don't have as much time to spend. They are also overexerting. If they are young, they are busy trying to publish in order not to perish, hanging by their fingernails onto a shrinking profession. If they are old and tenured, they are buried under the duties of administering departments—as departmental chairmen or members of committees—that have been thinned out by the budgetary axe.   30

Ultimately it will be the students' own business to break the circles in which they are trapped. They are too young to be prisoners of their parents' dreams and their classmates' fears. They must be jolted into believing in themselves as unique men and women who have the power to shape their own future.   31

"Violence is being done to the undergraduate experience," says Carlos Hortas. "College should be open-ended: at the end it should open many, many roads. Instead, students are choosing their goal in advance, and their choices narrow as they go along. It's almost as if they think that the country has been codified in the type of jobs that exist—that they've got to fit into certain slots. Therefore, fit into the best-paying slot.   32

"They ought to take chances. Not taking chances will lead to a life of colorless mediocrity. They'll be comfortable. But something in the spirit will be missing."   33

I have painted too drab a portrait of today's students, making them seem a solemn lot. That is only half of their story; if they were so dreary I wouldn't so thoroughly enjoy their company. The other half   34 is that they are easy to like. They are quick to laugh and to offer friendship. They are not introverts. They are unusually kind and are more considerate of one another than any student generation I have known.

Nor are they so obsessed with their studies that they avoid   35
sports and extracurricular activities. On the contrary, they juggle their crowded hours to play on a variety of teams, perform with musical and dramatic groups, and write for campus publications. But this in turn is one more cause of anxiety. There are too many choices. Academically, they have 1,300 courses to select from; outside class they have to decide how much spare time they can spare and how to spend it.

This means that they engage in fewer extracurricular pursuits   36
than their predecessors did. If they want to row on the crew and play in the symphony they will eliminate one; in the '60s they would have done both. They also tend to choose activities that are self-limiting. Drama, for instance, is flourishing in all twelve of Yale's residential colleges as it never has before. Students hurl themselves into these productions—as actors, directors, carpenters, and technicians—with a dedication to create the best possible play, knowing that the day will come when the run will end and they can get back to their studies.

They also can't afford to be the willing slave of organizations like   37
the *Yale Daily News*. . . . At the one-hundredth anniversary banquet of that paper—whose past chairmen include such once and future kings as Potter Stewart, Kingman Brewster, and William F. Buckley, Jr.—much was made of the fact that the editorial staff used to be small and totally committed and that "newsies" routinely worked fifty hours a week. In effect they belonged to a club; Newsies is how they defined themselves at Yale. Today's student will write one or two articles a week, when he can, and he defines himself as a student. I've never heard the word Newsie except at the banquet.

If I have described the modern undergraduate primarily as a   38
driven creature who is largely ignoring the blithe spirit inside who keeps trying to come out and play, it's because that's where the crunch is, not only at Yale but throughout American education. It's why I think we should all be worried about the values that are nurturing a generation so fearful of risk and so goal-obsessed at such an early age.

I tell students that there is no one "right" way to get ahead—   39
that each of them is a different person, starting from a different point and bound for a different destination. I tell them that change

is a tonic and that all the slots are not codified nor the frontiers closed. One of my ways of telling them is to invite men and women who have achieved success outside the academic world to come and talk informally with my students during the year. They are heads of companies or ad agencies, editors of magazines, politicians, public officials, television magnates, labor leaders, business executives, Broadway producers, artists, writers, economists, photographers, scientists, historians—a mixed bag of achievers.

I ask them to say a few words about how they got started. The   40
students assume that they started in their present profession and knew all along that it was what they wanted to do. Luckily for me, most of them got into their field by a circuitous route, to their surprise, after many detours. The students are startled. They can hardly conceive of a career that was not pre-planned. They can hardly imagine allowing the hand of God or chance to nudge them down some unforeseen trail.

Questions for Close Reading

1. What is the selection's thesis? Locate the sentence(s) in which Zinsser states his main idea. If he doesn't state the thesis explicitly, express it in your own words.
2. According to Zinsser, why are the pressures on college students today so harmful?
3. Zinsser says that some of the pressures are "intertwined." What does he mean? Give examples from the essay.
4. What actions or attitudes on the part of students can help free them from the pressures that Zinsser describes?
5. Refer to your dictionary as needed to define the following words used in the selection: *privy* (paragraph 3), *venerated* (6), *exhorted* (13), *tenacity* (15), *vacillates* (22), *furtively* (22), and *circuitous* (40).

Questions About the Writer's Craft

1. **The pattern.** When analyzing a subject, writers usually try to identify divisions and classifications that are—within reason—mutually exclusive. But Zinsser acknowledges that the four pressures he discusses can be seen as two distinct pairs, with each pair consisting of two "deeply intertwined" pressures. How does this overlapping of categories help Zinsser make his point?
2. **Other patterns.** In addition to using classification in this essay, what other pattern of development does Zinsser use? How does this additional pattern help him make his point?

3. Why do you suppose Zinsser uses the notes to Carlos as his essay's introduction? What profile of college students does the reader get from these notes?

4. In paragraph 4, the author writes that students want a map "they can follow unswervingly to career security, financial security, Social Security and, presumably, a prepaid grave." What tone is Zinsser using here? Where else does he use this tone?

Writing Assignments Using Division-Classification as a Pattern of Development

1. Zinsser writes as if all students are the same—panicky, overwrought, and materialistic. Take a position counter to his and write an essay explaining that campuses contain many students different from those Zinsser writes about. To support your point, categorize students into types, giving examples of what each type is like. Be sure that the categories you identify refute Zinsser's analysis of the typical student. The tone of your essay may be serious or playful. James Thurber's "University Days" (page 234) may give you some ideas for your essay, especially if you choose to approach your subject from a humorous or satiric perspective.

2. Is economic security the only kind of satisfaction that college students should pursue? Write an essay classifying the various kinds of satisfactions that students could aim for. At the end of the paper, include brief recommendations about ways that students could best spend their time preparing for these different kinds of satisfactions.

Writing Assignments Using Other Patterns of Development

3. Using Zinsser's analysis of the pressures on college students, write an essay explaining how these pressures can be reduced or eliminated. Give practical suggestions showing how students can avoid or get around the pressures. Also, indicate what society, parents, and college staff can do to help ease students' anxieties. You might benefit from gathering information on this topic in the library and/or on the Internet before writing.

4. Zinsser's essay indicates that today's students are "slotting" themselves into preordained careers and not leaving themselves open to later opportunities. Write an essay arguing that this tendency to specialize early in college is either beneficial *or* disastrous for students. Consider such issues as individual freedom, career confusion, changing job markets, changes in society, and the like.

Writing Assignments Using a Journal Entry as a Starting Point

5. Write an essay arguing in favor of *or* against the policy of requiring college students to take courses outside their major field. Take the ideas in your pre-reading journal entry and shape them into a convincing argument, remembering to cite the opposing point of view. To gain insight into the complexity of this issue, interview a variety of people having a broad range of viewpoints.

William Lutz

With a dash of humor, William Lutz (1941–), Professor of English at Rutgers University and former editor of the *Quarterly Review of Doublespeak*, writes about a subject he takes very seriously: doublespeak—the use of language to evade, deceive, and mislead. An expert on language, Lutz has appeared on many national television programs, among them the *Today Show*, the *Larry King Show*, and the *MacNeil-Lehrer News Hour*. Lutz, who has both a Ph.D. in English and a Doctor of Laws degree, has written over two dozen articles and is the author or coauthor of fourteen books, including the best-selling *Doublespeak: From Revenue Enhancement to Terminal Living* (1989) as well as its sequels, *Why No One Knows What Anyone's Saying Anymore* (1996) and *Doublespeak Defined: Cut Through the Bull★★★★ and Get to the Point* (1999). The following piece is from *Doublespeak*.

Pre-Reading Journal Entry

At one time or another, everyone twists language in order to avoid telling the full truth. In your journal, list several instances which demonstrate that indirect, partially-true language ("doublespeak") is sometimes desirable, even necessary. In each case, why was this evasive language used?

Doublespeak

There are no potholes in the streets of Tucson, Arizona, just 1 "pavement deficiencies." The Reagan Administration didn't propose any new taxes, just "revenue enhancement" through new "user's fees." Those aren't bums on the street, just "non-goal oriented members of society." There are no more poor people, just "fiscal underachievers." There was no robbery of an automatic teller machine, just an "unauthorized withdrawal." The patient didn't die because of medical malpractice, it was just a "diagnostic misadventure of a high magnitude." The U.S. Army doesn't kill the enemy anymore, it just "services the target." And the doublespeak goes on.

Doublespeak is language that pretends to communicate but 2 really doesn't. It is language that makes the bad seem good, the negative appear positive, the unpleasant appear attractive or at least tolerable. Doublespeak is language that avoids or shifts responsibility, language that is at variance with its real or purported meaning. It is language that conceals or prevents thought; rather than extending thought, doublespeak limits it. . . .

How to Spot Doublespeak

How can you spot doublespeak? Most of the time you will rec- 3
ognize doublespeak when you see or hear it. But, if you have any
doubts, you can identify doublespeak just by answering these questions: Who is saying what to whom, under what conditions and circumstances, with what intent, and with what results? Answering these questions will usually help you identify as doublespeak language that appears to be legitimate or that at first glance doesn't even appear to be doublespeak.

First Kind of Doublespeak

There are at least four kinds of doublespeak. The first is the 4
euphemism, an inoffensive or positive word or phrase used to avoid
a harsh, unpleasant, or distasteful reality. But a euphemism can also
be a tactful word or phrase which avoids directly mentioning a
painful reality, or it can be an expression used out of concern for the
feelings of someone else, or to avoid directly discussing a topic subject to a social or cultural taboo.

When you use a euphemism because of your sensitivity for 5
someone's feelings or out of concern for a recognized social or cultural taboo, it is not doublespeak. For example, you express your condolences that someone has "passed away" because you do not want to say to a grieving person, "I'm sorry your father is dead." When you use the euphemism "passed away," no one is misled. Moreover, the euphemism functions here not just to protect the feelings of another person, but to communicate also your concern for that person's feelings during a period of mourning. When you excuse yourself to go to the "restroom," or you mention that someone is "sleeping with" or "involved with" someone else, you do not mislead anyone about your meaning, but you do respect the social taboos about discussing bodily functions and sex in direct terms. You also indicate your sensitivity to the feelings of your audience, which is usually considered a mark of courtesy and good manners.

However, when a euphemism is used to mislead or deceive, it 6
becomes doublespeak. For example, in 1984 the U.S. State
Department announced that it would no longer use the word

"killing" in its annual report on the status of human rights in countries around the world. Instead, it would use the phrase "unlawful or arbitrary deprivation of life," which the department claimed was more accurate. Its real purpose for using this phrase was simply to avoid discussing the embarrassing situation of government-sanctioned killings in countries that are supported by the United States and have been certified by the United States as respecting the human rights of their citizens. This use of a euphemism constitutes doublespeak, since it is designed to mislead, to cover up the unpleasant. Its real intent is at variance with its apparent intent. It is language designed to alter our perception of reality.

The Pentagon, too, avoids discussing unpleasant realities when   7
it refers to bombs and artillery shells that fall on civilian targets as "incontinent ordnance." And in 1977 the Pentagon tried to slip funding for the neutron bomb unnoticed into an appropriations bill by calling it a "radiation enhancement device."

Second Kind of Doublespeak

A second kind of doublespeak is jargon, the specialized lan-   8
guage of a trade, profession, or similar group, such as that used by doctors, lawyers, engineers, educators, or car mechanics. Jargon can serve an important and useful function. Within a group, jargon functions as a kind of verbal shorthand that allows members of the group to communicate with each other clearly, efficiently, and quickly. Indeed, it is a mark of membership in the group to be able to use and understand the group's jargon.

But jargon, like the euphemism, can also be doublespeak. It can   9
be—and often is—pretentious, obscure, and esoteric terminology used to give an air of profundity, authority, and prestige to speakers and their subject matter. Jargon as doublespeak often makes the simple appear complex, the ordinary profound, the obvious insightful. In this sense it is used not to express but impress. With such doublespeak, the act of smelling something becomes "organoleptic analysis," glass becomes "fused silicate," a crack in a metal support beam becomes a "discontinuity," conservative economic policies become "distributionally conservative notions."

Lawyers, for example, speak of an "involuntary conversion" of   10
property when discussing the loss or destruction of property through theft, accident, or condemnation. If your house burns down or if your car is stolen, you have suffered an involuntary

conversion of your property. When used by lawyers in a legal situation, such jargon is a legitimate use of language, since lawyers can be expected to understand the term.

However, when a member of a specialized group uses its jargon 11 to communicate with a person outside the group, and uses it knowing that the nonmember does not understand such language, then there is doublespeak. For example, on May 9, 1978, a National Airlines 727 airplane crashed while attempting to land at the Pensacola, Florida airport. Three of the fifty-two passengers aboard the airplane were killed. As a result of the crash, National made an after-tax insurance benefit of $1.7 million, or an extra 18¢ a share dividend for its stockholders. Now National Airlines had two problems: It did not want to talk about one of its airplanes crashing, and it had to account for the $1.7 million when it issued its annual report to its stockholders. National solved the problem by inserting a footnote in its annual report which explained that the $1.7 million income was due to "the involuntary conversion of a 727." National thus acknowledged the crash of its airplane and the subsequent profit it made from the crash, without once mentioning the accident or the deaths. However, because airline officials knew that most stockholders in the company, and indeed most of the general public, were not familiar with legal jargon, the use of such jargon constituted doublespeak.

Third Kind of Doublespeak

A third kind of doublespeak is gobbledygook or bureaucratese. 12 Basically, such doublespeak is simply a matter of piling on words, of overwhelming the audience with words, the bigger the words and the longer the sentences the better. Alan Greenspan, then chair of President Nixon's Council of Economic Advisors, was quoted in *The Philadelphia Inquirer* in 1974 as having testified before a Senate committee that "It is a tricky problem to find the particular calibration in timing that would be appropriate to stem the acceleration in risk premiums created by falling incomes without prematurely aborting the decline in the inflation-generated risk premiums."

Nor has Mr. Greenspan's language changed since then. 13 Speaking to the meeting of the Economic Club of New York in 1988, Mr. Greenspan, now Federal Reserve chair, said, "I guess I should warn you, if I turn out to be particularly clear, you've probably misunderstood what I've said." Mr. Greenspan's doublespeak doesn't seem to have held back his career.

Sometimes gobbledygook may sound impressive, but when the   14
quote is later examined in print it doesn't even make sense. During
the 1988 presidential campaign, vice-presidential candidate Senator
Dan Quayle explained the need for a strategic-defense initiative by
saying, "Why wouldn't an enhanced deterrent, a more stable peace,
a better prospect to denying the ones who enter conflict in the first
place to have a reduction of offensive systems and an introduction
to defense capability? I believe this is the route the country will
eventually go."

The investigation into the Challenger disaster in 1986 revealed   15
the doublespeak of gobbledygook and bureaucratese used by too
many involved in the shuttle program. When Jesse Moore, NASA's
associate administrator, was asked if the performance of the shuttle
program had improved with each launch or if it had remained the
same, he answered, "I think our performance in terms of the liftoff
performance and in terms of the orbital performance, we knew more
about the envelope we were operating under, and we have been
pretty accurately staying in that. And so I would say the performance has not by design drastically improved. I think we have been
able to characterize the performance more as a function of our
launch experience as opposed to it improving as a function of time."
While this language may appear to be jargon, a close look will reveal
that it is really just gobbledygook laced with jargon. But you really
have to wonder if Mr. Moore had any idea what he was saying.

Fourth Kind of Doublespeak

The fourth kind of doublespeak is inflated language that is   16
designed to make the ordinary seem extraordinary; to make everyday things seem impressive; to give an air of importance to people,
situations, or things that would not normally be considered important; to make the simple seem complex. Often this kind of doublespeak isn't hard to spot, and it is usually pretty funny. While car
mechanics may be called "automotive internists," elevator operators
members of the "vertical transportation corps," used cars "pre-
owned" or "experienced cars," and black-and-white television sets
described as having "non-multicolor capability," you really aren't
misled all that much by such language.

However, you may have trouble figuring out that, when   17
Chrysler "initiates a career alternative enhancement program," it is

really laying off five thousand workers; or that "negative patient care outcome" means the patient died; or that "rapid oxidation" means a fire in a nuclear power plant.

The doublespeak of inflated language can have serious conse-   18 quences. In Pentagon doublespeak, "pre-emptive counterattack" means that American forces attacked first; "engaged the enemy on all sides" means American troops were ambushed; "backloading of augmentation personnel" means a retreat by American troops. In the doublespeak of the military, the 1983 invasion of Grenada was conducted not by the U.S. Army, Navy, Air Force, and Marines, but by the "Caribbean Peace Keeping Forces." But then, according to the Pentagon, it wasn't an invasion, it was a "predawn vertical insertion.". . .

The Dangers of Doublespeak

These . . . examples of doublespeak should make it clear that   19 doublespeak is not the product of carelessness or sloppy thinking. Indeed, most doublespeak is the product of clear thinking and is carefully designed and constructed to appear to communicate when in fact it doesn't. It is language designed not to lead but mislead. It is language designed to distort reality and corrupt thought. . . . When a fire in a nuclear reactor building is called "rapid oxidation," an explosion in a nuclear power plant is called an "energetic disassembly," the illegal overthrow of a legitimate government is termed "destabilizing a government," and lies are seen as "inoperative statements," we are hearing doublespeak that attempts to avoid responsibility and make the bad seem good, the negative appear positive, something unpleasant appear attractive; and which seems to communicate but doesn't. It is language designed to alter our perception of reality and corrupt our thinking. Such language does not provide us with the tools we need to develop, advance, and preserve our culture and our civilization. Such language breeds suspicion, cynicism, distrust, and, ultimately, hostility.

Questions for Close Reading

1. What is the selection's thesis? Locate the sentence(s) in which Lutz states his main idea. If he doesn't state the thesis explicitly, express it in your own words.

2. According to Lutz, four questions help people "spot" doublespeak. What are the questions? How do they help people distinguish between legitimate language and doublespeak?

3. Lutz's headings indicate simply "First Kind of Doublespeak," "Second Kind of Doublespeak," and so on. What terms does Lutz use to identify the four kinds of doublespeak? Cite one example of each kind.

4. What, according to Lutz, are the dangers of doublespeak?

5. Refer to your dictionary as needed to define the following words used in the selection: *variance* (paragraph 6), *esoteric* (9), *profundity* (9), *dividend* (11), and *initiative* (14).

Questions About the Writer's Craft

1. **The pattern.** Does Lutz make his four categories of doublespeak mutually exclusive, or does he let them overlap? Cite specific examples to support your answer. Why do you think Lutz took the approach he did?

2. **Other patterns.** What other patterns, besides division-classification, does Lutz use in this selection? Cite examples of at least two other patterns. Explain how each pattern reinforces Lutz's thesis.

3. Lutz quotes Alan Greenspan twice: first in paragraph 12 and again in paragraph 13. What is surprising about Greenspan's second comment (paragraph 13)? Why might Lutz have included this second quotation?

4. How would you characterize Lutz's tone in the essay? What key words indicate his attitude toward the material he discusses? Why do you suppose he chose this particular tone?

Writing Assignments Using Division-Classification as a Pattern of Development

∞ 1. According to Lutz, doublespeak "is language designed to alter our perception of reality." Using two of Lutz's categories (or any others you devise), analyze an advertisement or commercial that you think deliberately uses doublespeak to mislead consumers. Before writing your paper, read Ann McClintock's "Propaganda Techniques in Today's Advertising" (page 304). Feel free to include any of McClintock's interpretations in your paper.

2. Select *one* area of life that you know well. Possibilities include life in a college dormitory, the parent-child relationship, the dating scene, and sibling conflicts. Focus on a specific type of speech (for example, gossip, reprimands, flirtation, or criticism) that occurs in this area. Then identify the component parts of that type of speech. You might, for example, analyze dormitory gossip about individual students, couples, and professors. Reach some conclusions about the kinds of speech you discuss. Do you consider them funny, pathetic, or troubling? Your tone should be consistent with the conclusions you reach.

Writing Assignments Using Other Patterns of Development

∞ 3. Find a spoken or written example of doublespeak that disturbs you. Possibilities include a political advertisement, television commercial, newspaper article, or legal document. Write a letter of complaint to the appropriate person or office, using convincing examples to point out what is misleading about the communication. Caroline Rego's "The Fine Art of Complaining" (page 380) offers guidelines for writing effective letters of complaint.

∞ 4. In his essay, Lutz examines the relationship between language and perception. Identify two closely related terms, and contrast the different perceptions of reality represented by each term. For example, you might contrast "African-American" and "Negro," "Ms." and "Miss," "gay" and "homosexual," "dolls" and "action figures," or "pro-life" and "anti-abortion." Interviewing family, friends, and classmates will help you identify ideas to explore in the essay. For a discussion of the connection between language and perception, read at least one of the following: Alleen Pace Nilsen's "Sexism and Language" (page 225), Ann McClintock's "Propaganda Techniques in Today's Advertising" (page 304), Gloria Naylor's "Mommy, What Does 'Nigger' Mean?" (page 516), and Nat Hentoff's "Free Speech on Campus" (page 606).

Writing Assignments Using a Journal Entry as a Starting Point

∞ 5. Select from your pre-reading journal entry two or three compelling instances of *beneficial* doublespeak. Use these examples in an essay arguing that doublespeak isn't always harmful. For each example cited, contrast the positive effects of doublespeak with the potentially negative consequences of *not* using it. Brainstorming with others will help you generate convincing examples. Before you begin writing, consider reading at least two of the following essays, all of which illustrate varying instances of doublespeak: Audre Lorde's "The Fourth of July" (page 160), Beth Johnson's "Bombs Bursting in Air" (page 242), and Gloria Naylor's "Mommy, What Does 'Nigger' Mean?" (page 516).

Ann McClintock

Ann McClintock (1946–) was educated at Temple University in Philadelphia and later earned an advanced degree from the University of Pennsylvania. Formerly Director of Occupational Therapy at Ancora State Hospital in New Jersey, she has also worked as a freelance editor and writer. A frequent speaker before community groups, McClintock is especially interested in the effects of advertising on American life. The following selection, revised for this text, is part of a work in progress on the way propaganda techniques are used to sell products and political candidates.

Pre-Reading Journal Entry

How susceptible are you to ads and commercials? Do you consider yourself an easy target, or are you a "hard sell"? Have you purchased any products simply because you were won over by effective advertising strategies? What products have you not purchased because you deliberately didn't let yourself be swayed by advertisers' tactics? In your journal, reflect on these questions.

Propaganda Techniques in Today's Advertising

Americans, adults and children alike, are being seduced. They are being brainwashed. And few of us protest. Why? Because the seducers and the brainwashers are the advertisers we willingly invite into our homes. We are victims, content—even eager—to be victimized. We read advertisers' propaganda messages in newspapers and magazines; we watch their alluring images on television. We absorb their messages and images into our subconscious. We all do it—even those of us who claim to see through advertisers' tricks and therefore feel immune to advertising's charm. Advertisers lean heavily on propaganda to sell products, whether the "products" are a brand of toothpaste, a candidate for office, or a particular political viewpoint. 1

Propaganda is a systematic effort to influence people's opinions, to win them over to a certain view or side. Propaganda is not 2 necessarily concerned with what is true or false, good or bad. Propagandists simply want people to believe the messages being sent. Often, propagandists will use outright lies or more subtle deceptions to sway people's opinions. In a propaganda war, any tactic is considered fair.

When we hear the word "propaganda," we usually think of a   3 foreign menace: anti-American radio programs broadcast by a totalitarian regime or brainwashing tactics practiced on hostages. Although propaganda may seem relevant only in the political arena, the concept can be applied fruitfully to the way products and ideas are sold in advertising. Indeed, the vast majority of us are targets in advertisers' propaganda war. Every day, we are bombarded with slogans, print ads, commercials, packaging claims, billboards, trademarks, logos, and designer brands—all forms of propaganda. One study reports that each of us, during an average day, is exposed to over *five hundred* advertising claims of various types. This saturation may even increase in the future since current trends include ads on movie screens, shopping carts, videocassettes, even public television.

What kind of propaganda techniques do advertisers use? There   4 are seven basic types:

1. *Name Calling* Name calling is a propaganda tactic in   5 which negatively charged names are hurled against the opposing side or competitor. By using such names, propagandists try to arouse feelings of mistrust, fear, and hate in their audiences. For example, a political advertisement may label an opposing candidate a "loser," "fence-sitter," or "warmonger." Depending on the advertiser's target market, labels such as "a friend of big business" or "a dues-paying member of the party in power" can be the epithets that damage an opponent. Ads for products may also use name calling. An American manufacturer may refer, for instance, to a "foreign car" in its commercial—not an "imported" one. The label of foreignness will have unpleasant connotations in many people's minds. A childhood rhyme claims that "names can never hurt me," but name calling is an effective way to damage the opposition, whether it is another car maker or a congressional candidate.

2. *Glittering Generalities* Using glittering generalities is the   6 opposite of name calling. In this case, advertisers surround their products with attractive—and slippery—words and phrases. They

use vague terms that are difficult to define and that may have different meanings to different people: *freedom, democratic, all-American, progressive, Christian,* and *justice.* Many such words have strong, affirmative overtones. This kind of language stirs positive feelings in people, feelings that may spill over to the product or idea being pitched. As with name calling, the emotional response may overwhelm logic. Target audiences accept the product without thinking very much about what the glittering generalities mean—or whether they even apply to the product. After all, how can anyone oppose "truth, justice, and the American way"?

The ads for politicians and political causes often use glittering   7
generalities because such "buzz words" can influence votes. Election slogans include high-sounding but basically empty phrases like the following:

> "He cares about people." (That's nice, but is he a better candidate than his opponent?)
> "Vote for progress." (Progress by *whose* standards?)
> "They'll make this country great again." (What does "great" mean? Does "great" mean the same thing to others as it does to me?)
> "Vote for the future." (What kind of future?)
> "If you love America, vote for Phyllis Smith." (If I don't vote for Smith, does that mean I don't love America?)

Ads for consumer goods are also sprinkled with glittering gen-   8
eralities. Product names, for instance, are supposed to evoke good feelings: *Luvs* diapers, *New Freedom* feminine hygiene products, *Joy* liquid detergent, *Loving Care* hair color, *Almost Home* cookies, *Yankee Doodle* pastries. Product slogans lean heavily on vague but comforting phrases: Kinney is "The Great American Shoe Store," General Electric "brings good things to life," and Dow Chemical "lets you do great things." Chevrolet, we are told, is the "heartbeat of America," and Chrysler boasts cars that are "built by Americans for Americans."

3. *Transfer*   In transfer, advertisers try to improve the image of   9
a product by associating it with a symbol most people respect, like the American flag or Uncle Sam. The advertisers hope that the prestige attached to the symbol will carry over to the product. Many

companies use transfer devices to identify their products: Lincoln Insurance shows a profile of the president; Continental Insurance portrays a Revolutionary War minuteman; Amtrak's logo is red, white, and blue; Liberty Mutual's corporate symbol is the Statue of Liberty; Allstate's name is cradled by a pair of protective, fatherly hands.

Corporations also use the transfer technique when they sponsor prestigious shows on radio and television. These shows function as symbols of dignity and class. Kraft Corporation, for instance, sponsored a "Leonard Bernstein Conducts Beethoven" concert, while Gulf Oil is the sponsor of *National Geographic* specials and Mobil supports public television's *Masterpiece Theater.* In this way, corporations can reach an educated, influential audience and, perhaps, improve their public image by associating themselves with quality programming. 10

Political ads, of course, practically wrap themselves in the flag. Ads for a political candidate often show either the Washington Monument, a Fourth of July parade, the Stars and Stripes, a bald eagle soaring over the mountains, or a white-steepled church on the village green. The national anthem or "America the Beautiful" may play softly in the background. Such appeals to Americans' love of country can surround the candidate with an aura of patriotism and integrity. 11

4. *Testimonial*   The testimonial is one of advertisers' most-loved and most-used propaganda techniques. Similar to the transfer device, the testimonial capitalizes on the admiration people have for a celebrity to make the product shine more brightly—even though the celebrity is not an expert on the product being sold. 12

Print and television ads offer a nonstop parade of testimonials: here's William Shatner for Priceline.com; here's basketball star Michael Jordan eating Wheaties; a slew of well-known people (including rap star LL Cool J and the rock group Aerosmith) advertise clothing from the Gap; and Jerry Seinfeld assures us he never goes anywhere without his American Express card. Testimonials can sell movies, too; newspaper ads for films often feature favorable comments by well-known reviewers. And, in recent years, testimonials have played an important role in pitching books; the backs of paperbacks frequently list complimentary blurbs by celebrities. 13

Political candidates, as well as their ad agencies, know the value of testimonials. Barbra Streisand lent her star appeal to the 14 presidential campaign of Bill Clinton, while Arnold Schwarzenegger endorsed George Bush. Even controversial social issues are debated by celebrities. The nuclear-freeze debate, for instance, starred Paul Newman for the pro side and Charlton Heston for the con.

As illogical as testimonials sometimes are (Pepsi's Michael   15
Jackson, for instance, is a health-food adherent who does not drink soft drinks), they are effective propaganda. We like the *person* so much that we like the *product* too.

5. *Plain Folks*   The plain folks approach says, in effect, "Buy   16
me or vote for me. I'm just like you." Regular folks will surely like Bob Evans's Down on the Farm Country Sausage or good old-fashioned Countrytime Lemonade. Some ads emphasize the idea that "we're all in the same boat." We see people making long-distance calls for just the reasons we do—to put the baby on the phone to Grandma or to tell Mom we love her. And how do these folksy, warmhearted (usually saccharine) scenes affect us? They're supposed to make us feel that AT&T—the multinational corporate giant—has the same values we do. Similarly, we are introduced to the little people at Ford, the ordinary folks who work on the assembly line, not to bigwigs in their executive offices. What's the purpose of such an approach? To encourage us to buy a car built by these honest, hardworking "everyday Joes" who care about quality as much as we do.

Political advertisements make almost as much use of the "plain   17
folks" appeal as they do of transfer devices. Candidates wear hard hats, farmers' caps, and assembly-line coveralls. They jog around the block and carry their own luggage through the airport. The idea is to convince voters that the candidates are average people, not the elite—not wealthy lawyers or executives but common citizens.

6. *Card Stacking*   When people say that "the cards were   18
stacked against me," they mean that they were never given a fair chance. Applied to propaganda, card stacking means that one side may suppress or distort evidence, tell half-truths, oversimplify the facts, or set up a "straw man"— a false target—to divert attention from the issue at hand. Card stacking is a difficult form of propaganda both to detect and to combat. When a candidate claims that an opponent has "changed his mind five times on this important issue," we tend to accept the claim without investigating whether the candidate had good reasons for changing his mind. Many

people are simply swayed by the distorted claim that the candidate is "waffling" on the issue.

Advertisers often stack the cards in favor of the products they   19
are pushing. They may, for instance, use what are called "weasel words." These are small words that usually slip right past us, but that make the difference between reality and illusion. The weasel words are underlined in the following claims:

> "Helps control dandruff symptoms." (The audience usually interprets this as *stops* dandruff.)
>
> "Most dentists surveyed recommend sugarless gum for their patients who chew gum." (We hear the "most dentists" and "for their patients," but we don't think about how many were surveyed or whether the dentists first recommended that the patients not chew gum at all.)
>
> "Sticker price $1,000 lower than most comparable cars." (How many is "most"? What car does the advertiser consider "comparable"?)

Advertisers also use a card stacking trick when they make an   20
unfinished claim. For example, they will say that their product has "twice as much pain reliever." We are left with a favorable impression. We don't usually ask, "Twice as much pain reliever as what?" Or advertisers may make extremely vague claims that sound alluring but have no substance: Toyota's "Oh, what a feeling!"; Vantage cigarettes' "The taste of success"; "The spirit of Marlboro"; Coke's "the real thing." Another way to stack the cards in favor of a certain product is to use scientific-sounding claims that are not supported by sound research. When Ford claimed that its LTD model was "400% quieter," many people assumed that the LTD must be quieter than all other cars. When taken to court, however, Ford admitted that the phrase referred to the difference between the noise level inside and outside the LTD. Other scientific-sounding claims use mysterious ingredients that are never explained as selling points: "Retsyn," "special whitening agents," "the ingredient doctors recommend."

7. *Bandwagon* In the bandwagon technique, advertisers   21
pressure, "Everyone's doing it. Why don't you?" This kind of

propaganda often succeeds because many people have a deep desire not to be different. Political ads tell us to vote for the "winning candidate." Advertisers know we tend to feel comfortable doing what others do; we want to be on the winning team. Or ads show a series of people proclaiming, "I'm voting for the Senator. I don't know why anyone wouldn't." Again, the audience feels under pressure to conform.

In the marketplace, the bandwagon approach lures buyers. Ads   22
tell us that "nobody doesn't like Sara Lee" (the message is that you must be weird if you don't). They tell us that "most people prefer Brand X two to one over other leading brands" (to be like the majority, we should buy Brand X). If we don't drink Pepsi, we're left out of "the Pepsi generation." To take part in "America's favorite health kick," the National Dairy Council asks us, "Got Milk?" And Honda motorcycle ads, praising the virtues of being a follower, tell us, "Follow the leader. He's on a Honda."

Why do these propaganda techniques work? Why do so many of   23
us buy the products, viewpoints, and candidates urged on us by propaganda messages? They work because they appeal to our emotions, not to our minds. Often, in fact, they capitalize on our prejudices and biases. For example, if we are convinced that environmentalists are radicals who want to destroy America's record of industrial growth and progress, then we will applaud the candidate who refers to them as "treehuggers." Clear thinking requires hard work: analyzing a claim, researching the facts, examining both sides of an issue, using logic to see the flaws in an argument. Many of us would rather let the propagandists do our thinking for us.

Because propaganda is so effective, it is important to detect it   24
and understand how it is used. We may conclude, after close examination, that some propaganda sends a truthful, worthwhile message. Some advertising, for instance, urges us not to drive drunk, to become volunteers, to contribute to charity. Even so, we must be aware that propaganda is being used. Otherwise, we have consented to handing over to others our independence of thought and action.

Questions for Close Reading

1. What is the selection's thesis? Locate the sentence(s) in which McClintock states her main idea. If she doesn't state the thesis explicitly, express it in your own words.
2. What is *propaganda?* What mistaken associations do people often have with this term?
3. What are "weasel words"? How do they trick listeners?
4. Why does McClintock believe we should be better informed about propaganda techniques?
5. Refer to your dictionary as needed to define the following words used in the selection: *seduced* (paragraph 1), *warmonger* (5), and *elite* (17).

Questions About the Writer's Craft

1. **The pattern and other patterns.**   Before explaining the categories into which propaganda techniques can be grouped, McClintock provides a definition of propaganda. Is the definition purely informative, or does it have a larger objective? If you think the latter, what is the definition's broader purpose?
2. In her introduction, McClintock uses loaded words such as *seduced* and *brainwashed*. What effect do these words have on the reader?
3. Locate places in the essay where McClintock uses questions. Which are rhetorical and which are genuine queries?
4. What kind of conclusion does McClintock provide for the essay?

Writing Assignments Using Division-Classification as a Pattern of Development

1. McClintock cautions us to be sensitive to propaganda in advertising. Young children, however, aren't capable of this kind of awareness. With pen or pencil in hand, watch some commercials aimed at children, such as those for toys, cereals, and fast food. Then analyze the use of propaganda techniques in these commercials. Using division-classification, write an essay describing the main propaganda techniques you observed. Support your analysis with examples drawn from the commercials. Remember to provide a thesis that indicates your opinion of the advertising techniques. For additional insight into this issue, read Ellen Goodman's "Family Counterculture" (page 6).
2. Like advertising techniques, television shows can be classified. Avoiding the obvious system of classifying according to game shows, detective shows, and situation comedies, come up with your own original division-classification principle. Possibilities include how family life is depicted, the way work is presented, how male-female relationships are portrayed.

Using one such principle, write an essay in which you categorize popular TV shows into three types. Refer to specific shows to support your classification system. Your attitude toward the shows being discussed should be made clear.

Writing Assignments Using Other Patterns of Development

3. McClintock says that card stacking "distort[s] evidence, tell[s] half-truths, oversimpli[fies] the facts" (paragraph 18). Focusing on an editorial, a political campaign, a print ad, or a television commercial, analyze the extent to which card stacking is used as a persuasive strategy. Reading William Lutz's "Doublespeak" (page 296) will deepen your understanding of the extent to which the truth can be distorted.

4. To increase further your sensitivity to the moral dimensions of propaganda, write a proposal outlining an ad campaign for a real or imaginary product or elected official. The introduction to your proposal should identify who or what is to be promoted, and the thesis or plan of development should indicate the specific propaganda techniques you suggest. In the paper's supporting paragraphs, explain how these techniques would be used to promote your product or candidate.

Writing Assignments Using a Journal Entry as a Starting Point

5. Write an essay showing that, on the whole, you are fairly susceptible to *or* are fairly immune to advertising ploys. Drawing upon your pre-reading journal entry, illustrate your position with lively details of advertising campaigns that won you over—or that failed to sway you. Draw upon some of McClintock's terminology when describing advertisers' techniques. Your essay may have a serious or a playful tone.

Deborah Tannen

The recipient of grants from the National Endowment for the Humanities, the Rockefeller Foundation, and the National Science Foundation, Deborah Tannen (1945–) is a linguistics professor at Georgetown University and has been a Distinguished McGraw Lecturer at Princeton University. She has shared her scholarly research with the general public through appearances on the *Today* show and CNN, through pieces in *The New York Times* and the *Washington Post,* and in popular books, including *That's Not What I Meant: How Conversational Style Makes or Breaks Relationships* (1987), her best-selling *You Just Don't Understand: Women and Men in Conversation* (1990), *Talking From 9 to 5: How Women's and Men's Conversational Styles Affect Who Gets Ahead, Who Gets Credit, and What Gets Done at Work* (1994), *Gender and Discourse* (1994), and *The Argument Culture: Moving from Debate to Dialogue* (1998). The following selection, adapted from *You Just Don't Understand,* appeared in *The New York Times* in June 1990.

Pre-Reading Journal Entry

It's been said that men and women communicate in different ways. Do you agree? Why or why not? Take a few moments to respond to this question in your journal, drawing upon your experiences and observations.

But What Do You Mean?

Conversation is a ritual. We say things that seem obviously the thing to say, without thinking of the literal meaning of our words, any more than we expect the question "How are you?" to call forth a detailed account of aches and pains. 1

Unfortunately, women and men often have different ideas about what's appropriate, different ways of speaking. Many of the conversational rituals common among women are designed to take the other person's feelings into account, while many of the conversational rituals common among men are designed to maintain the one-up position, or at least avoid appearing one-down. As a result, when men and women interact—especially at work—it's often 2 women who are at the disadvantage. Because women are not trying to avoid the one-down position, that is unfortunately where they may end up.

Here, the biggest areas of miscommunication.   3

1. Apologies

Women are often told they apologize too much. The reason   4
they're told to stop doing it is that, to many men, apologizing seems synonymous with putting oneself down. But there are many times when "I'm sorry" isn't self-deprecating, or even an apology; it's an automatic way of keeping both speakers on an equal footing. For example, a well-known columnist once interviewed me and gave me her phone number in case I needed to call her back. I misplaced the number and had to go through the newspaper's main switchboard. When our conversation was winding down and we'd both made ending-type remarks, I added, "Oh, I almost forgot—I lost your direct number, can I get it again?" "Oh, I'm sorry," she came back instantly, even though she had done nothing wrong and *I* was the one who'd lost the number. But I understood she wasn't really apologizing; she was just automatically reassuring me she had no intention of denying me her number.

Even when "I'm sorry" *is* an apology, women often assume it   5
will be the first step in a two-step ritual: I say "I'm sorry" and take half the blame, then you take the other half. At work, it might go something like this:

> A: When you typed this letter, you missed this phrase I inserted.
> B: Oh, I'm sorry. I'll fix it.
> A: Well, I wrote it so small it was easy to miss.

When both parties share blame, it's a mutual face-saving device.   6
But if one person, usually the woman, utters frequent apologies and the other doesn't, she ends up looking as if she's taking the blame for mishaps that aren't her fault. When she's only partially to blame, she looks entirely in the wrong.

I recently sat in on a meeting at an insurance company where   7
the sole woman, Helen, said "I'm sorry" or "I apologize" repeatedly. At one point she said, "I'm thinking out loud. I apologize." Yet the meeting was intended to be an informal brainstorming session, and *everyone* was thinking out loud.

The reason Helen's apologies stood out was that she was the 8
only person in the room making so many. And the reason I was concerned was that Helen felt the annual bonus she had received was
unfair. When I interviewed the colleagues, they said that Helen was
one of the best and most productive workers—yet she got one of the
smallest bonuses. Although the problem might have been outright
sexism, I suspect her speech style, which differs from that of her
male colleagues, masks her competence.

Unfortunately, not apologizing can have its price too. Since so 9
many women use ritual apologies, those who don't may be seen as
hard-edged. What's important is to be aware of how often you say
you're sorry (and why), and to monitor your speech based on the
reaction you get.

2. Criticism

A woman who cowrote a report with a male colleague was 10
hurt when she read a rough draft to him and he leapt into a critical response—"Oh, that's too dry! You have to make it snappier!"
She herself would have been more likely to say, "That's a really
good start. Of course, you'll want to make it a little snappier when
you revise."

Whether criticism is given straight or softened is often a mat- 11
ter of convention. In general, women use more softeners. I
noticed this difference when talking to an editor about an essay I'd
written. While going over changes she wanted to make, she said,
"There's one more thing. I know you may not agree with me. The
reason I noticed the problem is that your other points are so lucid
and elegant." She went on hedging for several more sentences
until I put her out of her misery: "Do you want to cut that part?"
I asked—and of course she did. But I appreciated her tentativeness. In contrast, another editor (a man) I once called summarily
rejected my idea for an article by barking, "Call me when you have
something new to say."

Those who are used to ways of talking that soften the impact of 12
criticism may find it hard to deal with the right-between-the-eyes
style. It has its own logic, however, and neither style is intrinsically
better. People who prefer criticism given straight are operating on
an assumption that feelings aren't involved: "Here's the dope. I
know you're good; you can take it."

3. Thank-Yous

A woman manager I know starts meetings by thanking everyone   13
for coming, even though it's clearly their job to do so. Her "thank-
you" is simply a ritual.

A novelist received a fax from an assistant in her publisher's   14
office; it contained suggested catalog copy for her book. She immediately faxed him her suggested changes and said, "Thanks for running this by me," even though her contract gave her the right to
approve all copy. When she thanked the assistant, she fully expected him to reciprocate: "Thanks for giving me such a quick
response." Instead, he said, "You're welcome." Suddenly, rather
than an equal exchange of pleasantries, she found herself positioned
as the recipient of a favor. This made her feel like responding,
"Thanks for nothing!"

Many women use "thanks" as an automatic conversation starter   15
and closer; there's nothing literally to say thank you for. Like many
rituals typical of women's conversation, it depends on the goodwill
of the other to restore the balance. When the other speaker doesn't
reciprocate, a woman may feel like someone on a seesaw whose partner abandoned his end. Instead of balancing in the air, she has
plopped to the ground, wondering how she got there.

4. Fighting

Many men expect the discussion of ideas to be a ritual fight—   16
explored through verbal opposition. They state their ideas in the
strongest possible terms, thinking that if there are weaknesses someone will point them out, and by trying to argue against those objections, they will see how well their ideas hold up.

Those who expect their own ideas to be challenged will respond   17
to another's ideas by trying to poke holes and find weak links—as a
way of *helping*. The logic is that when you are challenged you will
rise to the occasion: Adrenaline makes your mind sharper; you get
ideas and insights you would not have thought of without the spur
of battle.

But many women take this approach as a personal attack. Worse,   18
they find it impossible to do their best work in such a contentious
environment. If you're not used to ritual fighting, you begin to hear
criticism of your ideas as soon as they are formed. Rather than making you think more clearly, it makes you doubt what you know.

When you state your ideas, you hedge in order to fend off potential attacks. Ironically, this is more likely to *invite* attack because it makes you look weak.

Although you may never enjoy verbal sparring, some women   19
find it helpful to learn how to do it. An engineer who was the only woman among four men in a small company found that as soon as she learned to argue she was accepted and taken seriously. A doctor attending a hospital staff meeting made a similar discovery. She was becoming more and more angry with a male colleague who'd loudly disagreed with a point she'd made. Her better judgment told her to hold her tongue, to avoid making an enemy of this powerful senior colleague. But finally she couldn't hold it in any longer, and she rose to her feet and delivered an impassioned attack on his position. She sat down in a panic, certain she had permanently damaged her relationship with him. To her amazement, he came up to her afterward and said, "That was a great rebuttal. I'm really impressed. Let's go out for a beer after work and hash out our approaches to this problem."

5. Praise

A manager I'll call Lester had been on his new job six months   20
when he heard that the women reporting to him were deeply dissatisfied. When he talked to them about it, their feelings erupted; two said they were on the verge of quitting because he didn't appreciate their work, and they didn't want to wait to be fired. Lester was dumbfounded: He believed they were doing a fine job. Surely, he thought, he had said nothing to give them the impression he didn't like their work. And indeed he hadn't. That was the problem. He had said *nothing*—and the women assumed he was following the adage "If you can't say something nice, don't say anything." He thought he was showing confidence in them by leaving them alone.

Men and women have different habits in regard to giving praise.   21
For example, Deirdre and her colleague William both gave presentations at a conference. Afterward, Deirdre told William, "That was a great talk!" He thanked her. Then she asked, "What did you think of mine?" and he gave her a lengthy and detailed critique. She found it uncomfortable to listen to his comments. But she assured herself that he meant well, and that his honesty was a signal that she, too, should be honest when he asked for a critique of his performance. As a matter of fact, she had noticed quite a few ways in which he

could have improved his presentation. But she never got a chance to tell him because he never asked—and she felt put down. The worst part was that it seemed she had only herself to blame, since she *had* asked what he thought of her talk.

But had she really asked for his critique? The truth is, when she asked for his opinion, she was expecting a compliment, which she felt was more or less required following anyone's talk. When he responded with criticism, she figured, "Oh, he's playing 'Let's critique each other'"—not a game she'd initiated, but one which she was willing to play. Had she realized he was going to criticize her and not ask her to reciprocate, she would never have asked in the first place.

It would be easy to assume that Deirdre was insecure, whether she was fishing for a compliment or soliciting a critique. But she was simply talking automatically, performing one of the many conversational rituals that allow us to get through the day. William may have sincerely misunderstood Deirdre's intention—or may have been unable to pass up a chance to one-up her when given the opportunity.

6. Complaints

"Troubles talk" can be a way to establish rapport with a colleague. You complain about a problem (which shows that you are just folks) and the other person responds with a similar problem (which puts you on equal footing). But while such commiserating is common among women, men are likely to hear it as a request to *solve* the problem.

One woman told me she would frequently initiate what she thought would be pleasant complaint-airing sessions at work. She'd talk about situations that bothered her just to talk about them, maybe to understand them better. But her male office mate would quickly tell her how she could improve the situation. This left her feeling condescended to and frustrated. She was delighted to see this very impasse in a section in my book *You Just Don't Understand,* and showed it to him. "Oh," he said, "I see the problem. How can we solve it?" Then they both laughed, because it had happened again: He short-circuited the detailed discussion she'd hoped for and cut to the chase of finding a solution.

Sometimes the consequences of complaining are more serious: A man might take a woman's lighthearted griping literally, and she can get a reputation as a chronic malcontent. Furthermore, she may be seen as not up to solving the problems that arise on the job.

7. Jokes

I heard a man call in to a talk show and say, "I've worked for 27 two women and neither one had a sense of humor. You know, when you work with men, there's a lot of joking and teasing." The show's host and guest (both women) took his comment at face value and assumed the women this man worked for were humorless. The guest said, "Isn't it sad that women don't feel comfortable enough with authority to see the humor?" The host said, "Maybe when more women are in authority roles, they'll be more comfortable with power." But although the women this man worked for *may* have taken themselves too seriously, it's just as likely that they each had a terrific sense of humor, but maybe the humor wasn't the type he was used to. They may have been like the woman who wrote to me: "When I'm with men, my wit or cleverness seems inappropriate (or lost!) so I don't bother. When I'm with my women friends, however, there's no hold on puns or cracks and my humor is fully appreciated."

The types of humor women and men tend to prefer differ. 28 Research has shown that the most common form of humor among men is razzing, teasing, and mock-hostile attacks, while among women it's self-mocking. Women often mistake men's teasing as genuinely hostile. Men often mistake women's mock self-deprecation as truly putting themselves down.

Women have told me they were taken more seriously when they 29 learned to joke the way the guys did. For example, a teacher who went to a national conference with seven other teachers (mostly women) and a group of administrators (mostly men) was annoyed that the administrators always found reasons to leave boring seminars, while the teachers felt they had to stay and take notes. One evening, when the group met at a bar in the hotel, the principal asked her how one such seminar had turned out. She reported, " As soon as you left, it got much better." He laughed out loud at her response. The playful insult appealed to the men—but there was a trade-off. The women seemed to back off from her after this. (Perhaps they were put off by her using joking to align herself with the bosses.)

There is no "right" way to talk. When problems arise, the cul-   30
prit may be style differences—and *all* styles will at times fail with
others who don't share or understand them, just as English won't
do you much good if you try to speak to someone who knows only
French. If you want to get your message across, it's not a question
of being "right"; it's a question of using language that's shared—or
at least understood.

Questions for Close Reading

1. What is the selection's thesis? Locate the sentence(s) in which Tannen
   states her main idea. If she doesn't state the thesis explicitly, express it in
   your own words.
2. Describe the differences in the way men and women perceive women's
   use of apologies. According to Tannen, how does this difference in perception create a problem?
3. What is the difference between "straight" and "softened" criticism
   (paragraph 11)? Does Tannen like one style more than the other? Why
   or why not?
4. What is a "ritual fight" (paragraph 16)? How, according to Tannen, do
   men and women differ in their responses to ritual fighting?
5. Refer to your dictionary as needed to define the following words used in
   the selection: *synonymous* (paragraph 4), *self-deprecating* (4), *reciprocate*
   (14), *contentious* (18), *dumbfounded* (20), *soliciting* (23), *commiserating*
   (24), and *malcontent* (26).

Questions About the Writer's Craft

1. **The pattern.**   Are Tannen's seven categories of male-female miscommunication mutually exclusive, or do they overlap? Cite specific examples to support your view. Why do you think she divided them as she did?
2. **Other patterns.**   Besides identifying the differences in men's and
   women's conversation rituals, Tannen often analyzes the causes and
   effects of these differences. Trace the causal chain in Tannen's discussion
   of apologies (paragraphs 7–9). How does this causal chain help Tannen
   reinforce her thesis?
3. Social scientists like Tannen often write impersonally, relying on statistics
   and a third-person point of view. Why do you suppose Tannen writes
   from the first-person point of view? What advantage does this point of
   view offer?
4. How would you characterize Tannen's tone in this selection? How does
   Tannen's attitude toward her subject and readers reinforce the essay's
   purpose?

Writing Assignments Using Division-Classification as a Method of Development

∞ **1.** Tannen's essay shows how typical male-female conversational patterns may put women at a disadvantage. Focus on two other closely related groups whose relationship is imbalanced because the communication behaviors of one are at odds with the group's best self-interest. You might examine the relationship between parents and children, teachers and students, or employers and employees. Like Tannen, categorize the areas in which the imbalance is apparent, and be sure to explain the consequences as well as the origins of the counterproductive communication behavior. For more on miscommunication between people, you might read Dave Barry's "The Ugly Truth About Beauty" (page 422), a humorous take on gendered behaviors.

∞ **2.** Given gender differences in communication styles, it's not surprising that men and women sometimes get embroiled in serious disagreements. Think about an argument between the sexes that you participated in or observed. Write an essay comparing and contrasting the gender-based communication patterns that contributed to the argument. End, as Tannen does, with suggestions for avoiding future conflicts. For additional insights into gender-based miscommunication, read one or more of the following: Barbara Ehrenreich's "What I've Learned From Men" (page 249), Camille Paglia's "Rape: A Bigger Danger Than Feminists Know" (page 615), and Susan Jacoby's "Common Decency" (page 622).

Writing Assignments Using Other Patterns of Development

∞ **3.** Tannen discusses differences in men's and women's communication rituals. Extending her work, examine another area where you perceive significant gender differences. Possibilities include the way men and women eat, socialize, shop for clothes, furnish their rooms, or watch television. Write an essay comparing and contrasting the sexes' attitudes and behaviors in this area. Brainstorm with others to gather anecdotes that convincingly exemplify the behaviors you describe. Your essay may be serious, light-hearted, or both. Before writing, read Barbara Ehrenreich's "What I've Learned From Men" (page 249) and Alleen Pace Nilsen's "Sexism and Language" (page 225) for additional perspectives on gender issues. You may also want to read relevant portions of Tannen's *You Just Don't Understand* or *Talking from 9 to 5.*

4. In this selection, Tannen shows that verbal behavior can be misunderstood. Write an essay showing that nonverbal behaviors can also be misinterpreted. Before you write, research nonverbal communication in the library and/or on the Internet. Armed with background information, spend time observing people's nonverbal communication in a variety of campus settings. When you write, do more than provide instances of misunderstanding; be sure to offer explanations of why such communication breakdowns occur.

Writing Assignments Using a Journal Entry as a Starting Point

5. Write an essay in which you agree *or* disagree with the claim that women and men have different styles of communication. To defend your contention, select and develop the most persuasive examples from your prereading journal entry. Brainstorming with friends, family, and classmates will help you generate additional supporting examples. Remember, too, to acknowledge the opposing argument, dismantling as much of it as you can. You might also consult two other essays that speculate about the nature of specific human behaviors: Stephen King's "Why We Crave Horror Movies" (page 455) and James Gleick's "Life As Type A" (page 509).

Additional Writing Topics

DIVISION-CLASSIFICATION

General Assignments

Choose one of the following subjects and write an essay developed wholly or in part through division-classification. Start by determining the purpose of the essay. Do you want to inform, compare and contrast, or persuade? Apply a single, significant principle of division or classification to your subject. Don't switch the principle midway through your analysis. Also, be sure that the types or categories you create are as complete and mutually exclusive as possible.

Division

1. A shopping mall
2. A video and/or stereo system
3. A fruit, such as a pineapple, an orange, or a banana
4. A tax dollar
5. A particular kind of team
6. A word-processing system
7. A human hand
8. A meal
9. A meeting
10. A favorite poem, story, or play
11. A favorite restaurant
12. A school library
13. A basement
14. A playground, gym, or other recreational area
15. A church service
16. A wedding or funeral
17. An eventful week in your life
18. A college campus
19. A television show or movie
20. A homecoming or other special weekend

Classification

1. People in a waiting room
2. Holidays
3. Closets
4. Roommates
5. Salad bars
6. Divorces

7. Beds
8. Students in a class
9. Shoes
10. Summer movies
11. Teachers
12. Neighbors
13. College courses
14. Bosses
15. TV watchers
16. Mothers or fathers
17. Commercials
18. Vacations
19. Trash
20. Relatives

Assignments With a Specific Purpose and Audience

1. You are a dorm counselor. During orientation week, you'll be talking to students on your floor about the different kinds of problems they may have with roommates. Write out your talk, describing each kind of problem and explaining how to cope.

2. As a driving instructor, you decide to prepare a lecture on the types of drivers that your students are likely to encounter on the road. In your lecture, categorize drivers according to a specific principle and show the behaviors of each type.

3. You have been asked to write a pamphlet for "new recruits"—new workers on your job, new students in your college class, new members of your sports team, or the like. In the pamphlet, identify at least three general qualities needed for the recruits' success.

4. A seasoned camp counselor, you've been asked to prepare, for new counselors, an informational sheet on children's emotional needs. Categorizing those needs into types, explain what counselors can do to nurture youngsters emotionally.

5. As your college newspaper's TV critic, you plan to write a review of the fall shows, most of which—in your opinion—lack originality. To show how stereotypical the programs are, select one type (for example, situation comedies or crime dramas). Then use a specific division-classification principle to illustrate that the same stale formulas are trotted out from show to show.

6. Asked to write an editorial for the campus paper, you decide to do a half-serious piece on taking "mental health" days off from classes. Structure your essay around three kinds of occasions when "playing hooky" is essential for maintaining sanity.

7

PROCESS ANALYSIS

WHAT IS PROCESS ANALYSIS?

Perhaps you've noticed the dogged determination of small children when they learn how to do something new. Whether trying to tie their shoelaces or tell time, little children struggle along, creating knotted tangles, confusing the hour with the minute hand. But they don't give up. Mastering such basic skills makes them feel less dependent on the adults of the world—all of whom seem to know how to do everything. Actually, none of us is born knowing how to do very much. We spend a good deal of our lives learning—everything from speaking our first word to balancing our first bank statement. Indeed, the milestones in our lives are often linked to the processes we have mastered: how to cross the street alone; how to drive a car; how to make a speech without being paralyzed by fear.

Process analysis, a technique that explains the steps or sequence involved in doing something, satisfies our need to learn as well as our curiosity about how the world works. All the self-help books flooding the market today (*Managing Stress, How to Make a Million in Real Estate, Ten Days to a Perfect Body*) are examples of process analysis. The instructions on the federal tax form and the recipes in a cookbook are also process analyses. Several television classics, now seen in reruns, also capitalize on our desire to learn how things happen: *The Wild Kingdom* shows how animals survive in faraway lands, and *Mission: Impossible* has great fun detailing elaborate plans for preventing the triumph of evil. Process analysis can be more than merely interesting or entertaining, though; it can be of critical importance. Consider a waiter hurriedly skimming the "Choking Aid" instructions posted on a restaurant wall or an air-traffic controller following emergency procedures in an effort to prevent a midair collision. In these last examples, the consequences could be fatal if the process analyses were slipshod, inaccurate, or confusing.

Undoubtedly, all of us have experienced less dramatic effects of poorly written process analyses. Perhaps you've tried to assemble a bicycle and spent hours sorting through a stack of parts, only to end up with one or two extra pieces never mentioned in the instructions. Or maybe you were baffled when putting up a set of wall shelves because the instructions used unfamiliar terms such as *mitered cleat, wing nut,* and *dowel pin.* No wonder many people stay clear of anything that actually admits "assembly required."

HOW PROCESS ANALYSIS FITS YOUR PURPOSE AND AUDIENCE

You will use process analysis in two types of writing situations: (1) when you want to give step-by-step instructions to readers showing how they can do something, or (2) when you want readers to understand how something happens even though they won't actually follow the steps outlined. The first kind of process analysis is *directional;* the second is *informational.*

When you look at the cooking instructions on a package of frozen vegetables or follow guidelines for completing a job application, you're reading directional process analysis. A serious essay explaining how to select a college and a humorous essay telling readers how to get on the good side of a professor are also examples of directional process analysis. Using a variety of tones, informational process analyses can range over equally diverse subjects; they can describe mechanical, scientific, historical, sociological, artistic, or psychological processes: for example, how the core of a nuclear reactor melts down; how television became so important in political campaigns; how abstract painters use color; how to survive a blind date.

Process analysis, both directional and informational, is often appropriate in *problem-solving situations.* In such cases, you say,

"Here's the problem and here's what should be done to solve the problem." Indeed, college assignments frequently take the form of problem-solving process analyses. Consider these examples:

> Community officials have been accused of mismanaging recent unrest over the public housing ordinance. Describe the steps the officials took, indicating why you think their strategy was unwise. Then explain how you think the situation should have been handled.

> Over the years, there have been many reports citing the abuse of small children in day care centers. What can parents do to guard against the mistreatment of their children?

> Because many colleges and universities have changed the eligibility requirements for financial aid, fewer students can depend on loans or scholarships. How can students cope with the increasing costs of obtaining a higher education?

Note that the first assignment asks students to explain what's wrong with the current approach before they present their own step-by-step solution. Problem-solving process analyses are often organized in this way. You may also have noted that none of the assignments explicitly requires an essay response using process analysis. However, the wording of the assignments—"*Describe* the steps," "*How* can students *cope*," "*What* can parents *do*"—suggests that process analysis would be an appropriate strategy for developing the responses.

Assignments don't always signal the use of process analysis so clearly. But during the prewriting stage, as you generate material to support your thesis, you'll often realize that you can best achieve your purpose by developing the essay—or part of it—using process analysis.

Sometimes process analysis will be the primary strategy for organizing an essay; other times it will be used to help make a point in an essay organized according to another pattern of development. Let's take a look at process analysis as a supporting strategy.

Assume that you're writing a *causal analysis* examining the impact of television commercials on people's buying behavior. To help readers see that commercials create a need where none existed before, you might describe the various stages in an advertising campaign to pitch a new, completely frivolous product. In an essay *defining* a good boss, you could convey the point that effective managers must be skilled at settling disputes by explaining the steps your boss took to resolve a heated disagreement between two employees. If you write an *argumentation-persuasion* paper urging the funding of programs to ease the plight of the homeless, you would have to dramatize for readers the tragedy of these people's lives. To achieve your purpose, you could devote part of the paper to an explanation of how the typical street person goes about the desperate jobs of finding a place to sleep and getting food to eat.

SUGGESTIONS FOR USING PROCESS ANALYSIS IN AN ESSAY

The suggestions that follow will be helpful whether you use process analysis as a dominant or a supportive pattern of development.

1. Identify the desired outcome of the process analysis. Many papers developed primarily through process analysis have a clear-cut purpose—simply to *inform* readers as objectively as possible about a process: "Here's a way of making french fries at home that will surpass the best served in your favorite fast-food restaurant." But a process analysis essay may also have a *persuasive* edge, with the writer advocating a point of view about the process, perhaps even urging a course of action: "If you don't want your arguments to deteriorate into ugly battles, you should follow a series of foolproof steps for having disagreements that leave friendships intact." Before starting to write, you need to decide if the essay is to be purely factual or if it will include this kind of persuasive dimension.

2. Formulate a thesis that clarifies your attitude toward the process. Like the thesis in any other paper, the thesis in a process analysis should do more than announce your subject. ("Here's how the college's work-study program operates.") It should also state or imply your attitude toward the process: "Enrolling in the college's work-study program has become unnecessarily complicated. The procedure could be simplified if the college adopted the helpful guidelines prepared by the Student Senate."

3. Keep your audience in mind. Only when you gauge how much your readers already know (or don't know) about the process can you determine how much explanation you'll have to provide. Suppose you've been asked to write an article informing students of the best way to use the university computer center. The article will be published in a newsletter for computer science majors. You would seriously misjudge your audience—and probably put them to sleep—if you explained in detail how to transfer material from disk to disk or how to delete information from a file. However, an article on the same topic prepared for a general audience—your composition class, for instance—would probably require such detailed instructions.

To determine how much explanation is needed, put yourself in your readers' shoes. Don't assume readers will know something just because you do. Ask questions such as these about your audience: "Will my readers need some background about the process before I describe it in depth?" "Are there technical terms I should define?" "If my essay is directional, should I specify near the beginning the ingredients, materials, and equipment needed to perform the process?" (For more help in analyzing your audience, see the checklist on page 20.)

4. Use prewriting to identify the steps in the process. To explain a sequence to your readers, you need to think through the process thoroughly, identifying its major parts and subparts, locating possible missteps or trouble spots. With your purpose, thesis, and audience in mind, use the appropriate prewriting techniques (brainstorming and mapping should be especially helpful) to break down the process into its component parts. In prewriting, it's a good idea to start by generating more material than you expect to use. Then the raw material can be shaped and pruned to fit your purpose and the needs of your audience. The amount of work done during the prewriting stage will have a direct bearing on the clarity of your presentation.

5. Identify the directional and informational aspects of the process analysis. Directional and informational process analyses are not always distinct. In fact, they may be complementary. Your prewriting may reveal that you'll need to provide background information about a process before outlining its steps. For example, in a paper describing a step-by-step approach for losing weight, you might first need to explain how the body burns calories. Or, in a paper on gardening, you could provide some theory about the way organic fertilizers work before detailing a plan for growing vegetables. Although both approaches may be appropriate in a paper, one generally predominates.

The kind of process analysis chosen has implications for the way you will relate to your reader. When the process analysis is *directional,* the reader is addressed in the *second person:* "You should first rinse the residue from the radiator by . . . ," or "Wrap the injured person in a blanket and then. . . ." (In the second example, the pronoun *you* is implied.)

If the process analysis has an *informational* purpose, you won't address the reader directly but will choose from a number of other options. For example, you might use the *first-person* point of view. In a humorous essay explaining how not to prepare for finals, you could cite your own disastrous study habits: "Filled with good intentions, I sit on my bed, pick up a pencil, open my notebook, and promptly fall asleep." The *third-person singular or plural* can also be used in informational process essays: "The door-to-door salesperson walks up the front walk, heart pounding, more than a bit nervous, but also challenged by the prospect of striking a deal," or "The new recruits next underwent a series of important balance tests in what was called the 'horror chamber.'" Whether you use the first, second, or third person, avoid shifting point of view midstream.

You might have noticed that in the third-person examples, the present tense ("walks up") is used in one sentence, the past tense ("underwent") in the other. The past tense is appropriate for events already completed, whereas the present tense is used for habitual or ongoing actions. ("A dominant male goose usually flies at the head of the V-wedge during migration.") The present tense is also effective when you want to lend a sense of dramatic immediacy to a process, even if the steps were performed in the past. ("The surgeon gently separates the facial skin and muscle from the underlying bony skull.") As with point of view, be on guard against changing tenses in the middle of your explanation.

6. Explain the process, one step at a time. Prewriting helped you identify key stages and sort out the directional and informational aspects of the process. Now you're ready to organize your raw material into an easy-to-follow sequence. At times your purpose will be to explain a process with a *fairly fixed chronological sequence:* how to make pizza, how to pot a plant, how to change a tire. In such cases, you should include all necessary steps, in the correct chronological order. However, if a strict chronological ordering of steps means that a particularly important part of the sequence gets buried in the middle, the sequence probably should be juggled so that the crucial step receives the attention it deserves.

Other times your goal will be to describe a process having *no commonly accepted sequence.* For example, in an essay explaining how to discipline a child or how to pull yourself out of a blue mood, you will have to come up with your own definition of the key steps and then arrange those steps in some logical order. You may also use process analyses to *reject* or *reformulate* a traditional sequence. In this case, you would propose a more logical series of steps: "Our system for electing congressional representatives is inefficient and undemocratic; it should be reformed in the following ways."

Whether the essay describes a generally agreed-on process or one that is not commonly accepted, you must provide all the details needed to explain the process. Your readers should be able to understand, even visualize, the process. There should be no fuzzy patches or confusing cuts from one step to another. Don't, however, go into obsessive detail about minor stages or steps. If you dwell for several hundred words on how to butter the pan, your readers will never stay with you long enough to learn how to make the omelet.

It's not unusual, especially in less defined sequences, for some steps in a process to occur simultaneously and overlap. When this happens, you should present the steps in the most logical order, being sure to tell your readers that several steps are not perfectly distinct and may merge. For example, in an essay explaining how a species becomes extinct, you would have to indicate that overpopulation of hardy strains and destruction of endangered breeds are often simultaneous events. You would also need to clarify that the depletion of food sources both precedes and follows the demise of a species.

7. Provide readers with the help they need to follow the sequence. As you move through the steps of a process analysis, don't forget to *warn readers about difficulties* they might encounter. For example, when writing a paper on the artistry involved in butterflying a shrimp, you might say something like this:

Next, make a shallow cut with your sharpened knife along the convex curve of the shrimp's intestinal tract. The tract, usually a faint black line along the outside curve of the shrimp, is faintly visible beneath the translucent flesh. But some shrimp have a thick orange, blue, or gray line instead of a thin black one. In all cases, be careful not to slice too deeply, or you will end up with two shrimp halves instead of one butterflied shrimp.

You have told readers what to look for, citing the exceptions, and have warned them against making too deep a cut. Anticipating spots where communication might break down is a key part of writing an effective process analysis.

Transitional words and phrases are also critical in helping readers understand the order of the steps being described. Time signals such as *first, next, now, while, after, before,* and *finally* provide readers with a clear sense of the sequence. Entire sentences can also be used to link parts of the process, reminding your audience of what has already been discussed and indicating what will now be explained: "Once the panel of experts finishes its evaluation of the exam questions, randomly selected items are field-tested in schools throughout the country."

8. Maintain an appropriate tone. When writing a process analysis essay, be sure your tone is consistent with your purpose, your attitude toward your subject, and the effect you want to have on the reader. When explaining how fraternities and sororities recruit new members, do you want to use an objective, nonjudgmental tone? To decide, take into account readers' attitudes toward your subject. Does your audience have a financial or emotional investment in the process being described? Does your own interest in the process coincide or conflict with that of your audience? Awareness of your readers' stance can be crucial. Consider another example: Assume you're writing a letter to the director of the student health center proposing a new system to replace the currently chaotic one. You'd do well to be tactful in your criticisms. Offend your reader, and your cause is lost. If, however, the letter is slated for the college newspaper and directed primarily to other students, you could adopt a more pointed, even sarcastic tone. Readers, you would assume, will probably share your view and favor change.

Once you settle on the essay's tone, maintain it throughout. If you're writing a light piece on the way computers are taking over our lives, you wouldn't include a grim step-by-step analysis of the way confidential computerized medical records may become public.

9. Open and close the process analysis effectively. A paper developed primarily through process analysis should have a strong beginning. The introduction should state the process to be described and imply whether the essay has an informational or directional intent.

If you suspect readers are indifferent to your subject, use the introduction to motivate them, telling them how important the subject is:

> Do you enjoy the salad bars found in many restaurants? If you do, you probably have noticed that the vegetables are always crisp and fresh--no matter how many hours they have been exposed to the air. What are the restaurants doing to make the vegetables look so inviting? There's a simple answer. Many restaurants dip and spray the vegetables with potent chemicals to make them appetizing.

If you think your audience may be intimidated by your subject (perhaps because it's complex or relatively obscure), the introduction is the perfect spot to reassure them that the process being described is not beyond their grasp:

> Studies show that many people willingly accept a defective product just so they won't have to deal with the uncomfortable process of making a complaint. But once a few easy-to-learn basics are mastered, anyone can register a complaint that gets results.

Most process analysis essays don't end as soon as the last step in the sequence is explained. Instead, they usually include some brief final comments that round out the piece and bring it to a satisfying close. This final section of the essay may summarize the main steps in the process—not by repeating the steps verbatim but by rephrasing and condensing them in several concise sentences. The conclusion can also be an effective spot to underscore the significance of the process, recalling what may have been said in the introduction about the subject's importance. Or the essay can end by echoing the note of reassurance that may have been included at the start.

STUDENT ESSAY

The following student essay was written by Robert Barry in response to this assignment:

> In "How to Say Nothing in 500 Words," Paul Roberts makes fun of college students' addiction to an inflated, padded writing style. By observing people, identify another example of an obsessive behavior that borders on the addictive. Then write a light-spirited essay explaining the various stages in the addiction. Since your essay is humorous in tone, be sure to describe an addiction that doesn't have serious consequences.

While reading Robert's paper, try to determine how effectively it applies the principles of process analysis. The annotations on Robert's paper and the commentary following it will help you look at the essay more closely.

Becoming a Videoholic
by Robert Barry

Introduction

In the last several years, videocassette recorders (VCRs) have become popular additions in many American homes. A recent newspaper article notes that one in three households has a VCR, with sales continuing to climb every day. VCRs seem to be the most popular technological breakthrough since television itself. No consumer warning labels are attached to these rapidly multiplying VCRs, but they should be. VCRs can be dangerous. Barely

Start of two-sentence thesis

aware of what is happening, a person can turn into a compulsive videotaper. The descent from innocent hobby to full-blown addiction takes place in several stages.

Topic sentence

First stage in process (VCR addiction)

In the first innocent stage, the unsuspecting person buys a VCR for occasional use. I was at this stage when I asked my parents if they would buy me a VCR as a combined birthday and high school graduation gift. With the VCR, I could tape reruns of Star Trek and Miami Vice, shows I would otherwise miss on nights I was at work. The VCR was perfect.

1

2

I hooked it up to the old TV in my bedroom, record-ed the intergalactic adventures of Captain Kirk and the high-voltage escapades of Sonny Crockett, then watched the tapes the next day. Occasionally, I taped a movie which my friends and I watched over the weekend. I had just one cassette, but that was all I needed since I watched every show I recorded and simply taped over the preceding show when I recorded another. In these early days, my VCR was the equivalent of light social drinking.

Beginning of analogy to alcoholism

Topic sentence

Second stage in process

In the second phase on the road to videoholism, an individual uses the VCR more frequently and begins to stockpile tapes rather than watch them. My troubles began in July when my family went to the shore for a week's vacation. I programmed the VCR to tape all five episodes of Star Trek while I was at the beach perfecting my tan. Since I used the VCR's long-play mode, I could get all five Star Treks on one cassette. But that ended up creating a prob-lem. Even I, an avid Trekkie, didn't want to watch five shows in one sitting. I viewed two shows, but the three unwatched shows tied up my tape, mak-ing it impossible to record other shows. How did I resolve this dilemma? Very easily. I went out and bought several more cassettes. Once I had these additional tapes, I was free to record as many Star Treks as I wanted, plus I could tape reruns of clas-sics like The Honeymooners and Mission: Impossible. Very quickly, I accumulated six Star Treks, four Honeymooners, and three Mission: Impossibles. Then a friend--who shall go name-less--told me that only eighty-two episodes of Star Trek were ever made. Excited by the thought that I could acquire as impressive a collection of tapes as a Hollywood executive, I continued recording Star Trek, even taping shows while I watched them. Clearly, my once innocent hobby was getting out of control. I was now using the VCR on a regular basis--the equivalent of several stiff drinks a day.

Continuation of analogy

Topic sentence

Third stage in process

In the third stage of videoholism, the amount of taping increases significantly, leading to an even more irrational stockpiling of cassettes. The catalyst that propelled me into this third stage was my par-ents' decision to get cable TV. Selfless guy that I am,

3

4

Continuation of analogy

I volunteered to move my VCR and hook it up to the TV in the living room, where the cable outlet was located. Now I could tape all the most recent movies and cable specials. With that delightful possibility in mind, I went out and bought two six-packs of blank tapes. Then, in addition to my regulars, I began to record a couple of other shows every day. I taped Rocky III, Magnum Force, a James Bond movie, an HBO comedy special with Eddie Murphy, and an MTV concert featuring Mick Jagger. Where did I get time to watch all these tapes? I didn't. Taping at this point was more satisfying than watching. Reason and common sense were abandoned. Getting things on tape had become an obsession, and I was taping all the time.

Topic sentence

Fourth stage in process

Continuation of analogy

In the fourth stage, videoholism creeps into other parts of the addict's life, influencing behavior in strange ways. Secrecy becomes commonplace. One day, my mother came into my room and saw my bookcase filled with tapes--rather than with the paperbacks that used to be there. "Robert," she exclaimed, "isn't this getting a bit out of hand?" I assured her it was just a hobby, but I started hiding my tapes, putting them in a suitcase stored in my closet. I also taped at night, slipping downstairs to turn on the VCR after my parents had gone to bed and getting down first thing in the morning to turn off the VCR and remove the cassette before my parents noticed. Also, denial is not unusual during this stage of VCR addiction. At the dinner table, when my younger sister commented, "Robert tapes all the time," I laughingly told everyone--including myself--that the taping was no big deal. I was getting bored with it and was going to stop any day, I assured my family. Obsessive behavior also characterizes the fourth stage of videoholism. Each week, I pulled out the TV magazine from the Sunday paper and went through it carefully, circling in red all the shows I wanted to tape. Another sign of addiction was my compulsive organization of all the tapes I had stockpiled. Working more diligently than I ever had for any term paper, I typed up labels and attached them to each cassette. I also created an elaborate list that showed my tapes broken down

5

into categories such as Westerns, horror movies, and comedies.

Topic sentence ———→ In the final stage of an addiction, the individual 6
either succumbs completely to the addiction or is
Continuation of ____ able to break away from the habit. I broke my addic-
analogy   tion, and I broke it cold turkey. This total withdraw-
                        al occurred when I went off to college. There was no
Final stage in   point in taking my VCR to school because TVs were
process   not allowed in the freshman dorms. Even though
there were many things to occupy my time during
the school week, cold sweats overcame me whenever I thought about everything on TV I was not
taping. I even considered calling home and asking
members of my family to tape things for me, but I
knew they would think I was crazy. At the beginning of the semester, I also had to resist the overwhelming desire to travel the three hours home
every weekend so I could get my fix. But after a
while, the urgent need to tape subsided. Now,
months later, as I write this, I feel detached and
sober.

Conclusion   I have no illusions, though. I know that once a 7
videoholic, always a videoholic. Soon I will return
home for the holidays, which, as everyone knows,
can be a time for excess eating--and taping. But I
Final references ——— will cope with the pressure. I will take each day one
to analogy   at a time. I will ask my little sister to hide my blank
tapes. And if I feel myself succumbing to the temp-
tations of taping, I will pick up the telephone and
dial the videoholics' hotline: 1-800-VCR-TAPE. I will
win the battle.

COMMENTARY

Purpose, thesis, and tone.   Robert's essay is an example of *informational process analysis;* his purpose is to describe—rather than
teach—the process of becoming a "videoholic." The title, with its
coined term *videoholic,* tips us off that the essay is going to be entertaining. And the introductory paragraph clearly establishes the essay's
playful, mock-serious tone. The tone established, Robert briefly
defines the term *videoholic* as a "compulsive videotaper" and then

moves to the essay's *thesis:* "Barely aware of what is happening, a person can turn into a compulsive videotaper. The descent from innocent hobby to full-blown addiction takes place in several stages."

Throughout the essay, Robert sustains the introduction's humor by mocking his own motivations and poking fun at his quirks: "Selfless guy that I am, I volunteered to move my VCR" (paragraph 4), and "Working more diligently than I ever had for any term paper, I typed up labels" (5). Robert probably uses a bit of *dramatic license* when reporting some of his obsessive behavior, and we, as readers, understand that he's exaggerating for comic effect. Most likely he didn't break out in a cold sweat at the thought of the TV shows he was unable to tape, and he probably didn't hide his tapes in a suitcase. Nevertheless, this tinkering with the truth is legitimate because it allows Robert to create material that fits the essay's lightly satiric tone.

Organization and topic sentences.   To meet the requirements of the assignment, Robert needed to provide a *step-by-step* explanation of a process. And because he invented the term *videoholism,* Robert also needed to invent the stages in the progression of his addiction. During his prewriting, Robert discovered five stages in his videoholism: Presented *chronologically,* these stages provide the organizing focus for his paper. Specifically, each supporting paragraph is devoted to one stage, with the *topic sentence* for each paragraph indicating the stage's distinctive characteristics.

Transitions.   Although Robert's essay is playful, it is nonetheless a process analysis and so must have an easy-to-follow structure. Keeping this in mind, Robert wisely includes *transitions* to signal what happened at each stage of his videoholism: "*Once* I had these additional tapes, I was free to record" (paragraph 3); "*Then,* in addition to my regulars, I began to record" (4); "*One day,* my mother came into my room" (5); and "*But after a while,* the urgent need to tape subsided" (6). In addition to such transitions, Robert also uses crisp questions to move from idea to idea within a paragraph: "How did I resolve this dilemma? Very easily. I . . . bought several more cassettes" (3), and "Where did I get time to watch all these tapes? I didn't" (4).

Other patterns of development.   Even though Robert's essay is a process analysis, it contains elements of other patterns of development.

For example, his paper is unified by an *analogy*—a sustained *comparison* between Robert's video addiction and the obviously more serious addiction to alcohol. Handled incorrectly, the analogy could have been offensive, but Robert makes the comparison work to his advantage. The analogy is stated specifically in several spots: "In these early days, my VCR was the equivalent of light social drinking" (paragraph 2); "I was now using the VCR on a regular basis—the equivalent of several stiff drinks a day" (3). Another place where Robert touches wittily on the analogy occurs in the middle of the fourth paragraph: "I went out and bought two six-packs of blank tapes." To illustrate his progression toward video-holism, Robert depicts the *effects* of his addiction. Finally, he generates numerous lively details or *examples* to illustrate the different stages in his addiction.

Two unnecessary sentences.   Perhaps you noticed that Robert runs into a minor problem at the end of the fourth paragraph. Starting with the sentence "Reason and common sense were abandoned," he begins to ramble and repeat himself. The paragraph's last two sentences fail to add anything substantial. Take a moment to read paragraph 4 aloud, omitting the last two sentences. Note how much sharper the new conclusion is: "Where did I get time to watch all these tapes? I didn't. Taping at this point was more satisfying than watching." This new ending says all that needs to be said.

Revising the first draft.   When it was time to revise, Robert—in spite of his apprehension—showed his paper to his roommate and asked him to read it out loud. Robert knew this strategy would provide a more objective point of view on his work. His roommate, at first an unwilling recruit, nonetheless laughed as he read the essay aloud. That was just the response Robert wanted. But when his roommate got to the conclusion, Robert heard that the closing paragraph was flat and anticlimactic. Here is Robert's original conclusion.

Original Version of the Conclusion

I have no illusions, though, that I am over my videoholism. Soon I will be returning home for the holidays, which can be a time for excess taping. All I can do is ask my little sister to hide my blank tapes. After that, I will hope for the best.

Robert and his roommate brainstormed ways to make the conclusion livelier and more in spirit with the rest of the essay. They decided that the best approach would be to continue the playful, mock-serious tone that characterized earlier parts of the essay. Robert thus made three major changes in the conclusion. First, he tightened the first sentence of the paragraph ("I have no illusions, though, that I am over my videoholism"), making it crisper and more dramatic: "I have no illusions, though." Second, he added a few sentences to sustain the light, self-deprecating tone he had used earlier: "I know that once a videoholic, always a videoholic"; "But I will cope with the pressure"; "I will win the battle." Third, and perhaps most important, he returned to the alcoholism analogy: "I will take each day one at a time. . . . And if I feel myself succumbing to the temptations of taping, I will pick up the telephone and dial the videoholics' hotline. . . ."

These weren't the only changes Robert made while reworking his paper, but they give you some sense of how sensitive he was to the effect he wanted to achieve. Certainly, the recasting of the conclusion was critical to the overall success of this amusing essay.

ACTIVITIES: PROCESS ANALYSIS

Prewriting Activities

1. Imagine you're writing two essays: One *defines* the term "comparison shopping"; the other *contrasts* two different teaching styles. Jot down ways you might use process analysis in each essay.

2. Select *one* of the essay topics that follow and determine what your purpose, tone, and point of view would be for each audience indicated in parentheses. Then use brainstorming, questioning, mapping, or another prewriting technique to identify the points you'd cover for each audience. Finally, organize the raw material, noting the differences in emphasis and sequence for each group of readers.

   a. How to buy a car (*young people who have just gotten a driver's license; established professionals*)
   b. How children acquire their values (*first-time parents; elementary school teachers*)
   c. How to manage money (*grade-school children; college students*)

     d. How loans or scholarships are awarded to incoming students on your campus (*high school graduates applying for financial aid; high school guidance counselors*)

     e. How arguments can strengthen relationships (*preteen children; young adults*)

     f. How to relax (*college students; parents with young children*)

Revising Activities

3. Below is the brainstorming for a brief essay that describes the steps involved in making a telephone sales call. The paper has the following thesis: "Establishing rapport with customers is the most challenging and the most important part of phone sales." Revise the brainstormed material by deleting anything that undermines the paper's unity and organizing the steps in a logical sequence.

- Keep customers on the phone as long as possible to learn what they need
- The more you know about customers' needs the better
- The tone of the opening comments is very important
- Gently introduce the product
- Use a friendly tone in opening comments
- End on a friendly tone, too
- Don't introduce the product right away
- Growing rudeness in society. Some people hang up right away. Very upsetting.
- Try in a friendly way to keep the person on the phone
- Many people are so lonely they don't mind staying on the phone so they can talk to someone--anyone
- How sad that there's so much loneliness in the world
- Describe the product's advantages--price, convenience, installment plan
- If person is not interested, try in a friendly way to find out why
- Don't tell people that their reasons for not being interested are silly
- Don't push people if they're not interested
- Encourage credit card payment--the product will arrive earlier
- Explain payment--check, money order, or credit card payment

4. Reprinted here is a paragraph from the first draft of a humorous essay advising shy college students how to get through a typical day. Written as a process analysis, the paragraph outlines techniques for

surviving class. Revise the paragraph, deleting digressions that disrupt the paragraph's unity, eliminating unnecessary repetition, and sequencing the steps in the proper order. Also correct inappropriate shifts in person and add transitions where needed. Feel free to add any telling details.

Simply attending class can be stressful for shy people. Several strategies, though, can lessen the trauma. Shy students should time their arrival to coincide with that of most other class members--about two minutes before the class is scheduled to begin. If you arrive too early, you may be seen sitting alone, or, even worse, may actually be forced to talk with another early arrival. If you arrive late, all eyes will be upon you. Before heading to class, the shy student should dress in the least conspicuous manner possible--say, in the blue jeans, sweatshirt, and sneakers that 99.9 percent of your classmates wear. That way you won't stand out from everyone else. Take a seat near the back of the room. Don't, however, sit at the very back since professors often take sadistic pleasure in calling on students back there, assuming they chose those seats because they didn't want to be called on. A friend of mine who is far from shy uses just the opposite ploy. In an attempt to get in good with her professors, she sits in the front row and, incredibly enough, volunteers to participate. However, since shy people don't want to call attention to themselves, they should stifle any urge to sneeze or cough. You run the risk of having people look at you or offer you a tissue or cough drop. And of course, never, ever volunteer to answer. Such a display of intelligence is sure to focus all eyes on you. In other words, make yourself as inconspicuous as possible. How, you might wonder, can you be inconspicuous if you're blessed (or cursed) with great looks? Well, . . . have you ever considered earning your degree through the mail?

Bill Bryson

Bill Bryson (1951–) has kept audiences on both sides of the Atlantic chuckling by exposing, in rollicking, down-to-earth fashion, the humor inherent in the world around him. A native of Iowa who resided in England for almost twenty years, Bryson earned fame as a columnist and best-selling author in England before returning to live with his wife and four children in Hanover, New Hampshire. Bryson's cross-cultural sensibility and talent for unearthing the absurd are apparent in his books on language, including *The Mother Tongue* (1990), and in his travel writing, including *In a Sunburned Country* (2000) and *A Walk in the Woods,* his best-selling 1998 account of a hike along the Appalachian trail. The following selection first appeared in *I'm a Stranger Here Myself: Notes on Returning to America After 20 Years Away* (1999).

Pre-Reading Journal Entry

Like most people, you've probably found that today's sophisticated technologies often complicate life, rather than making it easier. Take a moment to list in your journal some of the technologies that have added stress to your life. Under each technology, jot down some specifics about the problems you've experienced.

Your New Computer

Congratulations. You have purchased an Anthrax[1]/2000 Multimedia 615X Personal Computer with Digital Doo-Dah Enhancer. It will give years of faithful service, if you ever get it up and running. Also included with your PC is a bonus pack of preinstalled software—Lawn Mowing Planner, Mr. Arty-Farty, Blank Screen Saver, and Antarctica Route Finder—which will provide hours of pointless diversion while using up most of your computer's spare memory. 1

So turn the page and let's get started! 2

---

[1]An infectious, sometimes fatal disease of warm-blooded animals, including humans (editors' note).

Getting Ready

Congratulations. You have successfully turned the page and are   3
ready to proceed.

Important meaningless note: The Anthrax/2000 is configured   4
to use 80386, 214J10, or higher processors running at 2472 Herz
on variable speed spin cycle. Check your electrical installations and
insurance policies before proceeding. Do not machine wash.

To prevent internal heat buildup, select a cool, dry environment   5
for your computer. The bottom shelf of the refrigerator is ideal.

Unpack the box and examine its contents. (Warning: Do not   6
open box if contents are missing or faulty, as this will invalidate your
warranty. Return all missing contents in their original packaging
with a note explaining where they have gone and a replacement will
be sent within twelve working months.)

The contents of the box should include some of the following: 7
monitor with mysterious De Gauss[2] button; keyboard; computer
unit; miscellaneous wires and cables not necessarily designed for this
model; 2,000-page Owner's Manual; Short Guide to the Owner's
Manual; Quick Guide to the Short Guide to the Owner's Manual;
Laminated Super-Kwik Set-Up Guide for People Who Are
Exceptionally Impatient or Stupid; 1,167 pages of warranties,
vouchers, notices in Spanish, and other loose pieces of paper; 292
cubic feet of Styrofoam packing material.

Something They Didn't Tell You at the Store

Because of the additional power needs of the preinstalled bonus   8
software, you will need to acquire an Anthrax/2000 auxiliary software upgrade pack, a 900-volt memory capacitator for the auxiliary
software pack, a 50-megaherz oscillator unit for the memory capacitator, 2,500 mega-gigabytes of additional memory for the oscillator, and an electrical substation.

Setting Up

Congratulations. You are ready to set up. If you have not yet   9
acquired a degree in electrical engineering, now is the time to do so.

---

[2]Refers to neutralizing a magnetic field (something a computer owner would not
want to happen to a hard drive) (editors' note).

Connect the monitor cable (A) to the portside outlet unit (D);   10
attach power offload unit suborbiter (Xii) to the coaxial AC/DC
servo channel (G); plug three-pin mouse cable into keyboard housing unit (make extra hole if necessary); connect modem (B2) to
offside parallel audio/video lineout jack. Alternatively, plug the
cables into the most likely looking holes, switch on, and see what
happens.

Additional important meaningless note: The wires in the   11
ampule modulator unit are marked as follows according to international convention: blue = neutral or live; yellow = live or blue; blue
and live = neutral and green; black = instant death. (Except where
prohibited by law.)

Switch the computer on. Your hard drive will automatically   12
download. (Allow three to five days.) When downloading is complete, your screen will say: "Yeah, what?"

Now it is time to install your software. Insert Disc A (marked   13
"Disk D" or "Disk G") into Drive Slot B or J, and type "Hello!
Anybody home?" At the DOS command prompt, enter you License
Verification Number. Your License Verification Number can be
found by entering your Certified User Number, which can be found
by entering your License Verification Number. If you are unable to
find your License Verification or Certified User numbers, call the
Software Support Line for assistance. (Please have your License
Verification and Certified User numbers handy as the support staff
cannot otherwise assist you.)

If you have not yet committed suicide, then insert Installation   14
Diskette 1 in drive slot 2 (or vice versa) and follow the instructions
on your screen. (Note: Owing to a software modification, some
instructions will appear in Turkish.) At each prompt, reconfigure the
specified file path, double-click on the button launch icon, select a
single equation default file from the macro selection register, insert
the VGA graphics card in the rear aerofoil, and type "C:\>" followed
by the birthdates of all the people you have ever known.

Your screen will now say: "Invalid file path. Whoa! Abort or   15
continue?" Warning: Selecting "Continue" may result in irreversible
file compression and a default overload in the hard drive. Selecting
"Abort," on the other hand, will require you to start the installation
process all over again. Your choice.

When the smoke has cleared, insert disc A2 (marked "Disc A1")   16
and repeat as directed with each of the 187 other discs.

When installation is complete, return to file path, and type your 17
name, address, and credit card numbers and press "SEND." This will
automatically register you for our free software prize, "Blank
Screensaver IV: Nighttime in Deep Space," and allow us to pass
your name to lots and lots of computer magazines, online services,
and other commercial enterprises, who will be getting in touch
shortly.

Congratulations. You are now ready to use your computer. 18
Here are some simple exercises to get you off to a flying start.

Writing a Letter

Type "Dear ——" and follow it with a name of someone you 19
know. Write a few lines about yourself, and then write, "Sincerely
yours" followed by your own name. Congratulations.

Saving a File

To save your letter, select File Menu. Choose Retrieve from 20
Sub-Directory A, enter a backup file number, and place an insertion
point beside the macro dialogue button. Select secondary text box
from the merge menu, and double-click on the supplementary
cleared document window. Assign the tile cascade to a merge file
and insert in a text equation box. Alternatively, write the letter out
in longhand and put it in a drawer.

Advice on Using the Spreadsheet Facility

Don't. 21

Troubleshooting Section

You will have many, many problems with your computer. Here 22
are some common problems and their solutions.

Problem: My computer won't turn on. 23
Solution: Check to make sure the computer is plugged in; check 24
to make sure the power button is in the ON position; check the
cables for damage; dig up underground cables in your yard and
check for damage; drive out into country and check electricity
pylons for signs of fallen wires; call hotline.

Problem: My keyboard doesn't seem to have any keys. 25
Solution: Turn the keyboard the right way up. 26

Problem: My mouse won't drink its water or go on the spinning 27
wheel.

Solution: Try a high-protein diet or call your pet shop support 28
line.

Problem: I keep getting a message saying: "Non-System General 29
Protection Fault."

Solution: This is probably because you are trying to use the 30
computer. Switch the computer to OFF mode and any annoying messages will disappear.

Problem: My computer is a piece of useless junk. 31

Correct—and congratulations. You are now ready to upgrade to 32
an Anthrax/3000 Turbo model, or go back to pen and paper.

Questions for Close Reading

1. What is the selection's thesis? Locate the sentence(s) in which Bryson
   states his main idea. If he doesn't state the thesis explicitly, express it in
   your own words.
2. Paragraphs 6 and 13 target a similar flaw in computer manuals. What
   unfortunate tendency do the paragraphs ridicule?
3. Using humor to make a serious point, in paragraph 8 Bryson levels a
   not-so-funny charge against computer manufacturers. What accusation
   does he make? What support for this accusation does he provide?
4. Which Anthrax model does Bryson cite at the beginning of the essay?
   Which does he refer to at the end? In what way do these two references
   reinforce Bryson's thesis?
5. Refer to your dictionary as needed to define the following words used in
   the selection: *diversion* (paragraph 1), *configured* (4), *invalidate* (6), *miscellaneous* (7), *auxiliary* (8), *convention* (11), and *pylons* (24).

Questions About the Writer's Craft

1. **The pattern.** Is Bryson's process analysis *directional* or *informational*
   (see pages 329–330)? How do you know? What *purpose* (see page 328)
   do you think Bryson had in mind when writing the piece? Explain.
2. Although Bryson voices serious complaints about computers, their manufacturers, and computer manuals, he uses wry humor to do so. Why do
   you think Bryson uses humor rather than angry accusation to voice his
   grievances?
3. Bryson's essay is a *parody;* it mimics and ridicules the instructional manuals that come with computers. How does Bryson's use of subheads contribute to the effectiveness of his parody?

4. Bryson repeats the word "Congratulations" several times in the essay. Identify each place the word appears. What effect do you think Bryson hoped this word would have each time he used it?

Writing Assignments Using Process Analysis as a Pattern of Development

∞ **1.** With lightly barbed humor, Bryson shows how needlessly frustrating it can be to set up a computer. Write a humorous essay of your own explaining to the uninitiated how to do something that is supposedly easy but in practice is unnecessarily complicated. You might explain how to correct an erroneous credit card charge, how to apply for a scholarship or loan, how to program a VCR, and so on. Like Bryson, devise several tongue-in-cheek headings that convey your attitude about the absurd complexities of the process. To see how another writer uses humor in a how-to piece, read Paul Roberts's "How to Say Nothing in 500 Words" (page 365).

∞ **2.** In his essay, Bryson ironically suggests actions that in reality should *not* be done in order to get a computer functioning—for example, typing "the birthdates of all the people you have ever known" (paragraph 14). Taking a similarly ironic stance, write your own how-*not*-to guide to doing something. You could, for example, explain how *not* to get a raise, how *not* to pass a college course, how *not* to pass a driver's test. Adopt whatever tone you wish, though a lighthearted one seems particularly appropriate for this essay. For another model of a how-*not*-to guide, see Paul Roberts's "How to Say Nothing in 500 Words" (page 365).

Writing Assignments Using Other Patterns of Development

∞ **3.** Write an essay exploring the impact that a relatively recent technological development has had on your life. You might focus on ATMs, answering machines, cell phones, beepers, or satellite television. To illustrate how this technology has affected you personally, contrast your life *before* and *after* the introduction of the innovation. Your essay may have a serious or a lighthearted tone. Before you begin writing, consider reading Jonathan Coleman's "Is Technology Making Us Intimate Strangers?" (page 482) and James Gleick's "Life As Type A" (page 509), two essays exploring technology's impact on daily life.

💻 **4.** Bryson uses humor to express his frustration with computers. But some people don't regard computers with amusement; they are upset about threats posed by computer technology. Brainstorm with others to identify some of the concerns people have about computers. They may, for example, be disturbed about unauthorized access to computerized personal information or about children's exposure to Internet pornography.

Review your brainstormed material and select *one* area of concern that seems especially compelling. Also consider doing some library and/or Internet research to gain further insight into the issue. Then write an essay in which you provide dramatic examples to illustrate the validity of people's concerns. End by briefly describing steps that could be taken to minimize these problems.

Writing Assignments Using a Journal Entry as a Starting Point

5. Write an essay showing how technologies that are supposed to make life easier actually create stress. Review your pre-reading journal entry, selecting one or two technologies to write about. Draw upon the material in your journal as well as discussions with other people about their frustrating encounters with today's technologies. Your essay may have a serious or a lighthearted tone.

Nikki Giovanni

Poet and essayist Nikki Giovanni (1943–) attended Fisk University, where she became passionately interested in the link between literature and politics. In 1967, she became involved in the Black Arts movement, an informal coalition of African-American intellectuals who wrote impassioned poetry to raise awareness of Black rights and to promote the struggle for racial equality. In the wake of the assassination of Malcolm X and the rise of the Black Panthers, Giovanni's poetry became yet more political. Giovanni is now a professor at Virginia Tech, where she teaches English. Her poetry collections include *My House* (1972), *Those Who Ride the Night Winds* (1983), *The Sun Is So Quiet* (1996), and *Love Poems* (1997); her nonfiction publications include *Gemini: An Extended Autobiographical Statement on My First Twenty-Five Years Being a Black Poet* (1971), *Sacred Cows . . . and Other Edibles* (1988), and *Racism 101* (1994). The following selection is from *Racism 101.*

Pre-Reading Journal Entry

Were you exposed to racial and/or ethnic diversity while you were growing up? Looking back, do you think that this exposure—or lack of exposure— worked to your advantage or disadvantage? Use your journal to respond to these questions.

Campus Racism 101

There is a bumper sticker that reads: TOO BAD IGNORANCE ISN'T 1
PAINFUL. I like that. But ignorance is. We just seldom attribute the pain to it or recognize it when we see it. Like the postcard on my corkboard. It shows a young man in a very hip jacket smoking a cigarette. In the background is a high school with the American flag waving. The caption says: "Too cool for school. Yet too stupid for the real world." Out of the mouth of the young man is a bubble enclosing the words "Maybe I'll start a band." There could be a postcard showing a jock in a uniform saying, "I don't need school. I'm going to the NFL or NBA." Or one showing a young man or

woman studying and a group of young people saying, "So you want to be white." Or something equally demeaning. We need to quit it.

I am a professor of English at Virginia Tech. I've been here for four years, though for only two years with academic rank. I am tenured, which means I have a teaching position for life, a rarity on a predominantly white campus. Whether from malice or ignorance, people who think I should be at a predominantly Black institution will ask, "Why are you at Tech?" Because it's here. And so are Black students. But even if Black students weren't here, it's painfully obvious that this nation and this world cannot allow white students to go through higher education without interacting with Blacks in authoritative positions. It is equally clear that predominantly Black colleges cannot accommodate the numbers of Black students who want and need an education.

Is it difficult to attend a predominantly white college? Compared with what? Being passed over for promotion because you lack credentials? Being turned down for jobs because you are not college-educated? Joining the armed forces or going to jail because you cannot find an alternative to the streets? Let's have a little perspective here. Where can you go and what can you do that frees you from interacting with the white American mentality? You're going to interact; the only question is, will you be in some control of yourself and your actions, or will you be controlled by others? I'm going to recommend self-control.

What's the difference between prison and college? They both prescribe your behavior for a given period of time. They both allow you to read books and develop your writing. They both give you time alone to think and time with your peers to talk about issues. But four years of prison doesn't give you a passport to greater opportunities. Most likely that time only gives you greater knowledge of how to get back in. Four years of college gives you an opportunity not only to lift yourself but to serve your people effectively. What's the difference when you are called nigger in college from when you are called nigger in prison? In college you can, though I admit with effort, follow procedures to have those students who called you nigger kicked out or suspended. You can bring issues to public attention without risking your life. But mostly, college is and always has been the future. We, neither less nor more than other people, need knowledge. There are discomforts attached to attending predominantly white colleges, though no more so than living in a racist world. Here are some rules to follow that may help:

Go to class. No matter how you feel. No matter how you think   5
the professor feels about you. It's important to have a consistent
presence in the classroom. If nothing else, the professor will know
you care enough and are serious enough to be there.

Meet your professors. Extend your hand (give a firm handshake)   6
and tell them your name. Ask them what you need to do to make
an A. You may never make an A, but you have put them on notice
that you are serious about getting good grades.

Do assignments on time. Typed or computer-generated. You have   7
the syllabus. Follow it, and turn those papers in. If for some reason
you can't complete an assignment on time, let your professor know
before it is due and work out a new due date—then meet it.

Go back to see your professor. Tell him or her your name again. If   8
an assignment received less than an A, ask why, and find out what
you need to do to improve the next assignment.

Yes, your professor is busy. So are you. So are your parents who   9
are working to pay or help with your tuition. Ask early what you
need to do if you feel you are starting to get into academic trouble.
Do not wait until you are failing.

Understand that there will be professors who do not like you; there   10
may even be professors who are racist or sexist or both. You must
discriminate among your professors to see who will give you the
help you need. You may not simply say, "They are all against me."
They aren't. They mostly don't care. Since you are the one who
wants to be educated, find the people who want to help.

Don't defeat yourself. Cultivate your friends. Know your ene-   11
mies. You cannot undo hundreds of years of prejudicial thinking.
Think for yourself and speak up. Raise your hand in class. Say what
you believe no matter how awkward you may think it sounds. You
will improve in your articulation and confidence.

Participate in some campus activity. Join the newspaper staff.   12
Run for office. Join a dorm council. Do something that involves you
on campus. You are going to be there for four years, so let your presence be known, if not felt.

You will inevitably run into some white classmates who are   13
troubling because they often say stupid things, ask stupid questions—and expect an answer. Here are some comebacks to some of
the most common inquiries and comments:

Q: What's it like to grow up in a ghetto?   14
A: I don't know.

Q: (from the teacher): Can you give us the Black perspective on   15
Toni Morrison[1], Huck Finn[2], slavery, Martin Luther King, Jr., and
others?
A: I can give you *my* perspective. (Do not take the burden of 22 million people on your shoulders. Remind everyone that you are an individual, and don't speak for the race or any other individual within it.)

Q: Why do all the Black people sit together in the dining hall?   16
A: Why do all the white students sit together?

Q: Why should there be an African-American studies course?   17
A: Because white Americans have not adequately studied the contributions of Africans and African-Americans. Both Black and white
students need to know our total common history.

Q: Why are there so many scholarships for "minority" students?   18
A: Because they wouldn't give my great-grandparents their forty
acres and the mule.[3]

Q: How can whites understand Black history, culture, literature, and 19
so forth?
A: The same way we understand white history, culture, literature,
and so forth. That is why we're in school: to learn.

Q: Should whites take African-American studies courses?   20
A: Of course. We take white-studies courses, though the universities
don't call them that.

Comment: When I see groups of Black people on campus, it's real-   21
ly intimidating.
Comeback: I understand what you mean. I'm frightened when I see
white students congregating.

---

[1]A Nobel prize-winning African-American author (editors' note).
[2]Reference to a novel by Mark Twain in which one of the main characters is a slave
(editors' note).
[3]After the Civil War, the Freedman's Bureau of the United States government
promised each newly freed male slave forty acres of land and a mule as part of a
plan to promote economic independence; very few, if any, ex-slaves received this
assistance (editors' note).

Comment: It's not fair. It's easier for you guys to get into college   22
than for other people.
Comeback: If it's so easy, why aren't there more of us?

Comment: It's not our fault that America is the way it is.   23
Comeback: It's not our fault, either, but both of us have a responsibility to make changes.

It's really very simple. Educational progress is a national con-   24
cern; education is a private one. Your job is not to educate white
people; it is to obtain an education. If you take the racial world on
your shoulders, you will not get the job done. Deal with yourself as
an individual worthy of respect, and make everyone else deal with
you the same way. College is a little like playing grown-up. Practice
what you want to be. You have been telling your parents you are
grown. Now is your chance to act like it.

Questions for Close Reading

1. What is the selection's thesis? Locate the sentence(s) in which Giovanni
   states her main idea. If she doesn't state the thesis explicitly, express it in
   your own words.
2. How does Giovanni respond to those who question why she is teaching
   at a predominantly White college? What reasons does she give for accepting a position there?
3. What, according to Giovanni, are the most difficult challenges facing
   minority students at primarily White institutions?
4. What does Giovanni mean when she warns readers, "Do not take the
   burden of 22 million people on your shoulders" (paragraph 15)?
5. Refer to your dictionary as needed to define the following words used in
   the selection: *tenured* (paragraph 2), *predominantly* (2), *malice* (2), *authoritative* (2), *articulation* (11), *inevitably* (13), and *congregating* (21).

Questions About the Writer's Craft

1. **The pattern.** Giovanni describes two separate processes: the steps that
   Black students need to take to succeed in college and the strategies they
   can use to respond to classmates' "stupid questions" (paragraph 13). To
   what extent does Giovanni have an informative or persuasive purpose
   when explaining each process?
2. **Other patterns.** Giovanni opens her essay with brief descriptions of a
   bumper sticker and a postcard. Why do you think she chose to begin
   with these two descriptions?

3. Why do you suppose Giovanni mentions her position at Virginia Tech? What purpose does the reference serve?
4. Starting in paragraph 3, Giovanni addresses the reader as "you" and makes several comments using the first-person plural pronouns "we" and "us." To whom is Giovanni addressing her recommendations? How do you know?

Writing Assignments Using Process Analysis as a Pattern of Development

1. Select *one* of the suggestions that Giovanni offers in paragraphs 5–12, and expand it in an essay of your own. Explain as specifically as you can the steps that beginning college students should take to accomplish the recommendation. Illustrate the steps with concrete examples from your own and other students' experience.
2. Giovanni's suggestions highlight some of the steps that minority college students should take to get a good education. In an essay of your own, explain, step by step, what another group of people should do to achieve a clear-cut goal. You might explain how shy people can succeed at parties, how high school students can get good summer jobs, how friends can disagree without jeopardizing their relationship. Your tone may be serious or humorous, as long as it is consistent with your overall purpose.

Writing Assignments Using Other Patterns of Development

3. Giovanni urges her readers not to "defeat" themselves, not to sell themselves short. At one time or another, all of us have sold not only ourselves short but someone else as well. Write an essay about a time you underestimated someone's character, ability, or actions. Begin by explaining how you initially judged the person; then narrate the event(s) that altered your assessment of that person.
4. Giovanni briefly touches on, and has strong opinions about, several controversial issues: Black studies programs (17, 20), minority scholarships (18), and affirmative action in college admissions policies (22). Select *one* of these issues and write an essay defending or disputing Giovanni's position. Remember to acknowledge opposing viewpoints, refuting as many of them as you can. Where appropriate, mention points made by essayists Roger Wilkins ("Racism Has Its Privileges," page 638) and Shelby Steele ("The Price of Preference," page 649), two writers having sharply divergent views on racial issues.

Writing Assignments Using a Journal Entry as a Starting Point

∞ 5. Write an essay arguing that it is *or* is not important to expose children to racial and ethnic diversity. The material you generated in your pre-reading journal entry will help you develop your position. You'll probably find it helpful to brainstorm with others about their experiences with multiculturalism and draw on this material for specific supporting examples. Part of your essay should acknowledge the views of those who don't adopt the stance you take. Before writing, consider reading Yuh Ji-Yeon's "Let's Tell the Story of All America's Cultures" (page 581), a compelling argument advocating multicultural education.

Jessica Mitford

Dubbed "Queen of the Muckrakers" by *Time,* English-born Jessica Mitford
(1917–96) came to the United States in 1939 at the age of twenty-one.
Mitford worked as a bartender and salesperson before becoming an investi-
gator for the Office of Price Administration in Washington. She didn't
begin her writing career until the age of thirty-eight. Her books include two
autobiographies, *Daughters and Rebels* (1960) and *A Fine Old Conflict*
(1976); an examination of the American penal system, *Kind and Usual
Punishment* (1974); a collection of essays, *Poison Penmanship* (1979); a critique of the birthing business, *The American Way of Birth* (1993); and a
novel about celebrities and the media, *Grace Had an English Heart* (1989).
The following selection is from the book *The American Way of Death*
(1963), which earned Mitford a national reputation as an investigative
writer. A scathing attack on the U.S. funeral industry, this book shocked
readers and enraged morticians.

Pre-Reading Journal Entry

If you've ever attended a funeral, you know that efforts are made to avoid
the appearance or even the mention of death. Many significant life experiences are also accompanied by elaborate rituals that obscure the real meaning of the events. List several such life events in your journal. For each,
describe briefly the rituals that typically mark the event.

The American Way of Death

Embalming is indeed a most extraordinary procedure, and one
must wonder at the docility of Americans who each year pay hundreds of millions of dollars for its perpetuation, blissfully ignorant of
what it is all about, what is done, how it is done. Not one in ten
thousand has any idea of what actually takes place. Books on the
subject are extremely hard to come by. They are not to be found in
most libraries or bookshops.

In an era when huge television audiences watch surgical operations in the comfort of their living rooms, when, thanks to the ani-
mated cartoon, the geography of the digestive system has become

1

2

familiar territory even to the nursery school set, in a land where the satisfaction of curiosity about almost all matters is a national pastime, the secrecy surrounding embalming can, surely, hardly be attributed to the inherent gruesomeness of the subject. Custom in this regard has within this century suffered a complete reversal. In the early days of American embalming, when it was performed in the home of the deceased, it was almost mandatory for some relative to stay by the embalmer's side and witness the procedure. Today, family members who might wish to be in attendance would certainly be dissuaded by the funeral director. All others, except apprentices, are excluded by law from the preparation room.

A close look at what does actually take place may explain in large   3
measure the undertaker's intractable reticence concerning a procedure that has become his major *raison d'être*. Is it possible he fears that public information about embalming might lead patrons to wonder if they really want this service? If the funeral men are loath to discuss the subject outside the trade, the reader may, understandably, be equally loath to go on reading at this point. For those who have the stomach for it, let us part the formaldehyde curtain. . . .

The body is first laid out in the undertaker's morgue—or rather,   4
Mr. Jones is reposing in the preparation room—to be readied to bid the world farewell.

The preparation room in any of the better funeral establish-   5
ments has the tiled and sterile look of a surgery, and indeed the embalmer-restorative artist who does his chores there is beginning to adopt the term "dermasurgeon" (appropriately corrupted by some mortician-writers as "demisurgeon") to describe his calling. His equipment, consisting of scalpels, scissors, augers, forceps, clamps, needles, pumps, tubes, bowls and basins, is crudely imitative of the surgeon's, as is his technique, acquired in a nine- or twelve-month post-high-school course in an embalming school. He is supplied by an advanced chemical industry with a bewildering array of fluids, sprays, pastes, oils, powders, creams, to fix or soften tissue, shrink or distend it as needed, dry it here, restore the moisture there. There are cosmetics, waxes and paints to fill and cover features, even plaster of Paris to replace entire limbs. There are ingenious aids to prop and stabilize the cadaver: a Vari-Pose Head Rest, the Edwards Arm and Hand Positioner, the Repose Block (to support the shoulders during the embalming), and the Throop Foot Positioner, which resembles an old-fashioned stocks.

Mr. John H. Eckles, president of the Eckles College of   6
Mortuary Science, thus describes the first part of the embalming
procedure: "In the hands of a skilled practitioner, this work may be
done in a comparatively short time and without mutilating the body
other than by slight incision—so slight that it scarcely would cause
serious inconvenience if made upon a living person. It is necessary
to remove the blood, and doing this not only helps in the disinfect-
ing, but removes the principal cause of disfigurements due to discoloration."

Another textbook discusses the all-important time element: 7
"The earlier this is done, the better, for every hour that elapses
between death and embalming will add to the problems and complications encountered. . . ." Just how soon should one get going
on the embalming? The author tells us, "On the basis of such scanty
information made available to this profession through its rudimentary and haphazard system of technical research, we must conclude
that the best results are to be obtained if the subject is embalmed
before life is completely extinct—that is, before cellular death has
occurred. In the average case, this would mean within an hour after
somatic death." For those who feel that there is something a little
rudimentary, not to say haphazard, about this advice, a comforting
thought is offered by another writer. Speaking of fears entertained
in early days of premature burial, he points out, "One of the effects
of embalming by chemical injection, however, has been to dispel
fears of live burial." How true; once the blood is removed, chances
of live burial are indeed remote.

To return to Mr. Jones, the blood is drained out through the   8
veins and replaced by embalming fluid pumped in through the
arteries. As noted in *The Principles and Practices of Embalming,*
"every operator has a favorite injection and drainage point—a fact
which becomes a handicap only if he fails or refuses to forsake his
favorites when conditions demand it." Typical favorites are the
carotid artery, femoral artery, jugular vein, subclavian vein. There
are various choices of embalming fluid. If Flextone is used, it will
produce a "mild, flexible rigidity. The skin retains a velvety softness,
the tissues are rubbery and pliable. Ideal for women and children."
It may be blended with B. and G. Products Company's Lyf-Lyk tint,
which is guaranteed to reproduce "nature's own skin texture . . . the
velvety appearance of living tissue." Suntone comes in three separate
tints: Suntan; Special Cosmetic Tint, a pink shade "especially

indicated for young female subjects"; and Regular Cosmetic Tint, moderately pink.

About three to six gallons of a dyed and perfumed solution of   9
formaldehyde, glycerin, borax, phenol, alcohol, and water is soon
circulating through Mr. Jones, whose mouth has been sewn together with a "needle directed upward between the upper lip and gum
and brought out through the left nostril," with the corners raised
slightly "for a more pleasant expression." If he should be buck-
toothed, his teeth are cleaned with Bon Ami and coated with colorless nail polish. His eyes, meanwhile, are closed with flesh-tinted eye
caps and eye cement.

The next step is to have at Mr. Jones with a thing called a trocar.   10
This is a long, hollow needle attached to a tube. It is jabbed into the
abdomen, poked around the entrails and chest cavity, the contents of
which are pumped out and replaced with "cavity fluid." This done,
and the hole in the abdomen sewn up, Mr. Jones's face is heavily
creamed (to protect the skin from burns which may be caused by
leakage of the chemicals), and he is covered with a sheet and left
unmolested for a while. But not for long—there is more, much more,
in store for him. He has been embalmed, but not yet restored, and
the best time to start the restorative work is eight to ten hours after
embalming, when the tissues have become firm and dry.

The object of all this attention to the corpse, it must be remem-   11
bered, is to make it presentable for viewing in an attitude of healthy
repose. "Our customs require the presentation of our dead in the
semblance of normality . . . unmarred by the ravages of illness, disease or mutilation," says Mr. J. Sheridan Mayer in his *Restorative
Art*. This is rather a large order since few people die in the full
bloom of health, unravaged by illness and unmarked by some dis-
figurement. The funeral industry is equal to the challenge: "In some
cases the gruesome appearance of a mutilated or disease-ridden subject may be quite discouraging. The task of restoration may seem
impossible and shake the confidence of the embalmer. This is the
time for intestinal fortitude and determination. Once the formative
work is begun and affected tissues are cleaned or removed, all
doubts of success vanish. It is surprising and gratifying to discover
the results which may be obtained."

The embalmer, having allowed an appropriate interval to elapse,   12
returns to the attack, but now he brings into play the skill and equipment of sculptor and cosmetician. Is a hand missing? Casting one in

plaster of Paris is a simple matter. "For replacement purposes, only a cast of the back of the hand is necessary; this is within the ability of the average operator and is quite adequate." If a lip or two, a nose or an ear should be missing, the embalmer has at hand a variety of restorative waxes with which to model replacements. Pores and skin texture are simulated by stippling with a little brush, and over this cosmetics are laid on. Head off? Decapitation cases are rather routinely handled. Ragged edges are trimmed, and head joined to torso with a series of splints, wires and sutures. It is a good idea to have a little something at the neck—a scarf or high collar—when time for viewing comes. Swollen mouth? Cut out tissue as needed from inside the lips. If too much is removed, the surface contour can easily be restored by padding with cotton. Swollen necks and cheeks are reduced by removing tissue through vertical incisions made down each side of the neck. "When the deceased is casketed, the pillow will hide the suture incisions . . . as an extra precaution against leakage, the suture may be painted with liquid sealer."

The opposite condition is more likely to present itself—that of   13
emaciation. His hypodermic syringe now loaded with massage cream, the embalmer seeks out and fills the hollowed and sunken areas by injection. In this procedure the backs of the hands and fingers and the under-chin area should not be neglected.

Positioning the lips is a problem that recurrently challenges the   14
ingenuity of the embalmer. Closed too tightly they tend to give a stern, even disapproving expression. Ideally, embalmers feel, the lips should give the impression of being ever so slightly parted, the upper lip protruding slightly for a more youthful appearance. This takes some engineering, however, as the lips tend to drift apart. Lip drift can sometimes be remedied by pushing one or two straight pins through the inner margin of the lower lip and then inserting them between the two front upper teeth. If Mr. Jones happens to have no teeth, the pins can just as easily be anchored in his Armstrong Face Former and Denture Replacer. Another method to maintain lip closure is to dislocate the lower jaw, which is then held in its new position by a wire run through holes which have been drilled through the upper and lower jaws at the midline. As the French are fond of saying, *il faut souffrir pour être belle.*[1]

---

[1]One has to suffer to be beautiful (editors' note).

If Mr. Jones has died of jaundice, the embalming fluid will very   15
likely turn him green. Does this deter the embalmer? Not if he has
intestinal fortitude. Masking pastes and cosmetics are heavily laid on,
burial garments and casket interiors are color-correlated with particular care, and Jones is displayed beneath rose-colored lights. Friends
will say, "How *well* he looks." Death by carbon monoxide, on the
other hand, can be rather a good thing from the embalmer's viewpoint: "One advantage is the fact that this type of discoloration is an
exaggerated form of a natural pink coloration." This is nice because
the healthy glow is already present and needs but little attention.

The patching and filling completed, Mr. Jones is now shaved,   16
washed and dressed. Cream-based cosmetic, available in pink, flesh,
suntan, brunette, and blond, is applied to his hands and face, his hair
is shampooed and combed (and, in the case of Mrs. Jones, set), his
hands manicured. For the horny-handed son of toil special care
must be taken; cream should be applied to remove ingrained grime,
and the nails cleaned. "If he were not in the habit of having them
manicured in life, trimming and shaping is advised for better appearance—never questioned by kin."

Jones is now ready for casketing (this is the present participle of   17
the verb "to casket"). In this operation his right shoulder should be
depressed slightly "to turn the body a bit to the right and soften the
appearance of lying flat on the back." Positioning the hands is a matter of importance, and special rubber positioning blocks may be
used. The hands should be cupped slightly for a more lifelike,
relaxed appearance. Proper placement of the body requires a delicate
sense of balance. It should lie as high as possible in the casket, yet
not so high that the lid, when lowered, will hit the nose. On the
other hand, we are cautioned, placing the body too low "creates the
impression that the body is in a box."

Jones is next wheeled into the appointed slumber room where a   18
few last touches may be added—his favorite pipe placed in his hand
or, if he was a great reader, a book propped into position. (In the case
of little Master Jones a Teddy bear may be clutched.) Here he will
hold open house for a few days, visiting hours 10 A.M. to 9 P.M.

Questions for Close Reading

1. What is the selection's thesis? Locate the sentence(s) in which Mitford
   states her main idea. If she doesn't state the thesis explicitly, express it in
   your own words.

2. Why, according to Mitford, do Americans know so little about the embalming process?
3. Mitford quotes from a textbook on embalming practices (paragraph 11). What does the passage reveal about the goals of mortuary science?
4. In what ways is the body made to look even better than it did when alive?
5. Refer to your dictionary as needed to define the following words used in the selection: *docility* (paragraph 1), *intractable* (3), *raison d'être* (3), *augers* (5), *distend* (5), *stippling* (12), and *jaundice* (15).

Questions About the Writer's Craft

1. **The pattern.** What are the main stages of the mortician's craft? What happens in each step? What words and phrases does Mitford use to indicate that she's moving from one step to the next?
2. Why does Mitford refer to the body being embalmed as Mr. Jones? What effect does this naming have on the reader?
3. Mitford interweaves her description of the embalming and restoring process with many quotations from mortuary science texts. Why do you suppose she does this? What do you notice about the writing style of the authors of these texts?
4. What is Mitford's tone in this essay? Do you feel she is being objective in her description of the funeral industry? Explain.

Writing Assignments Using Process Analysis as a Pattern of Development

1. Many important events in our lives are marked by celebrations or rituals. Often, the basic outlines of these rituals are established by tradition, but we can always personalize these traditions in one way or another. Select an important event that you will celebrate in the future and explain how you would like to experience the event. Your choice could include any of the following: your marriage, the birth of a child, your graduation, your parent's retirement, or some other notable occurrence. Before writing, you may find it helpful to read Judith Ortiz Cofer's "A Partial Remembrance of a Puerto Rican Childhood" (page 134), an essay about a shared family ritual.
2. Write a paper telling your survivors how you wish to be treated after death. Explain how they should conduct your funeral, whether they should embalm you, where they should put your remains, and, most important, what you would like said in your eulogy. Be as specific as possible as you outline the steps to be taken.

Writing Assignments Using Other Patterns of Development

3. Write an essay describing a funeral or viewing that you attended. Focus on what seems to you the most important scene. Your thesis should

express a dominant feeling about the scene: depression, grief, discomfort, fear, relief, or some other emotion. Alternatively, write an essay describing any other ceremony or ritual you have experienced (for example, a wedding, a bar or bat mitzvah, or a graduation). Your dominant feeling may be positive or negative.

4. Write an essay showing that Americans often pretend that death doesn't exist or isn't really happening. Give examples drawn from your own life, your family's life, or public events. You might consider the following: the expressions we use with children ("Grandpa's gone away"; "Kitty is sleeping"); the euphemistic language we have for death ("passed away"; "no longer with us"); our obsession with looking young and keeping fit; our beliefs about "eternal life"; people's resistance to making a will. William Lutz's "Doublespeak" (page 296) will deepen your understanding of the way language can be used to hide uncomfortable truths.

Writing Assignments Using a Journal Entry as a Starting Point

5. Review your pre-reading journal entry, and select *one* major life event whose genuine significance is somehow masked by its accompanying rituals. Then write an essay describing this event and its rituals. If you need to supplement the material in your journal, interview others about their experiences and observations. Your essay may have a serious or a light-hearted tone.

Paul Roberts

Paul Roberts (1917–67) was a scholar of linguistics and a respected teacher whose textbooks helped scores of high school and college students become better writers. Roberts's works include *English Syntax* (1954) and *Patterns of English* (1956). The following selection is from his best-known book, *Understanding English* (1958).

Pre-Reading Journal Entry

Many educators argue that first-year college students write bland essays because their high school English classes didn't teach them how to think clearly and creatively. Do you agree? Take some time to reflect in your journal about your best and worst high school English classes. For each class, focus on teaching style, classroom atmosphere, assignments, activities, and so on.

How to Say Nothing in 500 Words

Nothing About Something

It's Friday afternoon, and you have almost survived another 1 week of classes. You are just looking forward dreamily to the weekend when the English instructor says: "For Monday you will turn in a five-hundred-word composition on college football."

Well, that puts a good big hole in the weekend. You don't have 2 any strong views on college football one way or the other. You get rather excited during the season and go to all the home games and find it rather more fun than not. On the other hand, the class has been reading Robert Hutchins in the anthology and perhaps Shaw's "Eighty-Yard Run," and from the class discussion you have got the idea that the instructor thinks college football is for the birds. You are no fool, you. You can figure out what side to take.

After dinner you get out the portable typewriter that you got 3 for high school graduation. You might as well get it over with and enjoy Saturday and Sunday. Five hundred words is about two double-spaced pages with normal margins. You put in a sheet of paper, think up a title, and you're off:

Why College Football Should Be Abolished

College football should be abolished because it's bad for the school and also bad for the players. The players are so busy practicing that they don't have any time for their studies.

4

This, you feel, is a mighty good start. The only trouble is that it's only thirty-two words. You still have four hundred and sixty-eight to go, and you've pretty well exhausted the subject. It comes to you that you do your best thinking in the morning, so you put away the typewriter and go to the movies. But the next morning you have to do your washing and some math problems, and in the afternoon you go to the game. The English instructor turns up too, and you wonder if you've taken the right side after all. Saturday night you have a date, and Sunday morning you have to go to church. (You shouldn't let English assignments interfere with your religion.) What with one thing and another, it's ten o'clock Sunday night before you get out the typewriter again. You make a pot of coffee and start to fill out your views on college football. Put a little meat on the bones.

5

Why College Football Should Be Abolished

In my opinion, it seems to me that college football should be abolished. The reason why I think this to be true is because I feel that football is bad for the colleges in nearly every respect. As Robert Hutchins says in his article in our anthology in which he discusses college football, it would be better if the colleges had race horses and had races with one another, because then the horses would not have to attend classes. I firmly agree with Mr. Hutchins on this point, and I am sure that many other students would agree too.

6

One reason why it seems to me that college football is bad is that it has become too commercial. In the olden times when people played football just for the fun of it, maybe college football was all right, but they do not play football just for the fun of it now as they used to in the old

7

days. Nowadays college football is what you might call a big business. Maybe this is not true at all schools, and I don't think it is especially true here at State, but certainly this is the case at most colleges and universities in America nowadays, as Mr. Hutchins points out in his very interesting article. Actually the coaches and alumni go around to the high schools and offer the high school stars large salaries to come to their colleges and play football for them. There was one case where a high school star was offered a convertible if he would play football for a certain college.

Another reason for abolishing college football is that it is bad for the players. They do not have time to get a college education, because they are so busy playing football. A football player has to practice every afternoon from three to six, and then he is so tired that he can't concentrate on his studies. He just feels like dropping off to sleep after dinner, and then the next day he goes to his classes without having studied and maybe he fails the test.   8

(Good ripe stuff so far, but you're still a hundred and fifty-one words from home. One more push.)

Also I think college football is bad for the colleges and the universities because not very many students get to participate in it. Out of a college of ten thousand students only seventy-five or a hundred play football, if that many. Football is what you might call a spectator sport. That means that most people go to watch it but do not play it themselves.   9

(Four hundred and fifteen. Well, you still have the conclusion, and when you retype it, you can make the margins a little wider.)

These are the reasons why I agree with Mr. Hutchins that college football should be abolished in American colleges and universities.   10

On Monday you turn it in, moderately hopeful, and on Friday it comes back marked "weak in content" and sporting a big "D."   11

This essay is exaggerated a little, not much. The English instructor will recognize it as reasonably typical of what an assignment on   12 college football will bring in. He knows that nearly half of the class will contrive in five hundred words to say that college football is too commercial and bad for the players. Most of the other half will inform him that college football builds character and prepares one for life and brings prestige to the school. As he reads paper after paper all saying the same thing in almost the same words, all blood-less, five hundred words dripping out of nothing, he wonders how he allowed himself to get trapped into teaching English when he might have had a happy and interesting life as an electrician or a con-fidence man.

Well, you may ask, what can you do about it? The subject is one   13
on which you have few convictions and little information. Can you be expected to make a dull subject interesting? As a matter of fact, this is precisely what you are expected to do. This is the writer's essential task. All subjects, except sex, are dull until somebody makes them interesting. The writer's job is to find the argument, the approach, the angle, the wording that will take the reader with him. This is seldom easy, and it is particularly hard in subjects that have been much discussed: College Football, Fraternities, Popular Music, Is Chivalry Dead?, and the like. You will feel that there is nothing you can do with such subjects except repeat the old bromides. But there are some things you can do which will make your papers, if not throbbingly alive, at least less insufferably tedious than they might otherwise be.

Avoid the Obvious Content

Say the assignment is college football. Say that you've decided   14
to be against it. Begin by putting down the arguments that come to your mind: it is too commercial, it takes the students' minds off their studies, it is hard on the players, it makes the university a kind of circus instead of an intellectual center, for most schools it is finan-cially ruinous. Can you think of any more arguments just off hand? All right. Now when you write your paper, *make sure that you don't use any of the material on this list.* If these are the points that leap to your mind, they will leap to everyone else's too, and whether you get a "C" or a "D" may depend on whether the instructor reads your paper early when he is fresh and tolerant or late, when the sen-tence "In my opinion, college football has become too commer-cial," inexorably repeated, has brought him to the brink of lunacy.

Be against college football for some reason or reasons of your   15
own. If they are keen and perceptive ones, that's splendid. But even
if they are trivial or foolish or indefensible, you are still ahead so long
as they are not everybody else's reasons too. Be against it because
the colleges don't spend enough money on it to make it worth
while, because it is bad for the characters of the spectators, because
the players are forced to attend classes, because the football stars
hog all the beautiful women, because it competes with baseball and
is therefore un-American and possibly Communist inspired. There
are lots of more or less unused reasons for being against college
football.

Sometimes it is a good idea to sum up and dispose of the trite   16
and conventional points before going on to your own. This has the
advantage of indicating to the reader that you are going to be neither trite nor conventional. Something like this:

> We are often told that college football should be abol-   17
> ished because it has become too commercial or because it is
> bad for the players. These arguments are no doubt very
> cogent, but they don't really go to the heart of the matter.

Then you go to the heart of the matter.

Take the Less Usual Side

One rather simple way of getting interest into your paper is to   18
take the side of the argument that most of the citizens will want to
avoid. If the assignment is an essay on dogs, you can, if you choose,
explain that dogs are faithful and lovable companions, intelligent,
useful as guardians of the house and protectors of children, indispensable in police work—in short, when all is said and done, man's
best friends. Or you can suggest that those big brown eyes conceal,
more often than not, a vacuity of mind and an inconstancy of purpose; that the dogs you have known most intimately have been
mangy, ill-tempered brutes, incapable of instruction; and that only
your nobility of mind and fear of arrest prevent you from kicking the
flea-ridden animals when you pass them on the street.

Naturally, personal convictions will sometimes dictate your   19
approach. If the assigned subject is "Is Methodism Rewarding to the
Individual?" and you are a pious Methodist, you have really no

choice. But few assigned subjects, if any, will fall in this category. Most of them will lie in broad areas of discussion with much to be said on both sides. They are intellectual exercises and it is legitimate to argue now one way and now another, as debaters do in similar circumstances. Always take the side that looks to you hardest, least defensible. It will almost always turn out to be easier to write interestingly on that side.

This general advice applies where you have a choice of subjects.   20
If you are to choose among "The Value of Fraternities" and "My Favorite High School Teacher" and "What I Think About Beetles," by all means plump for the beetles. By the time the instructor gets to your paper, he will be up to his ears in tedious tales about the French teacher at Bloombury High and assertions about how fraternities build character and prepare one for life. Your views on beetles, whatever they are, are bound to be a refreshing change.

Don't worry too much about figuring out what the instructor   21
thinks about the subject so that you can cuddle up with him. Chances are his views are no stronger than yours. If he does have convictions and you oppose them, his problem is to keep from grading you higher than you deserve in order to show he is not biased. This doesn't mean that you should always cantankerously dissent from what the instructor says; that gets tiresome too. And if the subject assigned is "My Pet Peeve," do not begin, "My pet peeve is the English instructor who assigns papers on 'my pet peeve.'" This was still funny during the War of 1812, but it has sort of lost its edge since then. It is in general good manners to avoid personalities.

Slip Out of Abstraction

If you will study the essay on college football . . . you will perceive   22
that one reason for its appalling dullness is that it never gets down to particulars. It is just a series of not very glittering generalities: "football is bad for the colleges," "it has become too commercial," "football is a big business," "it is bad for the players," and so on. Such round phrases thudding against the reader's brain are unlikely to convince him, though they may well render him unconscious.

If you want the reader to believe that college football is bad for   23
the players, you have to do more than say so. You have to display the evil. Take your roommate, Alfred Simkins, the second-string center. Picture poor old Alfy coming home from football practice every evening, bruised and aching, agonizingly tired, scarcely able to

shovel the mashed potatoes into his mouth. Let us see him staggering up to the room, getting out his econ textbook, peering desperately at it with his good eye, falling asleep and failing the test in the morning. Let us share his unbearable tension as Saturday draws near. Will he fail, be demoted, lose his monthly allowance, be forced to return to the coal mines? And if he succeeds, what will be his reward? Perhaps a slight ripple of applause when the third-string center replaces him, a moment of elation in the locker room if the team wins, of despair if it loses. What will he look back on when he graduates from college? Toil and torn ligaments. And what will be his future? He is not good enough for pro football, and he is too obscure and weak in econ to succeed in stocks and bonds. College football is tearing the heart from Alfy Simkins and, when it finishes with him, will callously toss aside the shattered hulk.

24 This is no doubt a weak enough argument for the abolition of college football, but it is a sight better than saying, in three or four variations, that college football (in your opinion) is bad for the players.

25 Look at the work of any professional writer and notice how constantly he is moving from the generality, the abstract statement, to the concrete example, the facts and figures, the illustration. If he is writing on juvenile delinquency, he does not just tell you that juveniles are (it seems to him) delinquent and that (in his opinion) something should be done about it. He shows you juveniles being delinquent, tearing up movie theatres in Buffalo, stabbing high school principals in Dallas, smoking marijuana in Palo Alto. And more than likely he is moving toward some specific remedy, not just a general wringing of the hands.

26 It is no doubt possible to be *too* concrete, too illustrative or anecdotal, but few inexperienced writers err this way. For most the soundest advice is to be seeking always for the picture, to be always turning general remarks into seeable examples. Don't say, "Sororities teach girls the social graces." Say "Sorority life teaches a girl how to carry on a conversation while pouring tea, without sloshing the tea into the saucer." Don't say, "I like certain kinds of popular music very much." Say, "Whenever I hear Gerber Spinklittle play 'Mississippi Man' on the trombone, my socks creep up my ankles."

Get Rid of Obvious Padding

27 The student toiling away at his weekly English theme is too often tormented by a figure: five hundred words. How, he asks

himself, is he to achieve this staggering total? Obviously by never using one word when he can somehow work in ten.

He is therefore seldom content with a plain statement like "Fast 28 driving is dangerous." This has only four words in it. He takes thought, and the sentence becomes:

> In my opinion, fast driving is dangerous.

Better, but he can do better still:

> In my opinion, fast driving would seem to be rather dangerous.

If he is really adept, it may come out:

> In my humble opinion, though I do not claim to be an expert on this complicated subject, fast driving, in most circumstances, would seem to be rather dangerous in many respects, or at least so it would seem to me.

Thus four words have been turned into forty, and not an iota of content has been added.

Now this is a way to go about reaching five hundred words, and 29 if you are content with a "D" grade, it is as good a way as any. But if you aim higher, you must work differently. Instead of stuffing your sentences with straw, you must try steadily to get rid of the padding, to make your sentences lean and tough. If you are really working at it, your first draft will greatly exceed the required total, and then you will work it down, thus:

> It is thought in some quarters that fraternities do not contribute as much as might be expected to campus life.
> Some people think that fraternities contribute little to campus life.

> The average doctor who practices in small towns or in the country must toil night and day to heal the sick.
> Most country doctors work long hours.

> When I was a little girl, I suffered from shyness and embarrassment in the presence of others.

I was a shy little girl.

It is absolutely necessary for the person employed as a marine fireman to give the matter of steam pressure his undivided attention at all times.
The fireman has to keep his eye on the steam gauge.

You may ask how you can arrive at five hundred words at this   30
rate. Simply. You dig up more real content. Instead of taking a couple of obvious points off the surface of the topic and then circling warily around them for six paragraphs, you work in and explore, figure out the details. You illustrate. You say that fast driving is dangerous, and then you prove it. How long does it take to stop a car at forty and at eighty? How far can you see at night? What happens when a tire blows? What happens in a head-on collision at fifty miles an hour? Pretty soon your paper will be full of broken glass and blood and headless torsos, and reaching five hundred words will not really be a problem.

Call a Fool a Fool

Some of the padding in freshman themes is to be blamed not on   31
anxiety about the word minimum but on excessive timidity. The student writes, "In my opinion, the principal of my high school acted in ways that I believe every unbiased person would have to call foolish." This isn't exactly what he means. What he means is, "My high school principal was a fool." If he was a fool, call him a fool. Hedging the thing about with "in-my-opinion's" and "it-seems-to-me's" and "as-I-see-it's" and "at-least-from-my-point-of-view's" gains you nothing. Delete these phrases whenever they creep into your paper.

The student's tendency to hedge stems from a modesty that in   32
other circumstances would be commendable. He is, he realizes, young and inexperienced, and he half suspects that he is dopey and fuzzy-minded beyond the average. Probably only too true. But it doesn't help to announce your incompetence six times in every paragraph. Decide what you want to say and say it as vigorously as possible, without apology and in plain words.

Linguistic diffidence can take various forms. One is what we call   33
euphemism. This is the tendency to call a spade "a certain garden

implement" or women's underwear "unmentionables." It is stronger in some eras than others and in some people than others but it always operates more or less in subjects that are touchy or taboo: death, sex, madness, and so on. Thus we shrink from saying "He died last night" but say instead "passed away," "left us," "joined his Maker," "went to his reward." Or we try to take off the tension with a lighter cliché: "kicked the bucket," "cashed in his chips," "handed in his dinner pail." We have found all sorts of ways to avoid saying *mad:* "mentally ill," "touched," "not quite right upstairs," "feeble-minded," "innocent," "simple," "off his trolley," "not in his right mind." Even such a now plain word as *insane* began as a euphemism with the meaning "not healthy."

Modern science, particularly psychology, contributes many   34 polysyllables in which we can wrap our thoughts and blunt their force. To many writers there is no such thing as a bad schoolboy. Schoolboys are maladjusted or unoriented or misunderstood or in need of guidance or lacking in continued success toward satisfactory integration of the personality as a social unit, but they are never bad. Psychology no doubt makes us better men or women, more sympathetic and tolerant, but it doesn't make writing any easier. Had Shakespeare been confronted with psychology, "To be or not to be" might have come out, "To continue as a social unit or not to do so. That is the personality problem. Whether 'tis a better sign of integration at the conscious level to display a psychic tolerance toward the maladjustments and repressions induced by one's lack of orientation in one's environment or—" But Hamlet would never have finished the soliloquy.

Writing in the modern world, you cannot altogether avoid   35 modern jargon. Nor, in an effort to get away from euphemism, should you salt your paper with four-letter words. But you can do much if you will mount guard against those roundabout phrases, those echoing polysyllables that tend to slip into your writing to rob it of its crispness and force.

Beware of the Pat Expression

Other things being equal, avoid phrases like "other things   36 being equal." Those sentences that come to you whole, or in two or three doughy lumps, are sure to be bad sentences. They are no creation of yours but pieces of common thought floating in the community soup.

Pat expressions are hard, often impossible, to avoid, because   37
they come too easily to be noticed and seem too necessary to be dispensed with. No writer avoids them altogether, but good writers
avoid them more often than poor writers.

By "pat expressions" we mean such tags as "to all practical   38
intents and purposes," "the pure and simple truth," "from where I
sit," "the time of his life," "to the ends of the earth," "in the twin-
kling of an eye," "as sure as you're born," "over my dead body,"
"under cover of darkness," "took the easy way out," "when all is
said and done," "told him time and time again," "parted the best of
friends," "stand up and be counted," "gave him the best years of her
life," "worked her fingers to the bone." Like other clichés, these
expressions were once forceful. Now we should use them only when
we can't possibly think of anything else.

Some pat expressions stand like a wall between the writer and   39
thought. Such a one is "the American way of life." Many student writers feel that when they have said that something accords with the
American way of life or does not they have exhausted the subject.
Actually, they have stopped at the highest level of abstraction. The
American way of life is the complicated set of bonds between a hundred and eighty million ways. All of us know this when we think about
it, but the tag phrase too often keeps us from thinking about it.

So with many another phrase dear to the politician: "this great   40
land of ours," "the man in the street," "our national heritage."
These may prove our patriotism or give a clue to our political beliefs,
but otherwise they add nothing to the paper except words.

Colorful Words

The writer builds with words, and no builder uses a raw mate-   41
rial more slippery and elusive and treacherous. A writer's work is a
constant struggle to get the right word in the right place, to find
that particular word that will convey his meaning exactly, that will
persuade the reader or soothe him or startle or amuse him. He
never succeeds altogether—sometimes he feels that he scarcely succeeds at all—but such successes as he has are what make the thing
worth doing.

There is no book of rules for this game. One progresses through   42
everlasting experiment on the basis of ever-widening experience.
There are few useful generalizations that one can make about words
as words, but there are perhaps a few.

Some words are what we call "colorful." By this we mean that   43
they are calculated to produce a picture or induce an emotion. They
are dressy instead of plain, specific instead of general, loud instead
of soft. Thus, in place of "Her heart beat," we may write "Her heart
pounded, throbbed, fluttered, danced." Instead of "He sat in his
chair," we may say, "He *lounged, sprawled, coiled.*" Instead of "It
was hot," we may say, "It was *blistering, sultry, muggy, suffocating,
steamy, wilting.*"

However, it should not be supposed that the fancy word is   44
always better. Often it is as well to write "Her heart beat" or "It was
hot" if that is all it did or all it was. Ages differ in how they like their
prose. The nineteenth century liked it rich and smoky. The twentieth has usually preferred it lean and cool. The twentieth-century
writer, like all writers, is forever seeking the exact word, but he is
wary of sounding feverish. He tends to pitch it low, to understate it,
to throw it away. He knows that if he gets too colorful, the audience
is likely to giggle.

See how this strikes you: "As the rich, golden glow of the sun-   45
set died away along the eternal western hills, Angela's limpid blue
eyes looked softly and trustingly into Montague's flashing brown
ones, and her heart pounded like a drum in time with the joyous
song surging in her soul." Some people like that sort of thing, but
most modern readers would say, "Good grief," and turn on the television.

Colored Words

Some words we would call not so much colorful as colored—   46
that is, loaded with associations, good or bad. All words—except
perhaps structure words—have associations of some sort. We have
said that the meaning of a word is the sum of the contexts in which
it occurs. When we hear a word, we hear with it an echo of all the
situations in which we have heard it before.

In some words, these echoes are obvious and discussable. The   47
word *mother,* for example, has, for most people, agreeable associations. When you hear *mother* you probably think of home, safety,
love, food, and various other pleasant things. If one writes, "She was
like a mother to me," he gets an effect which he would not get in
"She was like an aunt to me." The advertiser makes use of the associations of *mother* by working it in when he talks about his product.
The politician works it in when he talks about himself.

So also with such words as *home, liberty, fireside, contentment,* 48
patriot, tenderness, sacrifice, childlike, manly, bluff, limpid. All of
these words are loaded with favorable associations that would be
rather hard to indicate in a straightforward definition. There is more
than a literal difference between "They sat around the fireside" and
"They sat around the stove." They might have been equally warm
and happy around the stove, but *fireside* suggests leisure, grace,
quiet tradition, congenial company, and *stove* does not.

Conversely, some words have bad associations. *Mother* suggests 49
pleasant things, but *mother-in-law* does not. Many mothers-in-law
are heroically lovable and some mothers drink gin all day and beat
their children insensible, but these facts of life are beside the point.
The thing is that *mother* sounds good and *mother-in-law* does not.

Or consider the word *intellectual.* This would seem to be a 50
complimentary term, but in point of fact it is not, for it has picked
up associations of impracticality and ineffectuality and general dopi-
ness. So also with such words as *liberal, reactionary, Communist,*
socialist, capitalist, radical, schoolteacher, truck driver, undertaker,
operator, salesman, huckster, speculator. These convey meanings on
the literal level, but beyond that—sometimes, in some places—they
convey contempt on the part of the speaker.

The question of whether to use loaded words or not depends 51
on what is being written. The scientist, the scholar, try to avoid
them; for the poet, the advertising writer, the public speaker, they
are standard equipment. But every writer should take care that they
do not substitute for thought. If you write, "Anyone who thinks
that is nothing but a Socialist (or Communist or capitalist)," you
have said nothing except that you don't like people who think that,
and such remarks are effective only with the most naïve readers. It
is always a bad mistake to think your readers more naïve than they
really are.

Colorless Words

But probably most student writers come to grief not with words 52
that are colorful or those that are colored but with those that have
no color at all. A pet example is *nice,* a word we would find it hard
to dispense with in casual conversation but which is no longer capable of adding much to a description. Colorless words are those of
such general meaning that in a particular sentence they mean nothing. Slang adjectives, like *cool* ("That's real cool") tend to explode

all over the language. They are applied to everything, lose their original force, and quickly die.

Beware also of nouns of very general meaning, like *circumstances, cases, instances, aspects, factors, relationships, attitudes, eventualities,* etc. In most circumstances you will find that those cases of writing which contain too many instances of words like these will in this and other aspects have factors leading to unsatisfactory relationships with the reader resulting in unfavorable attitudes on his part and perhaps other eventualities, like a grade of "D." Notice also what "etc." means. It means "I'd like to make this list longer, but I can't think of any more examples."   53

Questions for Close Reading

1. What is the selection's thesis? Locate the sentence(s) in which Roberts states his main idea. If he doesn't state the thesis explicitly, express it in your own words.
2. According to Roberts, what do students assume they have to do to get a good grade on an English composition?
3. How do "colorful words," "colored words," and "colorless words" differ? Which should be used in essay writing? Why?
4. What are Roberts's most important pieces of advice for the student writer?
5. Refer to the dictionary as needed to define the following words used in the selection: *bromides* (paragraph 13), *insufferably* (13), *inexorably* (14), *dissent* (21), *abolition* (24), *adept* (28), *euphemism* (33), and *insensible* (49).

Questions About the Writer's Craft

1. **The pattern.**   What two processes does Roberts analyze in this essay? Is each process informational, directional, or a combination of the two?
2. Why do you think Roberts uses the second person "you" throughout the essay? How does this choice of point of view affect your response to the essay?
3. What is Roberts's tone in the essay? Find some typical examples of his tone. How does Roberts achieve this tone? Considering the author's intended audience, is this tone a good choice? Explain.
4. Does Roberts "practice what he preaches" about writing? Review the section headings of the essay and find examples of each piece of advice in the essay.

Writing Assignments Using Process Analysis as a Pattern of Development

∞ 1. Write a humorous essay showing how to avoid doing schoolwork, household chores, or anything else most people tend to put off. You may use the second person as Roberts does. Or you may use the first person and describe your typical method of avoidance. Before writing, read Bill Bryson's "Your New Computer" (page 343), a humorous model for a how-*not*-to guide.

∞ 2. Borrowing some of Roberts's lively techniques, make a routine, predictable process interesting to read about. You might choose an activity such as how to register to vote, apply for a driver's license, sign up for college courses, take care of laundry, play a simple game, study for an exam, or some other familiar process. Caroline Rego's "The Fine Art of Complaining" (page 380) may give you some ideas on how to explain a process in a helpful yet entertaining way.

Writing Assignments Using Other Patterns of Development

3. Should a composition course be required of all first-year college students? Write an essay arguing the value—or lack of value—of such a course. Follow Roberts's advice for writing a lively composition: avoid obvious padding, choose unusual points, avoid abstractions, go to the heart of the matter, use colorful words.

4. Write a paper detailing your experiences as a student in English classes— from elementary school up to now. Using several examples, describe how successfully or unsuccessfully English has been taught, and recommend any specific reforms or changes you feel are needed.

Writing Assignments Using a Journal Entry as a Starting Point

5. Write an essay describing an ideal high school English class. What kind of teacher would be at the helm? What kind of learning atmosphere would prevail? What sorts of skills would be covered? How? To formulate your position, review your pre-reading journal entry, drawing upon your experiences as a guide. End the essay by briefly discussing the factors that might prevent English classes from being like the ideal one you've described. To broaden your perspective on the issues involved, consider discussing the topic with friends and classmates.

Caroline Rego

Caroline Rego was born in 1950 in Edmond, Oklahoma. A graduate of the University of Oklahoma, she began her journalistic career as a police reporter for a daily newspaper in Montana. Later, while filling in for a vacationing colleague in the features section of another newspaper, she found her true calling: writing consumer-affairs articles that teach readers how to protect themselves against shoddy service, dangerous products, and inefficiency. A sought-after public speaker, Rego talks frequently to students and community groups on strategies for becoming an informed consumer. The following selection is part of a work in progress on consumer empowerment.

Pre-Reading Journal Entry

When you're disappointed with someone or something, how do you typically react—passively, assertively, or in some other way? In your journal, list a few disappointments you've experienced. How did you respond on each occasion? In retrospect, are you happy with your responses? Why or why not?

The Fine Art of Complaining

You waited forty-five minutes for your dinner, and when it came 1
it was cold—and not what you ordered in the first place. You washed your supposedly machine-washable, preshrunk T-shirt (the one the catalogue claimed was "indestructible"), and now it's the size of a napkin. Your new car broke down a month after you bought it, and the dealer says the warranty doesn't apply.

Life's annoyances descend on all of us—some pattering down 2
like gentle raindrops, others striking with the bruising force of hailstones. We dodge the ones we can, but inevitably, plenty of them make contact. And when they do, we react fairly predictably. Many of us—most of us, probably—grumble to ourselves and take it. We scowl at our unappetizing food but choke it down. We stash the shrunken T-shirt in a drawer, vowing never again to order from a catalogue. We glare fiercely at our checkbooks as we pay for repairs that should have been free.

A few of us go to the other extreme. Taking our cue from the   3
crazed newscaster in the 1976 movie *Network,* we go through life
mad as hell and unwilling to take it anymore. In offices, we shout
at hapless receptionists when we're kept waiting for appointments.
In restaurants, we make scenes that have fellow patrons craning
their necks to get a look at us. In stores, we argue with salespeople for not waiting on us. We may notice after a while that our
friends seem reluctant to venture into public with us, but hey—
we're just standing up for our rights. Being a patsy doesn't get you
anywhere in life.

It's true—milquetoasts live unsatisfying lives. However, people   4
who go through the day in an eye-popping, vein-throbbing state of
apoplectic rage don't win any prizes either. What persons at both
ends of the scale need—what could empower the silent sufferer and
civilize the Neanderthal—is a course in the gentle art of *effective*
complaining.

Effective complaining is not apologetic and half-hearted. It's   5
not making one awkward attempt at protest—"Uh, excuse me, I
don't think I ordered the squid and onions"—and then slinking
away in defeat. But neither is it roaring away indiscriminately,
attempting to get satisfaction through the sheer volume of our
complaint.

Effective complainers are people who act businesslike and   6
important. Acting important doesn't mean puffing up your chest
and saying, "Do you know who I am?"—an approach that would
tempt anyone to take you down a peg or two. It doesn't mean
shouting and threatening— techniques that will only antagonize the
person whose help you need. It *does* mean making it clear that you
know your request is reasonable and that you are confident it will be
taken care of. People are generally treated the way they expect to be
treated. If you act like someone making a fair request, chances are
that request will be granted. Don't beg, don't explain. Just state
your name, the problem, and what you expect to have done. Remain
polite. But be firm. "My car has been in your garage for three days,
and a mechanic hasn't even looked at it yet," you might say. "I want
to know when it is going to be worked on." Period. Now it is up to
them to give you a satisfactory response. Don't say, "Sorry to bother you about this, but . . ." or "I, uh, was sort of expecting. . . ."
You're only asking people to remedy a problem, after all; that is not
grounds for apology.

If your problem requires an immediate response, try to make   7
your complaint in person; a real, live, in-the-flesh individual has to
be dealt with in some way. Complaining over the telephone, by contrast, is much less effective. When you speak to a disembodied voice,
when the person at the other end of the line doesn't have to face
you, you're more likely to get a runaround.

Most importantly, complain to the right person. One of the   8
greatest frustrations in complaining is talking to a clerk or recep-
tionist who cannot solve your problem and whose only purpose
seems to be to drive you crazy. Getting mad doesn't help; the person you're mad at probably had nothing to do with your actual
problem. And you'll have to repeat everything you've said to the
clerk once you're passed along to the appropriate person. So make
sure from the start that you're talking to someone who can help—a
manager or supervisor.

If your problem doesn't require an immediate response, com-   9
plaining by letter is probably the most effective way to get what you
want. A letter of complaint should be brief, businesslike, and to the
point. If you have a new vacuum cleaner that doesn't work, don't
spend a paragraph describing how your Uncle Joe tried to fix the
problem and couldn't. As when complaining in person, be sure you
address someone in a position of real authority. Here's an example
of an effective letter of complaint.

Ms. Anne Lublin   10
Manager
Mitchell Appliances
80 Front Street
Newton, MA 02159

Dear Ms. Lublin: 11

First section: Explain the problem. Include facts to back up your story.   12

On August 6, I purchased a new Perma-Kool freezer from your store (a   13
copy of my sales receipt is enclosed). In the two weeks I have owned
the freezer, I have had to call your repair department three times in an
attempt to get it running properly. The freezer ran normally when it was
installed, but since then it has repeatedly turned off, causing the food
inside to spoil. My calls to your repair department have not been
responded to promptly. After I called the first time, on August 10, I waited two days for the repair person to show up. It took three days to get
a repair person here after my second call, on August 15. The freezer

stopped yet again on August 20. I called to discuss this recent problem, but no one has responded to my call.

Second section: Tell how you trust the company and are confident that 14
your reader will fix the problem. This is to "soften up" the reader a bit.

I am surprised to receive such unprofessional service and poor quality 15
from Mitchell Appliances since I have been one of your satisfied customers for fifteen years. In the past, I have purchased a television, air
conditioner, and washing machine from your company. I know that you
value good relations with your customers, and I'm sure you want to see
me pleased with my most recent purchase.

Third section: Explain exactly what you want to be done—repair, 16
replacement, refund, etc.

Although your repair department initially thought that the freezer need- 17
ed only some minor adjustments, the fact that no one has been able to
permanently fix the problem convinces me that the freezer has some
serious defect. I am understandably unwilling to spend any more time
having repairs made. Therefore, I expect you to exchange the freezer
for an identical model by the end of this week (August 30). Please call
me to arrange for the removal of the defective freezer and the delivery
of the new one.

Sincerely, 18

Janice Becker

P.S. (Readers always notice a P.S.) State again when you expect the 19
problem to be taken care of, and what you will do if it isn't.

P.S. I am confident that we can resolve this problem by August 30. If the 20
defective freezer is not replaced by then, however, I will report this incident to the Better Business Bureau.

Notice that the P.S. says what you'll do if your problem isn't solved. 21
In other words, you make a threat—a polite threat. Your threat must
be reasonable and believable. A threat to burn down the store if
your purchase price isn't refunded is neither reasonable nor believable—or if it *were* believed, you could end up in jail. A threat to
report the store to a consumer-protection agency, such as the Better
Business Bureau, however, is credible.

Don't be too quick to make one of the most common—and   22
commonly empty—threats: "I'll sue!" A full-blown lawsuit is more
trouble, and more expensive, than most problems are worth. On the
other hand, most areas have a small-claims court where suits involving modest amounts of money are heard. These courts don't use
complex legal language or procedures, and you don't need a lawyer
to use them. A store or company will often settle with you—if your
claim is fair—rather than go to small-claims court.

Whether you complain over the phone, in person, or by letter,   23
be persistent. One complaint may not get results. In that case, keep
on complaining, and make sure you keep complaining to the same
person. Chances are he or she will get worn out and take care of the
situation, if only to be rid of you.

Someday, perhaps, the world will be free of the petty annoy-   24
ances that plague us all from time to time. Until then, however,
toasters will break down, stores will refuse to honor rainchecks, and
bills will include items that were never purchased. You can depend
upon it—there will be grounds for complaint. You might as well
learn to be good at it.

Questions for Close Reading

1. What is the selection's thesis? Locate the sentence(s) in which Rego
   states her main idea. If she doesn't state the thesis explicitly, express it in
   your own words.
2. In Rego's opinion, what types of actions and statements are *not* helpful
   when making a complaint?
3. What should be included in a letter of complaint? What should be omitted?
4. What does Rego suggest doing if a complaint is ignored?
5. Refer to your dictionary as needed to define the following words used in
   the selection: *hapless* (paragraph 3), *venture* (3), *patsy* (3), *milquetoasts*
   (4), *apoplectic* (4), *Neanderthal* (4), *indiscriminately* (5), *disembodied*
   (7), and *credible* (21).

Questions About the Writer's Craft

1. **The pattern.** Is Rego's process analysis primarily directional or primarily informational? Explain. To what extent does Rego try to persuade
   readers to follow her process?
2. **Other patterns.** Where does Rego include narrative elements in her
   essay? What do these brief narratives add to the piece?

3. **Other patterns.** Numerous oppositions occur throughout the essay. How do these contrasts enliven the essay and help Rego persuade readers to adopt her suggestions?

4. Reread the essay, noting where Rego shifts point of view. Where does she use the second-person (*you*), the first-person-plural (*we*), and the third-person-plural (*they*) points of view? How does her use of multiple points of view add to the essay's effectiveness?

Writing Assignments Using Process Analysis as a Pattern of Development

1. Write an essay explaining to college students how to register—with someone in a position of authority—an effective complaint about a campus problem. You could show, for example, how to complain to a professor about a course's grading policy, to the bookstore manager about the markup on textbooks, to security about the poorly maintained college parking lots. Feel free to adapt some of Rego's recommendations, but be sure to invent several strategies of your own. In either case, provide—as Rego does—lively examples to illustrate the step-by-step procedure for registering an effective complaint with a specific authority figure on campus.

2. Rego argues that "people who go through the day in an eye-popping, vein-throbbing state of apoplectic rage don't win any prizes." But sometimes, getting mad can be appropriate—even productive. Write an essay explaining the best process for expressing anger effectively. Explain how to vent emotion safely, communicate the complaint in a nonthreatening way, encourage more honest interaction, and prompt change for the better. Illustrate the process by drawing upon your own experiences and observations. Consider reading James Gleick's "Life As Type A" (page 509), which addresses the origins of high-intensity behavior, and Barbara Ehrenreich's "What I've Learned From Men" (page 249), which provides some insight into the dynamics of anger and resentment.

Writing Assignments Using Other Patterns of Development

3. Think about a service or product that failed to live up to your expectations. Perhaps you were disgruntled about your mechanic's car repair, a store's return policy, or a hotel's accommodations. Using Rego's suggestions, write a letter of complaint in which you describe the problem, convey confidence in the reader's ability to resolve the problem, and state your request for specific action. Remember that a firm but cordial tone will persuade your reader that you have legitimate grounds for seeking the resolution you propose.

∞ **4.** Rego shows that events often don't turn out as we had hoped. In an essay, contrast how you thought a specific situation would be with the way it actually turned out. Was the unexpected outcome better or worse than what you had expected? Did you have trouble adjusting, or did you adapt with surprising ease? Provide vivid specifics about the unforeseen turn of events and your reaction to it. Before writing, you might read Audre Lorde's "The Fourth of July" (page 160), a professional writer's account of an experience that dramatically departed from her expectations.

Writing Assignments Using a Journal Entry as a Starting Point

∞ **5.** Write an essay contrasting the way you reacted to a specific disappointment with the way you wish you had reacted. Reread your pre-reading journal entry, and select *one* incident that illustrates this discrepancy most dramatically. Use vigorous narrative details to make the contrast vivid and real. In your conclusion, indicate what you've learned in hindsight. Before writing, consider reading two other essays that document personal reactions to life's minor—and major—calamities: Langston Hughes's "Salvation" (page 183) and Beth Johnson's "Bombs Bursting in Air" (page 242).

Additional Writing Topics

PROCESS ANALYSIS

General Assignments

Develop one of the following topics through process analysis. Explain the process one step at a time, organizing the steps chronologically. If there's no agreed-on sequence, design your own series of steps. Use transitions to ease the audience through the steps in the process. You may use any tone you wish, from serious to light.

Directional: How to Do Something

1. How to improve a course you have taken
2. How to drive defensively
3. How to get away with _____
4. How to succeed at a job interview
5. How to relax
6. How to show appreciation to others
7. How to get through school despite personal problems
8. How to be a responsible pet owner
9. How to conduct a garage or yard sale
10. How to look fashionable on a limited budget
11. How to protect a home from burglars
12. How to meet more people
13. How to improve the place where you work
14. How to gain or lose weight
15. How to get over a disappointment

Informational: How Something Happens

1. How a student becomes burned out
2. How a library's card catalog or computerized catalog organizes books
3. How a dead thing decays (or how some other natural process works)
4. How the college registration process works
5. How *Homo sapiens* chooses a mate
6. How a VCR (or some other machine) works
7. How a bad habit develops
8. How people fall into debt

Assignments With a Specific Purpose and Audience

1. As an author of books for elementary school children, you want to show children how to do something—take care of a pet, get along with siblings, keep a room clean. Explain the process in terms a child would understand yet not find condescending.

2. As a driver's education instructor in a high school, you decide to prepare a handout dealing with one of the following: making a three-point turn, parallel parking, handling a skid, or executing any other driving maneuver. Explain the process one step at a time. Remember, your audience consists of teens who are just learning how to drive.

3. Write an article for *Consumer Reports* on how to shop for a certain product. Give specific steps explaining how to save money, buy a quality product, and the like.

4. Write a process analysis showing how to save a life by CPR, rescue breathing, the Heimlich maneuver, or some other method. Your audience will be average, everyday people who are taking a first-aid class.

5. Your closest friend plans to move into his or her own apartment but doesn't know the first thing about how to choose one. Explain the process of selecting an apartment—where to look, what to investigate, what questions to ask before signing a lease.

6. You write an "advice to the lovelorn" column for the campus newspaper. A correspondent asks for advice on how to break up with a steady boyfriend (or girlfriend) without hurting the person. Give the writer guidance on how to end a meaningful relationship with a minimal amount of pain.

8

COMPARISON-CONTRAST

WHAT IS COMPARISON-CONTRAST?

We frequently try to make sense of the world by finding similarities and differences in our experiences. Seeing how things are alike (comparing) and seeing how they are different (contrasting) helps us impose meaning on experiences that otherwise might remain fragmented and disconnected. Barely aware of the fact that we're comparing and contrasting, we may think to ourselves, "I woke up in a great mood this morning, but now I feel uneasy and anxious. I wonder why I feel so different." This inner questioning, which often occurs in a flash, is just one example of the way we use comparison and contrast to understand ourselves and our world.

Comparing and contrasting also helps us make choices. We compare and contrast everything—from two brands of soap we might buy to two colleges we might attend. We listen to a favorite radio station, watch a preferred nightly news show, select a particular dessert from a menu— all because we have done some degree of comparing and contrasting. We often weigh these alternatives in an unstudied, casual manner, as when we flip from one radio station to another. But when we have to make important decisions, we tend to think rigorously about how things are alike or different: Should I live in a dorm or rent an apartment? Should I accept the higher-paying job or the lower-paying one that offers more challenges? Such a deliberate approach to comparison-contrast may also provide us with needed insight into complex contemporary issues: Is television's coverage of political campaigns more or less objective than it used to be? What are the merits of the various positions on abortion?

HOW COMPARISON-CONTRAST FITS YOUR PURPOSE AND AUDIENCE

When is it appropriate in writing to use the comparison-contrast method of development? Comparison-contrast works well if you want to demonstrate any of the following: (1) that one thing is better than another (the first example below); (2) that things which seem different are actually alike (the second example below); (3) that things which seem alike are actually different (the third example below).

> Compare and contrast the way male and female relationships are depicted in *Cosmopolitan, Ms., Playboy,* and *Esquire*. Which publication has the most limited view of men and women? Which has the broadest perspective?

> Football, basketball, and baseball differ in the ways they appeal to fans. Describe the unique drawing power of each sport, but also reach some conclusions about the appeals the three sports have in common.

> Studies show that both college students and their parents fell that post-secondary education should equip young people to succeed in the marketplace. Yet the same studies report that the two groups have a very different understanding of what it means to succeed. What differences do you think the studies identify?

Other assignments will, in less obvious ways, lend themselves to comparison-contrast. For instance, although words like *compare, contrast, differ,* and *have in common* don't appear in the following assignments, essay responses to the assignments could be organized around the comparison-contrast format:

The emergence of the two-career family is one of the major phenomena of our culture. Discuss the advantages and disadvantages of having both parents work, showing how you feel about such two-career households.

Some people believe that the 1950s, often called the golden age of television, produced several never-to-be-equaled comedy classics. Do you agree that such shows as *I Love Lucy* and *The Honeymooners* are superior to the situation comedies aired on television today?

There has been considerable criticism recently of the news coverage by the city's two leading newspapers, the *Herald* and the *Beacon*. Indicate whether you think the criticism is valid by discussing the similarities and differences in the two papers' news coverage.

Note: The last assignment shows that a comparison-contrast essay may cover similarities *and* differences, not just one or the other.

As you have seen, comparison-contrast can be the key strategy for achieving an essay's purpose. But comparison-contrast can also be a supplemental method used to help make a point in an essay organized chiefly around another pattern of development. A serious, informative essay intended for laypeople might *define* clinical depression by contrasting that state of mind with ordinary run-of-the-mill blues. Writing humorously about the exhausting *effects* of trying to get in shape, you might dramatize your plight for readers by contrasting the leisurely way you used to spend your day with your current rigidly compulsive exercise regimen. Or, in an urgent *argumentation-persuasion* essay on the need for stricter controls over drug abuse in the workplace, you might provide readers with background by comparing several companies' approaches to the problem.

SUGGESTIONS FOR USING COMPARISON-CONTRAST IN AN ESSAY

The following suggestions will be helpful whether you use comparison-contrast as a dominant or a supportive pattern of development.

1. Be sure your subjects are at least somewhat alike.   Unless you plan to develop an *analogy* (see below), the subjects you choose to compare or contrast should share some obvious characteristics or qualities. It makes sense to compare different parts of the country, two comedians, or several college teachers. But a reasonable paper wouldn't result from, let's say, a comparison of a television game show with a soap opera. Your subjects must belong to the same general group so that your comparison-contrast stays within good logical bounds and doesn't veer off into pointlessness.

2. Stay focused on your purpose.   When writing, remember that comparison-contrast isn't an end in itself. That is, your objective isn't to turn an essay into a mechanical list of "how A differs from B" or "how A is like B." Like the other patterns of development discussed in this book, comparison-contrast is a strategy for making a point or meeting a larger purpose.

Consider the assignment on page 391 about the two newspapers. Your purpose here might be simply to *inform*, to present information as objectively as possible: "This is what the *Herald*'s news coverage is like. This is what the *Beacon*'s news coverage is like."

More frequently, though, you'll use comparison-contrast to *evaluate* your subjects' pros and cons, your goal being to reach a conclusion or make a judgment: "Both the *Herald* and the *Beacon* spend too much time reporting local news," or "The *Herald*'s analysis of the recent hostage crisis was more insightful than the *Beacon*'s." Comparison-contrast can also be used to *persuade* readers to take action: "People interested in thorough coverage of international events should read the *Herald* rather than the *Beacon*." Persuasive essays may also propose a change, contrasting what now exists with a more ideal situation: "For the *Beacon* to compete with the *Herald*, it must assign more reporters to international stories."

Yet another purpose you might have in writing a comparison-contrast essay is to *clear up misconceptions* by revealing previously hidden similarities or differences. For example, perhaps your town's two newspapers are thought to be sharply different. However, a comparison-contrast analysis might reveal that—although one paper specializes in sensationalized stories while the other adopts a more muted approach—both resort to biased, emotionally charged analyses of local politics. Or the essay might illustrate that the tabloid's treatment of the local arts scene is surprisingly more comprehensive than that of its competitor.

Comparing and contrasting also make it possible to *draw an analogy* between two seemingly unrelated subjects. An analogy is an imaginative comparison that delves beneath the surface differences of subjects in order to expose their significant and often unsuspected similarities or differences. Your purpose may be to show that singles bars and zoos share a number of striking similarities. Or you may want to illustrate that wolves and humans raise their young in much the same way, but that wolves go about the process in a more civilized manner. The analogical approach can make a complex subject easier to understand—as when the national deficit is compared to a house-hold budget gone awry. Analogies are often dramatic and instructive, challenging you and your audience to consider subjects in a new light. But analogies don't speak for themselves. You must make clear to the reader how the analogy demonstrates your purpose.

3. Formulate a strong thesis. An essay developed primarily through comparison-contrast should be focused by a solid thesis. Besides revealing your attitude, the thesis will often do the following:

- Name the subjects being compared and contrasted.
- Indicate whether the essay focuses on the subjects' similarities, differences, or both.
- State the essay's main point of comparison or contrast.

Not all comparison-contrast essays need thesis statements as structured as those that follow. Even so, these examples can serve as models of clarity. Note that the first thesis statement signals similarities, the second differences, and the last both similarities and differences:

Middle-aged parents are often in a good position to empathize with adolescent children because the emotional upheavals experienced by the two age groups are much the same.

The priorities of most retired people are more conducive to health and happiness than the priorities of most young professionals.

College students in their thirties and forties face many of the same pressures as younger students, but they are better equipped to withstand these pressures.

4. Select the points to be discussed.   Once you have identified the essay's subjects, purpose, and thesis, you need to decide which aspects of the subjects to compare or contrast. College professors, for instance, could be compared and contrasted on the basis of their testing methods, ability to motivate students, confidence in front of a classroom, personalities, level of enthusiasm, and so forth.

Brainstorming, freewriting, and mapping are valuable for gathering possible points to cover. Whichever prewriting technique you use, try to produce more raw material than you'll need, so that you have the luxury of narrowing the material down to the most significant points.

When selecting points to cover, be sure to consider your audience. Ask yourself: "Will my readers be familiar with this item? Will I need it to get my message across? Will my audience find this item interesting or convincing?" What your readers know, what they don't know, and what you can predict about their reactions should influence your choices. And, of course, you need to select points that support your thesis. If your essay explains the differences between healthy, sensible diets and dangerous crash diets, it wouldn't be appropriate to talk about aerobic exercise. Similarly, imagine you want to write an essay making the point that, despite their differences, hard rock of the 1960s and punk rock of the 1970s both reflected young people's disillusionment with society. It wouldn't make much sense to contrast the long uncombed hairstyle of the 1960s with the short spikey cuts of the 1970s. But contrasting song lyrics (protest versus nihilistic messages) would help support your thesis and lead to interesting insights.

5. Organize the points to be discussed.   After deciding which points to include, you should use a systematic, logical plan for presenting those ideas. If the points aren't organized, your essay will be little more than a confusing jumble of ideas. There are two common ways to organize an essay developed wholly or in part by comparison-contrast: the one-side-at-a-time method and the point-by-point method. Although both strategies may be used in a paper, one method usually predominates.

In the *one-side-at-a-time method* of organization, you discuss everything relevant about one subject before moving to another subject. For example, responding to the earlier assignment that asked you to analyze the news coverage in two local papers, you might first talk about the *Herald's* coverage of international, national, and local news; then you would discuss the *Beacon's* coverage of the same categories. Note that the areas discussed should be the same for both newspapers. It wouldn't be logical to review the *Herald's* coverage of international, national, and local news and then to detail the *Beacon's* magazine supplements, modern living section, and comics page. Moreover, the areas compared and contrasted should be presented in the same order.

This is how you would organize the essay using the one-side-at-a-time method:

Everything about A	*Herald's* news coverage:
	• International
	• National
	• Local
Everything about B	*Beacon's* news coverage:
	• International
	• National
	• Local

In the *point-by-point method* of organization, you alternate from one aspect of the first subject to the same aspect of your other subject(s). For example, to use this method when comparing or contrasting the *Herald* and the *Beacon,* you would first discuss the *Herald's* international coverage, then the *Beacon's* international coverage; next the *Herald's* national coverage, then the *Beacon's*; and finally, the *Herald's* local coverage, then the *Beacon's*.

Using the point-by-point method, this is how the essay would be organized:

First aspect of A and B	*Herald:* International coverage
	Beacon: International coverage
Second aspect of A and B	*Herald:* National coverage
	Beacon: National coverage
Third aspect of A and B	*Herald:* Local coverage
	Beacon: Local coverage

Deciding which of these two methods of organization to use is largely a personal choice, though there are several factors to consider.

The one-side-at-a-time method tends to convey a more unified feeling because it highlights broad similarities and differences. It is, therefore, an effective approach for subjects that are fairly uncomplicated. This strategy also works well when essays are brief; the reader won't find it difficult to remember what has been said about subject A when reading about subject B.

Because the point-by-point method permits more extensive coverage of similarities and differences, it is often a wise choice when subjects are complex. This pattern is also useful for lengthy essays since readers would probably find it difficult to remember, let's say, ten pages of information about subject A while reading the next ten pages about subject B. The point-by-point approach, however, may cause readers to lose sight of the broader picture, so remember to keep them focused on your central point.

6. Supply the reader with clear transitions.   Although a well-organized comparison-contrast format is important, it doesn't guarantee that readers will be able to follow your line of thought easily. *Transitions*—especially those signaling similarities or differences—are needed to show readers where they have been and where they are going. Such cues are essential in all writing, but they're especially crucial in a paper using comparison-contrast. By indicating clearly when subjects are being compared or contrasted, the transitions help weave the discussion into a coherent whole.

The transitions (in boldface) in the following examples could be used to *signal similarities* in an essay discussing the news coverage in the *Herald* and the *Beacon:*

- The *Beacon* **also** allots only a small portion of the front page to global news.
- **In the same way**, the *Herald* tries to include at least three local stories on the first page.
- **Likewise**, the *Beacon* emphasizes the importance of up-to-date reporting of town meetings.
- The *Herald* is **similarly** committed to extensive coverage of high school and college sports.

The transitions (in boldface) in these examples could be used to *signal differences:*

- **By way of contrast**, the *Herald's* editorial page deals with national matters on the average of three times a week.
- **On the other hand**, the *Beacon* does not share the *Herald's* enthusiasm for interviews with national figures.
- The *Beacon*, **however**, does not encourage its reporters to tackle national stories the way the *Herald* does.
- **But** the *Herald's* coverage of the Washington scene is much more comprehensive than its competitor's.

STUDENT ESSAY

The following student essay was written by Carol Siskin in response to this assignment:

> In "That Lean and Hungry Look," Suzanne Britt contrasts two personality types, extolling the one normally considered less praiseworthy. In an essay of your own, contrast two personality types, lifestyles, or stages of life, showing that the one most people consider inferior is actually superior.

While reading Carol's paper, try to determine how well it applies the principles of comparison-contrast. The annotations on Carol's paper and the commentary following it will help you look at the essay more closely.

The Virtues of Growing Older
by Carol Siskin

The first of a two-paragraph introduction → Our society worships youth. Advertisements convince us to buy Grecian Formula and Oil of Olay so we can hide the gray in our hair and smooth the lines on our face. Television shows feature attractive young stars with firm bodies, perfect complexions, and thick manes of hair. Middle-aged folks work out in gyms and jog down the street, trying to delay the effects of age. 1

The second introductory paragraph → Wouldn't any person over thirty gladly sign with the devil just to be young again? Isn't aging an experience to be dreaded? Perhaps it is un-American to say so, but I believe the answer is "No." 2

Thesis ⟶ Being young is often pleasant, but being older has distinct advantages.

First half of ⟶ When young, you are apt to be obsessed with   3
topic sentence
for point 1:
Appearance

Start of what it's ⏤
like being young

your appearance. When my brother Dave and I were teens, we worked feverishly to perfect the bodies we had. Dave lifted weights, took megadoses of vitamins, and drank a half-dozen milk shakes a day in order to turn his wiry adolescent frame into some muscular ideal. And as a teenager, I dieted constantly. No matter what I weighed, though, I was never satisfied with the way I looked. My legs were too heavy, my shoulders too broad, my waist too big. When Dave and I were young, we begged and pleaded for the "right" clothes. If our parents didn't get them for us, we felt our world would fall apart. How could we go to school wearing loose-fitting blazers when everyone else would be wearing smartly tailored leather jackets? We would be considered freaks. I often wonder how my parents, and parents in general, manage to tolerate their children

Second half of
topic sentence for
point 1

Start of what it's ⏤
like being older

during the adolescent years. Now, however, Dave and I are beyond such adolescent agonies. My rounded figure seems fine, and I don't deny myself a slice of pecan pie if I feel in the mood. Dave still works out, but he has actually become fond of his tall lanky frame. The two of us enjoy wearing fashionable clothes, but we are no longer slaves to style. And women, I'm embarrassed to admit, even more than men, have always seemed to be at the mercy of fashion. Now my clothes--and my brother's--are attractive yet easy to wear. We no longer feel anxious about what others will think. As long as we feel good about how we look, we are happy.

First half of
topic sentence
for point 2:
Life choices

Being older is preferable to being younger in   4
another way. Obviously, I still have important choices to make about my life, but I have already made many of the critical decisions that confront those

Start of what it's
like being older

Second half of
topic sentence for
point 2

just starting out. I chose the man I wanted to marry. I decided to have children. I elected to return to college to complete my education. But when you are young, major decisions await you at every turn.

Start of what it's ⏤
like being
younger

"What college should I attend? What career should I pursue? Should I get married? Should I have children?" These are just a few of the issues facing

	young people. It's no wonder that, despite their
Topic sentence	carefree facade, they are often confused, uncertain,
for point 3:	and troubled by all the unknowns in their future.
Self-concept ─────→	But the greatest benefit of being forty is know- 5
Start of what it's ────	ing who I am. The most unsettling aspect of youth
like being	is the uncertainty you feel about your values, goals,
younger	and dreams. Being young means wondering what is
	worth working for. Being young means feeling
	happy with yourself one day and wishing you were
	never born the next. It means trying on new selves
	by taking up with different crowds. It means resent-
	ing your parents and their way of life one minute
	and then feeling you will never be as good or as
	accomplished as they are. By way of contrast, forty
Start of what it's ────	is sanity. I have a surer self-concept now. I don't
like being older	laugh at jokes I don't think are funny. I can make a
	speech in front of a town meeting or complain in a
	store because I am no longer terrified that people
	will laugh at me; I am no longer anxious that every-
	one must like me. I no longer blame my parents for
	my every personality quirk or keep a running score
	of everything they did wrong raising me. Life has
	taught me that I, not they, am responsible for who I
	am. We are all human beings--neither saints nor
	devils.
Conclusion	Most Americans blindly accept the idea that 6
	newer is automatically better. But a human life con-
	tradicts this premise. There is a great deal of happi-
	ness to be found as we grow older. My own parents,
	now in their sixties, recently told me that they are
	happier now than they have ever been. They would
	not want to be my age. Did this surprise me? At
	first, yes. Then it gladdened me. Their contentment
	holds out great promise for me as I move into the
	next--perhaps even better--phase of my life.

COMMENTARY

Purpose and thesis.   In her essay, Carol disproves the widespread belief that being young is preferable to being old. The *comparison-contrast* pattern allows her to analyze the drawbacks of one and the merits of the other, thus providing the essay with an *evaluative purpose*. Using the title to indicate her point of view, Carol places the *thesis* at the end of her two-paragraph introduction: "Being young is often pleasant, but being older has distinct advantages." Note that the thesis accomplishes several things. It names the two subjects to be discussed and clarifies Carol's point of view about her subjects. The thesis also implies that the essay will focus on the contrasts between these two periods of life.

Points of support and overall organization.   To support her assertion that older is better, Carol supplies examples from her own life and organizes the examples around three main points: attitudes about appearance, decisions about life choices, and questions of self-concept. Using the *point-by-point method* to organize the overall essay, she explores each of these key ideas in a separate paragraph. Each paragraph is further focused by one or two sentences that serve as a topic sentence.

Sequence of points, organizational cues, and paragraph development.   Let's look more closely at the way Carol presents her three central points in the essay. She obviously considers appearance the least important of a person's worries, life choices more important, and self-concept the most critical. So she uses *emphatic order* to sequence the supporting paragraphs, with the phrase "But the greatest benefit" signaling the special significance of the last issue. Carol is also careful to use *transitions* to help readers follow her line of thinking: "*Now, however,* Dave and I are beyond such adolescent agonies" (paragraph 3); "*But* when you are young, major decisions await you at every turn" (4); and "*By way of contrast,* forty is sanity" (5).

Although Carol has worked hard to write a well-organized paper—and has on the whole been successful—she doesn't feel compelled to make the paper fit a rigid format. As you've seen, the essay as a whole uses the point-by-point method, but each supporting paragraph uses the *one-side-at-a-time* method—that is, everything about one age group is discussed before there is a shift to the other age group. Notice too that the third and fifth paragraphs start with young people and then move to adults, whereas the fourth paragraph reverses the sequence by starting with older people.

Other patterns of development.   Carol uses the comparison-contrast format to organize her ideas, but other patterns of development also come into play. To illustrate her points, she makes extensive use of *exemplification,* and her discussion also contains elements typical of *causal analysis.* Throughout the essay, for instance, she traces the effect of being a certain age on her brother, herself, and her parents.

A problem with unity.   As you read the third paragraph, you might have noted that Carol's essay runs into a problem. Two sentences in the paragraph disrupt the *unity* of Carol's discussion: "I often wonder how my parents, and parents in general, manage to tolerate their children during the adolescent years," and "women, I'm embarrassed to admit . . . have always seemed to be at the mercy of fashion." These sentences should be deleted because they don't develop the idea that adolescents are overly concerned with appearance.

Conclusion.   Carol's final paragraph brings the essay to a pleasing and interesting close. The conclusion recalls the point made in the introduction: Americans overvalue youth. Carol also uses the conclusion to broaden the scope of her discussion. Rather than continuing to focus on herself, she briefly mentions her parents and the pleasure they take in life. By bringing her parents into the essay, Carol is able to make a gently philosophical observation about the promise that awaits her as she grows older. The implication is that a similarly positive future awaits us, too.

Revising the first draft.   To help guide her revision, Carol asked her husband to read her first draft aloud. As he did, Carol took notes on what she sensed were the paper's strengths and weaknesses. She then jotted down her observations, as well as her husband's, on the draft. Keeping these comments in mind, Carol made a number of changes in her paper. You'll get a good sense of how she proceeded if you compare the original introduction reprinted here with the final version in the full essay.

Original Version of the Introduction

America is a land filled with people who worship youth. We admire dynamic young achievers; our middle-aged citizens work out in gyms; all of us wear tight tops and colorful sneakers--clothes that look fine on the young but ridiculous on aging bodies. Television shows revolve around perfect-looking young stars, while commercials entice us with products that will keep us young.

Wouldn't every older person want to be young again? Isn't aging to be avoided? It may be slightly unpatriotic to say so, but I believe the answer is "No." Being young may be pleasant at times, but I would rather be my forty-year-old self. I no longer have to agonize about my physical appearance, I have already made many of my crucial life decisions, and I am much less confused about who I am.

After hearing her original two-paragraph introduction read aloud, Carol was dissatisfied with what she had written. Although she wasn't quite sure how to proceed, she knew that the paragraphs were flat and that they failed to open the essay on a strong note. She decided to start by whittling down the opening sentence, making it crisper and more powerful: "Our society worships youth." That done, she eliminated two bland statements ("We admire dynamic young achievers" and "all of us wear tight tops and colorful sneakers") and made several vague references more concrete and interesting. For example, "Commercials entice us with products that will keep us young" became "Grecian Formula and Oil of Olay . . . hide the gray in our hair and smooth the lines on our face"; "perfect-looking young stars" became "attractive young stars with firm bodies, perfect complexions, and thick manes of hair." With the addition of these specifics, the first paragraph became more vigorous and interesting.

Carol next made some subtle changes in the two questions that opened the second paragraph of the original introduction. She replaced "Wouldn't every older person want to be young again?" and "Isn't aging to be avoided?" with two more emphatic questions: "Wouldn't any person over thirty gladly sign with the devil just to be young again?" and "Isn't aging an experience to be dreaded?" Carol also made some changes at the end of the original second paragraph. Because the paper is relatively short and the subject matter easy to understand, she decided to omit her somewhat awkward *plan of development* ("I no longer have to agonize about my physical appearance, I have already made many of my crucial life decisions, and I am much less confused about who I am"). This deletion made it possible to end the introduction with a clear statement of the essay's thesis.

Once these revisions were made, Carol was confident that her essay got off to a stronger start. Feeling reassured, she moved ahead and made changes in other sections of her paper. Such work enabled her to prepare a solid piece of writing that offers food for thought.

ACTIVITIES: COMPARISON-CONTRAST

Prewriting Activities

1. Imagine you're writing two essays: One explores the *effects* of holding a job while in college; the other explains a *process* for budgeting money wisely. Jot down ways you might use comparison-contrast in each essay.

2. Using your journal or freewriting, jot down the advantages and disadvantages of two ways of doing something (for example, watching movies in the theater versus watching them on a VCR at home; following trends versus ignoring them; dating one person versus playing the field; and so on). Reread your prewriting and determine what your thesis, purpose, audience, tone, and point of view might be if you were to write an essay. Make a scratch list of the main ideas you would cover. Would a point-by-point or a one-side-at-a-time method of organization work more effectively?

Revising Activities

3. Of the statements that follow, which would *not* make effective thesis statements for comparison-contrast essays? Identify the problem(s) in the faulty statements and revise them accordingly.

   a. Although their classroom duties often overlap, teacher aides are not as equipped as teachers to handle disciplinary problems.

   b. This college provides more assistance to its students than most schools.

   c. During the state's last congressional election, both candidates relied heavily on television to communicate their messages.

   d. There are many differences between American and foreign cars.

4. The following paragraph is from the draft of an essay detailing the qualities of a skillful manager. How effective is this comparison-contrast paragraph? What revisions would help focus the paragraph on the point made in the topic sentence? Where should details be added or deleted? Rewrite the paragraph, providing necessary transitions and details.

   A manager encourages creativity and treats employees courteously, while a boss discourages staff resourcefulness and views it as a threat. At the hardware store where I work, I got my boss's approval to develop a system for organizing excess stock in the storeroom. I shelved items in roughly the same order as they were displayed in the store. The system was helpful to all the salespeople, not just to me, since everyone was stymied by the boss's helter-skelter system. What he did was store overstocked items according to each wholesaler, even though most of us weren't there long enough to know which items came from which wholesaler. His supposed system created chaos. When he saw what I had done, he was furious and insisted that we continue to follow the old slapdash system. I had assumed he would welcome my ideas the way my manager did last summer when I worked in a drugstore. But he didn't and I had to scrap my work and go back to his eccentric system. He certainly could learn something about employee relations from the drugstore manager.

Rachel Carson

Once accused of being a fearmonger, biologist Rachel Carson (1907–64) is now recognized as one of the country's first environmentalists. She was the author of three popular books about the marine world: *The Sea Around Us* (1951), *Under the Sea Wind* (1952), and *The Edge of the Sea* (1955). But it was the publication of *Silent Spring* (1962), Carson's alarming study of the use of pesticides and herbicides, that brought her special attention and established her reputation as a passionate advocate for a clean environment. The following selection is taken from *Silent Spring*.

Pre-Reading Journal Entry

Take a few minutes to record in your journal your impressions of a place that has special meaning for you—but that is being threatened in one way or another. Jot down sensory details about the place, focusing on those specifics that capture its unique qualities.

A Fable for Tomorrow

There was once a town in the heart of America where all life 1
seemed to live in harmony with its surroundings. The town lay in the midst of a checkerboard of prosperous farms, with fields of grain and hillsides of orchards where, in spring, white clouds of bloom drifted above the green fields. In autumn, oak and maple and birch set up a blaze of color that flamed and flickered across a backdrop of pines. Then foxes barked in the hills and deer silently crossed the fields, half hidden in the mists of the fall mornings.

Along the roads, laurel, viburnum and alder, great ferns and 2
wildflowers delighted the traveler's eye through much of the year. Even in winter the roadsides were places of beauty, where countless birds came to feed on the berries and on the seed heads of the dried weeds rising above the snow. The countryside was, in fact, famous for the abundance and variety of its bird life, and when the flood of migrants was pouring through in spring and fall people traveled from great distances to observe them. Others came to fish the streams, which flowed clear and cold out of the hills and contained

shady pools where trout lay. So it had been from the days many years ago when the first settlers raised their houses, sank their wells, and built their barns.

Then a strange blight crept over the area and everything began to change. Some evil spell had settled on the community: mysterious maladies swept the flocks of chickens; the cattle and sheep sickened and died. Everywhere was a shadow of death. The farmers spoke of much illness among their families. In the town the doctors had become more and more puzzled by new kinds of sickness appearing among their patients. There had been several sudden and unexplained deaths, not only among adults but even among children, who would be stricken suddenly while at play and die within a few hours.

There was a strange stillness. The birds, for example—where had they gone? Many people spoke of them, puzzled and disturbed. The feeding stations in the backyards were deserted. The few birds seen anywhere were moribund; they trembled violently and could not fly. It was a spring without voices. On the mornings that had once throbbed with the dawn chorus of robins, catbirds, doves, jays, wrens, and scores of other bird voices there was now no sound; only silence lay over the fields and woods and marsh.

On the farms the hens brooded, but no chicks hatched. The farmers complained that they were unable to raise any pigs—the litters were small and the young survived only a few days. The apple trees were coming into bloom but no bees droned among the blossoms, so there was no pollination and there would be no fruit.

The roadsides, once so attractive, were now lined with browned and withered vegetation as though swept by fire. These, too, were silent, deserted by all living things. Even the streams were now lifeless. Anglers no longer visited them, for all the fish had died.

In the gutters under the eaves and between the shingles of the roofs, a white granular powder still showed a few patches; some weeks before it had fallen like snow upon the roofs and the lawns, the fields and streams.

No witchcraft, no enemy action had silenced the rebirth of new life in this stricken world. The people had done it themselves.

This town does not actually exist, but it might easily have a thousand counterparts in America or elsewhere in the world. I know of no community that has experienced all the misfortunes I describe. Yet every one of these disasters has actually happened somewhere, and many real communities have already suffered a substantial number of them. A grim specter has crept upon us almost unnoticed, and this imagined tragedy may easily become a stark reality we all shall know.

Questions for Close Reading

1. What is the selection's thesis? Locate the sentence(s) in which Carson states her main idea. If she doesn't state the thesis explicitly, express it in your own words.
2. What are some of the delights of Carson's beautiful, healthy countryside?
3. When Carson writes of "a strange blight," an "evil spell" (paragraph 3), whose point of view is she adopting?
4. What are the effects of the blight?
5. Refer to your dictionary as needed to define the following words used in the selection: *viburnum* (paragraph 2), *alder* (2), *moribund* (4), and *specter* (9).

Questions About the Writer's Craft

1. **The pattern.**   To develop her essay, Carson uses the one-side-at-a-time method of comparison-contrast. What does this method enable her to do that the point-by-point approach would not?
2. **Other patterns.**   Throughout the essay, Carson appeals to the reader's senses of sight and hearing. Which paragraphs are developed primarily through visual or auditory description? How do the sensory images in these paragraphs reinforce Carson's thesis?
3. Carson's diction (word choice) and sentence rhythm often resemble those of the Bible. For example, we read, "So it had been from the days many years ago" (paragraph 2), "a strange blight crept over the area" (3), and "Everywhere was a shadow of death" (3). Why do you suppose Carson chose to echo the Bible in this way?
4. How does Carson's approach to her subject change in the last paragraph? What is the effect of this change?

Writing Assignments Using Comparison-Contrast as a Pattern of Development

1. Carson imagines a fictional town that has changed for the worse. Consider a place you know well that has changed for the *better.* You might focus on a renovated school, a rehabilitated neighborhood, a newly-preserved park. Write an essay contrasting the place before and after the change. At the end of your essay, describe briefly the effects of the change.

2. In her essay, Carson provides descriptive details unique to particular seasons. For example, she writes that "in autumn, oak and maple and birch set up a blaze of color that flamed and flickered across a backdrop of pines" (paragraph 1). Choosing a place you know well, contrast its sights, sounds, and smells during one season with those you've noticed during another time of year. Use rich sensory details to convey the differences between the two seasons. Consider first reading Joan Didion's "The Santa Ana" (page 688), which recounts, in vivid detail, a specific natural phenomenon and its impact on regional inhabitants.

Writing Assignments Using Other Patterns of Development

3. Carson cites "white granular powder" (paragraph 7) as the cause of the blight. Write an essay about a time you noticed a visible environmental problem—say, smog blurring a city skyline, soot coating a window, or medical syringes discarded on the beach. Use vivid narrative details to capture the effect of the experience on you.

4. Carson graphically shows the effects of herbicides and pesticides on the environment. Focus on some other less global environmental problem: graffiti on a public building; vandalized trees and shrubs; beer cans thrown in a neighborhood park, for example. Discuss the effects of this situation on the physical environment and on people's attitudes and actions. Conclude with suggestions about possible ways to remedy the problem. Gordon Parks's "Flavio's Home" (page 98) will help you appreciate the interaction between the environment and human behavior.

Writing Assignments Using a Journal Entry as a Starting Point

5. Write an essay describing an endangered place that is very important to you. Describe the potential threat either at the beginning or at the end of the essay, and paint such a vivid picture of the place in the rest of the essay that readers understand why the potential threat is so unfortunate. Select from your pre-reading journal entry only those details that convey the special qualities of the place, adding more texture and specifics where needed.

Suzanne Britt

Freelance writer and textbook author Suzanne Britt studied at Salem College and Washington University and now teaches at Meredith College. Her work has been published in the *Baltimore Sun, Long Island Newsday,* the *Boston Globe,* and *The New York Times.* A regular columnist for *North Carolina Gardens and Homes* and for a newsletter devoted to the works of Charles Dickens, Britt contributes to Duke University's *Books and Religion,* a publication featuring religious and social commentary. Britt's first book, *Skinny People Are Dull and Crunchy Like Carrots* (1982), is an expansion of the following essay, which was first published in *Newsweek's* "My Turn" column. Her second book, *Show and Tell,* was published in 1983.

Pre-Reading Journal Entry

When was the last time you or someone you know complained about being overweight or underweight? In your journal, consider our culture's stereotyped attitudes about weight. What qualities does society typically attribute to thin people? To heavy people? List as many qualities as you can for each. To what extent does your experience support these generalizations?

That Lean and Hungry Look[1]

Caesar was right. Thin people need watching. I've been watching them for most of my adult life, and I don't like what I see. When these narrow fellows spring at me, I quiver to my toes. Thin people come in all personalities, most of them menacing. You've got your "together" thin person, your mechanical thin person, your condescending thin person, your tsk-tsk thin person, your efficiency-expert thin person. All of them are dangerous. 1

In the first place, thin people aren't fun. They don't know how to goof off, at least in the best, fat sense of the word. They've always 2

---

[1]Britt's title is a reference to a line from Shakespeare's *Julius Caesar.* In the play, Caesar says he distrusts Cassius because Cassius has "a lean and hungry look; . . . such men are dangerous." Later in the play, Cassius helps assassinate Caesar, proving Caesar's fears were justified (editors' note).

got to be adoing. Give them a coffee break, and they'll jog around the block. Supply them with a quiet evening at home, and they'll fix the screen door and lick S&H green stamps. They say things like "there aren't enough hours in the day." Fat people never say that. Fat people think the day is too damn long already.

Thin people make me tired. They've got speedy little metabo-   3 lisms that cause them to bustle briskly. They're forever rubbing their bony hands together and eyeing new problems to "tackle." I like to surround myself with sluggish, inert, easygoing fat people, the kind who believe that if you clean it up today, it'll just get dirty again tomorrow.

Some people say the business about the jolly fat person is a   4 myth, that all of us chubbies are neurotic, sick, sad people. I disagree. Fat people may not be chortling all day long, but they're a hell of a lot *nicer* than the wizened and shriveled. Thin people turn surly, mean, and hard at a young age because they never learn the value of a hot-fudge sundae for easing tension. Thin people don't like gooey soft things because they themselves are neither gooey nor soft. They are crunchy and dull, like carrots. They go straight to the heart of the matter while fat people let things stay all blurry and hazy and vague, the way things actually are. Thin people want to face the truth. Fat people know there is no truth. One of my thin friends is always staring at complex, unsolvable problems and saying, "The key thing is . . ." Fat people never say that. They know there isn't any such thing as the key thing about anything.

Thin people believe in logic. Fat people see all sides. The sides   5 fat people see are rounded blobs, usually gray, always nebulous and truly not worth worrying about. But the thin person persists. "If you consume more calories than you burn," says one of my thin friends, "you will gain weight. It's that simple." Fat people always grin when they hear statements like that. They know better.

Fat people realize that life is illogical and unfair. They know very   6 well that God is not in his heaven and all is not right with the world. If God is up there, fat people could have two doughnuts and a big orange drink anytime they wanted it.

Thin people have a long list of logical things they are always   7 spouting off to me. They hold up one finger at a time as they reel off these things, so I won't lose track. They speak slowly as if to a young child. The list is long and full of holes. It contains tidbits like "get a grip on yourself," "cigarettes kill," "cholesterol clogs," "fit as

a fiddle," "ducks in a row," "organize," and "sound fiscal management." Phrases like that.

They think these 2,000-point plans lead to happiness. Fat peo- 8
ple know happiness is elusive at best and even if they could get the
kind thin people talk about, they wouldn't want it. Wisely, fat people see that such programs are too dull, too hard, too off the mark.
They are never better than a whole cheesecake.

Fat people know all about the mystery of life. They are the ones 9
acquainted with the night, with luck, with fate, with playing it by
ear. One thin person I know once suggested that we arrange all the
parts of a jigsaw puzzle into groups according to size, shape, and
color. He figured this would cut the time needed to complete the
puzzle by at least 50 percent. I said I wouldn't do it. One, I like to
muddle through. Two, what good would it do to finish early?
Three, the jigsaw puzzle isn't the important thing. The important
thing is the fun of four people (one thin person included) sitting
around a card table, working a jigsaw puzzle. My thin friend had no
use for my list. Instead of joining us, he went outside and mulched
the boxwoods. The three remaining fat people finished the puzzle
and made chocolate, double-fudged brownies to celebrate.

The main problem with thin people is they oppress. Their good 10
intentions, bony torsos, tight ships, neat corners, cerebral machinations, and pat solutions loom like dark clouds over the loose, comfortable, spread-out, soft world of the fat. Long after fat people have
removed their coats and shoes and put their feet up on the coffee
table, thin people are still sitting on the edge of the sofa, looking
neat as a pin, discussing rutabagas. Fat people are heavily into fits of
laughter, slapping their thighs and whooping it up, while thin people are still politely waiting for the punch line.

Thin people are downers. They like math and morality and rea- 11
soned evaluation of the limitations of human beings. They have
their skinny little acts together. They expound, prognose, probe,
and prick.

Fat people are convivial. They will like you even if you're irreg- 12
ular and have acne. They will come up with a good reason why you
never wrote the great American novel. They will cry in your beer
with you. They will put your name in the pot. They will let you off
the hook. Fat people will gab, giggle, guffaw, galumph, gyrate, and
gossip. They are generous, giving, and gallant. They are gluttonous
and goodly and great. What you want when you're down is soft and

jiggly, not muscled and stable. Fat people know this. Fat people have plenty of room. Fat people will take you in.

Questions for Close Reading

1. What is the selection's thesis? Locate the sentence(s) in which Britt states her main idea. If she doesn't state the thesis explicitly, express it in your own words.
2. Into what personality types does Britt categorize thin people? What do these personality types have in common?
3. Britt writes that thin people use their free time for such activities as jogging, fixing a screen door, and pasting in green stamps. How are these activities similar?
4. Why does Britt approve of fat people's tendency to "let things stay all blurry and hazy and vague"?
5. Refer to your dictionary as needed to define the following words used in the selection: *wizened* (paragraph 4), *nebulous* (5), *fiscal* (7), *mulch* (9), *machinations* (10), *expound* (11), and *convivial* (12).

Questions About the Writer's Craft

1. **The pattern.** Which comparison-contrast format does Britt use to develop her essay? Why might she have chosen this format?
2. How does Britt's choice of words and sentence structure establish an informal, lighthearted tone?
3. Why is Britt's carrot simile especially apt?
4. Where in the last paragraph does Britt use *alliteration* (the repetition of initial consonant sounds)? What might have been her reason for using this technique?

Writing Assignments Using Comparison-Contrast as a Pattern of Development

1. Write an essay contrasting two people who represent markedly dissimilar types. Perhaps one person is messy, the other neat. Or maybe one is worldly wise while the other is unsophisticated. Or one might be punctual while the other is always late. Use the one-side-at-a-time or the point-by-point method to highlight the differences between the two people. Adopting a light, waggish tone, argue—as Britt does—that one type is superior to the other. Similarly, Dave Barry, in "The Ugly Truth About Beauty" (page 422), explores with perceptive good humor the stereotypically conflicting behaviors of two groups: men and women.

2. Britt scoffs at thin people who "believe in logic." Take two decisions you made recently—one fairly logical, the other more emotional. Contrast how you went about making the decisions, the outcomes of the decisions, and so on. Reach some conclusion about the value of logic and emotion in your life.

Writing Assignments Using Other Patterns of Development

∞ **3.** Britt enjoys the pleasures of good food and company. In an essay, recall a gathering where the food and company were especially satisfying. Through sensory details, convey the aroma, taste, and appearance of the food, as well as the social atmosphere. For inspiration, you might read Judith Ortiz Cofer's "A Partial Remembrance of a Puerto Rican Childhood" (page 134), an essay that evokes the pleasures of shared family time.

4. Britt takes issue with the notion that thin is better than plump. What other prejudicial assumptions do you see at work in contemporary society? Select one and write an essay persuading readers that this idea is unfounded. Your tone may be serious or playful like Britt's.

Writing Assignments Using a Journal Entry as a Starting Point

5. Write an essay illustrating our culture's unfair stereotyping of either thin *or* heavy people. Review the ideas generated in your pre-reading journal entry, and select the stereotypes that inspire a lively rebuttal. Brainstorming with others will help you generate ideas worth exploring. Support your claims with research gathered by reading magazines, watching TV, and searching the Internet.

Richard Rodriguez

In his autobiographical work *Hunger of Memory* (1981), from which the following selection is taken, Richard Rodriguez describes his experiences growing up in America as a first-generation Mexican-American. Born in 1944 in San Francisco, Rodriguez spoke only Spanish for the first six years of his life. After winning a scholarship to a private high school, Rodriguez attended Stanford, Columbia, and the University of California at Berkeley, where he earned a Ph.D. in English literature. Rodriguez now writes for a variety of publications (*The Wall Street Journal* and *Time*, to name just two), serves as an editor at Pacific News Service in San Francisco, and regularly appears on PBS's *NewsHour*. In 1997, he won the Peabody Award for achievement in broadcasting. His books include *Mexico's Children* (1991) and *Movements* (1996). The critically acclaimed *Days of Obligation: An Argument With My Mexican Father* (1992) is Rodriguez's second autobiographical book.

Pre-Reading Journal Entry

Young people often find themselves being lectured by adults claiming that kids nowadays want it easy and aren't willing to do unglamorous "real work." Do you agree with these claims? Why or why not? Drawing upon your experiences and observations, respond to these questions in your journal.

Workers

It was at Stanford, one day near the end of my senior year, that 1
a friend told me about a summer construction job he knew was available. I was quickly alert. Desire uncoiled within me. My friend said that he knew I had been looking for summer employment. He knew I needed some money. Almost apologetically he explained: It was something I probably wouldn't be interested in, but a friend of his, a contractor, needed someone for the summer to do menial jobs. There would be lots of shoveling and raking and sweeping. Nothing too hard. But nothing more interesting either. Still, the pay would be good. Did I want it? Or did I know someone who did?

I did. Yes, I said, surprised to hear myself say it. 2

In the weeks following, friends cautioned that I had no idea 3
how hard physical labor really is. ("You only *think* you know what it
is like to shovel for eight hours straight.") Their objections seemed
to me challenges. They resolved the issue. I became happy with my
plan. I decided, however, not to tell my parents. I wouldn't tell my
mother because I could guess her worried reaction. I would tell my
father only after the summer was over, when I could announce that,
after all, I did know what "real work" is like.

The day I met the contractor (a Princeton graduate, it turned 4
out), he asked me whether I had done any physical labor before. "In
high school, during the summer," I lied. And although he seemed to
regard me with skepticism, he decided to give me a try. Several days
later, expectant, I arrived at my first construction site. I would take
off my shirt to the sun. And at last grasp desired sensation. No longer
afraid. At last become like a *bracero*. "We need those tree stumps out
of here by tomorrow," the contractor said. I started to work.

I labored with excitement that first morning—and all the days 5
after. The work was harder than I could have expected. But it was
never as tedious as my friends had warned me it would be. There was
too much physical pleasure in the labor. Especially early in the day, I
would be most alert to the sensations of movement and straining.
Beginning around seven each morning (when the air was still damp
but the scent of weeds and dry earth anticipated the heat of the sun),
I would feel my body resist the first thrusts of the shovel. My arms,
tightened by sleep, would gradually loosen; after only several minutes,
sweat would gather in beads on my forehead and then—a short while
later—I would feel my chest silky with sweat in the breeze. I would
return to my work. A nervous spark of pain would fly up my arm and
settle to burn like an ember in the thick of my shoulder. An hour, two
passed. Three. My whole body would assume regular movements; my
shoveling would be described by identical, even movements. Even
later in the day, my enthusiasm for primitive sensation would survive
the heat and the dust and the insects pricking my back. I would strain
wildly for sensation as the day came to a close. At three-thirty, quitting time, I would stand upright and slowly let my head fall back, luxuriating in the feeling of tightness relieved.

Some of the men working nearby would watch me and laugh. 6
Two or three of the older men took the trouble to teach me the
right way to use a pick, the correct way to shovel. "You're doing it
wrong, too fucking hard," one man scolded. Then proceeded to

show me—what persons who work with their bodies all their lives quickly learn—the most economical way to use one's body in labor.

"Don't make your back do so much work," he instructed. I 7 stood impatiently listening, half listening, vaguely watching, then noticed his work-thickened fingers clutching the shovel. I was annoyed. I wanted to tell him that I enjoyed shoveling the wrong way. And I didn't want to learn the right way. I wasn't afraid of back pain. I liked the way my body felt sore at the end of the day.

I was about to, but, as it turned out, I didn't say a thing. Rather 8 it was at that moment I realized that I was fooling myself if I expected a few weeks of labor to gain me admission to the world of the laborer. I would not learn in three months what my father had meant by "real work." I was not bound to this job; I could imagine its rapid conclusion. For me the sensations were to be feared. Fatigue took a different toll on their bodies—and minds.

It was, I know, a simple insight. But it was with this realization 9 that I took my first step that summer toward realizing something even more important about the "worker." In the company of carpenters, electricians, plumbers, and painters at lunch, I would often sit quietly, observant. I was not shy in such company. I felt easy, pleased by the knowledge that I was casually accepted, my presence taken for granted by men (exotics) who worked with their hands. Some days the younger men would talk and talk about sex, and they would howl at women who drove by in cars. Other days the talk at lunchtime was subdued; men gathered in separate groups. It depended on who was around. There were rough, good-natured workers. Others were quiet. The more I remember that summer, the more I realize that there was no single *type* of worker. I am embarrassed to say I had not expected such diversity. I certainly had not expected to meet, for example, a plumber who was an abstract painter in his off hours and admired the work of Mark Rothko. Nor did I expect to meet so many workers with college diplomas. (They were the ones who were not surprised that I intended to enter graduate school in the fall.) I suppose what I really want to say here is painfully obvious, but I must say it nevertheless: The men of that summer were middle-class Americans. They certainly didn't constitute an oppressed society. Carefully completing their work sheets; talking about the fortunes of local football teams; planning Las Vegas vacations; comparing the gas mileage of various makes of campers—they were not *los pobres* my mother had spoken about.

On two occasions, the contractor hired a group of Mexican   10
aliens. They were employed to cut down some trees and haul off
debris. In all, there were six men of varying age. The youngest in his
late twenties; the oldest (his father?) perhaps sixty years old. They
came and they left in a single old truck. Anonymous men. They were
never introduced to the other men at the site. Immediately upon
their arrival, they would follow the contractor's directions, start
working—rarely resting—seemingly driven by a fatalistic sense that
work which had to be done was best done as quickly as possible.

I watched them sometimes. Perhaps they watched me. The only   11
time I saw them pay me much notice was one day at lunchtime when
I was laughing with the other men. The Mexicans sat apart when
they ate, just as they worked by themselves. Quiet. I rarely heard
them say much to each other. All I could hear were their voices calling out sharply to one another, giving directions. Otherwise, when
they stood briefly resting, they talked among themselves in voices
too hard to overhear.

The contractor knew enough Spanish, and the Mexicans—or at   12
least the oldest of them, their spokesman—seemed to know enough
English to communicate. But because I was around, the contractor
decided one day to make me his translator. (He assumed I could
speak Spanish.) I did what I was told. Shyly I went over to tell the
Mexicans that the *patrón* wanted them to do something else before
they left for the day. As I started to speak, I was afraid with my old
fear that I would be unable to pronounce the Spanish words. But it
was a simple instruction I had to convey. I could say it in phrases.

The dark sweating faces turned toward me as I spoke. They   13
stopped their work to hear me. Each nodded in response. I stood
there. I wanted to say something more. But what could I say in
Spanish, even if I could have pronounced the words right? Perhaps
I just wanted to engage them in small talk, to be assured of their
confidence, our familiarity. I thought for a moment to ask them
where in Mexico they were from. Something like that. And maybe I
wanted to tell them (a lie, if need be) that my parents were from the
same part of Mexico.

I stood there.   14

Their faces watched me. The eyes of the man directly in front of   15
me moved slowly over my shoulder, and I turned to follow his
glance toward *el patrón* some distance away. For a moment I felt
swept up by that glance into the Mexicans' company. But then I

heard one of them returning to work. And then the others went back to work. I left them without saying anything more.

When they had finished, the contractor went over to pay them in cash. (He later told me that he paid them collectively—"for the job," though he wouldn't tell me their wages. He said something quickly about the good rate of exchange "in their own country.") I can still hear the loudly confident voice he used with the Mexicans. It was the sound of the *gringo* I had heard as a very young boy. And I can still hear the quiet, indistinct sounds of the Mexican, the oldest, who replied. At hearing that voice I was sad for the Mexicans. Depressed by their vulnerability. Angry at myself. The adventure of the summer seemed suddenly ludicrous. I would not shorten the distance I felt from *los pobres* with a few weeks of physical labor. I would not become like them. They were different from me.   16

After that summer, a great deal—and not very much really—changed in my life. The curse of physical shame was broken by the sun; I was no longer ashamed of my body. No longer would I deny myself the pleasing sensations of my maleness. During those years when middle-class black Americans began to assert with pride, "Black is beautiful," I was able to regard my complexion without shame. I am today darker than I ever was as a boy. I have taken up the middle-class sport of long-distance running. Nearly every day now I run ten or fifteen miles, barely clothed, my skin exposed to the California winter rain and wind or the summer sun of late afternoon. The torso, the soccer player's calves and thighs, the arms of the twenty-year-old I never was, I possess now in my thirties. I study the youthful parody shape in the mirror: the stomach lipped tight by muscle; the shoulders rounded by chin-ups; the arms veined strong. This man. A man. I meet him. He laughs to see me, what I have become.   17

The dandy. I wear double-breasted Italian suits and custom-made English shoes. I resemble no one so much as my father—the man pictured in those honeymoon photos. At that point in life when he abandoned the dandy's posture, I assume it. At the point when my parents would not consider going on vacation, I register at the Hotel Carlyle in New York and the Plaza Athenée in Paris. I am as taken by the symbols of leisure and wealth as they were. For my parents, however, those symbols became taunts, reminders of all they could not achieve in one lifetime. For me those same symbols are reassuring reminders of public success. I tempt vulgarity to be   18 reassured. I am filled with the gaudy delight, the monstrous grace of the nouveau riche.

In recent years I have had occasion to lecture in ghetto high   19
schools. There I see students of remarkable style and physical grace. (One can see more dandies in such schools than one ever will find in middle-class high schools.) There is not the look of casual assurance I saw students at Stanford display. Ghetto girls mimic high-fashion models. Their dresses are of bold, forceful color; their figures elegant, long; the stance theatrical. Boys wear shirts that grip at their overdeveloped muscular bodies. (Against a powerless future, they engage images of strength.) Bad nutrition does not yet tell. Great disappointment, fatal to youth, awaits them still. For the moment, movements in school hallways are dancelike, a procession of postures in a sexual masque. Watching them, I feel a kind of envy. I wonder how different my adolescence would have been had I been free. . . . But no, it is my parents I see—their optimism during those years when they were entertained by Italian grand opera.

The registration clerk in London wonders if I have just been to   20
Switzerland. And the man who carries my luggage in New York guesses the Caribbean. My complexion becomes a mark of my leisure. Yet no one would regard my complexion the same way if I entered such hotels through the service entrance. That is only to say that my complexion assumes its significance from the context of my life. My skin, in itself, means nothing. I stress the point because I know there are people who would label me "disadvantaged" because of my color. They make the same mistake I made as a boy, when I thought a disadvantaged life was circumscribed by particular occupations. That summer I worked in the sun may have made me physically indistinguishable from the Mexicans working nearby. (My skin was actually darker because, unlike them, I worked without wearing a shirt. By late August my hands were probably as tough as theirs.) But I was not one of *los pobres.* What made me different from them was an attitude of *mind*, my imagination of myself.

I do not blame my mother for warning me away from the sun   21
when I was young. In a world where her brother had become an old man in his twenties because he was dark, my complexion was something to worry about. "Don't run in the sun," she warns me today. I run. In the end, my father was right—though perhaps he did not know how right or why—to say that I would never know what real work is. I will never know what he felt at his last factory job. If

tomorrow I worked at some kind of factory, it would go differently
for me. My long education would favor me. I could act as a public
person—able to defend my interests, to unionize, to petition, to
speak up—to challenge and demand. (I will never know what real
work is.) I will never know what the Mexicans knew, gathering their
shovels and ladders and saws.

Their silence stays with me now. The wages those Mexicans   22
received for their labor were only a measure of their disadvantaged
condition. Their silence is more telling. They lack a public identity.
They remain profoundly alien. Persons apart. People lacking a union
obviously, people without grounds. They depend upon the relative
good will or fairness of their employers each day. For such people,
lacking a better alternative, it is not such an unreasonable risk.

Their silence stays with me. I have taken these many words to   23
describe its impact. Only: the quiet. Something uncanny about it.
Its compliance. Vulnerability. Pathos. As I heard their truck rumbling away, I shuddered, my face mirrored with sweat. I had finally
come face to face with *los pobres*.

Questions for Close Reading

1. What is the selection's thesis? Locate the sentence(s) in which Rodriguez
   states his main idea. If he doesn't state the thesis explicitly, express it in
   your own words.
2. What does Rodriguez find appealing about the construction job when
   his friend first offers it to him?
3. Once on the job, how long does it take Rodriguez to realize he will
   never be a "laborer"? Why does he feel this way?
4. According to Rodriguez, what makes him different from *los pobres*? Is
   poverty the only thing that makes them distinctive?
5. Refer to your dictionary as needed to define the following words used in
   the selection: *menial* (paragraph 1), *skepticism* (4), *luxuriating* (5),
   diversity (9), *ludicrous* (16), *nouveau riche* (18), and *pathos* (23).

Questions About the Writer's Craft

1. **The pattern.** One way Rodriguez develops his essay is by comparing
   and contrasting himself to the two groups of workers. Which group is he
   more like? What specifics does Rodriguez provide to show his similarity
   to this group and his dissimilarity to the other?
2. **Other patterns.** Rodriguez uses narration to develop his comparison-
   contrast of the two groups of workers. How many narrative segments
   appear in the essay? Why do you think Rodriguez puts the story about
   the Mexican workers last?

3. **Other patterns.** Rodriguez uses especially vivid language to describe the sun, his sweat, and the sensation of digging. Locate some examples of these descriptions. Which ones particularly stand out? Why?
4. Why does Rodriguez include some Spanish words in his essay? How is the use of these words related to the essay's overall theme?

Writing Assignments Using Comparison-Contrast as a Pattern of Development

1. Write an essay comparing and/or contrasting a part-time or summer job you've had with your (or someone else's) full-time or "real" job. Use examples, description, anecdotes, and illustrations to clarify the points of comparison or contrast.
2. Write an essay in which you compare and/or contrast the job you hope to have after graduation with a job you now have or have had in the past. Your analysis should reach conclusions about your interests, skills, and values.

Writing Assignments Using Other Patterns of Development

3. In an essay, define what you mean by the term *real work*. Support your definition by citing experiences you have had and/or have heard about. Jacques D'Amboise's "Showing What Is Possible" (page 460) and Virginia Woolf's "Professions for Women" (page 669) should prompt some interesting thoughts about work.
4. Former talk-show host Phil Donahue once did a show on people who had "terrible jobs." The guests included a garbage man, a toll collector, a car repossessor, an IRS auditor, and a diaper-service truck driver. Write an essay explaining what would be terrible work for you. It might be one or more of the jobs held by Donahue's guests or some other type of job. Provide abundant reasons why you would never want to do such work, and reach some conclusions about your priorities.

Writing Assignments Using a Journal Entry as a Starting Point

5. Write an essay comparing and/or contrasting the work habits of earlier generations with those of the current generation. Consider kinds of work, working conditions, benefits, hours on the job, and so on. In addition to drawing upon ideas from your pre-reading journal entry, interview an equal number of people of both generations to get their opinions. Where appropriate, include their views in your essay. Begin or end the essay with a statement indicating which generation's work habits you respect more. For additional insight into generational differences, read Russell Baker's "In My Day" (page 108).

Dave Barry

Pulitzer-Prize winning humorist Dave Barry (1947–) began his writing career covering—as he puts it—"incredibly dull municipal meetings" for *The Daily Local News* of West Chester, Pennsylvania. Next came an eight-year stint trying to teach businesspeople not to write sentences like "Enclosed please find the enclosed enclosures." In 1983, Barry joined the staff of the *Miami Herald,* where his rib-tickling commentary on the absurdities of everyday life quickly brought him a legion of devoted fans. Barry's column is now syndicated in more than 150 newspapers. A popular guest on television and radio, Barry has written many books, including *Dave Barry's Complete Guide to Guys* (1995), *Dave Barry in Cyberspace* (1996), and *Big Trouble* (1999). The essay below first appeared in the *Miami Herald* in 1998.

Pre-Reading Journal Entry

To what extent would you say our images of personal attractiveness are influenced by TV commercials and magazine advertisements? Think of commercials and ads you've seen recently. What physical traits are typically identified as attractive in women? In men? List as many as you can. What assumptions does each trait suggest? Use your journal to respond to these questions.

The Ugly Truth About Beauty

If you're a man, at some point a woman will ask you how she looks. 1

"How do I look?" she'll ask. 2

You must be careful how you answer this question. The best technique is to form an honest yet sensitive opinion, then collapse on the floor with some kind of fatal seizure. Trust me, this is the easiest way out. Because you will never come up with the right answer. 3

The problem is that women generally do not think of their looks in the same way that men do. Most men form an opinion of how they look in the seventh grade, and they stick to it for the rest of their lives. Some men form the opinion that they are irresistible 4 stud muffins, and they do not change this opinion even when their faces sag and their noses bloat to the size of eggplants and their eyebrows grow together to form what appears to be a giant forehead-dwelling tropical caterpillar.

Most men, I believe, think of themselves as average-looking. 5 Men will think this even if their faces cause heart failure in cattle at a range of 300 yards. Being average does not bother them; average is fine, for men. This is why men never ask anybody how they look. Their primary form of beauty care is to shave themselves, which is essentially the same form of beauty care that they give to their lawns. If, at the end of his four-minute daily beauty regimen, a man has managed to wipe most of the shaving cream out of his hair and is not bleeding too badly, he feels that he has done all he can, so he stops thinking about his appearance and devotes his mind to more critical issues, such as the Super Bowl.

Women do not look at themselves this way. If I had to express, 6 in three words, what I believe most women think about their appearance, those words would be: "not good enough." No matter how attractive a woman may appear to be to others, when she looks at herself in the mirror, she thinks: woof. She thinks that at any moment a municipal animal-control officer is going to throw a net over her and haul her off to the shelter.

Why do women have such low self-esteem? There are many 7 complex psychological and societal reasons, by which I mean Barbie. Girls grow up playing with a doll proportioned such that, if it were human, it would be seven feet tall and weigh 81 pounds, of which 53 pounds would be bosoms. This is a difficult appearance standard to live up to, especially when you contrast it with the standard set for little boys by their dolls . . . excuse me, by their action figures. Most of the action figures that my son played with when he was little were hideous-looking. For example, he was very fond of an action figure (part of the He-Man series) called "Buzz-Off," who was part human, part flying insect. Buzz-Off was not a looker. But he was extremely self-confident. You could not imagine Buzz-Off saying to the other actions figures: "Do you think these wings make my hips look big?"

But women grow up thinking they need to look like Barbie, 8 which for most women is impossible, although there is a multibillion-dollar beauty industry devoted to convincing women that they must try. I once saw an Oprah show wherein supermodel Cindy Crawford dispensed makeup tips to the studio audience. Cindy had all these middle-aged women applying beauty products to their faces; she stressed how important it was to apply them in a certain way, using the tips of their fingers. All the women dutifully did this, even though it was obvious to any sane observer that, no matter how carefully they applied these products, they would never look remotely like Cindy Crawford, who is some kind of genetic mutation.

I'm not saying that men are superior. I'm just saying that you're 9 not going to get a group of middle-aged men to sit in a room and apply cosmetics to themselves under the instruction of Brad Pitt, in hopes of looking more like him. Men would realize that this task was pointless and demeaning. They would find some way to bolster their self-esteem that did not require looking like Brad Pitt. They would say to Brad: "Oh YEAH? Well what do you know about LAWN CARE, pretty boy?"

Of course many women will argue that the reason they become 10 obsessed with trying to look like Cindy Crawford is that men, being as shallow as a drop of spit, WANT women to look that way. To which I have two responses:

1. Hey, just because WE'RE idiots, that does not mean YOU have 11 to be; and

2. Men don't even notice 97 percent of the beauty efforts you 12 make anyway. Take fingernails. The average woman spends 5,000 hours per year worrying about her fingernails; I have never once, in more than 40 years of listening to men talk about women, heard a man say, "She has a nice set of fingernails!" Many men would not notice if a woman had upward of four hands.

Anyway, to get back to my original point: If you're a man, and a 13 woman asks you how she looks, you're in big trouble. Obviously, you can't say she looks bad. But you also can't say that she looks great, because she'll think you're lying, because she has spent countless hours, with the help of the multibillion-dollar beauty industry, obsessing about the differences between herself and Cindy Crawford. Also, she suspects that you're not qualified to judge anybody's appearance. This is because you have shaving cream in your hair.

Questions for Close Reading

1. What is the selection's thesis? Locate the sentence(s) in which Barry states his main idea. If he doesn't state the thesis explicitly, express it in your own words.

2. Barry tells us that most men consider themselves to be "average-looking" (paragraph 5). Why, according to Barry, do men feel this way?

3. When Barry writes that most women think of themselves as "not good enough" (6), what does he mean? What, according to Barry, causes women to develop low opinions of themselves?

4. Barry implies that women could have a more rational response to the "difficult appearance standard" that pervades society (7). What would that response be?

5. Refer to your dictionary as needed to define the following words used in the selection: *regimen* (paragraph 5), *municipal* (6), *societal* (7), *dispensed* (8), *genetic* (8), *mutation* (8), *demeaning* (9), and *bolster* (9).

Questions About the Writer's Craft

1. **The pattern.** Which comparison-contrast method of organization (point-by-point or one-side-at-a-time) does Barry use to develop his essay? Why might he have chosen this pattern?

2. Barry uses exaggeration, a strategy typically associated with humorous writing. Locate instances of exaggeration in the selection. Why do you think he uses this strategy?

3. **Other patterns.** Barry demonstrates a series of cause-effect chains in his essay. Locate some of the cause-effect series. How do they help Barry reinforce his thesis?

4. Barry's title involves an *oxymoron*—a contradiction in terms. What does this title imply about Barry's attitude toward his subject?

Writing Assignments Using Comparison-Contrast as a Pattern of Development

1. Examine the pitches made in magazines and on TV for the male and female versions of *one* kind of grooming product. Possibilities include deodorant, hair dye, soap, and so on. Then write an essay contrasting the persuasive appeals that the product makes to men with those it make to women. (Don't forget to examine the assumptions behind the appeals.) To gain insight into advertising techniques, you'll find it helpful to read Ann McClintock's "Propaganda Techniques in Today's Advertising" (page 304). For useful perspectives on gender issues, consider reading Alleen Pace Nilsen's "Sexism and Language" (page 225), Barbara Ehrenreich's "What I've Learned From Men" (page 249), and Deborah Tannen's "But What Do You Mean?" (page 313).

2. Barry contrasts women's preoccupation with looking good to men's lack of concern about their appearance. Now consider the flip side—something men care about deeply that women virtually ignore. Write an essay contrasting men's stereotypical fascination with *one* area to women's indifference. You might, for example, examine male and female attitudes

toward sports, cars, tools, even lawn care. Following Barry's example, adopt a playful tone in your essay, illustrating the absurdity of the obsession you discuss.

Writing Assignments Using Other Patterns of Development

3. Barry implies that most men, unaffected by the "multibillion-dollar beauty industry," are content to "think of themselves as average looking." Do you agree? Conduct your own research into whether or not Barry's assertions about men are true. Begin by interviewing several male friends, family members, and classmates to see how these men feel about their physical appearance. In addition, in the library or online, research magazines such as *People, Gentlemen's Quarterly,* or *Men's Health* for articles describing how everyday men as well as male celebrities view their looks. Then write an essay refuting or defending the view that being average-looking doesn't bother most men. Start by acknowledging the opposing view; then support your assertion with convincing evidence drawn from your research.

4. Barry blames Barbie dolls for setting up "a difficult appearance standard" for girls to emulate. Many would argue that the toys that *boys* play with also teach negative, ultimately damaging values. Write an essay exploring the values that are conveyed to boys through their toys. Brainstorm with others, especially males, about the toys of their youth or the toys that boys have today. Identify two to three key negative values to write about, illustrating each with several examples of toys.

Writing Assignments Using a Journal Entry as a Starting Point

5. Review your pre-reading journal entry. Focusing on the characteristics of male *or* female attractiveness conveyed by the mass media, identify two to three assumptions suggested by these standards. Illustrate each assumption with examples from TV commercials and/or magazine advertisements. Be sure to make clear how you feel about these assumptions.

Stephen Chapman

Stephen Chapman was an associate editor for *The New Republic,* the publication for which he wrote "The Prisoner's Dilemma" in 1980. Since then, he has joined the staff of the *Chicago Tribune,* where his twice-weekly syndicated column on national and international affairs originates. Born in Texas in 1954, Chapman graduated *cum laude* from Harvard University in 1976 and did graduate work in business administration at the University of Chicago. He has contributed articles to national magazines including *Atlantic, Harper's, Reason,* and the *American Spectator.* Chapman lives with his family outside Chicago.

Pre-Reading Journal Entry

Should wrongdoing be punished in public? Why or why not? Use your journal to consider the pros and cons of public punishment for illegal actions. Think of three or four wrongdoings (from lesser offenses like shoplifting to serious crimes like armed robbery). For each offense, list possible forms of public punishment as well as the advantages and disadvantages of each form.

The Prisoner's Dilemma

One of the amusements of life in the modern West is the opportunity to observe the barbaric rituals of countries that are attached to the customs of the dark ages. Take Pakistan, for example. . . . President Zia, in harmony with the Islamic fervor that is sweeping his part of the world, revived the traditional Moslem practice of flogging lawbreakers in public. In Pakistan, this qualified as mass entertainment, and no fewer than 10,000 law-abiding Pakistanis turned out to see justice done to 26 convicts. To Western sensibilities the spectacle seemed barbaric—both in the sense of cruel and in the sense of pre-civilized. In keeping with Islamic custom each of the unfortunates—who had been caught in prostitution raids the previous night and summarily convicted and sentenced—was stripped down to a pair of white shorts, which were painted with a red stripe across the buttocks (the target). Then he was shackled against an easel, with pads thoughtfully placed over the kidneys to

1

prevent injury. The floggers were muscular, fierce-looking sorts—convicted murderers, as it happens—who paraded around the flogging platform in colorful loincloths. When the time for the ceremony began, one of the floggers took a running start and brought a five-foot stave down across the first victim's buttocks, eliciting screams from the convict and murmurs from the audience. Each of the 26 received from five to 15 lashes. One had to be carried from the stage unconscious.

Flogging is one of the punishments stipulated by Koranic law, 2 which has made it a popular penological device in several Moslem countries, including Pakistan, Saudi Arabia, and, most recently, the ayatollah's Iran. Flogging, or *ta'zir*, is the general punishment prescribed for offenses that don't carry an explicit Koranic penalty. Some crimes carry automatic *hadd* punishments—stoning or scourging (a severe whipping) for illicit sex, scourging for drinking alcoholic beverages, amputation of the hands for theft. Other crimes—as varied as murder and abandoning Islam—carry the death penalty (usually carried out in public). Colorful practices like these have given the Islamic world an image in the West, as described by historian G. H. Jansen, "of blood dripping from the stumps of amputated hands and from the striped backs of malefactors, and piles of stones barely concealing the battered bodies of adulterous couples." Jansen, whose book *Militant Islam* is generally effusive in its praise of Islamic practices, grows squeamish when considering devices like flogging, amputation, and stoning. But they are given enthusiastic endorsement by the Koran itself.

Such traditions, we all must agree, are no sign of an advanced 3 civilization. In the West, we have replaced these various punishments (including the death penalty in most cases) with a single device. Our custom is to confine criminals in prison for varying lengths of time. In Illinois, a reasonably typical state, grand theft carries a punishment of three to five years; armed robbery can get you from six to 30. The lowest form of felony theft is punishable by one to three years in prison. Most states impose longer sentences on habitual offenders. In Kentucky, for example, habitual offenders can be sentenced to life in prison. Other states are less brazen, preferring the more genteel sounding "indeterminate sentence," which allows parole boards to keep inmates locked up for as long as life. It was under an indeterminate sentence of one to 14 years that George Jackson served 12 years in California prisons for committing a $70 armed robbery. Under a Texas law imposing an automatic life sentence for a third felony conviction, a man was sent to jail for life last year because of three thefts adding up to less than $300 in property value. Texas also is famous for occasionally imposing extravagantly long sentences, often running into hundreds or thousands of years. This gives Texas a leg up on Maryland, which used to sentence some criminals to life plus a day—a distinctive if superfluous flourish. . . .

What are the advantages of being a convicted criminal in an advanced culture? First there is the overcrowding in prisons. One Tennessee prison, for example, has a capacity of 806, according to accepted space standards, but it houses 2300 inmates. One Louisiana facility has confined four and five prisoners in a single six-foot-by-six-foot cell. Then there is the disease caused by overcrowding, unsanitary conditions, and poor or inadequate medical care. A federal appeals court noted that the Tennessee prison had suffered frequent outbreaks of infectious diseases like hepatitis and tuberculosis. But the most distinctive element of American prison life is its constant violence. In his book *Criminal Violence, Criminal Justice,* Charles Silberman noted that in one Louisiana prison, there were 211 stabbings in only three years, 11 of them fatal. There were 15 slayings in a prison in Massachusetts between 1972 and 1975. According to a federal court, in Alabama's penitentiaries (as in many others), "robbery, rape, extortion, theft and assault are everyday occurrences."

At least in regard to cruelty, it's not at all clear that the system of punishment that has evolved in the West is less barbaric than the grotesque practices of Islam. Skeptical? Ask yourself: would you rather be subjected to a few minutes of intense pain and considerable public humiliation, or be locked away for two or three years in a prison cell crowded with ill-tempered sociopaths? Would you rather lose a hand or spend 10 years or more in a typical state prison? I have taken my own survey on this matter. I have found no one who does not find the Islamic system hideous. And I have found no one who *given the choices* mentioned above, would not prefer its penalties to our own. . . .

Imprisonment is now the universal method of punishing criminals in the United States. It is thought to perform five functions, each of which has been given a label by criminologists. First, there is simple *retribution:* punishing the lawbreaker to serve society's sense of justice and to satisfy the victims' desire for revenge. Second, there is *specific deterrence:* discouraging the offender from misbehaving in the future. Third, *general deterrence:* using the offender as an example to discourage others from turning to crime. Fourth, *prevention:* at least during the time he is kept off the streets, the criminal cannot victimize other members of society. Finally, and most important, there is *rehabilitation:* reforming the criminal so that when he returns to society he will be inclined to obey the laws and able to make an honest living.

How satisfactorily do American prisons perform by these criteria? Well, of course, they do punish. But on the other scores they don't do so well. Their effect in discouraging future criminality by the prisoner or others is the subject of much debate, but the soaring rates of the last 20 years suggest that prisons are not a dramatically effective deterrent to criminal behavior. Prisons do isolate convicted criminals, but only to divert crime from ordinary citizens to prison guards and fellow inmates. Almost no one contends any more that prisons rehabilitate their inmates. If anything, they probably impede rehabilitation by forcing inmates into prolonged and almost exclusive association with other criminals. And prisons cost a lot of money. Housing a typical prisoner in a typical prison costs far more than a stint at a top university. This cost would be justified if prisons did the job they were intended for. But it is clear to all that prisons fail on the very grounds—humanity and hope of rehabilitation—that caused them to replace earlier, cheaper forms of punishment. . . .

So the debate continues to rage in all the same old ruts. No one, of course, would think of copying the medieval practices of Islamic nations and experimenting with punishments such as flogging and amputation. But let us consider them anyway. How do they compare with our American prison system in achieving the ostensible objectives of punishment? First, do they punish? Obviously they do, and in a uniquely painful and memorable way. Of course any sensible person, given the choice, would prefer suffering these punishments to years of incarceration in a typical American prison. But presumably no Western penologist would criticize Islamic punishments on the grounds that they are not barbaric enough. Do they deter crime? Yes, and probably more effectively than sending convicts off to prison. Now we read about a prison sentence in the newspaper, then think no more about the criminal's payment for his crimes until, perhaps, years later we read a small item reporting his release.

By contrast, one can easily imagine the vivid impression it would leave to be wandering through a local shopping center and to stumble onto the scene of some poor wretch being lustily flogged. And the occasional sight of an habitual offender walking around with a bloody stump at the end of his arm no doubt also would serve as a forceful reminder that crime does not pay.

Do flogging and amputation discourage recidivism? No one   9
knows whether the scars on his back would dissuade a criminal from risking another crime, but it is hard to imagine that corporal measures could stimulate a higher rate of recidivism than already exists. Islamic forms of punishment do not serve the favorite new right goal of simply isolating criminals from the rest of society, but they may achieve the same purpose of making further crimes impossible. In the movie *Bonnie and Clyde,* Warren Beatty successfully robs a bank with his arm in a sling, but this must be dismissed as artistic license. It must be extraordinarily difficult, at the very least, to perform much violent crime with only one hand.

Do these medieval forms of punishment rehabilitate the crim-   10
inal? Plainly not. But long prison terms do not rehabilitate either. And it is just as plain that typical Islamic punishments are no crueler to the convict than incarceration in the typical American state prison.

Of course there are other reasons besides its bizarre forms of   11
punishment that the Islamic system of justice seems uncivilized to the Western mind. One is the absence of due process. Another is the long list of offenses—such as drinking, adultery, blasphemy, "profiteering," and so on—that can bring on conviction and punishment. A third is all the ritualistic mumbo-jumbo in pronouncements of Islamic law. . . . Even in these matters, however, a little cultural modesty is called for. The vast majority of American criminals are convicted and sentenced as a result of plea bargaining, in which due process plays almost no role. It has been only half a century since a wave of religious fundamentalism stirred this country to outlaw the consumption of alcoholic beverages. Most states also still have laws imposing austere constraints on sexual conduct. The *Washington Post* reported that the FBI had spent two and a half years and untold amounts of money to break up a nationwide pornography ring. Flogging the clients of prostitutes, as the Pakistanis did, does seem silly. But only a few months ago Mayor Koch of New York was proposing that clients caught in his own city have their names broadcast

by radio stations. We are not so far advanced on such matters as we often like to think. Finally, my lawyer friends assure me that the rules of jurisdiction for American courts contain plenty of petty requirements and bizarre distinctions that would sound silly enough to foreign ears.

Perhaps it sounds barbaric to talk of flogging and amputation, 12 and perhaps it is. But our system of punishment also is barbaric, and probably more so. Only cultural smugness about their system and willful ignorance about our own make it easy to regard the one as cruel and the other as civilized. We inflict our cruelties away from public view, while nations like Pakistan stage them in front of 10,000 onlookers. Their outrages are visible; ours are not. Most Americans can live their lives for years without having their peace of mind disturbed by the knowledge of what goes on in our prisons. To choose imprisonment over flogging and amputation is not to choose human kindness over cruelty, but merely to prefer that our cruelties be kept out of sight, and out of mind.

Public flogging and amputation may be more barbaric forms of 13 punishment than imprisonment, even if they are not more cruel. Society may pay a higher price for them, even if the particular criminal does not. Revulsion against officially sanctioned violence and infliction of pain derives from something deeply ingrained in the Western conscience, and clearly it is something admirable. Grotesque displays of the sort that occur in Islamic countries probably breed a greater tolerance for physical cruelty, for example, which prisons do not do precisely because they conceal their cruelties. In fact it is our admirable intolerance for calculated violence that makes it necessary for us to conceal what we have not been able to do away with. In a way this is a good thing, since it holds out the hope that we may eventually find a way to do away with it. But in another way it is a bad thing, since it permits us to congratulate ourselves on our civilized humanitarianism while violating its norms in this one area of our national life.

Questions for Close Reading

1. What is the selection's thesis? Locate the sentence(s) in which Chapman states his main idea. If he doesn't state the thesis explicitly, express it in your own words.
2. Chapman calls Islamic punishment practices "barbaric." What are some of these practices? Why would they seem barbaric to most Americans?

3. According to our society's philosophy of punishment, what goals is imprisonment supposed to accomplish? How successful, in Chapman's view, are U.S. prisons in meeting these goals?

4. For Chapman, what is the core difference between the U.S. punishment system and that of Islamic nations like Pakistan? Which system does he find preferable? Why?

5. Refer to your dictionary as needed to define the following words used in the selection: *barbaric* (paragraph 1), *stipulated* (2), *penological* (2), *malefactors* (2), *effusive* (2), *brazen* (3), *genteel* (3), *indeterminate* (3), *superfluous* (3), *extortion* (4), *criteria* (7), *ostensible* (8), *recidivism* (9), *corporal* (9), *blasphemy* (11), and *sanctioned* (13).

Questions About the Writer's Craft

1. **The pattern.** In paragraphs 8 through 10, Chapman contrasts the success of the American and Islamic systems in meeting the five goals of punishment cited in paragraph 6. How does Chapman help readers keep those goals in mind as he develops his contrast?

2. **Other patterns.** In paragraphs 1, 2, and 6, Chapman provides a number of definitions. How do these definitions help him convince readers to accept key points in his argument?

3. **Other patterns.** Examine the examples that Chapman provides in paragraphs 3 and 4. Why do you think he sequences each set of examples as he does?

4. Examine Chapman's tone, especially in paragraphs 3, 4, 5, and 8 to 9. Where does he shift from a fairly neutral tone to a more sarcastic and mocking one? How does this change help Chapman convince readers of the seriousness of the problems in U.S. justice?

Writing Assignments Using Comparison-Contrast as a Pattern of Development

1. Select one situation in which people are, in your opinion, ineffectively punished for violating a law or regulation. For example, you might focus on the punishment typically imposed for driving while intoxicated, plagiarizing a school paper, or habitually coming to work late. Write an essay describing the violation and its customary punishment. Then contrast this punishment with a more effective way of correcting the offending behavior. Whether you choose the one-side-at-a-time or the point-by-point method, be sure to provide clear signals, as Chapman does, to help readers follow your ideas.

2. Chapman contrasts two cultures' approaches to criminal punishment. Write an essay comparing and/or contrasting two cultures' approaches to another aspect of life. To structure your paper, use either the one-side-at-a-time or point-by-point method of development. The cultures

you discuss need not be nationalities or ethnicities. You might, for example, focus on parents' and teenagers' preferences in music, male and female expectations in a relationship, or high school teachers' and college professors' attitudes toward student responsibility. If appropriate, consider using a humorous tone to make fun of both sides—or to convey which side's approach you find preferable.

Writing Assignments Using Other Patterns of Development

3. Chapman states that there is "universal acknowledgment that prisons do not rehabilitate." Conduct research in the library and/or on the Internet on recent developments in criminal rehabilitation. Bibliographic sources like *The New York Times Index,* the *Social Sciences Index,* and *Criminal Justice Abstracts* will help you locate relevant information. Then write an essay refuting *or* defending the common view that the rehabilitation of prisoners is a futile goal. Start by acknowledging the opposing view, and then support your argument with convincing evidence drawn from your research.

4. Chapman describes people in Islamic cultures flocking to gawk at the misfortunes of others. People in our country are also fascinated, even entertained, by others' problems. They slow down to inspect traffic accidents, follow celebrities' troubles in tabloid publications, and glue themselves to the television when a natural disaster strikes. Write an essay in which you account for the causes of our fascination with others' misfortunes. Begin with one or two dramatic examples of this phenomenon, and then explain why you think people are so attracted to the troubles of others. Consider reading Stephen King's "Why We Crave Horror Movies" (page 455) and Mark Twain's "The Damned Human Race" (page 587) for some helpful insights into this morbid human tendency.

Writing Assignments Using a Journal Entry as a Starting Point

5. Write an essay arguing that public punishment would *or* would not be appropriate for a specific transgression. From your pre-reading journal entry, select *one* crime and its most realistic form of public punishment. Supplement the material in your journal by interviewing friends, classmates, and family members. Be sure to seek out and acknowledge the views of those who don't agree with the position you take.

Additional Writing Topics

COMPARISON-CONTRAST

General Assignments

Using comparison-contrast, write an essay on one of the following topics. Your thesis should indicate whether the two subjects are being compared, contrasted, or both. Organize the paper by arranging the details in a one-side-at-a-time or point-by-point pattern. Remember to use organizational cues to help the audience follow your analysis.

1. Two-career family versus one-career family
2. Two approaches for dealing with problems
3. Children's pastimes today and yesterday
4. Two rooms where you spend a good deal of time
5. Neighborhood stores versus shopping malls
6. Two characters in a novel or other literary work
7. Living at home versus living in an apartment or dorm
8. Two attitudes toward money
9. A sports team then and now
10. Watching a movie on television versus viewing it in a theater
11. Two attitudes about a controversial subject
12. Two approaches to parenting
13. Walking or biking versus driving a car
14. Marriage versus living together
15. The atmosphere in two classes
16. Two approaches to studying
17. The place where you live and the place where you would like to live
18. Two comedians
19. The coverage of an event on television versus the coverage in a newspaper
20. Significant trend versus passing fad
21. Two horror or adventure movies
22. Typewriter versus word processor
23. Two candidates for an office
24. Your attitude before and after getting to know someone
25. Two friends with different lifestyles

Assignments With a Specific Purpose and Audience

1. You would like to change your campus living arrangements. Perhaps you want to move from a dormitory to an off-campus apartment or

from home to a dorm. Before you do, though, you'll have to convince your parents (who are paying most of your college costs) that the move will be beneficial. Write out what you would say to your parents. Contrast your current situation with your proposed one, explaining why the new arrangement would be better.

2. As store manager, you decide to write a memo to all sales personnel explaining how to keep customers happy. Compare and/or contrast the needs and shopping habits of several different consumer groups (by age, spending ability, or sex), and show how to make each comfortable in your store.

3. As a member of the College Orientation Committee, you volunteer to write a guide entitled "Passing Exams" for first-year college students. You decide to contrast the right and wrong ways to prepare for and take exams. Although your purpose is basically serious, leaven the section with some humor on how *not* to approach exams.

4. You work as a volunteer for a mental health hot line. Many people call simply because they feel "stressed out." Prepare a brochure for these people, recommending a Type B approach to stressful situations. Focus the brochure on the contrast between Type A and Type B personalities: the former is nervous, hard-driving, competitive; the latter is relaxed and noncompetitive. Give specific examples of how each type tends to act in stressful situations.

5. As president of your student senate, you're concerned about the way your school is dealing with a particular situation (for example, advisement, parking, financial assistance). Write a letter to your college president contrasting the way your school handles the situation with another school's approach. In your conclusion, point out the advantages of adopting the other college's strategy.

6. Your old high school has invited you back to make a speech before an audience of seniors. The topic will be "how to choose the college that is right for you." Write your speech in the form of a comparison-contrast analysis. Focus on the choices available (two-year versus four-year schools, large versus small, local versus faraway, and so on), showing the advantages and/or disadvantages of each.

9

CAUSE-EFFECT

WHAT IS CAUSE-EFFECT?

Superstition has it that curiosity killed the cat. Maybe so. Yet our science, technology, storytelling, and fascination with the past and future all spring from our determination to know "Why" and "What if." Seeking explanations, young children barrage adults with endless questions: "Why do trees grow tall?" "What would happen if the sun didn't shine?" But children aren't the only ones who wonder in this way. All of us think in terms of cause and effect, sometimes consciously, sometimes unconsciously: "Why did they give me such an odd look?" we wonder, or "How would I do at another college?" we speculate. This exploration of reasons and results is also at the heart of most professions: "What led to our involvement in Vietnam?" historians question; "What will happen if we administer this experimental drug?" scientists ask.

Cause-effect writing, often called *causal analysis,* is rooted in this elemental need to make connections. Because the drive to understand reasons and results is so fundamental, causal analysis is a common kind of writing. An article analyzing the unexpected outcome of an election, a report linking poor nutrition to low academic achievement, an editorial analyzing the impact of a proposed tax cut—all are examples of cause-effect writing.

Done well, cause-effect pieces can uncover the subtle and often surprising connections between events or phenomena. By rooting out causes and projecting effects, causal analysis enables us to make sense of our experiences, revealing a universe that is somewhat less arbitrary and chaotic.

HOW CAUSE-EFFECT FITS YOUR PURPOSE AND AUDIENCE

Many assignments and exam questions in college involve writing essays that analyze causes, effects, or both. Sometimes, as in the following examples, you'll be asked to write an essay developed primarily through the cause-effect pattern:

> Although divorces have leveled off in the last few years, the number of marriages ending in divorce is still greater than it was a generation ago. What do you think are the causes of this phenomenon?

> Political commentators were surprised that so few people voted in the last election. Discuss the probable causes of this weak voter turnout.

> Americans never seem to tire of gossip about the rich and famous. What effect has this fascination with celebrities had on U.S. culture?

> The federal government is expected to pass legislation that will significantly reduce the funding of student loans. Analyze the possible effects of such a cutback.

Other assignments and exam questions may not explicitly ask you to address causes and effects, but they may use words that suggest causal analysis would be appropriate. Consider these examples, paying special attention to the words in boldface:

> In contrast to the socially involved youth of the 1960s, many young people today tend to remove themselves from

political issues. What do you think are the **sources** of the political apathy found among 18- to 25-year-olds? *(cause)*

A number of experts forecast that drug abuse will be the most significant factor affecting U.S. productivity in the coming decade. Evaluate the validity of this observation by discussing the **impact** of drugs in the workplace. *(effect)*

According to school officials, a predictable percentage of entering students drop out of college at some point during their first year. What **motivates** students to drop out? What **happens** to them once they leave? *(cause and effect)*

In addition to serving as the primary strategy for achieving an essay's purpose, causal analysis can also be a supplemental method used to help make a point in an essay developed chiefly through another pattern of development. Assume, for example, that you want to write an essay *defining* the term *the homeless.* To help readers see that unfavorable circumstances can result in nearly anyone becoming homeless, you might discuss some of the unavoidable, everyday factors causing people to live on streets and in subway stations. Similarly, in a *persuasive* proposal urging your college administration to institute an honors program, you would probably spend some time analyzing the positive effect of such a program on students and faculty.

SUGGESTIONS FOR USING CAUSE-EFFECT IN AN ESSAY

The following suggestions will be helpful whether you use causal analysis as a dominant or a supportive pattern of development.

1. Stay focused on the purpose of your analysis.   When writing a causal analysis, don't lose sight of your overall purpose. Consider, for example, an essay on the causes of widespread child abuse. If you're concerned primarily with explaining the problem of child abuse to your readers, you might take a purely *informative* approach:

Although parental stress is the immediate cause of child abuse, the more compelling reason for such behavior lies in the way parents were themselves mistreated in their own families.

Or you might want to *persuade* the audience about some point or idea concerning child abuse:

> The tragic consequences of child abuse provide strong support for more aggressive handling of such cases by social workers and judges.

Then again, you could choose a *speculative* approach, your main purpose being to suggest possibilities:

> Psychologists disagree about the potential effect on youngsters of all the media attention to child abuse. Will children exposed to this media coverage grow up assertive, self-confident, and able to protect themselves? Or will they become fearful and distrustful?

These examples illustrate that an essay's causal analysis may have more than one purpose. For instance, although the last example points to a paper with a primarily speculative purpose, the essay would probably start by informing readers of experts' conflicting views. The paper would also have a persuasive slant if it ended by urging readers to complain to the media about their sensationalized treatment of the child-abuse issue.

2. Adapt content and tone to your purpose and readers.   Your purpose and audience determine what supporting material and what tone will be most effective in a cause-effect essay. Assume you want to direct your essay on child abuse to general readers who know little about the subject. To *inform* readers, you might use facts, statistics, and expert opinion to provide an objective discussion of the causes of child abuse. Your analysis might show the following: (1) adults who were themselves mistreated as children tend to abuse their own offspring; (2) marital stress contributes to the mistreatment of children; and (3) certain personality disorders increase the likelihood of child abuse. Sensitive to what your readers would and wouldn't understand, you would stay away from a technical or formal tone. Rather than writing "Pathological preabuse symptomatology predicts adult transference of high aggressivity," you would say

"Psychologists can often predict, on the basis of family histories, who will abuse children."

Now imagine that your purpose is to *convince* future social workers that the failure of social service agencies to act authoritatively in child-abuse cases often has tragic consequences. Hoping to encourage more responsible behavior in the prospective social workers, you would adopt a more emotional tone in the essay, perhaps citing wrenching case histories that dramatize what happens when child abuse isn't taken seriously.

3. Think rigorously about causes and effects.   To write a meaningful causal analysis, you should do some careful thinking about the often complex relationship between causes and effects. Children tend to oversimplify causes and effects ("Mommy and Daddy are getting divorced because I was bad the other day"), and adults' arguments can be characterized by hasty, often slipshod thinking ("All these immigrants willing to work cheaply have made us lose our jobs"). But imprecise thinking has no place in essay writing. You should be willing to dig for causes, to think creatively about effects. You should examine your subject in depth, looking beyond the obvious and superficial.

Brainstorming, freewriting, and mapping will help you explore causes and effects thoroughly. No matter which prewriting technique you use, generate as many explanations as possible by asking yourself questions like these:

> *Causes:* What happened? What are the possible reasons? Which are most likely? Who was involved? Why?
>
> *Effects:* What happened? Who was involved? What were the observable results? What are some possible future consequences? Which consequences are negative? Which are positive?

If you remain open and look beyond the obvious, you'll discover that a cause may have many effects. Imagine that you're writing a paper on the effects of cigarette smoking. Prewriting would probably generate a number of consequences that could be discussed, some less obvious but perhaps more interesting than others: increased risk of lung cancer and heart disease, harm traced to secondhand smoke, legal battles regarding the rights of smokers and nonsmokers, lower birth weights in babies of mothers who smoke, and developmental problems experienced by such underweight infants.

In the same way, prewriting will help you see that an effect may have multiple causes. An essay analyzing the reasons for world hunger could discuss many causes, again some less evident but perhaps more thought-provoking than others: climatic changes, inefficient use of land, cultural predispositions for large families, and poor management of international relief funds.

Your analysis may also uncover a *causal chain* in which one cause (or effect) brings about another, which, in turn, brings about another, and so on. Here's an example of a causal chain: Prohibition went into effect; bootleggers and organized crime stepped in to supply public demand for alcoholic beverages; ordinary citizens began breaking the law by buying illegal alcohol and patronizing speakeasies; disrespect for legal authority became widespread and acceptable. As you can see, a causal chain often leads to interesting points. In this case, the subject of Prohibition leads not just to the obvious (illegal consumption of alcohol) but also to the more complex issue of society's decreasing respect for legal authority.

Don't grapple with so complex a chain, however, that you become hopelessly entangled. If your subject involves multiple causes and effects, limit what you'll discuss. Identify which causes and effects are *primary* and which are *secondary*. How extensively you cover secondary factors will depend on your purpose and audience. In an essay intended to inform a general audience about the harmful effects of pesticides, you would most likely focus on everyday dangers—polluted drinking water, residues in food, and the like. You probably wouldn't include a discussion of more long-range consequences (evolution of resistant insects, disruption of the soil's acid-alkaline balance).

Similarly, decide whether to focus on *immediate,* more obvious causes and effects, or on less obvious, more *remote* ones. Or perhaps you need to focus on both. In an essay about a faculty strike at your college, should you attribute the strike simply to the faculty's failure to receive a salary increase? Or should you also examine other factors: the union's failure to accept a salary package that satisfied most professors; the administration's inability to coordinate its negotiating efforts? It may be more difficult to explore more remote causes and effects, but it can also lead to more original and revealing essays. Thoughtful analyses take these less obvious considerations into account.

When developing a causal analysis, be careful to avoid the *post hoc fallacy*. Named after the Latin phrase *post hoc, ergo propter hoc,* meaning "after this, therefore because of this," this kind of faulty thinking occurs when you assume that simply because one event *followed* another, the first event *caused* the second. For example, if the Republicans win a majority of seats in Congress and, several months later, the economy collapses, can you conclude that the Republicans caused the collapse? A quick assumption of "Yes" fails the test of logic, for the timing of events could be coincidental and not indicative of any cause-effect relationship. The collapse may have been triggered by uncontrolled inflation that began well before the congressional elections. (For more information on the *post hoc* fallacy, see page 560.)

Also, be careful not to mistake *correlation* for *causation*. Two events correlate when they occur at about the same time. Such co-occurrence, however, doesn't guarantee a cause-effect relationship. For instance, while the number of ice cream cones eaten and the instances of heat prostration both increase during the summer months, this doesn't mean that eating ice cream causes heat prostration! A third factor—in this case, summer heat—is the actual cause. When writing causal analyses, then, use with caution words that imply a causal link (such as *therefore* and *because*). Words that express simply time of occurrence (like *following* and *previously*) are safer and more objective.

Finally, keep in mind that a rigorous causal analysis involves more than loose generalizations about causes and effects. Creating plausible connections may require library research, interviewing, or both. Often you'll need to provide facts, statistics, details, personal observations, or other corroborative material if readers are going to accept the reasoning behind your analysis.

4. Write a thesis that focuses the paper on causes, effects, or both.   The thesis in an essay developed through causal analysis often indicates whether the essay will deal mostly with causes, effects, or both. Here, for example, are three thesis statements for causal analyses dealing with the public school system. You'll see that each thesis signals that essay's particular emphasis:

> Our school system has been weakened by an overemphasis on trendy electives. *(causes)*

An ineffectual school system has led to crippling teachers' strikes and widespread disrespect for the teaching profession. *(effects)*

Bureaucratic inefficiency has created a school system unresponsive to children's emotional, physical, and intellectual needs. *(causes and effects)*

Note that the thesis statement—in addition to signaling whether the paper will discuss causes or effects or both—may also point to the essay's plan of development. Consider the last thesis statement; it makes clear that the paper will discuss children's emotional needs first, their physical needs second, and their intellectual needs last.

The thesis statement in a causal analysis doesn't have to specify whether the essay will discuss causes, effects, or both. Nor does the thesis have to be worded in such a way that the essay's plan of development is apparent. But when first writing cause-effect essays, you may find that a highly focused thesis will keep your analysis on track.

5. Choose an organizational pattern. There are two basic ways to organize the points in a cause-effect essay: You may use a chronological or an emphatic sequence. If you select a *chronological order,* you discuss causes and effects in the order in which they occur or will occur. Suppose you're writing an essay on the causes for the popularity of imported cars. These causes might be discussed in chronological sequence: American plant workers became frustrated and dissatisfied on the job; some workers got careless while others deliberately sabotaged the production of sound cars; a growing number of defective cars hit the market; consumers grew dissatisfied with American cars and switched to imports.

Chronology might also be used to organize a discussion about effects. Imagine you want to write an essay about the need to guard against disrupting delicate balances in the country's wildlife. You might start the essay by discussing what happened when the starling, a non-native bird, was introduced into the American environment. Because the starling had few natural predators, the starling population soared out of control; the starlings took over food sources and habitats of native species; the bluebird, a native species, declined and is now threatened with extinction.

Although a chronological pattern can be an effective way to organize material, a strict time sequence can present a problem if your primary cause or effect ends up buried in the middle of the sequence. In such a case, you might use *emphatic order,* reserving the most significant cause or effect for the end. For example, time order could be used to present the reasons behind a candidate's unexpected victory: Less than a month after the candidate's earlier defeat, a full-scale fund-raising campaign for the next election was started; the candidate spoke to many crucial power groups early in the campaign; the candidate did exceptionally well in the pre-election debates; good weather and large voter turnout on election day favored the candidate. However, if you believe that the candidate's appearance before influential groups was the key factor in the victory, it would be more effective to emphasize that point by saving it for the end. This is what is meant by emphatic order—saving the most important point for last.

Emphatic order is an especially effective way to sequence cause-effect points when readers hold what, in your opinion, are mistaken or narrow views about a subject. To encourage readers to look more closely at the issues, you present what you consider the erroneous or obvious views first, show why they are unsound or limited, then present what you feel to be the actual causes and effects. Such a sequence nudges the audience into giving further thought to the causes and effects you have discovered. Here are informal outlines for two causal analyses using this approach.

Subject: The causes of the riot at a rock concert

1. Some commentators blame the excessively hot weather.
2. Others cite drug use among the concertgoers.
3. Still others blame the liquor sold at the concessions.
4. But the real cause of the disaster was poor planning by the concert promoters.

Subject: The effects of campus crime

1. Immediate problems
   a. Students feel insecure and fearful.
   b. Many nighttime campus activities have been curtailed.
2. More significant long-term problems
   a. Unfavorable publicity about campus crime will affect future student enrollments.
   b. Hiring faculty will become more difficult.

When using emphatic order in a causal analysis, you might want to word the thesis in such a way that it signals which point your essay will stress. Look at the following thesis statements:

Although many immigrants arrive in this country without marketable skills, their most pressing problem is learning how to make their way in a society whose language they don't know.

The space program has led to dramatic advances in computer technology and medical science. Even more important, though, the program has helped change many people's attitudes toward the planet we live on.

These thesis statements reflect an awareness of the complex nature of cause-effect relationships. While not dismissing secondary issues, the statements establish which points the writer considers most noteworthy. The second thesis, for instance, indicates that the paper will touch on the technological and medical advances made possible by the space program but will emphasize the way the program has changed people's attitudes toward the earth.

Whether you use a chronological or emphatic pattern to organize your essay, you'll need to provide clear *signals* to identify when you're discussing causes and when you're discussing effects. Expressions such as "Another reason" and "A final outcome" help readers follow your line of thought.

6. Use language that hints at the complexity of cause-effect relationships.   Because it's difficult—if not impossible—to identify causes and effects with certainty, you should avoid such absolutes as "It must be obvious" and "There is no doubt." Instead, try phrases like "Most likely" or "It's probable that." Using such language is not indecisive; rather, it reflects your understanding of the often tangled nature of causes and effects. Be careful, though, of going to the other extreme and being reluctant to take a stand on the issues. If you've thought carefully about causes and effects, you have a right to state your analysis with conviction. Don't undercut the hard work you've done by writing as if your ideas were unworthy of your reader's attention.

STUDENT ESSAY

The following student essay was written by Carl Novack in response to this assignment:

> In "Is Technology Making Us Intimate Strangers?" Jonathan Coleman examines the way cell phones, e-mail, and other technologies affect the way we relate to each other. Think of another aspect of everyday life that has changed recently, and discuss those factors that you believe are responsible for the change.

While reading Carl's paper, try to determine how well it applies the principles of causal analysis. The annotations on Carl's paper and the commentary following it will help you look at the essay more closely.

Americans and Food
by Carl Novack

Introduction   An offbeat but timely cartoon recently   1
appeared in the local newspaper. The single panel
showed a gravel-pit operation with piles of raw
earth and large cranes. Next to one of the cranes
stood the owner of the gravel pit--a grizzled, tough-
looking character, hammer in hand, pointing proudly to the new sign he had just tacked up. The sign
read, "Fred's Fill Dirt and Croissants." The cartoon
illustrates an interesting phenomenon: the changing food habits of Americans. Our meals used to
consist of something like home-cooked pot roast,
mashed potatoes laced with butter and salt, a thick
slice of apple pie topped with a healthy scoop of
vanilla ice cream--plain, heavy meals, cooked from
Thesis ─────── scratch, and eaten leisurely at home. But America
has changed, and as it has, so have what we
Americans eat and how we eat it.

    We used to have simple, unsophisticated tastes   2
and looked with suspicion at anything more exotic
than hamburger. Admittedly, we did adopt some
foods from the various immigrant groups who
flocked to our shores. We learned to eat Chinese

Topic sentence: Background paragraph	food, pizza, and bagels. But in the last few years, the international character of our diet has grown tremendously. We can walk into any mall in Middle America and buy pita bread, quiche, and tacos. Such foods are often changed on their journey from exotic imports to ordinary "American" meals (no Pakistani, for example, eats frozen-on-a-stick boysenberry-flavored yogurt), but the imports are still a long way from hamburger on a bun.
Topic sentence: Three causes answer the question	Why have we become more worldly in our tastes? For one thing, television blankets the country with information about new food products and trends. Viewers in rural Montana know that the latest craving in Washington, D.C., is Cajun cooking or
First cause	that something called tofu is now available in the
Second cause	local supermarket. Another reason for the growing international flavor of our food is that many young Americans have traveled abroad and gotten hooked on new tastes and flavors. Backpacking students and young professionals vacationing in Europe come home with cravings for authentic French bread or German beer. Finally, continuing waves of
Third cause	immigrants settle in the cities where many of us live, causing significant changes in what we eat. Vietnamese, Haitians, and Thais, for instance, bring their native foods and cooking styles with them and eventually open small markets or restaurants. In time, the new food will become Americanized enough to take its place in our national diet.
Topic sentence: Another cause	Our growing concern with health has also affected the way we eat. For the last few years, the media have warned us about the dangers of our traditional diet, high in salt and fat, low in fiber. The media also began to educate us about the dangers of processed foods pumped full of chemical additives.
Start of a causal chain	As a result, consumers began to demand healthier foods, and manufacturers started to change some of their products. Many foods, such as lunch meat, canned vegetables, and soups, were made available in low-fat, low-sodium versions. Whole-grain cereals and higher-fiber breads also began to appear on the grocery shelves. Moreover, the food industry started to produce all-natural products--everything from potato chips to ice

3

4

cream--without additives and preservatives. Not surprisingly, the restaurant industry responded to this switch to healthier foods, luring customers with salad bars, broiled fish, and steamed vegetables.

Topic sentence: ⟶ Our food habits are being affected, too, by the 5
Another cause
rapid increase in the number of women working outside the home. Sociologists and other experts believe that two important factors triggered this phenomenon: the women's movement and a changing economic climate. Women were assured that it was acceptable, even rewarding, to work outside the home; many women also discovered that they had to work just to keep up with the cost of living. As the traditional role of homemaker changed, so did the way families ate. With Mom working, there wasn't time for her to prepare the traditional three square meals a day. Instead, families began looking

Start of a causal _____ for alternatives to provide quick meals. What was
chain
the result? For one thing, there was a boom in fast-food restaurants. The suburban or downtown strip that once contained a lone McDonald's now features Wendy's, Roy Rogers, Taco Bell, Burger King, and Pizza Hut. Families also began to depend on frozen foods as another time-saving alternative. Once again, though, demand changed the kind of frozen food available. Frozen foods no longer consist of foil trays divided into greasy fried chicken, watery corn niblets, and lumpy mashed potatoes. Supermarkets now stock a range of supposedly gourmet frozen dinners--from fettucini in cream sauce to braised beef en brochette.

Conclusion
It may not be possible to pick up a ton of fill dirt 6
and a half-dozen croissants at the same place, but America's food habits are definitely changing. If it is true that "you are what you eat," then America's identity is evolving along with its diet.

COMMENTARY

Title and introduction.   Asked to prepare a paper analyzing the reasons behind a change in our lives, Carl decided to write about a shift he had noticed in Americans' eating habits. The title of the essay, "Americans and Food," identifies Carl's subject but could be livelier and more interesting.

Despite his rather uninspired title, Carl starts his *causal analysis* in an engaging way—with the vivid description of a cartoon. He then connects the cartoon to his subject with the following sentence: "The cartoon illustrates an interesting phenomenon: the changing food habits of Americans." To back up his belief that there has been a revolution in our eating habits, Carl uses the first paragraph to summarize the kind of meal that people used to eat. He then moves into his *thesis:* "But America has changed, and as it has, so have what Americans eat and how we eat it." The thesis implies that Carl's paper will focus on both causes and effects.

Purpose.   Carl's *purpose* was to write an *informative* causal analysis. But before he could present the causes of the change in eating habits, he needed to show that such a change had, in fact, taken place. He therefore uses the second paragraph to document one aspect of this change—the internationalization of our eating habits.

Topic sentences.   At the beginning of the third paragraph, Carl uses a question—"Why have we become more worldly in our tastes?"—to signal that his discussion of causes is about to begin. This question also serves as the paragraph's *topic sentence,* indicating that the paragraph will focus on reasons for the increasingly international flavor of our food. The next two paragraphs, also focused by topic sentences, identify two other major reasons for the change in eating habits: "Our growing concern with health has also affected the way we eat" (paragraph 4), and "Our food habits are being affected, too, by the rapid increase in the number of women working outside the home" (5).

Other patterns of development.   Carl draws on two patterns—comparison-contrast and exemplification—to develop his causal analysis. At the heart of the essay is a basic *contrast* between the way we used to eat and the way we eat now. And throughout his essay, Carl provides convincing *examples* to demonstrate the validity of his points. Consider for a moment the third paragraph. Here Carl asserts that one reason for our new eating habits is our growing exposure to international foods. He then presents concrete evidence to show that we have indeed become more familiar with international cuisine: Television exposes rural Montana to Cajun cooking; students traveling abroad take a liking to French bread; urban dwellers enjoy the exotic fare served by numerous immigrant groups. The fourth and fifth paragraphs use similarly specific evidence (for example, "low-fat, low-sodium versions" of "lunch meat, canned vegetables, and soups") to illustrate the soundness of key ideas.

Causal chains.   Let's look more closely at the evidence in the essay. Not satisfied with obvious explanations, Carl thought through his ideas carefully and even brainstormed with friends to arrive at as comprehensive an analysis as possible. Not surprisingly, much of the evidence Carl uncovered took the form of *causal chains*. In the fourth paragraph, Carl writes, "The media also began to educate us about the dangers of processed foods pumped full of chemical additives. As a result, consumers began to demand healthier foods, and manufacturers started to change some of their products." And the next paragraph shows how the changing role of American women caused families to search for alternative ways of eating. This shift, in turn, caused the restaurant and food industries to respond with a wide range of food alternatives.

Making the paper easy to follow.   Although Carl's analysis digs beneath the surface and reveals complex cause-effect relationships, he wisely limits his pursuit of causal chains to *primary causes and effects*. He doesn't let the complexities distract him from his main purpose: to show why and how the American diet is changing. Carl is also careful to provide his essay with abundant *connecting devices*, making it easy for readers to see the links between points. Consider the use of *transitions* (signaled by italics) in the following sentences: "*Another* reason for the growing international flavor of our food is that many young Americans have traveled abroad" (paragraph 3); "*As a result,* consumers began to demand healthier foods" (4); and "*As* the traditional role of homemaker changed, so did the way families ate" (5).

A problem with the essay's close.   When reading the essay, you probably noticed that Carl's conclusion is a bit weak. Although his reference to the cartoon works well, the rest of the paragraph limps to a tired close. Ending an otherwise vigorous essay with such a slight conclusion undercuts the effectiveness of the whole paper. Carl spent so much energy developing the body of his essay that he ran out of the stamina needed to conclude the piece more forcefully. Careful budgeting of his time would have allowed him to prepare a stronger concluding paragraph.

Revising the first draft.   When Carl was ready to revise, he showed the first draft of his essay to several classmates. Listening carefully to what they said, he jotted down their most helpful comments and eventually transferred them, numbered in order of importance, to his draft. Comparing Carl's original version of his fourth paragraph (shown here) with his final version in the essay will show you how he went about revising.

Original Version of the Fourth Paragraph

A growing concern with health has also affected the way we eat, especially because the media have sent us warnings the last few years about the dangers of salt, sugar, food additives, high-fat and low-fiber diets. We have started to worry that our traditional meals may have been shortening our lives. As a result, consumers demanded healthier foods and manufacturers started taking some of the salt and sugar out of canned foods. "All-natural" became an effective selling point, leading to many preservative-free products. Restaurants, too, adapted their menus, luring customers with light meals. Because we now know about the link between overweight and a variety of health problems, including heart attacks, we are counting calories. In turn, food companies made fortunes on diet beer and diet cola. Sometimes, though, we seem a bit confused about the health issue; we drink soda that is sugar-free but loaded with chemical sweeteners. Still, we believe we are lengthening our lives through changing our diets.

On the advice of his classmates, Carl decided to omit all references to the way our concern with weight has affected our eating habits. It's true, of course, that calorie-counting has changed how we eat. But as soon as Carl started to discuss this point, he got involved in a causal chain that undercut the paragraph's unity. He ended up describing the paradoxical situation in which we find ourselves. In an attempt to eat healthy, we stay away from sugar and use instead artificial sweeteners that probably aren't very good for us. This is an interesting issue, but it detracts from the point Carl wants to make: that our concern with health has affected our eating habits in a *positive* way.

Carl's editing team also pointed out that the fourth paragraph's first sentence contained too much material to be an effective topic sentence. Carl corrected the problem by breaking the overlong sentence into two short ones: "Our growing concern with health has also affected the way we eat. For the last few years, the media have warned us about the dangers of our traditional diet, high in salt and fat, low in fiber." The first of these sentences serves as a crisp topic sentence that focuses the rest of the paragraph.

Finally, Carl agreed with his classmates that the fourth paragraph lacked convincing specifics. When revising, he changed "manufacturers started taking some of the salt and sugar out of canned foods" to the more specific "Many foods, such as lunch meats, canned vegetables, and soups, were made available in low-fat, low-sodium versions." Similarly, generalizations about "light meals" and "all-natural products" gained life through the addition of concrete examples: restaurants lured "customers with salad bars, broiled fish, and steamed vegetables," and the food industry produced "everything from potato chips to ice cream—without additives and preservatives."

Carl did an equally good job revising other sections of his paper. With the exception of the weak spots already discussed, he made the changes needed to craft a well-reasoned essay, one that demonstrates his ability to analyze a complex phenomenon.

ACTIVITIES: CAUSE-EFFECT

Prewriting Activities

1. Imagine you're writing two essays: One *argues* the need for high school courses in personal finance (how to budget money, balance a checkbook, and the like); the other explains a *process* for showing appreciation. Jot down ways you might use cause-effect in each essay.

2. Use mapping, collaborative brainstorming, or another prewriting technique to generate possible causes and/or effects for *one* of the topics below. Be sure to keep in mind the audience indicated in parentheses. Next, devise a thesis and decide whether your purpose would be informative, persuasive, speculative, or some combination of these. Finally, organize your raw material into a brief outline, with related causes and effects grouped in the same section.

   a. Pressure on students to do well (*high school students*)

b. Children's access to pornography on the Internet (*parents*)
c. Being physically fit (*those who are out of shape*)
d. Spiraling costs of a college education (*college officials*)

Revising Activities

3. Explain how the following statements demonstrate *post hoc* thinking and confuse correlation and cause-effect.

a. Our city now has many immigrants from Latin American countries. The crime rate in our city has increased. Latin American immigrants are the cause of the crime wave.
b. The divorce rate has skyrocketed. More women are working outside the home than ever before. Working outside the home destroys marriages.
c. A high percentage of people in Dixville have developed cancer. The landfill, used by XYZ Industries, has been located in Dixville for twenty years. The XYZ landfill has caused cancer in Dixville residents.

4. The following paragraph is from the first draft of an essay arguing that technological advances can diminish the quality of life. How solid is the paragraph's causal analysis? Which causes and/or effects should be eliminated? Where is the analysis simplistic? Where does the writer make absolute claims even though cause-effect relationships are no more than a possibility? Keeping these questions in mind, revise the paragraph.

How did the banking industry respond to inflation? It simply introduced a new technology--the automated teller machine (ATM). By making money more available to the average person, the ATM gives people the cash to buy inflated goods--whether or not they can afford them. Not surprisingly, automatic teller machines have had a number of negative consequences for the average individual. Since people know they can get cash at any time, they use their lunch hours for something other than going to the bank. How do they spend this new-found time? They go shopping, and machine-vended money means more impulse buying, even more than with a credit card. Also, because people don't need their checkbooks to withdraw money, they can't keep track of their accounts and therefore develop a casual attitude toward financial matters. It's no wonder children don't appreciate the value of money. Another problem is that people who would never dream of robbing a bank try to trick the machine into dispensing money "for free." There's no doubt that this kind of fraud contributes to the immoral climate in the country.

Stephen King

Probably the best-known living horror writer, Stephen King (1947–) is the author of more than thirty books. Before earning fame through his vastly popular books, including *Carrie* (1974), *The Shining* (1977), *Cujo* (1981), and *Tommyknockers* (1987), King worked as a high school English teacher and an industrial laundry worker. Much of King's prolific output has been adapted for the screen; movies based on King's work include *Misery* (1990), *Stand By Me* (1986), and *The Green Mile* (1999). His most recent book, *On Writing: A Memoir of the Craft* (2000), offers insight into the writing process and examines the role that writing has played in King's own life— especially following a near-fatal accident in 1999. King lives with his family in Bangor, Maine. The following essay first appeared in *Playboy* in 1982.

Pre-Reading Journal Entry

Several forms of entertainment, besides horror movies, are highly popular despite what many consider a low level of quality. In your journal, list as many "lowbrow" forms of entertainment as you can. Possibilities include professional wrestling, aggressive video games, Internet chat rooms, and so on. Review your list, and respond to the following question in your journal: What is it about each form of entertainment that attracts such popularity— and inspires such criticism?

Why We Crave Horror Movies

I think that we're all mentally ill: those of us outside the asylums only hide it a little better—and maybe not all that much better, after all. We've all known people who talk to themselves, people who sometimes squinch their faces into horrible grimaces when they believe no one is watching, people who have some hysterical fear— of snakes, the dark, the tight place, the long drop . . . and, of course, those final worms and grubs that are waiting so patiently underground. 1

When we pay our four or five bucks and seat ourselves at tenth-row center in a theater showing a horror movie, we are daring the nightmare. 2

Why? Some of the reasons are simple and obvious. To show that   3
we can, that we are not afraid, that we can ride this roller coaster.
Which is not to say that a really good horror movie may not surprise
a scream out of us at some point, the way we may scream when the
roller coaster twists through a complete 360 or plows through a lake
at the bottom of the drop. And horror movies, like roller coasters,
have always been the special province of the young; by the time one
turns 40 or 50, one's appetite for double twists or 360-degree loops
may be considerably depleted.

We also go to re-establish our feelings of essential normality; the   4
horror movie is innately conservative, even reactionary. Freda
Jackson as the horrible melting woman in *Die, Monster, Die!* confirms for us that no matter how far we may be removed from the
beauty of a Robert Redford or a Diana Ross, we are still light-years
from true ugliness.

And we go to have fun.   5

Ah, but this is where the ground starts to slope away, isn't it?   6
Because this is a very peculiar sort of fun indeed. The fun comes
from seeing others menaced—sometimes killed. One critic has suggested that if pro football has become the voyeur's version of combat, then the horror film has become the modern version of the
public lynching.

It is true that the mythic, "fairytale" horror film intends to take   7
away the shades of gray. . . . It urges us to put away our more civilized and adult penchant for analysis and to become children again,
seeing things in pure blacks and whites. It may be that horror
movies provide psychic relief on this level because this invitation to
lapse into simplicity, irrationality and even outright madness is
extended so rarely. We are told we may allow our emotions a free
rein . . . or no rein at all.

If we are all insane, then sanity becomes a matter of degree. If   8
your insanity leads you to carve up women like Jack the Ripper or the
Cleveland Torso Murderer, we clap you away in the funny farm (but
neither of those two amateur-night surgeons was ever caught, heh-
heh-heh); if, on the other hand your insanity leads you only to talk to
yourself when you're under stress or to pick your nose on the morning bus, then you are left alone to go about your business . . . though
it is doubtful that you will ever be invited to the best parties.

The potential lyncher is in almost all of us (excluding saints, past   9
and present; but then, most saints have been crazy in their own

ways), and every now and then, he has to be let loose to scream and roll around in the grass. Our emotions and our fears form their own body, and we recognize that it demands its own exercise to maintain proper muscle tone. Certain of these emotional muscles are accepted—even exalted—in civilized society; they are, of course, the emotions that tend to maintain the status quo of civilization itself. Love, friendship, loyalty, kindness—these are all the emotions that we applaud, emotions that have been immortalized in the couplets of Hallmark cards. . . .

When we exhibit these emotions, society showers us with positive reinforcement; we learn this even before we get out of diapers. When, as children, we hug our rotten little puke of a sister and give her a kiss, all the aunts and uncles smile and twit and cry, "Isn't he the sweetest little thing?" Such coveted treats as chocolate-covered graham crackers often follow. But if we deliberately slam the rotten little puke of a sister's fingers in the door, sanctions follow—angry remonstrance from parents, aunts and uncles; instead of a chocolate-covered graham cracker, a spanking. 10

But anticivilization emotions don't go away, and they demand periodic exercise. We have such "sick" jokes as, "What's the difference between a truckload of bowling balls and a truckload of dead babies?" (You can't unload a truckload of bowling balls with a pitchfork . . . a joke, by the way, that I heard originally from a ten-year-old.) Such a joke may surprise a laugh or a grin out of us even as we recoil, a possibility that confirms the thesis: If we share a brotherhood of man, then we also share an insanity of man. None of which is intended as a defense of either the sick joke or insanity but merely as an explanation of why the best horror films, like the best fairy tales, manage to be reactionary, anarchistic, and revolutionary all at the same time. 11

The mythic horror movie, like the sick joke, has a dirty job to do. It deliberately appeals to all that is worst in us. It is morbidity unchained, our most base instincts let free, our nastiest fantasies realized . . . and it all happens, fittingly enough, in the dark. For those reasons, good liberals often shy away from horror films. For myself, I like to see the most aggressive of them—*Dawn of the Dead,* for instance—as lifting a trap door in the civilized forebrain and throwing a basket of raw meat to the hungry alligators swimming around in that subterranean river beneath. 12

Why bother? Because it keeps them from getting out, man. It keeps them down there and me up here. It was Lennon and 13

McCartney who said that all you need is love, and I would agree with that.

    As long as you keep the gators fed.   14

Questions for Close Reading

1. What is the selection's thesis? Locate the sentence(s) in which King states his main idea. If he doesn't state the thesis explicitly, express it in your own words.
2. In what ways do King's references to "Jack the Ripper" and the "Cleveland Torso Murderer" (paragraph 8) support his thesis?
3. What does King mean in paragraph 4 when he says that horror movies are "innately conservative, even reactionary"? What does he mean in paragraph 11 when he calls them "anarchistic, and revolutionary"?
4. In paragraphs 12 and 14, King refers to "alligators" and "gators." What does the alligator represent? What does King mean when he says that all the world needs is love—"[a]s long as you keep the gators fed"?
5. Refer to your dictionary as needed to define the following words used in the selection: *hysterical* (paragraph 1), *reactionary* (4), *voyeur's* (6), *lynching* (6), *penchant* (7), *immortalized* (9), *anarchistic* (11), and *morbidity* (12).

Questions About the Writer's Craft

1. **The pattern.** Does King's causal analysis have an essentially informative, speculative, or persuasive (see pages 439–40) purpose? What makes you think so? How might King's profession as a horror writer have influenced his purpose?
2. **Other patterns.** King compares and contrasts horror movies to roller coasters (3), public lynchings (6), and sick jokes (11–12). How do these comparisons and contrasts reinforce King's thesis about horror movies?
3. **Other patterns.** Throughout the essay, King uses several examples involving children. Identify these instances. How do these examples help King develop his thesis?
4. What is unusual about paragraphs 2, 5, and 14? Why do you think King might have designed these paragraphs in this way?

Writing Assignments Using Cause-Effect
as a Pattern of Development

1. King argues that horror movies have "a dirty job to do": they feed the hungry monsters in our psyche. Write an essay in which you put King's thesis to the test. Briefly describe the first horror movie you ever saw;

then explain its effect on you. Like King, speculate about the nature of your response—your feelings and fantasies—while watching the movie.

2. Many movie critics claim that horror movies nowadays are more violent and bloody than they used to be. Write an essay about *one* other medium of popular culture that you think has changed for the worse. You might consider action movies, televised coverage of sports, men's or women's magazines, radio talk shows, TV sitcoms, and so on. Briefly describe key differences between the medium's past and present forms. Analyze the reasons for the change, and, at the end of the essay, examine the effects of the change.

Writing Assignments Using Other Patterns of Development

3. King advocates the horror movie precisely because "It deliberately appeals to all that is worst in us." Write an essay in which you rebut King. Argue instead that horror movies should be avoided precisely *because* they satisfy monstrous feelings in us. To refute King, provide strong examples drawn from your own and other people's experience. Consider supplementing your informal research with material gathered in the library and/or on the Internet.

4. Write an essay in which you illustrate, contrary to King, that humans are by nature essentially benevolent and kind. Brainstorm with others to generate vivid examples in support of your thesis. Consider referring in your paper to points made by Lewis Thomas in "The Lie Detector" (page 477).

Writing Assignments Using a Journal Entry as a Starting Point

5. King believes that horror movies involve "a very peculiar sort of fun." Review your pre-reading journal entry, and select *one* other form of popular entertainment that you think provides its own strange kind of enjoyment. Like King, write an essay in which you analyze the causes of people's enjoyment of this type of entertainment. Brainstorm with others to identify convincing examples. You may, like King, endorse the phenomenon you examine—or you may condemn it. For discussion of another strange source of people's enjoyment, read Stephen Chapman's "The Prisoner's Dilemma" (page 427).

Jacques D'Amboise

When Jacques D'Amboise (1934–) was growing up in a tough, gang-infested New York City neighborhood, his French-Canadian mother wanted to give her children a glimpse into a world of beauty. She enrolled D'Amboise's sister in a ballet class and, hoping to protect her son from the dangers of street life, insisted that her son take the class, too. It was there that D'Amboise discovered his love of dance. While still in his teens, D'Amboise joined the New York City Ballet and became one of the foremost dancers of his day. In 1976, he founded the National Dance Institute (NDI), which offers dance classes to public school students, most from underprivileged backgrounds. Through NDI, hundreds of children have experienced the joy and discipline of dance. D'Amboise's NDI experience provided the basis of a book he coauthored, *Teaching the Magic of Dance* (1983), and his contributions to the arts led to his being honored at the Kennedy Center in 1995. The following selection originally appeared in *Parade* magazine in 1989.

Pre-Reading Journal Entry

While you were growing up, to what extent were you exposed to the arts: music, dance, drawing, painting, and so forth? Looking back, do you think that this exposure—or lack of exposure—worked to your advantage or to your disadvantage? Use your journal to respond to these questions.

Showing What Is Possible

When I was 7 years old, I was forced to watch my sister's ballet   1
classes. This was to keep me off the street and away from my pals,
who ran with gangs like the ones in *West Side Story*. The class was
taught by Madame Seda, a Georgian-Armenian[1] who had a school
at 181st Street and St. Nicholas Avenue in New York City. As she
taught the little girls, I would sit, fidget and diabolically try to disrupt the class by making irritating little noises.

---

[1]A person from the neighboring republics of Georgia and Armenia, formerly of the
Soviet Union (editors' note).

But she was very wise, Madame Seda. She let me get away with 2
it, ignoring me until the end of the class, when everybody did the
big jumps, a series of leaps in place, called *changements.*

At that point, Madame Seda turned and, stabbing a finger at 3
me, said, "All right, little brother, if you've got so much energy, get
up and do these jumps. See if you can jump as high as the girls." So
I jumped. And loved it. I felt like I was flying. And she said, "Oh,
that was wonderful! From now on, if you are quiet during the class,
I'll let you join in the *changements.*"

After that, I'd sit quietly in the class and wait for the jumps. A 4
few classes later, she said, "You've got to learn how to jump and not
make any noise when you come down. You should learn to do the
pliés [graceful knee bends] that come at the beginning of the class."
So I would do *pliés*, then wait respectfully for the end of class to do
the jumps.

Finally she said, "You jump high, and you are landing beautifully, 5
but you look awful in the air, flaying your arms about. You've got to
take the rest of the class and learn how to do beautiful hands and arms."

I was hooked. 6

An exceptional teacher got a bored little kid, me, interested in 7
ballet. How? She challenged me to a test, complimented me on my
effort and then immediately gave me a new challenge. She set up an
environment for the achievement of excellence and cared enough to
invite me to be part of it. And, without realizing it fully at the time,
I made an important discovery.

Dance is the most immediate and accessible of the arts because it 8
involves your own body. When you learn to move your body on a note
of music, it's exciting. You have taken control of your body and, by
learning to do that, you discover that you can take control of your life.

I took classes with Madame Seda for six months, once a week, 9
but at the end of spring, in June 1942, she called over my mother,
my sister and me and did an unbelievably modest and generous
thing. She said, "You and your sister are very talented. You should
go to a better teacher." She sent us to George Balanchine's school—
the School of American Ballet.

Within a few years, I was performing children's roles. At 15, I 10
became part of a classical ballet company. What an extraordinary
thing for a street boy from Washington Heights, with friends in
gangs. Half grew up to become policemen and the other half gang-
sters—and I became a ballet dancer!

I had dreamed of being a doctor or an archaeologist or a priest. 11
But by the time I was 17, I was a principal dancer performing major
roles in the ballets, and by the time I was 21, I was doing movies,
Broadway shows and choreography. I then married a ballerina from
New York City Ballet, Carolyn George, and we were (and still are)
blessed with two boys and twin daughters.

It was a joyful career that lasted four decades. That's a long time 12
to be dancing and, inevitably, a time came when I realized that there
were not many years left for me as a performer. I wasn't sure what
to do next, but then I thought about how I had become a dancer,
and the teachers who had graced my life. Perhaps I could engage
young children, especially boys, in the magic of the arts—in dance
in particular. Not necessarily to prepare them to be professional performers, but to create an awareness by giving them a chance to
experience the arts. So I started National Dance Institute.

That was 13 years ago. Since then, with the help of fellow teach- 13
ers and staff at NDI, I have taught dance to thousands of inner-city
children. And in each class, I rediscover why teaching dance to children is so important.

Each time I can use dance to help a child discover that he can 14
control the way he moves, I am filled with joy. At a class I recently
taught at P.S. 59 in Brooklyn, there was one boy who couldn't get
from his right foot to his left. He was terrified. Everyone was
watching. And what he had to do was so simple: take a step with
his left foot on a note of music. All his classmates could do it, but
he couldn't.

He kept trying, but he kept doing it wrong until finally he was 15
frozen, unable to move at all. I put my arm around him and said,
"Let's do it together. We'll do it in slow motion." We did it. I
stepped back and said, "Now do it alone, and fast." With his face
twisted in concentration. he slammed his left foot down correctly on
the note. He did it!

The whole class applauded. He was so excited. But I think I was 16
even happier, because I knew what had taken place. He had discovered he could take control of his body, and from that he can learn
to take control of his life. If I can open the door to show a child that
that is possible, it is wonderful.

Dance is the art to express time and space. That is what our uni- 17
verse is about. We can hardly make a sentence without signifying
some expression of distance, place or time: "See you later." "Meet
you at the corner in five minutes."

Dance is the art that human beings have developed to express   18
that we live, right now, in a world of movement and varying tempos.

Dance, as an art, has to be taught. However, when teaching, it's   19
important to set up an environment where both the student and
teacher can discover together. Never teach something you don't
love and believe in. But how to set up that environment?

When I have a new group of young students and I'm starting a   20
class, I use Madame Seda's technique. I say, "Can you do this test?
I'm going to give all 100 of you exactly 10 seconds to get off your
seats and be standing and spread out all over the stage floor. And do
it silently. Go!" And I start a countdown. Naturally, they run, yelling
and screaming, and somehow arrive with several seconds to spare. I
say, "Freeze. You all failed. You made noise, and you got there too
soon. I said 'exactly 10 seconds'—not 6 or 8 or 11. Go back to your
seats, and we'll do it again. And if you don't get it, we'll go back and
do it again until you do. And if, at the end of the hour, you still
haven't gotten it, I'm not going to teach you."

They usually get it the second time. Never have I had to do it   21
more than three.

Demand precision, be clear and absolutely truthful. When they   22
respond—and they will—congratulate them on the extraordinary
control they have just exhibited. Why is that important? Because it's
the beginning of knowing yourself, knowing that you can manage
yourself if you want. And it's the beginning of dance. Once the children see that we are having a class of precision, order and respect,
they are relieved, and we have a great class.

I've taught dance to Russian children, Australian children,   23
Indian children, Chinese children, fat children, skinny children,
handicapped children, groups of Australian triathletes, New York
City police, senior citizens and 3-year-olds. The technique is the
same everywhere, although there are cultural differences.

For example, when I was in China, I would say to the children,   24
"I want everybody to come close and watch what I am going to
do." But in China they have had to deal with following a teacher
when there are masses of them. And they discovered that the way to
see what the teacher does is not to move close but to move away. So
100 people moved back to watch the one—me.

I realized they were right. How did they learn that? Thousands   25
of years of masses of people having to follow one teacher.

There are cultural differences and there are differences among   26
people. In any group of dancers, there are some who are ready and

excel more than others. There are many reasons—genetic, environment, the teachers they had. People blossom at different times.

But whatever the differences, someone admiring you, encouraging you, works so much better than the reverse. "You can do it, you are wonderful," works so much better than, "You're no good, the others are better than you, you've got to try harder." That never works.   27

I don't think there are any untalented children. But I think there are those whose talents never get the chance to flower. Perhaps they were never encouraged. Perhaps no one took the time to find out how to teach them. That is a tragedy.   28

However, the single most terrible thing we are doing to our children, I believe, is polluting them. I don't mean just with smog and crack, but by not teaching them the civilizing things we have taken millions of years to develop. But you cannot have a dance class without having good manners, without having respect. Dance can teach those things.   29

I think of each person as a trunk that's up in the attic. What are you going to put in the trunk? Are you going to put in machine guns, loud noises, foul language, dirty books and ignorance? Because if you do, that's what is going to be left after you, that's what your children are going to have, and that will determine the world of the future. Or are you going to fill that trunk with music, dance, poetry, literature, good manners and loving friends?   30

I say, fill your trunk with the best that is available to you from the wealth of human culture. Those things will nourish you and your children. You can clean up your own environment and pass it on to the next generation. That's why I teach dance.   31

Questions for Close Reading

1. What is the selection's thesis? Locate the sentence(s) in which D'Amboise states his main idea. If he doesn't state the thesis explicitly, express it in your own words.
2. In paragraph 2, D'Amboise says that Madame Seda "was very wise." In what ways was she wise?
3. D'Amboise believes that dance has to be taught in a particular kind of environment. What, according to D'Amboise, are the most important qualities of that environment?
4. What does D'Amboise mean in paragraph 29 when he says that we pollute our children? What does D'Amboise consider the possible consequences of such pollution?

5. Refer to your dictionary as needed to define the following words used in the selection: *diabolically* (paragraph 1), *flaying* (5), *accessible* (8), *choreography* (11), *inevitably* (12), and *triathletes* (23).

Questions About the Writer's Craft

1. **The pattern.** Writers often organize cause-effect pieces using either a chronological or an emphatic sequence—or perhaps a combination of the two. Identify the organizational pattern that D'Amboise uses.
2. **Other patterns.** D'Amboise begins his essay with a narrative that tells the story of his first experience with Madame Seda. What is the purpose of this opening narrative? How does it prepare readers for what follows?
3. Reread paragraphs 20–21. The two short sentences in paragraph 21 could have concluded paragraph 20. Why do you think D'Amboise placed these two sentences in a separate paragraph?
4. In the last two paragraphs, D'Amboise uses an *analogy* (a comparison between two objects or people that seem to have little in common). Identify the analogy, and explain its relevance to the essay's central idea.

Writing Assignments Using Cause-Effect as a Pattern of Development

1. According to D'Amboise, a good teacher is one who provides a classroom of precision and order. Without structure and clear expectations, D'Amboise suggests, children will not flourish in the classroom. Do you think the same might be said of children in the home? Write a paper analyzing the effect on children of *one* of the following: a parenting style that imposes a reasonable number of boundaries, one that imposes too many limits, one that imposes too few restrictions. When writing, draw upon your own experiences and observations as well as those of friends, classmates, and family members. The following essays provide insight into different parenting styles: Russell Baker's "In My Day" (page 108), E. B. White's "Once More to the Lake" (page 125), Judith Ortiz Cofer's "A Partial Remembrance of a Puerto Rican Childhood" (page 134), and Audre Lorde's "The Fourth of July" (page 160).
2. D'Amboise asserts that "the single most terrible thing we are doing to our children . . . is polluting them . . . by not teaching them the civilizing things we have taken millions of years to develop." Among the pollutants he lists are drugs, violence, and pornography. Select one of these negative influences (or another you consider important), and write an essay analyzing how it pollutes children. You might show how this factor affects children's behavior, self-concept, and attitudes toward others. Before preparing your paper, interview classmates, friends, and family members to learn in what ways they think this factor influences children.

Writing Assignments Using Other Patterns of Development

3. D'Amboise attributes his love of dance to Madame Seda, whom he calls an "exceptional teacher." Very likely, you too at some point in your life experienced the influence of a special adult—perhaps a teacher, coach, parent, grandparent, neighbor, or religious instructor. Using one extended example or a series of shorter examples, write an essay showing how your interaction with this person taught you important lessons that shaped your life. Before you begin writing, consider reading Maya Angelou's "Sister Flowers" (page 116), a loving portrait of a childhood mentor.

4. D'Amboise's opening narrative illustrates how he became interested in dance. Consider the career path you have chosen or are thinking about choosing. What experiences pointed you in that direction? Write an essay in which you explain why you are interested in that particular career. Recount at least two experiences that helped you feel this work would be interesting and rewarding. Use vivid dialogue to dramatize the intensity of the experiences.

Writing Assignments Using a Journal Entry as a Starting Point

5. Write an essay arguing that it is *or* is not important for schools to expose children to the arts. The material you generated in your pre-reading journal entry will help you develop your position. You'll probably also find it helpful to talk to others about their experiences with the arts. Since the issue of arts-education funding is currently being debated, you should have little trouble researching this topic in the library and/or on the Internet. No matter which position you take, be sure to acknowledge opposing viewpoints.

Alice Walker

The eighth child of Georgia sharecroppers, Alice Walker (1944–) has built a reputation as a sensitive chronicler of the Black experience in America. After studying at Spelman College in Atlanta, Walker graduated from Sarah Lawrence College in New York. Soon after that, she worked in the civil rights movement helping to register Black voters and teaching in Mississippi's Head Start program. The recipient of numerous writing fellowships and the founder of her own publishing company, Walker has written extensively: a biography, *Langston Hughes, American Poet* (1973); poetry, *Revolutionary Petunias and Other Poems* (1973); short stories, collected in *In Love & Trouble* (1973) and *You Can't Keep a Good Woman Down* (1981); essays, gathered in *Living by the Word* (1988) and *Alice Walker Banned* (1996); children's fiction, *To Hell with Dying* (1991); and novels for adults, including *Meridian* (1976), *The Color Purple* (1982), *The Temple of My Familiar* (1989), *By the Light of My Father's Smile* (1998), and *The Way Forward Is With a Broken Heart* (2000). *The Color Purple* won both the Pulitzer Prize and the American Book Award and was made into a feature film. The following selection comes from Walker's 1983 collection of essays, *In Search of Our Mothers' Gardens.*

Pre-Reading Journal Entry

It's easy to become discouraged when we're told we can't have—or be—something we want. That's when we most need the support of others. Who are the people in your life who have helped you focus not on your limitations but on your strengths? What specifically did each person do to encourage you? Use your journal to respond to these questions.

Beauty: When the Other Dancer Is the Self

It is a bright summer day in 1947. My father, a fat, funny man   1
with beautiful eyes and a subversive wit, is trying to decide which of
his eight children he will take with him to the county fair. My mother, of course, will not go. She is knocked out from getting most of

us ready: I hold my neck stiff against the pressure of her knuckles as she hastily completes the braiding and then beribboning of my hair.

My father is the driver for the rich old white lady up the road. 2 Her name is Miss Mey. She owns all the land for miles around, as well as the house in which we live. All I remember about her is that she once offered to pay my mother thirty-five cents for cleaning her house, raking up piles of her magnolia leaves, and washing her family's clothes, and that my mother—she of no money, eight children, and a chronic earache—refused it. But I do not think of this in 1947. I am two and a half years old. I want to go everywhere my daddy goes. I am excited at the prospect of riding in a car. Someone has told me fairs are fun. That there is room in the car for only three of us doesn't faze me at all. Whirling happily in my starchy frock, showing off my biscuit-polished patent-leather shoes and lavender socks, tossing my head in a way that makes my ribbons bounce, I stand, hands on hips, before my father. "Take me, Daddy," I say with assurance; "I'm the prettiest!"

Later, it does not surprise me to find myself in Miss Mey's shiny 3 black car, sharing the back seat with the other lucky ones. Does not surprise me that I thoroughly enjoy the fair. At home that night I tell the unlucky ones all I can remember about the merry-go-round, the man who eats live chickens, and the teddy bears, until they say: that's enough baby Alice. Shut up now, and go to sleep.

It is Easter Sunday, 1950. I am dressed in a green, flocked, scal- 4 loped-hem dress (handmade by my adoring sister, Ruth) that has its own smooth satin petticoat and tiny hot-pink roses tucked into each scallop. My shoes, new T-strap patent leather, again highly biscuit-polished. I am six years old and have learned one of the longest Easter speeches to be heard that day, totally unlike the speech I said when I was two: "Easter lilies / pure and white / blossom in / the morning light." When I rise to give my speech I do so on a great wave of love and pride and expectation. People in the church stop rustling their new crinolines. They seem to hold their breath. I can tell they admire my dress, but it is my spirit, bordering on sassiness (womanishness), they secretly applaud.

"That girl's a little *mess*," they whisper to each other, pleased. 5

Naturally I say my speech without stammer or pause, unlike 6 those who stutter, stammer, or, worst of all, forget. This is before the word "beautiful" exists in people's vocabulary, but "Oh, isn't she the *cutest* thing?" frequently floats my way. "And got so much sense!" they gratefully add . . . for which thoughtful addition I thank them to this day.

It was great fun being cute. But then, one day, it ended. 7

I am eight years old and a tomboy. I have a cowboy hat, cow- 8
boy boots, checkered shirt and pants, all red. My playmates are my brothers, two and four years older than I. Their colors are black and green, the only difference in the way we are dressed. On Saturday nights we all go to the picture show, even my mother; Westerns are her favorite kind of movie. Back home, "on the ranch," we pretend we are Tom Mix, Hopalong Cassidy, Lash LaRue (we've even named one of our dogs Lash LaRue); we chase each other for hours rustling cattle, being outlaws, delivering damsels from distress. Then my parents decide to buy my brothers guns. These are not "real" guns. They shoot "BBs," copper pellets my brothers say will kill birds. Because I am a girl, I do not get a gun. Instantly I am rele-gated to the position of Indian. Now there appears a great distance between us. They shoot and shoot at everything with their new guns. I try to keep up with my bow and arrows.

One day while I am standing on top of our makeshift 9
"garage"—pieces of tin nailed across some poles—holding my bow and arrow and looking out toward the fields, I feel an incredible blow in my right eye. I look down just in time to see my brother lower his gun.

Both brothers rush to my side. My eye stings, and I cover it with 10
my hand. "If you tell," they say, "we will get a whipping. You don't want that to happen, do you?" I do not. "Here is a piece of wire," says the older brother, picking it up from the roof; "say you stepped on one end of it and the other flew up and hit you." The pain is beginning to start. "Yes," I say. "Yes, I will say that is what hap-pened." If I do not say this is what happened, I know my brothers will find ways to make me wish I had. But now I will say anything that gets me to my mother.

Confronted by our parents we stick to the lie agreed upon. They 11
place me on a bench on the porch and I close my left eye while they examine the right. There is a tree growing from underneath the porch that climbs past the railing to the roof. It is the last thing my right eye sees. I watch as its trunk, its branches, and then its leaves are blotted out by the rising blood.

I am in shock. First there is intense fever, which my father tries 12
to break using lily leaves bound around my head. Then there are chills: my mother tries to get me to eat soup. Eventually, I do not

know how, my parents learn what has happened. A week after the "accident" they take me to see a doctor. "Why did you wait so long to come?" he asks, looking into my eye and shaking his head. "Eyes are sympathetic," he says. "If one is blind, the other will likely become blind too."

This comment of the doctor's terrifies me. But it is really how I   13
look that bothers me most. Where the BB pellet struck there is a glob of whitish scar tissue, a hideous cataract, on my eye. Now when I stare at people—a favorite pastime, up to now—they will stare back. Not at the "cute" little girl, but at her scar. For six years I do not stare at anyone, because I do not raise my head.

Years later, in the throes of a mid-life crisis, I ask my mother and   14
sister whether I changed after the "accident." "No," they say, puzzled. "What do you mean?"

What do I mean?   15

I am eight, and, for the first time, doing poorly in school, where   16
I have been something of a whiz since I was four. We have just moved to the place where the "accident" occurred. We do not know any of the people around us because this is a different county. The only time I see the friends I knew is when we go back to our old church. The new school is the former state penitentiary. It is a large stone building, cold and drafty, crammed to overflowing with boisterous, ill-disciplined children. On the third floor there is a huge circular imprint of some partition that has been torn out.

"What used to be here?" I ask a sullen girl next to me on our   17
way past it to lunch.

"The electric chair," says she.   18

At night I have nightmares about the electric chair; and about   19
all the people reputedly "fried" in it. I am afraid of the school, where all the students seem to be budding criminals.

"What's the matter with your eye?" they ask, critically.   20

When I don't answer (I cannot decide whether it was an "acci-   21
dent" or not), they shove me, insist on a fight.

My brother, the one who created the story about the wire,   22
comes to my rescue. But then brags so much about "protecting" me, I become sick.

After months of torture at the school, my parents decide to send   23
me back to our old community, to my old school. I live with my grandparents and the teacher they board. But there is no room for

Phoebe, my cat. By the time my grandparents decide there *is* room, and I ask for my cat, she cannot be found. Miss Yarborough, the boarding teacher, takes me under her wing, and begins to teach me to play the piano. But soon she marries an African—a "prince," she says—and is whisked away to his continent.

At my old school there is at least one teacher who loves me. She is the teacher who "knew me before I was born" and bought my first baby clothes. It is she who makes life bearable. It is her presence that finally helps me turn on the one child at the school who continually calls me "one-eyed bitch." One day I simply grab him by his coat and beat him until I am satisfied. It is my teacher who tells me my mother is ill. 24

My mother is lying in bed in the middle of the day, something I have never seen. She is in too much pain to speak. She has an abscess in her ear. I stand looking down on her, knowing that if she dies, I cannot live. She is being treated with warm oils and hot bricks held against her cheeks. Finally a doctor comes. But I must go back to my grandparents' house. The weeks pass but I am hardly aware of it. All I know is that my mother might die, my father is not so jolly, my brothers still have their guns, and I am the one sent away from home. 25

"You did not change," they say. 26
Did I imagine the anguish of never looking up? 27

I am twelve. When relatives come to visit I hide in my room. My cousin Brenda, just my age, whose father works in the post office and whose mother is a nurse, comes to find me. "Hello," she says. And then she asks, looking at my recent school picture, which I did not want taken, and on which the "glob," as I think of it, is clearly visible, "You still can't see out of that eye?" 28

"No," I say, and flop back on the bed over my book. 29
That night, as I do almost every night, I abuse my eye. I rant and rave at it, in front of the mirror. I plead with it to clear up before morning. I tell it I hate and despise it. I do not pray for sight. I pray for beauty. 30

"You did not change," they say. 31
I am fourteen and baby-sitting for my brother Bill, who lives in Boston. He is my favorite brother and there is a strong bond between us. Understanding my feelings of shame and ugliness he 32

and his wife take me to a local hospital, where the "glob" is removed by a doctor named O. Henry. There is still a small bluish crater where the scar tissue was, but the ugly white stuff is gone. Almost immediately I become a different person from the girl who does not raise her head. Or so I think. Now that I've raised my head I win the boyfriend of my dreams. Now that I've raised my head I have plenty of friends. Now that I've raised my head classwork comes from my lips as faultlessly as Easter speeches did, and I leave high school as valedictorian, most popular student, and *queen,* hardly believing my luck. Ironically, the girl who was voted most beautiful in our class (and was) was later shot twice through the chest by a male companion, using a "real" gun, while she was pregnant. But that's another story in itself. Or is it?

"You did not change," they say.   33

It is now thirty years since the "accident." A beautiful journalist   34
comes to visit and to interview me. She is going to write a cover story for her magazine that focuses on my latest book. "Decide how you want to look on the cover," she says. "Glamorous, or whatever."

Never mind "glamorous," it is the "whatever" that I hear.   35
Suddenly all I can think of is whether I will get enough sleep the night before the photography session: if I don't, my eye will be tired and wander, as blind eyes will.

At night in bed with my lover I think up reasons why I should   36
not appear on the cover of a magazine. "My meanest critics will say I've sold out," I say. "My family will now realize I write scandalous books."

"But what's the real reason you don't want to do this?" he asks.   37

"Because in all probability," I say in a rush, "my eye won't be   38
straight."

"It will be straight enough," he says. Then, "Besides, I thought   39
you'd made your peace with that."

And I suddenly remember that I have.   40

I remember: 41

I am talking to my brother Jimmy, asking if he remembers any-   42
thing unusual about the day I was shot. He does not know I consider that day the last time my father, with his sweet home remedy of cool lily leaves, chose me, and that I suffered and raged inside because of this. "Well," he says, "all I remember is standing by the side of the highway with Daddy, trying to flag down a car. A white man stopped, but when Daddy said he needed somebody to take his little girl to the doctor, he drove off."

I remember: 43

I am in the desert for the first time. I fall totally in love with it.   44
I am so overwhelmed by its beauty, I confront for the first time, consciously, the meaning of the doctor's words years ago: "Eyes are sympathetic. If one is blind, the other will likely become blind too." I
realize I have dashed about the world madly, looking at this, looking
at that, storing up images against the fading of the light. *But I might
have missed seeing the desert!* The shock of that possibility—and gratitude for over twenty-five years of sight—sends me literally to my
knees. Poem after poem comes—which is perhaps how poets pray.

On Sight   45

> *I am so thankful I have seen*
> *The Desert*
> *And the creatures in the desert*
> *And the desert Itself.*
>
> *The desert has its own moon*
> *Which I have seen*
> *With my own eye.*
> *There is no flag on it.*
>
> *Trees of the desert have arms*
> *All of which are always up*
> *That is because the moon is up*
> *The sun is up*
> *Also the sky*
> *The stars*
> *Clouds*
> *None with flags.*
>
> *If there were flags, I doubt*
> *the trees would point.*
> *Would you?*

But mostly, I remember this: 46

I am twenty-seven, and my baby daughter is almost three. Since   47
her birth I have worried about her discovery that her mother's eyes
are different from other people's. Will she be embarrassed? I think.
What will she say? Every day she watches a television program called
"Big Blue Marble." It begins with a picture of the earth as it appears
from the moon. It is bluish, a little battered-looking, but full of
light, with whitish clouds swirling around it. Every time I see it I

weep with love, as if it is a picture of Grandma's house. One day when I am putting Rebecca down for her nap, she suddenly focuses on my eye. Something inside me cringes, gets ready to try to protect myself. All children are cruel about physical differences, I know from experience, and that they don't always mean to be is another matter. I assume Rebecca will be the same.

But no-o-o-o. She studies my face intently as we stand, her inside   48
and me outside the crib. She even holds my face maternally between her dimpled little hands. Then, looking every bit as serious and lawyerlike as her father, she says, as if it may just possibly have slipped my attention: "Mommy, there's a *world* in your eye." (As in, "Don't be alarmed, or do anything crazy.") And then, gently, but with great interest: "Mommy, where did you *get* that world in your eye?"

For the most part, the pain left then. (So what, if my brothers   49
grew up to buy even more powerful pellet guns for their sons and to carry real guns themselves. So what, if a young "Morehouse man" once nearly fell off the steps of Trevor Arnett Library because he thought my eyes were blue.) Crying and laughing I ran to the bathroom, while Rebecca mumbled and sang herself off to sleep. Yes indeed, I realized, looking into the mirror. There *was* a world in my eye. And I saw that it was possible to love it: that in fact, for all it had taught me of shame and anger and inner vision, I *did* love it. Even to see it drifting out of orbit in boredom, or rolling up out of fatigue, not to mention floating back at attention in excitement (bearing witness, a friend has called it), deeply suitable to my personality, and even characteristic of me.

That night I dream I am dancing to Stevie Wonder's song   50
"Always" (the name of the song is really "As," but I hear it as "Always"). As I dance, whirling and joyous, happier than I've ever been in my life, another bright-faced dancer joins me. We dance and kiss each other and hold each other through the night. The other dancer has obviously come through all right, as I have done. She is beautiful, whole and free. And she is also me.

Questions for Close Reading

1. What is the selection's thesis? Locate the sentence(s) in which Walker states her main idea. If she doesn't state the thesis explicitly, express it in your own words.

2. How does Walker's injury affect her ability to express herself and relate to others?

3. What is the connection between the loss of young Alice's cat and her teacher's marriage (paragraph 23)?

4. How do you interpret the essay's title—"Beauty: When the Other Dancer Is the Self"? How does the title reinforce Walker's thesis?

5. Refer to your dictionary as needed to define the following words used in the selection: *subversive* (paragraph 1), *chronic* (2), *flocked* (4), *crinolines* (4), *cataract* (13), and *abscess* (25).

Questions About the Writer's Craft

1. **The pattern.** Walker's essay is structured around a causal chain that shows the interaction between the external and the internal. Explain how Walker develops this chain throughout the essay.

2. **Other patterns.** Although Walker narrates incidents occurring from infancy to midlife, she writes in the present tense. Why do you think she does this?

3. How does Walker signal the ages at which she experiences a crisis or some other major event? What technique does she use?

4. The refrain "You did not change" occurs in differing contexts throughout Walker's essay. What is the effect of this repetition?

Writing Assignments Using Cause-Effect as a Pattern of Development

1. An event initially viewed as handicapping can prove, as Walker shows, to be a blessing. Write a paper showing the effect on your life of an experience that at first seemed negative but turned out for the best.

2. Walker expects her daughter to react with revulsion to her eye injury. To her surprise, her daughter's reaction is tender and gentle. Think of a time you expected someone to treat you with kindness, but instead you were treated harshly, or, conversely, you expected severity but were met with generosity. In an essay, trace the causes of your faulty expectation as well as the possible reasons for the other person's unexpected behavior. Draw some conclusions about human nature.

Writing Assignments Using Other Patterns of Development

3. Walker writes of an experience in which joyful, exuberant play turned—in an instant—to terror. Write about a time in your own or in someone else's life when there was a sudden reversal of events—a positive experience that became negative or vice versa. Use vivid images, varied sentence structure, and dialogue to capture what happened. Did the event leave a lasting impression? If so, end by writing briefly about this effect.

∞ **4.** Walker mentions two elementary school teachers who responded to her in a loving, supportive way. Write a letter to beginning grade school teachers outlining the steps they should (and should not) take to make their students' school experience a positive one. Sophronia Liu's "So Tsi-Fai" (page 188) will help you appreciate the powerful influence that teachers can exert on children.

Writing Assignments Using a Journal Entry as a Starting Point

∞ **5.** Review your pre-reading journal entry and select *one* person who encouraged you to believe in yourself. Then write an essay showing how this individual helped you shift your focus from what you couldn't do to what you could do. Start by describing briefly how you thought and felt before this person influenced you. Then use several dramatic examples to show how this person helped you develop a more optimistic and affirming mindset. You might first consider reading Maya Angelou's "Sister Flowers" (page 116), a warm, nostalgic portrait of a childhood mentor.

Lewis Thomas

Lewis Thomas (1913–94) earned a reputation as an outstanding scientist and physician. A graduate of Princeton University and Harvard Medical School, Thomas held both the deanship of Yale University's medical school and the presidency of Sloan-Kettering Memorial Cancer Center. But more remarkable than Thomas's professional accomplishments was his gift for communicating the wonder of medicine and biology to the average reader. His essays, many of which first appeared in the *New England Journal of Medicine*, are less about medicine than they are about what he called the "mystery of being." Thomas published many books: a memoir, *The Youngest Science* (1983); and five essay collections, *Lives of a Cell* (1974), which won a National Book Award; *The Medusa and the Snail* (1979); *Late Night Thoughts on Listening to Mahler's Ninth Symphony* (1984); *Etcetera, Etcetera* (1990); and *The Fragile Species* (1992). The following selection is from *Late Night Thoughts*.

Pre-Reading Journal Entry

It's been argued that many technological developments of the last century reflect the worst in human nature. Consider the flip side of this claim. What three inventions of the last hundred years do you find reflect *positively* on human nature? List them in your journal, jotting down what about each invention inspires optimism about human beings.

The Lie Detector

Every once in a while the reasons for discouragement about the human prospect pile up so high that it becomes difficult to see the way ahead, and it is then a great blessing to have one conspicuous and irrefutable good thing to think about ourselves, something solid enough to step onto and look beyond the pile. 1

Language is often useful for this, and music. A particular painting, if you have the right receptors, can lift the spirits and hold them high enough to see a whole future for the race. The sound of laughter in the distance in the dark can be a marvelous encouragement. But these are chancy stimuli, ready to work only if you happen to be ready to receive them, which takes a bit of luck. 2

I have been reading magazine stories about the technology of   3
lie detection lately, and it occurs to me that this may be the thing
I've been looking for, an encouragement propped up by genuine,
hard scientific data. It is promising enough that I've decided to take
as given what the articles say, uncritically, and to look no further. For
a while, anyway.

Lying Is a Strain

As I understand it, a human being cannot tell a lie, even a small   4
one, without setting off a kind of smoke alarm somewhere deep in
a dark lobule of the brain, resulting in the sudden discharge of nerve
impulses, or the sudden outpouring of neurohormones of some
sort, or both. The outcome, recorded by the lie-detector gadgetry,
is a highly reproducible cascade of changes in the electrical conduc-
tivity of the skin, the heart rate, and the manner of breathing, similar to the responses to various kinds of stress.

Lying, then, is stressful, even when we do it for protection, or   5
relief, or escape, or profit, or just for the pure pleasure of lying and
getting away with it. It is a strain, distressing enough to cause the
emission of signals to and from the central nervous system warning
that something has gone wrong. It is, in a pure physiological sense,
an unnatural act.

Now I regard this as a piece of extraordinarily good news,   6
meaning, unless I have it all balled up, that we are a moral species
by compulsion, at least in the limited sense that we are biologically
designed to be truthful to each other. Lying doesn't hurt, mind you,
and perhaps you could tell lies all day and night for years on end
without being damaged, but maybe not—maybe the lie detector
informs us that repeated, inveterate untruthfulness will gradually
undermine the peripheral vascular system, the sweat glands, the
adrenals, and who knows what else. Perhaps we should be looking
into the possibility of lying as an etiologic agent for some of the
common human ailments still beyond explaining, recurrent head
colds, for instance, or that most human of all unaccountable disorders, a sudden pain in the lower mid-back.

Truth: Genetically Required?

It makes a sort of shrewd biological sense, and might therefore   7
represent a biological trait built into our genes, a feature of humanity

as characteristic for us as feathers for birds or scales for fish, enabling us to live, at our best, the kinds of lives we are designed to live. This is, I suppose, the "sociobiological" view to take, with the obvious alternative being that we are brought up this way as children in response to the rules of our culture. But if the latter is the case, you would expect to encounter, every once in a while, societies in which the rule does not hold, and I have never heard of a culture in which lying was done by everyone as a matter of course, all life through, nor can I imagine such a group functioning successfully. Biologically speaking, there is good reason for us to restrain ourselves from lying outright to each other whenever possible. We are indeed a social species, more interdependent than the celebrated social insects; we can no more live a solitary life than can a bee; we are obliged, as a species, to rely on each other. Trust is a fundamental requirement for our kind of existence, and without it all our linkages would begin to snap loose.

The restraint is a mild one, so gentle as to be almost impercep- 8
tible. But it is there; we know about it from what we call guilt, and now we have a neat machine to record it as well.

It seems a trivial thing to have this information, but perhaps it 9
tells us to look again, and look deeper. If we had better instruments, designed for profounder probes, we might see needles flipping, lines on charts recording quantitative degrees of meanness of spirit, or a lack of love. I do not wish for such instruments, I hope they will never be constructed; they would somehow belittle the issues involved. It is enough, quite enough, to know that we cannot even tell a plain untruth, betray a trust, without scaring some part of our own brains. I'd rather guess at the rest.

Questions for Close Reading

1. What is the selection's thesis? Locate the sentence(s) in which Thomas states his main idea. If he doesn't state the thesis explicitly, express it in your own words.
2. For what reasons does Thomas call lying an "unnatural act"? How does he feel about its being "unnatural"?
3. Thomas writes that receptivity to language, music, art, and laughter "takes a bit of luck" (paragraph 2). What do you think he means by this statement?
4. To his "sociobiological" view of truth telling, Thomas contrasts another viewpoint. What is this other interpretation? Does he give this other interpretation equal support? Why or why not?

5. Refer to your dictionary as needed to define the following words used in the selection: *irrefutable* (paragraph 1), *receptors* (2), *stimuli* (2), *lobule* (4), *neurohormones* (4), *inveterate* (6), and *etiologic* (6).

Questions About the Writer's Craft

1. **The pattern.** At the heart of Thomas's essay is a causal chain consisting of a series of interwoven causes and effects. What is this causal chain?
2. Thomas mixes technical terms from neuroscience with a rather informal style, involving contractions, the first-person ("I") point of view, colloquial expressions ("unless I have it all balled up"), and sentence fragments. Why might he have chosen to blend two such contrasting styles?
3. When presenting his viewpoint, Thomas uses a number of qualifiers: "it occurs to me" (paragraph 3), "as I understand it" (4), "unless I have it all balled up" (6), and "I suppose" (7). What is the effect of these qualifiers? Do they contribute to or detract from his credibility?
4. Thomas's next-to-last paragraph is shorter than any other in the essay. What function does this brief paragraph serve?

Writing Assignments Using Cause-Effect as a Pattern of Development

1. Reasons for lying, Thomas writes, include profit, protection, pleasure, and kindness. Write an essay tracing the reasons for a lie that you or someone else (a parent, friend, or public figure) once told. Also analyze the effect of the lie. Langston Hughes's "Salvation" (page 183) and William Lutz's "Doublespeak" (page 296) may provide some insight into the psychology of lying. End the paper with some conclusions about when lying is and is not acceptable.
2. Thomas welcomes the use of the lie detector but has qualms about the development of similar technologies. Focus on one technological breakthrough (word processors, cell phone, DVDs, handheld computers) and discuss its negative and positive effects. Although your analysis may be serious or playful, it should have a basically persuasive intent. You might read Jonathan Coleman's "Is Technology Making Us Intimate Strangers?" (page 482) for an additional perspective on the human impact of technology.

Writing Assignments Using Other Patterns of Development

3. Thomas claims, "Trust is a fundamental requirement for our . . . existence." In an essay, define the word *trust*. Consider dramatic examples, brief anecdotes, or a comparison of two people when developing the definition. Your essay should illustrate Thomas's point that without trust "all our linkages would . . . snap loose."

∞ **4.** According to Thomas, "We are a moral species by compulsion." Write an essay in which you argue for or against this contention. Remembering to consider the opposing opinion, develop your argument by citing several examples of human behavior. Before writing the paper, you might want to read Stephen King's "Why We Crave Horror Movies" (page 455) and Mark Twain's "The Damned Human Race" (page 587), two essays that present a point of view very different from Thomas's.

Writing Assignments Using a Journal Entry as a Starting Point

5. Write an essay showing that the very existence of a specific invention provides evidence of higher-level human attributes. From your pre-reading journal entry, select the *one* invention that you think offers the most compelling proof. Brainstorming with others will help you identify reasons and examples worth developing.

Jonathan Coleman

Jonathan Coleman (1951–), a frequent contributor to *Time* and *The New York Times,* was born in Allentown, Pennsylvania, and graduated from the University of Virginia. He was an editor with Alfred A. Knopf and Simon & Schuster before moving to CBS News in the early 1980s. While at CBS, Coleman began investigating the story that led to his first book, *At A Mother's Request* (1985). A bestseller, the book provided the basis for a popular CBS miniseries. Coleman is also the author of *Exit the Rainmaker* (1989) and *Long Way to Go: Black and White in America* (1997). A lecturer on the subject of race at universities across the country, Coleman has been interviewed on most major television and radio shows. He makes his home in Charlottesville, Virginia. The following selection first appeared in *Newsweek* in 2000.

Pre-Reading Journal Entry

You've probably observed that people today have such full schedules, they often do several things at once. What examples of "multi-tasking" have you seen in yourself and in others? What do you think about this tendency to multi-task? Do you consider it productive? Do you think it overcomplicates life? Use your journal to respond to these questions.

Is Technology Making Us Intimate Strangers?

Every day when I walk out of my house I feel surrounded. 1 Surrounded by mere civilians so loaded down with the latest equipment that any military commander would be envious. Cell phones, beepers, headsets, watches that both tell time and give good e-mail—smart, sleek, technological fashion statements that enable you to be reached any time, anywhere; devices that allow you to keep up and keep track and that keep you tethered to the daily grind. America is on the move, utterly self-absorbed, multi-tasking, busy, busy, busy.

So what's the matter with me, daring to go about the streets 2 without any of these things, a dinosaur sorely out of step with the times? Why can't I just capitulate, go along with The Program? After all, it might make me more efficient and productive, perhaps even give me a sense of power and importance.

Frankly, I worry about the freedom we give up, the time to 3 think and reflect, the time to consider where we've been in order to see where we are—or want to be—going. For many people these are painful things they don't necessarily want to dwell on. Self-reflection is far different—and far more difficult—than self-absorption, but the pain that self-absorption can inflict on others is acute.

Last summer, on as lovely an evening as one can hope for in 4 central Virginia, I was at my daughter's lacrosse practice. Standing next to me was a father more intent on the cell-phone conversation he was having (which did not sound terribly pressing) than on watching his daughter play. Time and again, she would look toward him, craving his attention, but he never saw her. Nor, for that matter, did another girl's mother see her child, focused as she was on her laptop, merrily tapping away.

Before you get antsy (or feel too guilty), stop reading this and 5 zero in on the next dot-com start-up vying for your attention, some confessions are in order. I've had e-mail only for a little more than a year, and I worry that I'm starting to become obsessed with it. In the intoxicating game of popularity that we all play, e-mail has presented another way for others to reach out to us. If someone hasn't left us a phone message or a fax, there is always the chance that an e-mail awaits. I can't even finish this essay without checking—three times already—to see if another one came through. I have also checked my stocks and a favorite Web site—all because they are there and are so tantalizingly *available*. I am not proud of my lack of discipline, but there you have it. Nor am I proud of the fact that when I read to my 6-year-old daughter at night, I sometimes reach for the phone when it rings, only to have her admonish me— "Daddy, don't!"—a sharp rebuke for being so quick to interrupt our sacred time together.

Speaking of which, do you remember when you and your 6 friends would go to the beach to swim and sun and take leave of your lives for an afternoon or longer? These days, I go to the beach and see teenagers come out of the water and instantly get on their cell phones. They can't imagine a life without a cell phone, and they can't image coming to the beach without it. In their view of the world, I am just a guy from the old days. A guy who needs to chill.

Nonetheless, I still say: why not step back and view all this   7
progress from a different angle? Instead of trying to figure out ways
to do a hundred things at once, why not slow things down? After
all, the greatest gift you can offer another person is your ability to
listen, to let that person feel that you are intent on what he or she is
saying, that you have all the time in the world. (The individuals I
know who can do that are few, but they stand out conspicuously in
my mind.) Through interviewing people I write about, I have come
to learn how much people yearn to be understood, how much they
want and need to be able to explain themselves.

Technology, for the most part, creates the illusion of intimacy.   8
As marvelous as it can be, it also foils us. It keeps us from the best
of ourselves and enables us to avoid others. It makes us into intimate
strangers.

To me, the most splendid thing about a place like New York   9
City, where I lived for a long time, is that you can walk the streets
day after day, year after year, and always see something new, something that will astonish or touch you. It may be a detail on a building, or the way the light hits the magnificent public library at a particular time, or even the moment when your doorman has an extra
spring in his step. But if you're not open to these things, if you're
too busy walking down the street glued to your phone and cut off
from all that is around you, you're going to miss something. It may
seem intangible and, therefore, unimportant, but those somethings
have a way of adding up.

Questions for Close Reading

1. What is the selection's thesis? Locate the sentence(s) in which Coleman
   states his main idea. If he doesn't state the thesis explicitly, express it in
   your own words.
2. Early in his essay, Coleman lists some of the technological devices we rely
   upon nowadays. Name some of these devices. What, according to
   Coleman, are their advantages and disadvantages?
3. What, in Coleman's opinion, is the difference between "self-reflection"
   and "self-absorption" (paragraphs 1 and 3)? What does he suggest are
   the effects of each?
4. Where in the essay does Coleman admit that he, too, has trouble resist-
   ing the seductive quality of modern technology? Who, besides Coleman,
   is affected by his inability to resist? Explain.

5. Refer to your dictionary as needed to define the following words used in the selection: *tethered* (paragraph 1), *capitulate* (2), *vying* (5), *intoxicating* (5), *tantalizing* (5), *rebuke* (5), *conspicuously* (7), *yearn* (7), *illusion* (8), *foils* (8), and *intangible* (9).

Questions About the Writer's Craft

1. **The pattern.** What seems to be Coleman's purpose in pointing out the effects of technology on our day-to-day lives? Is his purpose mainly informative, speculative, or persuasive? How do you know?
2. Coleman organizes his essay around a causal chain showing technology's effect on our relationships with ourselves and with those around us. Trace the development of this causal chain.
3. At various points in his essay, Coleman poses a single question or a number of related questions. Identify these instances of question-asking. In each case, why do you think Coleman adopted this questioning strategy?
4. **Other patterns.** Reread the first and final paragraphs of Coleman's essay. What are the similarities between the two? What are the differences? Why do you suppose Coleman decided to open and close his essay this way?

Writing Assignments Using Cause-Effect as a Pattern of Development

1. Coleman expresses frustration with parents who are too engrossed in technological devices to notice their children. Increasingly, however, it's children and teenagers who are becoming addicted to such devices. Brainstorm with others about the devices that commonly lure young people. What is the appeal—and the downside—of each device? Review your brainstorming notes, and pick *one* device to focus on. Then write an essay explaining to parents the negative consequences of youngsters' overuse of the technology. Consider ending the essay with brief suggestions for scaling back kids' reliance on the device. You'll probably find it helpful to supplement your ideas with information gathered in the library and/or on the Internet.

2. In all likelihood, you know someone who hasn't been seduced by recent technological devices. Perhaps the person resists having voice mail, owning a cell phone, or using the Internet. Write an essay exploring possible reasons why this individual hasn't been lured by one or more technological advancements. Examine too the effect on others of the person's decision, as Coleman puts it, not to "go along with The Program." Your essay may be lighthearted or serious. In either case, indicate, explicitly or implicitly, how you feel about the person's

reluctance to embrace technology. For insight into why many people avoid computer technology, read Bill Bryson's spirited essay "Your New Computer" (page 343).

Writing Assignments Using Other Patterns of Development

3. Coleman believes that technology "enables us to avoid others." Focusing on one or two specific technologies, write an essay in which you argue against this view. Show instead that technology can enhance interpersonal relations. Acknowledge Coleman's viewpoint near the beginning of the essay. Like Coleman, support your position with vigorous images, heartfelt commentary, and lively examples.

4. Coleman observes that teenagers today, unlike those in the past, can't even go to the beach without their cell phones. Identify several activities that you participated in as a child and teenager but that you think young people experience differently nowadays because of technology's dominant role in the culture. Possibilities include dating, doing homework, shopping, celebrating holidays with family. Write an essay illustrating how technology has changed young people's experience of these activities. To illustrate the change, contrast your childhood *or* adolescent experience of these activities with the experience of children *or* teenagers today. Be sure to convey whether you think the change has or has not been for the better.

Writing Assignments Using a Journal Entry as a Starting Point

5. Write an essay illustrating the advantages and disadvantages of "multi-tasking"—doing more than one thing at a time. To develop your discussion, draw upon the examples in your pre-reading journal entry and upon the experiences and observations of others. Your essay should indicate whether, on the whole, you think multi-tasking is a positive or negative phenomenon. Before writing, you might read James Gleick's "Life As Type A" (page 509), an essay that speculates about the consequences of today's high-intensity lifestyles.

Additional Writing Topics

CAUSE-EFFECT

General Assignments

Write an essay that analyzes the causes and/or effects of one of the following topics. Determine your purpose before beginning to write: Will the essay be informative, persuasive, or speculative? As you prewrite, think rigorously about causes and effects; try to identify causal chains. Provide solid evidence for the thesis and use either chronological or emphatic order to organize your supporting points.

1. Sleep deprivation
2. Having the parents you have
3. Lack of communication in a relationship
4. Overexercising or not exercising
5. A particular TV or rock star's popularity
6. Skill or ineptitude in sports
7. A major life decision
8. Stiffer legal penalties for drunken driving
9. Changing attitudes toward protecting the environment
10. A particular national crisis
11. The mass movement of women into the workforce
12. Choosing to attend this college
13. "Back to basics" movement in schools
14. Headaches
15. An act of violence
16. A natural event: leaves turning, birds migrating, animals hibernating, an eclipse occurring
17. Pesticide use
18. Use of computers in the classroom
19. Banning disposable cans and bottles
20. A bad habit
21. A fear of _____
22. Legalizing drugs
23. Abolishing the F grade
24. Joining a particular organization
25. Owning a pet

Assignments With a Specific Purpose and Audience

1. A debate about the prominence of athletics at colleges and universities is going to be broadcast on the local cable station. For this debate, prepare

a speech pointing out either the harmful or the beneficial effects of "big-time" college athletic programs.

2. Why do students "flunk out" of college? Write an article for the campus newspaper outlining the main causes of failure. Your goal is to steer students away from dangerous habits and situations that lead to poor grades or dropping out.

3. Write a letter to the editor of your favorite newspaper, analyzing the causes of the country's current "trash crisis." Be sure to mention the nationwide love affair with disposable items and the general disregard of the idea of thrift.

4. Employed by your college's work-study office, you've been asked to write a brief pamphlet: "Things to Keep in Mind If You Plan to Work While Attending College." The pamphlet will be given to your fellow students, and it will focus on the effects—both negative and positive—of combining a part-time job with college studies.

5. Why do you think teenage suicide is on the rise? Write a fact sheet for parents of teenagers and for high school guidance counselors, describing the factors that could make a young person desperate enough to attempt suicide. At the end, suggest what parents and counselors can do to help confused, unhappy young people.

6. Some communities have conducted campaigns encouraging residents to give up television for a fixed period of time. You feel your community should participate in such an experiment. Write a letter to your mayor encouraging a public relations effort in favor of "Turn Off the TV Month." Cite specifically the positive effects such a program would have on parents, children, and the community in general.

10

DEFINITION

WHAT IS DEFINITION?

In Lewis Carroll's wise and whimsical tale, *Through the Looking Glass,* Humpty Dumpty proclaims, "When *I* use a word . . ., it means just what I choose it to mean—neither more nor less." If the world were filled with characters like Humpty Dumpty, all of them bending words to their own purposes and accepting no challenges to their personal definitions, communication would be an exercise in frustration. You would say a word, and it would mean one thing to you but perhaps something completely different to a close friend. Without a common understanding, the two of you would talk at cross-purposes, missing each other's meanings as you blundered through a conversation.

For language to communicate, words must have accepted *definitions*. Dictionaries, the sourcebooks for accepted definitions, are compilations of current word meanings, enabling speakers of a language to understand one another. But as you might suspect, things are not as simple as they first appear. We all know that a word like *discipline* has a standard dictionary definition. We also know, though, that parents argue over what constitutes "discipline" and that controversies about the meaning of "discipline" rage within school systems year after year. Moreover, many of the wrenching moral debates of our time also boil down to questions of definition. Much of the controversy over abortion, for instance, centers on what is meant by "life" and when it "begins."

Words can, in short, be slippery. Each of us has unique experiences, attitudes, and values that influence the way we use words and the way we interpret the words of others. Lewis Carroll may have been exaggerating, but Humpty Dumpty's attitude exists—in a very real way—in all of us.

In addition to the idiosyncratic interpretations that may attach to words, some words may shift in meaning over time. The word *pedagogue,* for instance, originally meant "a teacher or leader of children." However, with time, *pedagogue* has come to mean "a dogmatic, pedantic teacher." And, of course, we invent other words (*modem, byte*) as the need arises.

Writing a definition, then, is no simple task. Primarily, the writer tries to answer basic questions: "What does _____ mean?" and "What is the special or true nature of _____?" The word to be defined may be an object, a concept, a type of person, a place, or a phenomenon. Potential subjects might be the "user-friendly" computer, animal rights, a model teacher, cabin fever. As you will see, there are various strategies for expanding definitions far beyond the single-word synonyms or brief phrases that dictionaries provide.

HOW DEFINITION FITS YOUR PURPOSE AND AUDIENCE

Many times, short-answer exam questions call for definitions. Consider the following examples:

Define the term *mob psychology.*

What is the difference between a metaphor and a simile?

How would you explain what a religious cult is?

In such cases, a good response might involve a definition of several sentences or several paragraphs.

Other times, definition may be used in an essay organized mainly around another pattern of development. In this situation, all that's needed is a brief formal definition or a short definition given in your own words. For instance, a *process analysis* showing readers how computers have revolutionized the typical business office might start with a textbook definition of the term *artificial intelligence*. In an *argumentation-persuasion* paper urging students to support recent efforts to abolish fraternities and sororities, you could refer to the definitions of *blackballing* and *hazing* found in the university handbook. Or your personal definition of *hero* could be the starting point for a *causal analysis* that explains to readers why there are few real heroes in today's world.

But the most complex use of definition, and the one we are primarily concerned with in this chapter, involves exploring a subject through an *extended definition*. Extended definition allows you to apply a personal interpretation to a word, to make a case for a revisionist view of a commonly accepted meaning, to analyze words representing complex or controversial issues. "Pornography," "gun control," "secular humanism," and "right-to-life" would be excellent subjects for extended definition—each is multifaceted, often misunderstood, and fraught with emotional meaning. "Junk food," "anger," "leadership," "anxiety" could make interesting subjects, especially if the extended definition helped readers develop a new understanding of the word. You might, for example, define "anxiety" not as a negative state to be avoided but as a positive force that propels us to take action.

An extended definition could perhaps run several paragraphs or a few pages. Keep in mind, however, that an extended definition may require a chapter or even an entire book to develop. If this seems unlikely, remember that theologians, philosophers, and pop psychologists have devoted entire texts to such concepts as "evil" and "love."

SUGGESTIONS FOR USING DEFINITION IN AN ESSAY

The following suggestions will be helpful whether you use definition as a dominant or a supportive pattern of development.

1. Stay focused on the essay's purpose, audience, and tone. Since your purpose for writing an extended definition shapes the entire paper, you need to keep that objective in mind when developing your definition. Suppose you decide to write an essay defining *jazz*. The essay could be purely *informative* and discuss the origins of jazz, its characteristic tonal patterns, and some of the great jazz musicians of the past. Or the essay could move beyond pure information and take on a *persuasive* edge. It might, for example, argue that jazz is the only contemporary form of music worth considering seriously.

Just as your purpose in writing will vary, so will your tone. A strictly informative definition will generally assume a detached, objective tone ("Apathy is an emotional state characterized by listlessness and indifference"). By way of contrast, a definition essay with a persuasive slant might be urgent in tone ("To combat student apathy, we must design programs that engage students in campus life"), or it might take a satiric approach ("An apathetic stance is a wise choice for any thinking student").

As you write, keep thinking about your audience as well. Not only do your readers determine what terms need to be defined (and in how much detail), but they also keep you focused on the essay's purpose and tone. For instance, you probably wouldn't write a serious, informative piece for the college newspaper about the "mystery meat" served in the campus cafeteria. Instead, you would adopt a light tone as you defined the culinary horror and might even make a persuasive pitch about improving the food prepared on campus.

2. Formulate an effective definition. A definition essay sometimes begins with a brief *formal definition*—the dictionary's, a textbook's, or the writer's—and then expands that initial definition with supporting details. Formal definitions are traditionally worded as three-part statements that consist of the following: the *term,* the *class* to which the term belongs, and the *characteristics* that distinguish the term from other members of its class.

Term	Class	Characteristics
The peregrine falcon,	an endangered bird,	is the world's fastest flyer.
A bodice-ripper	is a paperback book,	usually read by women, that deals with highly charged romance in exotic places and faraway times.
Back to basics	is a trend in education	that emphasizes skill mastery through rote learning.

A definition that meets these guidelines will clarify what your subject *is* and what it *is not*. These guidelines also establish the boundaries of your definition, removing unlike items from consideration in your (and your reader's) mind. For example, defining "back to basics" as a trend that emphasizes rote learning signals a certain boundary; it lets readers know that other educational trends, such as those that emphasize children's social or emotional development, will not be part of the essay's definition.

If you decide to include a formal definition, avoid tired openers like "the dictionary says" or "according to Webster." Such weak starts are just plain boring and often herald an unimaginative essay. You should also keep in mind that a strict dictionary definition may actually confuse readers. Suppose you're writing a paper on the way all of us absorb ideas and values from the media. Likening this automatic response to the process of osmosis, you decide to open the paper with a dictionary definition. If you write, "Osmosis is the tendency of a solvent to disperse through a semipermeable membrane into a more concentrated medium," readers are apt to be baffled, even hostile. Remember: The purpose of a definition is to clarify meaning, not obscure it.

You should also stay clear of ungrammatical "is when" definitions: "Blind ambition is when you want to get ahead, no matter how much other people are hurt." Instead, write "Blind ambition is wanting to get ahead, no matter how much other people are hurt." A final pitfall to avoid in writing formal definitions is *circularity,* saying the same thing twice and therefore defining nothing: "A campus tribunal is a tribunal composed of various members of the university community." Circular definitions like this often repeat the term being defined (*tribunal*) or use words having the same meaning (*campus; university community*). In this case, we learn nothing about what a campus tribunal is; the writer says only that "X is X."

3. Develop the extended definition. You can choose from a variety of patterns when formulating an extended definition. Description, narration, process analysis, and comparison-contrast can be used—alone or in combination. Imagine that you're planning to write an extended definition of "robotics." You might develop the term by providing *examples* of the ways robots are currently being used in scientific research; by *comparing* and *contrasting* human and robot capabilities; or by *classifying* robots, starting with the most basic and moving to the most advanced or futuristic models.

Which patterns of development to use will often become apparent during the prewriting stage. Here is a list of prewriting questions as well as the pattern of development implied by each question.

Question	Pattern of Development
How does X look, taste, smell, feel, and sound?	Description
What does X do? When? Where?	Narration
What are some typical instances of X?	Exemplification
What are X's component parts? What different forms can X take?	Division-classification
How does X work?	Process analysis
What is X like or unlike?	Comparison-contrast
What leads to X? What are X's consequences?	Cause-effect

Those questions yielding the most material often suggest the effective pattern(s) for developing an extended definition.

4. Organize the material that develops the definition.   If you use a single pattern to develop the extended definition, apply the principles of organization suited to that pattern, as described in the appropriate chapter of this book. Assume that you're defining "fad" by means of *process analysis.* You might organize your paragraphs according to the steps in the process: a fad's slow start as something avant-garde or eccentric; its wildfire acceptance by the general public; the fad's demise as it becomes familiar or tiresome. If you want to define "character" by means of a single *narration,* you would probably organize paragraphs chronologically.

In a definition essay using several methods of development, you should devote separate paragraphs to each pattern. A definition of "relaxation," for instance, might start with a paragraph that *narrates* a particularly relaxing day; then it might move to a paragraph that describes several *examples* of people who find it difficult to unwind; finally, it might end with a paragraph that explains a *process* for relaxing the mind and body.

5. Write an effective introduction.   It can be helpful to provide—near the beginning of a definition essay—a brief formal definition of the term you're going to develop in the rest of the paper.

Beyond this basic element, the introduction may include a number of other features. You might explain the *origin* of the term being defined: "Acid rock is a term first coined in the 1960s to describe music that was written or listened to under the influence of the drug LSD." Similarly, you could explain the *etymology*, or linguistic origin, of the key word that focuses the paper. "The term *vigilantism* is derived from the Latin word meaning 'to watch and be awake.'"

You may also use the introduction to clarify what the subject is *not*. Such *definition by negation* can be an effective strategy at the beginning of a paper, especially if readers don't share your view of the subject. In such a case, you might write something like this: "The gorilla, far from being the vicious killer of jungle movies and popular imagination, is a sedentary, gentle creature living in a closely knit family group." Such a statement provides the special focus of your essay and signals some of the misconceptions or fallacies soon to be discussed.

In addition, you may include in the introduction a *stipulative definition*, one that puts special restrictions on a term: "Strictly defined, a mall refers to a one- or two-story enclosed building containing a variety of retail shops and at least two large anchor stores. Highway-strip shopping centers or downtown centers cannot be considered true malls." When a term has multiple meanings, or when its meaning has become fuzzy through misuse, a stipulative definition sets the record straight right at the start, so that readers know exactly what is, and is not, being defined.

Finally, the introduction may end with a *plan of development* that indicates how the definition essay will unfold. A student who returned to school after having raised a family decided to write a paper defining the *midlife crisis* that led to her enrollment in college. After providing a brief formal definition of "midlife crisis," the student rounded off her introduction with this sentence: "Such a midlife crisis starts with vague misgivings, turns into depression, and ends with a significant change in lifestyle."

STUDENT ESSAY

The following student essay was written by Laura Chen in response to this assignment:

> In "Entropy," K. C. Cole takes a scientific term from physics and gives it a broader definition and a wider

application. Choose another specialized term and define it in such a way that you reveal something significant about contemporary life.

While reading Laura's paper, try to determine how well it applies the principles of definition. The annotations on Laura's paper and the commentary following it will help you look at the essay more closely.

Physics in Everyday Life
by Laura Chen

Introduction

A boulder sits on a mountainside for a thousand   1
years. The boulder will remain there forever unless
an outside force intervenes. Suppose a force does
affect the boulder--an earthquake, for instance.
Once the boulder begins to thunder down the
mountain, it will remain in motion and head in one
direction only--downhill--until another force interrupts its progress. If the boulder tumbles into a
gorge, it will finally come to rest as gravity anchors

Formal definition   it to the earth once more. In both cases, the boulder
is exhibiting the physical principle of inertia: the
tendency of matter to remain at rest or, if moving, to
keep moving in one direction unless affected by an

Thesis   outside force. Inertia, an important factor in the
world of physics, also plays a crucial role in the

Plan of   human world. Inertia affects our individual lives as
development   well as the direction taken by society as a whole.

Topic sentence   Inertia often influences our value systems and   2
personal growth. Inertia is at work, for example,
when people cling to certain behaviors and views.
Like the boulder firmly fixed to the mountain, most
people are set in their ways. Without thinking, they
vote Republican or Democratic because they have
always voted that way. They regard with suspicion
a couple having no children, simply because everyone else in the neighborhood has a large family. It is

Start of a series of   only when an outside force--a jolt of some sort--
causes and effects   occurs that people change their views. A white
American couple may think little about racial discrimination, for instance, until they adopt an Asian
child and must comfort her when classmates tease

her because she looks different. Parents may consider promiscuous any unmarried teenage girl who has a baby until their seventeen-year-old honor student confesses that she is pregnant. Personal jolts like these force people to think, perhaps for the first time, about issues that now affect them directly.

Topic sentence ⟶ To illustrate how inertia governs our lives, it is helpful to compare the world of television with real life. On TV, inertia does not exist. Television shows and commercials show people making all kinds of drastic changes. They switch brands of coffee or try a new hair color with no hesitation. In one car commercial, an ambitious young accountant abandons her career with a flourish and is seen driving off into the sunset as she heads for a small cabin by the sea to write poetry. In a soap opera, a character may progress from homemaker to hooker to nun in a single year. But in real life, inertia rules. People tend to stay where they are, to keep their jobs, to be loyal to products. A second major difference between television and real life is that, on television, everyone takes prompt and dramatic action to solve problems. The construction worker with a thudding headache is pain-free at the end of the sixty-second commercial; the police catch the murderer within an hour; the family learns to cope with their son's life-threatening drug addiction by the time the made-for-TV movie ends at eleven. But in the real world, inertia persists, so that few problems are solved neatly or quickly. Illnesses drag on, few crimes are solved, and family conflicts last for years.

3

Start of a series of contrasts

Topic sentence ⟶ Inertia is, most importantly, a force at work in the life of our nation. Again, inertia is two-sided. It keeps us from moving and, once we move, it keeps us pointed in one direction. We find ourselves mired in a certain path, accepting the inferior, even the dangerous. We settle for toys that break, winter coats with no warmth, and rivers clogged with pollution. Inertia also compels our nation to keep moving in one direction--despite the uncomfortable suspicion that it is the wrong direction. We are not sure if manipulating genes is a good idea, yet we continue to fund scientific projects in genetic engineering. More than fifty years ago, we were shaken

4

Start of a series of examples

Conclusion

when we saw the devastation caused by an atomic bomb. But we went on to develop weapons hundreds of times more destructive. Although warned that excessive television viewing may be harmful, we continue to watch hours of television each day.

We have learned to defy gravity, one of the basic laws of physics; we fly high above the earth, even float in outer space. But most of us have not learned to defy inertia. Those special individuals who are able to act when everyone else seems paralyzed are rare. But the fact that such people do exist means that inertia is not all-powerful. If we use our reasoning ability and our creativity, we can conquer inertia, just as we have conquered gravity.

5

COMMENTARY

Introduction. As the title of her essay suggests, Laura has taken a scientific term (*inertia*) from a specialized field and drawn on the term to help explain some everyday phenomena. Using the *simple-to-complex* approach to structure the introduction, she opens with a vivid *descriptive* example of inertia. This description is then followed by a *formal definition* of inertia: "the tendency of matter to remain at rest or, if moving, to keep moving in one direction unless affected by an outside force." Laura wisely begins the paper with the easy-to-understand description rather than with the more-difficult-to-grasp scientific definition. Had the order been reversed, the essay would not have gotten off to nearly as effective a start. She then ends her introductory paragraph with a *thesis*, "Inertia, an important factor in the world of physics, also plays a crucial role in the human world," and with a *plan of development*, "Inertia affects our individual lives as well as the direction taken by society as a whole."

Organization. To support her definition of inertia and her belief that it can rule our lives, Laura generates a number of compelling examples. She organizes these examples by grouping them into three major points, each point signaled by a *topic sentence* that opens each of the essay's three supporting paragraphs (2–4).

A definite organizational strategy determines the sequence of Laura's three central points. The essay moves from the way inertia affects the individual to the way it affects the nation. The phrase "most importantly" at the beginning of the fourth paragraph shows that Laura has arranged her points emphatically, believing that inertia's impact on society is most critical.

A weak example.   When reading the fourth paragraph, you might have noticed that Laura's examples aren't sequenced as effectively as they could be. To show that we, as a nation, tend to keep moving in the same direction, Laura discusses our ongoing uneasiness about genetic engineering, nuclear arms, and excessive television viewing. The point about nuclear weapons is most significant, yet it gets lost because it's sandwiched in the middle. The paragraph would be stronger if it ended with the point about nuclear arms. Moreover, the example about excessive television viewing doesn't belong in this paragraph since, at best, it has limited bearing on the issue being discussed.

Other patterns of development.   In addition to using numerous *examples* to illustrate her points, Laura draws on several other patterns of development to show that inertia can be a powerful force. In the second and fourth paragraphs, she uses *causal analysis* to explain how inertia can paralyze people and nations. The second paragraph indicates that only "an outside force—a jolt of some sort—" can motivate inert people to change. To support this view, Laura provides two examples of parents who experience such jolts. Similarly, in the fourth paragraph, she contends that inertia causes the persistence of specific national problems: shoddy consumer goods and environmental pollution.

Another pattern, *comparison-contrast,* is used in the third paragraph to highlight the differences between television and real life: on television, people zoom into action, but in everyday life, people tend to stay put and muddle through. The essay also contains a distinct element of *argumentation-persuasion,* since Laura clearly wants readers to accept her definition of inertia and her view that it often governs human behavior.

Conclusion.   Laura's *conclusion* rounds off the essay nicely and brings it to a satisfying close. Laura refers to another law of physics, one with which we are all familiar—gravity. By creating an *analogy* between gravity and inertia, she suggests that our ability to defy gravity should encourage us to defy inertia. The analogy enlarges the scope of the essay; it allows Laura to reach out to her readers by challenging them to action. Such a challenge is, of course, appropriate in a definition essay having a persuasive bent.

Revising the first draft. When it was time to rework her essay, Laura began by reading her paper aloud. She noted in the margin of her draft the problems she detected, numbering them in order of importance. After reviewing her notes, she started to revise in earnest, paying special attention to her third paragraph. The first draft of that paragraph is reprinted here:

Original Version of the Third Paragraph

The ordinary actions of daily life are, in part, determined by inertia. To understand this, it is helpful to compare the world of television with real life, for, in the TV-land of ads and entertainment, inertia does not exist. For example, on television, people are often shown making all kinds of drastic changes. They switch brands of coffee or try a new hair color with no hesitation. In one car commercial, a young accountant leaves her career and sets off for a cabin by the sea to write poetry. In a soap opera, a character may progress from homemaker to hooker to nun in a single year. In contrast, inertia rules in real life. People tend to stay where they are, to keep their jobs, to be loyal to products (wives get annoyed if a husband brings home the wrong brand or color of bathroom tissue from the market). Middle-aged people wear the hairstyles or makeup that suited them in high school. A second major difference between television and real life is that, on TV, everyone takes prompt and dramatic action to solve problems. A woman finds the solution to dull clothes at the end of a commercial; the police catch the murderer within an hour; the family learns to cope with a son's disturbing lifestyle by the time the movie is over. In contrast, the law of real-life inertia means that few problems are solved neatly or quickly. Things, once started, tend to stay as they are. Few crimes are actually solved. Medical problems are not easily diagnosed. Messy wars in foreign countries seem endless. National problems are identified, but Congress does not pass legislation to solve them.

After rereading what she had written, Laura realized that her third paragraph rambled. To give it more focus, she removed the last two sentences ("Messy wars in foreign countries seem endless" and "National problems are identified, but Congress does not pass legislation. . . .") because they referred to national affairs but were

located in a section focusing on the individual. Then, she eliminated two flat, unconvincing examples: wives who get annoyed when
their husbands bring home the wrong brand of bathroom tissue and
middle-aged people whose hairstyles and makeup are outdated.
Condensing the two disjointed sentences that originally opened the
paragraph also helped tighten this section of the essay. Note how
much crisper the revised sentences are: "To illustrate how inertia
rules our lives, it is helpful to compare the world of television with
real life. On TV, inertia does not exist."

Laura also worked to make the details and the language in the
paragraph more specific and vigorous. The vague sentence "A
woman finds the solution to dull clothes at the end of the commercial" is replaced by the more dramatic "The construction worker
with a thudding headache is pain-free at the end of the sixty-second
commercial." Similarly, Laura changed a "son's disturbing lifestyle"
to a "son's life-threatening drug addiction"; "by the time the movie
is over" became "by the time the made-for-TV movie ends at
eleven"; and "a young accountant leaves her career and sets off for
a cabin by the sea to write poetry" was changed to "an ambitious
young accountant abandons her career with a flourish and is seen
driving off into the sunset as she heads for a small cabin by the sea
to write poetry."

After making these changes, Laura decided to round off the
paragraph with a powerful summary statement highlighting how
real life differs from television: "Illnesses drag on, few crimes are
solved, and family conflicts last for years."

These third-paragraph revisions are similar to those that Laura
made elsewhere in her first draft. Her astute changes enabled her to
turn an already effective paper into an especially thoughtful analysis
of human behavior.

ACTIVITIES: DEFINITION

Prewriting Activities

1. Imagine you're writing two essays: one explains the *process* for reg-
    istering a complaint that gets results; the other *contrasts* the styles
    of two stand-up comics. Jot down ways you might use definition in
    each essay.

2. Select a term whose meaning varies from person to person or one for which you have a personal definition. Some possibilities include:

    | success | femininity | a liberal |
    | patriotism | affirmative action | a housewife |
    | individuality | pornography | intelligence |

    Brainstorm with others to identify variations in the term's meaning. Then examine your prewriting material. What thesis comes to mind? If you were writing an essay, would your purpose be informative, persuasive, or both? Finally, prepare a scratch list of the points you might cover.

Revising Activities

3. Explain why each of the following is an effective or ineffective definition. Rewrite those you consider ineffective.

    a. *Passive aggression* is when people show their aggression passively.
    b. A *terrorist* tries to terrorize people.
    c. *Being assertive* means knowing how to express your wishes and goals in a positive, noncombative way.
    d. *Pop music* refers to music that is popular.
    e. *Loyalty* is when someone stays by another person during difficult times.

4. The following introductory paragraph is from the first draft of an essay contrasting walking and running as techniques for reducing tension. Although intended to be a definition paragraph, it actually doesn't tell us anything we don't already know. It also relies on the old-hat "*Webster's* says." Rewrite the paragraph so it is more imaginative. You might use a series of anecdotes or one extended example to define *tension* and introduce the essay's thesis more gracefully.

    According to Webster's, tension is "mental or nervous strain, often accompanied by muscular tightness or tautness." Everyone feels tense at one time or another. It may occur when there's a deadline to meet. Or it could be caused by the stress of trying to fulfill academic, athletic, or social goals. Sometimes it comes from criticism by family, bosses, or teachers. Such tension puts wear and tear on our bodies and on our emotional well-being. Although some people run to relieve tension, research has found that walking is a more effective tension reducer.

K. C. Cole

K. C. Cole's writings about science, especially physics, have made a great deal of specialized knowledge available to the general public. A graduate of Barnard College, Cole has contributed numerous articles to such publications as the *New York Times,* the *Washington Post,* and *Long Island Newsday,* and writes a regular column for *Discover* magazine. Her work with the Exploratorium, a San Francisco science museum, led her to write several books on the exhibits there. In 1985, Cole published a collection of essays, *Sympathetic Vibrations: Reflections on Physics as a Way of Life.* Other books include *What Only a Mother Can Tell You About Having a Baby* (1986), *The Universe and the Teacup* (1998), *First You Build a Cloud* (1999), and *The Hole in the Universe* (2000). She is currently a science writer and editor at the *L.A. Times.* The following selection was first published as a "Hers" column in *The New York Times* in 1982.

Pre-Reading Journal Entry

Do you consider yourself an orderly or a disorderly person? What about those around you? What are the benefits and the drawbacks of being orderly? Of being disorderly? Use your journal to reflect on these questions.

Entropy

It was about two months ago when I realized that entropy was getting the better of me. On the same day my car broke down (again), my refrigerator conked out and I learned that I needed root-canal work in my right rear tooth. The windows in the bedroom were still leaking every time it rained and my son's baby sitter was still failing to show up every time I really needed her. My hair was turning gray and my typewriter was wearing out. The house needed paint and I needed glasses. My son's sneakers were developing holes and I was developing a deep sense of futility. 1

After all, what was the point of spending half of Saturday at the Laundromat if the clothes were dirty all over again the following Friday? 2

Disorder, alas, is the natural order of things in the universe.   3
There is even a precise measure of the amount of disorder, called
entropy. Unlike almost every other physical property (motion, gravity, energy), entropy does not work both ways. It can only increase.
Once it's created it can never be destroyed. The road to disorder is
a one-way street.

Because of its unnerving irreversibility, entropy has been called   4
the arrow of time. We all understand this instinctively. Children's
rooms, left on their own, tend to get messy, not neat. Wood rots,
metal rusts, people wrinkle and flowers wither. Even mountains wear
down; even the nuclei of atoms decay. In the city we see entropy in
the rundown subways and worn-out sidewalks and torn-down buildings, in the increasing disorder of our lives. We know, without asking, what is old. If we were suddenly to see the paint jump back on
an old building, we would know that something was wrong. If we
saw an egg unscramble itself and jump back into its shell, we would
laugh in the same way we laugh at a movie run backward.

Entropy is no laughing matter, however, because with every   5
increase in entropy energy is wasted and opportunity is lost. Water
flowing down a mountainside can be made to do some useful work
on its way. But once all the water is at the same level it can work no
more. That is entropy. When my refrigerator was working, it kept all
the cold air ordered in one part of the kitchen and warmer air in
another. Once it broke down the warm and cold mixed into a luke-
warm mess that allowed my butter to melt, my milk to rot and my
frozen vegetables to decay.

Of course the energy is not really lost, but it has diffused and   6
dissipated into a chaotic caldron of randomness that can do us no
possible good. Entropy is chaos. It is loss of purpose.

People are often upset by the entropy they seem to see in the   7
haphazardness of their own lives. Buffeted about like so many molecules in my tepid kitchen, they feel that they have lost their sense
of direction, that they are wasting youth and opportunity at every
turn. It is easy to see entropy in marriages, when the partners are too
preoccupied to patch small things up, almost guaranteeing that they
will fall apart. There is much entropy in the state of our country, in
the relationships between nations—lost opportunities to stop the
avalanche of disorders that seems ready to swallow us all.

Entropy is not inevitable everywhere, however. Crystals and   8
snowflakes and galaxies are islands of incredibly ordered beauty in

the midst of random events. If it was not for exceptions to entropy, the sky would be black and we would be able to see where the stars spend their days; it is only because air molecules in the atmosphere cluster in ordered groups that the sky is blue.

The most profound exception to entropy is the creation of life. 9 A seed soaks up some soil and some carbon and some sunshine and some water and arranges it into a rose. A seed in the womb takes some oxygen and pizza and milk and transforms it into a baby.

The catch is that it takes a lot of energy to produce a baby. It 10 also takes energy to make a tree. The road to disorder is all down-hill but the road to creation takes work. Though combating entropy is possible, it also has its price. That's why it seems so hard to get ourselves together, so easy to let ourselves fall apart.

Worse, creating order in one corner of the universe always cre- 11 ates more disorder somewhere else. We create ordered energy from oil and coal at the price of the entropy of smog.

I recently took up playing the flute again after an absence of sev- 12 eral months. As the uneven vibrations screeched through the house, my son covered his ears and said, "Mom, what's wrong with your flute?" Nothing was wrong with my flute, of course. It was my abil-ity to play it that had atrophied, or entropied, as the case may be. The only way to stop that process was to practice every day, and sure enough my tone improved, though only at the price of constant work. Like anything else, abilities deteriorate when we stop applying our energies to them.

That's why entropy is depressing. It seems as if just breaking 13 even is an uphill fight. There's a good reason that this should be so. The mechanics of entropy are a matter of chance. Take any ice-cold air molecule milling around my kitchen. The chances that it will wander in the direction of my refrigerator at any point are exactly 50-50. The chances that it will wander away from my refrigerator are also 50-50. But take billions of warm and cold molecules mixed together, and the chances that all the cold ones will wander toward the refrigerator and all the warm ones will wander away from it are virtually nil.

Entropy wins not because order is impossible but because there 14 are always so many more paths toward disorder than toward order. There are so many more different ways to do a sloppy job than a good one, so many more ways to make a mess than to clean it up. The obsta-cles and accidents in our lives almost guarantee that constant collisions will bounce us on to random paths, get us off the track. Disorder is the path of least resistance, the easy but not the inevitable road.

Like so many others, I am distressed by the entropy I see   15
around me today. I am afraid of the randomness of international events, of the lack of common purpose in the world; I am terrified that it will lead into the ultimate entropy of nuclear war. I am upset that I could not in the city where I live send my child to a public school; that people are unemployed and inflation is out of control; that tensions between sexes and races seem to be increasing again; that relationships everywhere seem to be falling apart.

Social institutions—like atoms and stars—decay if energy is not   16
added to keep them ordered. Friendships and families and economies all fall apart unless we constantly make an effort to keep them working and well oiled. And far too few people, it seems to me, are willing to contribute consistently to those efforts.

Of course, the more complex things are, the harder it is. If there   17
were only a dozen or so air molecules in my kitchen, it would be likely—if I waited a year or so—that at some point the six coldest ones would congregate inside the freezer. But the more factors in the equation—the more players in the game—the less likely it is that their paths will coincide in an orderly way. The more pieces in the puzzle, the harder it is to put back together once order is disturbed. "Irreversibility," said a physicist, "is the price we pay for complexity."

Questions for Close Reading

1. What is the selection's thesis? Locate the sentence(s) in which Cole states her main idea. If she doesn't state the thesis explicitly, express it in your own words.
2. How does entropy differ from the other properties of the physical world? Is the image "the arrow of time" helpful in establishing this difference?
3. Why is the creation of life an exception to entropy? What is the relationship between entropy and energy?
4. Why does Cole say that entropy "is no laughing matter"? What is so depressing about the entropy she describes?
5. Refer to your dictionary as needed to define the following words used in the selection: *futility* (paragraph 1), *dissipated* (6), *buffeted* (7), *tepid* (7), and *atrophied* (12).

Questions About the Writer's Craft

1. **The pattern.**   What is Cole's underlying purpose in defining the scientific term *entropy*? What gives the essay its persuasive edge?

2. What tone does Cole adopt to make reading about a scientific concept more interesting? Identify places in the essay where her tone is especially prominent.

3. Cole uses such words as *futility, loss,* and *depressing.* How do these words affect you? Why do you suppose she chose such terms? Find similar words in the essay.

4. **Other patterns.**   Many of Cole's sentences follow a two-part pattern involving a contrast: "The road to disorder is all downhill but the road to creation takes work" (paragraph 10). Find other examples of this pattern in the essay. Why do you think Cole uses it so often?

Writing Assignments Using Definition as a Pattern of Development

1. Write an essay in which you define *order* or *disorder* by applying the term to a system that you know well—for example, your school, dorm, family, or workplace. Develop your definition through any combination of writing patterns: by supplying examples, by showing contrasts, by analyzing the process underlying the system.

2. Choose, as Cole does, a technical term that you think will be unfamiliar to most readers. In a humorous or serious paper, define the term as it is used technically; then show how the term can shed light on some aspect of your life. For example, the concept in astronomy of a *supernova* could be used to explain your sudden emergence as a new star on the athletic field, in your schoolwork, or on the social scene. Here are a few suggested terms:

symbiosis	volatility	resonance
velocity	erosion	catalyst
neutralization	equilibrium	malleability

Writing Assignments Using Other Patterns of Development

3. Can one person make much difference in the amount of entropy—disorder and chaos—in the world? Share your view in an essay. Use examples of people who have tried to overcome the tendency of things to "fall apart." Make clear whether you think these people succeeded or failed in their attempts. To inform your perspective before writing, consider reading James Gleick's "Life As Type A" (page 509), an evaluation of the factors that influence people's compulsion for order.

4. Cole claims that we humans are "buffeted about like so many molecules." Write an essay arguing that people either do or do not control their own fates. Support your point with a series of specific examples. For different perspectives on the issue, you might want to read "Sister Flowers" (page 116) by Maya Angelou, "So Tsi-Fai" (page 188) by

Sophronia Liu, and "Campus Racism 101" (page 350) by Nikki Giovanni.

Writing Assignments Using a Journal Entry as a Starting Point

5. Write an essay arguing that disorder can be liberating *or* that it can be sti-fling. Review your pre-reading journal entry, and select strong, compelling examples that support your position. Aim to refute as many opposing arguments as possible. Your essay may have a serious or a humorous tone.

James Gleick

After graduating from Harvard College in 1976, James Gleick helped found *Metropolis,* an alternative newspaper in Minneapolis. He then spent ten years as a reporter and editor with *The New York Times,* where he now writes a Sunday column, titled "Fast Forward," about the impact of science and technology on modern life. His earlier books, *Chaos: Making a New Science* (1987) and *Genius: The Life and Science of Richard Feynman* (1992), were both finalists for the National Book Award and Pulitzer Prize. Formerly McGraw Distinguished Lecturer at Princeton University, Gleick lives with his wife, writer Cynthia Crossen, in New York. The following piece is taken from Gleick's most recent book, *Faster: The Acceleration of Just About Everything* (1999).

Pre-Reading Journal Entry

Like many people, you may feel harried and under pressure at least some of the time. Use your journal to reflect on the sources of stress in your everyday life. List several examples. For each, consider the factors leading to this frenzied feeling.

Life As Type A

Everyone knows about Type A. This magnificently bland coinage, put forward by a pair of California cardiologists in 1959, struck a collective nerve and entered the language. It is a token of our confusion: are we victims or perpetrators of the crime of haste? Are we living at high speed with athleticism and vigor, or are we stricken by hurry sickness?   1

The cardiologists, Meyer Friedman and Ray Rosenman, listed a set of personality traits which, they claimed, tend to go hand in hand with one another and also with heart disease. They described these traits rather unappealingly, as characteristics about and around the theme of impatience. Excessive competitiveness. Aggressiveness. "A harrying sense of time urgency." The Type A idea emerged in technical papers and then formed the basis of a popular book and made its way into dictionaries. The canonical Type A, as these doctors portrayed him, was "Paul":   2

A very disproportionate amount of his emotional energy is consumed in struggling against the normal constraints of time. "How can I move faster, and do more and more things in less and less time?" is the question that never ceases to torment him.

Paul hurries his thinking, his speech and his movements. He also strives to hurry the thinking, speech, and movements of those about him; they must communicate rapidly and relevantly if they wish to avoid creating impatience in him. Planes must arrive and depart precisely on time for Paul, cars ahead of him on the highway must maintain a speed he approves of, and there must never be a queue of persons standing between him and a bank clerk, a restaurant table, or the interior of a theater. In fact, he is infuriated whenever people talk slowly or circuitously, when planes are late, cars dawdle on the highway, and queues form.

Let's think . . . Do we know anyone like "Paul"?

This was the first clear declaration of *hurry sickness*—another   3
coinage of Friedman's. It inspired new businesses: mind-body workshops; videotapes demonstrating deep breathing; anxiety-management retreats; seminars on and even institutes of stress medicine. "I drove all the way in the right-hand lane," a Pacific Gas and Electric Company executive said proudly one morning in 1987 to a group of self-confessed hurriers, led by Friedman himself, by then seventy-six years old. In the battle against Type A jitters, patients tried anything and everything—the slow lane, yoga, meditation, visualization: "Direct your attention to your feet on the floor. . . . Be aware of the air going in your nostrils cool and going out warm. . . . Visualize a place you like to be. . . . Experience it and see the objects there, the forms and shadows. Take another deep breath and experience the sounds, the surf, the wind, leaves, a babbling brook." Some hospital television systems now feature a "relaxation channel," with hour after hour of surf, wind, leaves, and babbling brooks.

We believe in Type A—a triumph for a notion with no particu-   4
lar scientific validity. The Friedman-Rosenman claim has turned out to be both obvious and false. Clearly some heart ailments do result from, or at least go along with, stress (itself an ill-defined term), both chronic and acute. Behavior surely affects physiology, at least once in a while. Sudden dashes for the train, laptop computer in one

hand and takeout coffee in the other, can accelerate heartbeats and raise blood pressure. That haste makes coronaries was already a kind of folk wisdom—that is, standard medical knowledge untainted by research. "Hurry has a clearly debilitating effect upon the tissues and may in time injure the heart," admonished Dr. Cecil Webb-Johnson in *Nerve Troubles,* an English monograph of the early 1900s. "The great men of the centuries past were never in a hurry," he added sanctimoniously, "and that is why the world will never forget them in a hurry." It might be natural—even appealing—to expect certain less-great people to receive their cardiovascular come-uppance. But in reality, three decades of attention from cardiologists and psychologists have failed to produce any carefully specified and measurable set of character traits that predict heart disease—or to demonstrate that people who change their Type A behavior will actually lower their risk of heart disease.

Indeed, the study that started it all—Friedman and Rosenman's 5 "Association of Specific Overt Behavior Pattern with Blood and Cardiovascular Findings"—appears to have been a wildly flawed piece of research. It used a small sample—eighty-three people (all men) in what was then called "Group A." The selection process was neither random nor blind. White-collar male employees of large businesses were rounded up by acquaintances of Friedman and Rosenman on a subjective basis—they fit the type. The doctors further sorted the subjects by interviewing them personally and observing their appearance and behavior. Did a man gesture rapidly, clench his teeth, or exhibit a "general air of impatience"? If so, he was chosen. It seems never to have occurred to these experienced cardiologists that they might have been consciously or unconsciously selecting people whose physique indicated excess weight or other markers for incipient heart disease. The doctors' own data show that the final Group A drank more, smoked more, and weighed more than Group B. But the authors dismissed these factors, asserting, astonishingly, that there was no association between heart disease and cigarette smoking.

In the years since, researchers have never settled on a reliable 6 method for identifying Type A people, though not for want of trying. Humans are not reliable witnesses to their own impatience. Researchers have employed questionnaires like the Jenkins Activity Survey, and they have used catalogues of grimaces and frowns—Ekman and Friesen's Facial Action Coding System, for example, or the Cook-Medley Hostility Inventory. In the end, nothing conclusive emerges.

Some studies have found Type A people to have *lower* blood pressure. The sedentary and obese have cardiac difficulties of their own.

The notion of Type A has expanded, shifted, and flexed to suit   7 the varying needs of different researchers. V.A. Price adds *hypervig-ilance* to the list of traits. Some doctors lose patience with the incon-clusive results and shift their focus to anger and hostility—mere sub-sets of the original Type A grab-bag. Cynthia Perry finds that Type A people have fewer daydreams. How does she know? She asks them to monitor lines flashing across a computer screen for forty painful-ly boring minutes and finds that, when interrupted by a beep (1000 hertz at 53 decibels), they are less likely to press a black button to confess that irrelevant thoughts had strayed into their minds. Studies have labeled as Type A not only children (those with a ten-dency to interrupt and to play competitively at games) but even babies (those who cry more). Meanwhile, researchers interested in pets link the Type A personality to petlessness; a National Institutes of Health panel reports: "The description of a 'coronary-prone behavior pattern,' or Type A behavior, and its link to the probabili-ty of developing overt disease provided hope that, with careful train-ing, individuals could exercise additional control over somatic illness by altering their lifestyle. . . . Relaxation, meditation, and stress management have become recognized therapies. . . . It therefore seems reasonable that pets, who provide faithful companionship to many people, also might promote greater psychosocial stability for their owners, and thus a measure of protection from heart disease." This is sweet, but it is not science.

Typically a Type A study will begin with researchers who assume   8 that there are some correlations to be found, look for a wide variety of associations, fail to find some and succeed in finding others. For example, a few dozen preschool children are sorted according to their game-playing styles and tested for blood pressure. No correla-tion is found. Later, however, when performing a certain "memory game," the supposed Type A children rank somewhat higher in, specifically, systolic pressure. Interesting? The authors of various pub-lished papers evidently think so, but they are wrong, because if their technique is to keep looking until they find some correlation, some-where, they are bound to succeed. Such results are meaningless.

The categorizations are too variable and the prophecies too self-   9 fulfilling. It is never quite clear which traits *define* Type A and which are fellow travelers. The "free-floating, but well-rationalized form of hostility"? The "deep-seated insecurity"? "Their restlessness, their tense facial muscles, their tics, or their strident-staccato manner of speaking"? If you are hard-driving yet friendly, chafing yet self-assured—if you race for the airport gate and then settle *happily* into your seat—are you Type A or not? If you are driven to walk briskly, briskly, all the time, isn't that good for your heart?

Most forget that there is also supposed to be a Type B, defined not by the personality traits its members possess but by the traits they lack. Type B people are the shadowy opposites of Type A people. They are those who are not so very Type A. They do *not* wear out their fingers punching that elevator button. They do *not* allow a slow car in the fast lane to drive their hearts to fatal distraction; in fact, they are at the wheel of that slow car. Type B played no real part in that mass societal gasp of recognition in the 1970's. Type B-ness was just a foil. Doctors Friedman and Rosenman actually claimed to have had trouble finding eighty men in all San Francisco who were not under any time pressure. They finally came up with a few, they wrote solemnly, "in the municipal clerks' and the embalmers' unions." 10

Even more bizarrely, that first Friedman-Rosenman study also included a Group C, comprising forty-six unemployed blind men. Not much haste in Group C. "The primary reason men of Group C exhibited little ambition, drive, or desire to compete," the doctors wrote, "was the presence of total blindness for ten or more years and the lack of occupational deadlines because none was gainfully employed." No wonder they omitted Type C from the subsequent publicity. 11

If the Type A phenomenon made for poor medical research, it stands nonetheless as a triumph of social criticism. Some of us yield more willingly to impatience than others, but on the whole Type A is who we are—not just the coronary-prone among us, but all of us, as a society and as an age. No wonder the concept has proven too rich a cultural totem to be dismissed. 12

Questions for Close Reading

1. What is the selection's thesis? Locate the sentence(s) in which Gleick states his main idea. If he doesn't state the thesis explicitly, express it in your own words.
2. What is Gleick's opinion of the study Friedman and Rosenman conducted? List at least two elements of the study that Gleick uses to support his assessment.

3. In paragraph 7, Gleick observes that the concept of Type A has changed since Friedman and Rosenman's study first chronicled it. How has it changed? What accounts for this change?

4. According to Gleick, how do Friedman and Rosenman define the Type B personality? Why does Gleick find fault with their definition of this personality type?

5. Refer to your dictionary as needed to define the following words used in the selection: *coinage* (paragraph 1), *harrying* (2), *canonical* (2), *circuitously* (2), *sanctimoniously* (4), *overt* (5), *incipient* (5), *sedentary* (6), *hypervigilance* (7), *correlations* (8), *strident* (9), *staccato* (9), *foil* (10), and *totem* (12).

Questions About the Writer's Craft

1. **The pattern.** In their work, Friedman and Rosenman use a description of Paul to define "canonical Type A" behavior (paragraph 2). Why do you suppose that Gleick, who criticizes Friedman and Rosenman's research, quotes their portrait of Paul at such length?

2. **The pattern.** Gleick uses a sequence of three fragments when discussing (in paragraph 2) how Type A has been defined. Identify these fragments. What effect do you think Gleick wanted the fragments to have?

3. Locate places where Gleick uses the first-person pronouns "we," "us," and "our." What do you think Gleick's purpose is in using these pronouns?

4. In paragraph 1, Gleick sarcastically refers to the phrase *Type A* as "magnificently bland." Find other places in the essay where he uses sarcasm. Why might he have chosen to employ such language?

Writing Assignments Using Definition as a Pattern of Development

1. Write an essay offering a fuller definition of the Type B personality than Gleick's essay provides. Rather than defining Type B through negation, as Friedman and Rosenman do, marshal convincing evidence that illustrates the validity of the Type B phenomenon. Brainstorming with friends, family, and classmates will help you generate strong examples of this personality type. At some point in the essay, you might offer a brief personality sketch of the "canonical" Type B as well as discuss the factors that shape the Type B personality as you define it.

2. Gleick notes that, like *Type A, stress* is an ill-defined term. Brainstorm with others to identify as many examples of different kinds of stress as you can. Review the brainstormed material, and select a specific type of stress to focus on. Then write an essay providing a *clear* definition of that particular stress. Possibilities include "dating stress," "workplace stress," "online stress," "fitness stress." Near the end of the essay, you might

provide concise hints for managing the stress you define. Your essay may have a humorous or a serious tone—whichever seems appropriate to your subject.

Writing Assignments Using Other Patterns of Development

3. Write an essay contrasting situations in which being Type A would be beneficial with situations in which it would be counterproductive. Under what circumstances would Type A characteristics be desirable? Under what circumstances would they be undesirable? Drawing upon your own experiences and observations, reach some conclusions about the advantages and/or limitations of the Type A personality.

4. Gleick observes that "hurry sickness" is a trait induced by society at large. Identify a trait of yours that you think is also a reflection of the society in which you live. You might discuss your tendency to be aggressive or non-assertive, materialistic or idealistic, studious or fun-loving. Write an essay illustrating this character trait at work in your everyday behavior. Explain whether you think this trait works to your advantage or disadvantage.

Writing Assignments Using a Journal Entry as a Starting Point

5. Gleick claims that the Type A phenomenon is pervasive in our society. Write an essay of your own illustrating the extent to which your life reflects this phenomenon. Draw upon the most dramatic examples in your pre-reading journal entry. At the end of the essay, describe steps that you or anyone with similar pressures could take to slow down the frenetic pace of everyday life. Gathering information in the library and/or on the Internet might be helpful when you develop the final section of your paper.

Gloria Naylor

A native of New York City, Gloria Naylor (1950–) attended first Brooklyn College and then Yale University, where she earned a master's degree in African-American studies. Naylor is perhaps best known as the author of *The Women of Brewster Place* (1982), a novel made into a television drama starring Oprah Winfrey. *Brewster Place* was awarded the American Book Award for First Fiction in 1983. Naylor has also written the novels *Linden Hills* (1985), *Mama Day* (1988), *Bailey's Café* (1992), and *The Men of Brewster Place* (1998), as well as edited *Children of the Night: The Best Short Stories by Black Writers* (1996). The following selection first appeared in the *New York Times* in 1986.

Pre-Reading Journal Entry

How do adults respond to children's questions when the questions are painful? Consider this predicament by listing, in your journal, some of the uncomfortable questions that you asked as a child. Alternatively, list some of the jarring questions that children have asked you. In either case, think about the responses given to children's questions. Were the responses truthful—or did they shade the truth? Were the responses appropriate? Why or why not?

"Mommy, What Does 'Nigger' Mean?"

Language is the subject. It is the written form with which I've 1 managed to keep the wolf away from the door and, in diaries, to keep my sanity. In spite of this, I consider the written word inferior to the spoken, and much of the frustration experienced by novelists is the awareness that whatever we manage to capture in even the most transcendent passages falls far short of the richness of life. Dialogue achieves its power in the dynamics of a fleeting moment of sight, sound, smell and touch.

I'm not going to enter the debate here about whether it is lan- 2 guage that shapes reality or vice versa. That battle is doomed to be waged whenever we seek intermittent reprieve from the chicken and egg dispute. I will simply take the position that the spoken word, like the written word, amounts to a nonsensical arrangement of sounds or letters without a consensus that assigns "meaning." And building from the meanings of what we hear, we order reality. Words themselves are innocuous; it is the consensus that gives them true power.

I remember the first time I heard the word nigger. In my third- 3 grade class, our math tests were being passed down the rows, and as I handed the papers to a little boy in back of me, I remarked that once again he had received a much lower mark than I did. He snatched his test from me and spit out that word. Had he called me a nymphomaniac or a necrophiliac, I couldn't have been more puzzled. I didn't know what a nigger was, but I knew that whatever it meant, it was something he shouldn't have called me. This was verified when I raised my hand, and in a loud voice repeated what he had said and watched the teacher scold him for using a "bad" word. I was later to go home and ask the inevitable question that every black parent must face—"Mommy, what does 'nigger' mean?"

And what exactly did it mean? Thinking back, I realize that this 4 could not have been the first time the word was used in my presence. I was part of a large extended family that had migrated from the rural South after World War II and formed a close-knit network that gravitated around my maternal grandparents. Their ground-floor apartment in one of the buildings they owned in Harlem was a weekend mecca for my immediate family, along with countless aunts, uncles and cousins who brought along assorted friends. It was a bustling and open house with assorted neighbors and tenants popping in and out to exchange bits of gossip, pick up an old quarrel or referee the ongoing checkers game in which my grandmother cheated shamelessly. They were all there to let down their hair and put up their feet after a week of labor in the factories, laundries and shipyards of New York.

Amid the clamor, which could reach deafening proportions— 5 two or three conversations going on simultaneously, punctuated by the sound of a baby's crying somewhere in the back rooms or out on the street—there was still a rigid set of rules about what was said and how. Older children were sent out of the living room when it was time to get into the juicy details about "you-know-who" up on the third floor who had gone and gotten herself "p-r-e-g-n-a-n-t!" But my parents, knowing that I could spell well beyond my years, always demanded that I follow the others out to play. Beyond sexual misconduct and death, everything else was considered harmless for our young ears. And so among the anecdotes of the triumphs and disappointments in the various workings of their lives, the word nigger was used in my presence, but it was set within contexts and inflections that caused it to register in my mind as something else.

In the singular, the word was always applied to a man who had   6
distinguished himself in some situation that brought their approval for his strength, intelligence or drive:

"Did Johnny really do that?"   7

"I'm telling you, that nigger pulled in $6,000 of overtime last   8
year. Said he got enough for a down payment on a house."

When used with a possessive adjective by a woman—"my nig-   9
ger"—it became a term of endearment for husband or boyfriend. But it could be more than just a term applied to a man. In their mouths it became the pure essence of manhood—a disembodied force that channeled their past history of struggle and present survival against the odds into a victorious statement of being: "Yeah, that old foreman found out quick enough—you don't mess with a nigger."

In the plural, it became a description of some group within the   10
community that had overstepped the bounds of decency as my family defined it: Parents who neglected their children, a drunken couple who fought in public, people who simply refused to look for work, those with excessively dirty mouths or unkempt households were all "trifling niggers." This particular circle could forgive hard times, unemployment, the occasional bout of depression—they had gone through all of that themselves—but the unforgivable sin was lack of self-respect.

A woman could never be a "nigger" in the singular, with its   11
connotation of confirming worth. The noun girl was its closest equivalent in that sense, but only when used in direct address and regardless of the gender doing the addressing. "Girl" was a token of respect for a woman. The one-syllable word was drawn out to sound like three in recognition of the extra ounce of wit, nerve or daring that the woman had shown in the situation under discussion.

"G-i-r-l, stop. You mean you said that to his face?"   12

But if the word was used in a third-person reference or short-   13
ened so that it almost snapped out of the mouth, it always involved some element of communal disapproval. And age became an

important factor in these exchanges. It was only between individuals of the same generation, or from an older person to a younger (but never the other way around), that "girl" would be considered a compliment.

I don't agree with the argument that use of the word nigger at   14
this social stratum of the black community was an internalization of racism. The dynamics were the exact opposite: the people in my grandmother's living room took a word that whites used to signify worthlessness or degradation and rendered it impotent. Gathering there together, they transformed "nigger" to signify the varied and complex human beings they knew themselves to be. If the word was to disappear totally from the mouths of even the most racist of white society, no one in that room was naïve enough to believe it would disappear from white minds. Meeting the word head-on, they proved it had absolutely nothing to do with the way they were determined to live their lives.

So there must have been dozens of times that the word "nig-   15
ger" was spoken in front of me before I reached the third grade. But I didn't "hear" it until it was said by a small pair of lips that had already learned it could be a way to humiliate me. That was the word I went home and asked my mother about. And since she knew that I had to grow up in America, she took me in her lap and explained.

Questions for Close Reading

1. What is the selection's thesis? Locate the sentence(s) in which Naylor states her main idea. If she doesn't state the thesis explicitly, express it in your own words.
2. Why, when her classmate called her "nigger," did Naylor not understand the word's meaning?
3. What meanings of the word *girl* did Naylor pick up from her family? How did the context affect the word's meaning?
4. In paragraph 14, Naylor writes that she doesn't accept the view that the Black community's use of the word *nigger* is an example of internalized racism. What evidence does she offer to disprove this theory?
5. Refer to your dictionary as needed to define the following words used in the selection: *transcendent* (paragraph 1), *dynamics* (1), *intermittent* (2), *reprieve* (2), *consensus* (2), *innocuous* (2), *nymphomaniac* (3), *necrophiliac* (3), *gravitated* (4), *mecca* (4), *anecdotes* (5), *inflections* (5), *disembodied* (9), *unkempt* (10), *trifling* (10), *connotation* (11), *communal* (13), *internalization* (14), *degradation* (14), and *impotent* (14).

Questions About the Writer's Craft

1. **The pattern.** Locate some of the contrasts that Naylor establishes to illustrate the various ways the word *nigger* is used. How do these contrasts help her build her definition of "nigger"? How does this definition reinforce her thesis?

2. **Other patterns.** Throughout the essay, Naylor uses dialogue, a technique typically associated with narration. Identify several examples of dialogue, and explain why Naylor might have chosen to include direct quotations in each case.

3. Why do you think Naylor discusses at such length the "close-knit network" of family that surrounded her when she grew up? Why, for example, might she have mentioned that her grandparents owned the building where they lived, that the visiting adults worked in "factories, laundries, and shipyards," and that children were restricted from hearing certain conversations? How does Naylor's choice of details show her awareness of the reader?

4. Examine the essay's two concluding paragraphs. How does paragraph 14 enlarge the reader's understanding of the word *nigger?* What would have been lost if Naylor had ended the essay with paragraph 14?

Writing Assignments Using Definition as a Pattern of Development

1. Naylor illustrates her attempt to arrive at a personally meaningful interpretation of an emotionally charged word. Choose a word, phrase, or expression whose meaning you have struggled to understand. Possible words or phrases include *loyalty, morality, family values,* or *sexual harassment.* Write an essay in which you present both your definition and the personal experiences that led to your definition. You may provide the definition and then move to the personal examples, or you may begin with the examples and lead up to the definition. In either case, consider using dialogue—as Naylor does—to enliven and clarify your examples.

2. Choose a term or expression that you think is often misused or misunderstood. Possible examples include *feminism, adolescent, illiteracy, academic honesty, heavy metal, new age philosophy,* or *senior citizen.* Write an essay presenting what you believe to be the correct definition of this term. Begin with several illustrations showing how the word is commonly misused or misunderstood, and point out the errors in these interpretations. Then provide your own definition, using clear examples to convey why your understanding of the word is more accurate.

Writing Assignments Using Other Patterns of Development

∞ 3. The child who called the author "nigger" failed to recognize Naylor's individual worth. In an essay, tell about a time you had trouble viewing someone as an individual—either because of something about the person or because of something about you or the way you were raised. In an essay, explore what happened when you treated this person inappropriately or unjustly. How did you act? How did the other person respond? What did you learn from the experience? Before writing, consider reading "The Fourth of July" (page 160), in which Audre Lorde narrates an incident when prejudicial ignorance shattered a child's innocent beliefs. And for insight into the way preconceptions influence behavior, you might read William Raspberry's "The Handicap of Definition" (page 529) and Shelby Steele's "Affirmative Action: The Price of Preference" (page 649).

🖳 4. The boy who spit out the hateful term *nigger* undoubtedly acquired his prejudiced attitudes at home. Focus on one group that is often the object of prejudice (for example, the elderly, the physically handicapped, the overweight, or a particular ethnic or racial group), and write an essay illustrating the steps that parents *or* schools might take to develop children's appreciation of diversity in general and of that group in particular. To illustrate the need for such an approach, open with a dramatic example of children's prejudiced thinking about the group in question. Before writing the essay, brainstorm ideas with friends and classmates. Also consider doing research in the library and/or on the Internet about programs that encourage children's tolerance.

Writing Assignments Using a Journal Entry as a Starting Point

∞ 5. Review the examples you listed in your pre-reading journal entry, and identify two or three *kinds* of difficult questions that children often ask. Then write an essay presenting adults with a how-to guide for responding to these kinds of questions Draw upon your own and other people's experiences in preparing your guidelines. You might also look at some parenting guides in the library and/or on the Internet for help in devising your own suggestions. Before writing, consider reading Audre Lorde's "The Fourth of July" (page 160), Beth Johnson's "Bombs Bursting in Air" (page 242), and Yuh Ji-Yeon's "Let's Tell the Story of All America's Cultures" (page 581), all of which address the difficulty of communicating with children about life's darker truths.

Marie Winn

Born in Czechoslovakia and brought by her family to New York, Marie Winn was educated at Radcliffe College. The author or editor of ten children's books, Winn developed a special interest in the effect of television on children. She has contributed numerous articles to such publications as the *New York Times* and *Village Voice.* Winn's provocative and influential study, *The Plug-In Drug: Television, Children and Family,* was originally published in 1977 and revised in 1985. The selection that follows is from that book. Other books by Winn include *Children Without Childhood* (1983), *Unplugging the Plug-In Drug* (1987), *The Secret Life of Central Park* (1997), and *Red-Tails in Love: A Wildlife Drama in Central Park* (1998).

Pre-Reading Journal Entry

In all probability, you know children who watch more television than you think they should. What makes you think these children's TV viewing is excessive? Why do they spend so much time in front of the TV? What else might they be doing if they weren't watching TV? Respond to these questions in your journal, using your experiences and observations as a point of departure.

TV Addiction

Cookies or Heroin?

The word "addiction" is often used loosely and wryly in conversation. People will refer to themselves as "mystery book addicts" or "cookie addicts." E. B. White wrote of his annual surge of interest in gardening: "We are hooked and are making an attempt to kick the habit." Yet nobody really believes that reading mysteries or ordering seeds by catalogue is serious enough to be compared with addictions to heroin or alcohol. The word "addiction" is here used jokingly to denote a tendency to overindulge in some pleasurable activity.

People often refer to being "hooked on TV." Does this, too, fall into the lighthearted category of cookie eating and other pleasures that people pursue with unusual intensity, or is there a kind of television viewing that falls into the more serious category of destructive addiction?

When we think about addiction to drugs or alcohol we fre- 3
quently focus on negative aspects, ignoring the pleasures that
accompany drinking or drug-taking. And yet the essence of any serious addiction is a pursuit of pleasure, a search for a "high" that normal life does not supply. It is only the inability to function without
the addictive substance that is dismaying, the dependence of the
organism upon a certain experience and an increasing inability to
function normally without it. Thus people will take two or three
drinks at the end of the day not merely for the pleasure drinking
provides, but also because they "don't feel normal" without them.

Real addicts do not merely pursue a pleasurable experience one 4
time in order to function normally. They need to *repeat* it again and
again. Something about that particular experience makes life without it less than complete. Other potentially pleasurable experiences
are no longer possible, for under the spell of the addictive experience, their lives are peculiarly distorted. The addict craves an experience and yet is never really satisfied. The organism may be tem-
porarily sated, but soon it begins to crave again.

Finally, a serious addiction is distinguished from a harmless 5
pursuit of pleasure by its distinctly destructive elements. Heroin
addicts, for instance, lead a damaged life: their increasing need for
heroin in increasing doses prevents them from working, from maintaining relationships, from developing in human ways. Similarly
alcoholics' lives are narrowed and dehumanized by their dependence on alcohol.

Let us consider television viewing in the light of the conditions 6
that define serious addictions.

Not unlike drugs or alcohol, the television experience allows the 7
participant to blot out the real world and enter into a pleasurable
and passive mental state. The worries and anxieties of reality are as
effectively deferred by becoming absorbed in a television program as
by going on a "trip" induced by drugs or alcohol. And just as alcoholics are only vaguely aware of their addiction, feeling that they
control their drinking more than they really do ("I can cut it out any
time I want—I just like to have three or four drinks before dinner"),
people similarly overestimate their control over television watching.
Even as they put off other activities to spend hour after hour watching television, they feel they could easily resume living in a different,
less passive style. But somehow or other, while the television set is
present in their homes, the click doesn't sound. With television

pleasures available, those other experiences seem less attractive, more difficult somehow.

A heavy viewer (a college English instructor) observes: 8

"I find television almost irresistible. When the set is on, I can-   9
not ignore it. I can't turn it off. I feel sapped, will-less, enervated. As I reach out to turn off the set, the strength goes out of my arms. So I sit there for hours and hours."

Self-confessed television addicts often feel they "ought" to do   10
other things—but the fact that they don't read and don't plant their garden or sew or crochet or play games or have conversations means that those activities are no longer as desirable as television viewing. In a way the lives of heavy viewers are as imbalanced by their television "habit" as a drug addict's or an alcoholic's. They are living in a hold-ing pattern, as it were, passing up the activities that lead to growth or development or a sense of accomplishment. This is one reason peo-ple talk about their television viewing so ruefully, so apologetically. They are aware that it is an unproductive experience, that almost any other endeavor is more worthwhile by any human measure.

Finally it is the adverse effect of television viewing on the lives   11
of so many people that defines it as a serious addiction. The televi-sion habit distorts the sense of time. It renders other experiences vague and curiously unreal while taking on a greater reality for itself. It weakens relationships by reducing and sometimes eliminating normal opportunities for talking, for communicating.

And yet television does not satisfy, else why would the viewer   12
continue to watch hour after hour, day after day? "The measure of health," writes Lawrence Kubie, "is flexibility . . . and especially the freedom to cease when sated." But heavy television viewers can never be sated with their television experiences—they do not pro-vide the true nourishment that satiation requires—and thus they find that they cannot stop watching.

A former heavy watcher (filmmaker) describes such a syndrome: 13

"I remember when we first got the set I'd watch for hours and   14
hours, whenever I could, and I remember that feeling of tiredness and anxiety that always followed those orgies, a sense of time terribly wasted. It was like eating cotton candy; television promised so much richness, I couldn't wait for it, and then it just evaporated into air. I remember feeling terribly drained after watching for a long time."

Similarly a nursery school teacher remembers her own child-   15
hood television experience:

"I remember bingeing on television when I was a child and hav-   16
ing that vapid feeling after watching hours of TV. I'd look forward
to watching whenever I could, but it just didn't give back a real feeling of pleasure. It was like no orgasm, no catharsis, very frustrating.
Television just wasn't giving me the promised satisfaction, and yet I
kept on watching. It filled some sort of need, or had to do with an
inability to get something started."

The testimonies of ex-television addicts often have the evangel-   17
istic overtones of stories heard at Alcoholics Anonymous meetings.

A handbag repair shop owner says: 18

"I'd get on the subway home from work with the newspaper   19
and immediately turn to the TV page to plan out my evening's
watching. I'd come home, wash, change my clothes, and tell my
wife to start the machine so it would be warmed up. (We had an old-
fashioned set that took a few seconds before an image appeared.)
And then we'd watch TV for the rest of the evening. We'd eat our
dinner in the living room while watching, and we'd only talk every
once in a while, during the ads, if at all. I'd watch anything, good,
bad, or indifferent.

"All the while we were watching I'd feel terribly angry at myself   20
for wasting all that time watching junk. I could never go to sleep
until at least the eleven o'clock news, and then sometimes I'd still
stay up for the late-night talk show. I had a feeling that I *had* to
watch the news programs, that I *had* to know what was happening,
even though most of the time nothing much was happening and I
could easily find out what was by reading the paper the next morning. Usually my wife would fall asleep on the couch while I was
watching. I'd get angry at her for doing that. Actually, I was angry
at myself. I had a collection of three years of back issues of different
magazines that I planned to read sometime, but I never got around
to reading them. I never got around to sorting or labeling my collection of slides I had made when traveling. I only had time for television. We'd take the telephone off the hook while watching so we
wouldn't be interrupted! We like classical music, but we never listened to any, never!

"Then one day the set broke. I said to my wife, 'Let's not fix it.   21
Let's just see what happens.' Well, that was the smartest thing we
ever did. We haven't had a TV in the house since then.

"Now I look back and I can hardly believe we could have lived   22
like that. I feel that my mind was completely mummified for all

those years. I was glued to that machine and couldn't get loose, somehow. It really frightens me to think of it. Yes, I'm frightened of TV now. I don't think I could control it if we had a set in the house again. I think it would take over no matter what I did."

A further sign of addiction is that "an exclusive craving for   23 something is accompanied by a loss of discrimination towards the object which satisfies the craving . . . the alcoholic is not interested in the taste of liquor that is available; likewise the compulsive eater is not particular about what he eats when there is food around," write the authors of a book about the nature of addiction. And just so, for many viewers the process of *watching* television is far more important than the actual contents of the programs being watched. The knowledge that the act of watching is more important than *what* is being watched lies behind the practice of "roadblocking," invented by television advertisers and adopted by political candidates who purchase the same half-hour on all three channels in order to force-feed their message to the public. As one prominent candidate put it, "People will watch television no matter what is on, and if you allow them no other choice they will watch your show."

Questions for Close Reading

1. What is the selection's thesis? Locate the sentence(s) in which Winn states her main idea. If she doesn't state the thesis explicitly, express it in your own words.
2. Why, according to Winn, is a gardening addiction or a mystery book addiction a humorous kind of habit? What does she call "the essence of any serious addiction"?
3. In paragraph 7, the author says that television allows the viewer "to enter into a pleasurable . . . mental state," and later that "television does not satisfy." How does Winn prepare you earlier in the essay for this seeming contradiction?
4. Since television does "not provide the true nourishment that satiation requires," what activities does Winn suggest as truly nourishing alternatives?
5. Refer to your dictionary as needed to define the following words used in the selection: *wryly* (paragraph 1), *ruefully* (10), *adverse* (11), and *satiation* (12).

Questions About the Writer's Craft

1. **The pattern.** At the beginning of the essay, Winn uses definition by negation to clarify her interpretation of the term *television addiction*. What kinds of things does Winn say are *not* the equivalents of TV addiction? Why does she use this strategy of definition by negation?

2. How does Winn organize the two extended definitions of addiction and TV addiction? How does this organizational pattern help Winn persuade readers to accept her point that TV is addicting?
3. What do the quotations from TV addicts add to Winn's argument? Why do you think Winn chooses quotations from these people?
4. How does the lengthy discussion of addiction (paragraphs 3–5) help Winn to convince readers that television is indeed addicting?

Writing Assignments Using Definition as a Pattern of Development

1. In her introduction, Winn describes how people often use a very serious term—*addiction*—when referring to a light or harmless experience. Think of another term that you feel is serious, but that people use lightly and apply loosely. Your choice could be *friendship, love, hate,* or another word. Begin with an example that shows how the word is misused, and then provide an extended definition clarifying the proper use of the term.
2. TV addiction is only one of many forms of addiction. Write an essay on another activity that you feel meets the definition of an addiction. You might consider addictions to gambling, baseball games, cars, bingo, chocolate, and the latest clothing styles. Your essay may be serious or playful. If appropriate, support your claim with information gathered in the library and/or on the Internet.

Writing Assignments Using Other Patterns of Development

3. Many kinds of television shows come in for criticism—"tabloid TV" talk shows, sitcoms, game shows, children's cartoons, news broadcasts, and so forth. Pick one kind of TV show and write an essay defending the genre. Or argue that this type of show has no merit. Your essay may be serious or playful. Stephen King's defense of horror films "Why We Crave Horror Movies" (page 455) may spur you to imaginative thinking of your own.
4. You have probably heard from older relatives (or may yourself know) what life was like before TV. Write an essay for your future children or grandchildren describing what life was like before one or several of these new technologies: VCRs, cable TV, computers, microwave ovens, cash cards, and the like. Persuade your descendants that life was better *or* worse before these items were invented.

Writing Assignments Using a Journal Entry as a Starting Point

5. Drawing upon the material in your pre-reading journal entry, write an essay urging parents to combat their children's TV addiction. Begin the

essay with one or more dramatic examples illustrating both the extent of the problem and its effect. Then describe steps that parents can take to help their children break the TV habit. Interviewing others (especially parents) as well as conducting research in the library and/or on the Internet will help you gain insight into the complexities of the issue.

William Raspberry

Journalist William Raspberry was born in Okolona, Mississippi. From his mother, an English teacher and poet, Raspberry learned to care "about the rhythm and grace of words." His father, a shop teacher, taught him "that neither end tables nor arguments are worthwhile unless they stand solidly on all four legs." Raspberry graduated from Indiana Central College and later joined the staff of the Indianapolis *Recorder* as a reporter and editor. Following a two-year stint in the army, he was hired by the *Washington Post*, where his nationally syndicated column has originated since 1971. His coverage of the Watts race riots in 1965 won him the Capital Press Club Journalist of the Year award, and he later went on to win the Pulitzer Prize for commentary in 1994. *Looking Backward at Us*, a collection of Raspberry's columns, was published in 1991. The following selection appeared in Raspberry's *Washington Post* column in 1982.

Pre-Reading Journal Entry

Which do you think plays a more important role in determining what a person accomplishes: innate talent or belief in oneself? Take a few minutes to respond to this question in your journal, jotting down examples drawn from your experiences and observations.

The Handicap of Definition

I know all about bad schools, mean politicians, economic deprivation and racism. Still, it occurs to me that one of the heaviest burdens black Americans—and black children in particular—have to bear is the handicap of definition: the question of what it means to be black. 1

Let me explain quickly what I mean. If a basketball fan says that the Boston Celtics' Larry Bird plays "black," the fan intends it—and Bird probably accepts it—as a compliment. Tell pop singer Tom Jones he moves "black" and he might grin in appreciation. Say to Teena Marie or the Average White Band that they sound "black" and they'll thank you. 2

But name one pursuit, aside from athletics, entertainment or sexual performance, in which a white practitioner will feel 3 complimented to be told he does it "black." Tell a white broadcaster he talks "black" and he'll sign up for diction lessons. Tell a white reporter he writes "black" and he'll take a writing course. Tell a white lawyer he reasons "black" and he might sue you for slander.

What we have here is a tragically limited definition of blackness, and it isn't only white people who buy it.   4

Think of all the ways black children can put one another down   5
with charges of "whiteness." For many of these children, hard study and hard work are "white." Trying to please a teacher might be criticized as acting "white." Speaking correct English is "white." Scrimping today in the interest of tomorrow's goals is "white." Educational toys and games are "white."

An incredible array of habits and attitudes that are conducive to   6
success in business, in academia, in the nonentertainment professions are likely to be thought of as somehow "white." Even economic success, unless it involves such "black" undertakings as numbers banking, is defined as "white."

And the results are devastating. I wouldn't deny that blacks   7
often are better entertainers and athletes. My point is the harm that comes from too narrow a definition of what is black.

One reason black youngsters tend to do better at basketball, for   8
instance, is that they assume they can learn to do it well, and so they practice constantly to prove themselves right.

Wouldn't it be wonderful if we could infect black children with   9
the notion that excellence in math is "black" rather than white, or possibly Chinese? Wouldn't it be of enormous value if we could create the myth that morality, strong families, determination, courage and love of learning are traits brought by slaves from Mother Africa and therefore quintessentially black?

There is no doubt in my mind that most black youngsters could   10
develop their mathematical reasoning, their elocution and their attitudes, the way they develop their jump shots and their dance steps: by the combination of sustained, enthusiastic practice and the unquestioned belief that they can do it.

In one sense, what I am talking about is the importance of   11
developing positive ethnic traditions. Maybe Jews have an innate talent for communication; maybe the Chinese are born with a gift for mathematical reasoning; maybe blacks are naturally blessed with athletic grace. I doubt it. What is at work, I suspect, is assumption, inculcated early in their lives, that this is a thing our people do well.

Unfortunately, many of the things about which blacks make this 12
assumption are things that do not contribute to their career success—except for that handful of the truly gifted who can make it as
entertainers and athletes. And many of the things we concede to
whites are the things that are essential to economic security.

So it is with a number of assumptions black youngsters make 13
about what it is to be a "man": physical aggressiveness, sexual
prowess, the refusal to submit to authority. The prisons are full of
people who, by this perverted definition, are unmistakably men.

But the real problem is not so much that the things defined as 14
"black" are negative. The problem is that the definition is much too
narrow.

Somehow, we have to make our children understand that they 15
are intelligent, competent people, capable of doing whatever they
put their minds to and making it in the American mainstream, not
just in a black subculture.

What we seem to be doing, instead, is raising up yet another 16
generation of young blacks who will be failures—by definition.

Questions for Close Reading

1. What is the selection's thesis? Locate the sentence(s) in which Raspberry
   states his main idea. If he doesn't state the thesis explicitly, express it in
   your own words.
2. In paragraph 14, Raspberry emphasizes that the word *black* presents a
   problem not because it's negative but because it has become "much too
   narrow." According to Raspberry, what limitations have become associated with the term *black*? What negative consequences does he see
   resulting from these limitations?
3. In paragraph 11, Raspberry talks about "positive ethnic traditions."
   What does he mean by this term? What examples does he provide?
4. In Raspberry's opinion, what needs to be done to ensure the future success of African-American children?
5. Refer to your dictionary as needed to define the following words used in
   the selection: *diction* (paragraph 3), *scrimping* (5), *array* (6), *quintessentially* (9), *elocution* (10), *inculcated* (11), and *concede* (12).

Questions About the Writer's Craft

1. **The pattern.** Raspberry is primarily concerned with showing how limited the definition of *black* has come to be in our society. In the course
   of the essay, though, he also defines three other terms. Locate these
   terms and their definitions. How do the definitions and the effects of the

definitions help Raspberry make his point about the narrowness of the term *black?*

2. **Other patterns.** In his opening paragraph, Raspberry uses the argumentation technique of refutation. What does he refute? What does he achieve by using this strategy at the very beginning of the essay?

3. A Black journalist, Raspberry writes a nationally syndicated column that originates in the *Washington Post,* a major newspaper serving the nation's capital and the nation as a whole. Consider these facts when examining Raspberry's use of the pronouns *I, we,* and *our* in the essay. What do these pronouns seem to imply about Raspberry's intended audience? What is the effect of these pronouns?

4. Raspberry has chosen a relatively abstract topic to write about—the meaning of the term *black.* What techniques does he use to draw in readers and keep them engaged? Consider his overall tone, choice of examples, and use of balanced sentence structure.

Writing Assignments Using Definition as a Pattern of Development

1. Raspberry points out how restrictive the definitions of *black* and *white* can be. Do you think that the definitions of *male* and *female* can be equally restrictive? Focusing on the term *male* or *female,* write an essay showing how the term was defined as you were growing up. Considering the messages conveyed by your family, the educational system, and society at large, indicate whether you came to perceive the term as limiting or liberating. Before planning your paper, you may want to read one or more of the following essays, all of which deal with the way gender roles influence behavior: Alleen Pace Nilsen's "Sexism and Language" (page 225), Barbara Ehrenreich's "What I've Learned From Men" (page 249), Deborah Tannen's "But What Do You Mean?" (page 313), and Virginia Woolf's "Professions for Women" (page 669).

2. In paragraph 15, Raspberry seems to define *success* as "making it in the American mainstream," but not everyone would agree that this is what constitutes success. Write an essay in which you offer your personal definition of *success.* One way to proceed might be to contrast what you consider success with what you consider failure. Or you might narrate the success story of a person you respect highly. No matter how you proceed, be sure to provide telling specifics that support your definition.

Writing Assignments Using Other Patterns of Development

3. Like most people, you've probably had a "defining" term applied to you at one time or another. Perhaps you've been called "shy" or "stubborn" or "the class clown" or "the athlete in the family." Focusing on one such

label that's been applied to you, write an essay showing the effect of this term on your life. Be sure to explain why you got the label and how you felt about it. The following essays will give you additional perspectives on the ways that labels and names affect people's lives and self-image: Alice Walker's "Beauty: When the Other Dancer Is the Self" (page 467), Gloria Naylor's "Mommy, What Does 'Nigger' Mean?" (page 516), and Shelby Steele's "Affirmative Action: The Price of Preference (page 649).

∞ 4. In his conclusion, Raspberry makes a plea for providing the younger generation with a more positive, more expansive definition of *black*. Consider the beliefs and principles that today's older generation seems to impart to the younger generation. Write an essay showing which aspects of this value system seem helpful and valid and which do not. Also explain what additional values and convictions the older generation should be passing on. How should parents, teachers, and others convey these precepts? For a discussion of some obstacles to children's moral instruction, read Ellen Goodman's "Family Counterculture" (page 6).

Writing Assignments Using a Journal Entry as a Starting Point

∞ 5. Developing the material in your pre-reading journal entry, write an essay arguing that an individual's innate talent *or* self-confidence is the critical factor in determining achievement. Consider brainstorming with others to generate examples in support of your contention. At some point in the essay, you should acknowledge the opposing viewpoint, dismantling as much of it as you can. For an inspirational account of personal achievement despite the odds, read Jacques D' Amboise's "Showing What Is Possible" (page 460).

Additional Writing Topics

DEFINITION

General Assignments

Use definition to develop any of the following topics. Once you fix on a limited subject, decide if the essay has an informative or a persuasive purpose. The paper might begin with the etymology of the term, a stipulative definition, or a definition by negation. You may want to use a number of writing patterns—such as description, comparison, narration, process analysis—to develop the definition. Remember, too, that the paper doesn't have to be scholarly and serious. There is no reason it can't be a lighthearted discussion of the meaning of a term.

1. Fads
2. A family fight
3. Helplessness
4. An epiphany
5. A workaholic
6. A Pollyanna
7. A con artist
8. A stingy person
9. A team player
10. A Yiddish term like *mensch, klutz, chutzpah,* or *dreck,* or a term from some other ethnic group
11. Adolescence
12. Fast food
13. A perfect day
14. Hypocrisy
15. Inner peace
16. Obsession
17. Generosity
18. Exploitation
19. Depression
20. A double bind

Assignments With a Specific Purpose and Audience

1. *Newsweek* magazine runs a popular column called "My Turn," consisting of readers' opinions on subjects of general interest. Write a piece for this column defining *today's college students.* Use the piece to dispel

some negative stereotypes (for example, that college students are apathetic, ill-informed, self-centered, and materialistic).

2. You're an attorney arguing a case of sexual harassment—a charge your client has leveled against her boss, a business executive. To win the case, you must present to the jury a clear definition of exactly what *sexual harassment* is and isn't. Write such a definition for your opening remarks in court.

3. You have been asked to write part of a pamphlet for students who come to the college health clinic. For this pamphlet, define *one* of the following conditions and its symptoms: *depression, stress, burnout, test anxiety, addiction* (to alcohol, drugs, or TV), *workaholism*. Part of the pamphlet should describe ways to cope with the condition described.

4. A new position has opened in your company. Write a job description to be sent to employment agencies that will screen candidates. Your description should define the job's purpose, state the duties involved, and outline essential qualifications.

5. Part of your job as peer counselor in your college's counseling center involves helping people communicate more effectively. To assist students, write a definition of some term that you think represents an essential component of a strong interpersonal relationship. You might, for example, define *respect, sharing, equality,* or *trust*. Part of the definition should employ definition by negation, a discussion of what the term is *not*.

6. Having waited on tables for several years at a resort hotel, you've been asked by the hotel manager to give some pointers to this year's new dining hall staff. Prepare a talk in which you define *courtesy*, the quality you consider most essential to the job. Use specific examples to illustrate your definition.

11
ARGUMENTATION-PERSUASION

WHAT IS ARGUMENTATION-PERSUASION?

"You can't possibly believe what you're saying."
"Look, I know what I'm talking about, and that's that."

Does this heated exchange sound familiar? Probably. When we hear the word *argument*, most of us think of a verbal battle propelled by stubbornness and irrational thought, with one person pitted against the other.

Argumentation in writing, though, is a different matter. Using clear thinking and logic, the writer tries to convince readers of the soundness of a particular opinion on a controversial issue. If, while trying to convince, the writer uses emotional language and dramatic appeals to readers' concerns, beliefs, and values, then the piece is called *persuasion*. Besides encouraging acceptance of an opinion, per-suasion often urges readers (or another group) to commit themselves to a course of action. Assume you're writing an essay protesting the federal government's policy of offering aid to those suffering from hunger in other countries while many Americans go hungry. If your purpose is to document, coolly and objectively, the presence of hunger in the United States, you would prepare an argumentation essay. Such an essay would be filled with statistics, report findings, and expert opinion to demonstrate how widespread hunger is nation-wide. If, however, your purpose is to shake up readers, even motivate them to write letters to their congressional representatives and push for a change in policy, you would write a persuasive essay. In this case, your essay might contain emotional accounts of undernourished children, ill-fed pregnant women, and nearly starving elderly people.

Because people respond rationally *and* emotionally to situations, argumentation and persuasion are usually *combined*. Suppose you decide to write an article for the campus newspaper advocating a pre-Labor Day start for the school year. Your audience includes the college administration, students, and faculty. The article might begin by *arguing* that several schools starting the academic year earlier were able to close for the month of January and thus reduce heating and other maintenance expenses. Such an argument, supported by documented facts and figures, would help convince the administration. Realizing that you also have to gain student and faculty support for your idea, you might argue further that the proposed change would mean that students and faculty could leave for winter break with the semester behind them—papers written, exams taken, grades calculated and recorded. To make this part of your argument especially compelling, you could adopt a *persuasive* strategy by using emotional appeals and positively charged language: "Think how pleasant it would be to sleep late, spend time with family and friends, toast the New Year—without having to worry about work awaiting you back on campus."

When argumentation and persuasion blend in this way, emotion *supports* rather than *replaces* logic and sound reasoning. Although some writers resort to emotional appeals to the exclusion of rational thought, when you prepare argumentation-persuasion essays, you should advance your position through a balanced appeal to reason and emotion.

HOW ARGUMENTATION-PERSUASION FITS YOUR PURPOSE AND AUDIENCE

You probably realize that argumentation, persuasion, or a combination of the two is everywhere: an editorial urging the overhaul

of an ill-managed literacy program; a commercial for a new shampoo; a scientific report advocating increased funding for AIDS
research. Your own writing involves argumentation-persuasion as
well. When you prepare a *causal analysis, descriptive piece, narrative,* or *definition essay,* you advance a specific point of view:
MTV has a negative influence on teens' view of sex; Cape Cod in
winter is imbued with a special kind of magic; a disillusioning
experience can teach people much about themselves; *character*
can be defined as the willingness to take unpopular positions on
difficult issues. Indeed, an essay organized around any of the patterns of development described in this book may have a persuasive intent. You might, for example, encourage readers to try out
a *process* you've explained, or to see one of the two movies you've
compared.

Argumentation-persuasion, however, involves more than presenting a point of view and providing evidence. Unlike other forms
of writing, it assumes controversy and addresses opposing viewpoints. Consider the following assignments, all of which require the
writer to take a position on a controversial issue:

> In parts of the country, communities established for older
> citizens or childless couples have refused to rent to families
> with children. How do you feel about this situation? What
> do you think are the rights of the parties involved?

> Citing the fact that the highest percentage of automobile
> accidents involve young men, insurance companies consis-
> tently charge their highest rates to young males. Is this
> policy fair? Why or why not?

> Some colleges and universities have instituted a "no pass,
> no play" policy for athletes. Explain why this practice is or
> is not appropriate.

It's impossible to predict with absolute certainty what will make
readers accept the view you advance or take the action you propose.
But the ancient Greeks, who formulated our basic concepts of logic,
isolated three factors crucial to the effectiveness of argumentation-
persuasion: *logos, pathos,* and *ethos.*

Your main concern in an argumentation-persuasion essay
should be with the *logos,* or soundness, of your argument: the facts,

statistics, examples, and authoritative statements you gather to support your viewpoint. This supporting evidence must be unified, specific, sufficient, accurate, and representative (see pages 39–44). Imagine, for instance, you want to convince people that a popular charity misappropriates the money it receives from the public. Your readers, inclined to believe in the good works of the charity, will probably dismiss your argument unless you can substantiate your claim with valid, well-documented evidence that enhances the *logos* of your position.

Sensitivity to *pathos,* or the emotional power of language, is another key consideration for writers of argumentation-persuasion essays. *Pathos* appeals to readers' needs, values, and attitudes, encouraging them to commit themselves to a viewpoint or course of action. The *pathos* of a piece derives partly from the writer's language. *Connotative* language—words with strong emotional overtones—can move readers to accept a point of view and may even spur them to act.

Advertising and propaganda generally rely on *pathos* to the exclusion of logic, using emotion to influence and manipulate. Consider the following pitches for a man's cologne and a woman's perfume. The language—and the attitudes to which it appeals—is different in each case:

> Brawn: Experience the power. Bold. Yet subtle. Clean. Masculine. The scent for the man who's in charge.

> Black Lace is for you—the woman who dresses for success but who dares to be provocative, slightly naughty. Black Lace. Perfect with pearls by day and with diamonds by night.

The appeal to men plays on the impact that words like *Brawn, bold, power,* and *in charge* may have for some males. Similarly, the charged words *Black Lace, provocative, naughty,* and *diamonds* are intended to appeal to business women who—in the advertiser's mind, at least—may be looking for ways to reconcile sensuality and professionalism. (For more on slanted language, read Ann McClintock's "Propaganda Techniques in Today's Advertising," page 304.)

Like an advertising copywriter, you must select language that reinforces your message. In a paper supporting an expanded immigration policy, you might use evocative phrases like "land of liberty," "a nation of immigrants," and "America's open-door policy." However, if you were arguing for strict immigration quotas, you might use language like "save jobs for unemployed Americans," "flood of unskilled labor," and "illegal aliens." Remember, though: Such language should support, not supplant, clear thinking.

Finally, whenever you write an argumentation-persuasion essay, you should establish your *ethos,* or credibility and integrity. You cannot expect readers to accept or act on your viewpoint unless you convince them that you know what you're talking about and that you're worth listening to. Be sure, then, to tell readers about any experiences you've had that make you knowledgeable about the issue being discussed. You will also come across as knowledgeable and trustworthy if you present a logical, reasoned argument that takes opposing views into account. And make sure that your appeals to emotion aren't excessive. Overwrought emotionalism undercuts credibility. Remember, too, that *ethos* isn't constant. A writer may have credibility on one subject but not on another: An army general might be a reliable source for information on military preparedness but not for information on federal funding of day care.

Writing an effective argumentation-persuasion essay involves an interplay of *logos, pathos,* and *ethos.* The exact balance among these factors is determined by your audience and purpose (that is, whether you want the audience simply to agree with your view or whether you also want them to take action). More than any other kind of writing, argumentation-persuasion requires that you *analyze your readers* and tailor your approach to them. You need to determine how much they know about the issue, how they feel about you and your position, what their values and attitudes are, what motivates them.

In general, most readers will fall into one of three broad categories: supportive, wavering, or hostile. Each type of audience requires a different blend of *logos, pathos,* and *ethos* in an argumentation-persuasion essay.

1. A supportive audience.   If your audience agrees with your position and trusts your credibility, you don't need a highly reasoned argument dense with facts, examples, and statistics. Although you may want to solidify support by providing additional information (*logos*), you can rely primarily on *pathos*—a strong emotional appeal—to reinforce readers' commitment to your shared viewpoint. Assume that you belong to a local fishing club and have volunteered to write an article encouraging members to support threatened fishing rights in state parks. You might begin by stating that fishing strengthens the fish population by thinning out overcrowded streams. Since your audience would certainly be familiar with this idea, you wouldn't need to devote much discussion to it. Instead, you would attempt to move them emotionally. You might evoke the camaraderie in the sport, the pleasure of a perfect cast, the beauty of the outdoors, and perhaps conclude with "If you want these enjoyments to continue, please make a generous contribution to our fund."

2. A wavering audience.   At times, readers may be open to what you have to say but may not be committed fully to your viewpoint. Or perhaps they're not as informed about the subject as they should be. In either case, you don't want to risk alienating them with a heavy-handed emotional appeal. Concentrate instead on *ethos* and *logos,* bolstering your image as a reliable source and providing the evidence needed to advance your position. If you want to convince an audience of high school seniors to take a year off to work between high school and college, you might establish your credibility by recounting the year you spent working and by showing the positive effects it had on your life (*ethos*). In addition, you could cite studies indicating that delayed entry into college is related to higher grade point averages. A year's savings, you would explain, allows students to study when they might otherwise need to hold down a job to earn money for tuition (*logos*).

3. A hostile audience.   An apathetic, skeptical, or hostile audience is obviously most difficult to convince. With such an audience, you should avoid emotional appeals because they might seem irrational, sentimental, or even comical. Instead, weigh the essay heavily in favor of logical reasoning and hard-to-dispute facts (*logos*). Assume your college administration is working to ban liquor from the student pub. You plan to submit to the campus newspaper an open letter supporting this generally unpopular effort. To sway other students, you cite the positive experiences of schools that have gone dry. Many colleges, you explain, have found their tavern revenues actually increase because all students—not just those of drinking age—can now support the pub. With the greater revenues, some schools have upgraded the food served in the pubs and have hired disc jockeys or musical groups to provide entertainment. Many schools have also seen a sharp reduction in alcohol-related vandalism. Readers may not be won over to your side, but your sound, logical argument may encourage them to be more tolerant of your viewpoint. Indeed, such increased receptivity may be all you can reasonably expect from a hostile audience. (For more help in analyzing your audience, see pages 19–20.)

SUGGESTIONS FOR USING ARGUMENTATION-PERSUASION IN AN ESSAY

1. At the beginning of the paper, identify the controversy surrounding the issue and state your position in the thesis.   Your introduction should clarify the controversy about the issue. In addition, it should provide as much background information as your readers are likely to need.

The thesis of an argumentation-persuasion paper is often called the *assertion* or *proposition*. Occasionally, the proposition appears at the paper's end, but it is usually stated at the beginning. If you state the thesis right away, your audience knows where you stand and is better able to evaluate the evidence presented.

Remember: Argumentation-persuasion assumes conflicting viewpoints. Be sure your proposition focuses on a controversial issue and indicates your view. Avoid a proposition that is merely factual; what is demonstrably true allows little room for debate. To see the difference between a factual statement and an effective thesis, examine the two statements that follow:

Fact: In the past decade, the nation's small farmers have suffered financial hardships.

Thesis: Inefficient management, rather than competition from agricultural conglomerates, is responsible for the financial plight of the nation's small farmers.

The first statement is certainly true. It would be difficult to find anyone who believes that these are easy times for small farmers. Because the statement invites little opposition, it can't serve as the focus of an argumentation-persuasion essay. The second statement, though, takes a controversial stance on a complex issue. Such a proposition is a valid starting point for a paper intended to argue and persuade. However, don't assume that such advice means that you should take a highly opinionated position in your thesis. A dogmatic, overstated proposition ("Campus security is staffed by overpaid, badge-flashing incompetents") is bound to alienate some readers.

Remember also to keep the proposition narrow and specific, so you can focus your thoughts in a purposeful way. Consider the following statements:

> *Broad thesis:* The welfare system has been abused over the years.

> *Narrow thesis:* Welfare payments should be denied to unmarried teenage girls who have more than one child out of wedlock.

If you tried to write a paper based on the first statement, you would face an unmanageable task—showing all the ways that welfare has been abused. Your readers would also be confused about what to expect in the paper: Will it discuss unscrupulous bureaucrats, fraudulent bookkeeping, dishonest recipients? In contrast, the revised thesis is limited and specific. It signals that the paper will propose severe restrictions on welfare payments. Such a proposal will surely have opponents and is thus appropriate for argumentation-persuasion.

The thesis in an argumentation-persuasion essay can simply state your opinion about an issue, or it can go a step further and call for some action:

> *Opinion:* The lack of affordable day care centers discriminates against lower-income families.

> *Call for action:* The federal government should support the creation of more day care centers in low-income neighborhoods.

In either case, your stand on the issue must be clear to your readers.

2. Provide readers with strong support for the thesis. Finding evidence that relates to the readers' needs, values, and experience is a crucial part of writing an effective argumentation-persuasion essay. Readers will be responsive to evidence that is *unified, adequate,* *specific, accurate,* and *representative* (see pages 39–44). It might consist of personal experiences or observations. Or it could be gathered from outside sources—statistics; facts; examples; or expert authority taken from books, articles, reports, interviews, and documentaries. A paper arguing that elderly Americans are better off than they used to be might incorporate the following kinds of evidence:

- *Personal observation or experience:* A description of the writer's grandparents who are living comfortably on Social Security and pensions.
- *Statistics from a report:* A statement that the per capita after-tax income of older Americans is $335 greater than the national average.
- *Fact from a newspaper article:* The point that the majority of elderly Americans do not live in nursing homes or on the streets; rather, they have their own houses or apartments.
- *Examples from interviews:* Accounts of several elderly couples living comfortably in well-managed retirement villages in Florida.
- *Expert opinion cited in a documentary:* A statement by Dr. Marie Sanchez, a specialist in geriatrics: "An over-sixty-five American today is likely to be healthier, and have a longer life expectancy, than a fifty-year-old living only a decade ago."

As you seek outside evidence, you may—perhaps to your dismay—come across information that undercuts your argument. Resist the temptation to ignore such material; instead, use the evidence to arrive at a more balanced, perhaps somewhat qualified viewpoint. Conversely, don't blindly accept points made by sources agreeing with you. Retain a healthy skepticism, analyzing the material as rigorously as if it were advanced by the opposing side.

Also, keep in mind that outside sources aren't infallible. They may have biases that cause them to skew evidence. So be sure to evaluate your sources. If you're writing an essay supporting a woman's right to abortion, the National Abortion Rights Action League (NARAL) can supply abundant statistics, case studies, and reports. But realize that NARAL most likely won't give you the complete picture; it will probably present evidence that supports its "pro-choice" position only. To counteract such bias, you should review what those with differing opinions have to say. You should, for example, examine material published by such "pro-life" organizations as the National Right-to-Life Committee—keeping in mind, of course, that this material is also bound to present support for its viewpoint only. Remember, too, that there are more than two sides to a complex issue. To get as broad a perspective as possible, you should also track down sources that have no axe to grind—that is, sources that make a deliberate effort to examine all sides of the issue. For example, published proceedings from a debate on abortion or an in-depth article that aims to synthesize various views on abortion would broaden your understanding of this controversial subject.

Whatever sources you use, be sure to *document* (give credit to) that material. Otherwise, readers may dismiss your evidence as nothing more than your subjective opinion, or they may conclude that you have *plagiarized*—tried to pass off someone else's ideas as your own. (Documentation isn't necessary when material is commonly known or is a matter of historical or scientific record.) In brief informal papers, documentation may consist of simple citations like "Psychologist Aaron Beck believes depression is the result of distorted thoughts" or "*Time* (Dec. 4, 2000) reports a decline in the enrollment of male students in colleges across the country." In longer, more formal papers, documentation is more detailed (see the Appendix, "A Concise Guide to Finding and Documenting Sources"). One additional point: Because documentation lends a note of objectivity to writing, it may not be appropriate in a paper that cites sources to use the first-person point of view ("I, like many college students, agree with the government report that . . ."). To be on the safe side, check with your instructor to see if you should use the third-person point of view ("Many college students agree with the government report that . . .") instead.

3. Seek to create goodwill.   To avoid alienating readers with views different from your own, stay away from condescending expressions like "Anyone can see that . . ." or "It's obvious that . . ." Also, guard against personalizing the debate and being confrontational: "*My opponents* find the law ineffective" sounds adversarial, whereas "*Those opposed* to the law find it ineffective" or "*Opponents* of the law find it ineffective" is more evenhanded. The last two statements also focus—as they should—on the issue, not on the people involved in the debate.

Goodwill can also be established by finding a *common ground*—some points on which all sides can agree, despite their differences.

Assume a township council has voted to raise property taxes. The additional revenues will be used to preserve, as parkland, a wooded area that would otherwise be sold to developers. Before introducing its tax-hike proposal, the council would do well to remind home-owners of everyone's shared goals: maintaining the town's beauty and preventing the community's overdevelopment. This reminder of the common values shared by the town council and homeowners will probably make residents more receptive to the tax hike. (For more on establishing common ground, see pages 548–50.)

4. Organize the supporting evidence. The support for an argu-mentation-persuasion paper can be organized in a variety of ways. Any of the patterns of development described in this book (descrip-tion, narration, definition, causal analysis, and so on) may be used—singly or in combination—to develop the essay's proposition. Imagine you're writing a paper arguing that car racing should be banned from television. Your essay might contain a *description* of a horrifying accident that was televised in graphic detail; you might devote part of the paper to a *causal analysis* showing that the broad-cast of such races encourages teens to drive carelessly; you could include a *process analysis* to explain how young drivers "soup up" their cars in a dangerous attempt to imitate the racers seen on tele-vision. If your essay includes several patterns, you may need a sepa-rate paragraph for each.

When presenting evidence, arrange it so you create the strongest possible effect. In general, you should end with your most compelling point, leaving readers with dramatic evidence that underscores your proposition's validity.

5. Use Rogerian strategy to acknowledge differing view-points. If your essay has a clear thesis and strong logical support, you've taken important steps toward winning readers over. However, because argumentation-persuasion focuses on controver-sial issues, you should also consider contrary points of view. A good argument seeks out and acknowledges conflicting viewpoints. Such a strategy strengthens your argument in several ways. It helps you anticipate objections, alerts you to flaws in your own position, and makes you more aware of the other sides' weaknesses. Further, by acknowledging dissenting views, you come across as reasonable and thorough—qualities that may disarm readers and leave them more receptive to your argument. You may not convince them to surrender their views, but you can enlarge their perspectives and encourage them to think about your position.

Psychologist Carl Rogers took the idea of acknowledging contrary viewpoints a step further. He believed that argumentation's goal should be to *reduce conflict,* rather than to produce a "winner" and a "loser." But he recognized that people identify so strongly with their opinions that they experience any challenge to those opinions as highly threatening. Such a challenge feels like an attack on their very identity. And what's the characteristic response to such a perceived attack? People become defensive; they dig in their heels and become more adamant than ever about their position. Indeed, when confronted with solid information that calls their opinion into question, they devalue that evidence rather than allow themselves to be persuaded. The old maxim about the power of first impressions demonstrates this point. Experiments show that after people form a first impression of another person, they are unlikely to let future conflicting information affect that impression. If, for example, they initially perceive someone to be unpleasant and disagreeable, they tend to reject subsequent evidence that casts the person in a more favorable light.

Taking into account this tendency to cling tenaciously to opinions in the face of a challenge, Rogerian strategy rejects the adversarial approach that often characterizes argumentation. It adopts, instead, a respectful, conciliatory posture—one that demonstrates a real understanding of opposing views, one that emphasizes shared interests and values. Such an approach makes it easier to negotiate differences and arrive at—ideally—a synthesis: a new position that both parties find at least as acceptable as their original positions.

How can you apply Rogerian strategy in your writing? Simply follow these steps:

- Begin by making a conscientious effort to *understand* the viewpoints of those with whom you disagree. As you listen to or read about their opinions, try to put yourself in their shoes; focus on *what they believe* and *why they believe* it, rather than on how you will challenge their beliefs.
- Open your essay with an unbiased, even-handed *restatement of opposing points of view.* Such an objective summary shows that you're fair and open-minded—and not so blinded by the righteousness of your own position that you can't consider any other. Typically, people respond to such a respectful

approach by lowering their defenses. Because they appreciate your ability to understand what they have to say, they become more open to your point of view.

- When appropriate, *acknowledge the validity* of some of the arguments raised by those with differing views. What should you do if they make a well-founded point? You'll enhance your credibility if you concede that point while continuing to maintain that, overall, your position is stronger.
- Point out areas of *common ground* (see pages 546–47) by focusing on interests, values, and beliefs that you and those with opposing views share. When you say to them, "Look at the beliefs we share. Look at our common concerns," you communicate that you're not as unlike them as they first believed.
- Finally, *present evidence* for your position. Since those not agreeing with you have been "softened up" by your non-combative stance and disarmed by the realization that you and they share some values and beliefs, they're more ready to consider your point of view.

Let's consider, more specifically, how you might draw upon essentially Rogerian strategy when writing an argumentation-persuasion essay. In the following paragraphs, we discuss three basic strategies. As you read about each strategy, keep in mind this key point: The earlier you acknowledge alternate viewpoints, the more effective your argument will be. Establishing—right at the outset—your awareness of opposing positions shows you to be fair-minded and helps reduce resistance to what you have to say.

First, you may acknowledge the opposing viewpoint in a two-part proposition consisting of a subordinate clause followed by a main clause. The *first part of the proposition* (the subordinate clause) *acknowledges opposing opinions;* the *second part* (the main clause) *states your opinion* and implies that your view stands on more solid ground. (When using this kind of proposition, you may, but don't have to, discuss opposing opinions.) The following thesis illustrates this strategy (the opposing viewpoint is underlined once; the writer's position is underlined twice):

> Although some instructors think that standardized finals restrict academic freedom, such exams are preferable to those prepared by individual professors.

Second, *in the introduction,* you may provide—separate from the proposition—a *one- or two-sentence summary of the opposing viewpoint.* Suppose you're writing an essay advocating a ten-day waiting period before an individual can purchase a handgun. Before presenting your proposition at the end of the introductory paragraph, you might include sentences like these: "Opponents of the waiting period argue that the ten-day delay is worthless without a nationwide computer network that can perform background checks. Those opposed also point out that only a percentage of states with a waiting period have seen a reduction in gun-related crime."

Third, you can take *one or two body paragraphs* near the beginning of the essay to *present in greater detail arguments raised by opposing viewpoints.* After that, you *grant* (when appropriate) the validity of some of those points ("It may be true that . . .," "Granted, . . ."). Then you go on to *present evidence* for your position ("Even so . . .," "Nevertheless . . ."). Imagine you're preparing an editorial for your student newspaper arguing that fraternities and sororities on your campus should be banned. Realizing that many students don't agree with you, you "research" the opposing viewpoint by seeking out supporters of Greek organizations and listening respectfully to the points they raise. When it comes time to write the editorial, you decide not to begin with arguments for your position; instead, you start by summarizing the points made by those supporting fraternities and sororities. You might, for example, mention their argument that Greek organizations build college spirit, contribute to worthy community causes, and provide valuable contacts for entry into the business world. Following this summary of the opposing viewpoint, you might concede that the point about the Greeks' contributions to community causes is especially valid; you could then reinforce this conciliatory stance by stressing some common ground you share—perhaps you acknowledge that you share your detractors' belief that enjoyable social activities with like-minded people are an important part of campus life. Having done all that, you would be in a good position to present arguments why you nevertheless think fraternities and sororities should be banned. Because you prepared readers to listen to your opinion, they would tend to be more receptive to your argument.

6. Refute differing viewpoints.   There will be times, though, that acknowledging opposing viewpoints and presenting your own case won't be enough. Particularly when an issue is complex and when readers strongly disagree with your position, you may have to refute all or part of the *dissenting views*. *Refutation* means pointing out the problems with opposing viewpoints, thereby highlighting your own position's superiority. You may focus on the opposing sides' inaccurate or inadequate evidence, or you may point to their faulty logic. (Some common types of illogical thinking are discussed on pages 553, 555–56, and 559–62.)

Let's consider how you could refute a competing position in an essay you're writing that supports sex education in public schools. Adapting the Rogerian approach to suit your purposes, you might start by acknowledging the opposing viewpoint's key argument: "Sex education should be the prerogative of parents." After granting the validity of this view in an ideal world, you might show that many parents don't provide such education. You could present statistics on the number of parents who avoid discussing sex with their children because the subject makes them uncomfortable; you could cite studies revealing that children in single-parent homes are apt to receive even less parental guidance about sex; and you could give examples of young people whose parents provided sketchy, even misleading information.

There are various ways to develop a paper's refutation section. The best method to use depends on the paper's length and the complexity of the issue. Two possible sequences are outlined here:

First Strategy	**Second Strategy**
• State your proposition.	• State your proposition.
• Cite opposing viewpoints and the evidence for those views.	• Cite opposing viewpoints and the evidence for those views.
• Refute opposing viewpoints by presenting counterarguments.	• Refute opposing viewpoints by presenting counterarguments.
	• Present additional evidence for your proposition.

In the first strategy, you simply refute all or part of the opposing positions' arguments. The second strategy takes the first one a step further by presenting *additional evidence* to support your proposition. In such a case, the additional evidence *must be different* from the points made in the refutation. The additional evidence may appear at the essay's end (as in the preceding outline), or it may be given near the beginning (after the proposition); it may also be divided between the beginning and end.

No matter which strategy you select, you may refute opposing views *one side at a time* or *one point at a time*. When using the one-side-at-a-time approach, you cite all the points raised by the opposing side and then present your counterargument to each point. When using the one-point-at-a-time strategy, you mention the first point made by the opposing side, refute that point, then move on to the second point and refute that, and so on. (For more on comparing and contrasting the sides of an issue, see pages 392–97.)

Throughout the essay, be sure to provide clear signals so that readers can distinguish your arguments from the other sides': "Despite the claims of those opposed to the plan, many think that . . ." and "Those not in agreement think that . . ."

7. Use induction or deduction to think logically about your argument. The line of reasoning used to develop an argument is the surest indicator of how rigorously you have thought through your position. There are two basic ways to think about a subject: *inductively* and *deductively*. Though the following discussion treats induction and deduction as separate processes, the two often overlap and complement each other.

Inductive reasoning involves examination of specific cases, facts, or examples. Based on these specifics, you then draw a conclusion or make a generalization. This is the kind of thinking scientists use when they examine evidence (the results of experiments, for example) and then draw a *conclusion:* "Smoking increases the risk of cancer." All of us use inductive reasoning in everyday life. We might think the following: "My head is aching" (evidence); "My nose is stuffy" (evidence); "I'm coming down with a cold" (conclusion). Based on the conclusion, we might go a step further and take some action: "I'll take an aspirin."

With inductive reasoning, the conclusion reached can serve as the proposition for an argumentation essay. (Of course, the essay will most likely include elements of persuasion since strict argumentation—with no appeal to emotions—is uncommon.) If the paper advances a course of action, the proposition often mentions the action, signaling an essay with a distinctly persuasive purpose.

Let's suppose that you're writing a paper about a crime wave in the small town where you live. You might use inductive thinking to structure the essay's argument:

> Several people were mugged last month while shopping in
> the center of town. (*evidence*)

Several homes and apartments were burglarized in the past few weeks. (*evidence*)

Several cars were stolen from people's driveways over the weekend. (*evidence*)

The police force hasn't adequately protected town residents. (*conclusion, or proposition, for an argumentation essay with probable elements of persuasion*)

The police force should take steps to upgrade its protection of town residents. (*conclusion, or proposition, for an argumentation essay with a clearly persuasive intent*)

This inductive sequence highlights a possible structure for the essay. After providing a clear statement of your proposition, you might detail recent muggings, burglaries, and car thefts. Then you could move to the opposing viewpoint: a description of the steps the police say they have taken to protect town residents. At that point, you would refute the police's claim, citing additional evidence that shows the measures taken have not been sufficient. Finally, if you wanted your essay to have a decidedly persuasive purpose, you could end by recommending specific action the police should take to improve its protection of the community.

As in all essays, your evidence should be *specific, unified, sufficient,* and *representative* (see pages 39–44). These last two characteristics are critical when you think inductively; they guarantee that your conclusion would be equally valid even if other evidence were presented. Insufficient or atypical evidence often leads to *hasty generalizations* that mar the essay's logic. For example, you might think the following: "Some elderly people are very wealthy and do not need Social Security checks" (evidence), and "Some Social Security recipients illegally collect several checks" (evidence). If you then conclude, "Social Security is a waste of taxpayers' money," your conclusion is invalid and hasty because it's based on only a few atypical examples. Millions of Social Security recipients aren't wealthy and don't abuse the system. If you've failed to consider the full range of evidence, any action you propose ("The Social Security system should be disbanded") will probably be considered suspect by thoughtful readers. It's possible, of course, that Social Security should be disbanded, but the evidence leading to such a conclusion must be sufficient and representative.

When reasoning inductively, you should also be careful that the evidence you collect is both *recent* and *accurate*. No valid conclusion can result from dated or erroneous evidence. To ensure that your evidence is sound, you also need to evaluate the reliability of your sources. When a person who is legally drunk claims to have seen a flying saucer, the evidence is shaky, to say the least. But if two respected scientists, both with 20–20 vision, saw the saucer, their evidence is worth considering.

Finally, it's important to realize that there's always an element of uncertainty in inductive reasoning. The conclusion can never be more than an *inference*, involving what logicians call an *inductive leap*. There could be other explanations for the evidence cited and thus other positions to take and actions to advocate. For example, given a small town's crime wave, you might conclude not that the police force has been remiss but that residents are careless about protecting themselves and their property. In turn, you might call for a different kind of action—perhaps that the police conduct public workshops in self-defense and home security. In an inductive argument, your task is to weigh the evidence, consider alternative explanations, then choose the conclusion and course of action that seem most valid.

Unlike inductive reasoning, which starts with a specific case and moves toward a generalization or conclusion, *deductive reasoning* begins with a generalization that is then applied to a specific case. This movement from general to specific involves a three-step form of reasoning called a *syllogism*. The first part of a syllogism is called the *major premise*, a general statement about an entire group. The second part is the *minor premise*, a statement about an individual within that group. The syllogism ends with a *conclusion* about that individual.

Just as you use inductive thinking in everyday life, you use deductive thinking—often without being aware of it—to sort out your experiences. When trying to decide which car to buy, you might think as follows:

Major premise: In an accident, large cars are safer than small cars.

Minor premise: The Turbo Titan is a large car.

Conclusion: In an accident, the Turbo Titan will be safer than a small car.

Based on your conclusion, you might decide to take a specific action, buying the Turbo Titan rather than the smaller car you had first considered.

To create a valid syllogism and thus arrive at a sound conclusion, you need to avoid two major pitfalls of deductive reasoning. First, be sure not to start with a *hasty generalization* (see page 553) as your *major premise*. Second, don't accept as truth a *faulty conclusion.* Let's look at each problem.

Sweeping major premise.   Perhaps you're concerned about a trash-to-steam incinerator scheduled to open near your home. Your thinking about the situation might follow these lines:

Major premise: Trash-to-steam incinerators have had serious problems and pose significant threats to the well-being of people living near the plants.

Minor premise: The proposed incinerator in my neighborhood will be a trash-to-steam plant.

Conclusion: The proposed trash-to-steam incinerator in my neighborhood will have serious problems and pose significant threats to the well-being of people living near the plant.

Having arrived at this conclusion, you might decide to join organized protests against the opening of the incinerator. But your thinking is somewhat illogical. Your *major premise* is a *sweeping* one because it indiscriminately groups all trash-to-steam plants into a single category. It's unlikely that you're familiar with the operations of all trash-to-steam incinerators in this country and abroad; it's probably not true that *all* such plants have had serious difficulties that endangered the public. For your argument to reach a valid conclusion, the major premise must be based on repeated observations or verifiable facts. You would have a better argument, and thus reach a more valid conclusion, if you restricted or qualified the major premise, applying it to some, not all, of the group:

Major premise: A number of trash-to-steam incinerators have had serious problems and posed significant threats to the well-being of people living near the plants.

Minor premise: The proposed incinerator in my neighborhood will be a trash-to-steam plant.

Conclusion: It's possible that the proposed trash-to-steam incinerator in my neighborhood will run into serious problems and pose significant threats to the well-being of people living near the plant.

This new conclusion, the result of more careful reasoning, would probably encourage you to learn more about trash-to-steam incinerators in general and about the proposed plant in particular. If further research still left you feeling uncomfortable about the plant, you would probably decide to join the protest. On the other hand, your research might convince you that the plant has incorporated into its design a number of safeguards that have been successful at other plants. This added information could reassure you that your original fears were unfounded. In either case, the revised deductive process would lead to a more informed conclusion and course of action.

Faulty conclusion. Your syllogism—and thus your reasoning—would also be invalid if your *conclusion reverses the "if . . . then" relationship implied in the major premise.* Assume you plan to write a letter to the college newspaper urging the resignation of the student government president. Perhaps you pursue a line of reasoning that goes like this:

> *Major premise:* Students who plagiarize papers must appear before the Faculty Committee on Academic Policies and Procedures.
>
> *Minor premise:* Yesterday, Jennifer Kramer, president of the student government, appeared before the Faculty Committee on Academic Policies and Procedures.
>
> *Conclusion:* Jennifer must have plagiarized a paper.
>
> *Action:* Jennifer should resign her position as president of the student government.

Such a chain of reasoning is illogical and unfair. Here's why. *If* students plagiarize their papers and are caught, *then* they must appear before the committee. However, the converse isn't necessarily true—that *if* students appear before the committee, *then* they must have plagiarized. In other words, not *all* students appearing before the committee have been called up on plagiarism charges. For example, Jennifer could have been speaking on behalf of another student; she could have been protesting some action taken by the committee; she could have been seeking the committee's help on an article she plans to write about academic honesty. The conclusion doesn't allow for these other possible explanations.

Now that you're aware of potential problems associated with deductive reasoning, let's look at the way you can use a syllogism to structure an argumentation-persuasion essay. Suppose you decide to write a paper advocating support for a projected space mission. You know that controversy surrounds the space program, especially since seven astronauts died in a 1986 launch. Confident that the tragedy has led to more rigorous controls, you want to argue that the benefits of an upcoming mission outweigh its risks. A deductive pattern could be used to develop your argument. In fact, outlining your thinking as a syllogism might help you formulate a proposition, organize your evidence, deal with opposing viewpoints, and—if appropriate—propose a course of action:

Major premise:	Space programs in the past have led to important developments in technology, especially in medical science.
Minor premise:	The Cosmos Mission is the newest space program.
Proposition (essay might be persuasive):	The Cosmos Mission will most likely lead to important developments in technology, especially in medical science.
Proposition (essay clearly is persuasive):	Congress should continue its funding of the Cosmos Mission.

Having outlined the deductive pattern of your thinking, you might begin by stating your proposition and then discuss some new procedures developed to protect the astronauts and the rocket system's structural integrity. With that background established, you could detail the opposing claim that little of value has been produced by the space program so far. You could then move to your refutation, citing significant medical advances derived from former space missions. Finally, the paper might conclude on a persuasive note, with a plea to Congress to continue funding the latest space mission.

8. Use Toulmin logic to establish a strong connection between your evidence and your thesis.   Whether you use an essentially inductive or deductive approach, your argument depends on strong evidence. In *The Uses of Argument*, Stephen Toulmin describes a useful approach for strengthening the connection between evidence and thesis. Toulmin divides a typical argument into three parts:

- **Claim**—The thesis, proposition, or conclusion.
- **Data**—The evidence (facts, statistics, examples, observations, expert opinion) used to convince readers of the claim's validity.
- **Warrant**—The underlying assumption that justifies moving from evidence to claim.

| The train engineer was under the influence of drugs when the train crashed.

(Data) | Transportation employees entrusted with the public's safety should be tested for drug use.

(Claim) |

Transportation employees entrusted with
the public's safety should not be allowed
on the job if they use drugs.
(Warrant)

As Toulmin explains in his book, readers are more apt to consider your argument valid if they know what your warrant is. Sometimes your warrant will be so obvious that you won't need to state it explicitly; an *implicit warrant* will be sufficient. Assume you want to argue that the use of live animals to test product toxicity should be outlawed. To support your claim, you cite the following evidence: first, current animal tests are painful and usually result in the animal's death; second, human cell cultures frequently offer more reliable information on how harmful a product may be to human tissue; and third, computer simulations often can more accurately rate a substance's toxicity. Your warrant, although not explicit, is nonetheless clear: "It is wrong to continue product testing on animals when more humane and valid test methods are available."

Other times, you'll do best to make your warrant *explicit*. Suppose you plan to argue that students should be involved in deciding which faculty members are granted tenure. To develop your claim, you present some evidence. You begin by noting that, currently, only faculty members and administrators review candidates for tenure. Next, you call attention to the controversy surrounding two professors, widely known by students to be poor teachers, who were nonetheless granted tenure. Finally, you cite a decision, made several years ago, to discontinue using student evaluations as part of the tenure process; you emphasize that since that time complaints about teachers' incompetence have risen dramatically. Some readers, though, still might wonder how you got from your evidence to your claim. In this case, your argument could be made stronger by stating your warrant explicitly: "Since students are as knowledgeable as the faculty and administrators about which professors are competent, they should be involved in the tenure process."

The more widely accepted your warrant, Toulmin explains, the more likely it is that readers will accept your argument. If there's no consensus about the warrant, you'll probably need to *back it up*. For the preceding example, you might mention several reports that found students evaluate faculty fairly (most students don't, for example, use the ratings to get back at professors against whom they have a personal grudge); further, students' ratings correlate strongly with those given by administrators and other faculty.

Toulmin describes another way to increase receptivity to an argument: *qualify the claim*—that is, explain under what circumstances it might be invalid or restricted. For instance, you might grant that most students know little about their instructors' research activities, scholarly publications, or participation in professional committees. You could, then, qualify your claim this way: "Because students don't have a comprehensive view of their instructors' professional activities, they should be involved in the tenure process but play a less prominent role than faculty and administrators."

As you can see, Toulmin's approach provides strategies for strengthening an argument. So, when prewriting or revising, take a few minutes to ask yourself the following questions:

- What data (*evidence*) should I provide to support my claim (*thesis*)?
- Is my warrant clear? Should I state it explicitly? What backup can I provide to justify my warrant?
- Would qualifying my claim make my argument more convincing?

Your responses to these questions will help you structure a convincing and logical argument.

9. Recognize logical fallacies.   When writing an argumentation-persuasion essay, you need to recognize *logical fallacies* both in your own argument and in points raised by opposing sides. Work to eliminate such gaps in logic from your own writing and, when they appear in opposing arguments, try to expose them in your refutation. Logicians have identified many logical fallacies—including the sweeping or hasty generalization and the faulty conclusion discussed on pages 553 and 556. Other logical fallacies are described in Ann McClintock's "Propaganda Techniques in Today's Advertising" (page 304) and in the paragraphs that follow.

The *post hoc fallacy* (short for a Latin phrase meaning "after this, therefore because of this") occurs when you conclude that a cause-effect relationship exists simply because one event preceded another. Let's say you note the growing number of immigrants settling in a nearby city, observe the city's economic decline, and conclude that the immigrants' arrival caused the decline. Such a chain of thinking is faulty because it assumes a cause-effect relationship based purely on co-occurrence. Perhaps the immigrants' arrival was a factor in the economic slump, but there could also be other reasons: the lack of financial incentives to attract business to the city, restrictions on the size of the city's manufacturing facilities, citywide labor disputes that make companies leery of settling in the area. Your argument should also consider these possibilities. (For more on the *post hoc* fallacy, see page 443.)

The *non sequitur fallacy* (Latin for "it does not follow") is an even more blatant muddying of cause-effect relationships. In this case, a conclusion is drawn that has no logical connection to the evidence cited: "Millions of Americans own cars, so there is no need to fund public transportation." The faulty conclusion disregards the millions of Americans who don't own cars; it also ignores pollution and road congestion, both of which could be reduced if people had access to safe, reliable public transportation.

An *ad hominem argument* (from the Latin meaning "to the man") occurs when someone attacks a person rather than a point of view. Suppose your college plans to sponsor a physicians' symposium on the abortion controversy. You decide to write a letter to the school paper opposing the symposium. Taking swipes at two of the invited doctors who disapprove of abortion, you mention that one was recently involved in a messy divorce and that the other is alleged to have a drinking problem. By hurling personal invective, you avoid discussing the issue. Mudslinging is a poor substitute for reasoned argument.

Appeals to questionable or faulty authority also weaken an argument. Most of us have developed a healthy suspicion of phrases like *sources close to, an unidentified spokesperson states, experts claim,* and *studies show.* If these people and reports are so reliable, they should be clearly identified.

Begging the question involves failure to establish proof for a debatable point. The writer expects readers to accept as given a premise that's actually controversial. For instance, you would have trouble convincing readers that prayer should be banned from public schools if you based your argument on the premise that school prayer violates the U.S. Constitution. If the Constitution does, either explicitly or implicitly, prohibit prayer in public education, your essay must demonstrate that fact. You can't build a strong argument if you pretend there's no controversy surrounding your premise.

A *false analogy* wrongly implies that because two things share *some* characteristics, they are therefore *alike in all respects.* You might, for example, compare nicotine and marijuana. Both, you could mention, involve health risks and have addictive properties. If, however, you go on to conclude, "Driving while smoking a cigarette isn't illegal, so driving while smoking marijuana shouldn't be illegal either," you're employing a false analogy. You've overlooked a major difference between tobacco and marijuana: Marijuana impairs perception and coordination—important aspects of driving—while there's no evidence that tobacco does the same.

The *either-or fallacy* occurs when you assume that a particular viewpoint or course of action can have only one of two diametrically opposed outcomes—either totally this or totally that. Say you argue as follows: "Unless colleges continue to offer scholarships based solely on financial need, no one who is underprivileged will be able to attend college." Such a statement ignores the fact that bright, underprivileged students could receive scholarships based on their potential or their demonstrated academic excellence.

Finally, a *red herring argument* is an intentional digression from the issue—a ploy to deflect attention from the matter being discussed. Imagine that you're arguing that condoms shouldn't be dispensed to high school students. You would introduce a red herring if you began to rail against parents who fail to provide their children with any information about sex. Most people would agree that parents *should* provide such information. However, the issue being discussed is not parents' irresponsibility but the pros and cons of schools' distributing condoms to students.

STUDENT ESSAY

The following student essay was written by Mark Simmons in response to this assignment:

> Mary Sherry's "In Praise of the 'F' Word" invites contro-versy by attacking the popular notion that failing students is a harmful practice. Select another controversial issue, one that you feel strongly about. Conduct library research to gather evidence in support of your position, and brain-storm with others to identify some points that might be raised by those who oppose your view. Then, using logic and formal, documented evidence, convince readers that your viewpoint is valid.

Your instructor may not ask you to include research in your essay. But, if you're asked—as Mark was—to research your paper and to provide *formal documentation,* you'll want to pay special attention to the way Mark credits his sources. (In *your* paper, the Works Cited list should be double-spaced—along with the rest of the paper—and placed at the end on a separate page.) You'll also find it helpful to refer to the Appendix, "A Concise Guide to Finding and Documenting Sources" (page 691). If your instructor wants you to research your paper but will accept *informal docu-mentation,* the material on page 546 should come in handy.

Whether or not you include research in your paper, the annota-tions on Mark's essay and the comments following it will help you determine how well it applies the principles of argumentation-persuasion.

Compulsory National Service
by Mark Simmons

Beginning of two-paragraph introduction	Our high school history class spent several weeks studying the events of the 1960s. The most interesting thing about that decade was the spirit of service and social commitment among young peo-ple. In the '60s, young people thought about issues

1

beyond themselves; they joined the Peace Corps, worked in poverty-stricken Appalachian communities, and participated in freedom marches against segregation. Most young people today, despite their concern with careers and getting ahead, would also like an opportunity to make a worthwhile contribution to society.

Common knowledge: No need to document

Convinced that many young adults are indeed 2
eager for such an opportunity, President Clinton's administration implemented in 1994 a pilot program of voluntary national service. The following year, the program was formalized, placed under the management of the Corporation for National Service (CNS), and given the name AmeriCorps. In the years

Parenthetic citation of unpaged anonymous material obtained through the Internet

1994–2000, approximately 175,000 AmeriCorps volunteers provided varied assistance in communities across the country ("President Releases"). The program holds out so much promise that it seems only natural to go one step further and make young people's participation in this or some kind of national

Start of two-sentence thesis

service mandatory. By instituting a program of compulsory national service, the country could tap youth's idealistic desire to make a difference. Such a system would yield significant benefits.

Definition paragraph

What exactly is meant by compulsory national 3
service? Traditionally, it has tended to mean that everyone between the ages of seventeen and twenty-five would serve the country for two years. These young people could choose between two major options: military service or a public-service corps. They could serve their time at any point within an eight-year span. The unemployed or the uncertain could join immediately after high school; college-bound students could complete their education before joining the national service. Years ago, Senator Sam Nunn and Representative Dave McCurdy gave a new twist to the definition of com-

Beginning of summary of a source's ideas

pulsory national service. They proposed a plan that would require all high school graduates applying for federal aid for college tuition to serve either in the military or in a Citizens Corps. Anyone in the Citizens Corps would be required to work full-time at public-service duties for one or two years. During that time, participants would receive a weekly

<table>
<tr><td>

Parenthetic
citation—page
number *and*
author are given
since the author
is not cited earlier
in the sentence

</td><td>

stipend, and, at the end, be given a voucher worth
$10,000 for each year of civilian service. The vouch-
er could then be applied toward college credit,
employment training, or a down payment on a
house (Sudo 9).

</td></tr>
</table>

The traditional plan for compulsory national
service and the one proposed by Nunn and
McCurdy are just two of many variations that have
been discussed over the years. While this country
debates the concept, some nations such as France
have gone ahead and accepted it enthusiastically.
The idea could be workable in this country too.
Topic sentence ⟶ Unfortunately, opponents are doing all they can to
prevent the idea from taking hold. They contend,
Beginning of ⟶ first of all, that the program would cost too much. A
summary of three great deal of money, they argue, would be spent
points made by administering the program, paying young people's
the opposing wages, and providing housing for participants.
viewpoint Another argument against compulsory national
service is that it would demoralize young people;
supposedly, the plan would prevent the young from
moving ahead with their careers and would make
them feel as though they were engaged in work that
offered no personal satisfaction. A third argument is
that compulsory service would lay the groundwork
for a dictatorship. The picture is painted of an army
of young people, controlled by the government,
much like the Hitler Youth of the Second World War.
Topic sentence: ⟶ Despite opponents' claims that compulsory
Refutation of national service would involve exorbitant costs, the
first point program would not have to be that expensive to run.
AmeriCorps has already provided an excellent
model for achieving substantial benefits at reasonable cost. For example, a study conducted by universities in Iowa and Michigan showed that each
dollar spent on AmeriCorps programs yielded $2.60
in reduced welfare costs, increased earnings, and
other benefits (Garland 120). Also, the sums
required for wages and housing could be reduced
considerably through payments made by the towns,
cities, and states using the corps' services. And the
economic benefits of the program could be significant. AmeriCorps's official website gives an idea of
the current scope of the program's activities.

Information comes from two sources. Sources, separated by a semicolon, are given in the order they appear in the Works Cited list. First source is unpaged electronic text. No page given for second source because it runs only one page.

Topic sentence: Refutation of second point

Attribution giving author's full name and area of expertise

Full-sentence quotation is preceded by a comma and begins with a capital letter

Where secondary source was quoted

Quotation is blended into the sentence (no comma and the quotation begins with a lowercased word)

Quotation with ellipsis

Just the page number is provided because the author's name is cited in the preceding attribution

Volunteers provide crucial services including building affordable homes for families, reducing crime in neighborhoods, responding to natural disasters, and tutoring children ("AmeriCorps"). A compulsory national corps could also clean up litter, provide day care services, staff libraries, immunize children, and care for the country's growing elderly population (Clinton; Eng). All these projects would help solve many of the problems that plague our nation, and they would probably cost less than if they were handled by often inefficient government bureaucracies. It's important to note, then, that AmeriCorps isn't administered by a complex, multi-tiered federal agency; rather it is run by the streamlined nonprofit CNS, whose efficiency and cost-control measures have been recognized by many major corporations (Garland 120).

Also, rather than undermining the spirit of young people, as opponents contend, the program would probably boost their morale. Many young people feel enormous pressure and uncertainty; they are not sure whether they want to find a job or further their education. Compulsory national service could give these young people much-needed breathing space. As Edward Lewis, president of St. Mary's College, says, "Many students are not ready for college at seventeen or eighteen. This kind of program responds to that need" (qtd. in Fowler 3). Richard Coles, psychiatrist and social activist, argues that a public service stint enriches participants' lives in yet another way. Coles points out that young people often have little sense of the job market. When they get involved in community service, though, they frequently "discover an area of interest . . . that launches them on a career" (93). Equally important, compulsory national service can provide an emotional boost for the young; all of them would experience the pride that comes from working hard, reaching goals, acquiring skills, and handling responsibilities (Waldman and Wofford). A positive mind-set would also result from the sense of community that would be created by serving in the national service. All young people--rich or poor, educated or not, regardless of sex and social class--would come together and perceive not their

6

Parenthetic citation for electronic source having two authors. No page given since electronic text is unpaged.

differences but their common interests and similarities (Waldman and Wofford). As President Clinton proclaimed at the Year 2000 swearing-in of AmeriCorps's recruits in Philadelphia, AmeriCorps gives volunteers a chance "to tear down barriers of distrust and misunderstanding and old-fashioned ignorance, and build a genuine American community" (Clinton).

Topic sentence: Refutation of third point

Finally, in contrast to what opponents claim, compulsory national service would not signal the start of a dictatorship. Although the service would be required, young people would have complete freedom to choose any two years between the ages of seventeen and twenty-five. They would also have complete freedom to choose the branch of the military or public service corps that suits them best. And the corps would not need to be outfitted in military uniforms or to live in barrack-like camps. It could be set up like a regular job, with young people living at home as much as possible, following a nine-to-five schedule, enjoying all the personal freedoms that would ordinarily be theirs. Also, a dictatorship would no more likely emerge from compulsory national service than it has from our present military system. We would still have a series of checks and balances to prohibit the taking of power by one group or individual. We should also keep in mind that our system is different from that of fascist regimes; our long tradition of personal liberty makes improbable the seizing of absolute power by one person or faction. A related but even more important point to remember is that freedom does not mean people are guaranteed the right to pursue only their individual needs. That is mistaking selfishness for freedom. And, as everyone knows, selfishness leads only to misery. The national service would not take away freedom. On the contrary, serving in the corps would help young people grasp this larger concept of freedom, a concept that is badly needed to counteract the deadly "look out for number one" attitude that is spreading like a poison across the nation.

7

Beginning of two-paragraph conclusion

Perhaps there will never be a time like the 1960s when so many young people were concerned with remaking the world. Still, a good many of

8

today's young people want meaningful work. They want to feel that what they do makes a difference. A program of compulsory national service would harness this idealism and help young people realize the best in themselves. Such a program would also help resolve some of the country's most critical social problems.

When President Bush was in office, political **9** commentator Donald Eberly expressed his belief in the power of national service. Urging the inauguration of such a program, Eberly wrote the following:

> The promise of national service can be manifested in many ways: in cleaner air and fewer forest fires, in well-cared-for infants and old folks; in a better-educated citizenry and better-satisfied work force; perhaps in a more peaceful world. National service has a lot of promise. It's a promise well worth keeping. (651)

Several years later, President Clinton took office, gave his support to the concept, and AmeriCorps was born. Although there was pressure to reduce AmeriCorps's funding, such efforts were motivated by a political agenda intent on undercutting the accomplishments of the Clinton administration (Molyneux 39). Indeed, even among conservative Republicans today, there is growing support for AmeriCorps; in September 2000, forty-nine of fifty U.S. governors sponsored a bipartisan letter urging Congress to extend national service ("49 Governors"). An efficient and successful program of voluntary service, AmeriCorps has paved the way. Now seems to be the perfect time to expand the concept and make compulsory national service a reality.

Works Cited

"AmeriCorps: Who We Are." AmeriCorps. The Corporation for National Service. May 2000: 5 pars. 26 Jan. 2001 <http://www.americorps.org/whoweare.html>.

Margin notes:

Attribution leading to a long quotation. Attribution is followed by a colon since the lead-in is a full sentence. If the lead-in isn't a full sentence, use a comma after the attribution.

Long quotation is indented ten spaces. Don't leave any extra space within, above, or below the quotation.

For an indented quotation, the period is placed *before* the parenthetic citation.

In *your* paper, the Works Cited list would be double-spaced like the rest of the paper, with no extra space after the heading or between entries. Also, in *your* paper, the Works Cited would start on a *separate* page.

Anonymous material obtained on the Internet. Names of website and of sponsoring organization appear. Electronic text is 5 paragraphs long. Web address always required.

Authored ————▸ Clinton, William. "Remarks by the President to
material on the   AmeriCorps." AmeriCorps. The Corporation
Internet. Dates   for National Service. 11 Oct. 2000: 28 pars. 7
the material was   Jan. 2001 <http://www.americorps.org/news/
published and
accessed both   pr/potus_remarks101100.html>.
provided.

Book by one ┘————▸ Coles, Robert. The Call of Service. Boston: Houghton
author   Mifflin, 1993.

Published ┘————▸ Eberly, Donald. "What the President Should Do About
speech   National Service." Vital Speeches of the Day 15
                           Aug. 1989: 561–63.

Newspaper ————▸ Eng, Lily. "Congressional Pressure Puts AmeriCorps
article whose text   Under the Gun." Philadelphia Inquirer 18 Apr.
is only one page   1996, late ed.: B1.

Internet ————————▸ "49 Governors Urge Congress to Extend National
article with   Service." National Service Newsletter. Office
unnumbered   of the Governor of the State of Montana. 20
paragraphs or   Sept. 2000. 26 Jan. 2001 <http://
pages   www.nationalservice.org/news/pr/
                           92000.html>.

                    Fowler, Margaret. "New Interest in National Youth
                           Corps." New York Times 16 May 1989, natl.
                           ed.: A25.

Article from ————▸ Garland, Susan B. "A Social Program CEOs Want to
weekly magazine   Save." Business Week 19 June 1996: 120–21.

                    Molyneux, Guy. "When Success Fails." Rolling Stone
                           4 May 1995: 38–39.

                    "President Releases Study on Success of
                           AmeriCorps Tutoring." AmeriCorps. The
                           Corporation for National Service. 11 Oct. 2000:
                           6 pars. 7 Jan. 2001 <http://
                           www.americorps.org/news/pr/101100.html>.

                    Sudo, Phil. "Mandatory National Service?" Scholastic
                           Update 23 Feb 1990: 9.

Article (by ————▸ Waldman, Steven, and Harris Wofford. "AmeriCorps
two authors)   the Beautiful? Habitat for Conservative Values."
from scholarly   Policy Review Sept.–Oct. 1997: 49 pars.
journal on CD-
ROM   CD-ROM. EBSCOhost.

COMMENTARY

Blend of argumentation and persuasion.   In his essay, Mark tackles a controversial issue. He takes the position that compulsory national service would benefit both the country as a whole and its young people in particular. Mark's essay is a good example of the way argumentation and persuasion often mix: Although the paper presents Mark's position in a logical, well-reasoned manner (argumentation), it also appeals to readers' personal values and suggests a course of action (persuasion).

Audience analysis.   When planning the essay, Mark realized that his audience—his composition class—would consist largely of two kinds of readers. Some, not sure of their views, would be inclined to agree with him if he presented his case well. Others would probably be reluctant to accept his view. Because of this mixed audience, Mark knew he couldn't depend on *pathos* (an appeal to emotion) to convince readers. Rather, his argument had to rely mainly on *logos* (reason) and *ethos* (credibility). So Mark organized his essay around a series of logical arguments—many of them backed by expert opinion—and he evoked his own authority by drawing on his knowledge of history and his "inside" knowledge of young people.

Introduction and thesis.   Mark introduces his subject by discussing an earlier decade when large numbers of young people worked for social change. Mark's references to the Peace Corps, community work, and freedom marches reinforce his image as a knowledgeable source and establish a context for his position. These historical references, combined with the comments about AmeriCorps, the program of voluntary national service, lead into the two-sentence thesis at the end of the two-paragraph introduction: "By instituting a program of compulsory national service, the country could tap youth's idealistic desire to make a difference. Such a system would yield significant benefits."

The second paragraph in the introduction also illustrates Mark's first use of outside sources. Because the assignment called for research in support of an argument, Mark went to the library and identified sources that helped him defend his position. If Mark's instructor had required extensive investigation of an issue, Mark would have been obligated both to dig more deeply into his subject and to use more scholarly and specialized sources. But given the instructor's requirements, Mark proceeded just as he should have: He searched out expert opinion that supported his viewpoint; he presented that evidence clearly; he documented his sources carefully.

Background paragraph and use of outside sources.   The third paragraph provides a working *definition* of compulsory national service by presenting two common interpretations of the concept. Such background information guarantees that Mark's readers will share his understanding of the essay's central concept.

Acknowledging the opposing viewpoint.   Having explained the meaning of compulsory national service, Mark is now in a good position to launch his argument. Even though he wasn't required to research the opposing viewpoint, Mark wisely decided to get together with some friends to brainstorm some issues that might be raised by the dissenting view. He acknowledges this position in the *topic sentence* of the essay's fourth paragraph: "Unfortunately, opponents are doing all they can to prevent the idea from taking hold." Next he summarizes the main points the dissenting opinion might advance: compulsory national service would be expensive, demoralizing to young people, and dangerously authoritarian. Mark uses the rest of the essay to counter these criticisms.

Refutation.   The next three paragraphs (5–7) *refute* the opposing stance and present Mark's evidence for his position. Mark structures the essay so that readers can follow his *counterargument* with ease. Each paragraph argues against one opposing point and begins with a *topic sentence* that serves as Mark's response to the dissenting view. Note the way the italicized portion of each topic sentence recalls a dissenting point cited earlier: "Despite opponents' claims that *compulsory national service would involve exorbitant costs,* the program would not have to be that expensive to run" (paragraph 5); "Also, rather than *undermining the spirit of young people,* as opponents contend, the program would probably boost their morale" (6); "Finally, in contrast to what opponents claim, *compulsory national service would not signal the start of a dictatorship"* (7). Mark also guides the reader through the various points in the refutation by using *transitions* within paragraphs: "*And* the economic benefits . . . could be significant" (5); "*Equally important,* compulsory national service could provide an emotional boost . . ." (6); "*Also,* a dictatorship would no more likely emerge . . ." (7).

Throughout the three-paragraph refutation, Mark uses outside sources to lend power to his argument. If the assignment had called for in-depth research, he would have cited facts, statistics, and case studies to develop this section of his essay. Given the nature of the assignment, though, Mark's reliance on expert opinion is perfectly acceptable.

Mark successfully incorporates material from these outside sources into his refutation. He doesn't, for example, string one quotation numbingly after another; instead he usually develops his refutation by *summarizing* expert opinion and saves *direct quotations* for points that deserve emphasis. Moreover, whenever Mark quotes or summarizes a source, he provides clear signals to indicate that the material is indeed borrowed. (If you'd like some suggestions for citing outside sources in an essay of your own, see pages 558 and 706–711.)

Some problems with the refutation.   Overall, Mark's three-paragraph refutation is strong, but it would have been even more effective if the paragraphs had been resequenced. As it now stands, the last paragraph in the refutation (7) seems anticlimactic. Unlike the preceding two paragraphs, which are developed through fairly extensive reference to outside sources, paragraph 7 depends entirely on Mark's personal feelings and interpretations for its support. Of course, Mark was under no obligation to provide research in all sections of the paper. Even so, the refutation would have been more persuasive if Mark had placed the final paragraph in the refutation in a less emphatic position. He could, for example, have put it first or second in the sequence, saving for last either of the other two more convincing paragraphs.

You may also have felt that there's another problem with the third paragraph in the refutation. Here, Mark seems to lose control of his counterargument. Beginning with "And, as everyone knows . . .", Mark falls into the *logical fallacy* called *begging the question.* He shouldn't assume that everyone agrees that a selfish life inevitably brings misery. He also indulges in charged emotionalism when he refers—somewhat melodramatically—to the "deadly 'look out for number one' attitude that is spreading like a poison across the nation."

Inductive reasoning.   In part, Mark arrived at his position *inductively,* through a series of *inferences* or *inductive leaps.* He started with some personal *observations* about the nation and its young peo-ple. Then, to support those observations, he added his friends' insights as well as information gathered through research. Combined, all this material led him to the general *conclusion* that compulsory national service would be both workable and beneficial.

Other patterns of development.   To develop his argument, Mark draws on several patterns of development. The third paragraph relies on *definition* to clarify what is meant by compulsory national serv-ice. The first paragraph of both the introduction and conclusion *compares* and *contrasts* young people of the 1960s with those of today. And, to support his position, Mark uses a kind of *causal analysis;* he both speculates on the likely consequences of compul-sory national service and cites expert opinion to illustrate the valid-ity of some of those speculations.

Conclusion.   Despite some problems in the final section of his refutation, Mark comes up with an effective two-paragraph conclu-sion for his essay. In the first closing paragraph, he echoes the point made in the introduction about the 1960s and restates his thesis. That done, he moves to the second paragraph of his conclusion. There, he quotes a dramatic statement from a knowledgeable source, cites efforts to undermine AmeriCorps, and ends by pointing out that AmeriCorps has earned the respect of some unlikely supporters. All that Mark does in this final paragraph lends credibility to the crisp assertion and suggested course of action at the very end of his essay.

Revising the first draft.   Given the complex nature of his argu-ment, Mark found that he had to revise his essay several times. One way to illustrate some of the changes he made is to compare his final introduction with the original draft reprinted here:

Original Version of the Introduction

   "There's no free lunch." "You can't get something for nothing." "You have to earn your way." In America, these sayings are not really true. In America, we gladly take but give back little. In America, we receive economic opportunity, legal protection, the right to vote, and, most of all, a personal freedom unequaled throughout the world. How do we repay our country for such gifts? In most cases, we don't. This unfair relationship must be changed. The best way to make a start is to institute a system of national compulsory service for young people. This system would be of real benefit to the country and its citizens.

When Mark met with a classmate for a feedback session, he found that his partner had a number of helpful suggestions for revising various sections of the essay. But Mark's partner focused most of her comments on the essay's introduction because she felt it needed special attention. Following his classmate's suggestion, Mark deleted the original introduction's references to Americans in general. He made this change because he wanted readers to know—from the very start of the essay—that the paper would focus not on all Americans but on American youth. To reinforce this emphasis, he also added the point about the social commitment characteristic of young people in the 1960s. This reference to an earlier period gave the discussion an important historical perspective and lent a note of authority to Mark's argument. The decision to mention the '60s also helped Mark realize that his introduction should point out more recent developments—specifically, the promising start-up of AmeriCorps. Mark was pleased to see that adding this new material not only gave the introduction a sharper focus, but it also provided a smoother lead-in to his thesis.

These are just a few of the many changes Mark made while reworking his essay. Because he budgeted his time carefully, he was able to revise thoroughly. With the exception of some weak spots in the refutation, Mark's essay is well-reasoned and convincing.

ACTIVITIES: ARGUMENTATION-PERSUASION

Prewriting Activities

1. Imagine you're writing two essays: One *defines* hypocrisy; the other *contrasts* license and freedom. Identify an audience for each essay (college students, professors, teenagers, parents, employers, employees, or some other group). Then jot down how each essay might argue the merits of certain ways of behaving.

2. Following are several thesis statements for argumentation-persuasion essays. For each thesis, determine whether the three audiences

indicated in parentheses are apt to be supportive, wavering, or hostile. Then select *one* thesis and use group brainstorming to identify, for each audience, specific points you would make to persuade each group.

    a. Students should not graduate from college until they have passed a comprehensive exam in their majors (*college students, their parents, college officials*).

    b. Abandoned homes owned by the city should be sold to low-income residents for a nominal fee (*city officials, low-income residents, general citizens*).

    c. The town should pass a law prohibiting residents who live near the reservoir from using pesticides on their lawns (*environmentalists, homeowners, members of the town council*).

    d. Faculty advisors to college newspapers should have the authority to prohibit the publication of articles that reflect negatively on the school (*alumni, college officials, student journalists*).

Revising Activities

3. Each set of statements that follows contains at least one of the logical fallacies described earlier in the chapter and in Ann McClintock's essay "Propaganda Techniques in Today's Advertising" (page 304). Identify the fallacy or fallacies in each set and explain why the statements are invalid.

    a. Grades are irrelevant to learning. Students are in college to get an education, not good grades. The university should eliminate grading altogether.

    b. The best policy is to put juvenile offenders in jail so that they can get a taste of reality. Otherwise, they will repeat their crimes again and again.

    c. So-called sex education programs do nothing to decrease the rate of teenage pregnancy. Further expenditures on these programs should be curtailed.

    d. If we allow abortion, people will think it's acceptable to kill the homeless or pull the plug on sick people—two groups that are also weak and frail.

    e. The curfews that some towns impose on teenagers are as repressive as the curfews in totalitarian countries.

4. Following is the introduction from the first draft of an essay advocating the elimination of mandatory dress codes in public schools. Revise the paragraph, being sure to consider these questions: How

effectively does the writer deal with the opposing viewpoint? Does the paragraph encourage those who might disagree with the writer to read on? Why or why not? Do you see any logical fallacies in the writer's thinking? Where? Does the writer introduce anything that veers away from the point being discussed? Where? Before revising, you may find it helpful to do some brainstorming—individually or in a group—to find ways to strengthen the paragraph.

After reworking the paragraph, take a few minutes to consider how the rest of the essay might unfold. What persuasive strategies could be used? How could Rogerian argument win over readers? What points could be made? What action could be urged in the effort to build a convincing argument?

In three nearby towns recently, high school administrators joined forces to take an outrageously strong stand against students' constitutional rights. Acting like fascists, they issued an edict in the form of a preposterous dress code that prohibits students from wearing expensive jewelry, designer jeans, leather jackets--anything that the administrators, in their supposed wisdom, consider ostentatious. Perhaps the next thing they'll want to do is forbid students to play rock music at school dances. What prompted the administrators' dictatorial prohibition against certain kinds of clothing? Somehow or other, they got it into their heads that having no restrictions on the way students dress creates an unhealthy environment, where students vie with each other for the flashiest attire. Students and parents alike should protest this and any other dress code. If such codes go into effect, we might as well throw out the Constitution.

Mary Sherry

Following her graduation from Dominican University in 1962 with a degree in English, Mary Sherry (1940–) wrote freelance articles and advertising copy while raising her family. Over the years, a love of writing and an interest in education have been integral to all that Sherry does professionally. Founder and owner of a small research and publishing firm in Minnesota, she has taught creative and remedial writing to adults for more than sixteen years. The following selection first appeared as a 1991 "My Turn" column in *Newsweek*.

Pre-Reading Journal Entry

Imagine you had a son or daughter who didn't take school seriously. How would you go about motivating the child to value academic success? Would your strategies differ depending on the age and gender of the child? If so, how and why? What other factors might influence your approach? Use your journal to respond to these questions.

In Praise of the "F" Word

Tens of thousands of 18-year-olds will graduate this year and be 1
handed meaningless diplomas. These diplomas won't look any different from those awarded their luckier classmates. Their validity will be questioned only when their employers discover that these graduates are semiliterate.

Eventually a fortunate few will find their way into educational 2
repair shops—adult-literacy programs, such as the one where I teach basic grammar and writing. There, high-school graduates and high-school dropouts pursuing graduate-equivalency certificates will learn the skills they should have learned in school. They will also discover they have been cheated by our educational system.

As I teach, I learn a lot about our schools. Early in each session 3
I ask my students to write about an unpleasant experience they had in school. No writers' block here! "I wish someone would have had made me stop doing drugs and made me study." "I liked to party and no one seemed to care." "I was a good kid and didn't cause any

trouble, so they just passed me along even though I didn't read well and couldn't write." And so on.

I am your basic do-gooder, and prior to teaching this class I blamed the poor academic skills our kids have today on drugs, divorce and other impediments to concentration necessary for doing well in school. But, as I rediscover each time I walk into the classroom, before a teacher can expect students to concentrate, he has to get their attention, no matter what distractions may be at hand. There are many ways to do this, and they have much to do with teaching style. However, if style alone won't do it, there is another way to show who holds the winning hand in the classroom. That is to reveal the trump card[1] of failure.

I will never forget a teacher who played that card to get the attention of one of my children. Our youngest, a world-class charmer, did little to develop his intellectual talents but always got by. Until Mrs. Stifter.

Our son was a high-school senior when he had her for English. "He sits in the back of the room talking to his friends," she told me. "Why don't you move him to the front row?" I urged, believing the embarrassment would get him to settle down. Mrs. Stifter looked at me steely-eyed over her glasses. "I don't move seniors," she said. "I flunk them." I was flustered. Our son's academic life flashed before my eyes. No teacher had ever threatened him with that before. I regained my composure and managed to say that I thought she was right. By the time I got home I was feeling pretty good about this. It was a radical approach for these times, but, well, why not? "She's going to flunk you," I told my son. I did not discuss it any further. Suddenly English became a priority in his life. He finished out the semester with an A.

I know one example doesn't make a case, but at night I see a parade of students who are angry and resentful for having been passed along until they could no longer even pretend to keep up. Of average intelligence or better, they eventually quit school, concluding they were too dumb to finish. "I should have been held back" is a comment I hear frequently. Even sadder are those students who are high-school graduates who say to me after a few weeks of class, "I don't know how I ever got a high-school diploma."

Passing students who have not mastered the work cheats them and the employers who expect graduates to have basic skills. We

[1]In cards, an advantage held in reserve until it's needed (editors' note).

excuse this dishonest behavior by saying kids can't learn if they come from terrible environments. No one seems to stop to think that—no matter what environments they come from—most kids don't put school first on their list unless they perceive something is at stake. They'd rather be sailing.

Many students I see at night could give expert testimony on 9 unemployment, chemical dependency, abusive relationships. In spite of these difficulties, they have decided to make education a priority. They are motivated by the desire for a better job or the need to hang on to the one they've got. They have a healthy fear of failure.

People of all ages can rise above their problems, but they need 10 to have a reason to do so. Young people generally don't have the maturity to value education in the same way my adult students value it. But fear of failure, whether economic or academic, can motivate both.

Flunking as a regular policy has just as much merit today as it 11 did two generations ago. We must review the threat of flunking and see it as it really is—a positive teaching tool. It is an expression of confidence by both teachers and parents that the students have the ability to learn the material presented to them. However, making it work again would take a dedicated, caring conspiracy between teachers and parents. It would mean facing the tough reality that passing kids who haven't learned the material—while it might save them grief for the short term—dooms them to long-term illiteracy. It would mean that teachers would have to follow through on their threats, and parents would have to stand behind them, knowing their children's best interests are indeed at stake. This means no more doing Scott's assignments for him because he might fail. No more passing Jodi because she's such a nice kid.

This is a policy that worked in the past and can work today. A wise 12 teacher, with the support of his parents, gave our son the opportunity to succeed—or fail. It's time we return this choice to all students.

Questions for Close Reading

1. What is the selection's thesis? Locate the sentence(s) in which Sherry states her main idea. If she doesn't state the thesis explicitly, express it in your own words.
2. Sherry opens her essay with these words: "Tens of thousands of 18-year-olds will graduate this year and be handed meaningless diplomas." Why does Sherry consider these diplomas meaningless?

3. According to Sherry, what justification do many teachers give for "passing students who have not mastered the work" (paragraph 8)? Why does Sherry think that it is wrong to pass such students?

4. What does Sherry think teachers should do to motivate students to focus on school despite the many "distractions . . . at hand" (4)?

5. Refer to your dictionary as needed to define the following words used in the selection: *validity* (paragraph 1), *semiliterate* (1), *equivalency* (2), *impediments* (4), *composure* (6), *radical* (6), *priority* (6), *resentful* (7), *testimony* (9), *motivate* (10), *merit* (11), *conspiracy* (11), and *illiteracy* (11).

Questions About the Writer's Craft

1. **The pattern.** To write an effective argumentation-persuasion essay, writers need to establish their credibility. How does Sherry convince readers that she is qualified to write about her subject? What does this attempt to establish credibility say about Sherry's perception of her audience's point of view?

2. Sherry's title is deliberately misleading. What does her title lead you to believe the essay will be about? Why do you think Sherry chose this title?

3. Why do you suppose Sherry quotes her students rather than summarizing what they had to say? What effect do you think Sherry hopes the quotations will have on readers?

4. **Other patterns.** What example does Sherry provide to show that the threat of failure can work? How does this example reinforce her case?

Writing Assignments Using Argumentation-Persuasion as a Pattern of Development

1. Like Sherry, write an essay arguing your position on a controversial school-related issue. Possibilities include but need not be limited to the following: College students should *or* should not have to fulfill a physical education requirement; high school students should *or* should not have to demonstrate computer proficiency before graduating; elementary school students should *or* should not be grouped according to ability; a course in parenting should *or* should not be a required part of the high school curriculum. Once you select a topic, brainstorm with others to gather insight into varying points of view. When you write, restrict your argument to one level of education, and refute as many opposing arguments as you can. The following essays will help you identify educational issues worth writing about: Sophronia Liu's "So Tsi-Fai" (page 188), Charles Sykes's "The 'Values' Wasteland" (page 214), James Thurber's "University Days" (page 234), William Zinsser's "College Pressures" (page 285), Nikki Giovanni's "Campus Racism 101" (page 350), Paul Roberts's "How to Say Nothing in 500 Words" (page 365),

Jacques D'Amboise's "Showing What Is Possible" (page 460), and William Raspberry's "The Handicap of Definition" (page 529).

2. Sherry acknowledges that she used to blame students' poor academic skills on "drugs, divorce and other impediments." To what extent should teachers take these and similar "impediments" into account when grading students? Are there certain situations that call for leniency, or should out-of-school forces affecting students not be considered? To gain perspective on this issue, interview several friends, classmates, and instructors. Then write an essay in which you argue your position. Provide specific examples to support your argument, being sure to acknowledge and—when possible—to refute opposing viewpoints.

Writing Assignments Using Other Patterns of Development

3. You probably feel, as Sherry does, that Mrs. Stifter is a strong, committed professional. Write an essay illustrating the qualities you think a teacher needs to have to be effective. Ask friends, classmates, family members, and instructors for their opinions; however, in your paper, focus on only those attributes you believe are most critical. To highlight the importance of these qualities, begin with a dramatic example of an ineffective teacher—someone who lacks the attributes you consider most important. To gain insight into some of the factors that make teachers effective or ineffective, read Sophronia Liu's "So Tsi-Fai" (page 188) and Jacques D'Amboise's "Showing What Is Possible" (page 460).

4. Where else, besides in the classroom, do you see people acting irresponsibly, expending little effort, and taking the easy way out? You might consider the workplace, a school-related club or activity, family life, or interpersonal relationships. Select *one* area and write an essay illustrating the effects of this behavior on everyone concerned. For a broader perspective on the issue of personal responsibility, read Charles Sykes's "The 'Values' Wasteland" (page 214) and William Raspberry's "The Handicap of Definition" (page 529).

Writing Assignments Using a Journal Entry as a Starting Point

5. Write the text for a brochure presenting parents with a step-by-step guide for dealing with academically unmotivated students. Focus your discussion on a specific level of schooling. From your pre-reading journal entry, select those strategies you consider most realistic and productive. When presenting your ideas, take into account children's likely resistance to the strategies described, and instruct parents how to deal with this resistance. Interviewing others (especially parents) and doing some research in the library and/or on the Internet will broaden your understanding of the issues involved.

Yuh Ji-Yeon

At the age of five, Yuh Ji-Yeon (1965–) immigrated from Seoul, Korea, to the United States, settling in Chicago with her parents. After graduating from Stanford University, she worked as a reporter for the *Omaha World-Herald* and *New York Newsday*. Currently, she is writing her doctoral dissertation at the University of Pennsylvania. The dissertation examines the parallels between the experiences of Korean women immigrating to the United States as wives of U.S. soldiers and the larger context of United States-Korea relations. Nearly all of Yuh's writing reflects the concerns of people struggling for liberation in the face of oppression. The following selection first appeared in the *Philadelphia Inquirer* in 1991.

Pre-Reading Journal Entry

Which events in American history do you consider shameful? List these events in your journal. For each, jot down what your teachers taught you about the event when you were a child. Does what you were taught as a child differ from what you know now? In what way? If you did later on learn harsher truths about these events, how did you feel? Do you believe that you should have been told the truth from the beginning? Why or why not?

Let's Tell the Story of All America's Cultures

I grew up hearing, seeing and almost believing that America was white—albeit with a little black tinge here and there—and that white was best. 1

The white people were everywhere in my 1970s Chicago childhood: Founding Fathers, Lewis and Clark, Lincoln, Daniel Boone, Carnegie, presidents, explorers and industrialists galore. The only black people were slaves. The only Indians were scalpers. 2

I never heard one word about how Benjamin Franklin was so impressed by the Iroquois federation of nations that he adapted that model into our system of state and federal government. Or that the Indian tribes were systematically betrayed and massacred by a greedy young nation that stole their land and called it the United States. 3

I never heard one word about how Asian immigrants were   4
among the first to turn California's desert into fields of plenty. Or
about Chinese immigrant Ah Bing, who bred the cherry now on sale
in groceries across the nation. Or that plantation owners in Hawaii
imported labor from China, Japan, Korea and the Philippines to
work the sugar cane fields. I never learned that Asian immigrants
were the only immigrants denied U.S. citizenship, even though they
served honorably in World War I. All the immigrants in my textbook
were white.

I never learned about Frederick Douglass, the runaway slave   5
who became a leading abolitionist and statesman, or about black
scholar W.E.B. Du Bois. I never learned that black people rose up in
arms against slavery. Nat Turner wasn't one of the heroes in my
childhood history class.

I never learned that the American Southwest and California   6
were already settled by Mexicans when they were annexed after the
Mexican-American War. I never learned that Mexico once had a
problem keeping land-hungry white men on the U.S. side of the
border.

So when other children called me a slant-eyed chink and told   7
me to go back where I came from, I was ready to believe that I was-
n't really an American because I wasn't white.

America's bittersweet legacy of struggling and failing and get-   8
ting another step closer to democratic ideals of liberty and equality
and justice for all wasn't for the likes of me, an immigrant child from
Korea. The history books said so.

Well, the history books were wrong.   9

Educators around the country are finally realizing what I real-   10
ized as a teenager in the library, looking up the history I wasn't getting in school. America is a multicultural nation, composed of many
people with varying histories and varying traditions who have little
in common except their humanity, a belief in democracy and a desire
for freedom.

America changed them, but they changed America too.   11

A committee of scholars and teachers gathered by the New York   12
State Department of Education recognizes this in their recent
report, "One Nation, Many Peoples: A Declaration of Cultural
Interdependence."

They recommend that public schools provide a "multicultural   13
education, anchored to the shared principles of a liberal democracy."

What that means, according to the report, is recognizing that   14
America was shaped and continues to be shaped by people of diverse
backgrounds. It calls for students to be taught that history is an
ongoing process of discovery and interpretation of the past, and that
there is more than one way of viewing the world.

Thus, the westward migration of white Americans is not just a   15
heroic settling of an untamed wild, but also the conquest of indigenous peoples. Immigrants were not just white, but Asian as well.
Blacks were not merely passive slaves freed by northern whites, but
active fighters for their own liberation.

In particular, according to the report, the curriculum should   16
help children "to assess critically the reasons for the inconsistencies
between the ideals of the U.S. and social realities. It should provide
information and intellectual tools that can permit them to contribute to bringing reality closer to the ideals."

In other words, show children the good with the bad, and give   17
them the skills to help improve their country. What could be more
patriotic?

Several dissenting members of the New York committee publicly   18
worry that America will splinter into ethnic fragments if this multicultural curriculum is adopted. They argue that the committee's
report puts the focus on ethnicity at the expense of national unity.

But downplaying ethnicity will not bolster national unity. The   19
history of America is the story of how and why people from all over
the world came to the United States, and how in struggling to make
a better life for themselves, they changed each other, they changed
the country, and they all came to call themselves Americans.

E pluribus unum. Out of many, one.   20

This is why I, with my Korean background, and my childhood   21
tormentors, with their lost-in-the-mist-of-time European backgrounds, are all Americans.

It is the unique beauty of this country. It is high time we let all   22
our children gaze upon it.

Questions for Close Reading

1. What is the selection's thesis? Locate the sentence(s) in which Yuh states
   her main idea. If she doesn't state the thesis explicitly, express it in your
   own words.
2. Yuh makes the rather shocking claim that "the history books were
   wrong" (paragraph 9). Why does she make this statement? What evidence does she offer to support it?

3. According to Yuh, what changes are needed in U.S. history courses?

4. Why does Yuh feel it is critical that U.S. students receive more than the traditional whites-only version of our nation's history? Who will be served by making history books more multicultural?

5. Refer to your dictionary as needed to define the following words used in the selection: *albeit* (paragraph 1), *tinge* (1), *galore* (2), *multicultural* (10, 13, 18), *interdependence* (12), *indigenous* (15), *dissenting* (18), *ethnicity* (18), and *bolster* (19).

Questions About the Writer's Craft

1. **The pattern.** Where in her argument does Yuh present the opposing viewpoint? Why do you suppose she waits so long to deal with the dissenting opinion? What effect does this delay have on her argument's effectiveness?

2. **Other patterns.** Why might Yuh have decided to use so many examples in paragraphs 2 through 6? How do these examples contribute to the persuasiveness of her position? Why might she have placed these examples before her thesis statement?

3. Yuh mixes the subjective and the objective in her argument. Where does she use specifics from her own life? How do these personal details help persuade readers to accept her viewpoint?

4. Yuh often uses parallelism and repetition of phrases, particularly in paragraphs 1 through 6 and paragraph 15. What effect do you think she intended these two stylistic devices to have on her readers?

Writing Assignments Using Argumentation-Persuasion as a Pattern of Development

1. Using the resources of the library and/or Internet, read several articles about the ongoing debate over multiculturalism's role in contemporary education. You should find coverage of the 1991 New York State Department of Education Study (cited by Yuh in paragraph 12) and historian Arthur Schlesinger's *Time* essay "The Cult of Ethnicity: Good and Bad" (July 8, 1991) especially helpful. Review your research, and decide whether or not you support the idea of a multicultural curriculum. Then write an essay in which you argue your position, refuting as many of the opposing views as possible. Draw upon your own experiences as well as your research when developing your point of view.

2. Yuh cites a problem she encountered in her education. What problems or insufficiencies have you found in your own education? Perhaps you perceive an overemphasis on athletics, a reliance on rote memorization, a tendency to discourage female students from pursuing an interest in math and science. Select a single problem at one level of education, and brainstorm with others to gather material about the problem. Then write

an essay directed at those who think all is well in our educational system. Be sure your argument illustrates the inaccuracy of these individuals' overly positive view. Before writing your paper, you may want to read Charles Sykes's "The 'Values' Wasteland" (page 214) and William Zinsser's "College Pressures" (page 285) because they both offer critiques of U.S. education.

Writing Assignments Using Other Patterns of Development

3. Because the mainstream culture they lived in didn't recognize the presence of minorities, the author's classmates considered Yuh an outsider, almost a nonbeing. To what extent, in your opinion, does television contribute to the dehumanization of minorities? For several days, watch a variety of television shows, noting how a particular ethnic or minority group (such as African-Americans, Hispanic-Americans, or the elderly) is portrayed. Then write an essay showing that the depiction of this group on television is either accurate *or* distorted. Support your main idea with plentiful references to specific television shows, including newscasts, situation comedies, talk shows, and so forth.

4. In her essay, Yuh refers to a report issued by the New York State Department of Education. The report argues that curriculum should encourage students to examine "the reasons for the inconsistencies between the ideals of the U.S. and social realities." Like most people, you probably detected such disparities when you were growing up. Perhaps as a ten-year-old, you heard an admired neighbor brag about padding an expense account. As an eighth-grader, you may have visited your state legislature, where you saw chaos and rudeness instead of order and respect. As a high school student, you might have learned that an esteemed coach took kickbacks from college recruiters. Focus on one such clash between the ethical ideal and the everyday reality, and write about the incident's effect on you. Provide dramatic details to show how you reacted, what you did to explain the discrepancy to yourself, and whether you asked adults to help you understand the situation. At the end, reach some conclusions about the way children can be helped to deal with such collisions between ideals and reality. Before writing your paper, you may want to read Audre Lorde's "The Fourth of July" (page 160) and Langston Hughes's "Salvation" (page 183), two powerful essays that explore a child's disillusionment with adult realities.

Writing Assignments Using a Journal Entry as a Starting Point

5. Write an essay in which you argue for *or* against schools' revealing harsh historical realities to children. Review your pre-reading journal entry,

and select *one* historical event to focus on. Provide plentiful reasons to support your position, whenever possible pointing out weaknesses in opposing viewpoints. To deepen your understanding of the issue, consider reading Audre Lorde's "The Fourth of July" (page 160), Beth Johnson's "Bombs Bursting in Air" (page 242), and Gloria Naylor's "Mommy, What Does 'Nigger' Mean?" (page 516), essays exploring parents' quandary between protecting their children and educating them about life's painful realities.

Mark Twain

Mark Twain is a central figure in American literature. Published in 1884, *The Adventures of Huckleberry Finn,* Twain's finest work, recounts a journey down the Mississippi by two memorable figures: a White boy and a Black slave. Twain was born Samuel Langhorne Clemens in 1835 and was raised in Hannibal, Missouri. During his early years, he worked as a riverboat pilot, newspaper reporter, printer, and gold prospector. Although his popular image is as the author of such comic works as *The Adventures of Tom Sawyer* (1876), *Life on the Mississippi* (1883), and *The Prince and the Pauper* (1882), Twain had a darker side that may have resulted from the bitter experiences of his life: financial failure and the deaths of his wife and daughter. His last writings are savage, satiric, and pessimistic. The following selection is taken from *Letters From the Earth,* one of Twain's later works.

Pre-Reading Journal Entry

What would you identify as the major differences between human beings and other animals? What are the similarities? In your journal, list as many items for each as you can, from the obvious to the subtle. Be as specific as you can.

The Damned Human Race

1   I have been studying the traits and dispositions of the "lower animals" (so-called), and contrasting them with the traits and dispositions of man. I find the result humiliating to me. For it obliges me to renounce my allegiance to the Darwinian theory of the Ascent of Man from the Lower Animals; since it now seems plain to me that the theory ought to be vacated in favor of a new and truer one, this new and truer one to be named the *Descent* of Man from the Higher Animals.

2   In proceeding toward this unpleasant conclusion I have not guessed or speculated or conjectured, but have used what is commonly called the scientific method. That is to say, I have subjected every postulate that presented itself to the crucial test of actual experiment, and have adopted it or rejected it according to the result. Thus I verified and established each step of my course in its

turn before advancing to the next. These experiments were made in the London Zoological Gardens, and covered many months of painstaking and fatiguing work.

Before particularizing any of the experiments, I wish to state one or two things which seem to more properly belong in this place than further along. This in the interest of clearness. The massed experiments established to my satisfaction certain generalizations, to wit:

1. That the human race is of one distinct species. It exhibits slight variations—in color, stature, mental caliber, and so on—due to climate, environment, and so forth; but it is a species by itself, and not to be confounded with any other.
2. That the quadrupeds are a distinct family, also. This family exhibits variations—in color, size, food preferences and so on; but it is a family by itself.
3. That the other families—the birds, the fishes, the insects, the reptiles, etc.—are more or less distinct, also. They are in the procession. They are links in the chain which stretches down from the higher animals to man at the bottom.

Some of my experiments were quite curious. In the course of my reading I had come across a case where, many years ago, some hunters on our Great Plains organized a buffalo hunt for the entertainment of an English earl—that, and to provide some fresh meat for his larder. They had charming sport. They killed seventy-two of those great animals; and ate part of one of them and left the seventy-one to rot. In order to determine the difference between an anaconda and an earl—if any—I caused seven young calves to be turned into the anaconda's cage. The grateful reptile immediately crushed one of them and swallowed it, then lay back satisfied. It showed no further interest in the calves, and no disposition to harm them. I tried this experiment with other anacondas; always with the same result. The fact stood proven that the difference between an earl and an anaconda is that the earl is cruel and the anaconda isn't; and that the earl wantonly destroys what he has no use for, but the anaconda doesn't. This seemed to suggest that the anaconda was not descended from the earl. It also seemed to suggest that the earl was descended from the anaconda, and had lost a good deal in the transition.

I was aware that many men who have accumulated more millions of money than they can ever use have shown a rabid hunger for more, and have not scrupled to cheat the ignorant and the helpless out of their poor servings in order to partially appease that appetite. I furnished a hundred different kinds of wild and tame animals the opportunity to accumulate vast stores of food, but none of them would do it. The squirrels and bees and certain birds made accumulations, but stopped when they had gathered a winter's supply, and could not be persuaded to add to it either honestly or by chicanery. In order to bolster up a tottering reputation the ant pretended to store up supplies, but I was not deceived. I know the ant. These experiments convinced me that there is this difference between man and the higher animals: he is avaricious and miserly, they are not.

In the course of my experiments I convinced myself that among 6 the animals man is the only one that harbors insults and injuries, broods over them, waits till a chance offers, then takes revenge. The passion of revenge is unknown to the higher animals.

Roosters keep harems, but it is by consent of their concubines; 7 therefore no wrong is done. Men keep harems, but it is by brute force, privileged by atrocious laws which the other sex were allowed no hand in making. In this matter man occupies a far lower place than the rooster.

Cats are loose in their morals, but not consciously so. Man, in 8 his descent from the cat, has brought the cat's looseness with him but has left the unconsciousness behind—the saving grace which excuses the cat. The cat is innocent, man is not.

Indecency, vulgarity, obscenity—these are strictly confined to 9 man; he invented them. Among the higher animals there is no trace of them. They hide nothing; they are not ashamed. Man, with his soiled mind, covers himself. He will not even enter a drawing room with his breast and back naked, so alive are he and his mates to indecent suggestion. Man is "The Animal that Laughs." But so does the monkey, as Mr. Darwin pointed out; and so does the Australian bird that is called the laughing jackass. No—Man is the Animal that Blushes. He is the only one that does it—or has occasion to.

At the head of this article[1] we see how "three monks were burnt 10 to death" a few days ago, and a prior "put to death with atrocious cruelty." Do we inquire into the details? No; or we should find out

[1]Twain originally began his article with newspaper clippings containing telegrams that reported atrocities in Crete (editors' note).

that the prior was subjected to unprintable mutilations. Man—when he is a North American Indian—gouges out his prisoner's eyes; when he is King John, with a nephew to render untroublesome, he uses a red-hot iron; when he is a religious zealot dealing with heretics in the Middle Ages, he skins his captive alive and scatters salt on his back; in the first Richard's time he shuts up a multitude of Jew families in a tower and sets fire to it; in Columbus's time he captures a family of Spanish Jews and—but *that* is not printable; in our day in England a man is fined ten shillings for beating his mother nearly to death with a chair, and another man is fined forty shillings for having four pheasant eggs in his possession without being able to satisfactorily explain how he got them. Of all the animals, man is the only one that is cruel. He is the only one that inflicts pain for the pleasure of doing it. It is a trait that is not known to the higher animals. The cat plays with the frightened mouse; but she has this excuse, that she does not know that the mouse is suffering. The cat is moderate—unhumanly moderate: she only scares the mouse, she does not hurt it; she doesn't dig out its eyes, or tear off its skin, or drive splinters under its nails—man-fashion; when she is done playing with it she makes a sudden meal of it and puts it out of its trouble. Man is the Cruel Animal. He is alone in that distinction.

The higher animals engage in individual fights, but never in 11
organized masses. Man is the only animal that deals in that atrocity of atrocities, War. He is the only one that gathers his brethren about him and goes forth in cold blood and with calm pulse to exterminate his kind. He is the only animal that for sordid wages will march out, as the Hessians did in our Revolution, and as the boyish Prince Napoleon did in the Zulu war, and help to slaughter strangers of his own species who have done him no harm and with whom he has no quarrel.

Man is the only animal that robs his helpless fellow of his coun- 12
try—takes possession of it and drives him out of it or destroys him. Man has done this in all the ages. There is not an acre of ground on the globe that is in possession of its rightful owner, or that has not been taken away from owner after owner, cycle after cycle, by force and bloodshed.

Man is the only Slave. And he is the only animal who enslaves. 13
He has always been a slave in one form or another, and has always held other slaves in bondage under him in one way or another. In our day he is always some man's slave for wages, and does that man's

work; and this slave has other slaves under him for minor wages, and they do *his* work. The higher animals are the only ones who exclusively do their own work and provide their own living.

Man is the only Patriot. He sets himself apart in his own country, under his own flag, and sneers at the other nations, and keeps multitudinous uniformed assassins on hand at heavy expense to grab slices of other people's countries, and keep *them* from grabbing slices of *his*. And in the intervals between campaigns he washes the blood off his hands and works for "the universal brotherhood of man"—with his mouth. 14

Man is the Religious Animal. He is the only Religious Animal. He is the only animal that has the True Religion—several of them. He is the only animal that loves his neighbor as himself, and cuts his throat if his theology isn't straight. He has made a graveyard of the globe in trying his honest best to smooth his brother's path to happiness and heaven. He was at it in the time of the Caesars, he was at it in Mahomet's time, he was at it in the time of the Inquisition, he was at it in France a couple of centuries, he was at it in England in Mary's day, he has been at it ever since he first saw the light, he is at it today in Crete—as per the telegrams quoted above[2]—he will be at it somewhere else tomorrow. The higher animals have no religion. And we are told that they are going to be left out, in the Hereafter. I wonder why? It seems questionable taste. 15

Man is the Reasoning Animal. Such is the claim. I think it is open to dispute. Indeed, my experiments have proven to me that he is the Unreasoning Animal. Note his history, as sketched above. It seems plain to me that whatever he is he is *not* a reasoning animal. His record is the fantastic record of a maniac. I consider that the strongest count against his intelligence is the fact that with that record back of him he blandly sets himself up as the head animal of the lot: whereas by his own standards he is the bottom one. 16

In truth, man is incurably foolish. Simple things which the other animals easily learn, he is incapable of learning. Among my experiments was this. In an hour I taught a cat and a dog to be friends. I put them in a cage. In another hour I taught them to be friends with a rabbit. In the course of two days I was able to add a fox, a goose, a squirrel and some doves. Finally a monkey. They lived together in peace; even affectionately. 17

[2]See note, page 589 (editors' note).

Next, in another cage I confined an Irish Catholic from   18
Tipperary, and as soon as he seemed tame I added a Scotch
Presbyterian from Aberdeen. Next a Turk from Constantinople; a
Greek Christian from Crete; an Armenian; a Methodist from the wilds
of Arkansas; a Buddhist from China; a Brahman from Benares. Finally,
a Salvation Army Colonel from Wapping. Then I stayed away two
whole days. When I came back to note results, the cage of Higher
Animals was all right, but in the other, there was but a chaos of gory
odds and ends of turbans and fezzes and plaids and bones and flesh—
not a specimen left alive. These Reasoning Animals had disagreed on
a theological detail and carried the matter to a Higher Court.

One is obliged to concede that in true loftiness of character,   19
Man cannot claim to approach even the meanest of the Higher
Animals. It is plain that he is constitutionally incapable of approaching that altitude; that he is constitutionally afflicted with a Defect
which must make such approach forever impossible, for it is mani-
fest that this defect is permanent in him, indestructible, ineradicable.

I find this Defect to be *the Moral Sense.* He is the only animal   20
that has it. It is the secret of his degradation. It is the quality *which
enables him to do wrong.* It has no other office. It is incapable of performing any other function. It could never have been intended to
perform any other. Without it, man could do no wrong. He would
rise at once to the level of the Higher Animals.

Since the Moral Sense has but the one office, the one capacity—   21
to enable man to do wrong—it is plainly without value to him. It is
as valueless to him as is disease. In fact, it manifestly *is* a disease.
Rabies is bad, but it is not so bad as this disease. Rabies enables a
man to do a thing which he could not do when in a healthy state:
kill his neighbor with a poisonous bite. No one is the better man for
having rabies: The Moral Sense enables a man to do wrong. It
enables him to do wrong in a thousand ways. Rabies is an innocent
disease, compared to the Moral Sense. No one, then, can be the better man for having the Moral Sense. What, now, do we find the
Primal Curse to have been? Plainly what it was in the beginning: the
infliction upon man of the Moral Sense; the ability to distinguish
good from evil; and with it, necessarily, the ability to *do* evil; for
there can be no evil act without the presence of consciousness of it
in the doer of it.

And so I find that we have descended and degenerated, from   22
some far ancestor—some microscopic atom wandering at its pleasure

between the mighty horizons of a drop of water perchance—insect by insect, animal by animal, reptile by reptile, down the long highway of smirchless innocence, till we have reached the bottom stage of development—namable as the Human Being. Below us—nothing.

Questions for Close Reading

1. What is the selection's thesis? Locate the sentence(s) in which Twain states his main idea. If he doesn't state the thesis explicitly, express it in your own words.
2. Because of their intelligence, humans are usually called the highest animal. What, according to Twain, are the specific traits that make humans the lowest animal?
3. How does the story of the earl who hunted down seventy-two buffalo show that an anaconda is superior to an earl?
4. What does Twain mean when he points out that humankind is the only animal that "has occasion to" blush? What are some of the occasions for blushing that he highlights in the essay?
5. Refer to your dictionary as needed to define the following words used in the selection: *confounded* (paragraph 3), *anaconda* (4), *wantonly* (4), *chicanery* (5), *heretics* (10), *constitutionally* (19), *ineradicable* (19), and *smirchless* (22).

Questions About the Writer's Craft

1. **The pattern.** Most writers don't tell the reader outright the reasoning process they used to arrive at their essay's proposition. But Twain claims that he reached his conclusion about human beings inductively—through the use of the "scientific method." Why does Twain make this claim?
2. Where in the essay does Twain try to shock the audience? Why do you think he adopts this technique?
3. **Other patterns.** In some paragraphs, Twain provides numerous examples of political and religious atrocities. Why do you suppose he supplies so many examples?
4. Black humor is defined as "the use of the morbid and the absurd for comic purposes." What elements of the morbid and the absurd do you find in Twain's essay? Would you say "The Damned Human Race" is an example of black humor? Explain.

Writing Assignments Using Argumentation-Persuasion as a Pattern of Development

1. In an essay, argue that human beings are worthy of being considered the "highest animal." The paper should acknowledge and then refute

Twain's charges that people are miserly, vengeful, foolish, and so on. To support your proposition, use specific examples of how human beings can be kind, caring, generous, and peace-loving. You might find it helpful to read Lewis Thomas's "The Lie Detector" (page 477), an essay focusing on the potentially positive aspects of human nature.

2. Write an essay agreeing with Twain that it is our everyday meannesses, unkindnesses, and cruelties that make us the "lowest animal." Use compelling examples to support your argument, including description and dialogue whenever appropriate. You might focus on one of the following topics:

Violence toward children
Abuse of animals
Hurtful sarcasm
Insults of a racial, sexist, or religious nature
Indifference to the unfortunate

Somewhere in the essay, you should acknowledge the view that humans are capable of considerable kindness and compassion. To gain some insight into this more optimistic perspective, you might want to read Lewis Thomas's "The Lie Detector" (page 477). For a perspective more like Twain's, read Stephen King's "Why We Crave Horror Movies" (page 455).

Writing Assignments Using Other Patterns of Development

3. What failings of human decency do you see around you every day in your town, on your campus, or at your job? Write an essay showing that inhumanity resides not just in atrocities but also in ordinary acts of indifference. In your essay, you may use Twain's kind of bitter sarcasm, or you may adopt a more objective, less vitriolic tone.

4. How could humans become less cruel? Write an essay outlining a new process for raising children or "re-civilizing" adults—a process that, if instituted, would improve human morality.

Writing Assignments Using a Journal Entry as a Starting Point

5. Write an essay in which, unlike Twain, you illustrate the *similarities* between human beings and other species of animals. Using your pre-reading journal entry, select the most compelling similarities. Try to explore likenesses that go beyond such obvious ones as eating, sleeping, reproduction, etc.; focus instead on behaviors and traits that are elusive but telling. Your essays, which may be humorous or serious, should reveal your attitude toward the similarities you discuss. Do they reflect favorably or negatively on the human species?

Jonathan Swift

The foremost satirist in the English language, Jonathan Swift (1667–1745) is most famous as the author of *Gulliver's Travels* (1726), an often scorching indictment of human conduct. Born in Ireland, Swift moved to London at a young age and in 1694 was ordained an Anglican priest. In 1714 he was appointed the dean of St. Patrick's Cathedral in Dublin, a minor post the ambitious Swift accepted with reluctance. For most of his life, Swift was an outspoken public figure, writing satiric poems, plays, and essays aimed at political and religious targets. His works include *A Tale of a Tub* and *The Battle of the Books,* both published in 1704. More than two decades later, outraged by the British government's treatment of the Irish people, Swift wrote "A Modest Proposal," the classic essay reprinted here. Speaking not as himself but in the guise of an impartial observer, Swift suggested an outrageous solution to Ireland's problems, a solution in keeping with the inhumanity he saw rampant in Ireland.

Pre-Reading Journal Entry

Swift's epitaph reads, "He has gone where savage indignation can no longer lacerate his heart." In your journal, list several situations that arouse *your* "savage indignation." Under each, jot down what might be done to help rectify the problem.

A Modest Proposal

It is a melancholy object to those who walk through this great town[1] or travel in the country, when they see the streets, the roads, and cabin doors, crowded with beggars of the female sex, followed by three, four, or six children, all in rags and importuning every passenger for an alms. These mothers, instead of being able to work for their honest livelihood, are forced to employ all their time in

1

---

[1]Dublin. In 1729, Ireland was in its third year of devastating famine; poverty and hunger were widespread. The British government, which ruled Ireland, imposed high taxes on the already impoverished populace. Enraged by these injustices, Swift wrote this satire attacking the English and wealthy Irish for ignoring the suffering of the masses (editors' note).

strolling to beg sustenance for their helpless infants, who, as they grow up, either turn thieves for want of work, or leave their dear native country to fight for the Pretender in Spain, or sell themselves to the Barbadoes.[2]

I think it is agreed by all parties that this prodigious number of children in the arms, or on the backs, or at the heels of their mothers, and frequently of their fathers, is in the present deplorable state of the kingdom a very great additional grievance; and therefore whoever could find out a fair, cheap, and easy method of making these children sound, useful members of the commonwealth would deserve so well of the public as to have his statue set up for a preserver of the nation.

2

But my intention is very far from being confined to provide only for the children of professed beggars; it is of a much greater extent, and shall take in the whole number of infants at a certain age who are born of parents in effect as little able to support them as those who demand our charity in the streets.

3

As to my own part, having turned my thoughts for many years upon this important subject, and maturely weighed the several schemes of other projectors, I have always found them grossly mistaken in their computation. It is true, a child just dropped from its dam may be supported by her milk for a solar year, with little other nourishment; at most not above the value of two shillings, which the mother may certainly get, or the value in scraps, by her lawful occupation of begging; and it is exactly at one year old that I propose to provide for them in such a manner as instead of being a charge upon their parents or the parish, or wanting food and raiment for the rest of their lives, they shall on the contrary contribute to the feeding, and partly to the clothing, of many thousands.

4

There is likewise another great advantage in my scheme, that it will prevent those involuntary abortions, and that horrid practice of women murdering their bastard children, alas, too frequent among us, sacrificing the poor innocent babes, I doubt, more to avoid the expense than the shame, which would move tears and pity in the most savage and inhuman breast.

5

The number of souls in this kingdom being usually reckoned one million and a half, of these I calculate there may be about two hundred thousand couples whose wives are breeders, from which

6

[2]Many poor Irish were leaving the country to try to find a living elsewhere (editors' note).

number I subtract thirty thousand couples who are able to maintain their own children, although I apprehend there cannot be so many under the present distress of the kingdom; but this being granted, there will remain an hundred and seventy thousand breeders. I again subtract fifty thousand for those women who miscarry, or whose children die by accident or disease within the year. There only remain an hundred and twenty thousand children of poor parents annually born. The question therefore is, how this number shall be reared and provided for, which, as I have already said, under the present situation of affairs, is utterly impossible by all the methods hitherto proposed. For we can neither employ them in handicraft nor agriculture; we neither build houses (I mean in the country) nor cultivate land. They can very seldom pick up livelihood by stealing till they arrive at six years old, except where they are of towardly parts;[3] although I confess they learn the rudiments much earlier, during which time they can however be looked upon only as probationers, as I have been informed by a principal gentleman in the county of Cavan, who protested to me that he never knew above one or two instances under the age of six, even in a part of the kingdom so renowned for the quickest proficiency in that art.

I am assured by our merchants that a boy or a girl before twelve years old is no salable commodity; and even when they come to this age, they will not yield above three pounds, or three pounds and half a crown at most on the Exchange; which cannot turn to account either to the parents or the kingdom, the charge of nutriment and rags having been at least four times that value.   7

I shall now therefore humbly propose my own thoughts, which I hope will not be liable to the least objection.   8

I have been assured by a very knowing American of my acquaintance in London, that a young healthy child well nursed is at a year old a most delicious, nourishing, and wholesome food, whether stewed, roasted, baked, or boiled; and I make no doubt that it will equally serve in fricasee or a ragout.   9

I do therefore humbly offer it to public consideration that of the hundred and twenty thousand children, already computed, twenty thousand may be reserved for breed, whereof only one fourth part to be males, which is more than we allow to sheep, black cattle, or swine; and my reason is that these children are seldom the   10

---

[3]Prematurely developed (editors' note).

fruits of marriage, a circumstance not much regarded by our savages, therefore one male will be sufficient to serve four females. That the remaining hundred thousand may at a year old be offered in sale to the persons of quality and fortune through the kingdom, always advising the mother to let them suck plentifully in the last month, so as to render them plump and fat for a good table. A child will make two dishes at an entertainment for friends; and when the family dines alone, the fore or hind quarter will make a reasonable dish, and seasoned with a little pepper or salt will be very good boiled on the fourth day, especially in winter.

I have reckoned upon a medium that a child just born will   11
weigh twelve pounds, and in a solar year if tolerably nursed increaseth to twenty-eight pounds.

I grant this food will be somewhat dear, and therefore very   12
proper for landlords, who, as they have already devoured most of the parents, seem to have the best title to the children.

Infant's flesh will be in season throughout the year, but more   13
plentiful in March, and a little before and after. For we are told by a grave author, an eminent French physician,[4] that fish being a prolific diet, there are more children born in Roman Catholic countries about nine months after Lent, than at any other season; therefore, reckoning a year after Lent, the markets will be more glutted than usual, because the number of popish infants is at least three to one in this kingdom; and therefore it will have one other collateral advantage, by lessening the number of Papists among us.

I have already computed the charge of nursing a beggar's child   14
(in which list I reckon all cottagers, laborers, and four fifths of the farmers) to be about two shillings per annum, rags included; and I believe no gentleman would repine to give ten shillings for the carcass of a good fat child, which, as I have said, will make four dishes of excellent nutritive meat, when he hath only some particular friend or his own family to dine with him. Thus the squire will learn to be a good landlord, and grow popular among the tenants; the mother will have eight shillings net profit, and be fit for work till she produces another child.

Those who are more thrifty (as I must confess the times require)   15
may flay the carcass; the skin of which artificially[5] dressed will make admirable gloves for ladies, and summer boots for fine gentlemen.

[4]François Rabelais, a sixteenth-century comic writer (editors' note).
[5]Skillfully (editors' note).

As to our city of Dublin, shambles[6] may be appointed for this purpose in the most convenient parts of it, and butchers we may be assured will not be wanting; although I rather recommend buying the children alive, and dressing them hot from the knife as we do roasting pigs.

A very worthy person, a true lover of his country, and whose virtues I highly esteem, was lately pleased in discoursing on this matter to offer a refinement upon my scheme. He said that many gentlemen of his kingdom, having of late destroyed their deer, he conceived that the want of venison might be well supplied by the bodies of young lads and maidens, not exceeding fourteen years of age nor under twelve, so great a number of both sexes in every county being now ready to starve for want of work and service; and these to be disposed of by their parents, if alive, or otherwise by their nearest relations. But with due deference to so excellent a friend and so deserving a patriot, I cannot be altogether in his sentiments; for as to the males, my American acquaintance assured me from frequent experience that their flesh was generally tough and lean, like that of our schoolboys, by continual exercise, and their taste disagreeable; and to fatten them would not answer the charge. Then as to the females, it would, I think with humble submission, be a loss to the public, because they soon would become breeders themselves; and besides, it is not improbable that some scrupulous people might be apt to censure such a practice (although indeed very unjustly) as a little bordering upon cruelty; which, I confess, hath always been with me the strongest objection against any project, how well soever intended.

But in order to justify my friend, he confessed that this expedient was put into his head by the famous Psalmanazar,[7] a native of the island Formosa, who came from thence to London above twenty years ago, and in conversation told my friend that in his country when any young person happened to be put to death, the executioner sold the carcass to the persons of quality as a prime dainty; and that in his time the body of a plump girl of fifteen, who was crucified for an attempt to poison the emperor, was sold to his Imperial Majesty's prime minister of state, and other great mandarins of the

16

17

18

6Slaughterhouses (editors' note).
7A Frenchman, Georges Psalmanazar, who fooled London society into thinking he was from the exotic land of Formosa (editors' note).

court, in joints from the gibbet, at four hundred crowns. Neither indeed can I deny that if the same use were made of several plump young girls in this town, who without one single groat to their fortunes cannot stir abroad without a chair,[8] and appear at the playhouse and assemblies in foreign fineries which they never will pay for, the kingdom would not be the worse.

Some persons of a desponding spirit are in great concern about   19 that vast number of poor people who are aged, diseased, or maimed, and I have been desired to employ my thoughts what course may be taken to ease the nation of so grievous an encumbrance. But I am not in the least pain upon that matter, because it is very well known that they are every day dying and rotting by cold and famine, and filth and vermin, as fast as can be reasonably expected. And as to the younger laborers, they are now in almost as hopeful a condition. They cannot get work, and consequently pine away for want of nourishment to a degree that if any time they are accidentally hired to common labor, they have not strength to perform it; and thus the country and themselves are happily delivered from the evils to come.

I have too long digressed, and therefore shall return to my sub-   20 ject. I think the advantages by the proposal which I have made are obvious and many, as well as of the highest importance.

For first, as I have already observed, it would greatly lessen the   21 number of Papists, with whom we are yearly overrun, being the principal breeders of the nation as well as our most dangerous enemies; and who stay at home on purpose to deliver the kingdom to the Pretender, hoping to take their advantage by the absence of so many good Protestants, who have chosen rather to leave their country than to stay at home and pay tithes against their conscience to an Episcopal curate.

Secondly, the poorer tenants will have something valuable of   22 their own, which by law may be made liable to distress,[9] and help to pay their landlord's rent, their corn and cattle being already seized and money a thing unknown.

Thirdly, whereas the maintenance of an hundred thousand chil-   23 dren, from two years old and upwards, cannot be computed at less than ten shillings a piece per annum, the nation's stock will be thereby

[8]A groat was a coin worth several pennies; a chair was a sedan chair in which a person was carried by servants (editors' note).
[9]Seizure for the payment of debts (editors' note).

increased fifty thousand pounds per annum, besides the profit of a new dish introduced to the tables of all gentlemen of fortune in the kingdom who have any refinement in taste. And the money will circulate among ourselves, the goods being entirely of our own growth and manufacture.

Fourthly, the constant breeders, besides the gain of eight   24
shillings sterling per annum by the sale of their children, will be rid of the charge for maintaining them after the first year.

Fifthly, this food would likewise bring great custom to taverns,   25
where the vintners will certainly be so prudent as to procure the best receipts for dressing it to perfection, and consequently have their houses frequented by all the fine gentlemen, who justly value themselves upon their knowledge in good eating; and a skillful cook, who understands how to oblige his guests, will contrive to make it as expensive as they please.

Sixthly, this would be a great inducement to marriage, which   26
all wise nations have either encouraged by rewards or enforced by laws and penalties. It would increase the care and tenderness of mothers toward their children, when they were sure of a settlement for life to the poor babes, provided in some sort by the public, to their annual profit instead of expense. We should see an honest emulation among the married women, which of them could bring the fattest child to the market. Men would become as fond of their wives during the time of pregnancy as they are now of their mares in foal, their cows in calf, or sows when they are ready to farrow; nor offer to beat or kick them (as is too frequent a practice) for fear of a miscarriage.

Many other advantages might be enumerated. For instance, the   27
addition of some thousand carcasses in our exportation of barreled beef, the propagation of swine's flesh, and improvements in the art of making good bacon, so much wanted among us by the great destruction of pigs, too frequent at our tables, which are no way comparable in taste or magnificence to a well-grown, fat, yearling child, which roasted whole will make a considerable figure at a lord mayor's feast or any other public entertainment. But this and many others I omit, being studious of brevity.

Supposing that one thousand families in this city would be con-   28
stant customers for infants' flesh, besides others who might have it at merry meetings, particularly weddings and christenings, I compute that Dublin would take off annually about twenty thousand

carcasses, and the rest of the kingdom (where probably they will be sold somewhat cheaper) the remaining eighty thousand.

I can think of no one objection that will possibly be raised   29 against this proposal, unless it should be urged that the number of people will be thereby much lessened in the kingdom. This I freely own, and it was indeed one principal design in offering it to the world. I desire the reader will observe; that I calculate my remedy for this one individual kingdom of Ireland and for no other that ever was, is, or I think ever can be upon earth. Therefore, let no man talk to me of other expedients: of taxing our absentees at five shillings a pound: of using neither clothes nor household furniture except what is of our own growth and manufacture: of utterly rejecting the materials and instruments that promote foreign luxury: of curing the expensiveness of pride, vanity, idleness, and gaming in our women: of introducing a vein of parsimony, prudence, and temperance: of learning to love our country, in the want of which we differ even from Lowlanders and the inhabitants of Topinamboo:[10] of quitting our animosities and factions, nor acting any longer like the Jews,[11] who were murdering one another at the very moment their city was taken: of being a little cautious not to sell our country and conscience for nothing: of teaching landlords to have at least one degree of mercy toward their tenants: lastly, of putting a spirit of honesty, industry, and skill into our shopkeepers; who, if a resolution could now be taken to buy only our native goods, would immediately unite to cheat and exact upon us in the price, the measure, and the goodness, nor could ever yet be brought to make one fair proposal of just dealing, though often and earnestly invited to it.

Therefore, I repeat, let no man talk to me of these and the like   30 expedients, till he hath at least some glimpse of hope that there will ever be some hearty and sincere attempt to put them in practice.

But as to myself, having been wearied out for many years with   31 offering vain, idle, visionary thoughts, and at length utterly despairing of success, I fortunately fell upon this proposal, which, as it is wholly new, so it hath something solid and real, of no expense and little trouble, full in our own power, and whereby we can incur no danger in disobliging England. For this kind of commodity will not

---

[10]A place in the Brazilian jungle (editors' note).
[11]Rival factions were at war within Jerusalem when the city was seized by the Romans in 70 A.D. (editors' note).

bear exportation, the flesh being of too tender a consistence to admit a long continuance in salt, although perhaps I could name a country which would be glad to eat up our whole nation without it.

After all, I am not so violently bent upon my own opinion as to reject any offer proposed by wise men, which shall be found equally innocent, cheap, easy, and effectual. But before something of that kind shall be advanced in contradiction to my scheme, and offering a better, I desire the author or authors will be pleased maturely to consider two points. First, as things now stand, how they will be able to find food and raiment for an hundred thousand useless mouths and backs. And secondly, there being a round million of creatures in human figure throughout this kingdom, whose sole subsistence put into a common stock would leave them in debt two millions of pounds sterling, adding those who are beggars by profession to the bulk of farmers, cottagers, and laborers, with their wives and children who are beggars in effect; I desire those politicians who dislike my overture, and may perhaps be so bold to attempt an answer, that they will first ask the parents of these mortals whether they would not at this day think it a great happiness to have been sold for food at a year old in this manner I prescribe, and thereby have avoided such a perpetual scene of misfortunes as they have since gone through by the oppression of landlords, the impossibility of paying rent without money or trade, the want of common sustenance, with neither house nor clothes to cover them from the inclemencies of the weather, and the most inevitable prospect of entailing the like or greater miseries upon their breed forever. 32

I profess, in the sincerity of my heart, that I have not the least personal interest in endeavoring to promote this necessary work, having no other motive than the public good of my country, by advancing our trade, providing for infants, relieving the poor, and giving some pleasure to the rich. I have no children by which I can propose to get a single penny; the youngest being nine years old, and my wife past childbearing. 33

Questions for Close Reading

1. What is the selection's thesis? Locate the sentence(s) in which Swift states his main idea. If he doesn't state the thesis explicitly, express it in your own words.
2. Swift mentions several economic, social, and political realities in Ireland that prompted him to write this essay. Identify a few of them.

3. What twisted reasoning does the speaker use to argue that his proposal will improve relationships between husbands and wives and between parents and children?

4. What problems does the speaker contend the British government will solve if it permits the butchering and sale of infants from impoverished families?

5. Refer to your dictionary as needed to define the following words used in the selection: *importuning* (paragraph 1), *alms* (1), *prodigious* (2), *raiment* (4), *prolific* (13), *repine* (14), *discoursing* (17), *encumbrance* (19), and *vintners* (25).

Questions About the Writer's Craft

1. **The pattern.** *Satire* uses humor to criticize a situation and create awareness of the need for change; *irony,* often used in satire, occurs when a writer or speaker implies—rather than explicitly states—a discrepancy or incongruity. (*Verbal irony* involves a discrepancy between literal words and what's actually meant. In *situational irony,* the circumstances are themselves incongruous.) How do satire and irony help Swift accomplish what a more conventional approach to persuasion would not?

2. Swift uses language laden with emotion to convey a sarcastic, downright bitter tone. Locate several examples of emotionally charged language. How does this language support Swift's real purpose for writing "A Modest Proposal"?

3. In paragraph 20, the speaker apologizes for having "digressed" in the last few paragraphs. Do paragraphs 17, 18, and 19 really represent a digression, or are they germane to the issue? Explain.

4. **The pattern.** Writers of argumentation-persuasion essays often anticipate and then refute opposing opinions. In what paragraph does the speaker in "A Modest Proposal" refute the dissenting viewpoint? What is the real purpose of this refutation?

Writing Assignments Using Argumentation-Persuasion as a Pattern of Development

1. Select a subject that you feel strongly about—one that has an ethical or moral dimension to it. Then, like Swift, use an ironic approach to convince readers of your position. In other words, argue for one point of view while pretending to advance the other. For example, if you're concerned about some colleges' exemption of their star athletes from conventional academic requirements, you could write an essay arguing the "advantages" of letting student-athletes "coast" through college.

2. Swift focuses on the disenfranchised people of his time: the impoverished Irish. Write an essay in which you try to persuade skeptical readers that a particular group is the most disenfranchised of *our* time. Brainstorm

with others to generate possible subjects. When you write your essay, remember to acknowledge—and, if you can, to dismantle—dissenting opinions. Consider using the library and/or the Internet to gather evidence in support of your claim.

Writing Assignments Using Other Patterns of Development

3. At the beginning of "A Modest Proposal," Swift describes briefly the poverty he witnessed in his native land. How would *you* describe the face of poverty? Write an essay describing an impoverished, blighted area. What are its streets, houses, stores, and people like? Organizing the essay around a dominant impression, depict what you see, smell, hear, and feel. Gordon Parks's "Flavio's Home" (page 98) will help you see how you might approach such an essay.

4. Seeking to improve the Irish economy, Swift advocates boycotting foreign-made products. Do you believe the United States should impose restrictive tariffs and import limits on goods manufactured abroad? Write a paper in which you identify the positive and negative consequences of such protective measures. Gather information by brainstorming with others, and consider supplementing this informal research with material gathered in the library and/or on the Internet.

Writing Assignments Using a Journal Entry as a Starting Point

5 Write an essay about a situation that distresses you. Select from your pre-reading journal entry the one problem that especially concerns you. Begin the essay with a dramatic example illustrating the extent of the problem. Then describe in detail the steps that could be taken to remedy the situation. Save for last the step that you think is most important and about which you have most to say.

Nat Hentoff

Nat Hentoff was born in Boston in 1925. His writings for the *Village Voice* and the *New Yorker*, his columns for the *Washington Post*, and his more than twenty-five books of fiction and nonfiction have earned him the reputation as a respected voice of the political Left. Privacy, drug testing, racism, the draft, abortion, and educational reform have all come under Hentoff's keen observation. In 1987, Hentoff published his autobiography, *Boston Boy*, and 1989 saw the publication of his book *The First Freedom: The Tumultuous History of Free Speech in America. Free Speech for Me—But Not for Thee* (1993), *Listen to the Stories* (1996), *Speaking Freely: A Memoir* (1997), and *Living the Bill of Rights: How to Be an Authentic American* (1998) are his latest works. Despite his political stance as a leftist, Hentoff has criticized the zeal of the Left in suppressing speech it finds offensive. Such concerns led him to write the following essay, first published in the *Progressive* in May 1989.

Pre-Reading Journal Entry

How do you feel about freedom of speech on campus? In your journal, list several controversial issues that might be debated in a college setting. For each issue, indicate whether you feel that divergent, even inflammatory views should have an opportunity to be heard on campus—for example, in class, in the college newspaper, in a lecture series. Jot down why you feel as you do.

Free Speech on Campus

A flier distributed at the University of Michigan some months 1 ago proclaimed that blacks "don't belong in classrooms, they belong hanging from trees."

At other campuses around the country, manifestations of racism 2 are becoming commonplace. At Yale, a swastika and the words WHITE POWER! were painted on the building housing the University's Afro-American Cultural Center. At Temple University, a White Students Union has been formed with some 130 members.

Swastikas are not directed only at black students. The Nazi sym- 3 bol has been spray-painted on the Jewish Student Union at

Memphis State University. And on a number of campuses, women have been singled out as targets of wounding and sometimes frightening speech. At the law school of the State University of New York at Buffalo, several women students have received anonymous letters characterized by one professor as venomously sexist.

These and many more such signs of the resurgence of bigotry 4 and knownothingism throughout the society—as well as on campus—have to do solely with speech, including symbolic speech. There have also been physical assaults on black students and on black, white, and Asian women students, but the way to deal with physical attacks is clear: call the police and file a criminal complaint. What is to be done, however, about speech alone—however disgusting, inflammatory, and rawly divisive that speech may be?

At more and more colleges, administrators—with the enthusias- 5 tic support of black students, women students, and liberal students—have been answering that question by preventing or punishing speech. In public universities, this is a clear violation of the First Amendment. In private colleges and universities, suppression of speech mocks the secular religion of academic freedom and free inquiry.

The Student Press Law Center in Washington, D.C.—a vital 6 source of legal support for student editors around the country—reports, for example, that at the University of Kansas, the student host and producer of a radio news program was forbidden by school officials from interviewing a leader of the Ku Klux Klan. So much for free inquiry on that campus.

In Madison, Wisconsin, the *Capital Times* ran a story in January 7 about Chancellor Sheila Kaplan of the University of Wisconsin branch at Parkside, who ordered her campus to be scoured of "some anonymously placed white supremacist hate literature." Sounding like the legendary Mayor Frank ("I am the law") Hague of Jersey City, who booted "bad speech" out of town, Chancellor Kaplan said, "This institution is not a lamppost standing on the street corner. It doesn't belong to everyone."

Who decides what speech can be heard or read by everyone? 8 Why, the Chancellor, of course. That's what George III[1] used to say, too.

---

[1] King of England at the time of the American Revolution, George III reportedly lost his sanity in his later years (editors' note).

University of Wisconsin political science professor Carol Tebben   9
thinks otherwise. She believes university administrators "are getting
confused when they are acting as censors and trying to protect students from bad ideas. I don't think students need to be protected
from bad ideas. I think they can determine for themselves what ideas
are bad."

After all, if students are to be "protected" from bad ideas, how   10
are they going to learn to identify and cope with them? Sending such
ideas underground simply makes them stronger and more dangerous.

Professor Tebben's conviction that free speech means just that   11
has become a decidedly minority view on many campuses. At the
University of Buffalo Law School, the faculty unanimously adopted
a "Statement Regarding Intellectual Freedom, Tolerance, and
Political Harassment." Its title implies support of intellectual freedom, but the statement warned students that once they enter "this
legal community," their right to free speech must become tempered
"by the responsibility to promote equality and justice."

Accordingly, swift condemnation will befall anyone who   12
engages in "remarks directed at another's race, sex, religion, national origin, age, or sex preference." Also forbidden are "other remarks
based on prejudice and group stereotype."

This ukase is so broad that enforcement has to be alarmingly   13
subjective. Yet the University of Buffalo Law School provides no
due-process procedures for a student booked for making any of
these prohibited remarks. Conceivably, a student caught playing a
Lenny Bruce, Richard Pryor, or Sam Kinison[2] album in his room
could be tried for aggravated insensitivity by association.

When I looked into this wholesale cleansing of bad speech at   14
Buffalo, I found it had encountered scant opposition. One protest-
er was David Gerald Jay, a graduate of the law school and a cooper-
ating attorney for the New York Civil Liberties Union. Said the
appalled graduate: "Content-based prohibitions constitute prior
restraint and should not be tolerated."

You would think that the law professors and administration at this   15
public university might have known that. But hardly any professors
dissented, and among the students only members of the conservative

[2]Lenny Bruce was a stand-up comic popular in the 1950s and early 1960s. Bruce's
caustic social commentary and his use of language that many considered offensive
established the precedent for the confrontational style of many later comedians,
including Richard Pryor and Sam Kinison (editors' note).

Federalist Society spoke up for free speech. The fifty-strong chapter of the National Lawyers Guild was on the other side. After all, it was more important to go on record as vigorously opposing racism and sexism than to expose oneself to charges of insensitivity to these malignancies.

The pressures to have the "right" attitude—as proved by having   16
the "right" language in and out of class—can be stifling. A student who opposes affirmative action, for instance, can be branded a racist.

At the University of California at Los Angeles, the student news-   17
paper ran an editorial cartoon satirizing affirmative action. (A student stops a rooster on campus and asks how the rooster got into UCLA. "Affirmative action," is the answer.) After outraged complaints from various minority groups, the editor was suspended for violating a publication policy against running "articles that perpetuate derogatory or cultural stereotypes." The art director was also suspended.

When the opinion editor of the student newspaper at California   18
State University at Northridge wrote an article asserting that the sanctions against the editor and art director at UCLA amounted to censorship, he was suspended too.

At New York University Law School, a student was so disturbed   19
by the pall of orthodoxy at that prestigious institution that he wrote to the school newspaper even though, as he said, he expected his letter to make him a pariah among his fellow students.

Barry Endick described the atmosphere at NYU created by "a   20
host of watchdog committees and a generally hostile classroom reception regarding any student comment right of center." This "can be arguably viewed as symptomatic of a prevailing spirit of academic and social intolerance of . . . any idea which is not 'politically correct.'"

He went on to say something that might well be posted on cam-   21
pus bulletin boards around the country, though it would probably be torn down at many of them: "We ought to examine why students, so anxious to wield the Fourteenth Amendment, give short shrift to the First. Yes, Virginia, there are racist assholes. And you know what, the Constitution protects them, too."

Not when they engage in violence or vandalism. But when they   22
speak or write, racist assholes fall right into this Oliver Wendell Holmes[3] definition—highly unpopular among bigots, liberals, radicals, feminists, sexists, and college administrators: "If there is any

[3]Holmes was Associate Justice of the Supreme Court (1902–32) (editors' note).

principle of the Constitution that more imperatively calls for attachment than any other, it is the principle of free thought—not free only for those who agree with us, but freedom for the thought we hate."

The language sounds like a pietistic Sunday sermon, but if it   23
ever falls wholly into disuse, neither this publication nor any other journal of opinion—right or left—will survive.

Sometimes, college presidents and administrators sound as if   24
they fully understand what Holmes was saying. Last year, for example, when the *Daily Pennsylvanian*[4]—speaking for many at the University of Pennsylvania—urged that a speaking invitation to Louis Farrakhan[5] be withdrawn, University President Sheldon Hackney disagreed.

"Open expression," said Hackney, "is the fundamental principle   25
of a university." Yet consider what the same Sheldon Hackney did to the free-speech rights of a teacher at his own university. If any story distills the essence of the current decline of free speech on college campuses, it is the Ballad of Murray Dolfman.

For twenty-two years, Dolfman, a practicing lawyer in   26
Philadelphia, had been a part-time lecturer in the Legal Studies Department of the University of Pennsylvania's Wharton School. For twenty-two years, no complaint had ever been made against him; indeed his student course evaluations had been outstanding. Each year students competed to get into his class.

On a November afternoon in 1984, Dolfman was lecturing   27
about personal-service contracts. His style somewhat resembles that of Professor Charles Kingsfield in *The Paper Chase*.[6] Dolfman insists that students he calls on be prepared—or suffer the consequences. He treats all students this way—regardless of race, creed, or sex.

This day, Dolfman was pointing out that no one can be forced   28
to work against his or her will—even if a contract has been signed. A court may prevent the resister from working for someone else so long as the contract is in effect but, Dolfman said, there can "be nothing that smacks of involuntary servitude."

---

[4]The student newspaper at the University of Pennsylvania (editors' note).
[5]The leader of the Black Nation of Islam, Farrakhan holds controversial views that have been called anti-Semitic and racially inflammatory (editors' note).
[6]Charles Kingsfield was the demanding law professor in both the film and the television show *The Paper Chase*. The series, popular in the 1970s, chronicled the struggles of first-year law students at a prestigious university (editors' note).

Where does this concept come from? Dolfman looked around 29
the room. Finally, a cautious hand was raised: "The Constitution?"

"Where in the Constitution?" No hands. "The Thirteenth 30
Amendment," said the teacher. So, what does *it* say? The students
were looking everywhere but at Dolfman.

"We will lose our liberties," Dolfman often told his classes, "if 31
we don't know what they are."

On this occasion, he told them that he and other Jews, as ex- 32
slaves, spoke at Passover of the time when they were slaves under the
Pharaohs so that they would remember every year what it was like
not to be free.

"We have ex-slaves here," Dolfman continued, "who should 33
know about the Thirteenth Amendment." He asked black students
in the class if they could tell him what was in that amendment.

"I wanted them to really think about it," Dolfman told me 34
recently, "and know its history. You're better equipped to fight
racism if you know all about those post-Civil War amendments and
civil rights laws."

The Thirteenth Amendment provides that "neither slavery nor 35
involuntary servitude . . . shall exist within the United States."

The black students in his class did not know what was in that 36
amendment, and Dolfman had them read it aloud. Later, they complained to university officials that they had been hurt and humiliat-
ed by having been referred to as ex-slaves. Moreover, they said, they
had no reason to be grateful for a constitutional amendment which
gave them rights which should never have been denied them—and
gave them precious little else. They had not made these points in
class, although Dolfman—unlike Professor Kingsfield—encourages
rebuttal.

Informed of the complaint, Dolfman told the black students he 37
had intended no offense, and he apologized if they had been offended.

That would not do—either for the black students or for the 38
administration. Furthermore, there were mounting black-Jewish
tensions on campus, and someone had to be sacrificed. Who better
than a part-time Jewish teacher with no contract and no union? He
was sentenced by—George Orwell[7] would have loved this—the
Committee on Academic Freedom and Responsibility.

[7]British essayist and novelist, George Orwell often wrote about the fragile line separating democratic and despotic institutions (editors' note; for more information on
Orwell, see page 167).

On his way to the stocks, Dolfman told President Sheldon   39
Hackney that if a part-time instructor "can be punished on this kind
of charge, a tenured professor can eventually be booted out, then a
dean, and then a president."

Hackney was unmoved. Dolfman was banished from the cam-   40
pus for what came to be a year. But first he was forced to make a
public apology to the entire university and then he was compelled
to attend a "sensitivity and racial awareness" session. Sort of like a
Vietnamese reeducation camp.

A few conservative professors objected to the stigmatization of   41
Murray Dolfman. I know of no student dissent. Indeed, those students most concerned with making the campus more "sensitive" to
diversity exulted in Dolfman's humiliation. So did most liberals on
the faculty.

If my children were still of college age and wanted to attend the   42
University of Pennsylvania, I would tell them this story. But where
else could I encourage them to go?

Questions for Close Reading

1. What is the selection's thesis? Locate the sentence(s) in which Hentoff
   states his main idea. If he doesn't state the thesis explicitly, express it in
   your own words.
2. What evidence does Hentoff present to support his statement that
   there's a "resurgence of bigotry and knownothingism throughout the
   society"?
3. According to Hentoff, how have officials on campuses at the University
   of Kansas, the University of Wisconsin, and the University of California
   at Los Angeles interfered with free inquiry and free speech? What reasons did university officials give for their actions?
4. Why, in Hentoff's opinion, should college campuses permit all types of
   speech? According to Hentoff, what problems arise when free speech is
   curtailed?
5. Refer to your dictionary as needed to define the following words used in
   the selection: *venomously* (paragraph 3), *knownothingism* (4), *ukase* (13),
   dissented (15), *malignancies* (15), *sanctions* (18), *pall* (19), *pariah* (19),
   pietistic (23), *distills* (25), *stocks* (39), and *stigmatization* (41).

Questions About the Writer's Craft

1. **The pattern.** Writing on a complex and controversial issue, Hentoff
   wisely confronts the opposing viewpoint—in this case, the position that

the free speech of extremists should be suppressed. What strategies does Hentoff use to deal with this view?

2. **Other patterns.** Where in the selection does Hentoff use examples and a narrative account to support his argument? How do the examples and the narrative help him support his case?

3. What tone does Hentoff employ when describing those who believe that sometimes it is necessary to limit free speech? How do Hentoff's sentence structure and word choice help create this tone?

4. Examine the quotations in paragraphs 20 through 22. Why do you think Hentoff chooses to quote these two particular individuals—law student Barry Endick and Supreme Court Justice Oliver Wendell Holmes? What does he achieve by juxtaposing Endick's words with those of Holmes?

Writing Assignments Using Argumentation-Persuasion as a Pattern of Development

1. Consider the stereotyping, the economic deprivations, and the personal slurs that many members of minority groups continue to suffer. Then decide which you believe is more important: totally free speech or the protection of the rights, feelings, and status of groups that have been discriminated against. Write an essay in which you argue that on college campuses protecting "equality and justice" either is or isn't more important than protecting freedom of speech. Provide specific examples to defend your position, and don't forget to deal with opposing viewpoints.

2. Hentoff mentions that on one campus student journalists were punished for publishing a satirical cartoon that proved offensive to several minority groups. But satire and comedy, especially when they have some bite, often offend one group or another. Carefully consider the comedy and satire currently in vogue. Do they provide harmless entertainment? Do they perpetuate negative stereotypes? Do they open up helpful discussion and debate? Prepare an essay in which you argue your position, supporting it with a number of persuasive examples. And don't forget to acknowledge (and, if possible, to refute) opposing viewpoints at some point in your paper.

Writing Assignments Using Other Patterns of Development

3. What procedures has your college or university established so that people on campus—faculty, staff, and/or students—can file grievances if they feel they have been discriminated against in some way? In an essay, describe this process and indicate whether you feel it's adequate. If it isn't, explain what steps need to be taken to improve the procedures.

∞ 4. Stereotyping isn't restricted to minorities. Most of us have felt unfairly stereotyped at some time or another, perhaps because of gender, physical or intellectual abilities, even a hobby or interest. Write an essay about a time you were treated unfairly or cruelly because of some personal characteristic. Be sure to show how the event affected you. The following essays will provide insight into the potentially corrosive effect of labels and stereotypes: Audre Lorde's "The Fourth of July" (page 160), Alice Walker's "Beauty: When the Other Dancer Is the Self" (page 467), Gloria Naylor's "Mommy, What Does 'Nigger' Mean?" (page 516), William Raspberry's "The Handicap of Definition" (page 529), and Shelby Steele's "Affirmative Action: The Price of Preference" (page 649).

Writing Assignments Using a Journal Entry as a Starting Point

5. Write an editorial for your college newspaper arguing that a college campus is *or* is not the place to air conflicting, even inflammatory views about *one* of the controversial issues listed in your pre-reading journal entry. Perhaps you feel that the issue warrants a public forum in one campus setting but not another. If so, explain why. To lend authority to your position, interview students who don't share your point of view. Be sure to acknowledge their position in your editorial.

Camille Paglia

Before 1991, Camille Paglia, Professor of Humanities at Philadelphia's University of the Arts, was known primarily for her electrifying performance in the classroom. Then came the publication of Paglia's *Sexual Personae: Art and Decadence From Nefertiti to Emily Dickinson,* a sweeping book that moves with dizzying speed from the days of cave art to the nineteenth century. *Sexual Personae* makes the case that man creates art as a defensive response to woman's terrifying cosmic power—specifically, her sexual and procreative force. Suddenly Paglia became an international celebrity and had many opportunities to express her controversial views. She has been both revered and reviled for making statements like these: "Male aggression and lust are the energizing factors in culture" and "If I ever got into a dating situation where I was raped and overwhelmed, I would say, 'Oh well, I misread the signals.'" Born in 1947, Paglia earned her doctorate from Yale University, where her Ph.D. thesis was an early version of *Sexual Personae. Sex, Art, and American Culture: Essays* (1992), *Vamps and Tramps: New Essays* (1994), and *Alfred Hitchcock's "The Birds"* (1998) are Paglia's latest works. She is also a regular columnist for *Salon* online magazine. The following selection, written in Paglia's characteristically provocative style, first appeared in *Long Island Newsday* in 1988.

Pre-Reading Journal Entry

How would you define "date rape"? Use your journal to formulate a preliminary definition. Working as quickly as you can, jot down your preliminary thoughts about what it is and what it isn't.

Rape: A Bigger Danger Than Feminists Know

Rape is an outrage that cannot be tolerated in civilized society. 1
Yet feminism, which has waged a crusade for rape to be taken more seriously, has put young women in danger by hiding the truth about sex from them.

In dramatizing the pervasiveness of rape, feminists have told 2
young women that before they have sex with a man, they must give

consent as explicit as a legal contract's. In this way, young women have been convinced that they have been the victims of rape. On elite campuses in the Northeast and on the West Coast, they have held consciousness-raising sessions, petitioned administrations, demanded inquests. At Brown University, outraged, panicky "victims" have scrawled the names of alleged attackers on the walls of women's rest rooms. What marital rape was to the '70s, "date rape" is to the '90s.

The incidence and seriousness of rape do not require this kind   3
of exaggeration. Real acquaintance rape is nothing new. It has been a horrible problem for women for all of recorded history. Once, father and brothers protected women from rape. Once, the penalty for rape was death. I come from a fierce Italian tradition where, not so long ago in the motherland, a rapist would end up knifed, castrated, and hung out to dry.

But the old clans and small rural communities have broken   4
down. In our cities, on our campuses far from home, young women are vulnerable and defenseless. Feminism has not prepared them for this. Feminism keeps saying the sexes are the same. It keeps telling women they can do anything, go anywhere, say anything, wear anything. No, they can't. Women will always be in sexual danger.

One of my male students recently slept overnight with a friend   5
in a passageway of the Great Pyramid in Egypt. He described the moon and sand, the ancient silence and eerie echoes. I am a woman. I will never experience that. I am not stupid enough to believe I could ever be safe there. There is a world of solitary adventure I will never have. Women have always known these somber truths. But feminism, with its pie-in-the-sky fantasies about the perfect world, keeps young women from seeing life as it is.

We must remedy social injustice whenever we can. But there are   6
some things we cannot change. There are sexual differences that are based in biology. Academic feminism is lost in a fog of social constructionism. It believes we are totally the product of our environment. This idea was invented by Rousseau.[1] He was wrong. Emboldened by dumb French language theory, academic feminists repeat the same hollow slogans over and over to each other. Their view of sex is naive and prudish. Leaving sex to the feminists is like letting your dog vacation at the taxidermist's.

[1]A French political writer and philosopher (1712–78) (editors' note).

The sexes are at war. Men must struggle for identity against the 7
overwhelming power of their mothers. Women have menstruation
to tell them they are women. Men must do or risk something to be
men. Men become masculine only when other men say they are.
Having sex with a woman is one way a boy becomes a man.

College men are at their hormonal peak. They have just left 8
their mothers and are questing for their male identity. In groups,
they are dangerous. A woman going to a fraternity party is walking
into Testosterone Flats, full of prickly cacti and blazing guns. If she
goes, she should be armed with resolute alertness. She should arrive
with girlfriends and leave with them. A girl who lets herself get dead
drunk at a fraternity party is a fool. A girl who goes upstairs alone
with a brother at a fraternity party is an idiot. Feminists call this
"blaming the victim." I call it common sense.

For a decade, feminists have drilled their disciples to say, "Rape 9
is a crime of violence but not of sex." This sugar-coated Shirley
Temple nonsense has exposed young women to disaster. Misled by
feminism, they do not expect rape from the nice boys from good
homes who sit next to them in class.

Aggression and eroticism, in fact, are deeply intertwined. Hunt, 10
pursuit and capture are biologically programmed into male sexuality. Generation after generation, men must be educated, refined, and
ethically persuaded away from their tendency toward anarchy and
brutishness. Society is not the enemy, as feminism ignorantly claims.
Society is woman's protection against rape. Feminism, with its
solemn Carry Nation[2] repressiveness, does not see what is for men
the eroticism or fun element in rape, especially the wild, infectious
delirium of gang rape. Women who do not understand rape cannot
defend themselves against it.

The date-rape controversy shows feminism hitting the wall of its 11
own broken promises. The women of my '60s generation were the
first respectable girls in history to swear like sailors, get drunk, stay
out all night—in short, to act like men. We sought total sexual freedom and equality. But as time passed, we woke up to cold reality.
The old double standard protected women. When anything goes,
it's women who lose.

Today's young women don't know what they want. They see that 12
feminism has not brought sexual happiness. The theatrics of public

[2]A nineteenth-century reformer who advocated the abolition of alcohol (editors'
note).

rage over date rape are their way of restoring the old sexual rules that were shattered by my generation. Yet nothing about the sexes has really changed. The comic film *Where the Boys Are* (1960), the ultimate expression of '50s man-chasing, still speaks directly to our time. It shows smart, lively women skillfully anticipating and fending off the dozens of strategies with which horny men try to get them into bed. The agonizing date-rape subplot and climax are brilliantly done. The victim, Yvette Mimieux, makes mistake after mistake, obvious to the other girls. She allows herself to be lured away from her girlfriends and into isolation with boys whose character and intentions she misreads. *Where the Boys Are* tells the truth. It shows courtship as a dangerous game in which the signals are not verbal but subliminal.

Neither militant feminism, which is obsessed with politically correct language, nor academic feminism, which believes that knowledge and experience are "constituted by" language, can understand preverbal or nonverbal communication. Feminism, focusing on sexual politics, cannot see that sex exists in and through the body. Sexual desire and arousal cannot be fully translated into verbal terms. This is why men and women misunderstand each other.   13

Trying to remake the future, feminism cut itself off from sexual history. It discarded and suppressed the sexual myths of literature, art and religion. Those myths show us the turbulence, the mysteries and passions of sex. In mythology we see men's sexual anxiety, their fear of woman's dominance. Much sexual violence is rooted in men's sense of psychological weakness toward women. It takes many men to deal with one woman. Woman's voracity is a persistent motif. Clara Bow,[3] it was rumored, took on the USC[4] football team on weekends. Marilyn Monroe, singing "Diamonds Are a Girl's Best Friend," rules a conga line of men in tuxes. Half-clad Cher, in the video for "If I Could Turn Back Time," deranges a battleship of screaming sailors and straddles a pink-lit cannon. Feminism, coveting social power, is blind to woman's cosmic sexual power.   14

To understand rape, you must study the past. There never was and never will be sexual harmony. Every woman must be prudent and cautious about where she goes and with whom. When she makes a mistake, she must accept the consequences and, through self-criticism, resolve never to make that mistake again. Running to   15

[3]A movie star from the Roaring Twenties era (editors' note).
[4]University of Southern California (editors' note).

mommy and daddy on the campus grievance committee is unworthy of strong women. Posting lists of guilty men in the toilet is cowardly, infantile stuff.

The Italian philosophy of life espouses high-energy confronta- 16
tion. A male student makes a vulgar remark about your breasts? Don't slink off to whimper with the campus shrinking violets. Deal with it. On the spot. Say, "Shut up, you jerk! And crawl back to the barnyard where you belong!" In general, women who project this take-charge attitude toward life get harassed less often. I see too many dopey, immature, self-pitying women walking around like melting sticks of butter. It's the Yvette Mimieux syndrome: make me happy. And listen to me weep when I'm not.

The date-rape debate is already smothering in propaganda 17
churned out by the expensive Northeastern colleges and universities, with their overconcentration of boring, uptight academic feminists and spoiled, affluent students. Beware of the deep manipulativeness of rich students who were neglected by their parents. They love to turn the campus into hysterical psychodramas of sexual transgression, followed by assertions of parental authority and concern. And don't look for sexual enlightenment from academe, which spews out mountains of books but never looks at life directly.

As a fan of football and rock music, I see in the simple, swagger- 18
ing masculinity of the jock and in the noisy posturing of the heavy-metal guitarist certain fundamental, unchanging truths about sex. Masculinity is aggressive, unstable, combustible. It is also the most creative cultural force in history. Women must reorient themselves toward the elemental powers of sex, which can strengthen or destroy.

The only solution to date rape is female self-awareness and self- 19
control. A woman's number-one line of defense against rape is herself. When a real rape occurs, she should report it to the police. Complaining to college committees because the courts "take too long" is ridiculous. College administrations are not a branch of the judiciary. They are not equipped or trained for legal inquiry. Colleges must alert incoming students to the problems and dangers of adulthood. Then colleges must stand back and get out of the sex game.

Questions for Close Reading

1. What is the selection's thesis? Locate the sentence(s) in which Paglia states her main idea. If she doesn't state the thesis explicitly, express it in your own words.

2. In Paglia's opinion, why are women more "vulnerable and defenseless" now than in the past?

3. According to Paglia, what "truth about sex" has feminism hidden from young women?

4. What does Paglia believe is "the only solution to date rape"?

5. Refer to your dictionary as needed to define the following words used in the selection: *inquests* (paragraph 2), *testosterone* (8), *constituted* (13), *grievance* (15), and *judiciary* (19).

Questions About the Writer's Craft

1. The pattern. Examine the way Paglia develops her argument in paragraphs 6 and 8. Which of her assertions in these paragraphs can be assumed to be true without further proof? Why do you think Paglia includes these essentially incontestable statements? Conversely, which of her assertions in paragraphs 6 and 8 require further proof before their truth can be demonstrated? Does Paglia provide such support? Explain.

2. Other patterns. How does Paglia use the comparison-contrast pattern to develop her argument?

3. Paglia's style is frequently characterized by short sentences strung together with few transitions. Locate some examples of this style. Why might Paglia have chosen this style? What is its effect?

4. Where does Paglia use emotional, highly connotative language? Where does she employ strongly worded absolute statements? Do you think that this use of pathos makes Paglia's argument more or less convincing? Explain.

Writing Assignments Using Argumentation-Persuasion as a Pattern of Development

∞ 1. Read Susan Jacoby's "Common Decency" (page 622), an essay that takes exception to Paglia's view of date rape. Decide which writer presents her case more convincingly. Then write an essay arguing that the *other writer* has trouble making a strong case for her position. Consider the merits and flaws (including any logical fallacies) in the argument, plus such issues as the writer's credibility, strategies for dealing with the opposing view, and use of emotional appeals. Throughout, support your opinion with specific examples drawn from the selection. Keep in mind that you're critiquing the effectiveness of the writer's argument. It's not appropriate, then, simply to explain why you agree or disagree with the writer's position or merely to summarize what the writer says.

∞ 2. Paglia criticizes those who claim that the environment, or social climate, is primarily responsible for shaping gender differences. She believes that such differences "are based in biology." Write an essay arguing your own position about the role that environment and biology play in determining sex-role attitudes and behavior. Remembering to acknowledge opposing views, defend your own viewpoint with plentiful examples based on your experiences and observations. You may also need to conduct some library research to gather support for your position. The following essays will provide insights that you may want to draw upon in your paper: Alleen Pace Nilsen's "Sexism and Language" (page 225), Barbara Ehrenreich's "What I've Learned From Men" (page 249), Deborah Tannen's "But What Do You Mean?" (page 313), and Dave Barry's "The Ugly Truth About Beauty" (page 422).

Writing Assignments Using Other Patterns of Development

3. Paglia writes in paragraph 7 that "men become masculine only when other men say they are. Having sex with a woman is one way a boy becomes a man." Write an essay constructing your own definition of masculinity. Comment on the extent to which you feel being sexually active is an important criterion, but also include other hallmarks of masculinity.

4. Date rape seems to be on the rise. Brainstorm with others to identify what may be leading to its growing occurrence. Focusing on several related factors, write an essay showing how these factors contribute to the problem. Possible factors include the following: the way males and females are depicted in the media (advertisements, movies, television, rock videos); young people's use of alcohol; the emergence of coed college dorms. At the end of the essay, offer some recommendations about what can be done to create a safer climate for dating. You should consider supporting your speculations with information about date rape gathered in the library and/or on the Internet.

Writing Assignments Using a Journal Entry as a Starting Point

5. Drawing upon the material in your pre-reading journal entry, write an essay in which you present a carefully considered definition of the term "date rape." Explain clearly what constitutes date rape and what doesn't. To deepen your understanding of this thorny issue, consider brainstorming with others as well as conducting research in the library and/or on the Internet. One issue to consider: Do males and females define the term differently? If so, how do they define it, and why might their definitions differ?

Susan Jacoby

In her first job as a newspaper reporter, Susan Jacoby (1945–) carefully avoided doing "women's stories," believing that such features weren't worthy of a serious journalist. However, Jacoby's opinion changed with the times, especially as women's issues began to gain increasing attention. Indeed, many of her essays—including those in the *New York Times* and *McCall's*—have dealt with women's concerns. A good number of Jacoby's essays have been collected in *The Possible She* (1979) and *Money, Manners, and Morals* (1993). In 1994, she coauthored the biography *Soul to Soul: A Black Russian American Family 1865–1992*. Jacoby's most recent books include *Body* and *Geotrivia Sports*, both published in 1996, and *Half-Jew: A Daughter's Search for Her Family's Buried Past* (2000). The following selection, published in the *New York Times* in April 1991, was written in response to the book *Sexual Personae* by Camille Paglia (see page 615).

Pre-Reading Journal Entry

The phrase "boys will be boys" is often cited to explain certain types of male behavior. What kinds of actions typically fall into this category? List a few of these in your journal. Which behaviors are positive? Why? Which are negative? Why?

Common Decency

She was deeply in love with a man who was treating her badly. 1
To assuage her wounded ego (and to prove to herself that she could get along nicely without him), she invited another man, an old boyfriend, to a dinner *à deux* in her apartment. They were on their way to the bedroom when, having realized that she wanted only the man who wasn't there, she changed her mind. Her ex-boyfriend was understandably angry. He left her apartment with a not-so-politely phrased request that she leave him out of any future plans.

And that is the end of the story—except for the fact that he was 2
eventually kind enough to accept her apology for what was surely a classic case of "mixed signals."

I often recall this incident, in which I was the embarrassed 3
female participant, as the controversy over "date rape"—intensified

by the assault that William Kennedy Smith[1] has been accused of—heats up across the nation. What seems clear to me is that those who place acquaintance rape in a different category from "stranger rape"—those who excuse friendly social rapists on grounds that they are too dumb to understand when "no" means no—are being even more insulting to men than to women.

These apologists for date rape—and some of them are women—   4
are really saying that the average man cannot be trusted to exercise any impulse control. Men are nasty and men are brutes—and a woman must be constantly on her guard to avoid giving a man any excuse to give way to his baser instincts.

If this view were accurate, few women would manage to get   5
through life without being raped, and few men would fail to commit rape. For the reality is that all of us, men as well as women, send and receive innumerable mixed signals in the course of our sexual lives—and that is as true in marital beds at age fifty as in the back seats of cars at age fifteen.

Most men somehow manage to decode these signals without   6
using superior physical strength to force themselves on their partners. And most women manage to handle conflicting male signals without, say, picking up carving knives to demonstrate their displeasure at sexual rejection. This is called civilization.

Civilized is exactly what my old boyfriend was being when he   7
didn't use my muddleheaded emotional distress as an excuse to rape me. But I don't owe him excessive gratitude for his decent behavior—any more than he would have owed me special thanks for not stabbing him through the heart if our situations had been reversed. Most date rapes do not happen because a man honestly mistakes a woman's "no" for a "yes" or a "maybe." They occur because a minority of men—an ugly minority, to be sure—can't stand to take "no" for an answer.

This minority behavior—and a culture that excuses it on   8
grounds that boys will be boys—is the target of the movement against date rape that has surfaced on many campuses during the past year.

---

[1]William Kennedy Smith, the nephew of John, Robert, and Edward Kennedy, was accused of raping a woman in 1991. Kennedy was acquitted, but the trial, broadcast on television, created a national furor and generated heated debate on the issue of date rape (editors' note).

It's not surprising that date rape is an issue of particular impor-   9
tance to college-age women. The campus concentration of large
numbers of young people, in an unsupervised environment that
encourages drinking and partying, tends to promote sexual aggression and discourage inhibition. Drunken young men who rape a
woman at a party can always claim they didn't know what they were
doing—and a great many people will blame the victim for having
been there in the first place.

That is the line adopted by antifeminists like Camille Paglia,[2]   10
author of the controversial *Sexual Personae: Art and Decadence From
Nefertiti to Emily Dickinson.* Paglia, whose views strongly resemble
those expounded twenty years ago by Norman Mailer[3] in *The
Prisoner of Sex,* argues that feminists have deluded women by telling
them they can go anywhere and do anything without fear of rape.
Feminism, in this view, is both naïve and antisexual because it ignores
the power of women to incite uncontrollable male passions.

Just to make sure there is no doubt about a woman's place,   11
Paglia also links the male sexual aggression that leads to rape with
the creative energy of art. "There is no female Mozart," she has
declared, "because there is no female Jack the Ripper." According
to this "logic," one might expect to discover the next generation of
composers in fraternity houses and dorms that have been singled out
as sites of brutal gang rapes.

This type of unsubtle analysis makes no distinction between sex   12
as an expression of the will to power and sex as a source of pleasure.
When domination is seen as an inevitable component of sex, the act
of rape is defined not by a man's actions but by a woman's signals.

It is true, of course, that some women (especially the young)   13
initially resist sex not out of real conviction but as part of the elaborate persuasion and seduction rituals accompanying what was once
called courtship. And it is true that many men (again, especially the
young) take pride in the ability to coax a woman a step further than
she intended to go.

But these mating rituals do not justify or even explain date rape.   14
Even the most callow youth is capable of understanding the difference between resistance and genuine fear; between a halfhearted
"no, we shouldn't" and tears or screams; between a woman who is

---

[2]For information on Camille Paglia, see page 615 (editors' note).
[3]An American essayist and novelist (editors' note).

physically free to leave a room and one who is being physically restrained.

The immorality and absurdity of using mixed signals as an excuse for rape is cast in high relief when the assault involves one woman and a group of men. In cases of gang rape in a social setting (usually during or after a party), the defendants and their lawyers frequently claim that group sex took place but no force was involved. These upright young men, so the defense invariably contends, were confused because the girl had voluntarily gone to a party with them. Why, she may have even displayed sexual interest in *one* of them. How could they have been expected to understand that she didn't wish to have sex with the whole group? 15

The very existence of the term "date rape" attests to a slow change in women's consciousness that began with the feminist movement of the late 1960s. Implicit in this consciousness is the conviction that a woman has the right to say no at any point in the process leading to sexual intercourse—and that a man who fails to respect her wishes should incur serious legal and social consequences. 16

The other, equally important half of the equation is respect for men. If mixed signals are the real cause of sexual assault, it behooves every woman to regard every man as a potential rapist. 17

In such a benighted universe, it would be impossible for a woman (and, let us not forget, for a man) to engage in the tentative emotional and physical exploration that eventually produces a mature erotic life. She would have to make up her mind right from the start in order to prevent a rampaging male from misreading her intentions. 18

Fortunately for everyone, neither the character of men nor the general quality of relations between the sexes is that crude. By censuring the minority of men who use ordinary socializing as an excuse for rape, feminists insist on sex as a source of pure pleasure rather than as a means of social control. Real men want an eager sexual partner—not a woman who is quaking with fear or even one who is ambivalent. Real men don't rape. 19

Questions for Close Reading

1. What is the selection's thesis? Locate the sentence(s) in which Jacoby states her main idea. If she doesn't state the thesis explicitly, express it in your own words.
2. Why does Jacoby feel that she doesn't owe her old boyfriend a great deal of gratitude, even though she sent mixed signals about what type of relationship she wanted?

3. What does Jacoby mean in paragraph 6 by her comment, "This is called civilization"? How does this comment support her thesis?
4. Why does Jacoby think that it's insulting to men to accept Paglia's notion that men are ruled by uncontrollable passions?
5. Refer to your dictionary as needed to define the following words used in the selection: *apologists* (paragraph 4), *deluded* (10), *unsubtle* (12), *implicit* (16), *benighted* (18), *erotic* (18), *rampaging* (18), and *ambivalent* (19).

Questions About the Writer's Craft

1. **The pattern.** One way to refute an idea is to carry it to its logical extreme, thus revealing its inherent falsity or absurdity. This technique is called *reduction ad absurdum*. Examine paragraphs 4–5 and 15 and explain how Jacoby uses this technique to refute Paglia's position on date rape.
2. **Other patterns.** Locate places in the essay where Jacoby compares and contrasts male and female behavior or the behavior of rapists and non-rapists. How does her use of comparison-contrast help her build her argument?
3. What introduction technique (see pages 61–63) does Jacoby use to begin the essay? How does this type of introduction help her achieve her persuasive goal?
4. How would you characterize Jacoby's tone? Identify specific sentences and words that convey this tone. What effect might Jacoby have hoped this tone would have on readers?

Writing Assignments Using Argumentation-Persuasion as a Pattern of Development

∞ 1. Jacoby feels that Camille Paglia and others "excuse . . . rapists." If you haven't already done so, read "Rape: A Bigger Danger Than Feminists Know" (page 615) to see what Paglia says about who bears primary responsibility for preventing rape. Then decide to what degree you feel men who commit date rape should be held accountable for their actions. Argue your position in an essay, making reference to both Jacoby's and Paglia's ideas to support your case. Also include reasons and evidence of your own.
2. Determine what your campus is doing about date rape. Does it have a formal policy defining date rape, a hearing process, ongoing workshops, discussions during orientation for incoming students? Write a paper explaining how your college deals with date rape. Then argue either that more attention should be devoted to this issue or that your college has adopted fair and comprehensive measures to deal with the problem. If you feel the college should do more, indicate what additional steps should be taken.

Writing Assignments Using Other Patterns of Development

3. Jacoby acknowledges that males and females often send "mixed signals" and cause each other confusion. Select one time that you found "mixed signals" with a person of the opposite sex to be a problem. For example, you might have conflicted because of different ways of expressing anger or because of dissimilar styles in asking for support. Describe what happened and explain why you think such mixed signals occurred. Before writing the paper, you may want to read "But What Do You Mean?" (page 313) to see what Deborah Tannen has to say about some basic differences between men and women.

4. Interview some people, both males and females, to determine their definition of date rape. In an essay, discuss any differences between the two sexes' perspectives. That done, present your own definition of date rape, explaining what it is and what it isn't.

Writing Assignments Using a Journal Entry as a Starting Point

5. Some people believe that "boys-will-be-boys" behavior is potentially dangerous and therefore not acceptable. Others argue that it is perfectly innocent and therefore permissible. What do you think? Drawing upon your pre-reading journal entry, write an essay taking a position on this issue. Provide persuasive examples to support your viewpoint, refuting as much of the opposing argument as you can. Discussing the topic with others and doing some research in the library and/or on the Internet will broaden your understanding of this complex issue.

Daniel Kevles

Founder and director of the Science, Ethics, and Public Policy Program at the California Institute of Technology, Daniel Kevles received a B.A. in physics and a Ph.D. in history from Princeton University. Kevles has published widely here and abroad. His articles and essays which appear in scholarly as well as popular publications, address the impact of scientific developments on history, society, politics, and morality. His books include *The Code of Codes: Scientific and Social Issues in the Human Genome Project* (1992), *In the Name of Eugenics: Genetics and the Uses of Human Heredity* (1995), and *The Baltimore Case: A Trial of Politics, Science and Character* (1998). Kevles lives in Pasadena, California. The following essay first appeared in *The New York Times* in 1997.

Pre-Reading Journal Entry

Some people hold definite views on controversial issues, while others adopt a "wait and see" stance. In your journal, list several complex issues with which you have direct experience but on which you haven't yet taken a position. Consider personal, campus, and community issues. Under each issue, jot down concerns you have that keep you from taking a definitive position.

Study Cloning, Don't Ban It

In "Songs on Innocence," William Blake asked, "Little Lamb, 1 who made thee?"[1] The answer for Dolly the sheep is Dr. Ian Wilmut and his colleagues at the Roslin Institute near Edinburgh.[2] Dolly, as the world now knows, is a clone, a duplicate of one genetic parent. Her birth marks a milestone in our ability to engineer animals for food and medicine. It also signals that humans can, in principle, be

---

[1]English poet and artist, Blake (1757–1827) authored *Songs of Innocence,* a collection of poems with deceptively simple nursery-rhyme style. The poem quoted here, "The Lamb," concludes that "God made thee"—a certainty that no longer exists, thanks to cloning technology (editors' note).
[2]In 1997, Wilmut and his team produced Dolly the sheep, the first viable genetically cloned creature (editors' note).

cloned, too. That prospect troubles many people, but they ought not be too concerned about it at the moment.

Dolly has provoked widespread ethical foreboding. The Church 2 of Scotland suggested that cloning animals runs contrary to God's biodiversity. Dr. Wilmut himself said that cloning humans would be "ethically unacceptable." Carl Feldbaum, president of the Biotechnology Industry Organization, urged that human cloning be prohibited in the United States. (President Clinton asked a Federal bioethics commission for a speedy review of the implications of mammalian cloning.)

The outcry over Dolly calls to mind the great biologist J.B.S. 3 Haldane's "Daedalus," a slim book . . . published in 1924. Haldane held that Daedalus of Greek mythology was the first biological inventor (the first genetic engineer, we would say) . . . [responsible for] the pro-creation of the Minotaur[3]. . . . Daedalus escaped punishment from the gods for his hubris, Haldane noted, but he suffered "the agelong repro-bation of a humanity to whom biological inventions are abhorrent."

If Daedalus did not offend the gods of his day, many people 4 have indicted biotechnologists for affronting God in ours. Yet Haldane, for one, knew that although biological innovations are often initially seen as perversions, over time, they become accepted as "a ritual supported by unquestioned beliefs and prejudices." As technologies improve, people recognize them as advantageous. Society, through its legislatures and courts, figures out how to resolve the problems they posed at the outset.

In this way, artificial insemination of humans, considered tanta- 5 mount to adultery before World War II, has become widely accept-ed. So have reproductive methods like *in vitro* fertilization and sur-rogate motherhood. People abort fetuses with genetic disorders, administer growth hormones to smallish children, and use insulin made by bacteria injected with a human gene.

Scientist have long speculated about manipulating genes to 6 produce new Einsteins, Heifetzes, and Hemingways. Now impresa-rios can dream of cloning Kareem Abdul-Jabar and raising their own Dream Team.[4]

---

[3]The monster of Greek mythology was half human and half bull (editors' note).
[4]Albert Einstein (1879–1955) was a Nobel Prize-winning physicist, Jascha Heifetz (1901–87) a renowned violinist, Ernest Hemingway (1899–1961) a Nobel Prize-winning writer, and Kareem Abdul-Jabar (1947–) a famed basketball player (edi-tors' note).

The fantasies are endless, but they are just fantasies. People are 7 the products not only of their genes but of their environments. Today an Einstein clone might grow up to be Steven Spielberg.[5] Anyway, no one knows what genes contribute to the qualities we most admire and value, whether virtuosity of the pen, the pitch, or the piccolo.

Still, Dolly heralds wondrous innovations with huge economic 8 implications (that Dr. Wilmut held back the news of Dolly's birth until he could register a patent has been reported without comment). Someday an infertile couple might choose to have a child by cloning one or the other partner. A cancer victim might use his DNA to clone spare body parts—liver, pancreas, lungs, kidneys, bone marrow.

For now, cloning should rightly be confined to animals. But as 9 the technology evolves to invite human experimentation, it would be better to watch and regulate rather than prohibit. Outlaw the exploration of human cloning and it will surely go offshore, only to turn into bootleg science that will find its way back to our borders simply because people want it.

As with so many previous advances in biology, today's affront to 10 the gods may be tomorrow's highly regarded—and highly demanded—agent of self-gratification or health.

---

[5]Steven Spielberg (1947–) is a successful and respected filmmaker (editors' note).

Questions for Close Reading

1. What is the selection's thesis? Locate the sentence(s) in which Kevles states his main idea. If he doesn't state the thesis explicitly, express it in your own words.
2. Kevles argues that one reason for not overreacting to human cloning is that many initially rejected "biological innovations" are eventually accepted (paragraph 4). What once-contested but now commonplace practices does Kevles point to as evidence of this point?
3. Kevles invokes the name of Dr. Wilmut several times in his essay. Locate these instances. In each case, how does the reference contribute to Kevles's argument?
4. What does Kevles mean when he says, "Today an Einstein clone might grow up to be Steven Spielberg" (paragraph 7)?
5. Refer to your dictionary as needed to define the following words used in the selection: *foreboding* (paragraph 2), *bioethics* (2), *hubris* (3), *reprobation*

(3), *abhorrent* (3), *indicted* (4), *affronting* (4), *perversions* (4), *insemination* (5), *tantamount* (5), *in vitro* (5), *impresarios* (6), *virtuosity* (7), and *heralds* (8).

Questions About the Writer's Craft

1. **The pattern.** Where does Kevles acknowledge dissenting opinions? How does he refute these points of view?
2. **Other patterns.** In paragraphs 2, 5, and 8, Kevles presents a number of brief, undeveloped examples. Looking at each paragraph in turn, explain why you think Kevles chose not to develop his examples.
3. **Other patterns.** Discussing the Daedalus myth, Kevles contrasts the way Daedalus was treated by the gods with the way he was treated by humanity (paragraph 3). What larger point is Kevles trying to make in drawing this contrast?
4. **Other patterns.** When considering the implications of cloning research, Kevles identifies several causal relationships. What are some of them? How do they help Kevles advance his central point?

Writing Assignments Using Argumentation-Persuasion as a Pattern of Development

1. In paragraphs 5 and 8, Kevles mentions several reproductive technologies that people currently use—or will probably use in the future. Some would argue that these technologies raise fundamental issues about the morality of "designing" a child. Do you think that such interventions differ from other decisions that parents make—for example, the decision to send a child to preschool or the decision not to let the youngster eat at fast-food restaurants? Brainstorm this question with others. Then, focusing on *one* of the technologies Kevles mentions, write an essay arguing that this intervention is *or* is not different from other actions that parents take to mold their children. Keep in mind that some readers probably won't agree with you; try to anticipate and dismantle their reservations.
2. One objection to cloning that Kevles doesn't cite involves the possible future use of cloning technology to create a society of perfect citizens, all of whom conform to a socially determined ideal. Write an essay in which you argue that an already existing practice is also an example of conformity-inducing social engineering. Brainstorm with others to generate strong evidence that convinces even skeptical readers that your claim is valid. Your essay might focus on such trends as the burgeoning weight-loss industry, the widespread use of antidepressants, or the growing popularity of cosmetic surgery.

Writing Assignments Using Other Patterns of Development

3. Although Kevles and Charles Krauthammer (author of "Of Headless Mice . . . and Men," page 633) both write about cloning, they hold very different views. Study both selections; then write an essay showing that one author makes his case more convincingly than the other. To make your point, you'll need to evaluate the strength of the authors' reasoning, their avoidance of logical fallacies, their use of emotional appeals, and the effectiveness of their refutation strategies. Use either the one-side-at-a-time or point-by-point structure (see pages 394–95) to organize your essay.

4. Kevles cites several *medical* developments that initially were hotly contested but now are widely accepted. In an essay of your own, write about a single *cultural* development that you once regarded with suspicion but no longer do. You might focus, for example, on your changing attitude about two-career families, mandatory school dress codes, or interracial dating. At some point in the essay, indicate what caused you to change your viewpoint.

Writing Assignments Using a Journal Entry as a Starting Point

5. Kevles advocates a cautious watchfulness of human cloning, rather than an outright prohibition. Reread your pre-reading journal entry, and select a single issue that you think merits a "wait and see" attitude. Write an essay defending your tentative approach toward the issue. To achieve your goal, present various sides of the issue as well as your assessment of each side's arguments. Overall, the purpose of your essay is to show that, in this case, withholding judgment is a sign of intellectual honesty, not lazy indecision.

Charles Krauthammer

Born in New York and raised in Montreal, Charles Krauthammer (1950–)
earned an advanced degree in political science from Oxford University and
a medical degree in psychiatry from Harvard Medical School. Before turning to journalism in the early 1980s, he practiced medicine for three years
and served as science advisor to President Jimmy Carter and as speechwriter
for Vice President Walter Mondale. Krauthammer's career as a journalist
began at *The New Republic,* where he served as a writer and an editor. His
weekly column for the *Washington Post* and his monthly column for *Time*
magazine led to his receiving a Pulitzer Prize for distinguished commentary
in 1985. In the same year, *Cutting Edges,* a collection of his work, was published. The recipient of an honorary Doctorate of Letters from McGill
University, Krauthammer lives in Chevy Chase, Maryland, with his family.
The following selection first appeared in *Time* in 1998.

Pre-Reading Journal Entry

It's been argued that human beings will do anything in their power to deny
their mortality. What evidence exists that people will go to great lengths to
look and feel young forever—even to try to outwit death? In your journal,
list as many human actions as you can think of that reflect this impulse. For
each item, indicate whether you consider the action positive, negative, or
both—and why.

Of Headless Mice . . . and Men[1]

Last year Dolly the cloned sheep[2] was received with wonder, tit-   1
ters and some vague apprehension. Last week the announcement by
a Chicago physicist that he is assembling a team to produce the first
human clone occasioned yet another wave of Brave New World anxiety. But the scariest news of all—and largely overlooked—comes
from two obscure labs, at the University of Texas and at the

---

[1]A play on words of the title of John Steinbeck's 1937 novella, *Of Mice and Men*
(editors' note).
[2]The first viable genetically-cloned creature—a sheep—produced in 1997 by Dr.
Ian Wilmut and his team of biologists in Scotland (editors' note).

University of Bath. During the past four years, one group created headless mice; the other, headless tadpoles.

For sheer Frankenstein wattage, the purposeful creation of these 2 animal monsters has no equal. Take the mice. Researchers found the gene that tells the embryo to produce the head. They deleted it. They did this in a thousand mice embryos, four of which were born. I use the term loosely. Having no way to breathe, the mice died instantly.

Why then create them? The Texas researchers want to learn how 3 genes determine embryo development. But you don't have to be a genius to see the true utility of manufacturing headless creatures: for their organs—fully formed, perfectly useful, ripe for plundering.

Why should you be panicked? Because humans are next. "It 4 would almost certainly be possible to produce human bodies without a forebrain," Princeton biologist Lee Silver told the London *Sunday Times*. "These human bodies without any semblance of consciousness would not be considered persons, and thus it would be perfectly legal to keep them 'alive' as a future source of organs."

"Alive." Never have a pair of quotation marks loomed so ominously. Take the mouse-frog technology, apply it to humans, combine it with cloning, and you are become a god: with a single cell taken from, say, your finger, you produce a headless replica of yourself, a mutant twin, arguably lifeless, that becomes your own personal, precisely tissue-matched organ farm.

There are, of course, technical hurdles along the way. 6 Suppressing the equivalent "head" gene in man. Incubating tiny infant organs to grow into larger ones that adults could use. And creating artificial wombs (as per Aldous Huxley),3 given that it might be difficult to recruit sane women to carry headless fetuses to their birth/death.

It won't be long, however, before these technical barriers are 7 breached. The ethical barriers are already cracking. Lewis Wolpert, professor of biology at University College, London, finds producing headless humans "personally distasteful" but, given the shortage of organs, does not think distaste is sufficient reason not to go ahead with something that would save lives. And Professor Silver not only

3English novelist and essayist Aldous Huxley (1894–1963) is best known for his 1932 novel, *Brave New World*, a dark commentary about a future society in which technological expediency—rather than human relationships—reigns supreme. In Huxley's novel, embryos develop in bottles rather than in human wombs (editors' note).

sees "nothing wrong, philosophically or rationally," with producing headless humans for organ harvesting, he wants to convince a skeptical public that it is perfectly O.K.

When prominent scientists are prepared to acquiesce in—or indeed encourage—the deliberate creation of deformed and dying quasi-human life, you know we are facing a bioethical abyss. Human beings are ends, not means. There is no grosser corruption of biotechnology than creating a human mutant and disemboweling it at our pleasure for spare parts.   8

The prospect of headless human clones should put the whole debate about "normal" cloning in a new light. Normal cloning is less a treatment for infertility than a treatment for vanity. It is a way to produce an exact genetic replica of yourself that will walk the earth years after you're gone.   9

But there is a problem with a clone. It is not really you. It is but a twin, a perfect John Doe Jr., but still a junior. With its own independent consciousness, it is, alas, just a facsimile of you.   10

The headless clone solves the facsimile problem. It is a gateway to the ultimate vanity: immortality. If you create a real clone, you cannot transfer your consciousness into it to truly live on. But if you create a headless clone of just your body, you have created a ready source of replacement parts to keep you—your consciousness— going indefinitely.   11

Which is why one form of cloning will inevitably lead to the other. Cloning is the technology of narcissism, and nothing satisfies narcissism like immortality. Headlessness will be cloning's crowning achievement.   12

The time to put a stop to this is now. Dolly moved President Clinton to create a commission that recommended a temporary ban on human cloning. But with physicist Richard Seed threatening to clone humans, and with headless animals already here, we are past the time for toothless commissions and meaningless bans.   13

Clinton banned federal funding of human-cloning research, of which there is none anyway. He then proposed a five-year ban on cloning. This is not enough. Congress should ban human cloning now. Totally. And regarding one particular form, it should be draconian: the deliberate creation of headless humans must be made a crime, indeed a capital crime. If we flinch in the face of this high-tech barbarity, we'll deserve to live in the hell it heralds.   14

Questions for Close Reading

1. What is the selection's thesis? Locate the sentence(s) in which Krauthammer states his main idea. If he doesn't state the thesis explicitly, express it in your own words.
2. Krauthammer acknowledges that today's technology isn't sufficient to produce headless human clones. What, according to Krauthammer, are the technical obstacles that need to be overcome before this kind of cloning is possible?
3. What does Krauthammer mean when he describes headless cloning as "the ultimate vanity" (paragraph 11) and "the technology of narcissism" (12)?
4. In paragraph 8, Krauthammer writes, "Human beings are ends, not means." What does he mean? What does he imply about those who favor cloning?
5. Refer to your dictionary as needed to define the following words used in the selection: *plundering* (paragraph 3), *semblance* (4), *breached* (7), *acquiesce* (8), *abyss* (8), *disemboweling* (8), *facsimile* (10), *narcissism* (12), *draconian* (14), and *heralds* (14).

Questions About the Writer's Craft

1. **The pattern.** How would you characterize the tone of Krauthammer's argument? Is his language objective and neutral, or is it subjective and passionate? Cite examples to support your opinion.
2. Paragraph 6 includes a series of sentence fragments. Why do you think Krauthammer chose this technique? What is its effect?
3. **Other patterns.** In paragraphs 9–12, Krauthammer identifies a cause-effect relationship between "normal" cloning and "headless" cloning. What, according to Krauthammer, is the connection between the two? How does this causal connection reinforce Krauthammer's thesis?
4. Krauthammer ends his essay by proposing a course of action. What would have been lost if he had proposed the course of action at the beginning of the essay?

Writing Assignments Using Argumentation-Persuasion as a Pattern of Development

1. Krauthammer states, "Congress should ban human cloning now. Totally." Do you agree? Write an essay arguing that human cloning should or should not be prohibited. Before formulating your position, be sure to read Daniel Kevles's "Study Cloning, Don't Ban It" (page 628), an essay that takes a very different position from Krauthammer's.
2. According to Krauthammer, human cloning technology brings us to the brink of a "bioethical abyss." Brainstorm with others to identify several

contemporary technologies that pose serious ethical questions. Possibilities include the production of genetically-altered foods, the prescribing of behavioral medications to children, the prolonging of life via support machines. Select *one* technology, and write an essay arguing that this technology raises significant moral issues. Provide specific evidence to convince skeptical readers that your concerns are warranted. Gathering information in the library and/or on the Internet will help you prepare a persuasive argument.

Writing Assignments Using Other Patterns of Development

3. Recent technological developments have influenced in significant ways how we live our everyday lives. Brainstorm with others to identify a number of developments that have had a favorable impact. Focus on *one* of these technologies, and write an essay tracing its beneficial effects on *one* area of everyday life. For instance, you might examine the technology's effect on family life, leisure time, or the workplace. At the end of your essay, describe briefly possible future effects of the technology. Will they continue to be positive, or do they carry a potential for harm?

4. Twice in his essay, Krauthammer alludes to Aldous Huxley's *Brave New World,* a novel about life in a *dystopia*—a potentially ideal society gone terribly wrong. Consider a specific situation that you think has lost its moorings. Select a situation that you know well, one you've either observed or experienced firsthand. Possibilities include a classroom where no learning took place, a formerly close relationship gone awry, the decline of a once-vital neighborhood. Write an essay analyzing what went wrong and why. You might end your essay with suggestions for improving the situation, making it closer to the ideal.

Writing Assignments Using a Journal Entry as a Starting Point

5. Krauthammer suggests that the desire to produce human clones is evidence of the impulse to deny mortality. But cloning isn't the only way that humans pursue immortality. Reread your pre-reading journal entry, and select *one* mortality-denying activity that people undertake. Brainstorm with others to gather insight into this particular manifestation of the desire to live forever. Is it positive or not? Write an essay in which you support your conclusion with vivid examples drawn from your and other people's experiences. Carol Siskin's "The Virtues of Growing Older" (page 392) might spark some ideas worth exploring in your essay.

Roger Wilkins

Pulitzer Prize-winning journalist Roger Wilkins (1932–) is the author of many works, including *A Man's Life: An Autobiography* (1982), *Quiet Riots: Race and Poverty in the U.S.* (1988), and *Jefferson's Pillow* (2001). A member of the editorial board at *The Nation*, Wilkins is professor of history at George Mason University in Virginia. Senior advisor to Jesse Jackson during Jackson's presidential campaigns, Wilkins also served as national coordinator of the visit that South African president Nelson Mandela made to the United States in 1988. The following essay was first published in *The Nation* in 1995.

Pre-Reading Journal Entry

Do you thing schools should engage in discussions of racism, a sensitive and painful topic? Why do you feel as you do? Would such discussions be appropriate at some levels of schooling but not at others? Take some time to explore these questions in your journal.

Racism Has Its Privileges

The storm that has been gathering over affirmative action for 1 the past few years has burst. Two conservative California professors are leading a drive to place an initiative on the state ballot in 1996 that will ask Californians to vote affirmative action up or down.[1] Since the state is beloved in political circles for its electoral votes, advance talk of the initiative has put the issue high on the national agenda. Three Republican presidential contenders—Bob Dole, Phil Gramm and Lamar Alexander—have already begun taking shots at various equal opportunity programs. Congressional review of the Clinton Administration's enforcement of these programs has begun. The President has started his own review, promising adherence to principles of nondiscrimination and full opportunity while asserting the need to prune those programs that are unfair or malfunctioning.

[1]Approved by 54 percent of the voters in California, Proposition 209 took effect in August 1997, ending affirmative action efforts in the state (editors' note).

It is almost an article of political faith that one of the major influ- 2
ences in last November's election was the backlash against affirmative
action among "angry white men," who are convinced it has stacked the
deck against them. Their attitudes are shaped and their anger heightened by unquestioned and virtually uncheckable anecdotes about victimized whites flooding the culture. For example, *Washington Post*
columnist Richard Cohen recently began what purported to be a serious analysis and attack on affirmative action by recounting that he had
once missed out on a job someplace because they "needed a woman."

Well, I have an anecdote too, and it, together with Cohen's, 3
offers some important insights about the debate that has flared
recently around the issues of race, gender and justice. Some years
ago, after watching me teach as a visiting professor for two semesters,
members of the history department at George Mason University
invited me to compete for a full professorship and endowed chair.
Mason, like other institutions in Virginia's higher education system,
was under a court order to desegregate. I went through the appropriate application and review process and, in due course, was appointed. A few years later, not long after I had been honored as one of the
university's distinguished professors, I was shown an article by a
white historian asserting that he had been a candidate for that chair
but that at the last moment the job had been whisked away and
handed to an unqualified black. I checked the story and discovered
that this fellow had, in fact, applied but had not even passed the first
threshold. But his "reverse discrimination" story is out there polluting the atmosphere in which this debate is taking place.

Affirmative action, as I understand it, was not designed to pun- 4
ish anyone; it was, rather—as a result of a clear-eyed look at how
America actually works—an attempt to enlarge opportunity for
everybody. As amply documented in the 1968 Kerner Commission
report on racial disorders, when left to their own devices, American
institutions in such areas as college admissions, hiring decisions and
loan approvals had been making choices that discriminated against
blacks. That discrimination, which flowed from doing what came
naturally, hurt more than blacks: it hurt the entire nation, as the
riots of the late 1960s demonstrated. Though the Kerner report
focused on blacks, similar findings could have been made about
other minorities and women.

Affirmative action required institutions to develop plans enabling 5
them to go beyond business as usual and search for qualified people

in places where they did not ordinarily conduct their searches or their business. Affirmative action programs generally require some proof that there has been a good-faith effort to follow the plan and numerical guidelines against which to judge the sincerity and the success of the effort. The idea of affirmative action is *not* to force people into positions for which they are unqualified but to encourage institutions to develop realistic criteria for the enterprise at hand and then to find a reasonably diverse mix of people qualified to be engaged in it. Without the requirements calling for plans, good-faith efforts and the setting of broad numerical goals, many institutions would do what they had always done: assert that they had looked but "couldn't find anyone qualified," and then go out and hire the white man they wanted to hire in the first place.

Affirmative action has done wonderful things for the United 6 States by enlarging opportunity and developing and utilizing a far broader array of the skills available in the American population than in the past. It has not outlived its usefulness. It was never designed to be a program to eliminate poverty. It has not always been used wisely, and some of its permutations do have to be reconsidered, refined or, in some cases, abandoned. It is not a quota program, and those cases where rigid numbers are used (except under a court or administrative order after a specific finding of discrimination) are a bastardization of an otherwise highly beneficial set of public policies.

President Clinton is right to review what is being done under pres- 7 ent laws and to express a willingness to eliminate activities that either don't work or are unfair. Any program that has been in place for thirty years should be reviewed. Getting rid of what doesn't work is both good government and good politics. Gross abuses of affirmative action provide ammunition for its opponents and undercut the moral authority of the entire effort. But the President should retain—and strengthen where required—those programs necessary to enlarge social justice.

What makes the affirmative action issue so difficult is that it 8 engages blacks and whites exactly at those points where they differ the most. There are some areas, such as rooting for the local football team, where their experiences and views are virtually identical. There are others—sometimes including work and school—where their experiences and views both overlap and diverge. And finally, there are areas such as affirmative action and inextricably related notions about the presence of racism in society where the divergences draw out almost all the points of difference between the races.

This Land Is My Land

Blacks and whites experience America very differently. Though   9
we often inhabit the same space, we operate in very disparate psychic spheres.

Whites have an easy sense of ownership of the country; they feel   10
they are entitled to receive all that is best in it. Many of them believe
that their country—though it may have some faults—is superior to
all others and that, as Americans, they are superior as well. Many of
them think of this as a white country and some of them even experience it that way. They think of it as a land of opportunity—a good
place with a lot of good people in it. Some suspect (others *know*)
that the presence of blacks messes everything up. . . .

For most blacks, America is either a land of denied opportunity   11
or one in which the opportunities are still grudgingly extended and
extremely limited. For some—that one-third who are mired in poverty, many of them isolated in dangerous ghettos—America is a land of
desperadoes and desperation. In places where whites see a lot of idealism, blacks see, at best, idealism mixed heavily with hypocrisy.
Blacks accept America's greatness but are unable to ignore ugly warts
that many whites seem to need not to see. I am reminded here of
James Baldwin's searing observation from *The Fire Next Time:*

> The American Negro has the great advantage of having
> never believed that collection of myths to which white
> Americans cling: that their ancestors were all freedom-lov-
> ing heroes, that they were born in the greatest country the
> world has ever seen, or that Americans are invincible in bat-
> tle and wise in peace, that Americans have always dealt hon-
> orably with Mexicans and Indians and all other neighbors
> or inferiors, that American men are the world's most direct
> and virile, that American women are pure.

It goes without saying, then, that blacks and whites remember   12
America differently. The past is hugely important since we argue a
lot about who we are on the basis of who we think we have been,
and we derive much of our sense of the future from how we think
we've done in the past. In a nation in which few people know much
history these are perilous arguments, because in such a vacuum,
people tend to weave historical fables tailored to their political or
psychic needs.

Blacks are still recovering the story of their role in America,   13
which so many white historians simply ignored or told in a way that
made black people ashamed. But in a culture that batters us, learning
the real history is vital in helping blacks feel fully human. It also helps
us understand just how deeply American we are, how richly we have
given, how much has been taken from us and how much has yet to
be restored. Supporters of affirmative action believe that broad and
deep damage has been done to American culture by racism and sexism over the whole course of American history and that they are still
powerful forces today. We believe that minorities and women are still
disadvantaged in our highly competitive society and that affirmative
action is absolutely necessary to level the playing field. . . .

The Politics of Denial

The successful public relations assault on affirmative action   14
flows on a river of racism that is as broad, powerful and American as
the Mississippi. And, like the Mississippi, racism can be violent and
deadly and is a permanent feature of American life. But while
nobody who is sane denies the reality of the Mississippi, millions of
Americans who are deemed sane—some of whom are powerful and
some even thought wise—deny, wholly or in part, that racism exists.

It is critical to understand the workings of denial in this debate   15
because it is used to obliterate the facts that created the need for the
remedy in the first place. One of the best examples of denial was
provided recently by the nation's most famous former history professor, House Speaker Newt Gingrich. According to *The Washington
Post*, "Gingrich dismissed the argument that the beneficiaries of
affirmative action, commonly African Americans, have been subjected to discrimination over a period of centuries. 'That is true of virtually every American,' Gingrich said, noting that the Irish were discriminated against by the English, for example."

That is breathtaking stuff coming from somebody who should   16
know that blacks have been on this North American continent for
375 years and that for 245 the country permitted slavery. Gingrich
should also know that for the next hundred years we had legalized
subordination of blacks, under a suffocating blanket of condescen-
sion and frequently enforced by nightriding terrorists. We've had
only thirty years of something else.

That something else is a nation trying to lift its ideals out of a   17
thick, often impenetrable slough of racism. Racism is a hard word for

what over the centuries became second nature in America—preferences across the board for white men and, following in their wake,
white women. Many of these men seem to feel that it is un-American
to ask them to share anything with blacks—particularly their work,
their neighborhoods or "their" women. To protect these things—
apparently essential to their identity—they engage in all forms of
denial. For a historian to assert that "virtually every American" shares
the history I have just outlined comes very close to lying.

Denial of racism is much like the denials that accompany addic-   18
tions to alcohol, drugs or gambling. It is probably not stretching the
analogy too much to suggest that many racist whites are so addicted to their unwarranted privileges and so threatened by the prospect
of losing them that all kinds of defenses become acceptable. . . .

"Those People" Don't Deserve Help

Before the 1950s, whites who were busy denying that the nation   19
was unfair to blacks would simply assert that we didn't deserve equal
treatment because we were *inferior.* These days it is not permissible in
most public circles to say that blacks are inferior, but it is perfectly
acceptable to target the *behavior* of blacks, specifically poor blacks. . . .

While I don't hold the view that all blacks who behave badly are   20
blameless victims of a brutal system, I do believe that many poor
blacks have, indeed, been brutalized by our culture, and I know of
no blacks, rich or poor, who haven't been hurt in some measure by
the racism in this country. The current mood (and, in some cases
like the Speaker's, the cultivated ignorance) completely ignores the
fact that some blacks never escaped the straight line of oppression
that ran from slavery through the semislavery of sharecropping to
the late mid-century migration from Southern farms into isolated
pockets of urban poverty. Their families have always been excluded,
poor and without skills, and so they were utterly defenseless when
the enormous American economic dislocations that began in the
mid-1970s slammed into their communities, followed closely by
deadly waves of crack cocaine. One would think that the double-
digit unemployment suffered consistently over the past two decades
by blacks who were *looking for work* would be a permanent feature
of the discussions about race, responsibility, welfare and rights.

But people's attention is kept trained on the behavior of some   21
poor blacks by politicians and television news shows, reinforcing the
stereotypes of blacks as dangerous, as threats, as unqualified.

Frightened whites direct their rage at pushy blacks rather than at the corporations that export manufacturing operations to low-wage countries, or at the Federal Reserve, which imposes interest rate hikes that slow down the economy.

Who Benefits? We All Do

There is one final denial that blankets all the rest. It is that only 22 society's "victims"—blacks, other minorities and women (who should, for God's sake, renounce their victimological outlooks)— have been injured by white male supremacy. Viewed in this light, affirmative action remedies are a kind of zero-sum game in which only the "victims" benefit. But racist and sexist whites who are not able to accept the full humanity of other people are themselves badly damaged—morally stunted—people. The principal product of a racist and sexist society is damaged people and institutions—victims and victimizers alike. Journalism and education, two enterprises with which I am familiar, provide two good examples.

Journalistic institutions often view the nation through a lens 23 that bends reality to support white privileges. A recent issue of *U.S. News & World Report* introduced a package of articles on these issues with a question on its cover: "Does affirmative action mean NO WHITE MEN NEED APPLY?" The words "No white men need apply" were printed in red against a white background and were at least four times larger than the other words in the question. Inside, the lead story was illustrated by a painting that carries out the cover theme, with a wan white man separated from the opportunity ladders eagerly being scaled by women and dark men. And the story yielded up the following sentence: "Affirmative action poses a conflict between two cherished American principles: the belief that all Americans deserve equal opportunities and the idea that hard work and merit, not race or religion or gender or birthright, should determine who prospers and who does not."

Whoever wrote that sentence was in the thrall of one of the 24 myths that Baldwin was talking about. The sentence suggests—as many people do when talking about affirmative action—that America is a meritocratic society. But what kind of meritocracy excludes women and blacks and other minorities from all meaningful competition? And even in the competition among white men, money, family and connections often count for much more than merit, test results (for whatever they're worth) and hard work.

The *U.S. News* story perpetuates and strengthens the view that   25
many of my white students absorb from their parents: that white
men now have few chances in this society. The fact is that white men
still control virtually everything in America except the wealth held
by widows. According to the Urban Institute, 53 percent of black
men aged 25–34 are either unemployed or earn too little to lift a
family of four from poverty.

Educational institutions that don't teach accurately about why   26
America looks the way it does and why the distribution of winners
and losers is as it is also injure our society. Here is another anecdote.

A warm, brilliant young white male student of mine came in just   27
before he was to graduate and said that my course in race, law and culture, which he had just finished, had been the most valuable and the
most disturbing he had ever taken. I asked how it had been disturbing.

"I learned that my two heroes are racists," he said.   28

"Who are your heroes and how are they racists?" I asked.   29

"My mom and dad," he said. "After thinking about what I was   30
learning, I understand that they had spent all my life making me into
the same kind of racists they were."

Affirmative action had brought me together with him when he   31
was 22. Affirmative action puts people together in ways that make
that kind of revelation possible. Nobody is a loser when that happens. The country gains.

And that, in the end, is the case for affirmative action. The argu-   32
ments supporting it should be made on the basis of its broad contributions to the entire American community. It is insufficient to vilify white males and to skewer them as the whiners that journalism of
the kind practiced by *U.S. News* invites us to do. These are people
who, from the beginning of the Republic, have been taught that
skin color is destiny and that whiteness is to be revered. Listen to
Jefferson, writing in the year the Constitution was drafted:

> The first difference that strikes us is that of colour. . . . And
> is the difference of no importance? Is it not the foundation
> of a greater or less share of beauty in the two races? Are not
> the fine mixtures of red and white . . . in the one, preferable
> to that eternal monotony, which reigns in the counte-
> nances, that immoveable veil of black which covers all the
> emotions of the other race? Add to these, flowing hair, a
> more elegant symmetry of form, their own judgment in

favor of the whites, declared by their preference for them, as uniformly as is the preference of the Oran-ootan for the black women over those of his own species. The circumstance of superior beauty, is thought worthy attention in the propagation of our horses, dogs, and other domestic animals; why not in that of man?

In a society so conceived and so dedicated, it is understandable that white males would take their preferences as a matter of natural right and consider any alteration of that a primal offense. But a nation that operates in that way abandons its soul and its economic strength, and will remain mired in ugliness and moral squalor because so many people are excluded from the possibility of decent lives and from forming any sense of community with the rest of society. . . .

It may be that we will need affirmative action until most white   33
males are really ready for a color-blind society—that is, when they are ready to assume "the rank of a mere citizen." As a nation we took a hard look at that special favoritism thirty years ago. Though the centuries of cultural preference enjoyed by white males still overwhelmingly skew power and wealth their way, we have in fact achieved a more meritocratic society as a result of affirmative action than we have ever previously enjoyed in this country.

If we want to continue making things better in this society, we'd   34
better figure out ways to protect and defend affirmative action against the confused, the frightened, the manipulators and, yes, the liars in politics, journalism, education and wherever else they may be found. In the name of longstanding American prejudice and myths and in the service of their own narrow interests, power-lusts or blindness, they are truly victimizing the rest of us, perverting the ideals they claim to stand for and destroying the nation they pretend to serve.

Questions for Close Reading

1. What is the selection's thesis? Locate the sentences in which Wilkins states his main idea. If he doesn't state the thesis explicitly, express it in your own words.
2. How does Wilkins define *affirmative action*? What must an affirmative-action program include in order to be successful?
3. According to Wilkins, what "myths" do White people believe? How have these myths prevented White people from seeing the need for affirmative action?

4. How, in Wilkins's opinion, does affirmative action benefit *all* Americans?

5. Refer to your dictionary as needed to define the following words used in the selection: *initiative* (paragraph 1), *adherence* (1), *purported* (2), *permutations* (6), *bastardization* (6), *inextricably* (8), *disparate* (9), *invincible* (11), *obliterate* (15), *meritocratic* (24), *perpetuates* (25), *vilify* (32), and *skew* (33).

Questions About the Writer's Craft

1. **The pattern.** Where in his argument does Wilkins acknowledge conflicting viewpoints? What is his attitude toward these opposing views? How does this attitude help Wilkins reinforce his thesis?

2. **Other patterns.** Why do you suppose Wilkins places the anecdote about his being hired at George Mason University (paragraph 3) near the beginning of his essay? How does this anecdote add to the effectiveness of his argument?

3. **Other patterns.** Locate places in the essay where Wilkins uses comparison-contrast. How do these comparisons and contrasts help Wilkins develop his central argument?

4. Sometimes Wilkins uses provocative language, as when he refers to the beliefs of those opposed to affirmative action as "myths." What other emotionally loaded words does he use? What assumptions about his audience might have motivated Wilkins to employ this charged language?

Writing Assignments Using Argumentation-Persuasion as a Pattern of Development

∞ 1. Wilkins argues that "affirmative action is absolutely necessary to level the playing field" for minorities in this country. Do you agree? Focusing on a specific minority group, write an essay in which you support or challenge Wilkins's argument. To assure that your position is more than a reflexive opinion, conduct some library research on the group in question, and read Shelby Steele's "Affirmative Action: The Price of Preference" (page 649), an essay that is in sharp opposition to Wilkins's. No matter which side you take, assume that some readers are opposed to your point of view. Acknowledge and try to dismantle as many of their objections as possible. Refer, whenever it's relevant, to Steele's argument in your paper.

∞ 2. Wilkins suggests that it is appropriate for schools to celebrate the admirable and heroic aspects of our history. But, he believes, schools must also be willing to acknowledge the "ugly warts" in that history. Do you agree? Write an essay arguing that schools should *or* should not teach students about the non-heroic aspects of our national story. Your essay should acknowledge and refute as many opposing arguments as possible. To broaden your understanding of the issue, interview classmates, family members, friends, and instructors. Also read "Let's Tell the Story of All America's Cultures" (page 581) by Yuh Ji-Yeon.

Writing Assignments Using Other Patterns of Development

3. Wilkins believes that people who consider themselves victims should "renounce their victimological outlooks." Select a group that you believe perceives itself as being victimized. Possibilities include a specific racial, ethnic, or religious group; the disabled; the overweight; those in abusive relationships. Write an essay explaining the steps these individuals could take to overthrow their victimhood. End the paper by discussing the effects of abandoning a victimological perspective. What would be gained? What might be lost? Before writing, read one or more of the following essays to sharpen your understanding of the concept of victimhood: Maya Angelou's "Sister Flowers" (page 116), William Raspberry's "The Handicap of Definition" (page 529), and Camille Paglia's "Rape: A Bigger Danger Than Feminists Know" (page 615).

4. One student told Wilkins that the course Wilkins taught was "the most valuable . . . he had ever taken." Write an essay showing how a course or school experience made you, like Wilkins's student, realize something important about yourself, society, or life in general. Develop your essay by contrasting what you were like before with what you were like after the educational experience.

Writing Assignments Using a Journal Entry as a Starting Point

5. Write an essay arguing that schools should *or* should not encourage students to discuss the issue of racism. Review your pre-reading journal entry, and select a specific level of schooling to focus on before taking a position. Supplement the material in your journal by gathering the opinions, experiences, and observations of friends, family, and classmates. No matter which position you take, remember to cite opposing arguments, refuting as many of them as you can. Before writing, consider reading "Let's Tell the Story of All America's Cultures" (page 581), in which Yuh Ji-Yeon forcefully argues the need for honest discussion of race and ethnicity in the classroom.

Shelby Steele

Currently a professor of English at San Jose State University, Shelby Steele (1946–) was born in Chicago and earned his doctoral degree at the University of Utah. The recipient of a National Magazine Award in 1989, Steele has published widely. His writing on racial issues has appeared in publications including *Harper's*, the *New York Times*, the *Washington Post*, and *American Scholar*. One of his pieces on race was selected for *The Best American Essays 1989*, and a number of his most compelling essays were published in *The Content of Our Character: A New Vision of Race in America* (1990). Most recently, he wrote *A Dream Deferred: The Second Betrayal of Black Freedom in America* (1998). The following essay, which originally appeared in the *New York Times Magazine* (1990), is reprinted from *The Content of Our Character.*

Pre-Reading Journal Entry

What do you think would happen if college affirmative-action admission policies were ruled illegal and were subsequently outlawed? What positive effects might there be? What negative effects? Take some time to respond to these questions in your journal.

Affirmative Action:
The Price of Preference

In a few short years, when my two children will be applying to college, the affirmative-action policies by which most universities offer black students some form of preferential treatment will present me with a dilemma. I am a middle-class black, a college professor, far from wealthy, but also well removed from the kind of deprivation that would qualify my children for the label "disadvantaged." Both of them have endured racial insensitivity from whites. They have been called names, have suffered slights and have experienced first hand the peculiar malevolence that racism brings out of people. Yet they have never experienced racial discrimination, have never been stopped by their race on any path they have chosen to follow. Still,

1

their society now tells them that if they will only designate them-selves as black on their college applications, they will probably do better in the college lottery than if they conceal this fact. I think there is something of a Faustian[1] bargain in this.

Of course many blacks and a considerable number of whites   2
would say that I was sanctimoniously making affirmative action into a test of character. They would say that this small preference is the meagerest recompense for centuries of unrelieved oppression. And to these arguments other very obvious facts must be added. In America, many marginally competent or flatly incompetent whites are hired every day—some because their white skin suits the con-scious or unconscious racial preference of their employers. The white children of alumni are often grandfathered[2] into elite univer-sities in what can only be seen as a residual benefit of historic white privilege. Worse, white incompetence is always an individual matter, but for blacks it is often confirmation of ugly stereotypes. Given that unfairness cuts both ways, doesn't it only balance the scales of his-tory, doesn't this repay, in a small way, the systematic denial under which my children's grandfather lived out his days?

In theory, affirmative action certainly has all the moral symmetry   3
that fairness requires. It is reformist and corrective, even repentant and redemptive. And I would never sneer at these good intentions. Born in the late 1940s in Chicago, I started my education (a chari-table term, in this case) in a segregated school, and suffered all the indignities that come to blacks in a segregated society. My father, born in the South, made it only to the third grade before the white man's fields took permanent priority over his formal education. And though he educated himself into an advanced reader with an almost professorial authority, he could only drive a truck for a living, and never earned more than $90 a week in his entire life. So yes, it is cru-cial to my sense of citizenship, to my ability to identify with the spir-it and the interests of America, to know that this country, however imperfectly, recognizes its past sins and wishes to correct them.

Yet good intentions can blind us to the effects they generate   4
when implemented. In our society affirmative action is, among other things, a testament to white good will and to black power, and in the

[1]A reference to the legend of Faust, a scholar who sold his soul to the devil in
return for unlimited power. Faust later regretted the bargain (editors' note).
[2]Permitted to enter on the basis of longtime association with an institution without
having to satisfy existing entrance requirements (editors' note).

midst of these heavy investments its effects can be hard to see. But after 20 years of implementation I think that affirmative action has shown itself to be more bad than good and that blacks—whom I will focus on in this essay—now stand to lose more from it than they gain.

In talking with affirmative-action administrators and with blacks   5
and whites in general, I found that supporters of affirmative action focus on its good intentions and detractors emphasize its negative effects. It was virtually impossible to find people outside either camp. The closest I came was a white male manager at a large computer company who said, "I think it amounts to reverse discrimination, but I'll put up with a little of that for a little more diversity." But this only makes him a half-hearted supporter of affirmative action. I think many people who don't really like affirmative action support it to one degree or another anyway.

I believe they do this because of what happened to white and   6
black Americans in the crucible of the 1960s,[3] when whites were confronted with their racial guilt and blacks tasted their first real power. In that stormy time white absolution and black power coalesced into virtual mandates for society. Affirmative action became a meeting ground for those mandates in the law. At first, this meant insuring equal opportunity. The 1964 civil-rights bill was passed on the understanding that equal opportunity would not mean racial preference. But in the late 60's and early 70's, affirmative action underwent a remarkable escalation of its mission from simple antidiscrimination enforcement to social engineering by means of quotas, goals, timetables, set-asides and other forms of preferential treatment.

Legally, this was achieved through a series of executive orders and   7
Equal Employment Opportunity Commission guidelines that allowed racial imbalances in the workplace to stand as proof of racial discrimination. Once it could be assumed that discrimination explained racial imbalances, it became easy to justify group remedies to presumed discrimination rather than the normal case-by-case redress.

Even though blacks had made great advances during the 60's   8
without quotas, the white mandate to achieve a new racial innocence and the black mandate to gain power, which came to a head in the

---

[3]A decade characterized by both nonviolent and violent civil rights protests that forced mainstream America finally to acknowledge the injustices endured by Black Americans (editors' note).

very late 60's, could no longer be satisfied by anything less than racial preferences. I don't think these mandates, in themselves, were wrong, because whites clearly needed to do better by blacks and blacks needed more real power in society. But as they came together in affirmative action, their effect was to distort our understanding of racial discrimination. By making black the color of preference, these mandates have reburdened society with the very marriage of color and preference (in reverse) that we set out to eradicate. . . .

I think one of the most troubling effects of racial preferences for blacks is a kind of demoralization. Under affirmative action, the quality that earns us preferential treatment is an implied inferiority. However this inferiority is explained—and it is easily enough explained by the myriad deprivations that grew out of our oppression—it is still inferiority. There are explanations and then there is the fact. And the fact must be borne by the individual as a condition apart from the explanation, apart even from the fact that others like himself also bear this condition. In integrated situations in which blacks must compete with whites who may be better prepared, these explanations may quickly wear thin and expose the individual to racial as well as personal self-doubt. (Of course whites also feel doubt, but only personally, not racially.) 9

What this means in practical terms is that when blacks deliver themselves into integrated situations they encounter a nasty little reflex in whites, a mindless, atavistic reflex that responds to the color black with negative stereotypes, such as intellectual ineptness. I think this reflex embarrasses most whites today and thus it is usually quickly repressed. On an equally atavistic level, the black will be aware of the reflex his color triggers and will feel a stab of horror at seeing himself reflected in this way. He, too, will do a quick repression, but a lifetime of such stabbings is what constitutes his inner realm of racial doubt. Even when the black sees no implication of inferiority in racial preferences, he knows that whites do, so that—consciously or unconsciously—the result is virtually the same. The effect of preferential treatment—the lowering of normal standards to increase black representation—puts blacks at war with an expanded realm of debilitating doubt, so that the doubt itself becomes an unrecognized preoccupation that undermines their ability to perform, especially in integrated situations. 10

I believe another liability of affirmative action comes from the fact that it indirectly encourages blacks to exploit their own past 11 victimization. Like implied inferiority, victimization is what justifies preference, so that to receive the benefits of preferential treatment one must, to some extent, become invested in the view of one's self as a victim. In this way, affirmative action nurtures a victim-focused identity in blacks and sends us the message that there is more power in our past suffering than in our present achievements.

When power itself grows out of suffering, blacks are encouraged   12
to expand the boundaries of what qualifies as racial oppression, a situation that can lead us to paint our victimization in vivid colors even as we receive the benefits of preference. The same corporations and institutions that give us preference are also seen as our oppressors. At Stanford University, minority-group students—who receive at least the same financial aid as whites with the same need—recently took over the president's office demanding, among other things, more financial aid.

But I think one of the worst prices that blacks pay for preference   13
has to do with an illusion. I saw this illusion at work recently in the mother of a middle-class black student who was going off to his first semester of college: "They owe us this, so don't think for a minute that you don't belong there." This is the logic by which many blacks, and some whites, justify affirmative action—it is something "owed," a form of reparation. But this logic overlooks a much harder and less digestible reality, that it is impossible to repay blacks living today for the historic suffering of the race. If all blacks were given a million dollars tomorrow it would not amount to a dime on the dollar for three centuries of oppression, nor would it dissolve the residues of that oppression that we still carry today. The concept of historic reparation grows out of man's need to impose on the world a degree of justice that simply does not exist. Suffering can be endured and overcome, it cannot be repaid. To think otherwise is to prolong the suffering. . . .

But if not preferences, what? The impulse to discriminate is   14
subtle and cannot be ferreted out unless its many guises are made clear to people. I think we need social policies that are committed to two goals: the educational and economic development of disadvantaged people regardless of race and the eradication from our society—through close monitoring and severe sanctions—of racial, ethnic or gender discrimination. Preferences will not get us to either of these goals, because they tend to benefit those who are not disadvantaged—middle-class white women and middle-class

blacks—and attack one form of discrimination with another. Preferences are inexpensive and carry the glamour of good intentions—change the numbers and the good deed is done. To be against them is to be unkind. But I think the unkindest cut is to bestow on children like my own an undeserved advantage while neglecting the development of those disadvantaged children in the poorer sections of my city who will most likely never be in a position to benefit from a preference. Give my children fairness; give disadvantaged children a better shot at development—better elementary and secondary schools, job training, safer neighborhoods, better financial assistance for college and so on. A smaller percentage of black high school graduates go to college today than 15 years ago; more black males are in prison, jail or in some other way under the control of the criminal-justice system than in college. This despite racial preferences.

The mandates of black power and white absolution out of which   15 preferences emerged were not wrong in themselves. What was wrong was that both races focused more on the goals of those mandates than on the means to the goals. Blacks can have no real power without taking responsibility for their own educational and economic development. Whites can have no racial innocence without earning it by eradicating discrimination and helping the disadvantaged to develop. Because we ignored the means, the goals have not been reached and the real work remains to be done.

Questions for Close Reading

1. What is the selection's thesis? Locate the sentence(s) in which Steele states his main idea. If he doesn't state the thesis explicitly, express it in your own words.
2. Why doesn't Steele want his children to designate themselves as Black on their college applications? Why does he call such labeling "a Faustian bargain"?
3. Why does Steele believe that affirmative action "demoralizes" Blacks?
4. What does Steele suggest as an alternative to affirmative action in hiring and in education?
5. Refer to your dictionary as needed to define the following words used in the selection: *malevolence* (paragraph 1), *sanctimoniously* (2), *meagerest* (2), *recompense* (2), *residual* (2), *symmetry* (3), *diversity* (5), *absolution* (6), *mandates* (6), *eradicate* (8), *demoralization* (9), *myriad* (9), *ineptness* (10), *debilitating* (10), *reparation* (13), and *residues* (13).

Questions About the Writer's Craft

1. **The pattern.** Which of the two possible strategies for organizing a refutation (see pages 562–64) does Steele use in his essay? Do you consider the points he makes in the refutation sufficiently persuasive? Explain.
2. **Other patterns.** Why do you suppose Steele begins with the example of his own children? How does this example prepare readers for his argument?
3. Steele often uses "I think" or "I believe" when making his points. (One example is at the end of the first paragraph.) Find additional instances elsewhere in the essay. Why do you think he uses these expressions so frequently?
4. In paragraph 9, which two key words does Steele repeat? Why might he have used this repetition?

Writing Assignments Using Argumentation-Persuasion as a Pattern of Development

∞ 1. To support his argument that affirmative action has negative effects, Steele makes a number of key points, including the following:

- Preferential treatment implies an inherent inferiority and thus leads to corrosive self-doubt.
- Preferential treatment fosters a feeling of victimhood that strips people of the ability to take strong action on their own behalf.
- Preferential treatment creates a dangerous illusion of entitlement that ultimately works to the detriment of those who feel they are owed something.

Focusing on a specific minority group, write an essay defending or challenging *one* of these points (or any other that Steele makes). Remember to acknowledge and, when possible, to refute opposing opinions. Before formulating your position, read William Raspberry's "The Handicap of Definition" (page 529) and Roger Wilkins's "Racism Has Its Privileges" (page 638). Raspberry provides additional evidence for Steele's viewpoint, while Wilkins presents a sharply divergent point of view. Where appropriate, refer to Raspberry and/or Wilkins in your paper.

∞ 2. Choose another social program or common practice with which you are familiar, and write an essay arguing—as Steele does—that it has had an effect very different from that which was intended. Like Steele, include specific examples of the program's ill effects, making sure to acknowledge the views of those who support the program. For additional insight into the way practices can have unintended negative consequences, read

Nat Hentoff's "Free Speech on Campus" (page 606) and Jonathan Coleman's "Is Technology Making Us Intimate Strangers?" (page 482) before writing your paper.

Writing Assignments Using Other Patterns of Development

3. Imagine what your life might be like if you were a member of another race, religion, or ethnic group. Or consider what life might be like if you were the opposite sex. Then write an essay in which you provide examples showing how your life would or would *not* change if you did indeed have another identity. Reach some conclusions about whether life would be easier or more difficult with this other identity.

4. Steele states that "Blacks can have no real power without taking responsibility for their own . . . development." The same could be said for all people. Write an essay telling about a time that you took charge of your life at a difficult point. Perhaps you rallied your strength to end a painful relationship or insisted on furthering your education even though others believed additional schooling was unnecessary. Provide vivid narrative details to show how hard you worked to take responsibility for your life. End by explaining how this concerted effort on your own behalf affected you and those who are important to you. Maya Angelou's "Sister Flowers" (page 116) and William Raspberry's "The Handicap of Definition" (page 529) should spark ideas worth exploring.

Writing Assignments Using a Journal Entry as a Starting Point

5. Write an essay exploring the positive and negative consequences that might ensue if colleges nationwide were required to dismantle their affirmative-action admission programs. To develop your discussion, draw upon the material in your pre-reading journal entry as well as the opinions of friends, classmates, and family members. Consider supplementing your informal research with material gathered in the library and/or on the Internet. At the end of your essay, indicate whether you think disbanding affirmative-action admission policies would be a good idea or a bad one.

Additional Writing Topics

ARGUMENTATION-PERSUASION

General Assignments

Using argumentation-persuasion, develop one of the topics below in an essay. After choosing a topic, think about your purpose and audience. Remember that the paper's thesis should state the issue under discussion as well as your position on the issue. As you work on developing evidence, you might want to do some outside research. Keep in mind that effective argumentation-persuasion usually means that some time should be spent acknowledging and perhaps refuting opposing points of view. Be careful not to sabotage your argument by basing your case on a logical fallacy.

1. Mercy killing
2. Hiring quotas
3. Giving birth-control devices to teenagers
4. Prayer in the schools
5. Living off campus
6. The drinking age
7. Spouses sharing housework equally
8. Smoking in public places
9. Big-time sports in college
10. Music videos
11. Working mothers with young children
12. Acid rain
13. Drugs on campus
14. Political campaigns
15. Requiring college students to pass a comprehensive exam in their majors before graduating
16. Fifty-five-mile-per-hour speed limit
17. Putting elderly parents in nursing homes
18. An optional pass-fail system for courses
19. The homeless
20. Nonconformity in a neighborhood: allowing a lawn to go wild, keeping many pets, painting a house an odd color, or some other atypical behavior

Assignments With a Specific Purpose and Audience

1. A college has rejected your or your child's application on the basis of low SAT scores. Write to the college admissions director, arguing that

SAT scores are not a fair indicator of your or your child's abilities and potential.

2. As a staff writer for the college opinion magazine, you've been asked to nominate the "Outstanding Man or Woman on Campus," to be featured on the magazine's cover. Write a letter to your supervising editor in support of your nominee.

3. You and your parents don't agree on some aspect of your romantic life (you want to live with your partner and they don't approve; you want to get married and they want you to wait; they simply don't like your partner). Write your parents a letter explaining why your preference is reasonable. Try hard to win them over to your side, and remember not to be antagonistic.

4. As a high school teacher, you support some additional restriction on students. The restriction might be "no radios in school," "no T-shirts," "no food in class," "no smoking on school grounds." Write an article for the school newspaper, justifying this new rule to the student body.

5. Someone you know is convinced that the music you listen to is trashy or boring. Write a letter to the person arguing that your music has value. Support your contention with specific references to lyrics, musical structure, and performers' talent.

6. Assume you're a member of a racial, ethnic, religious, or social minority. You might, for example, be a Native American, an elderly person, a female executive. On a recent television show or in a TV commercial, you saw something that depicts your group in an offensive way. Write a letter (to the network or the advertiser) expressing your feelings and explaining why you feel the material should be taken off the air.

12

COMBINING THE PATTERNS

Throughout this book, you've studied the patterns of development—narration, process analysis, definition, and so on—in depth. You've seen how the patterns are used as strategies for generating, developing, and organizing ideas for essays. You've also learned that, in practice, most types of writing combine two or more patterns. The two sections that follow provide additional information about these important points. The rest of the chapter then gives you an opportunity to look more closely at the way several writers use the patterns of development in their work.

THE PATTERNS IN ACTION:
DURING THE WRITING PROCESS

The patterns of development come into play throughout the composing process. In the prewriting stage, awareness of the patterns encourages you to think about your subject in fresh, new ways. Assume, for example, that you've been asked to write an essay about the way children are disciplined in school. However, you draw a blank as soon as you try to limit this general subject. To break the logjam, you could apply one or more patterns of development to your subject. *Comparison-contrast* might prompt you to write an essay investigating the differences between your parents' and your own feelings about school discipline. *Division-classification* might lead you to another paper—one that categorizes the kinds of discipline used in school. And *cause-effect* might point to still another essay—one that explores the way students react to being suspended.

Further along in the writing process—after you've identified your limited subject and your thesis—the patterns of development can help you generate your paper's evidence. Imagine that your thesis is "Teachers shouldn't discipline students publicly just to make an example of them." You're not sure, though, how to develop this thesis. Calling upon the patterns might spark some promising possibilities. *Narration* might encourage you to recount the disastrous time you were singled out and punished for the misdeeds of an entire class. Using *definition,* you might explain what is meant by an *autocratic* disciplinary style. *Argumentation-persuasion* might prompt you to advocate a new plan for disciplining students fairly and effectively.

The patterns of development also help you organize your ideas by pointing the way to an appropriate framework for a paper. Suppose you plan to write an essay for the campus newspaper about the disturbingly high incidence of shoplifting among college students; your purpose is to persuade young people not to get involved in this tempting, supposedly victimless crime. You believe that many readers will be deterred from shoplifting if you tell them about the harrowing *process* set in motion once a shoplifter is detected. With this step-by-step explanation in mind, you can now map out the essay's content: what happens when a shoplifter is detained by a salesperson, questioned by store security personnel, led to a police car, booked at the police station, and tried in a courtroom.

THE PATTERNS IN ACTION: IN AN ESSAY

Although this book devotes a separate chapter to each of the nine patterns of development, all chapters emphasize the same important point: Most writing consists of several patterns, with the dominant pattern providing the piece's organizational framework. To reinforce this point, each chapter contains a section, "How [the Pattern] Fits Your Purpose and Audience," that shows how a writer's purpose often leads to a blending of patterns. You might also have noticed that one of the "Questions About the Writer's Craft" following each professional selection asks you to analyze the piece's combination of patterns. Further, the "Writing Assignments Using Other Patterns of Development" encourage you to discover for yourself which mix of patterns would work best in a given piece of writing. In short, all through *The Macmillan Reader* we emphasize that the patterns of development are far from being mechanical formulas. On the contrary: They are practical strategies that open up options in every stage of the composing process.

In this section of the book, you'll have a chance to focus on the way writers combine patterns in their essays. The following six selections are by three writers whose styles and subjects differ sharply. (Before reading the selections, you'll probably find it helpful to glance back at pages 27–28 so you can review the broad purpose of each pattern of development.) As you read each selection, ask yourself these questions:

1. What is the writer's *purpose* and *thesis?*
2. What *pattern of development dominates* the essay? How does this pattern help the writer support the essay's thesis and fulfill the essay's purpose?
3. What *other patterns appear* in the essay? How do these secondary patterns help the writer support the essay's thesis and fulfill the essay's purpose?

Your responses to these three questions will reward you with a richer understanding of the way writers work and with a deeper appreciation of three skilled prose stylists. To give you an even clearer sense of how writers mix patterns, we have annotated Virginia Woolf's "The Death of the Moth" (page 662), using the preceding three questions as a guide. By making your own annotations on Woolf's essay and then comparing them to ours, you can measure your ability to analyze Woolf's use of the patterns. You can further evaluate your analysis of the piece by answering the three questions on your own and then comparing your responses to ours on pages 666–68.

Virginia Woolf

Virginia Woolf is considered one of the most innovative writers of the twentieth century. Born in 1882 in London, Woolf was educated at home by her father, a well-known biographer, critic, and scholar. Along with her sister, Woolf became a key member of the Bloomsbury Group, a circle of writers and artists committed to the highest standards in art and literature. Woolf married a fellow Bloomsbury member, author and publisher Leonard Woolf. Together, they established Hogarth Press, which went on to publish Woolf's ground-breaking writings, including the novels *Mrs. Dalloway* (1923) and *To the Lighthouse* (1927), as well as the collection of essays *A Room of One's Own* (1920). Woolf's experimentation with point of view and her use of stream of consciousness earned her a place as a pivotal figure in English literature. Although Woolf's work met with critical acclaim and her collaboration with her husband was productive, Woolf was troubled all her life by severe depression. She committed suicide in 1941. The first of the following two selections by Woolf, "The Death of the Moth," appeared in the volume *The Death of the Moth and Other Essays* (1948); the second, "Professions for Women," was delivered as a speech to the Women's Service League in 1931.

The Death of the Moth

Description of
the moth

Definition (by
negation): How
this moth differs
from the usual
kind

Moths that fly by day are not properly to be   1
called moths; they do not excite that pleasant
sense of dark autumn nights and ivy-blossom
which the commonest yellow-underwing asleep
in the shadow of the curtain never fails to rouse
in us. They are hybrid creatures, neither gay like
butterflies nor sombre like their own species.
Nevertheless the present specimen, with his narrow hay-coloured wings, fringed with a tassel of
the same colour, seemed to be content with life.
It was a pleasant morning, mid-September, mild,
benignant, yet with a keener breath than that of
the summer months. The plough was already
scoring the field opposite the window, and where

the share had been, the earth was pressed flat and gleamed with moisture. Such vigour came rolling in from the fields and the down beyond that it was difficult to keep the eyes strictly turned upon the book. The rooks too were keeping one of their annual festivities; soaring round the tree tops until it looked as if a vast net with thousands of black knots in it had been cast up into the air; which, after a few moments, sank slowly down upon the trees until every twig seemed to have a knot at the end of it. Then, suddenly, the net would be thrown into the air again in a wider circle this time, with the utmost clamour and vociferation, as though to be thrown into the air and settle slowly down upon the tree tops were a tremendously exciting experience.

The same energy which inspired the rooks, the ploughmen, the horses, and even, it seemed, the lean bare-backed downs, sent the moth fluttering from side to side of his square of the window-pane. One could not help watching him. One was, indeed, conscious of a queer feeling of pity for him. The possibilities of pleasure seemed that morning so enormous and so various that to have only a moth's part in life, and a day moth's at that, appeared a hard fate, and his zest in enjoying his meagre opportunities to the full, pathetic. He flew vigorously to one corner of his compartment, and, after waiting there a second, flew across to the other. What remained for him but to fly to a third corner and then to a fourth? That was all he could do, in spite of the size of the downs, the width of the sky, the far-off smoke of houses, and the romantic voice, now and then, of a steamer out at sea. What he could do he did. Watching him, it seemed as if a fibre, very thin but pure, of the enormous energy of the world had been thrust into his frail and diminutive body. As often as he crossed the pane, I could fancy that a thread of vital light became visible. He was little or nothing but life.

Margin annotations:

Part of implied purpose/thesis: Nature's energy

Description of nature's energy here contrasts with description of nature in ¶5 (part of purpose/thesis)

Comparison between nature's energy and the moth's strong life force (part of purpose/thesis)

Start of narrative (main pattern) about the moth's plight

Start of narrative about Woolf's reaction to the moth's plight

Description of moth's strong life force—despite its small size (these two contrasting qualities are part of purpose/thesis)

Part of purpose/thesis: The moth represents life

2

Narrative about Woolf's reaction continues

Yet, because he was so small, and so simple a 3 form of the energy that was rolling in at the open window and driving its way through so many narrow and intricate corridors in my own brain and in those of other human beings, there was something marvellous as well as pathetic about him. It was as if someone had taken a tiny bead of pure life and decking it as lightly as possible with down and feathers, had set it dancing and zigzagging to show us the true nature of life. Thus displayed one could not get over the strangeness of it. One is apt to forget all about life, seeing it humped and bossed and garnished and cumbered so that it has to move with the greatest circumspection and dignity. Again, the thought of all that life might have been had he been born in any other shape caused one to view his simple activities with a kind of pity.

Restatement of part of purpose/ thesis: The moth's two contrasting qualities

Restatement of part of purpose/ thesis: The moth represents life

Narrative about the moth's plight continues; tension builds

After a time, tired by his dancing apparently, 4 he settled on the window ledge in the sun, and, the queer spectacle being at an end, I forgot about him. Then, looking up, my eye was caught by him. He was trying to resume his dancing, but seemed either so stiff or so awkward that he could only flutter to the bottom of the window-pane; and when he tried to fly across it he failed. Being intent on other matters I watched these futile attempts for a time without thinking, unconsciously waiting for him to resume his flight, as one waits for a machine, that has stopped momentarily, to start again without considering the reason of its failure. After perhaps a seventh attempt he slipped from the wooden ledge and fell, fluttering his wings, on to his back on the window sill. The helplessness of his attitude roused me. It flashed upon me that he was in difficulties; he could no longer raise himself; his legs struggled vainly. But, as I stretched out a pencil, meaning to help him to right himself, it came over me that the failure and awkwardness

Narrative about Woolf's reaction continues

Hint of the resolution of the *narrative* about the moth

were the approach of death. I laid the pencil down again.

The legs agitated themselves once more. I 5 looked as if for the enemy against which he struggled. I looked out of doors. What had happened there? Presumably it was midday, and work in the fields had stopped. Stillness and quiet had

Narrative about Woolf's reaction continues

Description of nature's indifference here *contrasts* with *description* of nature in ¶1 (part of purpose/ thesis)

replaced the previous animation. The birds had taken themselves off to feed in the brooks. The horses stood still. Yet the power was there all the same, massed outside, indifferent, impersonal, not attending to anything in particular. Somehow it was opposed to the little hay-coloured moth. It was useless to try to do anything. One could only

Restatement of part of purpose/ thesis: The strength of the moth's life force—despite small size

watch the extraordinary efforts made by those tiny legs against an oncoming doom which could, had it chosen, have submerged an entire city, not merely a city, but masses of human beings; noth-ing, I knew, had any chance against death.

Part of purpose/thesis: Death's inevitability

Nevertheless after a pause of exhaustion the legs fluttered again. It was superb, this last protest, and so frantic that he succeeded at last in righting himself. One's sympathies, of course, were all on the side of life. Also, when there was nobody to

Narrative about moth continues

care or to know, this gigantic effort on the part of an insignificant little moth, against a power of

Narrative about Woolf's reaction continues

such magnitude, to retain what no one else valued or desired to keep, moved one strangely. Again, somehow, one saw life, a pure bead. I lift-ed the pencil again, useless though I knew it to

Restatement of part of purpose/ thesis: The strength of the moth's life force—despite its size

be. But even as I did so, the unmistakable tokens of death showed themselves. The body relaxed, and instantly grew stiff. The struggle was over. The insignificant little creature now knew death. As I looked at the dead moth, this minute way-side triumph of so great a force over so mean an

Resolution of the *narrative* about the moth

antagonist filled me with wonder. Just as life had been strange a few minutes before, so death was now as strange. The moth having righted himself now lay most decently and uncomplainingly

Restatement of part of purpose/ thesis: Death's inevitability

composed. O yes, he seemed to say, death is stronger than I am.

The following answers to the questions on page 661 will help you analyze Virginia Woolf's use of the patterns of development in the essay "The Death of the Moth."

1. *What is the writer's purpose and thesis?*

Woolf's *purpose* is to show that the tiny moth's courageous but ultimately futile battle to cling to life embodies the struggle at the very heart of all existence. Woolf achieves her purpose by relating the story of the moth's efforts to resist death. Her *thesis* might be expressed this way: Although living creatures may make "extraordinary efforts" (paragraph 5) to hold onto life, these attempts aren't strong enough to defy death. Nothing, Woolf writes, has "any chance against death" (5).

Woolf's purpose and thesis first become apparent at the end of paragraph 2. There she shows that the moth, with his "frail and diminutive body," represents "nothing but life." Although "small . . . and . . . simple" (3), the moth is suffused with the same extraordinary energy that is evident in the natural world beyond Woolf's window. This energy, combined with the moth's tiny size, makes the creature both "marvellous" and "pathetic" (3)—two qualities that are particularly apparent during the moth's final struggles. During those moments, the moth makes a final "superb" (5) protest against death, but ultimately the "insignificant" (5) creature—like all forms of life—must cease his valiant struggle and die.

2. *What pattern of development dominates the essay? How does this pattern help the writer support the essay's thesis and fulfill the essay's purpose?*

Although the essay's first paragraph is largely descriptive, it becomes clear by paragraph 2 that the description is in service of a larger narrative about the moth's struggles. It's this narrative that dominates the essay.

At the beginning, the moth is imbued with vitality, as he flies "vigorously" (paragraph 2) and with "zest" (2) from one side of the window to the other. But narrative tension begins to build in paragraph 4. There Woolf writes that the moth tries once again to cross the windowpane, fails repeatedly, and slips "on to his back," seemingly defeated. However, even then, the moth doesn't abandon his hold on life, for—as Woolf relates in paragraph 5—he tries, despite exhaustion, to right himself.

Against all odds, he finally succeeds, but his frantic struggle to hold onto life takes its toll, and the tiny creature soon dies. This detailed story of the moth's futile battle against death is presented as an emblem of the fate of all life. Through this narrative, Woolf achieves her purpose and thesis: to convey the power of nature and the inability of living creatures—despite heroic efforts—to defy this power.

Paralleling the tale of the moth's struggle is another *narrative*: the story of Woolf's changing understanding of the event that unfolds before her. When the moth is "dancing" (3), energetic, and vital, Woolf "could not help watching him" (2) and feels a kind of wonderment at this "tiny bead of pure life" (3). Then in paragraph 4, Woolf writes that she forgets about the moth for a while until she happens to look up and see his "futile attempts" to "resume . . . dancing." For a few moments, she watches the moth's "stiff" and "awkward" efforts to fly, expecting him to demonstrate the same vitality as before. Suddenly, she understands that the moth is "in difficulties" and can no longer lift himself up. She tries to help but abandons her efforts when she realizes that the moth's labored efforts signify the "approach of death." Paragraph 5 presents the final stage of Woolf's interior narrative. She looks outside her window for an explanation of the moth's plight. But now she finds that the forces of nature—earlier so exuberant and vibrant—are, if anything, "opposed to the little hay-coloured moth." With that, her attention is once again drawn to the moth and the fluttering of his legs. Although drained, the tiny creature makes one last effort to resist death—and, improbably enough, picks himself up one more time. Struck by the sheer power of the moth's life force, Woolf is prompted, as before, to help the creature, even though she recognizes the futility. But then the "unmistakable tokens of death" appear, and the moth gives up his struggle, succumbing—as all forms of life must—to the forces of nature. With the moth lying "uncomplainingly composed," Woolf comes to accept the fact that death is stronger than life.

3. *What other patterns appear in the essay? How do these secondary patterns help the writer support the essay's thesis and fulfill the essay's purpose?*

Although the essay is predominantly a narrative, it also contains other patterns. The *descriptive* passage at the beginning of the essay includes a brief *definition by negation* in which Woolf explains how the creature she is observing differs from the usual, more colorful night moth. The rest of paragraph 1 draws upon description to evoke the sense of early autumn and nature's extraordinary energy. This description of the natural world's vibrancy and abundance, exemplified by the rooks and plowed earth, *contrasts* with Woolf's later characterization of the natural world in paragraph 5. There she writes, "Stillness and quiet . . . replaced the previous animation," and she senses not that nature fosters vitality, but that it is "indifferent, impersonal, not attending to anything in particular."

Shifting her focus in paragraph 2 from the natural world to the moth, Woolf exercises her *descriptive* powers to convey the moth's extraordinary zest as he flies across the windowpane. In this paragraph, Woolf also draws upon *comparison-contrast* to show that despite *differences* in their sizes, the tiny moth and the vast natural world embody the *same* primal energy. Woolf's consideration of this elemental similarity leads her to the basic *contrast* at the heart of the essay: While the moth's tiny size makes him "pathetic," his formidable life spirit makes him "marvellous." He may be small and lightweight, but he is abuzz with vitality. When contrasted to the enormous power of nature, the moth—like all forms of life—may be puny, but his impulse to defy such power inspires awe and reverence.

Virginia Woolf

Professions for Women[1]

When your secretary invited me to come here, she told me that your Society is concerned with the employment of women and she suggested that I might tell you something about my own professional experiences. It is true I am a woman; it is true I am employed; but what professional experiences have I had? It is difficult to say. My profession is literature; and in that profession there are fewer experiences for women than in any other, with the exception of the stage—fewer, I mean, that are peculiar to women. For the road was cut many years ago—by Fanny Burney, by Aphra Behn, by Harriet Martineau, by Jane Austen, by George Eliot[2]—many famous women, and many more unknown and forgotten, have been before me, making the path smooth, and regulating my steps. Thus, when I came to write, there were very few material obstacles in my way. Writing was a reputable and harmless occupation. The family peace was not broken by the scratching of a pen. No demand was made upon the family purse. For ten and sixpence one can buy paper enough to write all the plays of Shakespeare—if one has a mind that way. Pianos and models, Paris, Vienna and Berlin, masters and mistresses, are not needed by a writer. The cheapness of writing paper is, of course, the reason why women have succeeded as writers before they have succeeded in the other professions.

But to tell you my story—it is a simple one. You have only got to figure to yourselves a girl in a bedroom with a pen in her hand. She had only to move that pen from left to right—from ten o'clock to one. Then it occurred to her to do what is simple and cheap enough after all—to slip a few of those pages into an envelope, fix a

1

2

---

[1]The following is a speech delivered by Woolf to the Women's Service League in 1931 (editors' note).
[2]Fanny Burney (1752–1840), Aphra Behn (1640–89), Harriet Martineau (1802–76), Jane Austen (1775–1817), and Marian Evans (1819–80), whose pen name was George Eliot, were all English women of letters (editors' note).

penny stamp in the corner, and drop the envelope into the red box at the corner. It was thus that I became a journalist; and my effort was rewarded on the first day of the following month—a very glorious day it was for me—by a letter from an editor containing a cheque for one pound ten shillings and sixpence. But to show you how little I deserve to be called a professional woman, how little I know of the struggles and difficulties of such lives, I have to admit that instead of spending that sum upon bread and butter, rent, shoes and stockings, or butcher's bills, I went out and bought a cat—a beautiful cat, a Persian cat, which very soon involved me in bitter disputes with my neighbors.

What could be easier than to write articles and to buy Persian 3
cats with the profits? But wait a moment. Articles have to be about something. Mine, I seem to remember, was about a novel by a famous man. And while I was writing this review, I discovered that if I were going to review books I should need to do battle with a certain phantom. And the phantom was a woman, and when I came to know her better I called her after the heroine of a famous poem, "The Angel in the House." It was she who used to come between me and my paper when I was writing reviews. It was she who bothered me and wasted my time and so tormented me that at last I killed her. You who come of a younger and happier generation may not have heard of her—you may not know what I mean by the Angel in the House. I will describe her as shortly as I can. She was intensely sympathetic. She was immensely charming. She was utterly unselfish. She excelled in the difficult arts of family life. She sacrificed herself daily. If there was chicken, she took the leg; if there was a draught she sat in it—in short she was so constituted that she never had a mind or a wish of her own, but preferred to sympathize always with the minds and wishes of others. Above all—I need not say it—she was pure. Her purity was supposed to be her chief beauty—her blushes, her great grace. In those days—the last of Queen Victoria—every house had its Angel. And when I came to write I encountered her with the very first words. The shadow of her wings fell on my page; I heard the rustling of her skirts in the room. Directly, that is to say, I took my pen in hand to review that novel by a famous man, she slipped behind me and whispered: "My dear, you are a young woman. You are writing about a book that has been written by a man. Be sympathetic; be tender; flatter; deceive; use all the arts and wiles of our sex. Never let anybody guess that you have

a mind of your own. Above all, be pure." And she made as if to guide my pen. I now record the one act for which I take some credit to myself, though the credit rightly belongs to some excellent ancestors of mine who left me a certain sum of money—shall we say five hundred pounds a year?—so that it was not necessary for me to depend solely on charm for my living. I turned upon her and caught her by the throat. I did my best to kill her. My excuse, if I were to be had up in a court of law, would be that I acted in self-defence. Had I not killed her she would have killed me. She would have plucked the heart out of my writing. For, as I found, directly I put pen to paper, you cannot review even a novel without having a mind of your own, without expressing what you think to be the truth about human relations, morality, sex. And all these questions, according to the Angel in the House, cannot be dealt with freely and openly by women; they must charm, they must conciliate, they must—to put it bluntly—tell lies if they are to succeed. Thus, whenever I felt the shadow of her wing or the radiance of her halo upon my page, I took up the inkpot and flung it at her. She died hard. Her fictitious nature was of great assistance to her. It is far harder to kill a phantom than a reality. She was always creeping back when I thought I had despatched her. Though I flatter myself that I killed her in the end, the struggle was severe; it took much time that had better have been spent upon learning Greek grammar; or in roaming the world in search of adventures. But it was a real experience; it was an experience that was bound to befall all women writers at that time. Killing the Angel in the House was part of the occupation of a woman writer.

But to continue my story. The Angel was dead; what then 4 remained? You may say that what remained was a simple and common object—a young woman in a bedroom with an inkpot. In other words, now that she had rid herself of falsehood, that young woman had only to be herself. Ah, but what is "herself"? I mean, what is a woman? I assure you, I do not know. I do not believe that you know. I do not believe that anybody can know until she has expressed herself in all the arts and professions open to human skill. That indeed is one of the reasons why I have come here—out of respect for you, who are in process of showing us by your experiments what a woman is, who are in process of providing us, by your failures and successes, with that extremely important piece of information.

But to continue the story of my professional experiences. I 5
made one pound ten and six by my first review; and I bought a
Persian cat with the proceeds. Then I grew ambitious. A Persian cat
is all very well, I said; but a Persian cat is not enough. I must have
a motor car. And it was thus that I became a novelist—for it is a very
strange thing that people will give you a motor car if you will tell
them a story. It is a still stranger thing that there is nothing so
delightful in the world as telling stories. It is far pleasanter than writing reviews of famous novels. And yet, if I am to obey your secretary and tell you my professional experiences as a novelist, I must tell
you about a very strange experience that befell me as a novelist. And
to understand it you must try first to imagine a novelist's state of
mind. I hope I am not giving away professional secrets if I say that
a novelist's chief desire is to be as unconscious as possible. He has
to induce in himself a state of perpetual lethargy. He wants life to
proceed with the utmost quiet and regularity. He wants to see the
same faces, to read the same books, to do the same things day after
day, month after month, while he is writing, so that nothing may
break the illusion in which he is living—so that nothing may disturb
or disquiet the mysterious nosings about, feelings round, darts,
dashes and sudden discoveries of that very shy and illusive spirit, the
imagination. I suspect that this state is the same both for men and
women. Be that as it may, I want you to imagine me writing a novel
in a state of trance. I want you to figure to yourself a girl sitting with
a pen in her hand, which for minutes, and indeed for hours, she
never dips into the inkpot. The image that comes to my mind when
I think of this girl is the image of a fisherman lying sunk in dreams
on the verge of a deep lake with a rod held out over the water. She
was letting her imagination sweep unchecked round every rock and
cranny of the world that lies submerged in the depths of our unconscious being. Now came the experience, the experience that I
believe to be far commoner with women writers than with men. The
line raced through the girl's fingers. Her imagination had rushed
away. It had sought the pools, the depths, the dark places where the
largest fish slumber. And then there was a smash. There was an
explosion. There was foam and confusion. The imagination had
dashed itself against something hard. The girl was roused from her
dream. She was indeed in a state of the most acute and difficult distress. To speak without figure she had thought of something, something about the body, about the passions which it was unfitting for

her as a woman to say. Men, her reason told her, would be shocked. The consciousness of what men will say of a woman who speaks the truth about her passions had roused her from her artist's state of unconsciousness. She could write no more. The trance was over. Her imagination could work no longer. This I believe to be a very common experience with women writers—they are impeded by the extreme conventionality of the other sex. For though men sensibly allow themselves great freedom in these respects, I doubt that they realize or can control the extreme severity with which they condemn such freedom in women.

These then were two very genuine experiences of my own. 6 These were two of the adventures of my professional life. The first— killing the Angel in the House—I think I solved. She died. But the second, telling the truth about my own experiences as a body, I do not think I solved. I doubt that any woman has solved it yet. The obstacles against her are still immensely powerful—and yet they are very difficult to define. Outwardly, what is simpler than to write books? Outwardly, what obstacles are there for a woman rather than for a man? Inwardly, I think, the case is very different: she has still many ghosts to fight, many prejudices to overcome. Indeed it will be a long time still, I think, before a woman can sit down to write a book without finding a phantom to be slain, a rock to be dashed against. And if this is so in literature, the freest of all professions for women, how is it in the new professions which you are now for the first time entering?

Those are the questions that I should like, had I time, to ask 7 you. And indeed, if I have laid stress upon these professional experiences of mine, it is because I believe that they are, though in different forms, yours also. Even when the path is nominally open— when there is nothing to prevent a woman from being a doctor, a lawyer, a civil servant—there are many phantoms and obstacles, as I believe, looming in her way. To discuss and define them is, I think, of great value and importance; for thus only can the labour be shared, the difficulties be solved. But besides this, it is necessary also to discuss the ends and the aims for which we are fighting, for which we are doing battle with these formidable obstacles. Those aims cannot be taken for granted; they must be perpetually questioned and examined. The whole position, as I see it—here in this hall surrounded by women practicing for the first time in history I know not how many different professions—is one of extraordinary interest and importance. You have won rooms of your own in the house hitherto exclusively owned by men. You are able, though not without great labor and effort, to pay the rent. You are earning your five hundred pounds a year. But this freedom is only a beginning; the room is your own, but it is still bare. It has to be furnished; it has to be decorated; it has to be shared. How are you going to furnish it, how are you going to decorate it? With whom are you going to share it, and upon what terms? These, I think, are questions of the utmost importance and interest. For the first time in history you are able to ask them; for the first time you are able to decide for yourselves what the answers should be. Willingly would I stay and discuss those questions and answers—but not tonight. My time is up; and I must cease.

Martin Luther King, Jr.

More than thirty years after his assassination, Martin Luther King, Jr. (1929–68), is still recognized as the towering figure in the struggle for civil rights in the United States. Born in Atlanta, Georgia, King earned doctorates from Boston University and Chicago Theological Seminary and served as pastor of a Baptist congregation in Montgomery, Alabama. Advocating a philosophy of nonviolent resistance to racial injustice, he led bus boycotts, marches, and sit-ins that brought about passage of the 1964 Civil Rights Act and the Voting Rights Act of 1965. Dr. King was awarded the Nobel Peace Prize in 1964. The following two selections by King are taken from *Where Do We Go From Here: Community or Chaos?* (1967).

Where Do We Go From Here: Community or Chaos?

1 A final problem that mankind must solve in order to survive in the world house that we have inherited is finding an alternative to war and human destruction. Recent events have vividly reminded us that nations are not reducing but rather increasing their arsenals of weapons of mass destruction. The best brains in the highly developed nations of the world are devoted to military technology. The proliferation of nuclear weapons has not been halted, in spite of the limited-test-ban treaty.

2 In this day of man's highest technical achievement, in this day of dazzling discovery, of novel opportunities, loftier dignities and fuller freedoms for all, there is no excuse for the kind of blind craving for power and resources that provoked the wars of previous generations. There is no need to fight for food and land. Science has provided us with adequate means of survival and transportation, which make it possible to enjoy the fullness of this great earth. The question now is, do we have the morality and courage required to live together as brothers and not be afraid?

3 One of the most persistent ambiguities we face is that everybody talks about peace as a goal, but among the wielders of power peace is practically nobody's business. Many men cry "Peace! Peace!" but they refuse to do the things that make for peace.

The large power blocs talk passionately of pursuing peace while   4
expanding defense budgets that already bulge, enlarging already
awesome armies and devising ever more devastating weapons. Call
the roll of those who sing the glad tidings of peace and one's ears
will be surprised by the responding sounds. The heads of all the
nations issue clarion calls for peace, yet they come to the peace table
accompanied by bands of brigands each bearing unsheathed swords.

The stages of history are replete with the chants and choruses of   5
the conquerors of old who came killing in pursuit of peace.
Alexander, Genghis Khan, Julius Caesar, Charlemagne and
Napoleon were akin in seeking a peaceful world order, a world fashioned after their selfish conceptions of an ideal existence. Each
sought a world at peace which would personify his egotistic dreams.
Even within the life span of most of us, another megalomaniac
strode across the world stage. He sent his blitzkrieg-bent legions
blazing across Europe, bringing havoc and holocaust in his wake.
There is grave irony in the fact that Hitler could come forth, following nakedly aggressive expansionist theories, and do it all in the
name of peace.

So when in this day I see the leaders of nations again talking   6
peace while preparing for war, I take fearful pause. When I see our
country today intervening in what is basically a civil war, mutilating
hundreds of thousands of Vietnamese children with napalm, burning villages and rice fields at random, painting the valleys of that
small Asian country red with human blood, leaving broken bodies
in countless ditches and sending home half-men, mutilated mentally and physically; when I see the unwillingness of our government to
create the atmosphere for a negotiated settlement of this awful conflict by halting bombings in the North and agreeing unequivocally
to talk with the Vietcong—and all this in the name of pursuing the
goal of peace—I tremble for our world.[1] I do so not only from dire
recall of the nightmares wreaked in the wars of yesterday, but also
from dreadful realization of today's possible nuclear destructiveness
and tomorrow's even more calamitous prospects.

Before it is too late, we must narrow the gaping chasm between   7
our proclamations of peace and our lowly deeds which precipitate

[1]Only after more than 58,000 Americans had been killed did the United States
withdraw from Vietnam. The war then continued until the North Vietnamese,
aided by the Vietcong, took over all of Vietnam (editors' note).

and perpetuate war. We are called upon to look up from the quagmire of military programs and defense commitments and read the warnings on history's signposts.

One day we must come to see that peace is not merely a distant   8
goal that we seek but a means by which we arrive at that goal. We must pursue peaceful ends through peaceful means. How much longer must we play at deadly war games before we heed the plaintive pleas of the unnumbered dead and maimed of past wars?

President John F. Kennedy said on one occasion, "Mankind   9
must put an end to war or war will put an end to mankind." Wisdom born of experience should tell us that war is obsolete. There may have been a time when war served as a negative good by preventing the spread and growth of an evil force, but the destructive power of modern weapons eliminates even the possibility that war may serve any good at all. If we assume that life is worth living and that man has a right to survive, then we must find an alternative to war. In a day when vehicles hurtle through outer space and guided ballistic missiles carve highways of death through the stratosphere, no nation can claim victory in war. A so-called limited war will leave little more than a calamitous legacy of human suffering, political turmoil and spiritual disillusionment. A world war will leave only smoldering ashes as mute testimony of a human race whose folly led inexorably to ultimate death. If modern man continues to flirt unhesitatingly with war, he will transform his earthly habitat into an inferno such as even the mind of Dante[2] could not imagine.

Therefore I suggest that the philosophy and strategy of non-   10
violence become immediately a subject for study and for serious experimentation in every field of human conflict, by no means excluding the relations between nations. It is, after all, nation-states which make war, which have produced the weapons that threaten the survival of mankind and which are both genocidal and suicidal in character.

We have ancient habits to deal with, vast structures of power,   11
indescribably complicated problems to solve. But unless we abdicate our humanity altogether and succumb to fear and impotence in the presence of the weapons we have ourselves created, it is as possible and as urgent to put an end to war and violence between nations as it is to put an end to poverty and racial injustice.

[2]In *The Divine Comedy* (1321), Italian poet Dante depicts the burning torments of hell endured by a lost soul before it can attain salvation (editors' note).

The United Nations is a gesture in the direction of nonviolence   12
on a world scale. There, at least, states that oppose one another have
sought to do so with words instead of with weapons. But true nonviolence is more than the absence of violence. It is the persistent and
determined application of peaceable power to offenses against the
community—in this case the world community. As the United Nations
moves ahead with the giant tasks confronting it, I would hope that it
would earnestly examine the uses of nonviolent direct action.

I do not minimize the complexity of the problems that need to   13
be faced in achieving disarmament and peace. But I am convinced
that we shall not have the will, the courage and the insight to deal
with such matters unless in this field we are prepared to undergo a
mental and spiritual re-evaluation, a change of focus which will
enable us to see that the things that seem most real and powerful are
indeed now unreal and have come under sentence of death. We need
to make a supreme effort to generate the readiness, indeed the
eagerness, to enter into the new world which is now possible, "the
city which hath foundation, whose Building and Maker is God."

It is not enough to say, "We must not wage war." It is necessary   14
to love peace and sacrifice for it. We must concentrate not merely on
the eradication of war but on the affirmation of peace. A fascinating
story about Ulysses and the Sirens[3] is preserved for us in Greek literature. The Sirens had the ability to sing so sweetly that sailors could
not resist steering toward their island. Many ships were lured upon
the rocks, and men forgot home, duty and honor as they flung themselves into the sea to be embraced by arms that drew them down to
death. Ulysses, determined not to succumb to the Sirens, first decided to tie himself tightly to the mast of his boat and his crew stuffed
their ears with wax. But finally he and his crew learned a better way
to save themselves: They took on board the beautiful singer Orpheus,
whose melodies were sweeter than the music of the Sirens. When
Orpheus sang, who would bother to listen to the Sirens?

So we must see that peace represents a sweeter music, a cos-   15
mic melody that is far superior to the discords of war. Somehow
we must transform the dynamics of the world power struggle from
the nuclear arms race, which no one can win, to a creative contest
to harness man's genius for the purpose of making peace and

[3]Ulysses and the Sirens, as well as Orpheus (mentioned later in the paragraph), are
all figures in Greek mythology (editors' note).

prosperity a reality for all the nations of the world. In short, we must shift the arms race into a "peace race." If we have the will and determination to mount such a peace offensive, we will unlock hitherto tightly sealed doors of hope and bring new light into the dark chambers of pessimism.

Martin Luther King, Jr.

The World House

Some years ago a famous novelist died. Among his papers was 1
found a list of suggested plots for future stories, the most promi-
nently underscored being this one: "A widely separated family inher-
its a house in which they have to live together." This is the great new
problem of mankind. We have inherited a large house, a great
"world house" in which we have to live together—black and white,
Easterner and Westerner, Gentile and Jew, Catholic and Protestant,
Moslem and Hindu—a family unduly separated in ideas, culture and
interest, who, because we can never again live apart, must learn
somehow to live with each other in peace.

However deeply American Negroes are caught in the struggle 2
to be at last at home in our homeland of the United States, we cannot ignore the larger world house in which we are also dwellers.
Equality with whites will not solve the problems of either whites or
Negroes if it means equality in a world society stricken by poverty
and in a universe doomed to extinction by war.

All inhabitants of the globe are now neighbors. This worldwide 3
neighborhood has been brought into being largely as a result of the
modern scientific and technological revolutions. The world of today
is vastly different from the world of just one hundred years ago. A century ago Thomas Edison had not yet invented the incandescent lamp
to bring light to many dark places of the earth. The Wright brothers
had not yet invented that fascinating mechanical bird that would
spread its gigantic wings across the skies and soon dwarf distance and
place time in the service of man. Einstein had not yet challenged an
axiom and the theory of relativity had not yet been posited.

Human beings, searching a century ago as now for better 4
understanding, had no television, no radios, no telephones and no
motion pictures through which to communicate. Medical science
had not yet discovered the wonder drugs to end many dread
plagues and diseases. One hundred years ago military men had not

yet developed the terrifying weapons of warfare that we know today—
not the bomber, an airborne fortress raining down death; nor napalm,
that burner of all things and flesh in its path. A century ago there were
no skyscraping buildings to kiss the stars and no gargantuan bridges
to span the waters. Science had not yet peered into the unfathomable
ranges of interstellar space, nor had it penetrated oceanic depths. All
these new inventions, these new ideas, these sometimes fascinating
and sometimes frightening developments came later. Most of them
have come within the past sixty years, sometimes with agonizing slowness, more characteristically with bewildering speed, but always with
enormous significance for our future.

The years ahead will see a continuation of the same dramatic 5
developments. Physical science will carve new highways through the
stratosphere. In a few years astronauts and cosmonauts will probably walk comfortably across the uncertain pathways of the moon. In
two or three years it will be possible, because of the new supersonic
jets, to fly from New York to London in two and one-half hours. In
the years ahead medical science will greatly prolong the lives of men
by finding a cure for cancer and deadly heart ailments. Automation
and cybernation will make it possible for working people to have
undreamed-of amounts of leisure time. All this is a dazzling picture
of the furniture, the workshop, the spacious rooms, the new deco-
rations and the architectural pattern of the large world house in
which we are living.

Along with the scientific and technological revolution, we 6
have also witnessed a worldwide freedom revolution over the last
few decades. The present upsurge of the Negro people of the
United States grows out of a deep and passionate determination
to make freedom and equality a reality "here" and "now." In one
sense the civil rights movement in the United States is a special
American phenomenon which must be understood in the light of
American history and dealt with in terms of the American situation. But on another and more important level, what is happening in the United States today is a significant part of a world
development.

We live in a day, said the philosopher Alfred North Whitehead, 7
"when civilization is shifting its basic outlook; a major turning point
in history where the presuppositions on which society is structured
are being analyzed, sharply challenged, and profoundly changed."
What we are seeing now is a freedom explosion, the realization of

"an idea whose time has come," to use Victor Hugo's[1] phrase. The deep rumbling of discontent that we hear today is the thunder of disinherited masses, rising from dungeons of oppression to the bright hills of freedom. In one majestic chorus the rising masses are singing, in the words of our freedom song, "Ain't gonna let nobody turn us around." All over the world like a fever, freedom is spreading in the widest liberation movement in history. The great masses of people are determined to end the exploitation of their races and lands. They are awake and moving toward their goal like a tidal wave. You can hear them rumbling in every village street, on the docks, in the houses, among the students, in the churches and at political meetings. For several centuries the direction of history flowed from the nations and societies of Western Europe out into the rest of the world in "conquests" of various sorts. That period, the era of colonialism, is at an end. East is moving West. The earth is being redistributed. Yes, we are "shifting our basic outlooks."

These developments should not surprise any student of history.   8 Oppressed people cannot remain oppressed forever. The yearning for freedom eventually manifests itself. The Bible tells the thrilling story of how Moses stood in Pharaoh's court centuries ago and cried, "Let my people go." This was an opening chapter in a continuing story. The present struggle in the United States is a later chapter in the same story. Something within has reminded the Negro of his birthright of freedom, and something without has reminded him that it can be gained. Consciously or unconsciously, he has been caught up by the spirit of the times, and with his black brothers of Africa and his brown and yellow brothers in Asia, South America and the Caribbean, the United States Negro is moving with a sense of great urgency toward the promised land of racial justice.

Nothing could be more tragic than for men to live in these revolutionary times and fail to achieve the new attitudes and the new mental outlooks that the new situation demands. In Washington Irving's familiar story of Rip Van Winkle, the one thing that we usually remember is that Rip slept twenty years. There is another important point, however, that is almost always overlooked. It was the sign on the inn in the little town on the Hudson from which Rip departed and scaled the mountain for his long sleep. When he went up, the sign had a picture of King George III of England. When he came

---

[1]French poet, dramatist, and novelist (1802–85) (editors' note).

down, twenty years later, the sign had a picture of George Washington. As he looked at the picture of the first President of the United States, Rip was confused, flustered and lost. He knew not who Washington was. The most striking thing about this story is not that Rip slept twenty years, but that he slept through a revolution that would alter the course of human history.

One of the great liabilities of history is that all too many people   10
fail to remain awake through great periods of social change. Every society has its protectors of the status quo and its fraternities of the indifferent who are notorious for sleeping through revolutions. But today our very survival depends on our ability to stay awake, to adjust to new ideas, to remain vigilant and to face the challenge of change. The large house in which we live demands that we transform this worldwide neighborhood into a worldwide brotherhood. Together we must learn to live as brothers or together we will be forced to perish as fools.

We must work passionately and indefatigably to bridge the gulf   11
between our scientific progress and our moral progress. One of the great problems of mankind is that we suffer from a poverty of the spirit which stands in glaring contrast to our scientific and techno-logical abundance. The richer we have become materially, the poor-er we have become morally and spiritually.

Every man lives in two realms, the internal and the external.   12
The internal is that realm of spiritual ends expressed in art, litera-ture, morals, and religion. The external is that complex of devices, techniques, mechanisms, and instrumentalities by means of which we live. Our problem today is that we have allowed the internal to become lost in the external. We have allowed the means by which we live to outdistance the ends for which we live. So much of modern life can be summarized in that suggestive phrase of Thoreau:[2] "Improved means to an unimproved end." This is the serious predicament, the deep and haunting problem, confronting modern man. Enlarged material powers spell enlarged peril if there is not proportionate growth of the soul. When the external of man's nature subjugates the internal, dark storm clouds begin to form.

Western civilization is particularly vulnerable at this moment,   13
for our material abundance has brought us neither peace of mind

[2]American philosopher and essayist (1817–62) (editors' note).

nor serenity of spirit. An Asian writer has portrayed our dilemma in candid terms:

> You call your thousand material devices "labor-saving machinery," yet you are forever "busy." With the multiplying of your machinery you grow increasingly fatigued, anxious, nervous, dissatisfied. Whatever you have, you want more; and wherever you are you want to go somewhere else . . . your devices are neither time-saving nor soul-saving machinery. They are so many sharp spurs which urge you on to invent more machinery and to do more business.

This tells us something about our civilization that cannot be   14
cast aside as a prejudiced charge by an Eastern thinker who is jealous of Western prosperity. We cannot escape the indictment.

This does not mean that we must turn back the clock of scien-   15
tific progress. No one can overlook the wonders that science has wrought for our lives. The automobile will not abdicate in favor of the horse and buggy, or the train in favor of the stagecoach, or the tractor in favor of the hand plow, or the scientific method in favor of ignorance and superstition. But our moral and spiritual "lag" must be redeemed. When scientific power outruns moral power, we end up with guided missiles and misguided men. When we foolishly minimize the internal of our lives and maximize the external, we sign the warrant for our own day of doom.

Our hope for creative living in this world house that we have   16
inherited lies in our ability to reestablish the moral ends of our lives in personal character and social justice. Without this spiritual and moral reawakening we shall destroy ourselves in the misuse of our own instruments.

Joan Didion

Known for her taut prose style and sharp social commentary, Joan Didion (1934–) graduated from the University of California at Berkeley. Her essays have appeared in the *Saturday Evening Post,* the *American Scholar,* and the *National Review,* as well as in three collections: *Slouching Towards Bethlehem* (1969), *The White Album* (1979), and *After Henry* (1992). *Salvador* (1983) is a book-length essay about a 1982 visit to Central America. The coauthor of several screenplays (including *A Star Is Born* in 1976 and *Up Close and Personal* in 1996), Didion has also written novels, including *Run River* (1963), *A Book of Common Prayer* (1977), *Democracy* (1984), and *The Last Thing He Wanted* (1996). "On Going Home" and "The Santa Ana" are both from *Slouching Towards Bethlehem.*

On Going Home

I am home for my daughter's first birthday. By "home" I do not 1 mean the house in Los Angeles where my husband and I and the baby live, but the place where my family is, in the Central Valley of California. It is a vital although troublesome distinction. My husband likes my family but is uneasy in their house, because once there I fall into their ways, which are difficult, oblique, deliberately inarticulate, not my husband's ways. We live in dusty houses ("D-U-S-T," he once wrote with his finger on surfaces all over the house, but no one noticed it) filled with mementos quite without value to him (what could the Canton dessert plates mean to him? how could he have known about the assay scales, why should he care if he did know?), and we appear to talk exclusively about people we know who have been committed to mental hospitals, about people we know who have been booked on drunk-driving charges, and about property, particularly about property, land, price per acre and C-2 zoning and assessments and freeway access. My brother does not understand my husband's inability to perceive the advantage in the rather common real-estate transaction known as "sale-leaseback," and my husband in turn does not understand why so many of the people he hears about in my father's house have recently been committed to mental hospitals or booked on drunk-driving charges. Nor does he understand that when we talk about sale-leasebacks and right-of-way condemnations we are talking in code about the things we like best, the yellow fields and the cottonwoods and the rivers rising and falling and the mountain roads closing when the heavy snow comes in. We miss each other's points, have another drink and regard the fire. My brother refers to my husband, in his presence, as "Joan's husband." Marriage is the classic betrayal.

Or perhaps it is not any more. Sometimes I think that those of   2 us who are now in our thirties were born into the last generation to carry the burden of "home," to find in family life the source of all tension and drama. I had by all objective accounts a "normal" and a "happy" family situation, and yet I was almost thirty years old before I could talk to my family on the telephone without crying after I had hung up. We did not fight. Nothing was wrong. And yet some nameless anxiety colored the emotional charges between me and the place that I came from. The question of whether or not you could go home again was a very real part of the sentimental and largely literary baggage with which we left home in the fifties; I suspect that it is irrelevant to the children born of the fragmentation after World War II. A few weeks ago in a San Francisco bar I saw a pretty young girl on crystal take off her clothes and dance for the cash prize in an "amateur-topless" contest. There was no particular sense of moment about this, none of the effect of romantic degradation, of "dark journey," for which my generation strived so assiduously. What sense could that girl possibly make of, say, *Long Day's Journey into Night?*[1] Who is beside the point?

That I am trapped in this particular irrelevancy is never more   3 apparent to me than when I am home. Paralyzed by the neurotic lassitude engendered by meeting one's past at every turn, around every corner, inside every cupboard, I go aimlessly from room to room. I decide to meet it head-on and clean out a drawer, and I spread the contents on the bed. A bathing suit I wore the summer I was seventeen. A letter of rejection from *The Nation*,[2] an aerial photograph of the site for a shopping center my father did not build in 1954. Three teacups hand-painted with cabbage roses and signed "E.M.," my grandmother's initials. There is no final solution for letters of rejection from *The Nation* and teacups handpainted in 1900. Nor is there

[1]The 1956 (posthumously published) drama written by the American playwright Eugene O'Neill (1888–1953) (editors' note).
[2]A magazine of political commentary (editors' note).

any answer to snapshots of one's grandfather as a young man on skis, surveying around Donner Pass in the year 1910. I smooth out the snapshot and look into his face, and do and do not see my own. I close the drawer, and have another cup of coffee with my mother. We get along very well, veterans of a guerrilla war we never understood.

Days pass. I see no one. I come to dread my husband's evening 4
call, not only because he is full of news of what by now seems to me our remote life in Los Angeles, people he has seen, letters which require attention, but because he asks what I have been doing, suggests uneasily that I get out, drive to San Francisco or Berkeley. Instead I drive across the river to a family graveyard. It has been vandalized since my last visit and the monuments are broken, overturned in the dry grass. Because I once saw a rattlesnake in the grass I stay in the car and listen to a country-and-Western station. Later I drive with my father to a ranch he has in the foothills. The man who runs his cattle on it asks us to the roundup, a week from Sunday, and although I know that I will be in Los Angeles I say, in the oblique way my family talks, that I will come. Once home I mention the broken monuments in the graveyard. My mother shrugs.

I go to visit my great-aunts. A few of them think now that I am 5
my cousin, or their daughter who died young. We recall an anecdote about a relative last seen in 1948, and they ask if I still like living in New York City. I have lived in Los Angeles for three years, but I say that I do. The baby is offered a horehound drop, and I am slipped a dollar bill "to buy a treat." Questions trail off, answers are abandoned, the baby plays with the dust motes in a shaft of afternoon sun.

It is time for the baby's birthday party: a white cake, strawberry-marshmallow ice cream, a bottle of champagne saved from 6
another party. In the evening, after she has gone to sleep, I kneel beside the crib and touch her face, where it is pressed against the slats, with mine. She is an open and trusting child, unprepared for and unaccustomed to the ambushes of family life, and perhaps it is just as well that I can offer her little of that life. I would like to give her more. I would like to promise her that she will grow up with a sense of her cousins and of rivers and of her great-grandmother's teacups, would like to pledge her a picnic on a river with fried chicken and her hair uncombed, would like to give her *home* for her birthday, but we live differently now and I can promise her nothing like that. I give her a xylophone and a sundress from Madeira, and promise to tell her a funny story.

Joan Didion

The Santa Ana

There is something uneasy in the Los Angeles air this afternoon,   1
some unnatural stillness, some tension. What it means is that tonight
a Santa Ana will begin to blow, a hot wind from the northeast whining down through the Cajon and San Gorgonio Passes, blowing up
sandstorms out along Route 66, drying the hills and the nerves to
the flash point. For a few days now we will see smoke back in the
canyons, and hear sirens in the night. I have neither heard nor read
that a Santa Ana is due, but I know it, and almost everyone I have
seen today knows it too. We know it because we feel it. The baby
frets. The maid sulks. I rekindle a waning argument with the telephone company, then cut my losses and lie down, given over to
whatever is in the air. To live with the Santa Ana is to accept, consciously or unconsciously, a deeply mechanistic view of human
behavior.

I recall being told, when I first moved to Los Angeles and was   2
living on an isolated beach, that the Indians would throw themselves
into the sea when the bad wind blew. I could see why. The Pacific
turned ominously glossy during a Santa Ana period, and one woke
in the night troubled not only by the peacocks screaming in the
olive trees but by the eerie absence of surf. The heat was surreal. The
sky had a yellow cast, the kind of light sometimes called "earthquake
weather." My only neighbor would not come out of her house for
days, and there were no lights at night, and her husband roamed the
place with a machete. One day he would tell me that he had heard
a trespasser, the next a rattlesnake.

"On nights like that," Raymond Chandler[1] once wrote about   3
the Santa Ana, "every booze party ends in a fight. Meek little wives
feel the edge of the carving knife and study their husbands' necks.

---

[1]Chandler (1888–1959) was an American novelist, best known for his detective
novels featuring the character of Philip Marlowe (editors' note).

Anything can happen." That was the kind of wind it was. I did not know then that there was any basis for the effect it had on all of us, but it turns out to be another of those cases in which science bears out folk wisdom. The Santa Ana, which is named for one of the canyons it rushes through, is a *foehn* wind, like the *foehn* of Austria and Switzerland and the *hamsin* of Israel. There are a number of persistent malevolent winds, perhaps the best known of which are the mistral of France and the Mediterranean sirocco, but a *foehn* wind has distinct characteristics: it occurs on the leeward slope of a mountain range and, although the air begins as a cold mass, it is warmed as it comes down the mountain and appears finally as a hot dry wind. Whenever and wherever a *foehn* blows, doctors hear about headaches and nausea and allergies, about "nervousness," about "depression." In Los Angeles some teachers do not attempt to conduct formal classes during a Santa Ana, because the children become unmanageable. In Switzerland the suicide rate goes up during the *foehn*, and in the courts of some Swiss cantons the wind is considered a mitigating circumstance for crime. Surgeons are said to watch the wind, because blood does not clot normally during a *foehn*. A few years ago an Israeli physicist discovered that not only during such winds, but for the ten or twelve hours which precede them, the air carries an unusually high ratio of positive to negative ions. No one seems to know exactly why that should be; some talk about friction and others suggest solar disturbances. In any case the positive ions are there, and what an excess of positive ions does, in the simplest terms, is make people unhappy. One cannot get much more mechanistic than that.

Easterners commonly complain that there is no "weather" at all   4
in Southern California, that the days and the seasons slip by relentlessly, numbingly bland. That is quite misleading. In fact the climate is characterized by infrequent but violent extremes: two periods of torrential subtropical rains which continue for weeks and wash out the hills and send subdivisions sliding toward the sea; about twenty scattered days a year of the Santa Ana, which, with its incendiary dryness, invariably means fire. At the first prediction of a Santa Ana, the Forest Service flies men and equipment from northern California into the southern forests, and the Los Angeles Fire Department cancels its ordinary non-firefighting routines. The Santa Ana caused Malibu to burn the way it did in 1956, and Bel Air in 1961, and Santa Barbara in 1964. In the winter of 1966–67

eleven men were killed fighting a Santa Ana fire that spread through the San Gabriel Mountains.

Just to watch the front-page news out of Los Angeles during a   5 Santa Ana is to get very close to what it is about the place. The longest single Santa Ana period in recent years was in 1957, and it lasted not the usual three or four days but fourteen days, from November 21 until December 4. On the first day 25,000 acres of the San Gabriel Mountains were burning, with gusts reaching 100 miles an hour. In town, the wind reached Force 12, or hurricane force, on the Beaufort Scale; oil derricks were toppled and people ordered off the downtown streets to avoid injury from flying objects. On November 22 the fire in the San Gabriels was out of control. On November 24 six people were killed in automobile accidents, and by the end of the week the Los Angeles *Times* was keeping a box score of traffic deaths. On November 26 a prominent Pasadena attorney, depressed about money, shot and killed his wife, their two sons, and himself. On November 27 a South Gate divorcée, twenty-two, was murdered and thrown from a moving car. On November 30 the San Gabriel fire was still out of control, and the wind in town was blowing eighty miles an hour. On the first day of December four people died violently, and on the third the wind began to break.

It is hard for people who have not lived in Los Angeles to real-   6 ize how radically the Santa Ana figures in the local imagination. The city burning is Los Angeles's deepest image of itself: Nathanael West perceived that, in *The Day of the Locust;* and at the time of the 1965 Watts riots what struck the imagination most indelibly were the fires.[2] For days one could drive the Harbor Freeway and see the city on fire, just as we had always known it would be in the end. Los Angeles weather is the weather of catastrophe, of apocalypse, and, just as the reliably long and bitter winters of New England determine the way life is lived there, so the violence and the unpredictability of the Santa Ana affect the entire quality of life in Los Angeles, accentuate its impermanence, its unreliability. The wind shows us how close to the edge we are.

[2]Set in Hollywood, West's 1939 novel, *The Day of the Locust,* ends with a description of Los Angeles engulfed in flames. In 1965, the Watts section of Los Angeles experienced widespread riots, leaving much of the area devastated by fire (editors' note).

Appendix

A CONCISE GUIDE TO FINDING AND DOCUMENTING SOURCES

Many assignments in *The Macmillan Reader* suggest that you might want to do some research in the library and/or on the Internet. Such research enlarges your perspective and enables you to move beyond off-the-top-of-your-head opinions to those that are firmly supported. This appendix will be useful if you do decide to draw upon outside sources when preparing a paper. The appendix explains how to: (1) use the library to find books, reference works, and periodicals on a subject; (2) research a topic using the Internet; and (3) document print and electronic sources.

USING THE LIBRARY TO FIND BOOKS ON YOUR SUBJECT

To locate books on a specific topic, go to your college's *library catalog,* which lists all the books in the library. Although most college libraries have a *computerized catalog* of their book holdings, some use a *card catalog,* a list of alphabetically arranged cards in a series of drawers. Library technology is changing rapidly. With each passing year, a greater number of college (and local) libraries can be accessed online. That means that you can check—at any time of the day or night—a library's book holdings from your home or dorm computer.

Searching the Library Catalog by Author, Title, or Subject

Whether you use your own computer to visit a library's holdings online or use the library's computerized (or card) catalog, you need to familiarize yourself with the three ways to look up a book: by author, title, or subject. To locate a specific book, you can do either an *author* or a *title search.* To search by author, look up the book under the author's last name; to search by title, use the first word in the title, or the second word if the first is *A, An,* or *The.* To identify books on a specific topic, do a *subject search.* Following are some strategies for searching a computerized catalog by subject. (If your library's holdings aren't computerized, it's easy to adapt the suggestions to card-catalog research.) To do a subject search, type in a word or phrase that summarizes your topic. You may have to try several key terms to discover under which term(s) the computer lists sources on your topic. Assume you're conducting research to identify classroom strategies that undermine student success. You might start by typing the word *Education.* But that word would probably yield so many possibilities that you wouldn't know where to start. You might narrow your search by keying in "teaching techniques," "classroom practices," or "academic failure." For help in identifying appropriate key terms, speak with your college librarian. He or she will probably have you consult the *Library of Congress Subject Headings* or a bound or on-screen thesaurus of headings used in your library's database.

When you search for a book by subject, the screen usually indicates narrower subheadings under that topic. When you click on one of those subheads, a list of books on that subject will appear. To get complete bibliographic information about a specific book, follow the computer's instructions. The book's publisher, publication date, call number (see page 694), and so on will then appear on the screen. Most computerized catalogs also indicate the status of a book—whether it is available, on reserve, out on loan, overdue, lost, or available through an inter-library loan system. (If all copies of the book are checked out, fill out a form to be notified when the book is returned.) Here is one college's computerized catalog display for a book on education in the inner city:

Other subject headings to look under to find additional relevant books. The underlining indicates that these are links to related subjects in the computerized catalog.

AUTHOR:	Rathbone, Cristina.
TITLE:	**On the Outside Looking In: A Year at an Inner-City High School**
PUBLICATION INFO:	**New York: Atlantic Monthly Press, 1998.**
PAGING AND SIZE:	**387p.; 24 cm.**
SUBJECTS:	**Education, Urban, Case Studies—United States. Economically Disadvantaged Youth, Education (Secondary)—United States. New York City High Schools.**

1. CALL NUMBER: LC5131.R38 1998—STACKS—Checked Out

2. CALL NUMBER: LC5131.R38 1998—STACKS—Available

Indicates the book's call number, location, and availability in the library. In this case, the library owns two copies, one checked out, the other available.

Once the computer identifies books on your subject, you can copy down the authors, titles, and call numbers of promising books; or, in many libraries, you can direct the computer to print out a list. Mastering your library's computerized catalog enables you to identify in minutes sources that once might have taken you several hours to track down.

Locating Books in the Stacks

Most college libraries contain several floors of bookshelves (called *stacks*). There you'll find fiction, nonfiction, periodicals, microfilm and microfiche files, reserved books, government documents, reference works (see below), and special collections. To locate a book in the stacks, use its *call number* (a number used to classify a book and indicate its location in the library). The call number appears both in the catalog entry and on the spine of the book. There are two systems of call numbers in use in the United States—the *Dewey Decimal* and the *Library of Congress*. Once you have a book's call number, consult a map or list (usually posted near the front desk) to see where in the library you'll find the book. For example, to track down Cristina Rathbone's *On the Outside Looking In,* you'd need to find where the library shelves books with the call number *LC5131.R38.* If your library has closed stacks, make out a call slip, and a member of the staff will get the book for you.

USING THE LIBRARY TO FIND REFERENCE WORKS ON YOUR SUBJECT

Though they present highly condensed information, *reference works* can be helpful, especially in the early stages of your research. Some reference volumes cover a wide range of subjects (*Encyclopedia Britannica* and the *World Almanac and Book of Facts*), while others are more specialized (*Mathematics Dictionary* and *Dance Encyclopedia*). Many reference volumes are available on CD-ROM or can be accessed online. Those that aren't are most likely arranged on library shelves alphabetically by subject ("Art," "Economics," "History"), making it easy to browse for useful reference volumes. Keep in mind that reference materials can't be checked out; you must consult them while in the library. Here are representative reference books found in most college libraries. Check with the librarian to see if any you're interested in are available electronically.

> **Biography:** *International Who's Who, Who's Who in America*
>
> **Business/Economics:** *Dictionary of Banking and Finance, Encyclopedia of Economics*

Ethnic/Feminist Studies: *Encyclopedia of Feminism, Harvard Encyclopedia of American Ethnic Groups*

Fine Arts: *New Grove Dictionary of American Music, The Oxford Companion to Art*

Literature: *Benét's Reader's Encyclopedia, The Oxford Companion to American Literature*

History/Political Science: *Editorials on File, Facts on File, A Political Handbook of the World*

Philosophy/Religion: *The Encyclopedia of American Religions, An Encyclopedia of Philosophy*

Science/Technology/Mathematics: *McGraw-Hill Encyclopedia of Science and Technology, A Dictionary of Mathematics*

Psychology/Education: *Encyclopedia of Education, Encyclopedia of Psychology*

Social Sciences: *International Encyclopedia of the Social Sciences, Encyclopedia of Crime and Justice*

USING THE LIBRARY TO FIND ARTICLES ON YOUR SUBJECT

Periodicals are publications issued at intervals throughout the year. Generally, periodicals contain material that is more recent than that found in books or reference works. There are three broad types of periodicals: general, scholarly, and serious. Written for the average reader, *general periodicals* (daily newspapers and magazines such as *Time* and *Newsweek*) contain articles that provide background information rather than comprehensive coverage of a subject. Intended for readers with specialized knowledge, *scholarly publications* (such as the *Journal of Experimental Child Psychology* and the *Journal of Renaissance Drama*) provide in-depth analyses written by authorities in the field. Designed for well-educated lay people rather than those having specialized knowledge, *serious publications* (for example, *Scientific American* and *Smithsonian*) develop subjects with less depth than scholarly publications.

Using Periodical Indexes, Abstracts, and Bibliographies

Periodical indexes are cumulative directories that list articles published in specific journals, newspapers, and magazines. (Major newspapers, such as *The New York Times,* publish their own directories.) Most periodical indexes list articles under subject headings. Beneath the headings, individual articles are organized alphabetically by authors' last names.

When you were in high school, you may have used the *Readers' Guide to Periodical Literature,* which lists highly accessible, general-interest articles published by popular newsstand magazines like *U.S. News & World Report* and *Sports Illustrated.* The college equivalents of the *Readers' Guide* are the *Humanities Index* and the *Social Sciences Index.* To locate articles appropriate for college-level research, you'll need to consult these indexes as well as those listing articles from more academic, professional, and specialized publications.

Some specialized indexes provide brief descriptions of the articles they list. These indexes are usually called *abstracts.* Examples are *Abstracts of Folklore Studies* and *Psychological Abstracts.* Abstracts usually contain fewer listings than other types of indexes and are restricted to a limited field. In contrast to indexes that list only articles, *bibliographies* like the *Modern Language Association International Bibliography* list books as well as articles.

You shouldn't end your search for appropriate material until you've consulted the most pertinent indexes and bibliographies. For a paper on the psychology of child abuse, you might start with *The New York Times Index* and then move to more specialized volumes, such as *Psychological Abstracts, Child Development Abstracts,* and *Mental Health Book Review Index.* To ensure that you don't miss current developments in your subject area, start with the most recent years and work your way back.

Most college libraries offer computerized databases of the major periodical indexes, abstracts, and bibliographies. The databases, which group directories alphabetically by subject, can be accessed through the library's computer terminals—and often through a campus-wide computer network, making it possible for you to conduct part of your research from your own room. In some libraries, periodical databases are maintained in the same system as the computerized catalog for books. In other libraries, the databases are available at a separate bank of terminals. These terminals are usually hooked up to a CD-ROM player containing compact discs that contain periodical indexes. (If your school library isn't computerized, you'll probably find the periodical indexes located in the periodicals section, arranged alphabetically by title. Simply scan the shelves to find the index you want.)

Listed here is a small sample of the indexes, abstracts, and bibliographies found in most college libraries. Check with the librarian to see which can be accessed electronically.

General: *Academic Search FullTEXT, Dialog, EBSCOhost, Humanities Index, InfoTrac Academic Index, InfoTrac Magazine Index, InfoTrac National Newspaper Index, Magazine Index Plus, National Newspaper Index, Readers' Guide to Periodical Literature, Social Sciences Index*

Education: *Education Abstracts, Education Index, ERIC (Educational Resources Information Center)*

History, Political Science, Government: *Government Publications Index, Historical Abstracts, Monthly Index to United States Government Publications, Political Science Bibliographies, Public Affairs Information Service, Vertical File Index*

Philosophy/Religion: *Philosopher's Index, Religion Index*

Psychology/Sociology: *Psychological Abstracts, Sociological Abstracts*

Sciences: *Applied Science and Technology Index, Biological Abstracts, Botanical Bibliographies, Chemical Abstracts, Engineering Index Annual, Environment Index, International Computer Bibliography*

Women's and Ethnic Studies: *Bibliography on Women, Ethnic Newswatch, Hispanic American Periodicals Index, Index to Periodical Articles by and About Blacks*

Whether a periodicals directory is in computerized or print form, you identify titles of relevant articles by looking under keywords that describe your subject. If you don't find your subject listed in a printed index, or if a computerized database yields no titles when you type in keywords, try alternate terms for your topic. Suppose you're researching the subject of business ethics. In addition to using "Business ethics" as keywords, you might try "Bribery" or "Fraud" to find relevant articles. Computerized and print indexes also show cross-references. By looking under "Business ethics," you might see suggested search terms such as "Advertising ethics," "Banking, ethical aspects," and "Commercial crime." In many libraries, the computer terminals at which you view database listings are hooked up to printers, enabling you to print out the listings rather than record them from the screen. Some online

and CD-ROM databases offer access to the full text of selected articles or books. These texts may be read on screen and, if the computer terminal connects to a printer, printed out.

Here's an entry from the computerized database EBSCOhost.
The entry gives all the information you need to track down the article in the library.

EBSCOhost

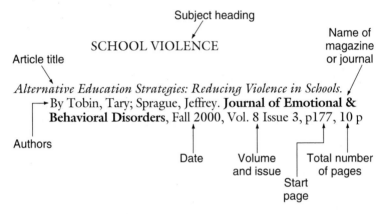

Locating a Specific Issue of a Periodical

If you don't have the option of printing out text of relevant
online articles, you'll need to obtain the original text. To do so, you
have to determine whether the library owns the specific periodicals
and issues you want. If your library catalogs its periodicals online,
search for a periodical by typing in its name. Does that particular
name appear on screen? If it does, your library owns issues of that
publication. With a few additional keystrokes, you can obtain more
detailed information—such as which issues of the periodical the
library holds and their location in the library.

If your library doesn't catalog its periodicals online, look for a
card catalog of holdings. The library probably has a separate periodicals card catalog in the periodicals section. Look up the periodicals by name. A periodical card will usually tell you the issues owned
by the library and their location.

Recent issues of magazines, newspapers, and journals are kept in
the library's periodicals section, where they are arranged alphabetically by title. Less current issues can be found in bound volumes in the

periodicals section, in the stacks, or on microfilm. Usually, periodicals must be read in the library. Back issues of major newspapers are generally stored on microfilm filed in cabinets in a separate location.

USING THE INTERNET TO RESEARCH YOUR SUBJECT

Computer technology isn't, of course, limited to college libraries. It's everywhere. Nothing demonstrates the staggering impact of the computer revolution more powerfully than the growth of the Internet. This global network of interlinked computer systems puts a massive storehouse of information within the reach of anyone with access to a personal computer and a modem. Such a wealth of material presents obvious research benefits to you as a student. However, when faced with the task of using the Internet, you may feel overwhelmed and unsure of how to proceed. The following pages will introduce you to the Internet, show you how to access its resources, and offer pointers on evaluating the material you find there.

The Internet is the catch-all term for the global network that links individual computers throughout the world. The *World Wide Web* refers to a global information system existing *within* the Internet. The Web consists of uncounted millions of *websites*. Some websites feature text only; others also contain graphics; still others include audio and video components. Although there's great variation in the content and design of websites, all contain a *home page* that provides the site's title, descriptive material about the site, and a menu consisting of *links* to the information that can be accessed at the site. A link is a stepping stone to other pages on the site or to a related website. You can jump from the first location to the next just by clicking on the link. (For more on links, see page 702.)

Accessing the Web

Access to the Web is provided through a software program called a *web browser.* Netscape, Internet Explorer, and Mosaic are several widely used browsers. If you attend one of the many colleges or universities providing Web access to students, you'll probably use one of these browsers. At these schools, you can do your research online by accessing the library's catalog of holdings, its databases, and other resources. If your school doesn't offer Web access and you have a computer and modem at home, you can subscribe to a commercial online service, such as America Online, Earthlink, Prodigy, or CompuServe, all of which have their own browsers.

The Advantages and Limitations of the Web

The World Wide Web offers a collection of data that surpasses anything else the world has seen. With the click of a mouse, you can read electronic versions of the *Washington Post* or the *London Times;* you can check the temperature in Cairo or get up-to-the-minute stock quotes; you can read reviews of a best-selling novel or learn about alternative treatments for arthritis. Because the Web (unlike a library) *doesn't have a centralized organizational structure,* you're automatically—and somewhat haphazardly—exposed to this staggering array of material.

Keep in mind, too, that anyone—from Nobel Prize winners to members of extreme fringe groups—can post material on the Web at any time. Not surprisingly, then, the quality of information found on the Web ranges from authoritative to speculative to fraudulent. Unlike sources in the library, which may be dated or even no longer accurate, online material is generally up-to-date because it can be posted on the Web as soon as it's created. Yet the instantaneous nature of Web postings can create problems. Library materials certainly aren't infallible, but most have gone through a process of editorial review before being published. This is often *not* the case with material on the Web. Given this basic limitation, it's a good idea not to rely solely on the Web when you research a topic. Consider using the Web as a supplement to, rather than a substitute for, library research. (For more about evaluating the currency and validity of material on the Web, see pages 704–705.)

Using Online Time Productively

Whether you access the Web through a university service or a commercial provider, the following suggestions will help you use online time productively. First, just as you do when conducting library research (see pages 691–99), be sure to record accurate and sufficient information about your online source so you can provide full documentation when it comes time to write your paper. Specifically, be sure to record the material's title and date, as well as the date of your retrieval. You also need to copy the source's full *URL* (*uniform resource locator*), or Internet *address*. Here, for example is the address for the *Boston Globe* newspaper: *www.boston.com/globe*. Having the address makes it possible for you—and the reader of your research paper—to return to this page in the future. Type the address *exactly* as it appears on the website's home page. Don't capitalize something that originally was in lowercase letters, and don't leave extra space between elements in the address. Typing even slight changes in the address usually makes it impossible to access the site. Second, when you find a helpful website that you may want to visit again, use your browser's *Bookmark* or *Favorite Places* option. After you "bookmark" a site, its address is saved in your personal file, so you can click on its name and instantly return to the site, without having to remember (or type) its address.

Using the Internet to Find Books on Your Topic

Assume that you've used your library's computerized catalog to track down several books on your subject. Now you'd like to go online to see if there are additional books you might find helpful. In such a case, you could access the site of one or both of the following national booksellers: Barnes and Noble (at *www.bn.com*) and Amazon (at *www.amazon.com*). At either site, you would use the "Browse Subjects" box on the bookseller's home page to identify relevant books. Let's say you want to investigate how the experience of childhood poverty affected the politics of certain American presidents. Using the "Browse Subjects" box, you note that one of the subject listings is "Biography." Clicking on "Biography," you see that one of the subcategories is "Presidents." Click on "Presidents," and a list of books on American presidents appears. By clicking on specific titles from the list, you obtain information about each book, including reviewer and reader comments. With this information, you can usually determine which books are appropriate for your purpose. At that point, you check the availability of those books in the library or, if you wish, purchase them online.

Online booksellers can also help you narrow your topic. Perhaps you want to research the topic of illiteracy. As soon as you type the word "illiteracy" in the "Key Words" box on the bookseller's home page, you receive a long list of books on the subject. Simply looking at the range of titles can help you narrow your research. You might, for example, decide to focus on illiteracy in the workplace, teenagers' declining reading scores, or programs that teach marginally literate parents how to read to their children.

Using the Internet to Find Articles and Other Materials on Your Topic

What do you do if you want to go online to track down articles, speeches, legislation, TV transcripts, and so on about your subject? How, given the array of online material, can you identify pertinent sources? Search directories and search engines will help.

Search Directories.   A *search directory*, a service that lists websites organized by categories, will point you in the right direction. If you're not sure how to narrow your topic, seeing the search directory's categories may help you by identifying directions you wouldn't have thought of on your own. New search directories crop up regularly, but one of the most popular and user-friendly is Yahoo! On page 703 is an approximation of what you'll see when you go to Yahoo's home page. (Bear in mind that websites change constantly. What appears on your computer screen will not be identical to what's presented here.)

As you see, Yahoo! divides websites into fourteen categories: Arts & Humanities, Business & Economy, and so on. Each category is presented as a *link* (see page 699). Typically, a link shows up as an underlined word or phrase that's a different color from the type elsewhere on the page. When you click on a link, you're automatically transported to a related site. There you're presented with a more focused list of websites to choose from. As you move from link to link, you go from the general topic to more specific aspects of the topic. For example, say you're researching the legal rights of the disabled. You notice that there's a section titled "Law" under the category "Government." Click on "Law" and you're presented with a screen that lists several dozen law-related links, from "arbitration and mediation" to "trade." (There's even a link for "lawyer jokes.") When you see the link "disabilities," you know you're on the right track. As soon as you click on "disabilities," links to related sites appear on screen. From those, you select the sites you think will be most useful in your research.

Search Engines.   Search directories are wonderful tools when you begin exploring your topic. But when you're refining your investigation, you'll want to use another kind of resource—the *search engine*. Search engines comb through the vast amount of information on the Web for sites that match your research needs. You activate a search engine by typing in key words or phrases that tell the engine what to

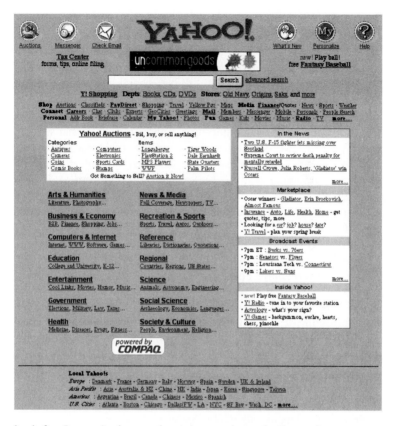

look for. Increasingly, search engines and search directories are combined, making it possible to access both from the site's home page. Here's a list of some popular search directories and search engines and their addresses.

About at *www.about.com*

AltaVista at *www.altavista.com*

Excite! at *www.excite.com*

Google at *www.google.com*

GoTo at *www.goto.com*

Lycos at *www.lycos.com*

Northern Light at *www.northernlight.com*

Refdesk at *www.refdesk.com*

Yahoo! at *www.yahoo.com*

Tips for Using Search Engines.   When you reach the home page of a search engine, it's a good idea to click on the "help" or "tips" button. When you do, you'll receive specific guidelines for using that particular search engine efficiently. As you proceed, don't forget to "bookmark" (see page 701) the search engines you use so you can return to them easily at a later date.

Return to the example of a Yahoo! home page (page 703). Note that at the top, there's an empty box beside "Search." That's where you type in keyword(s) describing your research topic. After you click on "Search" (or whatever your search engine calls its "search" command), the engine scans the Web for your keyword(s). It then provides you with a list of "hits," or links, to websites where your keyword is found. Most search engines also provide a brief description of each site.

The success of your search depends on how carefully you follow your search engine's guidelines and on how specific and descriptive your search terms are. For example, say you're doing research on animal-rights activism. Depending upon your search engine, if you simply enter the words *animal rights activism* in the search box, the engine may provide a list of *every* document that contains the word *animal* or *rights* or *activism*—hundreds of thousands of hits. To limit the number of hits you get, follow with great care your search engine's specific guidelines. For example, you might be told to enclose the keywords in quotation marks ("animal rights activism") or to place plus signs between the words (animal + rights + activism) to find documents in which all three words appear.

Evaluating Internet Materials

You need to take special care to evaluate the worth of material you find on the Web. Electronic documents often seem to appear out of nowhere and can disappear without a trace. And anyone— from scholar to con artist—can create a Web page. How, then, do you know if an Internet source is credible? Here are some questions to ask when you work with online material:

- Who is the author of the material? Does the author offer his or her credentials in a résumé or biographical note? Do these credentials qualify the author to provide reliable information on the topic? Does the author provide an e-mail address so you can request more information? The less you know about an author, the more suspicious you should be about using the data.

- Can you verify the accuracy of the information presented? Does the author refer to studies or to other authors you can investigate? If the author doesn't cite other works or other points of view, that may suggest the document is opinionated and one-sided. In such a case, it's important to track down material addressing alternative points of view.

- Who's sponsoring the website? Many sites are established by organizations—businesses, agencies, lobby groups—as well as by individuals. If a sponsor pushes a single point of view, you should use the material with great caution. Once again, make an extra effort to locate material addressing other sides of the issue.

- Is the cited information up-to-date? Being on the Internet doesn't guarantee that information is current. To assess the timeliness of Internet materials, check at the top or bottom of the document for copyright date, publication date, and/or revision date. Having those dates will help you determine whether the material is recent enough for your purposes.

DOCUMENTING SOURCES

In Chapter 11, you learned the importance of *documentation*—giving credit to the print and electronic sources whose words and idea you borrow in an essay (see page 546). That earlier discussion showed you how to document sources in informal papers. The following pages will show you how to use the documentation system in Modern Language Association (MLA)[1] when citing sources in more formal papers.

The discussion here covers key features of the MLA system. For more detailed coverage, you may want to consult a recent composition handbook or the latest edition of the *MLA Handbook for*

---

[1]MLA documentation is appropriate in papers written for humanities courses, such as your composition class. If you're writing a paper for a course in the social sciences (for example, psychology, economics, or sociology), your professor will probably expect you to use the citation format developed by the American Psychological Association (APA). For information about APA documentation, consult a composition handbook or the most recent edition of the *Publication Manual of the American Psychological Association*.

Writers of Research Papers. For a sample paper that uses MLA documentation, turn to the student essay on pages 562–69.

WHAT TO DOCUMENT

You may inadvertently fall into the trap of *plagiarizing*—passing off someone else's ideas as your own—if you're not sure when you need to acknowledge outside sources in an essay. To avoid plagiarism, you must provide documentation in the following situations:

- When you include *word-for-word quotation* from source.
- When you *summarize or restate in your own words* ideas or information from a source, unless that material is *commonly known* or is a *matter of historical or scientific record.*
- When you *combine a summary and a quotation.*

An important note: On the whole, you should try to state borrowed material in your own words. A string of quotations signals that you haven't sufficiently evaluated and distilled your sources. Use quotations sparingly; draw upon them only when they dramatically illustrate key points you want to make. Also, keep in mind that quotations won't, by themselves, make your case for you. You need to interpret and comment on them, showing how they support your points.

HOW TO DOCUMENT

The MLA documentation system uses the *parenthetic reference,* a brief note in parentheses inserted into the text after borrowed material. The parenthetic reference doesn't provide full bibliographic information but it presents enough so that readers can turn to the Works Cited list (see page 711) at the end of the paper for complete information. If the method of documentation you learned in high school involved footnotes or endnotes, you will be happy to know that parenthetic documentation—currently the preferred method— is much easier to use. While it is now accepted by most college professors, be sure to check with your professors to determine their documentation preferences.

Whenever you quote or summarize material from an outside source, you must do two things: (1) *identify the author* and (2) *specify the page(s)* in your source on which the material appears. The author's name may be given *either* in a lead-in sentence (often called the *attribution*) *or* in the parentheses following the borrowed material. The page number *always* appears in parentheses. The examples below illustrate the MLA documentation style and are based on the following excerpt from page 8 of Julian Stamp's book *The Homeless and History:*

> The key to any successful homeless program requires a clear understanding of just who make up the homeless in our country. Since fifty percent of shelter residents have drug and alcohol addictions, programs need to provide not only a place to sleep but also comprehensive substance-abuse treatment. Since roughly one-third of the homeless population is mentally ill, programs need to offer psychiatric care, even institutionalization, not just housing subsidies. Since the typical head of a homeless family often lacks the know-how needed to maintain a job and a home, programs need to supply employment and life skills training.
>
> When we switch our focus to larger *economic* issues, we see that homelessness cannot be resolved solely at the level of the individual. Since the 1980s, the gap between the rich and the poor has widened, buying power has stagnated, jobs have fled overseas, and funding for low-cost housing has been almost eliminated. Given these developments, homelessness begins to look like a product of history, and by addressing shifts in the American economy we can begin to find effective solutions.

Using Parentheses Only

Counseling and support services are not enough to solve the problem of homelessness; proposed solutions must also address the complex economic issues at the heart of homelessness (Stamp 8).

If we look beyond the problems of homelessness, to "larger *economic* issues, we see that homelessness cannot be resolved solely at the level of the individual" (Stamp 8).

Given the fact that a significant percentage of the homeless suffer from mental illness, "programs need to offer psychiatric care [. . .], not just housing subsidies" (Stamp 8).

Using Parentheses and Attributions

Historian Julian Stamp argues that homelessness must be addressed in terms of economics, not simply in terms of individual counseling, addiction therapy, or job training (8).

Because half of those taking refuge in shelters have problems with drugs and alcohol, Stamp argues that "programs need to provide not only a place to sleep but also comprehensive substance-abuse treatment" (8).

As Stamp states, "The key to any successful homeless program requires a clear understanding of just who make up the homeless [. . .]" (8).

Key Points to Remember

Take a moment to look again at the preceding examples and note the following points:

- The parenthetic reference is placed *immediately after* the borrowed material, at a natural pause in the sentence or at the end of the sentence.
- The parenthetic reference is placed *before* any *internal punctuation* (a comma or semicolon) as well as *before* any *terminal punctuation* (a period or question mark).
- If you want to call attention to a specific author, use an attribution indicating the author's name.
- When the author's name is provided in the attribution, the name is *not* repeated in the parentheses.
- The first time an author is referred to in an attribution, the author's *full name* is given; afterwards, only the *last name* is provided.
- Sometimes, to inform readers of an author's area of expertise, the person may be identified by profession ("Historian Julian Stamp argues that . . ."), title, or affiliation.
- When the author's name is provided in the parentheses, only the last name is given.
- The page number comes directly after the author's name. (If the source is only one page long, only the author's name is needed.)

- There is no punctuation between the author's name and the page number.
- There is no *p.* or *page* preceding the page number.
- Words may be deleted from a quotation as long as the author's original meaning isn't changed. In such a case, three spaced periods—called an *ellipsis* (. . .)—are inserted in place of the deleted words. To make it clear that the ellipsis stands for material that you rather than your source deleted, place brackets around the ellipsis.[2] An ellipsis is not needed when material is omitted from the start of a quotation.

Three Other Important Points

Here are three additional situations you may encounter when documenting sources.

1. More than one source by the same author.   When your paper includes references to more than one work by the same author, you must specify—either in the parentheses or in the attribution—the particular work being cited. You do this by providing the *title*, as well as the author's name and the page(s). As with the author's name, the title may be given in *either* the attribution *or* the parenthetic citation. Here are some examples:

In The Language and Thought of the Child, Jean Piaget states that "discussion forms the basis for a logical point of view" (240).

Piaget considers dialogue essential to the development of logical thinking (Language and Thought 240).

The Child's Conception of the World shows that young children think that the name of something can never change (Piaget 81).

Young children assume that everything has only one name and that no others are possible (Piaget, Child's Conception 81).

[2]The 1999 edition of the *MLA Handbook for Writers of Research Papers* was the first edition calling for the use of brackets with ellipsis points. Earlier editions required only the ellipses. To be consistent with the most recent guidelines, the examples here and on page 708 use brackets with the ellipses. Check with your instructors to see which guidelines they want you to follow.

Notice that when a work is named in the attribution, the full title appears; when a title is given in the parenthetic citation, though, only the first few significant words appear. (However, don't use the ellipsis to indicate that some words have been omitted from the title; the ellipsis is used only when quoting a source.)

2. Long quotations.   A quotation extending beyond four typed lines starts on a new line and is indented ten spaces from the left margin throughout. Since this so-called *block format* already indicates a quotation, quotation marks are unnecessary. Double-space the block quotation, as you do the rest of your paper. Don't leave extra space above or below the quotation. Long quotations, which should be used sparingly, require a lead-in. A lead-in that *isn't* a full sentence is followed by a comma, while a lead-in that *is* a full sentence (as in the accompanying example) is followed by a colon:

Stamp cites changing economic conditions as the key to a national homeless policy:

> Since the 1980s, the gap between the rich and the poor has widened, buying power has stagnated, jobs have fled overseas, and funding for low-cost housing has been almost eliminated. Given these developments, homelessness begins to look like a product of history, and only by addressing shifts in the American economy can we begin to find effective solutions. (8)

Notice that the page number appears in parentheses, just as in a short quotation. But in a long quotation, the parenthetic citation is placed two spaces *after* the period that ends the quotation.

3. Quoting or summarizing a source within a source.   If you quote or summarize a *secondhand source* (someone whose ideas come to you only through another source), you need to make this clear. The parenthetic documentation should indicate "as quoted in" with the abbreviation *qtd. in:*

According to Sherman, "Recycling has, in several communities, created unanticipated expenses" (qtd. in Pratt 3-4).

Sherman explains that recycling can be surprisingly costly (qtd. in Pratt 3-4).

Your Works Cited list would include the source you actually read (Pratt), rather than the source you refer to secondhand (Sherman).

LIST OF WORKS CITED

A documented paper ends with a list of Works Cited, which includes only those sources you actually acknowledge in the paper. Place on its own page, the Works Cited list provides the reader with full bibliographic information about the sources cited in the parenthetic references (see pages 706–708). By referring to the Works Cited list that appears at the end of the student essay on pages 567–69, you will notice the following:

- The list is organized alphabetically by authors' last names. Entries without an author are alphabetized by the first major word in the title (that is, not *A, An,* or *The*).
- Entries are not numbered.
- If an entry runs longer than one line, each additional line is indented five spaces. Entries are double-spaced with no extra space between entries.

Sample Works Cited Entries

Listed here are sample Works Cited entries for the most commonly used kinds of sources. Refer to these samples when you prepare your own Works Cited list, taking special care to reproduce the punctuation and spacing exactly. If you don't spot an entry for the kind of source you need to document, consult the *MLA Handbook* for more comprehensive examples.

CITING BOOKS

Book by One Author

List the author's last name followed by a comma and first name. Then type the title (underlined) and city of publication, followed by a colon and the shortened version of the publisher's name (for example, use *UP* for "University Press" and *Norton* for "W.W. Norton & Co."). End with the year of publication.

Young, Iris Marion. <u>Inclusion and Democracy</u>. New York: Oxford UP, 2000.

Book by Two or Three Authors

Provide all the authors' names in the order they appear on the title page of the book, but reverse only the first name.

Ward, Jeffrey C., and Ken Burns. Jazz: A History of America's Music. New York: Knopf, 2000.

Wallerstein, Judith S., Julia M. Lewis, and Sandra Blakeslee. The Unexpected Legacy of Divorce: A 25 Year Landmark Study. New York: Hyperion, 2000.

Book by Four or More Authors

For a work by four or more authors, give only the first author's name followed by a comma and *et al.* (Latin for "and others").

Frye, Northrop, et al. The Harper Handbook to Literature. New York: Longman, 1997.

Two or More Works by the Same Author

If you use more than one work by the same author, list each book separately. Give the author's name in the first entry only; begin the entries for other books by that author with three hyphens followed by a period. Arrange the works alphabetically by title.

Sommers, Christina Hoff. The War Against Boys: How Misguided Feminism Is Harming Our Young Men. New York: Simon & Schuster, 2000.

---. Who Stole Feminism?: How Women Have Betrayed Women. New York: Simon & Schuster, 1995.

Revised Edition

Indicate a revised edition (*Rev. ed., 2nd ed., 3rd ed., 4th ed.*, and so on) after the title.

Eagleton, Terry. Literary Theory: An Introduction. 2nd ed. Minneapolis: U of Minnesota P, 1996.

Kobliner, Beth. <u>Get a Financial Life: Personal Finance in Your Twenties and Thirties</u>. Rev. ed. New York: Simon & Schuster, 2000.

Book With an Editor or Translator

Following the title, type *Ed.* or *Trans.*, followed by the name of the editor or translator.

Jacobs, Harriet. <u>Incidents in the Life of a Slave Girl, Written by Herself</u>. Ed. Jean Fagan Yellin. Cambridge: Harvard UP, 2000.

Anthology or Compilation of Works by Different Authors

List anthologies according to the editor or editors' names, followed by *ed*.

Gates, Henry Louis, Jr., and Nellie Y. McKay, ed. <u>The Norton Anthology of African American Literature</u>. New York: Norton, 1997.

Section of an Anthology or Compilation

Begin this entry with the author and title of the selection (in quotation marks), followed by the title of the anthology. The editors' names are listed after the anthology title and are preceded by *Ed*. Note that the entry ends with the page numbers on which the selection appears.

Baldwin, James. "Everybody's Protest Novel." <u>The Norton Anthology of African American Literature</u>. Ed. Henry Louis Gates, Jr. and Nellie Y. McKay. New York: Norton, 1997. 1654-59.

Section or Chapter in a Book by One Author

Murphy, Tom. "Interactivity: Taking Control." <u>Web Rules: How the Internet Is Changing the Way Consumers Make Choices</u>. Chicago: Dearborn Trade, 2000. 77-89.

Reference Work

"Temperance Movements." Columbia Encyclopedia. 6th ed. New
    York: Columbia University Press, 2000.

Book by an Institution or Corporation

United Nations Commission on Women. The World's Women, 2000:
    Trends and Statistics. New York: United Nations, 2000.

CITING PERIODICALS

Article in a Weekly or Biweekly Magazine

Provide the author's name (if the article is signed), article title
(in quotation marks), periodical name (underlined), and date of
publication, followed by a colon and page number(s) of the article.

Mannix, Margaret. "The Web's Dark Side." U.S. News & World
    Report 28 Aug. 2000: 36-45.

Article in a Monthly or Bimonthly Magazine

Stone, Robin D. "Reading, Writing, Roulette." Essence Sep. 2000:
    153-62.

Article in a Daily Newspaper

If the article is printed on multiple, nonconsecutive pages, simply list the first page (including both section and page numbers or
letters) followed by a plus sign (+). (Note: Omit the initial *The* from
newspaper names.)

Zernike, Kate. "New Tactic on College Drinking: Play It Down." New
    York Times 3 Oct. 2000: A1+.

Editorial, Letter to the Editor, or Reply to a Letter

List as you would any signed or unsigned article, but indicate
the type of piece after the article's title.

Steele, Shelby. "A New Front in the Culture War." Editorial. Wall
    Street Journal 2 Aug. 2000: A22.

Article in a Scholarly Journal

Some journals are paged continuously; the first issue of each
year starts with page one, and each subsequent issue picks up where
the previous one left off. For such journals, use numerals to indicate
the volume number after the title, and then indicate the year in
parentheses. Note that neither *volume* nor *vol.* is used. The article's
page(s) appear at the end, separated from the year by a colon.

"Standing Up to School Bullies." Congressional Quarterly Researcher
    9 (1999): 604-11.

For a journal that pages each issue separately, use numerals to
indicate the *volume and issue numbers;* separate the two with a period but leave no space after the period.

Staples, J. Scott. "Violence in Schools: Rage Against a Broken World."
    Annals of the American Academy of Political & Social Science
    56.1 (2000): 30-42.

CITING ELECTRONIC SOURCES

Article in an Online Periodical

For an article obtained online, supply the same information you
would for printed text: author's name, selection's title, source, and
(when available) publication date and page or paragraph numbers.
When page or paragraph numbers are provided, list them after the
date of publication (using *pp.* for "pages" or *par.* for "paragraphs").
Complete your listing with the date on which you accessed the
material, followed by the exact address of the website (in angle
brackets) and then a final period. (Since online material can be
revised at any time, it's critical that you provide your date of access
to identify the version you retrieved.) Note that long web addresses
should be broken up only after slashes.

Nordland, Rod. "Sanctioning Starvation?" Newsweek Online 3 Aug.
    2000. 6 Feb. 2001 <http:www.msnbc.com/news/
    NW-front_Front.asp>.

Ramos, Dante. "Public Health vs. Private Medicine." Salon 31 July
    2000: 17 pars. 2 Mar. 2001 <http://salon.com/health/
    feature/2000/07/31/betrayaloftrust/index/html>.

Article in a Full-Text Online Periodicals Index

For full-text articles accessed through an online index (generally only available to libraries by subscription), begin with the same
information as for online periodicals. After the publication information (issue, date, and page numbers), list the title of the index
(underlined), its vendor, and the library through which you gained
access to it. Complete the entry with the date you accessed the index
and the index's Web address.

Casella, Ronnie. "The Benefits of Peer Mediation in the Context of
    Urban Conflict." Urban Education 35.3 (2000): 324-56.
    EBSCOhost. MasterFILE Premier. Camden County Library,
    Voorhees. 19 May 2001 <http://ehostvg.wl.epnet.com>.

Online Book

When it's available, include the book's original publication
information between the book's title and the underlined database
name. Also include (when available) the name of the site's editor, its
electronic publication date, its sponsoring organization, your date of
access, and the Web address.

Franklin, Benjamin. The Autobiography of Benjamin Franklin. London,
    1793. Electronic Text Center. Ed. David Seaman. 1998.
    University of Virginia Library. 16 July 2001 <http://
    etext.lib.virginia.edu>.

Online Reference Work

"Salem Witch Trials." Britannica.com. Apr. 2000. Encyclopedia
    Britannica. 29 Sep. 2000 <http://britannica.com/bcom/eb/
    article/html?/query=salem%20witch%20trials>.

Professional or Personal Website

<u>John Steinbeck's Life and Work</u>. Sep. 1999. San Jose Center for Steinbeck Studies, San Jose State University. 24 Jan. 2001 <http://www.sjsu.edu/depts/steinbec/steinbio.html>.

Mallen, Enrique. <u>Online Picasso Project</u>. 18 Apr. 2001 <http://www.tamu.edu/mocl/picasso>.

Article on CD-Rom

Supplement basic publication information with the title of the database (underlined), publication medium (CD-ROM), CD-ROM publisher, and CD-ROM publication date.

Krauss, Clifford. "Crime Statistics in the Big Apple." <u>New York Times</u> 12 Mar. 1998, late ed.: B1. <u>New York Times Ondisc</u>. CD-ROM. UMI-ProQuest. 11 Dec. 2000.

Computer Software

Cite the following information (when available); author of the software, title (underlined), medium (CD-ROM or diskette), version, publication city, publisher, and year of publication.

<u>Compton's Encyclopedia 2000 Deluxe</u>. CD-ROM. 2000 ed. Mindscape, 2000.

E-mail Message

Bernard, Lynn. "Regional Adult Literacy Seminar." E-mail to Ronnie Hotis. 30 Aug. 2001.

CITING OTHER NONPRINT SOURCES

Television or Radio Program

"Underground Culture Hits Main Street." <u>Nightline</u>. Narr. Robert Krulwich. Part 1 of 3. ABC. WPVI-TV, Philadelphia. 6 Sep. 2000.

Movie, Recording, Videotape, DVD, Filmstrip, or Slide Program

Provide the author or composer of the piece (if appropriate); title (underlined); director, conductor, or performer; medium; distributor; and year of release.

The Matrix. Dir. Andy Wachowski and Larry Wachowski. DVD.
    Warner Bros, 1999.

Personal or Phone Interview

Langdon, Paul. Personal interview. 26 Jan. 2001.

Lecture

Akers, Sharon. "Stock Market Savvy." Investing Made Easy Seminar.
    Camden County Adult Education Program. East Hills High
    School, New Jersey. 27 Mar. 2001.

GLOSSARY

Abstract and concrete language refers to two different qualities of words. Abstract words and phrases convey concepts, qualities, emotions, and ideas that we can think and talk about but not actually see or experience directly. Examples of abstract words are *conservatism, courage, avarice, joy,* and *hatred.* Words or phrases whose meanings are directly seen or experienced by the senses are concrete terms. Examples of phrases using concrete words are *split-level house, waddling penguin,* and *short pink waitress uniform.*

Adequate—see *Evidence.*

***Ad hominem* argument**—see *Logical fallacies.*

Analogy refers to an imaginative comparison between two subjects that seem to have little in common. Often a complex idea or topic can be made understandable by comparing it to a more familiar subject, and such an analogy can be developed over several paragraphs or even an entire essay. For example, to explain how the economic difficulties of farmers weaken an entire nation, a writer might create an analogy between failing farms and a cancer that slowly destroys a person's life.

Argumentation-persuasion tries to encourage readers to accept a writer's point of view on some controversial issue. In *argumentation,* a writer uses objective reasoning, facts, and hard evidence to demonstrate the soundness of a position. In *persuasion,* the writer uses appeals to the readers' emotions and value systems, often in the hope of encouraging them to take a specific action. Argumentation and persuasion are frequently used together in an essay. For example, a writer might argue for the construction of a highway through town by pointing out that the road would bring new business, create new jobs, and lighten traffic. The writer also might try to persuade readers to vote for a highway appropriations bill by appealing to their emotions, claiming that the highway would allow people to get home faster, thus giving them more time for family life and leisure activities. A whole essay can be organized around argumentation-persuasion, or an essay developed chiefly through another pattern may contain elements of argumentation-persuasion.

Assertion refers to the *thesis* of an *argumentation-persuasion* essay. The assertion, or *proposition,* is a point of view or opinion on a controversial issue or topic. The assertion cannot be merely a statement of a fact. Such statements as "Women still experience discrimination in the job market," "General Rabb would make an ideal mayor for our town," and "This university should devote more funds to raising the quality of the food services" are examples of assertions that could serve as theses for argumentation-persuasion essays.

Audience refers to a writer's intended readers. In planning the content and tone of an essay, you should identify your audience and consider its needs. How similar are the members of your audience to you in knowledge and point of view? What will they need to know for you to achieve your *purpose?* What *tone* will make them open to receiving your message? For example, if you were to write a description of a trip to Disney World, you would have to explain a lot more to an eighty-year-old grandmother who had never seen a theme park than to a young parent who has probably visited several. If you wrote about the high cost of clothing for an economics professor, you would choose a serious, analytic tone and supply statistical evidence for your points. If you write about the same topic for the college newspaper, you might use a tone tinged with humor and provide helpful hints on finding bargain clothing.

Begging the question—see *Logical fallacies.*

Brainstorming is a technique used in the *prewriting* stage. It helps you discover the limited subject you can successfully write about and also generates raw material—ideas and details—to develop that subject. In brainstorming, you allow your mind to play freely with the subject. You try to capture fleeting thoughts about it, no matter how random, minor, or tangential, and jot them down rapidly before they disappear from your mind.

Causal analysis—see *Cause-effect.*

Causal chain refers to a series of causes and effects, in which the result or effect of a cause becomes itself the cause of a further effect, and so on. For example, a person's alarm clock failing to buzz might begin a causal chain by causing the person to oversleep. Oversleeping then causes the person to miss the bus, and missing the bus causes the person to arrive late to work. Arriving late causes the person to miss an important phone call, which causes the person to lose a chance at a lucrative contract.

Cause-effect, sometimes called *causal analysis,* involves analyzing the reasons for or results of an event, action, decision, or phenomenon. Writers develop an essay through an analysis of causes whenever they attempt to answer such questions as "Why has this happened?" or "Why does this exist?" When writers explore such questions as "What happens or would happen if a certain change occurs?" or "What will happen if a condition continues?" their essays involve a discussion of effects. Some cause-effect essays concentrate on the causes of a situation, some focus on the effects, and others present both causes and effects. Causal analysis can be an essay's central pattern, or it can be used to help support a point in an essay developed primarily through another pattern.

Characteristics—see *Formal definition.*

Chronological sequence—see *Narrative sequence* and *Organization.*

Circularity is an error in *formal definition* resulting from using variations of the to-be-defined word in the definition. For example, "A scientific hypothesis is a hypothesis made by a scientist about the results of an experiment" is circular because the unknown term is used to explain itself.

Class—see *Formal definition.*

Coherence refers to the clear connection among the various parts of an essay. As a writer, you can draw upon two key strategies to make writing coherent. You can use a clear *organizational format* (for example, a chronological, spatial, emphatic, or simple-to-complex sequence). You can also provide *appropriate signaling* or *connecting devices* (transitions, bridging sentences, repeated words, synonyms, and pronouns).

Comparison-contrast means explaining the similarities and/or differences between events, objects, people, ideas, and so on. The comparison-contrast format can be used to meet a purely factual purpose ("This is how A and B are alike or different"). But usually writers use comparison-contrast to make a judgment about the relative merits of the subjects under discussion. Sometimes a writer will concentrate solely on similarities *or* differences. For instance, when writing about married versus single life, you would probably devote most of your time to discussing the differences between these lifestyles. Other times, comparison and contrast are found together. In an essay analyzing two approaches to U.S. foreign policy, you would probably discuss the similarities *and* the differences in the goals and methods characteristic of each approach. Comparison-contrast can be the dominant pattern in an essay, or it can help support a point in an essay developed chiefly through another pattern.

Conclusion refers to the one or more paragraphs that bring an essay to an end. Effective conclusions give the reader a sense of completeness and finality. Writers often use the conclusion as a place to reaffirm the *thesis* and to express a final thought about the subject. Methods of conclusion include summarizing main points, using a quotation, predicting an outcome, and recommending an action.

Conflict creates tension in the readers of a *narration*. It is produced by the opposition of characters or other forces in a story. Conflict can occur between individuals, between a person and society or nature, or within a person. Readers wonder how a conflict will be resolved and read on to find out.

Connotative and denotative language describe the ability of language to emphasize one or another aspect of a word's range of meaning. *Denotative language* stresses the dictionary meaning of words. *Connotative language* emphasizes the echoes of feeling that cluster around some words. For example, the terms *weep, bawl, break down,* and *sob* all denote the same thing: to cry. But they have different associations and call up different images. A writer employing the connotative resources of language would choose the term among these that suggested the appropriate image.

Controlling idea—see *Thesis.*

Deductive reasoning is a form of logical thinking in which general statements believed to be true are applied to specific situations or cases. The result of deduction is a conclusion or prediction about the specific situation. Deduction is often expressed in a three-step pattern called a *syllogism.* The first part of the syllogism is a general statement about a large class of items or situations, the *major premise.* The second part is the *minor premise,* a more limited statement about a specific item or case. The third part is the *conclusion,* drawn from the major premise, about that specific case or item. Deductive reasoning is very common in everyday thinking. For example, you might use deduction when car shopping:

In an accident, large cars are safer than small cars. (*major premise*)

The Turbo Titan is a large car. (*minor premise*)

In an accident, the Turbo Titan will be safer than a small car. (*conclusion*)

Definition explains the meaning of a word or concept. The brief formal definitions found in the dictionary can be useful if you need to clarify or restrict the meaning of a term used in an essay. In such cases, the definition is short and to the point. But you may also use an *extended definition* in an essay, taking several paragraphs, even the entire piece, to develop the meaning of a term. You may use extended definition to convey a personal slant on a well-known term, to refute a commonly held interpretation of a word, or to dissect a complex or controversial issue. Definition can be the chief method of development in an essay, or it can help support a point in an essay organized around another pattern.

Definition by negation is a method of defining a term by first explaining what the term is *not,* and then going on to explain what it is. For example, you might begin a critical essay about television with a definition by negation: "Television, far from being a medium that dispenses only light, insubstantial fare, actually disseminates a dangerously distorted view of family life." Definition by negation can provide a stimulating introduction to an essay.

Denotative language—see *Connotative and denotative language.*

Description involves the use of vivid word pictures to express what the five senses have experienced. The subject of a descriptive essay can be a person, a place, an object, or an event. Description can be the dominant pattern in an essay, or it can be used as a supplemental method in an essay developed chiefly through another pattern.

There are two main types of description. In an *objective description,* a writer provides details about a subject without conveying the emotions the subject arouses. For example, if you were involved in a traffic accident, your insurance agent might ask you to write an objective description of the events leading up to and during the crash. But in a *subjective description,* the writer's goal is to evoke in the reader the emotions felt during the experience. For example, in a cautionary letter to a friend who has a habit of driving dangerously, you might write a subjective description of your horrifyingly close call with death during a car accident.

Development—see *Evidence.*

Dialogue is the writer's way of directly presenting the exact words spoken by characters in a *narration.* By using dialogue, writers can convey people's individuality and also add drama and immediacy to an essay.

Directional process analysis—see *Process analysis.*

Division-classification refers to a logical method for analyzing a single subject or several related subjects. Though often used together in an essay, division and classification are separate processes. *Division* involves breaking a subject or idea into its component parts. For instance, the concept "an ideal vacation" could be divided according to its destination, accommodations, or cost. *Classification* involves organizing a number of related items into categories. For example, in an essay about the overwhelming flow of paper in our everyday lives, you might classify the typical kinds of mail most people receive: personal mail (letters, birthday cards, party invitations), business mail (bills, bank statements, charge-card receipts), and junk mail (flyers about bargain sales, solicitations to donate, contest announcements). Division-classification can be the dominant pattern in a paper, or it may be used to support a point in an essay organized chiefly around another pattern of development.

Dominant impression refers to the purpose of a descriptive essay. While some descriptive essays have a thesis, others do not; instead, they convey a dominant impression or main point. For example, one person writing a descriptive essay about New York City might use its architectural diversity as a focal point. Another person writing a description of Manhattan might concentrate on the overpowering sense of hustle and speed about everyone and everything in the city. Both writers would select only those details that supported their dominant impressions.

Dramatic license refers to the writer's privilege, when writing a narrative, to alter facts or details to strengthen the support of the *thesis* or *narrative point*. For example, a writer is free to flesh out the description of an event whose specific details may be partially forgotten or to modify or omit details of a narrative that do not contribute to the meaning the writer wishes to convey.

Either-or fallacy—see *Logical fallacies.*

Emphatic sequence—see *Organization.*

Ethos refers to a writer's reliability or credibility. Such an image of trustworthiness is particularly important to readers of an *argumentation-persuasion* essay or piece. Writers establish their *ethos* by using reason and logic, by being moderate in their appeals to emotions, by avoiding a hostile tone, and by demonstrating overall knowledgeability of the subject. The most effective argumentation-persuasion involves an interplay of *ethos, logos,* and *pathos.*

Etymology refers to the history of a word or term. All English words have their origins in other, often ancient, languages. Giving a brief etymology of a word can help a writer establish the context for developing an *extended definition* of the word. For example, the word *criminal* is derived from a Latin word meaning "accusation" or "accused." Today, our word *criminal* goes beyond the concept of "accused" to mean "guilty."

Evidence lends substance to a writer's main ideas and thus helps the reader to accept the writer's viewpoint. Evidence should meet several criteria. First of all, it should be *unified,* in the sense that all supporting ideas and details should relate directly to the key point the writer is making. Second, evidence should be *adequate;* there should be enough evidence to convince the reader to agree with the thesis. Third, evidence should be *specific;* that is, vivid and detailed rather than vague and general. Fourth, evidence must be *accurate* and not overstate or understate information. Fifth, evidence should be *representative,* relying on the typical rather than the atypical to make a point. The bulk of an essay is devoted to supplying evidence. Supporting the thesis with solid evidence is the third stage in the writing process.

Exemplification, at the heart of all effective writing, involves using concrete specifics to support generalizations. In exemplification, writers provide examples or instances that support or clarify broader statements. You might support the thesis statement "I have a close-knit family" by using such examples as the following: "We have a regular Sunday dinner at my grandmother's house with at least ten family members present"; "My sisters and brothers visit my parents every week"; "I spend so much time on the phone talking with my sisters that sometimes I have trouble finding time for my new college friends." Exemplification may be an essay's central pattern, or it may supplement an essay developed mainly around another pattern.

Extended definition—see *Definition.*

Fallacies—see *Logical fallacies.*

False analogy—see *Logical fallacies.*

Figures of speech are imaginative comparisons between two things usually thought of as dissimilar. Some major figures of speech are *simile, metaphor,* and *personification. Similes* are comparisons that use the signal words *like* or *as:* "Superman was as powerful as a locomotive." *Metaphors,* which do not use signal words, directly equate unlike things: "The boss is a tiger when it comes to landing a contract." "The high-powered pistons of the boxer's arms pummeled his opponent." *Personification* attributes human characteristics to inanimate things or nonhuman beings: "The angry clouds unleashed their fury on the town"; "The turtle shyly poked his head out of his shell."

First draft refers to the writer's first try at producing a basic, unpolished version of the whole essay. It is often referred to as the "rough" draft, and nothing about it is final or unchangeable. The process of writing the first draft often brings up new ideas or details. Writers sometimes break off writing the draft to *brainstorm* or *freewrite* as new ideas occur to them and then return to the draft with new inspiration. You shouldn't worry about spelling, grammar, or style in the first-draft stage; instead, you should keep focused on casting your ideas into sentence and paragraph form. Writing the first draft is the fifth stage in the writing process.

Flashback—see *Narrative sequence.*

Flashforward—see *Narrative sequence.*

Formal definition involves stating a definition in a three-part pattern of about one sentence in length. In presenting a formal definition, a writer puts the *term* in a *class* and then lists the *characteristics* that separate the term from other members of its class. For example, a formal definition of a word processor might be, "A word processor (term) is an electronic machine (class) that is used to write, edit, store, and produce typewritten documents (characteristics)." Writers often use a formal definition to prepare a reader for an extended definition that follows.

Freewriting is most often used during the *prewriting* stage to help writers generate ideas about a limited topic. To use this method, write nonstop for five or ten minutes about everything your topic brings to mind. Disregard grammar, spelling, and organization as you keep your pen and mind moving. Freewriting is similar to *brainstorming,* except that the result is a rambling, detail-filled paragraph rather than a list. Freewriting can also be used to generate ideas during later stages of the writing process.

Gender-biased language gives the impression that one sex is more important, powerful, or valuable than the other. When writing, you should work to replace such sexist language with *gender-neutral* or *nonsexist* terms that convey no sexual prejudice. First of all, try to avoid *sexist vocabulary* that demeans or excludes one of the sexes: *stud, jock, chick, fox,* and so on. Also, just as adult males should be called *men,* adult females should be referred to as *women,* not *girls.* And men shouldn't be empowered with professional and honorary titles (*President* Clinton) while professional women—such as congressional representatives—are assigned only personal titles (*Mrs.* Shroeder). Here are some examples of the way you can avoid words that exclude women: Change "chairman" to *chairperson,* "layman" to *layperson,* "congressman" to *congressional representative,* "workmen" to *workers,* the "average guy" to the *average person.* Second, be aware of the fact that indefinite singular nouns—those representing a general group of people consisting of both genders—can lead to *sexist pronoun use:* for example, "On *his* first day of school, a young child often experiences separation anxiety." This sentence excludes female children from consideration, although the situation being described applies equally to them. Third, recognize that indefinite pronouns like *anyone, each,* and *everybody* may also pave the way to sexist pronoun use. Although such pronouns often refer to a number of individuals, they're considered singular. So, wanting to be grammatically correct, you may write a sentence like the following: "Everybody wants *his* favorite candidate to win." The sentence, however, is sexist because *everybody* is certainly not restricted to men. One way to avoid this type of sexist construction is to use both male and female pronouns: "Everybody wants *his* or *her* favorite candidate to win." Another approach is to use *s/he* in place of *he*. A third possibility is to use the gender-neutral pronouns *they, their,* or *themselves:* "Everybody wants *their* favorite candidate to win." Be warned, though. Some people object to using these plural pronouns with singular indefinite pronouns, even though the practice is common in everyday speech. Two alternative strategies enable you to eliminate the need for *any* gender-marked singular pronouns. First, you can change singular general nouns or indefinite pronouns to their plural equivalents and then use nonsexist plural pronouns. For example, you may change "A *workaholic* feels anxious when *he* isn't busy" to "*Workaholics* feel anxious when *they're* not busy" and "*Everyone* in the room expressed *his* opinion freely" to "*Those* in the room expressed *their* opinions freely." Second, you can recast the sentence to omit the singular pronoun: For instance, you may change "A *manager* usually spends part of each day settling squabbles among *his* staff" to "A manager usually spends part of each day settling *staff squabbles*" and "No *one* wants *his* taxes raised" to "No one wants *to pay more taxes.*"

Hasty generalization—see *Logical fallacies.*

Inductive reasoning is a form of logical thinking in which specific cases and facts are examined to draw a wider-ranging conclusion. The result of inductive reasoning is a generalization that is applied to situations or cases similar to the ones examined. Induction is typical of scientific investigation and of everyday thinking. For example, on the basis of specific experiences, you may have concluded that when you feel chilly in a room where everyone else is comfortable, you are likely to develop a cold and fever in the next day or two. In an *argumentation-persuasion* essay, the conclusion reached by induction would be your *assertion* or *thesis.*

Inference is the term for a conclusion based on *inductive reasoning.* Because the reasoning behind specific cases may not be simple, there is usually an element of uncertainty in an inductive conclusion. Choosing the correct explanation for specific cases is a matter of carefully weighing and selecting alternative conclusions.

Informational process analysis—see *Process analysis.*

Introduction refers to the first paragraph or several paragraphs of an essay. The introduction serves three purposes. It informs readers of the general subject of the essay, it catches their attention, and it presents the controlling idea or thesis. The methods of introducing an essay include the use of an anecdote, a quotation or surprising statistic or fact, and questions. Or you may narrow your discussion down from a broad subject to a more limited one.

Irony occurs when a writer or speaker implies (rather than states directly) a discrepancy or incongruity of some kind. *Verbal irony,* which is often tongue- in-cheek, involves a discrepancy between the literal words and what's actually meant ("I know you must be unhappy about receiving the highest grade in the course"). If the ironic comment is designed to be hurtful or insulting, it qualifies as *sarcasm* ("Congratulations! You failed the final exam"). In *situational irony*, the circumstances are themselves incongruous. For example, although their constitutional rights were violated when the federal government detained them in internment camps, Japanese-Americans nevertheless played American football, sang American songs, and saluted the American flag during their imprisonment.

Journal writing is a form of prewriting in which writers make daily entries in a private journal, much as they would in a diary. Whether they focus on one topic or wander freely, journal writers jot down striking incidents, images, and ideas encountered in the course of a day. Such journal material can produce ideas for future essays.

Logical fallacies are easily committed mistakes in reasoning that writers must avoid, especially when writing *argumentation-persuasion* essays. There are many kinds of logical fallacies. Here are several:

Ad hominem argument occurs when someone attacks another person's point of view by criticizing that person, not the issue. Often called "mudslinging," *ad hominem* arguments try to invalidate a person's ideas by revealing unrelated, past or present, personal or ethical flaws. For example, to claim that a person cannot govern the country well because it can be proven he or she has little sense of humor is to use an *ad hominem* argument.

Begging the question is a fallacy in which the writer assumes the truth of something that needs to be proven. Imagine a writer argues the following: "A law should be passed requiring dangerous pets like German shepherds and Doberman pinschers to be restrained by fences, leashes, and muzzles." Such an argument begs the question since it assumes readers will automatically accept the view that such dogs are indeed dangerous.

Either-or fallacies occur when it's argued that a complex situation can be resolved in only one of two possible ways. Here's an example: "If the administration doesn't grant striking professors more money, the college will never be able to attract outstanding teachers in years ahead." Such an argument oversimplifies matters. Excellent teachers might be attracted to a college for a variety of reasons, not just because of good salaries: the school's location, research facilities, reputation for scholarship, hardworking students, and so on.

False analogy erroneously suggests that because two things are alike in some regards, they are similar in all ways. In the process, significant differences between the two are disregarded. If you argue that a woman prosecuting a rapist is subjected to a second rape in court, you're guilty of a false analogy. As embarrassing, painful, and hurtful as the court proceedings may be, the woman is not physically assaulted, as she was when she was raped. Also, as difficult as her decision to seek justice might be, she's in court by choice and not against her will.

Hasty generalizations are unsound *inductive inferences* based on too few instances of a behavior, situation, or process. For example, it would be a hasty generalization to conclude that you're allergic to a food such as curry because you once ate it and became ill. There are several other possible explanations for your illness, and only repetitions of this experience or a lab test could prove conclusively that you're allergic to this spice.

Non sequiturs are faulty conclusions about cause and effect. Here's an example: "Throughout this country's history, most physicians have been male. Women apparently have little interest in becoming doctors." The faulty conclusion accords one factor—the possible vocational preferences of women—the status of sole cause. The conclusion fails to consider pressures on women to devote themselves to homemaking and to avoid an occupation sexually stereotyped as "masculine."

Post hoc thinking results when it's presumed that one event caused another just because it occurred first. For instance, if your car broke down the day after you lent it to your brother, you would be committing the *post hoc* fallacy if you blamed him, unless you knew he did something to your car's engine.

Questionable authority, revealed by such phrases as "studies show" and "experts claim," undercuts a writer's credibility. Readers become suspicious of such vague and unsubstantial appeals to authority. Writers should demonstrate the reliability of their sources by citing them specifically.

Red herring arguments are deliberate attempts to focus attention on a peripheral matter rather than examine the merits of the issue under discussion. Imagine that a local environmental group advocates stricter controls for employees at a nearby chemical plant. The group points out that plant employees are repeatedly exposed to high levels of toxic chemicals. If you respond, "Many of the employees are illegal aliens and shouldn't be allowed to take jobs from native-born townspeople," you're throwing in a red herring. By bringing in immigration policies, you sidetrack attention from the matter at hand: the toxic level to which plant employees—illegal aliens or not—are exposed.

Logos is a major factor in creating an effective argument. It refers to the soundness of *argumentation,* as created by the use of facts, statistics, information, and commentary by authoritative sources. The most effective arguments involve an interplay among *logos, pathos,* and *ethos.*

Major premise—see *Deductive reasoning.*

Minor premise—see *Deductive reasoning*.

MLA documentation is the system developed by the Modern Language Association for citing sources in a paper. When you quote or summarize source material, you must do two things within your paper's text: (1) identify the author and (2) specify the pages on which the material appears. You may provide the author's name in a lead-in sentence or within parentheses following the borrowed material; the page number always appears in parentheses, inserted in the text after the borrowed material. The material in the parentheses is called a *parenthetic reference*. A paper using MLA documentation ends with a *Works Cited* list, which includes only those sources actually acknowledged in the paper. Entries are organized alphabetically by authors' last names. Entries without an author are alphabetized by the first major word in the title.

Narration means recounting an event or a series of related events to make a point. Narration can be an essay's principal pattern of development, or it can be used to supplement a paper organized primarily around another pattern. For instance, to persuade readers to avoid drug use, a writer might use the narrative pattern by recounting the story of an abuser's addiction and recovery.

Narrative point refers to the meaning the writer intends to convey to a reader by telling a certain story. This narrative point might be a specific message, or it might be a feeling about the situation, people, or place of the story. This underlying meaning is achieved by presenting details that support it and eliminating any that are nonessential. For example, in an essay about friendship, a writer's point might be that friendships change when one of the friends acquires a significant partner of the opposite sex. The writer would focus on the details of how her close female friend had less time for her, changed their usual times of getting together, and confided in her less. The writer would omit judgments of the friend's choice of boyfriend and her friend's declining grades because these details, while real for the writer, would distract the reader from the essay's narrative point.

Narrative sequence refers to the order in which a writer recounts events. When you follow the order of the events as they happened, you're using *chronological sequence*. This sequence, in which you begin at the beginning and end with the last event, is the most basic and commonly used narrative sequence. If you interrupt this flow to present an event that happened before the beginning of the narrative sequence, you're employing a *flashback*. If you skip ahead to an event later than the one that comes next in your narrative, you're using the *flashforward* technique.

Non sequiturs—see *Logical fallacies*.

Objective description—see *Description*.

One-side-at-a-time method refers to one of the two techniques for organizing a *comparison-contrast* essay. In using this method, a writer discusses all the points about one of the compared and contrasted subjects before going on to the other. For example, in an essay titled "Single or Married?" a writer might first discuss single life in terms of amount of independence, freedom of career choice, and companionship. Then the writer would, within reason, discuss married life in terms of these same three subtopics. The issues the writer discusses in each half of the essay would be identical and presented in the same order. See also *Point-by-point method.*

Organization refers to the process of arranging evidence to support a thesis in the most effective way. When organizing, a writer decides what ideas come first, next, and last. In *chronological* sequence, details are arranged according to occurrence in time. In *spatial* sequence, details appear in the order in which they occur in space. In *emphatic* order, ideas are sequenced according to importance, with the most significant, outstanding, or convincing evidence being reserved for last. In *simple-to-complex* order, easy-to-grasp material is presented before more-difficult-to-comprehend information. Organizing is the fourth stage of the writing process.

Outlining involves making a formal plan before writing a *first draft.* Writing an outline helps you determine whether your supporting evidence is logical and adequate. As you write, you can use the outline to keep yourself on track. Many writers use the indentation system of Roman numerals, letters, and Arabic numbers to outline; sometimes writers use a less formal system.

Paradox refers to a statement that seems impossible, contrary to common sense, or self-contradictory, yet that can—after consideration—be seen to be plausible or true. For example, Oscar Wilde produced a paradox when he wrote "When the gods wish to punish us, they answer our prayers." The statement doesn't contradict itself because often, Wilde believes, that which we wish for turns out to be the very thing that will bring us the most pain.

Parenthetic reference—see *MLA documentation.*

Pathos refers to the emotional power of an *argumentation-persuasion* essay. By appealing to the needs, values, and attitudes of readers and by using *connotative language,* writers can increase the chances that readers will come to agree with the ideas in an essay. Although *pathos* is an important element of persuasion, such emotional appeals should reinforce rather than replace reason. The most effective argumentation-persuasion involves an interplay among *pathos, logos,* and *ethos.*

Peer review is the critical reading of another person's writing with the intention of suggesting changes. To be effective, peer review calls for readers who are objective, skilled, and tactful enough to provide useful feedback. Begin by giving your readers a clear sense of what you expect from the review. To promote specific responses, ask the reviewers targeted (preferably written) questions. Following the review, rank the problems and solutions that the reviewers identified. Then enter your own notes for revising in the margins of your draft so that you'll know exactly what changes need to be made in your draft as you rework it.

Plan of development refers to a technique whereby the writer supplies the reader with a brief map of the main points to be covered in an essay. If used, the plan of development occurs as part of the *thesis* or in a sentence following the thesis. In it, the main ideas are mentioned in the order in which they'll appear in the supporting paragraphs. Longer essays and term papers usually need a plan of development to maintain unity, but shorter papers may do without one.

Point-by-point method refers to one of the two techniques for organizing a *comparison-contrast* essay. A writer using this method moves from one aspect of one subject to the same aspect of another subject before going on to the second aspect of each subject. For example, in an essay titled "Single or Married?" a writer might first discuss the amount of independence a person has when single and when married. Then, the writer might go on to discuss how much freedom of career choice a person has when single and when married. Finally, the writer might discuss, in turn, the amount of companionship available in each of the two lifestyles. See also *One-side-at-a-time method*.

Point of view refers to the perspective a writer chooses when writing about a subject. If you narrate events as you experience them, you're using the *first-person* point of view. You might say, for example, "*I* noticed jam on the child's collar and holes in her shirt." If you relate the events from a distance—as if you observed them but did not experience them personally— you're using the *third-person* point of view, for instance, "Jam splotched the child's collar, and her shirt had several holes in it." The point of view should be consistent throughout an essay.

Post hoc thinking—see *Logical fallacies*.

Prewriting is the first stage of the writing process. During prewriting, you jot down rough ideas about your subject without yet moving to writing a draft of your essay. Your goals at this stage are to (1) understand the boundaries of the assignment, (2) discover the limited subject you could write about, (3) generate raw material about the limited subject, and (4) organize the raw material into a very rough *scratch outline*. If you keep in mind that prewriting is "unofficial," it can be a low-pressure, even enjoyable activity.

Process analysis refers to writing that explains the steps involved in doing something or the sequence of stages in an event or behavior. There are two types of process analysis. In *directional process analysis,* readers are shown how to do something step by step. Cookbook recipes, tax form instructions, and how-to books are some typical uses of directional process analysis. In *informational process analysis,* the writer explains how something is done or occurs, without expecting the reader to attempt the process. "A Senator's Road to Political Power," "How a Bee Makes Honey," and "How a Convict Gets Paroled" would be titles of essays developed through informational process analysis. Process analysis can be the dominant mode in an essay, as in these examples, or it may help make a point in an essay developed chiefly through another pattern. For example, in a cause-effect essay that explores the impact of the two-career family, process analysis might be used to explain how parents arrange for day care.

Proofreading involves rereading a final draft carefully to catch any errors in spelling, grammar, punctuation, or typing that have slipped by. While such errors are minor, a significant number of them can seriously weaken the effectiveness of an essay. Proofreading is the last stage in the writing process.

Proposition—see *Assertion.*

Purpose is the reason a writer has for preparing a particular essay. Usually, writers frame their purposes in terms of the effect they wish to have on their *audience.* They may wish to explore the personal meaning of a subject or experience, explain an idea or process, provide information, influence opinion, or entertain. Many essays combine purposes, with one purpose predominating and providing the essay's focus.

Red herring argument—see *Logical fallacies.*

Refutation is an important strategy in *argumentation-persuasion.* In refutation, writers acknowledge that there are opposing views on the subject under discussion and then go on to do one of two things. Sometimes they may admit that the opposing views are somewhat valid but assert that their own position has more merit and devote their essay to demonstrating that merit. For example, a writer might assert, "Business majors often find interesting and lucrative jobs. However, in the long run, liberal arts graduates have many more advantages in the job market because the breadth of their background helps them think better, learn faster, and communicate more effectively." This writer would concentrate on proving the advantages that liberal arts graduates have. At other times, writers may choose to argue actively against an opposing position by dismantling that view point by point. Such refutation of opposing views can strengthen the writer's own arguments.

Repeated words, synonyms, and pronouns—see *Signaling devices.*

Revision means, literally, "reseeing" a *first draft* with a fresh eye, as if the writer had not actually prepared the draft. When revising, you move from more global issues (like clarifying meaning and organization) to more specific matters (like fine-tuning sentences and word choice). While revising, you make whatever changes are necessary to increase the essay's effectiveness. You might strengthen your thesis, resequence paragraph order, or add more transitions. Such changes often make the difference between mediocre and superior writing. Revision, itself a multi-stage process, is the last stage of the writing process.

Satire is a humorous form of social criticism usually aimed at society's institutions or human behavior. Often irreverent as well as witty, satire is serious in purpose: to point out evil, injustice, and absurdity and bring about change through an increase in awareness. Satire ranges widely in tone: it may be gentle or biting; it may sarcastically describe a real situation or use fictional characters and events to spoof reality. Satire often makes use of *irony*. In this book, Jonathan Swift's "A Modest Proposal" is an example of an essay that uses satire.

Scratch outline refers to your first informal plan for an essay, devised at the end of the *prewriting* stage. In making a scratch outline, you select ideas and details from your raw material for inclusion in your essay and discard the rest. You also arrange these ideas in an order that makes sense and that will help you achieve your *purpose*. A scratch outline is tentative and flexible, and can be reshaped as needed.

Sensory description vividly evokes the sights, smells, taste, sounds, and physical feelings of a scene or event. For example, if a writer carefully chooses words and images, readers can see the vibrant reds and oranges of falling leaves, taste the sourness of an underripe grapefruit, hear the growling of motorcycles as a gang sweeps through a town, smell the spicy aroma of a grandmother's homemade tomato soup, and feel the pulsing pain of a jaw after Novocain wears off. Sensory description is particularly important in writing *description* or *narration*.

Sentence variety adds interest to the style of an essay or paragraph. In creating sentence variety, writers mix different kinds of sentences and sentence patterns. For example, you might vary the way your sentences open or intersperse short sentences with long ones, simple sentences with complex ones. Repetitive sentence patterns tend to make readers lose interest.

Signaling devices indicate the relationships among ideas in an essay. They help the reader follow the train of thought from sentence to sentence and from paragraph to paragraph. There are three types of connectives. *Transitions* are words that clarify flow of meaning. They can signal an additional or contrasting point, an enumeration of ideas, the use of an example, or other movement of ideas. *Linking sentences* summarize a point just made and then introduce a follow-up point. *Repeated words, synonyms,* and *pronouns* create a sense of flow by keeping important concepts in the mind of the reader.

Spatial sequence—see *Organization.*

Specific—see *Evidence.*

Stipulative definition is a way of restricting a term for the purposes of discussion. Many words have multiple meanings that can get in the way of clarity when a writer is creating an *extended definition.* For example, you might stipulate the following definition of *foreign car:* "While many American automobiles use parts or even whole engines made by foreign car manufacturers, for the purposes of discussion, 'foreign car' refers only to those automobiles designed and manufactured wholly by a company based in another country. By this definition, a European vehicle made in Pennsylvania is *not* a foreign car."

Subjective description—see *Description.*

Support—see *Evidence.*

Syllogism—see *Deductive reasoning.*

Term—see *Formal definition.*

Thesis is the central idea in any essay, usually expressed in a one- or two-sentence *thesis statement.* Writers accomplish two things by providing a thesis statement in an essay: They indicate the essay's limited subject and express an attitude about that subject. Also called the *controlling idea,* the thesis statement consists of a particular slant, angle, or point of view about the limited subject. Stating the thesis is the second stage of the writing process.

Tone conveys your attitude toward yourself, your purpose, your topic, and your readers. As in speaking, tone in writing may be serious, playful, sarcastic, and so on. Generally, readers detect tone more by how you say something (that is, through your sentence structure and word choice) than by what you say.

Topic sentence is the term for the sentence(s) that convey the main idea of a paragraph. Such sentences are often, but not always, found at the start of a paragraph. They provide a statement of the subject to be discussed and an indication of the writer's attitude toward that subject. Writers usually concern themselves with topic sentences during the writing of the first draft, the fifth stage of the writing process.

Transitions—see *Signaling devices.*

Unified—see *Evidence.*

Works Cited—see *MLA documentation.*

ACKNOWLEDGMENTS

Angelou, Maya, "Sister Flowers." From *I Know Why the Caged Bird Sings* by Maya Angelou. Copyright © 1969 and renewed 1997 by Maya Angelou. Reprinted by permission of Random House, Inc.

Baker, Russell, "In My Day." Reprinted from *Growing Up* by Russell Baker, © 1982. Used with permission of NTC/Contemporary Publishing Company, Chicago.

Barry, Dave, "The Ugly Truth about Beauty." From *The Miami Herald*, copyright © 1998 by Dave Barry, reprinted with permission of the author.

Britt, Suzanne, "That Lean and Hungry Look." Reprinted by permission of the author.

Bryson, Bill, "Your New Computer." From *I'm a Stranger Here Myself* by Bill Bryson, copyright © 1999 by Bill Bryson. Used by permission of Broadway Books, a division of Random House, Inc.

Carson, Rachel, "A Fable for Tomorrow." From *Silent Spring* by Rachel Carson. Copyright © 1962 by Rachel L. Carson, renewed 1990 by Roger Christie. Reprinted by permission of Houghton Mifflin Co. All rights reserved.

Chapman, Stephen, "The Prisoner's Dilemma." Reprinted by permission of *The New Republic*, © 1980, The New Republic, Inc.

Cofer, Judith Ortiz, "A Partial Remembrance of a Puerto Rican Childhood." Reprinted with permission from the publisher of *Silent Dancing: A Partial Remembrance of a Puerto Rican Childhood,* Houston: Arte Publico Press—University of Houston, 1990.

Cole, K. C., "Entropy." From *The New York Times,* March 18, 1982. Copyright © 1982 by The New York Times Company. Reprinted by permission.

Coleman, Jonathan, "Is Technology Making Us Intimate Strangers?" From *Newsweek,* March 27, 2000, © by Newsweek, Inc. All rights reserved. Reprinted by permission.

Didion, Joan, "On Going Home" and "The Santa Ana" from *Slouching Towards Bethlehem* by Joan Didion. Copyright © 1966, 1968, renewed 1996 by Joan Didion. Reprinted by permission of Farrar, Straus and Giroux, LLC.

D'Amboise, Jacques, "Showing What Is Possible." From *Parade,* August 6, 1989. Reprinted with permission from *Parade,* copyright © 1989.

Dillard, Annie, "The Chase." From *An American Childhood* by Annie Dillard. Copyright © 1987 by Annie Dillard. Reprinted by permission of HarperCollins Publishers, Inc.

Ehrenreich, Barbara, "What I've Learned From Men." Reprinted by permission of *Ms.* Magazine, © 1985.

Giovanni, Nikki, "Campus Racism 101." From *Campus Racism 101* by Nikki Giovanni. Copyright © 1994 by Nikki Giovanni. Reprinted by permission of HarperCollins Publishers, Inc. William Morrow.

Gleick, James, "Life as Type A." From *Faster* by James Gleick. Copyright © 1999 by James Gleick. Reprinted by permission of Pantheon Books, a division of Random House, Inc.

Goodman, Ellen, "Family Counterculture." From *The Boston Globe,* August 16, 1991, © 1991, The Boston Globe Newspaper Company/Washington Post Writers Group. Reprinted with permission.

Hentoff, Nat, "Free Speech on campus." From *The Progressive,* May 1989. Reprinted by permission of the author.

Hughes, Langston, "Salvation." From *The Big Sea* by Langston Hughes. Copyright © 1940 by Langston Hughes. Renewal copyright © 1968 by Arna Bontemps and George Houston Bass. Reprinted by permission of Hill and Wang, a division of Farrar, Straus and Giroux, LLC.

Jacoby, Susan, "Common Decency." Copyright © 1991 by Susan Jacoby. Originally appeared in *The New York Times.* Reprinted by permission of Georges Borchardt, Inc. for the author.

Johnson, Beth, "Bombs Bursting in Air." Reprinted by permission of the author. Beth Johnson lives in Lederach, PA.

Kevles, Daniel, "Study Cloning, Don't Ban It." From *The New York Times,* February 16, 1997. Copyright © 1997 by the New York Times Company. Reprinted by permission.

King, Martin Luther, Jr., "Where Do We Go From Here: Community or Chaos?" and "The World House." Reprinted by arrangement with The Heirs to the Estate of Martin Luther King, Jr., c/o Writers House, Inc. as agent for the proprietor. Copyright 1967 by Martin Luther King, Jr., copyright renewed 1991 by Coretta Scott King.

King, Stephen, "Why We Crave Horror Movies." Originally appeared in *Playboy,* 1982. Reprinted by permission. © Stephen King. All rights reserved.

Krauthammer, Charles, "Of Headless Mice . . . and Men." From *Time,* January 19, 1998, © 1998 Time Inc. Reprinted by permission

Liu, Sophronia, "So Tsi-Fai." First published in *Hurricane Alice* 2, No. 4 (Fall 1986). Copyright © 1986 by Sophronia Liu. Reprinted by permission of the author.

Lorde, Audre, "The Fourth of July." From *Zami: A New Spelling of My Name* by Audre Lorde, copyright 1982. Published by the Crossing Press, Santa Cruz, CA.

Lutz, William, "Doublespeak." From *Doublespeak* by William Lutz. Copyright © 1989 by Blonde Bear, Inc. Reprinted by permission of HarperCollins Publishers, Inc.

McClintock, Ann, "Propaganda Techniques in Today's Advertising." Reprinted by permission of the author.

Mitford, Jessica, "The American Way of Death." Reprinted by permission of Jessica Mitford. Copyright © 1963, 1978 by Jessica Mitford, all rights reserved.

Naylor, Gloria, "Mommy, What Does 'Nigger' Mean"? From *The New York Times,* February 20, 1986. Reprinted by permission of Sterling Lord Literistic, Inc. Copyright © 1986 by Gloria Naylor.

Nilsen, Alleen Pace, "Sexism and Language." From "Sexism as Shown Through the English Vocabulary," from *Sexism and Language* by Alleen Pace Nilsen, Haig Bosmajian, H. Lee Gershuny, and Julia P. Stanley. Copyright 1977 by the National Council of Teachers of English. Reprinted with permission.

Orwell, George, "Shooting an Elephant." From *Shooting an Elephant and Other Stories* by George Orwell. Copyright 1950 by Sonia Brownell Orwell and renewed 1978 by Sonia Pitt-Rivers. Reprinted by permission of Harcourt, Inc.

Paglia, Camille, "Rape: A Bigger Danger Than Feminists Know." Reprinted by permission of the author.

Parks, Gordon, "Flavio's Home." From *Voices in the Mirror* by Gordon Parks. Copyright © 1990 by Gordon Parks. Used by permission of Doubleday, a division of Random House.

Raspberry, William, "The Handicap of Definition." © 1982, The Washington Post Writers Group. Reprinted with permission.

Rego, Caroline, "The Fine Art of Complaining." Reprinted with permission of the author.

Roberts, Paul, "How to Say Nothing in 500 Words." From *Understanding English* by Paul Roberts. Copyright © 1958 by Paul Roberts. Reprinted by permission of Addison-Wesley Educational Publishers, Inc.

Rodriguez, Richard, "Workers." From *Hunger of Memory* by Richard Rodriguez. Copyright © 1982 by Richard Rodriguez. Reprinted by permission of Georges Borchardt, Inc.

Sherry, Mary, "In Praise of the 'F' Word." From *Newsweek*, May 6, 1991. Reprinted with permission of the author.

Steele, Shelby, "Affirmative Action: The Price of Preference." From *The Content of Our Character: A New Vision of Race in America* by Shelby Steele. Copyright © 1990 by Shelby Steele. Reprinted by permission of St. Martin's Press, LLC.

Sykes, Charles, "The 'Values' Wasteland." From *Dumbing Down Our Kids: Why American Children Feel Good About Themselves but Can't Read, Write, or Add* by Charles Sykes. Copyright © 1995 by Charles Sykes. Reprinted by permission of St. Martin's Press, LLC.

Tannen, Deborah, "But What Do You Mean?" From *Talking From 9 to 5* by Deborah Tannen, copyright © 1994 by Deborah Tannen. Reprinted by permission of HarperCollins Publishers, Inc. William Morris.

Thomas, Lewis, "The Lie Detector." Copyright © 1980 by Lewis Thomas, from *Late Night Thoughts on Listening to Mahler's Ninth* by Lewis Thomas. Used by permission of Viking Penguin, a division of Penguin Putnam Inc.

Thurber, James, "University Days." From the book *My Life and Hard Times,* copyright © 1933, 1961 by James Thurber. Reprinted by arrangement with Rosemary A. Thurber and The Barbara Hogenson Agency. All rights reserved.

Twain, Mark, "The Damned Human Race." From *Letters from the Earth by Mark Twain,* edited by Bernard DeVoto. Copyright © 1938, 1944, 1946, 1959, 1962 by The Mark Twain Company. Reprinted by permission of HarperCollins Publishers, Inc.

Viorst, Judith, "Friends, Good Friends—And Such Good Friends." Copyright © 1977 by Judith Viorst. Originally appeared in *Redbook*. This usage granted by permission of Lescher & Lescher, Ltd.

Walker, Alice, "Beauty: When the Other Dancer Is the Self." From *In Search of Our Mothers' Gardens: Womanist Prose,* copyright © 1983 by Alice Walker, reprinted by permission of Harcourt, Inc.

White, E. B., "Once More to the Lake." From *One Man's Meat* by E. B. White. Text copyright © 1941 by E. B. White. Reprinted by permission of Tilbury House, Publishers, Gardiner, Maine.

Wilkins, Roger, "The Case for Affirmative Action: Racism Has Its Privileges." Reprinted with permission from the March 27, 1995, issue of *The Nation.*

Winn, Marie, "TV Addiction." From *The Plug-In Drug,* Revised Edition by Marie Winn. Copyright © 1977, 1985 by Marie Winn Miller. Used by permission of Viking Penguin, a division of Penguin Putnam Inc.

Woolf, Virginia, "The Death of the Moth" and "Professions for Women." From *The Death of the Moth and Other Essays* by Virginia Woolf, copyright 1942 by Harcourt, Inc. and renewed 1970 by Marjorie T. Parsons, Executrix, reprinted by permission of the publisher.

Yuh, Ji-Yeon, "Let's Tell the Story of All America's Cultures." From *The Philadelphia Inquirer,* June 30, 1991. Reprinted by permission from The Philadelphia Inquirer.

Zinsser, William, "College Pressures." Copyright © 1979 by William K. Zinsser. Reprinted by permission of the author.

INDEX

To the Student
From the Authors

By now, you realize that almost all writing goes through a series of revisions. The same was true for this book. *The Macmillan Reader,* sixth edition, has been reworked a number of times, with each revision taking into account students' and instructors' reactions to drafts of material.

Before we prepare the seventh edition of *The Macmillan Reader,* we'd like to know how you, the student, feel about the book. We hope you'll spend a few minutes completing this brief questionnaire. You can be sure that your responses will help shape subsequent editions. Please send your completed survey to the College English Editor, Longman Publishers, 1185 Avenue of the Americas, New York, NY 10036.

Thanks for your time.

College _____ City and state _____

Course title _____ Instructor_____

	I really liked it.	It was okay.	I didn't like it.	I didn't read it.
DESCRIPTION				
Parks, *Flavio's Home*	___	___	___	___
Baker, *In My Day*	___	___	___	___
Angelou, *Sister Flowers*	___	___	___	___
White, *Once More to the Lake*	___	___	___	___
Cofer, *A Partial Remembrance of a Puerto Rican Childhood*	___	___	___	___
NARRATION				
Lorde, *The Fourth of July*	___	___	___	___
Orwell, *Shooting an Elephant*	___	___	___	___
Dillard, *The Chase*	___	___	___	___
Hughes, *Salvation*	___	___	___	___
Liu, *So Tsi-Fai*	___	___	___	___

EXEMPLIFICATION

	I really liked it.	It was okay.	I didn't like it.	I didn't read it.
Sykes, *The "Values" Wasteland*	___	___	___	___
Nilsen, *Sexism and Language*	___	___	___	___
Thurber, *University Days*	___	___	___	___
Johnson, *Bombs Bursting in Air*	___	___	___	___
Ehrenreich, *What I've Learned From Men*	___	___	___	___

DIVISION-CLASSIFICATION

Viorst, *Friends, Good Friendsand Such Good Friends*	___	___	___	___
Zinsser, *College Pressures*	___	___	___	___
Lutz, *Doublespeak*	___	___	___	___
McClintock, *Propaganda Techniques in Today's Advertising*	___	___	___	___
Tannen, *But What Do You Mean?*	___	___	___	___

PROCESS ANALYSIS

Bryson, *Your New Computer*	___	___	___	___
Giovanni, *Campus Racism 101*	___	___	___	___
Mitford, *The American Way of Death*	___	___	___	___
Roberts, *How to Say Nothing in 500 Words*	___	___	___	___
Rego, *The Fine Art of Complaining*	___	___	___	___

COMPARISON-CONTRAST

Carson, *A Fable for Tomorrow*	___	___	___	___
Britt, *That Lean and Hungry Look*	___	___	___	___
Rodriguez, *Workers*	___	___	___	___
Barry, *The Ugly Truth About Beauty*	___	___	___	___
Chapman, *The Prisoner's Dilemma*	___	___	___	___

CAUSE-EFFECT

	I really liked it.	It was okay.	I didn't like it.	I didn't read it.
King, *Why We Crave Horror Movies*	___	___	___	___
D'Amboise, *Showing What Is Possible*	___	___	___	___
Walker, *Beauty: When the Other Dancer Is the Self*	___	___	___	___
Thomas, *The Lie Detector*	___	___	___	___
Coleman, *Is Technology Making Us Intimate Strangers?*	___	___	___	___

DEFINITION

Cole, *Entropy*	___	___	___	___
Gleick, *Life as Type A*	___	___	___	___
Naylor, *"Mommy, What Does 'Nigger' Mean?"*	___	___	___	___
Winn, *TV Addiction*	___	___	___	___
Raspberry, *The Handicap of Definition*	___	___	___	___

ARGUMENTATION-PERSUASION

Sherry, *In Praise of the "F" Word*	___	___	___	___
Yuh, *Let's Tell the Story of All America's Cultures*	___	___	___	___
Twain, *The Damned Human Race*	___	___	___	___
Swift, *A Modest Proposal*	___	___	___	___
Hentoff, *Free Speech on Campus*	___	___	___	___
Paglia, *Rape: A Bigger Danger Than Feminists Know*	___	___	___	___
Jacoby, *Common Decency*	___	___	___	___
Kevles, *Study Cloning, Don't Ban It*	___	___	___	___
Krauthammer, *Of Headless Mice . . . and Men*	___	___	___	___
Wilkins, *Racism Has Its Privileges*	___	___	___	___
Steele, *Affirmative Action: The Price of Preference*	___	___	___	___

COMBINING THE PATTERNS

	I really liked it.	It was okay.	I didn't like it.	I didn't read it.
Woolf, *The Death of the Moth*	_____	_____	_____	_____
Woolf, *Professions for Women*	_____	_____	_____	_____
King, *Where Do We Go From Here: Community or Chaos?*	_____	_____	_____	_____
King, *The World House*	_____	_____	_____	_____
Didion, *On Going Home*	_____	_____	_____	_____
Didion, *The Santa Ana*	_____	_____	_____	_____

Any general comments or suggestions?

Name_____ Date _____

Address _____

THANKS AGAIN!